ISTENING TO MUSIC

Listening to Music

RICHARD L. CROCKER

ANN P. BASART

University of California, Berkeley

McGRAW-HILL BOOK COMPANY

New York   San Francisco   St. Louis   Düsseldorf   London   Mexico   Panama   Sydney   Toronto

This book was set in Monophoto Times Roman by Holmes Typography, Inc., and printed on permanent paper and bound by Von Hoffman Press, Inc. The designer was Ronald Q. Lewton; the drawings were done by Reese Thornton. The editors were Robert P. Rainier and Michael A. Ungersma. Charles A. Goehring supervised production.

LISTENING TO MUSIC

Printed in the United States of America.

Library of Congress catalog card number: 77–118394

1234567890 VHVH 79876543210

13851

PREFACE

THIS BOOK grew out of the authors' experience in teaching an introductory course in music for college non-majors. The challenge of such a course is to give these students, in a few short weeks, something not just rudimentary but truly fundamental, something that might equip them for a lifetime of listening —since many of them will take no further course in music.

Only a limited number of things can be accomplished in such a course. A choice must be made on the basis of some one overriding purpose; we felt that purpose should be to help the students develop their ability to listen, in particular to listen to music's shapes and structures. The structure of a piece of music itself is at the center of the listener's concert experience. Structure seemed to us to provide the most convenient, most reliable context in which to develop skill and knowledge about music.

A careful selection of pieces for this book makes it possible to use a single piece as an example of several different aspects, thereby increasing the concentration on the overall shape of the piece as well as increasing the likelihood that it will become a rich part of the student's musical experience. The aspects of timbre, texture, rhythm, line, harmony, theme, and motive, which occupy Chapters 2 through 9, are each discussed within the context of a particular piece. What does a particular timbre contribute to the piece? How does its appearance at a particular spot shape the piece? What is the relationship of the whole pattern of timbres in the piece to its overall shape?

We have found in class testing that students can deal with this kind of question from the start with no training in notation—without, for that matter, even knowing the name of the instrument that produced the timbre—and that in answering they learn something decisive about music. This contextual approach works for rhythm and even harmony as well as for timbre and texture. Our experience in the course showed that concentration on listening produced results that easily compensate for the de-emphasis on traditional notation and musicianship. An important advantage is that students who are very literate in fields other than music can come to grips at once with pieces challenging enough to engage their attention.

Furthermore, we found that by concentrating on the intrinsic aspects of a few pieces, the beginning student listener can gain access more quickly to a wider spectrum of music. By learning to hear whatever he finds in a given piece (instead of learning merely to identify a limited set of historical or stylistic conventions), the student is better equipped to deal with the great variety of sounds now met under the name "music." At the same time, the basic listening skills he has acquired give him a better foundation for studies in history or repertory.

We do use a notation, but one designed to be used only by the listener, and only for listening to music. This notation has the sole purpose of showing in an immediately self-evident way the *relative* lengths and pitches of notes. It merely depicts on paper certain aspects of sound for easy reference. Ultimately the best use of student can make of the notation (and all the other diagrams) is to forget them—after their point has become part of his listening experience. This notation has advantages in courses where many of the students do not know traditional notation; for those students who do, we think there are advantages in working with a notation that attracts attention away from making sound and toward hearing it.

Since introductory courses are taught on many different schedules, the book is designed to be as flexible as possible. In general, Chapters 1 through 8 are designed to be taken in order as the basis for the first seven or eight weeks of the course, with a selection from Chapters 9 through 17 being used according to individual needs. The book is thus equally suitable for quarter or semester courses. Specific schedules by week and chapter are suggested in the *Instructor's Manual*.

Flexibility is further increased by the other materials in the book. Each of Chapters 2 through 10 includes a section called Exercises for Further Listening, designed as drill with which the reader can practice listening on his own for the aspects of musical organization discussed in each chapter. The material is programmed for self-instruction: the reader should check each of his answers before proceeding to the next question. Two self-tests are included for review, one following Chapter 7, another following Chapter 10.

While the exercises are intended to deepen the concentration on the works discussed in the text (and especially to ensure that the basic concepts are clearly understood), the Suggestions for Further Listening at the end of the text can be used to broaden the range of musical works studied, and to take into account parallel examples, if that is desired.

Several kinds of material are included to provide an easy transition to other kinds of courses or individual studies. An extensive glossary includes many terms commonly found in musical scores, as well as standard technical equivalents of the strictly pragmatic terms used in the text itself. An appendix called Notation and Nomenclature explains the conventional notation of rhythm and pitch and the corresponding standard nomenclature, up through the preliminary terms used in harmony. A historical outline of Western music from 700 to the present sketches the development of musical forms and styles during that period. The Suggestions For Further Listening, the historical outline, and the appendix on notation should be particularly useful for a two-term introductory course.

The music discussed in detail in the book is available on a specially prepared set of four long-playing records. The recorded items are musically complete and free of voice commentary so that they may be listened to as pieces of music; but where called for they are punctuated by slight pauses to make clear the larger sections, thus providing orientation to the sectional plans as discussed in the text.

We want to stress here that we developed this text to maximize listening skills in this particular course, for these particular students. We would not contemplate abandoning notation or musicianship for musicians; we do not advocate musical illiteracy. We do advocate listening for listeners; we wish to bring some of the advantages of a musical education to people who may never become musically literate. The realistic choice in such a course is between teaching on the one hand a little notation alongside a little listening, with no chance to relate the two in terms of modern concert life, and on the other hand no notation at all but enough listening to make a significant start with difficult works. And while no one would advocate *verbal* illiteracy, still it is possible for someone who cannot *read* English (and also for blind people) to experience and understand Shakespeare very profoundly when it is presented on the stage or in a recorded performance.

Richard L. Crocker

Ann P. Basart

TABLE OF CONTENTS

LIST OF WORKS

Gregorian Chant from the Easter Mass
(Missa in Dominica Resurrectionis)

"Resurrexi" (introit)
"Haec dies" (gradual)
"Alleluia pascha nostrum"
"Victimae paschali laudes" (prose)

Vocal music of Claudio Monteverdi (1562–1643)

"Chiome d'oro" (canzonetta)
"Si ch'io vorrei morire" (madrigal, Book IV)′
"Amor che deggio far" (canzonetta)

Johann Sebastian Bach (1685–1750)

Well-Tempered Clavier, Book II
    Prelude and Fugue No. 5 in D major
    Prelude and Fugue No. 12 in F minor

Joseph Haydn (1732–1809)

Symphony No. 100 in G major ("Military")
    Adagio—Allegro
    Allegretto
    Menuetto and Trio: Moderato
    Finale: Presto

Wolfgang Amadeus Mozart (1756–1791)

Le Nozze di Figaro ("The Marriage of Figaro")
    Act II, Finale

Ludwig van Beethoven (1770–1827)

Symphony No. 7 in A major, op. 92
    Poco sostenuto—Vivace
    Allegretto
    Presto/Assai meno presto
    Allegro con brio

Franz Schubert (1797–1828)

Die schöne Müllerin (a song cycle, "The Maid of the Mill")

Richard Wagner (1813–1883)

Tristan und Isolde (a music drama)
    Prelude (Vorspiel)

Igor Stravinsky (1882–   )

Les Noces (Svadyebka, "The Wedding")

Béla Bartók (1881–1945)

String Quartet No. 6
    I. Mesto—Pesante—Vivace
    II. Mesto—Marcia
    III. Mesto—Burletta
    IV. Mesto

Krzysztof Penderecki (1933–   )

To the Victims of Hiroshima, Threnody

Mario Davidovsky (1934–   )

Synchronisms No. 3 for Cello and Electronic Sounds

LISTENING TO MUSIC

LISTENING FOR WHAT'S THERE. People who want to know more about music frequently ask, "What should I listen for?" There was a time, not so long ago, when several clear-cut answers could be given. The beginner might be told about the symphony orchestra and taught to identify its various instruments. Or he might be taught the rudiments of chords and scales and what they do or how certain standard forms could be expected to behave. Now, however, the listener may encounter at any time in his day-to-day musical experience a piece that does not use chords or scales or traditional forms. A piece may not be for symphony orchestra or for traditional instruments; it may use sounds unlike those ever heard before. It may come from so far away or long ago, or be so new, as to have nothing to do with what the listener has traditionally been taught to listen for.

There is another answer to the question. It takes a while to see that this answer is not whimsical or irresponsible, but rather is the only one truly responsive to the reality of modern musical life. The answer is "Listen for what is there."

Anyone can listen for what is there; it takes no special talent or previous training, but it does take a great deal of concentration. We all listen instinctively for what we want to hear, not for what the composer wants to tell us. We project ourselves into the piece. We do this on first hearing, when we still have no idea what the composer intends. We do it on repeated hearings, gradually building up in our minds a set of relationships in the piece, an image of its structure, which may have less and less to do with the composer's original image. All too often we let slip the unrepeatable opportunity, afforded by a first hearing, to grasp a new musical idea. All too often we must depend on some chance insight to strip away years of self-conditioning to a masterpiece to discover what it really is.

Provided he concentrates on what is there, any alert, attentive listener can perceive something of what is really in a piece, even on first hearing. That something may be very simple or very obvious. But the first thing to learn about listening is to accept—as important—the simple and obvious features of a musical experience.

CHAPTER *1* INTRODUCTION

THE LARGER SHAPE. The most obvious thing about a piece of music is that it begins and ends. What comes between beginning and end is, of course, the music itself. Yet, in a way that is far more than trivial, beginnings and endings make us aware that the music is there. By giving a piece a beginning and end, the composer does something significant. Furthermore, the way in which he does it is an important aspect of his piece.

Beginnings and endings offer one approach to understanding music. They can be found *within* many pieces, as pauses or breaks marking off sections of the basic shape. These inner divisions are one of the most important means of grasping the composer's thought.

Everyone hears such divisions—at least, the more decisive ones; what takes practice is bringing the awareness of them to full consciousness. To grasp fully the structure and meaning of a piece, the ear must not only note the divisions as they occur but also sense their relationship to one another and their cumulative effect. The ear has to learn to gauge the relative importance of successive breaks, grouping the sections as the composer grouped them to add up to the whole piece.

Breaks or pauses in the interior are less decisive than the beginning and end of the whole piece; if not, the piece would be several pieces rather than one. Inner breaks vary in strength along a continuum, from those almost as clear as the beginning and end, to subdivisions so subtle, so close to continuity, that one person may hear them and another may not. Sometimes only the beginning and end of a piece will be perceptible as breaks, joined by one unbroken surge of sound. But by that very avoidance of division the composer would tell us something important.

There is no commonly accepted terminology to describe various degrees of division and subdivision in all kinds of music. The largest divisions of an opera are called *acts*. Symphonies and several other kinds of instrumental music are usually divided into a few large sections called *movements*; that is, each section has a different kind of musical motion, or movement. The movements of a traditional symphony are apt to be self-contained. At the end of the movement, the conductor relaxes for a moment; the musicians may wipe their brows or their eyeglasses; the listeners look at the program or perhaps stretch. We can usually take the movement itself as a basic artistic unit, regarding the whole symphony as a compound form. We will discuss such forms later as multimovement forms.

Self-contained divisions of a work have their own divisions and subdivisions. There can be as many levels of division as the composer chooses—or as he can cause us to hear. We will speak of two main levels of division: we will identify the *sections* of a piece or of a movement and the *phrases* within each section, as shown in Ex. 1-1.

Phrases are perhaps more difficult to describe and to identify, for a phrase is not just a small subdivision

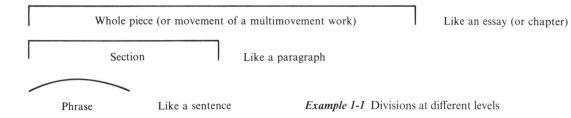

Whole piece (or movement of a multimovement work)　　Like an essay (or chapter)

Section　　Like a paragraph

Phrase　　Like a sentence

Example 1-1 Divisions at different levels

but a very basic, yet very subtle, musical unit. A musical phrase is like a sentence; or a phrase is what you can sing in one breath; or a phrase is what makes sense as the smallest complete unit. These are very rough definitions—indeed, not definitions at all. As we discuss specific works we can develop a more concrete idea of what phrasing means in music. Besides the phrase, we will also discuss the *phrase group*, as something larger than a phrase and smaller than a section, and the *subphrase*, as a very small subdivision.

Ludwig van Beethoven (1770–1827)

**SYMPHONY NO. 7
PRESTO/ASSAI MENO PRESTO
(THIRD MOVEMENT)**

The larger shape of a work, then, can be approached through a perception of its most decisive sectional divisions. The larger shape is an extremely important aspect of the work; indeed, in the broadest sense this is the way the work is—this is the primary form the work takes in our awareness. In some cases, the composer uses the larger shape to convey a basic meaning of the work. As an example, listen to the third movement of Beethoven's Symphony No. 7, in many ways a complex piece (and, of course, itself a part of a larger piece, the whole symphony) but easy to follow in its main divisions and the sections they create.

While listening to this movement through from the beginning for the first time, take note of the major divisions of the movement. *How many* divisions are there, and how many sections do they make within the piece? Do not go looking for the divisions; rather, let them come to you. If Beethoven wants you to hear a division, he will see to it that you do.

One of the most important ways Beethoven—or any composer—has of making the listener hear sections is by creating a strong contrast between them. In this particular piece, the contrasts are so strong that they may soak up all your attention. You may become deeply involved in the qualities of sound in one section, as compared to the highly contrasting sounds of the next. This is what Beethoven intended; yet it is even more important to hear how the points of high contrast divide the piece into sections. Remember that we are interested only in large sections and strong contrast. How many times in this piece do you have a feeling (a feeling that is often keenest on first hearing) of one thing finished and another just begun? Is there a pattern of contrasting sections?

After one or two hearings, it should be clear that the whole piece has five main sections. (If these five sections are not clear, this is probably due to your listening too minutely, allowing an awareness of too much detail to obscure the more obvious outlines of the piece.)

Furthermore, these five sections, resulting from four major contrasts, present themselves to the ear as *A B A B A*, rather than simply as *A B C D E*. The composer has done more, in other words, than just make sections; he has established an order among these sections, and that order is what should really interest the listener.

One of the obvious ways in which these sections are differentiated is by change of pace: the *B* sections go slower than the *A* sections. This is the meaning of the Italian terms used to identify the movement. *Presto*, the label for the *A* section, means "fast," and *assai meno presto*, the label for the *B* section, means "rather less fast."

The basic divisions in this movement are simple, but the grasping of the whole can be difficult because of the length of the sections. Beethoven frequently asks that attention be sustained for long periods until he gets to the point. Different listeners, of course, have different comprehension spans: for some the sections in this piece may seem much longer than for others. But Beethoven has a way of challenging anyone's powers of comprehension.

Identifying a pattern of sections is only the first step in discovering its meaning. We need to ask, "What is the effect of this *A B A B A* form?" During the third section, when *A B A* has been heard, the order and meaning of events is perhaps most clear: one thing (*A*) has been stated, then something different (*B*) occurs, then there is a return and confirmation (*A*). The shape of the experience has been simple, its meaning clear: the piece is basically about *A*, with *B* as episodic relief. How would the piece be different if it stopped after *A B A*? What is the effect, in other words, of continuing with another *B*, then another *A*?

We should also consider the way in which *A* and *B* return. The repetitions seem literal; at least, if there are changes, they are not obtrusive, playing no obvious role in the overall shape. What would happen if the repetitions were somehow different— varied or extended in some significant way? What is the effect of having *un*varied repetitions? Answers to these questions can and should reflect not mere personal taste but something intrinsic to the piece itself.

It is possible to agree, perhaps, that there is something noteworthy in the form Beethoven gave to this particular piece. There would have been nothing unusual as far as *A B A*, with only one literal repeat of the *A*. But in a piece that is otherwise rich and elaborate, is there not something striking, obstinate perhaps, about the ensuing literal repeat of the whole *B* section, then yet another literal repeat of the whole *A* section?

There are other questions to ask about the relationship between *A* and *B*. Do they differ drastically in length? Does one go significantly faster than the other? The answers to these questions may depend somewhat on which performance is heard. (Eventually one can use conclusions about the nature of a piece to help decide which performance best reveals that nature.) While performances of this particular piece vary, especially in the tempo and character of the *B* section, still the two sections seem generally to be comparable in dimensions.

What about their relative weight or importance? Does the *B* section seem like a mere interlude, a relief to *A*? Or does the *A* section only provide a frame for *B*? Judged at this high level, and making allowances for different performances, the two sections are remarkably balanced. One does not seem to be a frame for the other. The form is neither *a B a B a* nor *A b A b A*. We could show the same thing by asking, "Could the piece end after *A B A B*?" In most ways no, but in some ways yes; there is structural ambiguity, which Beethoven has carefully prepared and exploited.

This piece can be thought of as a study in larger form, a play on structural expectations developed as the piece unfolds. If we can recapture the uncertainty of first hearing, we can see that the piece is successively *A B*, then *A B A*, then *A B A B*, then *A B A B A*—and then at the last moment *A B A B A b*, and finally *A B A B A b a*! The brief recall of *B* in the closing seconds of the piece is no section in itself; but because of the way the piece has been constructed—the literal, insistent repetitions—a brief recall is all that is needed to make a brilliant point.

FROM OVERALL PLAN TO DETAIL. Great pieces of music communicate something of their basic nature even on first hearing. An awareness of the larger structure, the order of sections, in Beethoven's Presto reveals the main point the composer was trying to make. You probably feel, however, that your perception of the work is still only dim, that the *A B A B A* plan is, perhaps, too abstract to be really meaningful. This feeling exists because the plan needs to be filled in with an awareness of concrete detail.

Not all the details of a piece require close attention, nor did the composer intend that they should. Some notes or groups of notes are more important than others, depending on their kind or their degree of participation in the larger plan. Some understanding

of the larger plan should therefore precede a study of detail; the plan is a guide to the important details, giving them a deeper meaning.

In this book we will be concerned extensively with musical details, because they are such an important source of animation and interest. But we will try to relate details, as we go, to the larger shape in which we find them.

VARIOUS ASPECTS OF MUSIC. One of the most challenging things about music is that it presents the ear with many different but related aspects at once—such as the qualities of voices or instruments, the ways they are combined, the rhythm, melody, or harmony of a work. Ideally, perhaps, we should try to study all aspects at once, just as they come to us in an actual work. Most listeners, however, seem to prefer studying these aspects one at a time, raising each to consciousness separately in order to become more acutely sensitive to it. The chapters in Part One of this book take up separate aspects of music, considering each within the context of one or more particular pieces. In Part Two, we will attempt to deal with all aspects—or at any rate, all the more obvious aspects—of each of several complete pieces.

DIALOG WITH THE AUTHORS. When the authors teach courses using the materials of this book, they are usually confronted after the introductory lecture (on the material discussed here up to this point) with many questions about what will *not* be included. Here are some of the best and most frequently asked questions, with our answers.

WHAT ABOUT THE WAY MUSIC MAKES ME FEEL? This important question deserves a lengthy discussion. We all respond to music with feelings—sometimes with strong feelings; if we did not, we would not be more than casually concerned with music. This book will not discuss music in terms of personal feelings or associations, but that should not be taken as an assertion that such feelings are unimportant or irrelevant.

A piece of music can have a broad range of meanings, all the way from meanings shared by all listeners, whoever they may be, to meanings shared

only by the composer and one other person. In addition, there is the kind of meaning a piece of music has for each of us alone—unshared and unsharable because of our different individual personalities. If we succeed in articulating and communicating to another person one of these special meanings, we have the curious feeling that some essential quality of the meaning has been lost in transmission. In being specifically described, the meaning has necessarily lost those hidden, implied connections with one's whole inner experience that made it seem so rich.

As soon as we try to articulate and communicate our innermost responses to music, then, we are dissatisfied with the result—and so too, usually, are the people with whom we are trying to communicate. Accounts of other people's inner responses to music are apt to make dull reading. A poet (by way of exception) may embody his responses to a piece of music in a beautiful poem; but a poet is a privileged character, and anyway we value his poem (if it is valuable) more for its own sake than for what it tells us about the piece.

Does not the composer succeed in communicating his innermost experience in his piece? Sometimes he seems to, and therein lies one of the mysteries of music. But of what interest would the composer's feelings be if he had not succeeded in giving them artistic shape? We are primarily interested in the shape, the completed art work; and that shape is what we can most profitably discuss, in a class or in a book. If the unsharable is to be shared, we do so through the magic of music itself, in listening to it, hearing it together.

Some listeners see mental pictures—or would like to see mental pictures—when they listen to music. Such pictures are a form of inner response. Sometimes the composer encourages us to make this kind of response; more often he does not. In either event, these mental pictures, like other personal responses, are responses *to* something in the music—something that is more "in the music" than the picture is. That something has to do with the specific shape the piece of music takes as it is performed in our hearing. As you concentrate on the way pieces actually sound, when considered from the point of view of their overall shape, you may well find that the problem of pictures—and of musical "meaning" in general—begins to take care of itself.

This book will discuss the outward, objective shapes of pieces of music; these are what you hear. By hearing them with a trained, sensitive ear and a reflective mind, you keep the way open to expanding realms of feeling. A book such as this cannot tell you what those feelings are to be; it can only suggest how to open yourself to them.

WHY IS THERE NOTHING ABOUT THE COMPOSERS? By "something about the composers," listeners usually mean biographical sketches, including especially the circumstances under which a given piece was composed, as well as interpretations of the significance of individual pieces in a composer's life and work. In a broader sense, the question would refer to a general description of the cultural and social background of a composer and his compositions, to the chronology and history of music.

We do not feel that this information is prerequisite to understanding the kind of discussion we wanted to present. On the contrary, we feel that learning to hear what is there in the music is prerequisite to assimilating intelligently the wealth of biographical and historical material now available. In this sense, the book *is* about the composers—that is, about their pieces, which in the long run are the most important things one can know about them.

A very brief outline of the history of music is included as Appendix D, for those readers who desire a point of departure for further historical or biographical reading.

WHY NO ROCK OR FOLK MUSIC? The authors have nothing against rock or folk—or jazz either. We just don't know enough about these repertories to write informatively about them, and an ignorant discussion would be worse than none.

Beyond that, the book is not about repertories *as repertories* but rather about aspects of all kinds of music and ways to hear them. Examples of most aspects discussed in the book could be provided from folk, rock, and jazz; we hope that people who know enough will provide such examples.

WHY NO ETHNIC MUSIC? Again, our answer is that we have selected our examples from the kind of music we know best. Ethnic or non-Western repertories are especially treacherous for unqualified people to discuss—and very few *are* qualified, except musicians indigenous to a particular repertory. The danger (to teachers and students alike) is that when we listen to sounds from another culture we hear patterns that may be meaningful to us but that are not meaningful within the culture that produced the piece. This danger can be reduced by close study of the culture as a whole, or of its history. In this book, however, we are concentrating exclusively on pieces, not on cultural repertories.

In spite of the cultural gap that separates us from various ethnic musics (a gap we should be conscious of and should try to bridge), still we can say that if a composer consciously put something into a piece of music, then anyone, from any culture, should be able to hear it in some degree. If we are successful in hearing what is really there in one repertory, then we should be able—putting aside preconception and prejudice—to hear what is there in any repertory. As with folk or rock, examples of many things in this book might well be drawn from ethnic repertories.

WHY SO MUCH MODERN MUSIC? To begin with, we do not think the amount of modern music is disproportionate, if "modern" means "twentieth century." Of twelve works used for core pieces, four are from the twentieth century, three from the nineteenth, three from the eighteenth, one from the seventeenth—and only the chant represents the first millenium of the Christian era. (Again, our primary purpose was not a well-balanced representation of repertories.)

The word "modern" means different things to different people, of course. If "modern" means "recent," then only two of the twentieth-century composers qualify, for Stravinsky's *Les Noces* was composed in the period 1914–1917, before most of us were born, and Bartók's Sixth Quartet was composed in 1939. Only the works by Penderecki and Davidovsky were written in the second half of the century.

If by "modern" is meant "difficult, challenging, obscure, unfamiliar, or disturbing," then the question

must be answered differently. Too often, "understanding" music has meant "getting used" to it. The music of Beethoven—even of Mozart—can sometimes be all of those things, if only we learn to hear it the way it is. From new music of our own time we can learn something of how new music of any time sounded to its original audience; we can come up against the restless searching of creative imagination and feel the sting of a new musical idea. Perhaps we understand music of the past only after we have learned this essential aspect of music from the present.

Then, too, twentieth-century pieces provide useful, convincing examples of several specific aspects of music that we wanted to study. But these reasons are all argumentative—and less than positive. The simple, positive answer to the question is that the twentieth century has produced pieces as good as any found elsewhere in Western music, pieces no listener should miss. Some of them had to be included in this book.

WHY IS THE BOOK SO TECHNICAL? A distinction should be made between "technical" and "specific." This book is more or less free of unnecessary technicalities—at least, we have scrutinized everything in it to discover technicalities that should be omitted. We take "technical" to refer to special nomenclature and notation used in the craft of music by composers and performers; to the physics of music; to the construction of musical instruments and apparatus; to theoretical systems and explanations about the nature of music in general; to accounts of how music should be composed, or how a particular piece was composed; or to instructions in how to perform pieces on instruments. If we have alluded to any of these technical matters in the course of the book, the allusions are matters of passing interest, not essential steps in learning to hear music. Some of these technicalities are included in the appendices, because many readers who are just becoming acquainted with music may want to know the meanings of some commonly found notation and nomenclature. While such technical matters are very interesting and for some purposes are important or even essential, we do not think they are needed for intelligent listening.

On the other hand, many listeners want information that is far more *specific* than that generally available to them in nontechnical form. Listeners want to be guided to specific important aspects of a piece; they want to be able to hear specific relationships spanning broad stretches of a piece. Listeners with no technical knowledge can—and frequently do—hear very detailed and complex matters of musical construction. We have tried to discuss such matters in nontechnical terms, making sure that in all such discussions the point at issue is something that can be clearly and distinctly heard by anyone— musician or layman—who cares to concentrate.

I HAVE TAKEN PIANO [PLAYED IN THE BAND] FOR YEARS, BUT I CANNOT FOLLOW ANYTHING YOU SAY. This is a frequent complaint from students trained in musical performance. We have become steadily more aware, in teaching listeners, that listening and performing are two distinct skills. Listening is not rudimentary performing; performing is not advanced listening. A student who can play an instrument has not thereby leapfrogged training in listening. On the other hand, many people have found that they could become perceptive listeners without being able to play a note. And, unfortunately, skilled performers sometimes do not learn how to listen.

The attitude of a performer, intent upon execution of notes, is sometimes an obstacle to the wide-open approach needed for intelligent listening. Someone who plays in a band or an orchestra is at a particular disadvantage in this respect, since he approaches a piece from the point of view of a single instrumental line. A trained performer can learn to listen just like anyone else; but it requires a little more effort for him to overcome his performing approach. Above all he must realize that in learning to listen he is embarking on a different kind of activity.

PART ONE

Aspects of musical shape

WHEN WE ENCOUNTER a piece of music for the first time in a live performance, we watch the performers, noticing their appearance and gestures. Similarly, our ears are drawn to the kinds of sounds they are making. If the sounds are good, we notice that fact right away; if the sounds are not good—if the singer has a cold, or if an instrument is badly out of tune—we notice that fact even sooner. If the performance is a recorded one, our first impressions will have to do with the quality of the recorded sound; scratches or poor reproduction can so monopolize our attention that we cannot hear the piece at all.

Such circumstances show the importance of the qualities of sound for our first impressions of a piece. If the sound is good and if the piece contains many rich sounds, our first impressions may be totally taken up with the profusion of sonorous details. Hearing them may be so rewarding in itself that we do not hear any features of the shape of the piece—indeed, we may have no interest in that shape.

Total absorption in the sheer sound of music is probably an experience familiar to many listeners. It is an important part of the musical experience: you should be alert to it, ready to enter into it. A piece whose sound is not in some degree intense or interesting will not seem to have a significant shape.

Nevertheless, you should be just as ready to proceed from absorption in rich sounds to perception of the larger design. The sounds themselves will not sustain interest indefinitely; a piece that offers nothing but rich sounds will eventually reveal its limitations. The concern of this book will be the understanding of the sounds of any piece in terms of its overall design. The first step toward this understanding is to hear individual sounds as clearly, as specifically, as possible; to distinguish various kinds of sound from each other.

Be assured, once for all, that listening closely and analytically to a piece in order to make sharp distinctions among its sounds does not forever preclude your chance to hear that piece again with the original sense of wonder. Many listeners, rightly cherishing the richness of a first hearing, wrongly refuse to listen more closely for fear of losing that initial sense of openness, of unlimited possibility—a sense especially associated with the quality of sound and

CHAPTER  QUALITIES OF SOUND

the feeling of immediacy it can produce. Many people rely upon total absorption in the quality of sound to maintain this openness; they thereby miss the chance to discover all the other dimensions of the piece, which may lead much further than can possibly be imagined at the start. And in music the freshness of first hearing can mysteriously return at any moment, needing only the stimulus of, say, a new, unfamiliar performance or recording.

Igor Stravinsky (1882–   )

**LES NOCES
FIRST TABLEAU**

Stravinsky's *Les Noces* ("The Wedding") has a sense of luxuriance in its sounds; their various qualities strike the ear immediately, and absorb the listener's attention. Less obvious, perhaps, is the degree to which the various qualities of sound help to shape the piece as a whole. Aspects of music such as rhythm or melody can hardly be ignored in listening to a piece; but by way of beginning with the obvious, concentrate exclusively for a while on the qualities of sound in *Les Noces*. *Les Noces* has a text, and ordinarily you would begin with the text in order to find a proper approach to the piece. The discussion here, however, is concerned with what you hear in a piece even before you absorb the meaning and implications of the text. (The full text of Stravinsky's *Les Noces*, in Russian transliteration and in parallel English translation, appears at the end of Chapter 13, where it will be used

in connection with our study of the piece as a whole.)

Listen to the First Tableau of *Les Noces* (about 5 minutes), keeping a rough mental inventory of the different kinds of sounds you hear. Your first attempt may well be confusing—it is hard to find ways to keep track of the different combinations of sound. The following discussion will suggest some ways to identify sounds in the First Tableau and will trace the shapes that emerge.

Voices are immediately prominent in *Les Noces*. There are instruments too (pianos and various percussion instruments), but the voices are predominant; the ear follows the lead of the voices, noticing the instruments mainly when they obtrude. There is an overall progression of sound within the First Tableau, from solo female voice to full chorus and back again. This buildup of vocal resources can almost be said to produce the shape of the Tableau—the movement toward the climax and away from it—all by itself. In the next few pages, we will follow the buildup in detail.

BEGINNING OF THE TABLEAU TO REHEARSAL NUMBER 9. During the first minute or so of *Les Noces*, there are three different qualities of voices, singing in turn. First, a high, bright female voice singing alone; her voice type is called *soprano* (Italian, "upper"), and since no one else is singing exactly her notes at the same time her part is described as a *soprano solo*.

The second quality of voice comes from a chorus

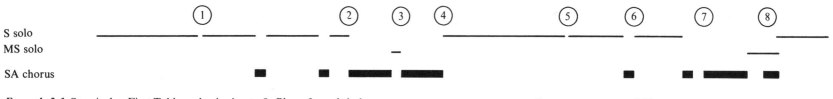

 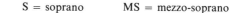

Example 2-1 Stravinsky, First Tableau, beginning to 9: Plan of vocal timbres   S = soprano   MS = mezzo-soprano   A = alto

of women, who first enter briefly after the soprano solo, drop out, then sing at greater length, as shown in Ex. 2-1. (The numbers used here are for reference only; they are taken from the score, where they are also used for reference, and are called *rehearsal numbers*.) Everyone in the women's chorus sings the same notes here; the chorus part, in other words, could have been sung by a solo singer—except that then there would be an important difference in the quality of sound between a solo and a chorus. The chorus sounds less bright and hard; it is richer, more fuzzy. This kind of difference is included under the broad heading *timbre*, a general term for "quality of sound": there is an important difference in timbre between a solo voice and a chorus.

Women's voices in general are divided into *soprano* (higher) and *alto* (lower) voices. The chorus includes both sopranos and altos, but since here they are all singing the same notes—singing in *unison*, as it is called—you cannot distinguish the sopranos from the altos (later on you can). The *range* of a soprano, that is, how high and how low she can sing, overlaps the range of an alto, which is what makes it possible for them to sing the same notes (Ex. 2-2).

In fact, the differences among various types of

women's voices (and among men's) are more a matter of timbre than of range. If you listen carefully, you can hear a third quality of voice briefly toward the middle of the chorus section (as shown in Ex. 2-1). It is a solo voice and therefore contrasts in timbre with the chorus. This solo voice happens to be singing in a lower part of the women's range, that is, in a different *register* than the soprano had in her opening solo (see Ex. 2-3); the difference in register makes the sound subtly different. Even more subtle are the differences in timbre that are due to the fact that this is a different voice type and a different person: this voice is a *mezzo-soprano* (Italian, *mezzo*, "middle"), one with a typically "darker" timbre than would be found in a higher soprano. Timbre often seems to be a matter of tone "color."

Different singers appear in different performances, of course. Each singer has his or her special timbre, just as everyone has in his speaking voice a special timbre, by which his friends can recognize him. But all performances of *Les Noces* will use the same general voice types, because the composer has so directed. Here are listed the types you will meet in *Les Noces* (see entry "voice type" in the Glossary, Appendix B, for a more general list of voice types).

	Solo voices	Chorus
Women	Soprano / Mezzo-soprano	Soprano / Alto
Men	Tenor / Bass	Tenor / Bass

The ranges of tenor and bass overlap just as do those of soprano and alto; and even where tenor and bass sing in the same register, they produce different timbres. The three voice timbres heard between the beginning and rehearsal number 4 (soprano solo, chorus, mezzo-soprano, chorus) are heard again in order between 4 and 9. Actually, the whole block of music from 1 through 4 is repeated between 4 and 8, but you might not notice that—you might only notice the repetition in terms of the voice types. Timbre is one of the obvious features by which the composer can immediately communicate an approximate sense of the structure. Later, on repeated hearings, you would be more likely to perceive the more refined aspects, such as exact returns of melody.

TIMBRE AND LINE. The voice timbres described so far present musical material in a form that can conveniently be called *line*. "Line" is a term we will use throughout the book, in several contexts.

When considered in the simplest way, line is intimately related to timbre. We already noticed how the First Tableau goes from a single solo timbre (soprano) to a complex combination of solo timbres (soprano, mezzo-soprano, tenor, bass) and chorus at the climax. It is as if the vocal lines at the beginning were replaced later by masses of sound at the climax; "mass" is not a word we will use in a specifically musical sense, but we will introduce other terms to

Example 2-2 Relation of soprano and alto ranges

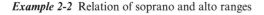

Higher

Lower

Soprano range

Alto range

Example 2-3   Registers within a soprano range

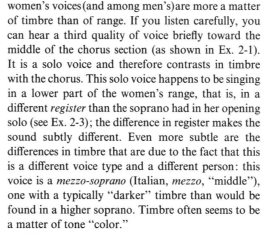

Range of a soprano

} A higher register

} A lower register

As used here, register means "part of the range." In a more general sense, "in a high register" means simply "high(er) in pitch," and "in a low register" means "low(er) in pitch."

help describe musical effects that contrast with line.

A line performed in a solo timbre is easy to follow. At the beginning, all the notes the soprano solo sings are linked into a line simply by the fact that she sings them one after another. You may or may not hear in these notes a tune you could imitate or remember; but you will hear them as a vocal line. Some of the same notes are scattered around the accompaniment provided by piano and percussion, but you probably do not hear a line in the accompaniment here, merely isolated notes. At rehearsal number 1, however, notes appear in the piano part with enough consistency of timbre to be heard easily as a line; the piano line duplicates, or *doubles*, the soprano line at that point.

Line is a concept more subtle than it may first appear, because it is a metaphorical concept. There is no real line in the music; there are only individual pitches. The ear connects the pitches it hears in many different ways, one of these ways being line. Example 2-4 represents the notes of the soprano's part by means of wedgelike marks. The connection into a line is represented by the line drawn through the wedges, going in general from left to right, but bending up or down to go through higher or lower pitches.

Such a line has a shape—a very important kind of shape for music. The line drawn in the example, however, is there only to call your attention to the fact that you hear a line in the music. Determine the qualities of the musical line from the way it sounds, not from the way it looks on the page. Listen to the soprano part several times while following Ex. 2-4 in order to understand how the diagram works.

The soprano's line is the form in which her music comes to us; on this line we can hang a number of other details that have to do with qualities of sound. Not all these details are important, but some of them are prominent and will have attracted your attention if you listened carefully.

MUSICAL DYNAMICS. In addition to singing in a high, bright timbre, the solo soprano sings very loudly and in a highly accented manner. Different degrees of intensity—loud and soft—come under the general heading of musical *dynamics*, which are most conveniently described by the standard Italian terms

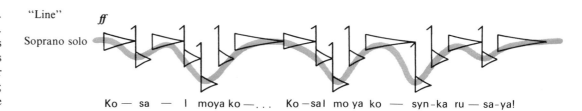

"Line" *ff*
Soprano solo

Ko — sa — I moya ko —. . . Ko —sal mo ya ko — syn-ka ru — sa-ya!

Detail: A wedge is shown for every note in the soprano part.

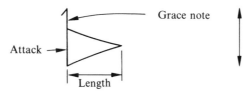

Grace note

Attack →

Wedges are placed higher or lower to indicate relative pitch.

Length

Example 2-4 Stravinsky, First Tableau:
Beginning of soprano line

listed here (some of these are by now in English usage).

Fortissimo	Very loud	*ff*
Forte	Loud	*f*
Mezzo-forte	Moderately loud	*mf*
Mezzo-piano	Moderately soft	*mp*
Piano	Soft	*p*
Pianissimo	Very soft	*pp*
Crescendo	Getting louder	cresc.
Decrescendo	Getting softer	decresc.
Diminuendo	Getting softer	dim.
Sforzando	Forcing (a sudden loud accent)	*sf*

Loud and soft—the two ends of a continuum—can be sometimes very important aspects of the shape of a piece. When the composer has chosen to make deliberate, consistent use of loud and soft, these qualities may be among the most significant features of a piece. Perception of loud and soft on an absolute scale is extremely dependent upon the conditions under which a listener hears a piece—obviously so, in the case of a recorded performance, but also (in more subtle ways) in a live performance. *Relative* effects of loud and soft are what we have to deal with.

ARTICULATION. The listener's impression of the soprano part is that the soloist is accenting all her

notes strongly; musicians say she is singing each note with a strong *attack*. The way a singer (or a player) attacks and releases notes affects us immediately. Even though we often cannot detect the precise details of what the soprano is doing to individual notes, still we are aware of the results of what she is doing, just as we are aware of the way a speaker articulates his words. Attack and release, which go under the heading *articulation*, are a prominent factor in the sound of a piece, and when they are used by the composer in a significant way, they play an important role in the shape of the piece.

One detail of the soprano's part you probably have noticed is the way certain notes are approached through another very quick subsidiary note—as if her voice were breaking (although the effect as intended is stylized, not realistic). These subsidiary notes are called *grace notes*, even though the effect here is not a graceful one; they are shown in Ex. 2-4 as little vertical marks attached to the notes they precede. So short that they do not affect the line, these grace notes merely intensify the attack, the feeling of accent.

COMBINED EFFECTS UP TO NUMBER 9. Changes in register, timbre, dynamics, and articulation can be matters of detail, but when such changes are synchronized, they add up to a gross change that is immediately perceptible, even though at first you may not be able to perceive the ingredients of the change. Listen again from the beginning up to 9, following Ex. 2-1, and notice the combined effect of factors we have considered separately.

When the chorus sings at 2, their choral timbre is in a lower register and mostly at a reduced dynamic level (piano); these features contrast with the high solo timbre of the soprano, who sang fortissimo. In addition, the chorus has accents only occasionally; but these are very strong accents, achieved by singing forte for a couple of notes and supported by blasts of sound from the accompaniment.

The other, softer notes are sung by the chorus in a detached kind of articulation called *staccato* (Italian, "detached"). The opposite of staccato is *legato* (Italian, "bound" or "connected"). Different performances of *Les Noces* might have different degrees of detachment at this point. Three different degrees of articulation—legato, slightly staccato, more staccato —are shown in Ex. 2-5. The mezzo-soprano line is somewhat more legato that that of the chorus.

For every section so far, the accompaniment provides a different kind of sound, helping to project the differences in voice types. Up to 1, the soprano solo is accompanied by isolated bits of sound; the thin accompaniment, with its sharply differentiated timbres of piano and cymbal, throws the solo voice into relief, making the whole sound dry and brittle. At 1, the solo is accompanied by a more continuous thrumming. When the chorus enters at 2, a subtle accompaniment of percussion in a lower register helps change the overall timbre. The mezzo-soprano

Example 2-5 Stravinsky, First Tableau, chorus at 2: Degrees of articulation

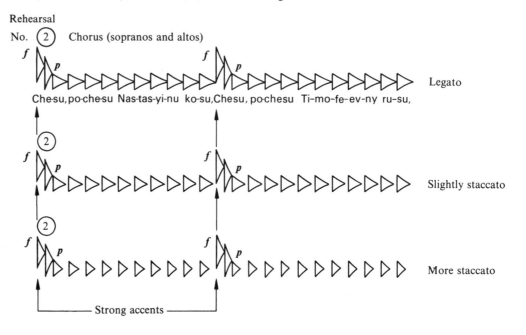

has no percussion accompaniment, the pianos doubling in a sonorous but straightforward way.

In addition to helping set off one voice type from another, the accompaniment reinforces the accents of the vocal line (as when the chorus sings at 2) or even provides accents of its own at various times. All these things the accompaniment does throughout the First Tableau; but, generally speaking, the accompaniment does not have its own sense of line, except

where it is merely doubling a vocal line (as that of the mezzo-soprano).

FROM 9 THROUGH THE CLIMAX. After 9, changes in voice types, as well as in some other qualities of sound, are more striking and occur more quickly. Listen from 9 through 17, following Ex. 2-6; or, better yet, listen from the beginning, so as to appreciate the change that takes place at 9, when the chorus enters.

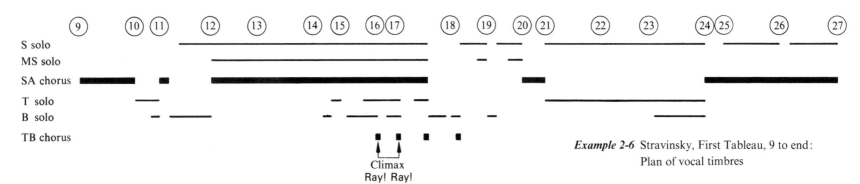

Example 2-6 Stravinsky, First Tableau, 9 to end: Plan of vocal timbres

Here the chorus of women sings not just one line in unison, but several lines at once—enough lines so that you probably cannot keep them distinct in your ear. The music is abruptly thicker. The division of the chorus into higher and lower groups of voices is now apparent, with sopranos singing the higher parts, altos the lower. All together they produce a rich, full sound that is very different from that of either the solo soprano or the solo mezzo-soprano. They sing in a relatively legato manner, with no strong accents, at a mezzo-forte level.

A special accent by the tambourine announces a new timbre—a solo tenor—at rehearsal number 10 (Ex. 2-6). This is the first time a male voice appears in the piece. He sings very legato, and his notes are bound even more tightly together by the way the syllables are placed. Example 2-7 shows the tenor line with the syllables as sung. When two or more notes are sung to a single syllable, they can be joined together by the singer in an especially smooth manner; such notes are said to be *slurred*. Curved lines called *slurs* show this super-legato effect in Ex. 2-7.

As the tenor repeats the close of his phrase, he is joined by the bass solo. Because both tenor and bass are here strong, solo timbres, you can easily follow their two distinct lines—whereas you could not so easily follow separate lines in the chorus of sopranos

and altos. Similarly, when the bass reenters at 11 (Ex. 2-6), you can follow both his line and that of the solo soprano, who soon joins him. Different both in timbre and range, the soprano and bass lines stand out in sharp contrast to each other. But the chorus, when it reenters at 12, is again a blended sound, having a unified timbre; only the top part is audible as a distinct line.

At 12, incidentally, the soprano and mezzo-soprano soloists are singing along with the top two choral parts. These solo timbres, elsewhere so distinctive, are blended with the chorus, so that only very close listening will detect their presence—and then only in certain performances.

The reinforcement of the chorus with solo voices is part of the continuing buildup of timbre that leads to the climax of the First Tableau. From solo soprano or unison chorus at the beginning, the music has moved first to a thicker choral sound, then to an enrichment of timbre through the addition of tenor and bass. Tenor has appeared in combination with bass, and bass with soprano. Soprano and mezzo-soprano have now joined the women's chorus, and that ensemble sings continuously to the climax. After 14, tenor and bass sing more and more, at first standing out in contrast to the women, then blending in.

The climax is reached at 16 and 17, with the great

shouts of "Ray! Ray!" ("Come! Come!"). The men's chorus joins in on these accented, sharply detached fortissimo sounds. Here the full vocal resources of the piece are used all together. Any sense of individual solo timbres is lost; instead we hear the full-bodied timbre of a mass chorus (Ex. 2-8). The shouts themselves are examples of *chords*: in Ex. 2-8 each chord is represented by a shaded block that includes several pitches sounding simultaneously.

We often use the term *tutti* (Italian, "all," "everyone") to describe this kind of full-bodied sound in opposition to solo timbres. The term "tutti" is relative: "everyone" means everyone who is singing or playing in a particular piece. In this case we use it to refer to all the singers, as distinct from one singer or a few. In a piece for string ensemble, we use "tutti" to mean all the strings, as opposed to, for example, a solo violin. In a piece for full orchestra, "tutti" means the whole orchestra, which includes a wide variety of instruments—strings, winds, and percussion. Note that solo parts seem to have a more distinctive timbre than tuttis. In a tutti, the individual differences of timbre are blended into a more neutral timbre.

FROM THE CLIMAX TO THE END OF THE TABLEAU.
After the climax, timbre changes continue to shape the piece, now providing greater variety. Shortly after rehearsal number 17, the tutti gives way abruptly to solo timbres—bass (joined briefly by basses from the chorus), then soprano and mezzo-soprano. Thereafter to the end of the Tableau, there are no more tuttis, so that the climax is left standing clear in the center of the Tableau. But increasingly intricate combinations of timbres serve to maintain interest after the climax.

At 21 (with a sudden reduction of dynamics to pianissimo) soprano and tenor soloists are combined, each with a distinct line. Later, they are joined by the solo bass, who sings a line exactly parallel to that of the tenor but lower in pitch. A distant murmuring accompaniment in pianos and percussion helps set the passage off from what preceded.

Finally, the music first assigned to the women's chorus returns; but this time the solo soprano sings simultaneously with the chorus, instead of in alter-

Example 2-7 Stravinsky, First Tableau, 10: Slurs

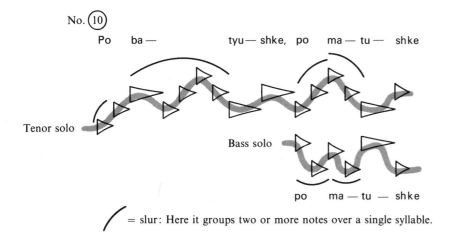

No. ⑩

Po   ba —   tyu — shke, po   ma — tu — shke

Tenor solo

Bass solo

po   ma — tu — shke

⟋ = slur: Here it groups two or more notes over a single syllable.

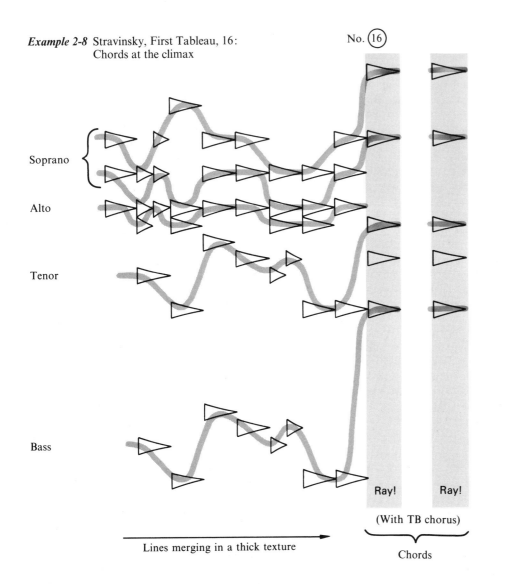

Example 2-8 Stravinsky, First Tableau, 16: Chords at the climax

No. ⑯

Soprano

Alto

Tenor

Bass

Ray!　Ray!

(With TB chorus)

Lines merging in a thick texture

Chords

nation. Here, too, the soprano's line is distinct; two lines—solo and choral—can be followed. The end of the Tableau is marked by a change in timbre from women's voices to men's, when the men's chorus enters at 27 for its first sustained appearance.

So far, you have listened without preconceptions for what is there in the First Tableau. We have tried, in the discussion, to make you aware of qualities of

sound many listeners absorb automatically. The qualities of sound have a large share in shaping this particular piece, so it has been possible to perceive the overall shape from even this preliminary survey.

Such a survey, no matter how casual, may tell you more than you might think. If you were to begin with the text of *Les Noces* (as given in Chapter 13), you would discover that in this first scene of a work about

a wedding in old rural Russia, the bride has sung her ritual lament with her bridesmaids, who then sing an invitation to the wedding, with a return to the lament at the end of the Tableau. This important information makes much of the context of the piece more concrete. It does not, however, make the purely musical shape more concrete, nor could one imagine just from the text how the music would actually sound.

Claudio Monteverdi (1567–1643)
"CHIOME D'ORO" (CANZONETTA)

In listening to a piece of music, a listener almost automatically takes stock of its different timbres. Even without thinking, he forms a rough idea about how many timbres can be distinguished throughout the piece and about which timbre or combination of timbres constitutes the main body of the piece.

In some pieces, certain timbres are clearly present throughout. In *Les Noces*, for example, the voices and the pianos are heard continuously, while the percussion instruments—even though prominent when used—are heard only intermittently. However, even though the pianos are heard continuously, they are not the leading part but are rather accompaniment to the voices.

In Monteverdi's "Chiome d'oro" (a kind of song called a *canzonetta*), voices are dominant, but instruments have a very prominent role; more than accompaniment, they have sections to play while the voices are silent. The instruments are more differentiated than in *Les Noces*, and in order to refer to them we need to introduce a few terms comparable to the terms used for voice types.

A PRELIMINARY CLASSIFICATION OF INSTRUMENTS.
Generally speaking, each instrument has its own characteristic timbre—characteristic enough that with practice you can learn to identify each instrument by its timbre. Many instruments, however, can produce more than one characteristic timbre, depending on how they are played. When played forte, for example, an instrument may have a very different timbre than when played piano; it may have very

different timbres when played in different registers, higher or lower; and its timbre may be altered by different kinds of attack. Finally, one instrument of a given kind sounds different in timbre from many instruments of that same kind all playing together.

Knowledge of as many instruments as possible, of their capabilities, ranges, and characteristic timbres under all the varying conditions just summarized, is an essential part of a composer's craft; such knowledge is called *instrumentation*, or—when referring to the combination of timbres—*orchestration*. From the listener's point of view, however, it makes less sense to approach timbre from a knowledge of the many instruments and conditions that produce the timbre, than to concentrate on perceiving the function of timbres—however produced—within the context of the piece being heard.

Actually you will meet various timbres in mixed combinations (as in an orchestra or instrumental ensemble) far more frequently than you will have the opportunity of absorbing the sound of a single solo instrument. The main problem a listener faces is understanding how timbres go together, not how they are produced separately. As far as identifying various instruments goes, you need to be able to name them only for purposes of discussion. It is usually sufficient to distinguish among *strings* (for example, violins or cellos), *woodwinds* (for example, flutes, oboes, clarinets), *brasses* (for example, trumpets, French horns), and *percussion*. The classification given here, although sketchy, will serve our purposes. The instruments listed in the next column are merely the most common representatives of the various classes. Many instruments—familiar as well as unfamiliar, do not fit well into this or any other classification. A saxophone is both a woodwind (reed) and a brass instrument. A piano is both a stringed instrument and—since the strings are struck by "hammers" —a percussion instrument.

Listen to the whole of "Chiome d'oro" to hear as many of the voices and instruments as you can. There are not many; and some of them are clearly audible, but others are less so. Notice that all the purely instrumental sounds used throughout the piece appear in the first minute of instrumental introduction that precedes the entry of the voices.

I. WOODWIND
　A. *Without reeds*
　　Piccolo
　　Flute
　　Recorder
　B. *Single reed*
　　Clarinet, bass clarinet
　　Saxophone
　C. *Double reed*
　　Oboe
　　English horn
　　Bassoon, contrabassoon
II. BRASS
　　Horn (French horn)
　　Trumpet, cornet
　　Trombone
　　Tuba
III. KEYBOARD
　　Piano
　　Clavichord
　　Harpsichord
　　Organ
IV. PERCUSSION
　A. *With pitch*
　　Timpani (kettledrums)
　　Xylophone
　　Vibraphone
　　Glockenspiel
　　Tubular bells
　　Celeste
　B. *Without pitch*
　　Tenor drum, bass drum
　　Tam-tam
　　Rattles, woodblocks
　　Gong, cymbals
　　Snare drum
V. STRINGED
　A. *Plucked and strummed*
　　Guitar
　　Lute
　　Harp
　B. *Bowed*
　　Violin
　　Viola
　　Cello (violoncello)
　　Double bass (contrabass, bass viol)

INSTRUMENTS IN THE INTRODUCTION. At the bottom of the sound a strong, distinctive timbre forms a line—a *bass line*, as if a bass voice were singing (Ex. 2-9). (The vocal term "bass" is often used to refer to the lowest sounding instrumental part.) This bass line is played by a stringed instrument (a cello).

Above the bass line things are not so clear. There are three distinct timbres, and at some times during the first minute two different timbres chase each other in two clearly perceptible lines. One of these lines is played by a stringed instrument (a violin), the other by a woodwind (a recorder). Each of these instruments plays only one note at a time; each produces a line as clear, as easy to follow, as the line of a solo voice. Considered by itself, each of these two lines is located in a single register or at most moves from one register to a neighboring one.

The third timbre is more difficult to localize. You may be most aware of it as a very high, almost bell-like timbre, above the violin and recorder. But the closer you listen, the more you will be aware that this third timbre does not form a clearly perceptible line (like violin or recorder) because of the complexity of each sound. Components of the sound seem to be distributed simultaneously through several registers, instead of in just one at a time, as is the case with either violin or recorder.

This third timbre actually consists of chords, which sound both above and below the violin and recorder lines. The timbre of the chords is produced by a harpsichord, which resembles a piano in external appearance but is an instrument whose strings are plucked (not struck) so that its timbre is closer to that of a guitar than a piano.

Sometimes it is easier to distinguish these four timbres than at other times; the same timbres go together in more than one subtle combination. These particular changes affect the violin and the recorder, the cello and the harpsichord remaining the same.

VOICES. Once you have the instrumental timbres of the introduction clearly in mind, listen to the whole piece, comparing the sound of the vocal sections to that of the instrumental ones. The first entrance of

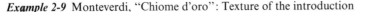

Example 2-9 Monteverdi, "Chiome d'oro": Texture of the introduction

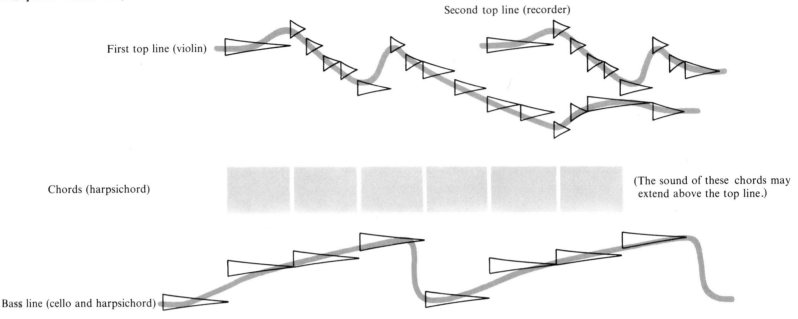

Second top line (recorder)

First top line (violin)

Chords (harpsichord)

(The sound of these chords may extend above the top line.)

Bass line (cello and harpsichord)

the voices produces the most striking change of timbre in the whole piece.

There are two voices, both high male ones; one is a tenor, the other a *countertenor*—a kind of voice infrequently met and one that varies greatly in timbre from one performance to another. The range of a countertenor extends above that of a tenor.

More important than the timbres of the individual voices, however, is their relation to each other and to the shape of the piece. The two voices go together very closely—so closely that it may at first be hard to distinguish them or to be sure how many there are. In this respect the vocal sections of the piece are different from the instrumental sections; in general, it is easier to keep distinct the two upper instrumental lines than the two vocal lines. Two factors are involved. First, timbre: the two voices are more alike in timbre than are the violin and recorder. Second, spacing: if the two vocal lines were played by violin and recorder instead of sung, they would still be very close—generally closer than the lines actually played by violin and recorder.

While the voices are singing, violin and recorder are silent; cello and harpsichord continue, accompanying the voices. The music alternates, in other words, between pairs of vocal and instrumental lines over the accompaniment.

MELISMAS. During the first vocal section a subtle change takes place—not a change in timbre, exactly, but still a change in the quality of the sound. The voices begin by singing one note for each syllable of text: "Chiome d'oro bel thesoro/tu mi leghi in mille modi."(Example 2-10 shows notes for the top voice: the countertenor.) Then, at the end of the word "modi" both voices sing a series of notes on the one syllable, the syllable "-di." A group of many notes (not just three or four) on one syllable is sometimes called a *melisma*; the passage can be called *melismatic* in opposition to the music before and after, which is *syllabic*. Both "melismatic" and "syllabic" apply to the relationship of text and music in a vocal part (not to instrumental parts). Sometimes (as in many places in *Les Noces*) the text setting is neither

melismatic nor strictly syllabic but instead consists of just a few notes to a single syllable here and there. In "Chiome d'oro," however, the contrast between syllabic and melismatic passages is marked; it tends to appear at the same point—toward the end—of each vocal section. Where the change to melismatic setting appears more than once in a section, it works together with other factors (yet to be discussed) to set that section off from the others.

The change from syllabic to melismatic setting is akin to a change from staccato to legato. No matter how performed, the notes in a syllabic passage are separated from each other by the consonants in a way that notes in a melisma are not separated. For example, a new syllable provides a fresh attack for a note even though it is the same pitch as the preceding note. A change from syllabic to melismatic setting is often very obvious, as in "Chiome d'oro." When it occurs in two or more voices simultaneously, it tends to link the voices more strongly together—especially when the voices are exactly synchronized in the syllabic portions, as they are here.

16

Top voice only (countertenor)

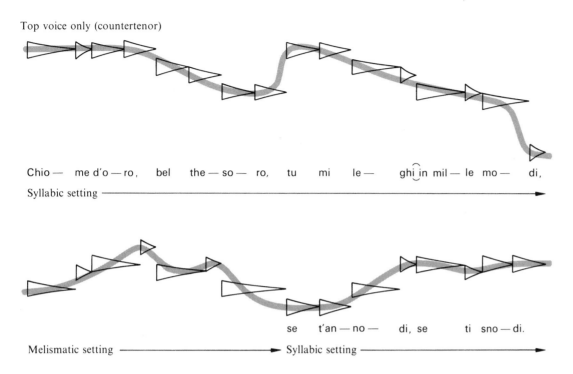

Chio — me d'o — ro, bel the — so — ro, tu mi le — ghi in mil — le mo — di,

Syllabic setting

se t'an — no — di, se ti sno — di.

Melismatic setting ———→ Syllabic setting

Example 2-10 Monteverdi, "Chiome d'oro": Syllabic and melismatic setting

Chiome d'oro, bel thesoro,
tu mi leghi in mille modi,
se t'annodi, se ti snodi.

Candidette perle elette,
se le rose che coprite,
discoprite mi ferite.

Vive stelle, che sì belle
e se vaghe risplendete,
se ridete m'ancidete.

Preziose, amorose,
coralline labbra amate,
se parlate mi beate.

O bel nodo per cui godo,
O soave uscir di vita,
O gradita mia ferita.

Tresses golden, gilded treasure, how you bind me
In a thousand modes: tied or untied, knotted
Or unknotted, done or undone, I am undone.

Clear perfected pearls, O gems of the elect! If those
Protecting roses covering them uncover them to
Your lover I, confounded, shall be wounded.

Living starlight, lovely charming rays and splendid,
Should you gaze in candid laughter, I disarmed,
    shall be slain.

And those lovely lips of coral,
If they, speaking, once address me, blessed I.

Knot of beauty, maze of wonder, bind me: through
    you I find
A sweet egress from living, a loveliness, my wound.

English translation © 1956 by Chester Kallman. Used by permission.

VOICES AND INSTRUMENTS IN THE OVERALL SHAPE.

As you can tell from even a first hearing of "Chiome d'oro," the two combinations, vocal and instrumental, alternate throughout in clearly defined sections. Indeed, the alternation of timbres is the most obvious feature of the shape of the piece. Listen again to the whole piece in order to keep track of the vocal and instrumental sections as sections, and to compare their relative lengths.

One of the charming features of "Chiome d'oro" is the deliberate disarray in order of the instrumental sections. The introduction is clear enough: there are three sections, each repeated (1, 1, 2, 2, 3, 3). Clear enough, we should say, after one has heard the whole piece a few times, for in the introduction the sections follow one another without a break. You may not be able to distinguish them clearly until you realize that first one and then another of these sections return between vocal sections, both marking off the vocal sections and being marked off by them. Once you are aware of the identity of the instrumental sections in the introduction, you may puzzle over the unexpected order in which they return. The whole plan of vocal and instrumental sections is shown in Ex. 2-11.

The alternation of voices and instruments helps make vivid the impression of relative length of the sections. The instrumental sections (1, 2, 3) are all the same length. Some of the vocal sections are the same length as the instrumental ones; some of the vocal sections, however, are longer, and with the help of repetition of material in successive vocal sections the ear hears the greater length as an extension beyond a norm. Example 2-11 shows the extended sections. The way of making the extension will be discussed soon; first, be sure you hear that these sections are extended and that the others are the normal ones.

Each vocal section presents one stanza of text. The musical length of a normal section is the length required for a relatively straightforward presentation of the text: the first, second, and fourth stanzas have no repetition of words and only one melisma. Listen to the whole piece while following the complete text, laid out in stanzas on this page.

In this particular piece, we should notice the

17

Example 2-11 Monteverdi, "Chiome d'oro": Plan of vocal and instrumental sections

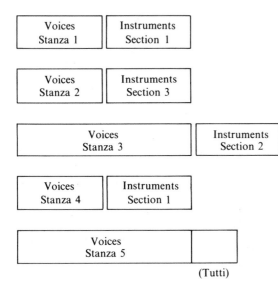

| Instruments Section 1 | Instruments Section 1 | Instruments Section 2 | Instruments Section 2 | Instruments Section 3 | Instruments Section 3 |

(Introduction)

| Voices Stanza 1 | Instruments Section 1 |

| Voices Stanza 2 | Instruments Section 3 |

| Voices Stanza 3 | Instruments Section 2 |

| Voices Stanza 4 | Instruments Section 1 |

| Voices Stanza 5 | |

(Tutti)

quality of sound of the poetry itself. Internal rhymes come thick and fast; it seems as though almost every sound in some lines of the poem was controlled by an overall idea of verbal sonority.

Chio-me d'o-ro	Kyoh-may daw-ro
bel the-so-ro	bel tay-saw-roh
tu mi le-ghi in	too mee lay-gin
mil-le mo-di	mee-lay maw-dee
se t'an-no-di	say tahn-naw-dee
se ti sno-di	say tee snaw-dee

Clearly the composer felt the verbal sonority was an important aspect of the piece, for he took pains that the quality of sound of the words should be plainly audible through the syllabic setting and the synchronized movement of the two voices.

As you become aware of the length of the normal stanza, you will sense more acutely the extension in the third stanza. This vocal section is more than

twice as long as usual. At the point where we would expect it to end, another melisma is tacked on; then another syllabic phrase; then another, even longer melisma; and yet another syllabic phrase. The syllabic phrases repeat the last line of text. The section seems much longer than it actually is because of the contrasts (syllabic and melismatic) and their simple block-by-block addition. In any case, this section stands out in the piece as the most extended section—aside from the opening introduction, which is probably perceived as six sections rather than one.

The fifth stanza is also extended; here, however, the usual melisma is suppressed in favor of the exclamation "O." Repetitions of text follow immediately, and only then the melismatic extension. On the last repetition of text, the upper instruments, violin and recorder, join the voices; this, the only tutti sound of the piece, is reserved as something different with which to close.

The listener can hear and follow several distinct timbres and can come to understand their various functions in a piece of music, without knowing the names of the instruments that produce them, without even having heard them—or of them—before. The ensemble for "Chiome d'oro" (violin, recorder, harpsichord, cello, tenor, and countertenor) is not a standard performing group in any standard repertory. It includes two timbres (harpsichord, countertenor) that are unfamiliar to many listeners. Yet the musical shape of the whole piece is just as clear as if the timbres were standard and familiar.

In dealing with "Chiome d'oro" (as with *Les Noces*), you went through only the first stages of getting to know the piece. With the basic shape of the piece in mind, you are now in a position to grasp other aspects—in particular, aspects related to the meaning of the text. Part Two of this book will explore relationships between text and music in greater detail.

Ludwig van Beethoven (1770–1827)

SYMPHONY NO. 7
PRESTO/ASSAI MENO PRESTO
(THIRD MOVEMENT)

In "Chiome d'oro," contrasts of timbres expressed themselves at a relatively high level, marking off sections of the whole piece. There was plenty of time to hear and identify each new combination of timbres as it came along. As further study, we will identify timbres as they change at lower levels—at the level of phrase or of subphrase. Identifying, again, is not a matter of naming but of hearing clearly and distinctly the differences between one combination of timbres and a contrasting one.

We have already discussed the Presto (third movement) from Beethoven's Symphony No. 7 at its highest level, the level of sectional divisions (Ex. 2-12). Now we will follow changes in timbre and other qualities of sound throughout the Presto and the Assai meno presto.

Example 2-12 Beethoven, Presto/Assai meno presto: High-level sectional divisions

| Presto | Assai meno presto | Presto | Assai meno presto | Presto |

(In Chapter 1 these sections were labeled *A B A B A*.)

Within the Presto itself, it is possible to perceive (without reference to any particular aspect, such as timbre) an overall shape, produced simply by the repetition of music. The first brief section, lasting

Example 2-13 Beethoven: Sections within the Presto and Assai meno presto

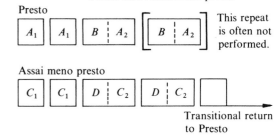

Presto

| A_1 | A_1 | B | A_2 | B | A_2 |

This repeat is often not performed.

Assai meno presto

| C_1 | C_1 | D | C_2 | D | C_2 | |

Transitional return to Presto

only a few seconds, is immediately and exactly repeated (section A_1 in Ex. 2-13). The repeat is followed by a longer section, B, which in turn is followed—without a break—by something that proceeds much as A_1 did. We will identify some of the subtle differences, specifically those in timbre, that make section A_2 different from A_1. The Assai meno presto has a sectional plan similar to that of the Presto, except that group D C_2 is always repeated (the repeat of B A_2 is often not performed).

THE A_1 SECTION OF THE PRESTO. After you can follow the sectional plan of the Presto shown in Ex. 2-13, listen for changes of timbre, dynamics, and articulation in the short A_1 section, which is immediately repeated. You will notice first, perhaps, the high contrast of dynamics, a contrast that by itself shapes the section. The Presto begins forte, but the opening blast is very brief, being followed immediately by a much softer passage (piano). After a crescendo, the forte returns to close the short section. A very simple framelike shape results from the use of dynamics (Ex. 2-14a).

At the beginning of *Les Noces*, there was no necessary connection between degrees of loudness and the number of performers; the solo soprano sang forte, while the women's chorus responded more softly. In Beethoven's Presto, however, there happens to be a

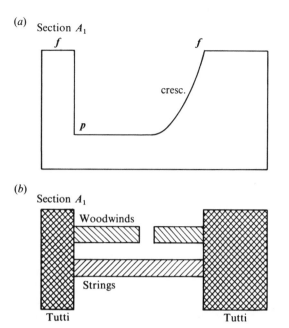

(a) Section A_1

(b) Section A_1

Example 2-14 Beethoven, Presto, section A_1: Dynamics and timbre

close connection between dynamics and the grouping of performers—in this case, the instruments of the orchestra.

In section A_1, the opening forte is played by the whole orchestra, producing a characteristic orchestral tutti sound. The reduction to piano is accomplished not just by directing the instruments to play softly, but by actually reducing the number of instruments to selected woodwinds (flutes and oboes) and strings. The crescendo, when it comes, is produced in part by again augmenting the instruments by adding the rest of the winds (both woodwinds and brass). The brass in particular adds body to the center of the sonority, as well as bite and brightness (Ex. 2-14b).

For one brief moment in the softer part of section A_1, the woodwinds drop out completely, leaving the strings sounding alone. This moment may be hard to detect on a recording, for during this passage the woodwinds play the same melody as the violins. The woodwinds, however, are playing in a range different from that of the violins—the flutes higher, the bassoons lower. When the woodwinds pause, you may hear a slight discontinuity in the line, as suggested in Ex. 2-15.

When woodwinds and strings are both playing, their melodies run exactly parallel. In Ex. 2-15, the parallel lines indicate the two melodies (the dotted lines show the two lines leaping upward between two

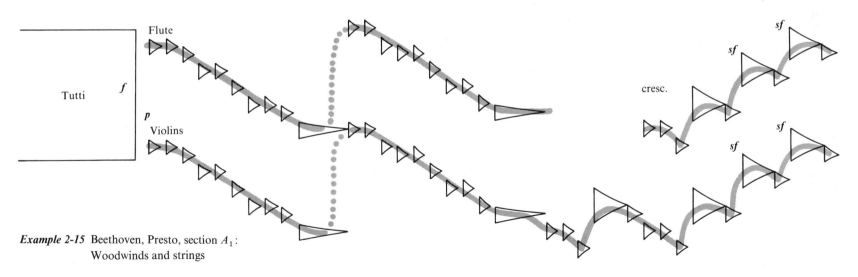

Example 2-15 Beethoven, Presto, section A_1: Woodwinds and strings

subphrases). The pause in the woodwinds provides a freshening of the timbre—a detail, but of a potentially important kind.

Several different kinds of articulation occur in the A_1 section. You can hear them all with the help of Ex. 2-16, which shows the notes (but without any up-and-down placement for pitch) for the leading line throughout the A_1 section. You may hear this line in tutti, winds, or strings, but it is always at the top of the sound.

The opening tutti consists of two presentations of a simple slurred pattern (Ex. 2-16): the second and third notes are slurred together, as are the fifth and sixth. The effect of such slurring is more apparent when compared with notes that are not slurred—as in the softer passage immediately following, for woodwinds and strings. Here the notes are staccato, no two being connected by slurs. The only difference made in the softer passage is between the many short notes and the two longer ones; this is a difference of rhythm, not articulation. The contrast in articulation between the two passages reinforces the contrasts in dynamics and timbre.

At the moment the strings sound alone, another slurred pattern appears (Ex. 2-16). This pattern is repeated several times, at first in alternation with three staccato notes, then by itself; it is given very strong accents. Everything about the use of the

slurred pattern at this point gives impetus to the crescendo welling up in the orchestra.

The A_1 section is brief; its features go by so fast it may be difficult at first to hear all the details discussed. Once you have these details in mind, however, you will find the rest of the Presto much easier to follow, for its changes in timbre, dynamics, and articulation are often leisurely and more obvious.

NOTES AN OCTAVE APART. At the very beginning of the B section is an excellent example of a puzzling phenomenon—the appearance of what seem to be the same notes in different registers. Listen to the beginning of section B while following Ex. 2-17; the example is very short. In the opening phrase, the same pattern of notes appears four times, as numbered 1 through 4 in the diagram. We say instinctively, "the same notes," even though it is obvious that the three notes at 1 are *not* exactly the same as the three notes at 2 (or 3 or 4). The three notes are higher in pitch at each numbered appearance: they appear in successively higher registers. Yet something about the four appearances is the same, something important. The three notes at 2 are very similar to those at 1—much more similar than any other notes *near* those at 2. (A musician can demonstrate this for you at a piano.) It is as if the notes at group 1 were sung in a bass register, the notes at 2 in a tenor

register, the notes at 3 in an alto register, and those at 4 in a soprano register; yet all voices would be singing, in some sense, "the same notes." This curious effect has called forth comment from theorists since the days of Pythagoras, the ancient Greek philosopher—if not from even earlier times.

The technical term *octave* is useful as a label for the distance in pitch between groups 1 and 2, 2 and 3, 3 and 4. Each note in group 2 is an *octave higher* than its counterpart in group 1. Notes an octave apart sound "the same"—not exactly the same because one is higher, but "the same" in the special sense just described. The two lines shown in Ex. 2-15—one in woodwinds, one in strings—are an octave apart; the woodwinds are an octave higher than the strings. When notes an octave apart are combined in this fashion, they often sound so much "the same" that we seem to hear only one note or one line; but that note or line has a different timbre than a note or line sounding without its octave.

At the end of section A_2 the same slurred pattern just studied occurs again, first in successively higher octaves, just as in Ex. 2-17, then in all of these octaves simultaneously for four more times with yet another octave added at the top in the winds. (For complete accuracy, we should note that another octave *below* is sounded at group 1 and also in the reiterated simultaneous octaves, but this octave is not easy to

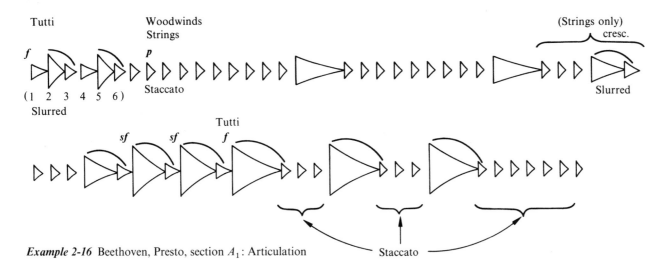

Example 2-16 Beethoven, Presto, section A_1: Articulation

discern because of the timpani sounding against it.) The simultaneous octaves occur in conjunction with the great tutti that ends the first presentation of the Presto, with the simple group of three notes resonating through the entire depth of the orchestra and culminating in the single long note that leads to the Assai meno presto.

You can profitably listen to the whole Presto just for the sake of hearing these octave passages at the beginning of the *B* section and the end of the A_2 section. In ways we cannot discuss yet, these passages are important for the shape of the whole; Beethoven used the duplication in octaves to make a point.

CHANGES OF TIMBRE IN B AND A₂. The following discussion will go through the *B* section and the start of A_2, taking up all the significant changes in timbre. Examples 2-18, 2-19, and 2-20 include all this material in order.

At the beginning of the *B* section, the fourfold repetition of the slurred pattern (Ex. 2-17) is followed by three distinctly different combinations of timbres; these combinations follow one another in progres-

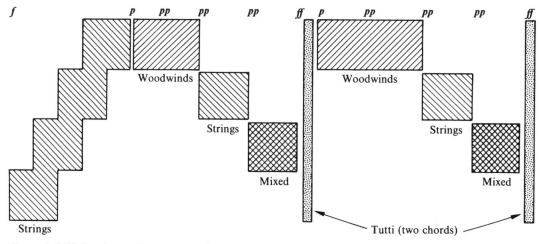

Example 2-18 Beethoven, Presto, start of section *B*: Timbre

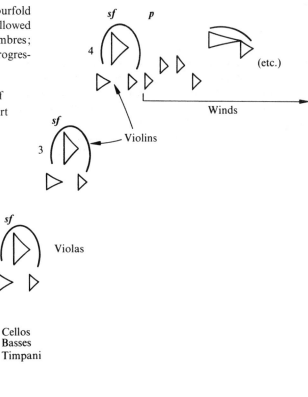

Example 2-17 Beethoven, Presto, beginning of section *B*: Notes an octave apart

Same notes repeated in four different registers

sively *lower* registers (but not at the distance of an octave). First comes a phrase for woodwinds alone (flutes and clarinets). This very distinctive combination of timbres is easily identified, standing out sharply from its surroundings (Ex. 2-18). The phrase is first piano, then pianissimo, in sharp dynamic contrast to the preceding forte. The next combination is strings, also pianissimo. Finally comes a mixed group consisting of horn and bassoons in a middle register and cellos and basses in a low register. The passage is punctuated by two tutti chords, fortissimo, then the succession of timbres is repeated. This part of the Presto, from the beginning of section *B*, presents the clearest examples of the different string timbres (in the four ascending groups), as well as the purest expression of woodwinds, encountered so far in this book.

The next stretch of the *B* section includes the combination of a solo woodwind (oboe) against string accompaniment (Ex. 2-19); bassoons are also sounding, sometimes doubling, sometimes accompanying. The timbre of the solo oboe easily cuts through the sound of the thirty or forty instruments accompanying it (that is, all the stringed instruments and the bassoons). As mentioned before (page 13), solo timbres have a much more distinctive quality than groups of timbres.

You can also hear easily the entrance of the flute playing along with the oboe. First the flute sounds below the oboe, then the oboe below the flute, with very subtle effects upon the resulting timbre. While this is going on, however, a torrential crescendo is building up in the orchestra, and soon solo timbres are obliterated in a return of the tutti sound. This marks the beginning of the A_2 section.

The music of section A_2 is similar to that of A_1; but first the orchestration is different, then something is interpolated. The whole passage is a good exercise for practice in tenaciously following a line as it skips from one timbre to another—as you might, watching a play, follow a speech delivered by several different actors alternating in rapid succession.

At the start of section A_2, focus on the first violins, through the clamor of the tutti. The line in the first violins descends twice, sounding—in melody, though not in timbre—like the beginning of the A_1 section (Ex. 2-20). The next passage has been added to the material as it appeared in A_1: now the woodwinds (flute and oboe) are heard *ascending* twice; the passage is soft. The line has passed from violins to woodwinds. (In some performances, your attention might be drawn during this soft passage to the bassoons, which echo the descending lines just played forte by the violins; in most performances, however, these bassoons are not prominent.)

Now the line returns to the violins, which are playing their slurred pattern (Ex. 2-16); the strings play alone for a moment, as in section A_1. Then, instead of woodwinds joining the strings (as before in A_1), the woodwinds play alone while the strings pause. The result is a sudden discontinuity in timbre right in the middle of a phrase—an arresting effect.

What happens here in a relatively clear way, happens frequently in more obscure or complex ways, when a single line of melody is presented in varying timbres. The ear must be trained to listen over and through changes of timbre, while taking note of their immediate effects.

The remainder of the A_2 section is more like A_1, except for the great octave passage at the end, already discussed. After you understand the details of B and A_2 that we have discussed, listen straight through the Presto while following Ex. 2-14 (or 2-16), then 2-18, 2-19, and 2-20. You should eventually gain a sense of unity of timbre that overrides

Example 2-19 Beethoven, Presto, section *B* (cont.): Timbre

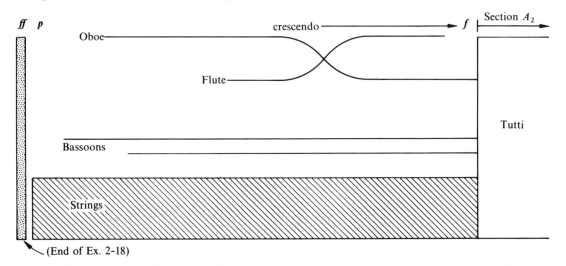

(End of Ex. 2-18)

all the varied details pointed out in the Presto and contrasts with the new timbres characteristic of the next section.

TIMBRES IN THE ASSAI MENO PRESTO. The change at the start of the Assai meno presto is striking, partly because a combination of timbres new to the movement is introduced, partly because the new combination persists for a relatively long time. The new combination consists mainly of mixed winds (clarinets, horns, bassoons—Ex. 2-21). They make a smoothly blended ensemble; only with difficulty can the ear separate and follow the different instruments.

Against the compact combination of winds, the violins sustain a single long high note—actually, two long notes an octave apart, another instance in which the two notes are "the same," or so similar that we seem to hear only one. In Ex. 2-21, the upper violin note, in a high register, is represented by a solid line. The lower violin note (an octave lower) is shown by a dotted line. Here, as before, the octaves stress an important note.

Soon the winds are increased, first by the addition of oboes to the original group, then by the flutes answering the enlarged group. A dialog between different performance groups (in this case flutes

against the other winds) is sometimes called *antiphony* ("sounding against"); the flutes here are said to be sounding in an *antiphonal* manner.

With slight changes, the wind timbre combination continues through the *D* section. Then, after a crescendo from the prevailing piano to a fortissimo (for the start of C_2), the tutti plays what the winds played at first, while the trumpets blare out the long note previously sustained by the violins. Trumpet

Example 2-21 Beethoven, Assai meno presto: Timbre

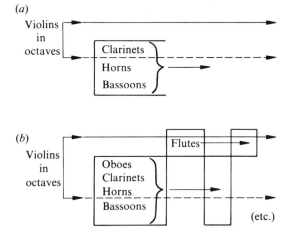

Example 2-20 Beethoven, Presto, start of section A_2: Timbre

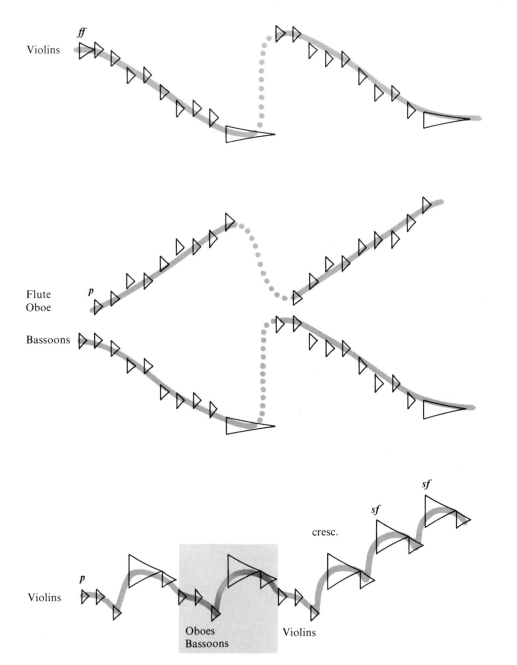

timbre is very bright and resonant; two trumpet parts in octaves make a full sound almost as rich as a tutti. In some performances, you will hear the brazen rattle characteristic of brasses when they attack a note fortissimo—as at the quick repetitions between phrases of the tutti. This rattle is an example of certain aspects of timbre that, while seemingly not "musical" in themselves, add immeasurably to the *éclat* of a musical sound.

Between the end of the Assai meno presto (section C_2, the second time) and the resumption of the Presto (section A_1) there is a soft transition. The strings play in sustained chords, while a solo horn reiterates a simple slurred pattern.

DYNAMICS IN THE SECOND PRESTO. The second presentation of the Presto (see the plan in Ex. 2-12) is the same as the first, except for some changes in dynamics. In the first A_1 section, everything is as it was. But in the second A_1 section, Beethoven directs all the performers to play piano—not just in the usual places but throughout, including the tutti passages that frame the A_1 section. In the B section as well, the short tutti blasts are now pianissimo. There is nothing louder than piano until the crescendo to fortissimo for the return of A_2. When they were fortissimo, the short tutti blasts in the B section had the effect of reminding us of the massive orchestral power latent throughout much of the movement, ready to erupt at any moment. When even these brief blasts are suppressed, as they are throughout the middle of the second Presto, the effect is even more ominous.

Mario Davidovsky (1934–   )

SYNCHRONISMS NO. 3, FOR CELLO AND ELECTRONIC SOUNDS (ORIGINAL VERSION)

In the pieces discussed so far, differences of timbre have often helped mark off the larger sections of a piece. In Davidovsky's *Synchronisms No. 3 for Cello and Electronic Sounds*, the sectional structure is much less clear; but on the other hand the interplay between two kinds of sound—string and electronic—provides much of the content of the piece.

This work is performed as a duet between a cellist

23

and a tape recorder, playing a tape on which the composer has recorded sounds generated by electronic means. In a concert performance, it is relatively easy to keep track of the two kinds of sounds, since the listener can coordinate by observation the cello's sounds with the cellist's gestures; indeed, in line and rhythm the cello part has a very gestic quality. In listening to a recorded performance, however, it may be more difficult to distinguish the cello from the electronic sounds on the tape. Listen to the whole piece very carefully several times to identify the two kinds of sound.

The distinction is made more difficult (as you will quickly discover on listening) by the behavior of the cello on the one hand and that of the tape on the other. The cello produces a great variety of sounds, including some you might not expect. The tape, for its part, sometimes imitates the cello. While it sometimes succeeds in resembling the cello's "gesture," the tape almost always retains its characteristic electronic quality; but you may have to listen closely to catch the difference.

Once you can distinguish the cello from the tape, try to hear how the piece is laid out in terms of the kinds of sounds, as suggested in Ex. 2-22. Since the cello plays practically all the time, while the tape plays intermittently, the cello might seem clearly dominant. However, even though the cello often leads the dialog (especially in starting off after a pause), the tape is not merely a passive background and sometimes shows a strength of response that surpasses the cello.

Determining sections is not a completely objective matter in this piece. As shown in Ex. 2-22, we have divided it into five sections, using different aspects as bases for the division. Section 1 runs up to the first entrance of the tape, hence consists of a monolog for cello. Besides the change of timbre at the tape's entrance, there seems to be a certain finality in the cello's part just before this entrance, marking the end of a section.

Sections 2 and 3 conclude with a long note for cello followed by a long pause. (There are other long notes and other pauses, but these seem to be the most decisive.) The end of section 4 is marked not by such a pause, but rather by a feeling of return

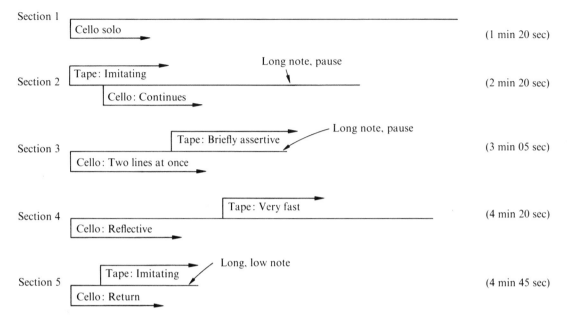

Example 2-22 Davidovsky, Synchronisms No. 3: Sectional plan

to the cello's opening monolog of section 1. The return is not exact; unlike section 1, the tape joins in but there is just enough similarity to provide the feeling of return and with it a fifth section.

In the overall shape of this piece, the content of the sections is more important than their divisions, and the content can be heard most easily in terms of the relationship between the cello and the tape. Each of these two kinds of sound seems to acquire an identity, possibly even a personality, as the piece proceeds; each seems to respond to the other in well-defined but varying ways.

The cello establishes its identity in its monolog during the opening 1 minute and 20 seconds. In this brilliant, flamboyant passage, the cello sets forth such a stunning display of timbres as to make further exploration seem superfluous. The effect of flamboyance results from compressing such a wide variety of sounds into a relatively short time. The cello plays very low notes and very high ones; very long notes and extremely short ones; very loud notes (not trusting ordinary indications, the composer writes *fff* and *ffff*), and barely audible notes.

At one point, the cellist neither bows nor plucks, but simply presses the fingers of his left hand down hard on the strings to evoke a ghost of a normal sound. Plucked (*pizzicato*) notes often alternate with notes bowed in the normal manner. More unusual sounds result from bowing with the wooden part of the bow instead of the hair, which produces a peculiarly brittle sound, or from bowing on an unusual part of the strings to make squeaky sounds in a much higher register. During one intense series of pizzicatos, the performer is instructed to knock on the instrument with his hand. On other pizzicato notes, he performs a *glissando* ("slide"). What is remarkable about the cello's opening monolog is the rapidity with which these effects follow one another— a profusion of utterance, as if the cello were determined to say everything there was to say on the subject.

One aspect of the pitch organization of the piece can be discussed briefly here under the heading "quality of sound." Most of the sounds in the piece have a determinate pitch (although some—such as the knock—may not). But more important is the fact that the pitch of some notes is much more perceptible than that of others, so much more as to constitute a real difference in quality of sound. The very long notes (especially when they are very loud) impress their "pitchness" upon the ear, while the extremely rapid notes (and the scratchy ones) often scuttle by, leaving little or no impression of pitch.

After the cello has come to its forceful conclusion at the end of section 1, the electronic sounds commence with relative diffidence. The cello soon joins in (after such an opening, it could hardly be expected to remain silent for long); in fact, the tape seems to be imitating the cello. At any rate, together they reproduce some of the effects of section 1, and the dialog between them is intense. At the end of the section, the cello introduces a kind of sound new to the argument, a sweetly persuasive legato.

Purely in terms of the kind of sound, then, a subtle shift in the roles of cello and tape has taken place. The cello's new, softer tone persists through some of section 3, although other sounds appear, too: shortly after the start of section 3 the cello briefly plays two lines at once. Then, after a very sweet, very high note (in seeming harmony with the tape), a brief but animated passage follows, in which the tape seems more insistent, perhaps more independent, and certainly more percussive. However, the section is ended by the cello, recalling softly some earlier sounds.

Section 4 is begun by the cello in its most reflective mood; only occasional strong pizzicato notes recall its original vehemence. The tape seems to remain silent longer than usual; but the tape's response, when it comes, is profuse, soon drowning the cello in a flood of rapid, high, chattering sounds. The cello plays rapid pizzicato notes of its own, but clearly the tape dominates in the production of this kind of sound. The dynamic level of the passage is not very loud, but the competition between tape and cello seems to be at its most intense.

From one section to the next, the relationship between the two kinds of sound has gradually increased in complexity. This relationship, and the roles of the cello and the tape, could be expressed or interpreted in various ways; but, however they are interpreted, perception of the relationship makes possible a grasp of the sense of the piece.

In section 5 the roles of the cello and the tape become even more closely intertwined. It is difficult to tell exactly what is going on. By returning to sounds from its opening monolog, the cello seems to reassert its original leadership. By joining in immediately, the tape, now imitating the cello more closely than ever, seems determined to maintain a dialog between equals. But what happens on the very low note just before the end? And does one or the other have the last word, or are they completely merged at the end? Starting from two opposed elements, the dialectic of the piece seems to have led, indeed, to a synchronism.

Exercises for further listening

I. BEETHOVEN: SYMPHONY NO. 7. POCO SOSTENUTO (INTRODUCTION)

Listen from the beginning up to the entrance of the fast, rising figures. Answer questions 1 through 5.

1. The first four sounds heard in the Poco sostenuto involve
___ a. A sudden change of dynamics from soft to loud (*pf*)
___ b. A sudden change of dynamics from loud to soft (*fp*)
___ c. A gradual crescendo
___ d. A gradual decrescendo

1. b

2. The loud-soft (*fp*) dynamic pattern
___ a. Does not occur again in the beginning of the Poco sostenuto
___ b. Is immediately repeated one time
___ c. Is immediately repeated several times

2. c

3. The loud (forte) passages in this opening section are played by
___ a. Strings only ___ b. Woodwinds only ___ c. Brasses only ___ d. Tutti

3. d

4. The soft (piano) passages in this opening section are played principally by   **4.** b
_____ **a.** Strings   _____ **b.** Woodwinds and horns
_____ **c.** Trumpets and percussion   _____ **d.** Tutti

5. The slow, four-note figure that is heard throughout this passage   **5.** b
_____ **a.** Always carries the same timbre, because it is played by the same group of
instruments
_____ **b.** Moves around from instrument to instrument, with a resulting change in timbre
_____ **c.** Has no recognizable timbre

Listen through the section with the fast rising figures. Answer questions 6 through 11.

6. In this section, the first large change in dynamics is   **6.** b
_____ **a.** A rapid decrescendo, to _pp_
_____ **b.** A rapid crescendo, to _ff_
_____ **c.** A rapid alternation between piano and forte

7. Before and after the crescendo to _ff_, the rising scale figures are played by   **7.** c
_____ **a.** Winds   _____ **b.** Brasses
_____ **c.** Strings   _____ **d.** Tutti

8. During the crescendo to _ff_,   **8.** c
_____ **a.** Only the strings play
_____ **b.** The strings drop out and only the winds play
_____ **c.** The winds join forces with the strings

9. Just after the crescendo, beginning with the point of arrival at the _ff_, the slow four-note figure   **9.** a
from the opening is heard again, played by
_____ **a.** Strings only
_____ **b.** Woodwinds only
_____ **c.** Strings and woodwinds alternately

10. In addition to the slow four-note figure and the fast rising figure, a new sonority—sustained   **10.** a
chords—is heard in the
_____ **a.** Woodwinds and horns   _____ **b.** Brasses   _____ **c.** Strings

11. At the end of this section there is a change of dynamics   **11.** b
_____ **a.** From _p_ to _ff_   _____ **b.** From _ff_ to _p_
_____ **c.** From _ff_ to _fff_   _____ **d.** From _p_ to _ppp_

Listen to the new tuneful interlude, until the fast rising figures begin again. Answer questions 12 through 16.

12. The tune of the interlude occurs twice. At first it is played by   12.   a
___ **a.** Woodwinds   ___ **b.** Brass   ___ **c.** Strings   ___ **d.** Tutti

13. Its accompaniment is played by   13.   d
___ **a.** Woodwinds only
___ **b.** Strings only
___ **c.** Horns only
___ **d.** Woodwinds and strings

14. In its second occurrence, the melody is played by   14.   c
___ **a.** Woodwinds   ___ **b.** Brass   ___ **c.** Strings   ___ **d.** Tutti

15. The accompaniment is played by   15.   c
___ **a.** Woodwinds only
___ **b.** Strings only
___ **c.** Strings and woodwinds
___ **d.** Tutti

16. The dynamics in this interlude   16.   d
___ **a.** Remain loud throughout
___ **b.** Remain soft throughout
___ **c.** Remain loud until the end of the interlude, then decrease suddenly
___ **d.** Remain soft until the end of the interlude, then increase suddenly

Listen to the passage with fast, rising figures, between the two interludes. Answer questions 17, 18, and 19.

17. The entire passage is played by   17.   d
___ **a.** Woodwinds and percussion
___ **b.** Woodwinds and brass
___ **c.** Strings and brass
___ **d.** Tutti

18. The dynamic level   18.   c
___ **a.** Remains loud throughout
___ **b.** Remains soft throughout
___ **c.** Remains loud until the end of the passage, where a decrescendo occurs
___ **d.** Remains soft until the end of the passage, where a crescendo occurs

19. The slow four-note figure from the opening is now heard   **19.** d
___ **a.** In the woodwinds only   ___ **b.** In the brass and percussion only
___ **c.** In the strings only   ___ **d.** In all the groups of instruments

Listen to the second interlude, to the end of the Poco sostenuto. Answer questions 20, 21, and 22.

20. When the melody of the interlude first appears this time, it is played by   **20.** a
___ **a.** Woodwinds   ___ **b.** Strings
___ **c.** Woodwinds and strings in alternation   ___ **d.** Brass

21. In its second (shortened) appearance, the melody is played by   **21.** b
___ **a.** Woodwinds   ___ **b.** Strings
___ **c.** Woodwinds and strings in alternation   ___ **d.** Brass

22. At the end of the Poco sostenuto, as the musical material gradually breaks up, the principal   **22.** c
tone color is that of
___ **a.** Woodwinds   ___ **b.** Strings
___ **c.** Woodwinds and strings in alternation   ___ **d.** Brass

Listen to the entire Poco sostenuto. Answer questions 23 and 24.

23. The two principal groups of instruments in this Introduction are the   **23.** c
___ **a.** Woodwinds and brass   ___ **b.** Woodwinds and percussion
___ **c.** Woodwinds and strings   ___ **d.** Brass and percussion
___ **e.** Brass and strings

24. The first two large crescendos lead up to   **24.** b
___ **a.** The beginnings of the two interludes
___ **b.** The two repeats of the opening material (with fast rising figures)
___ **c.** Neither of these

II. WAGNER: PRELUDE TO TRISTAN UND ISOLDE

Listen to the first phrase group at beginning of the Prelude. Answer questions 1, 2, and 3.

1. In this section of the Prelude   **1.** b
___ **a.** The sound is continuous, without internal groupings
___ **b.** There are several groups of sounds

2. The sounds are heard as separate groups because

____ **a.** There are pauses between the groups

____ **b.** There is a change of the quality of sound from each group to the next

____ **c.** Both *a* and *b*

____ **d.** Neither *a* nor *b*

2. c

3. How many groups of sounds are there?

____ **a.** Three ____ **b.** Seven ____ **c.** Five ____ **d.** Ten

3. b

Listen to groups 1 through 3. Use the following diagram as a guide to groupings. Answer questions 4 through 12.

1	2	3	4	5	6	7

4. Group 1 consists of

____ **a.** One timbre in one register

____ **b.** Two separate timbres in one register

____ **c.** Two separate timbres in two separate registers

4. c

5. The two timbres in group 1

____ **a.** Start together and end together

____ **b.** Begin separately and end together

____ **c.** Begin separately and end separately, overlapping in the middle

5. c

6. The first timbre in group 1 is

____ **a.** Strings ____ **b.** Brass ____ **c.** Woodwinds ____ **d.** Tutti

6. a

7. This string timbre is in a

____ **a.** Very high register

____ **b.** Very low register

____ **c.** Medium register

7. c

8. The second timbre, which overlaps the first, is

____ **a.** Strings ____ **b.** Brass ____ **c.** Woodwinds ____ **d.** Tutti

8. c

9. The woodwind melody extends

____ **a.** Higher in pitch than the preceding strings

____ **b.** Lower in pitch than the preceding strings

9. a

10. Groups 2 and 3   **10.** a
____ **a.** Have the same timbre pattern as group 1
____ **b.** Have different timbre patterns than group 1

11. The register of groups 1 through 3 as a whole   **11.** b
____ **a.** Steadily descends   ____ **b.** Steadily rises   ____ **c.** Stays the same

12. The dynamic pattern within each of the three groups is   **12.** c
____ **a.** *p*, growing steadily softer to *pp*
____ **b.** *pp*, growing steadily louder to *ff*
____ **c.** *pp*, increasing towards the middle of the group and growing softer towards the end

Listen to groups 4 through 6. Answer questions 13 through 18.

13. Groups 4 through 6 differ from the end of group 3 in   **13.** c
____ **a.** Register
____ **b.** Timbre
____ **c.** Both *a* and *b*
____ **d.** Neither *a* nor *b*

14. Group 4 is played by   **14.** c
____ **a.** Strings
____ **b.** Brass
____ **c.** Woodwinds
____ **d.** Tutti

15. Group 4 is in a   **15.** a
____ **a.** Higher register than group 3
____ **b.** Lower register than group 3

16. Group 5 is played by   **16.** a
____ **a.** Strings
____ **b.** Brass
____ **c.** Woodwinds
____ **d.** Tutti

17. Group 5 is in a   **17.** b
____ **a.** Higher register than group 4
____ **b.** Lower register than group 4

18. Group 6 is played by   **18.** c
___ **a.** Strings
___ **b.** Brass
___ **c.** Woodwinds
___ **d.** Tutti

Listen to the beginning of the Prelude again (groups 1 through 7). Answer questions 19 and 20.

19. The final group, 7, is played by   **19.** d
___ **a.** Strings ___ **b.** Brass ___ **c.** Woodwinds ___ **d.** Tutti

20. Where do the loudest dynamics occur?   **20.** d
___ **a.** In groups 1 through 3 as a whole
___ **b.** In groups 4 through 6 as a whole
___ **c.** On the first note of group 7
___ **d.** Toward the end of group 7

Under the group diagram preceding question 4, indicate the dynamics throughout the Prelude. Use the following symbols:

p = piano   *f* = forte   ◁———◁ = crescendo
pp = pianissimo   *ff* = fortissimo ———▷ = decrescendo

Your diagram might look something like this:

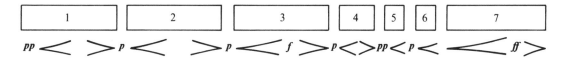

III. MOZART: LE NOZZE DI FIGARO. ACT II, SECTION 8 (ALLEGRO ASSAI)

Listen to the Finale, from the beginning of the Allegro assai to the end of Act II (sections 8 and 9). Do not follow the text. Answer question 1.

1. In this part of the Finale, the vocal sonority   **1.** b
___ **a.** Does not change appreciably from beginning to end
___ **b.** Is dominated at the beginning by solos, at the end by ensembles
___ **c.** Is dominated at the beginning by ensembles, at the end by solos

Listen to section 8 (Allegro assai) as you follow the Italian text given here. Answer questions 2 through 8.

1	Voi signor, che giusto siete	_____	1 E
2	Ci dovete or ascoltar	_____	2 E
3	Son venuti, son venuti a {sconcertarmi / vendicarmi	_____	3 S/E
4	{io mi sento a consolar. / qual rimedio ritrovar.	_____	4 S/E
5	Son tre stolidi, tre pazzi	_____	5 S
[: 6	Cosa mai vengono a far. :]	_____	6 S
7	Pian, pianin, senza schiamazzi	_____	7 S
[: 8	dica ogn'un quel che gli par. :]	_____	8 S
9	Un impegno nuzziale	_____	9 S
10	ha costui con me contratto	_____	10 S
11	e prefendo ch'il contratto	_____	11 S
12	deva meco effetuar	_____	12 S
13	Come? come?	_____	13 E
14	Olà! Silenzio! silenzio! silenzio!	_____	14 S
15	Io son quì per giudicar.	_____	15 S
16	Io da lei scelto avvocato,	_____	16 S
17	vengo a far le sue difese	_____	17 S
18	le legitime pretese	_____	18 S
19	io vivengo a palesar.	_____	19 S
[:20	È un birbante! :]	_____	20 E
21	Olà! Silenzio! silenzio! silenzio!	_____	21 S
22	Io son quì per giudicar.	_____	22 S
23	Io com' uom al mondo cognito,	_____	23 S
24	vengo quì per testimonio	_____	24 S
25	del promesso matrimonio	_____	25 S
26	con prestanza di danar.	_____	26 S
[:27	Son tre matti, son tre matti :]	_____	27 S
28	Olà! Silenzio! lo vedremo,	_____	28 S
29	il contratto leggeremo	_____	29 S
30	tutto in ordin deve andar.	_____	30 S

2. Indicate each change of vocal timbre by marking an "E" to the right of the appropriate line of text above for each new entrance of an ensemble, an "S" for each new entrance of a soloist. [: :] indicates a repeat.

2. See above

3. Which two lines are sung simultaneously by a solo voice and an ensemble? _____ **3.** Lines 3 and 4

4. Which lines are sung by a high solo female voice (soprano)? _____ **4.** Lines 9 through 12

5. Which lines are sung by a high solo male voice (tenor)? _____ **5.** Lines 23 through 26

6. At the beginning of the Allegro assai and again after line 1, short instrumental passages are played by   **6.** d
___ **a.** Woodwinds
___ **b.** Brass
___ **c.** Strings
___ **d.** Tutti

7. The woodwinds are prominent in the accompaniment of line   **7.** b
___ **a.** 3
___ **b.** 15
___ **c.** 21
___ **d.** 28

8. Lines 28, 29, and 30 are separated by short instrumental passages played by   **8.** c
___ **a.** Woodwinds
___ **b.** Brass
___ **c.** Strings
___ **d.** Tutti

CHAPTER 3 TEXTURE

LINE AND TEXTURE. If we extend the metaphor implicit in the term "line" (as used in the preceding chapter), we can develop the concept of musical *texture*. This, too, is a metaphor—a particularly useful one for describing the overall quality of musical sound. The concept of texture will help distinguish qualities of sound that cannot be clearly distinguished on the basis of timbre alone.

If the notes sung or played in succession by one voice or instrument can be said to form a single line, then musical texture is the way several lines are combined to form a more complex sound, just as many threads may be woven together in various designs to form a fabric. We often speak metaphorically of the "fabric" of a piece of music; the texture is the way the fabric is woven at any particular point in the piece.

A piece of music may have one texture throughout, or it may change texture at any time. Texture can be thick or thin; that is, it can consist of many lines or threads or only a few. Texture can be compact or diffuse, depending on whether the threads are woven together tightly or loosely. It can be simple or complex, according to whether the threads are of similar or disparate color and quality. As a result of the interaction of these and other factors, the woven fabric will have a pattern—uniform or varied, perhaps very intricate.

Thickness or thinness is one of the simplest aspects of texture and can be determined very easily by observing the number of instrumental or vocal lines sounding at any given time. Timbre and quality of line, however, tend to enter into perception of any texture, sometimes decisively: four simultaneous lines may sound thicker when played by brasses than when played by solo strings. Often combinations of disparate timbres (strings, woodwinds, brasses) make a texture more complex than it would be when played in one timbre.

The element of texture tends to bring with it a sense of "vertical distance" or "space" between various strands. We speak of texture as compact or diffuse, depending on whether the strands lie closely knit, with little or no space between them, or whether, on the contrary, they are widely spaced. The dimension of space involved here is the difference in pitch between two lines: if one line is much higher in pitch than the other (as a soprano above a bass), they are widely spaced; two tenors singing a duet, on the other hand, may have lines so closely spaced that they can be distinguished only with difficulty. Thus, even though this chapter concentrates on texture, we will need to refer to the timbres involved—and also to pitch, but only in a general sense of higher and lower, not in more specific ways to be discussed in Chapter 6.

Some textural designs recur so frequently that we give them standardized names, such as *melody and accompaniment*. Other designs may be infrequent, or even unique, woven by a particular composer for a particular spot in one and only one piece. We describe such textures as best we can with whatever words seem appropriate. In fact, there are relatively few standard technical terms for kinds of texture.

MONOPHONIC TEXTURE. Some music consists of only one line. For example, Gregorian chant (as in the music for the Easter Mass), consists of only one note at a time in a single vocal line. Even though there may be many singers in the choir, they all sing the same notes; there is a difference in *timbre* between the sound of a solo voice and a chorus singing the same note, but not a difference in *texture*. Texture that consists of a single line is called *monophonic* texture (*mono-phonic*, "single-sounding"; *monophony* is music consisting of a single line). All Gregorian chant is monophonic in texture, as are many other kinds of music.

While a piece of Gregorian chant is a good illustration of monophonic texture, it does not offer a good chance to study the effect of texture upon the shape of a piece, simply because the texture remains constant throughout a piece of chant. It is, of course, important for the shape of a piece if its texture remains the same, for the sameness produces unity and continuity throughout the piece. But any aspect that remains more or less the same is harder to perceive than one that changes in some obvious way. To become familiar with the concept of musical texture, we should start with a piece that has some striking changes of texture.

Béla Bartók (1881–1945)
STRING QUARTET NO. 6
MESTO—PESANTE
(FIRST MOVEMENT, BEGINNING)

The String Quartet No. 6 by Béla Bartók is a difficult, challenging piece—it will offer material for several discussions in this book. Right now, we will use only the first minute of the quartet as a conveniently compact example of monophonic and polyphonic textures and of a transition between them.

The quartet begins with an expressive line for solo viola; no other instrument plays. This passage is unique in the quartet: at no other time does one instrument play alone for such a long stretch. This introduction is labeled *Mesto*, or "sad."

Throughout the rest of the quartet, generally speaking, more instruments than one are playing at a time and more notes than one are sounding at a time. That is, the instruments do not usually all perform the same pitch at once (as do the singers in a Gregorian chant choir). Hence, of the quartet as a whole, only the slow introduction is monophonic.

POLYPHONIC TEXTURE. The generic name for textures in which two or more pitches are consistently sounding is *polyphonic* (meaning "many-sounding"; *polyphony* is music consisting of more than one pitch at a time). Much of the music we hear is polyphonic in texture—to the degree that we ordinarily do not bother to say so, as we do not bother to describe as prose most of what we say or write. Very often we are concerned primarily with how one kind of polyphonic texture differs from another. In polyphony, texture can articulate the shape through its differences, as well as provide continuity through its sameness.

In the course of the first minute of Bartók's quartet, the texture changes from monophonic to polyphonic, eventually assuming a variety of polyphonic textures. On first hearing, merely note the overall difference in texture between the monophonic beginning and the polyphonic continuation.

FROM MONOPHONIC TO POLYPHONIC TEXTURE IN THE PESANTE. Drastic as the change in texture is, it does not occur suddenly; rather, the polyphonic texture appears gradually in a brief passage (about 20 seconds long) that comes after the end of the Mesto section and before the start of the Vivace (Ex. 3-1). This passage is labeled *Più mosso, pesante*—"faster, heavily"; it begins abruptly louder than the viola solo that precedes it and soon gets very loud, ending with a long sustained note. During this Pesante passage, all four instruments play; and the texture changes from monophonic to polyphonic. You can get a more precise idea of the difference between monophonic and polyphonic sound by following the Pesante in detail.

Example 3-2 shows all the individual notes played in the Pesante section. Listen to the beginning of the quartet several times until you can find where the Mesto dies softly away; then match up the wedges in Ex. 3-2 with the notes in the Pesante immediately

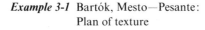

Example 3-1 Bartók, Mesto—Pesante: Plan of texture

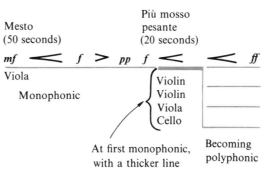

following. *Work only with the left-to-right succession numbered 1 through 15; you probably will not be able to hear right away how the up-and-down arrangement of wedges is manifest in the music.*

At the points numbered 1 through 10 in Ex. 3-2, the texture is midway between monophonic and polyphonic. You should hear that the sound at the start of the Pesante is immediately richer and fuller than in the preceding Mesto (in addition to being louder), and that more than one instrument is playing. Yet there seems to be only one line sounding, just as in the Mesto. Before trying to pick out individual instruments in the portion numbered 1 through 10 of the Pesante, listen to the overall effect, hearing how the beginning of the Pesante, with its single line, is basically different from the portion numbered 11 through 15.

The lines played by different instruments from 1 through 10 reproduce the same series of notes but in different *registers*. At 1 and 2, the violins and viola are playing an octave higher than the cello—as if men and women were singing the same tune in two different registers. As far as real pitches go, these are two lines (as shown in Ex. 3-2), but they sound like one. The upper instruments double at the octave above. The doubling continues to 10; at one point, 3, the line is doubled in two octaves. The doubling effect is shown in Ex. 3-2 by a vertical line connecting the wedges.

At 11, the notes in the upper instruments no longer double the lower. There the texture becomes different—it is polyphonic instead of expanded monophonic. Since the instruments continue to play in the same rhythm and pace through 15, the change is not startling; clearly, the composer has intended a smooth transition from a monophonic to a polyphonic texture. Still, by 15 there are four different lines sounding instead of one.

With concentration, you should be able to hear the difference in texture, even if you cannot actually follow the four separate lines (which is very difficult). Probably, you will hear only the top violin going up and the cello going down, while the inner parts will be indistinct. The first important aspect is the difference in texture between the two portions (1 through 10 and 11 through 15).

CHORDAL OR HOMOPHONIC TEXTURE. During the polyphonic passage at the close of the Pesante (Ex. 3-2), the individual qualities of the lines combine to form enveloping sonorities. The lines do not have distinct motions that stand out from those sonorities because the polyphonic texture here is *chordal* (as shown in Ex. 3-2b). We tend to hear the notes in blocklike groups or *chords*, instead of hearing and following the motions of four independent lines.

Chordal texture (sometimes called *homophonic*, meaning "same-sounding," texture) is one special kind of polyphonic texture. Often the appearance of a chordal texture is a striking event in a piece; just as often, chordal texture is used in more subtle ways.

Texture is chordal when it *seems* chordal; that is, when attention is drawn to the overall blocks of sound rather than to the individual lines. For this reason, different people may hear the texture of a passage such as the Pesante differently: one listener may be more aware of individual lines; another may be more aware of the chordal dimension.

Also, subtle differences of timbre can determine whether a passage sounds more chordal or more linear. Played as they are by four stringed instruments, the lines of the Pesante blend together into chords. If they were played by a mixture of contrasting strings and winds, the individual lines might be much more distinct.

35

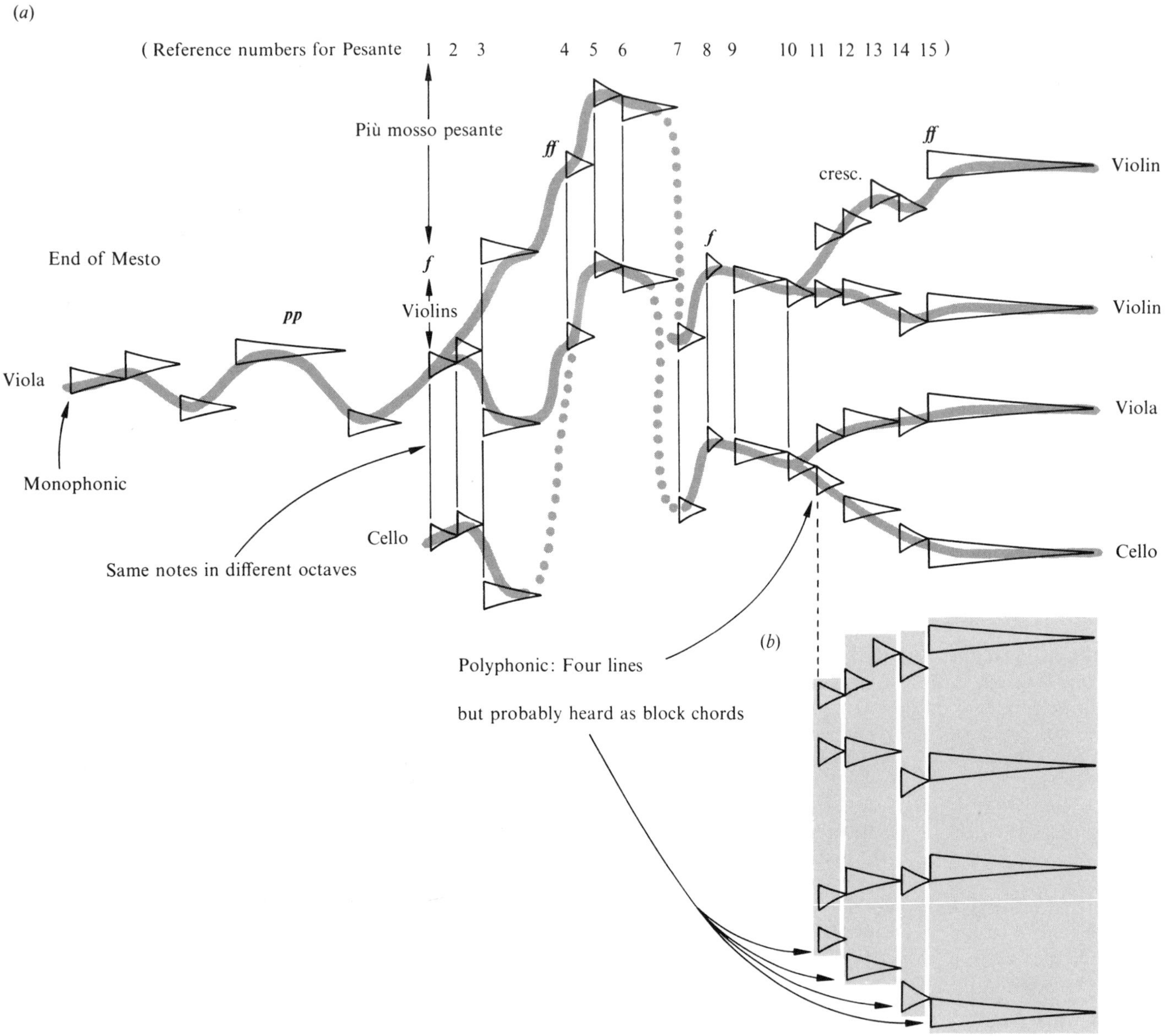

(a)

(Reference numbers for Pesante 1 2 3   4 5 6   7 8 9   10 11 12 13 14 15)

Più mosso pesante

ff

ff

End of Mesto

cresc.

Violin

pp

f

f

Violins

Violin

Viola

Viola

Monophonic

Cello

Viola

Same notes in different octaves

Cello

Cello

Polyphonic: Four lines

(b)

but probably heard as block chords

Example 3-2 Bartók, Pesante

In a fragment as small as the beginning of Bartok's quartet, you could not hear how the changes in texture shaped the piece as a whole. In the next example, you will be able to hear how the changes in texture are correlated with the largest sections in the piece. In some pieces, texture and its changes are the main shaping factor. More often, texture changes reinforce sectional divisions that are produced in other ways.

The texture of "Der Neugierige" ("The Question"), the sixth song in Schubert's cycle *Die schöne Müllerin,* is intimately related to its being a song and to its timbre. Its texture is *melody and accompaniment*—an awkward but accurate designation for which no more convenient equivalent is available. In this case, the voice sings the melody; the piano provides the accompaniment. The distinguishing feature of melody-and-accompaniment texture is the prominence of a single line in a polyphonic context. Often, but not always, the accompaniment takes the form of chords. The melody can be made prominent in many ways; a contrast in timbre (as between voice and piano) is one of the most obvious.

First listen to "Der Neugierige" just to hear the prevailing texture, disregarding subtle variations and brief changes in texture. On first hearing, the vocal line will certainly be the song's most prominent feature: the vocal line will seem so important that it could almost stand by itself as an independent, unaccompanied melody. Yet an unobtrusive accompaniment such as this is responsible for much of the total shape and effect of the song. Nevertheless, the vocal line of "Der Neugierige" is clearly the song's leading element. The piano part takes a variety of forms, but they all seem to depend upon the vocal line for forward direction and continuity. The ear follows the vocal line, referring the piano accompaniment to it. This, at least, is a first impression; we will refine it to account for a few exceptions.

For a more specific discussion of "Der Neugierige" we need to refer to its text. To the right of the original German text appears a summary of the different textures in the song. A translation will be found at the end of Chapter 11.

Ich frage keine Blume,
Ich frage keinen Stern;
Sie können mir alle nicht sagen,
Was ich erführ' so gern.

Ich bin ja auch kein Gärtner,
Die Sterne steh'n zu hoch;
Mein Bächlein will ich fragen,
Ob mich mein Herz belog.

O Bächlein meiner Liebe,
Wie bist du heut' so stumm!
Will ja nur Eines wissen,
Ein Wörtchen um und um,
Ein Wörtchen um und um.

Ja, heisst das eine Wörtchen,
Das andre heisset Nein,
Die beiden Wörtchen schliessen
Die ganze Welt mir ein,
Die beiden Wörtchen schliessen
Die ganze Welt mir ein.

O Bächlein meiner Liebe,
Was bist du wunderlich!
Will's ja nicht weiter sagen.
Sag', Bächlein, liebt sie mich?
Sag', Bächlein, liebt sie mich?

Piano introduction:
melody and accompaniment (chordal)

Stanza 1:
melody and accompaniment ("um-pah")
chordal at end

Stanza 2:
(like stanza 1)

Short piano interlude:
melody and accompaniment (chordal)

Stanza 3:
melody and accompaniment (chords and a figure; later a line in the bass)

Stanza 4:
declamation over sustained chords
homophonic

Stanza 5:
(like stanza 3)

Short piano postlude:
melody and accompaniment (chords and a figure)

MELODY AND ACCOMPANIMENT. Stanza 1 of the text is preceded by a short introduction for piano alone; and after stanza 2 there is a very short interlude, again for piano alone. At the end of the song, the piano plays a brief postlude. At these three spots, the piano takes over the singer's role in providing the melody, as well as continuing to supply an accompaniment. The whole texture of melody and accompaniment can be located in the piano part, as heard most easily in the introduction to stanza 1 (shown in Ex. 3-3).

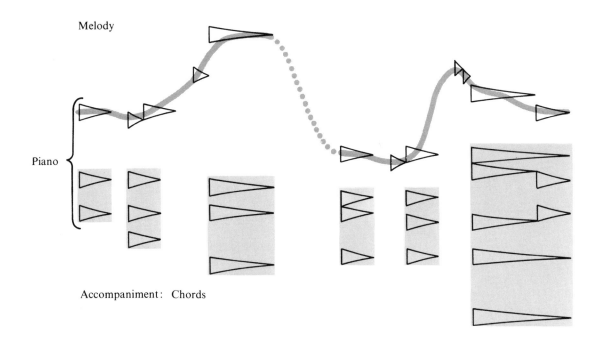

Melody

Piano

Accompaniment: Chords

Example 3-3 Schubert, "Der Neugierige," piano introduction

The fact that both the melody and the accompaniment can be played by the piano alone shows that we are indeed dealing with texture, not timbre. The difference in timbre between voice and piano will project the melody forcefully, making it seem far more prominent than the accompaniment. But the piano introduction shows that difference in timbre only highlights the melody; it is not solely responsible for making the melody distinct from the accompaniment. Many other factors, having to do with the relative motions of the melody and the accompaniment, are responsible for the clear distinction. These factors will be studied in the chapters on rhythm, melody, and harmony. For now, you should hear that there is a clear distinction between the melody and the accompaniment and that the distinction is independent of timbre, even though accentuated by it.

Although an accompaniment to a melody often takes the form of chords, it can take many other

forms also; and even chords can be treated in different ways. When the voice starts stanza 1 ("Ich frage . . ."), the piano relinquishes the melody and merely accompanies—still in chords, but chords expressed in a slightly more complex pattern. If you can listen only to the accompaniment during stanza 1, you will hear that the piano plays a single note in alternation with a chord (see Ex. 3-4). The single notes are always lower than the chords. (The popular name for this accompaniment texture is "um-pah.") This texture persists up to the last line of the stanza ("Was ich erführ' so gern") when it is replaced by a completely chordal texture in the accompaniment, as shown at the end of Ex. 3-4. This slight change in texture— along with several other factors not yet discussed— helps mark the end of the first stanza. The "um-pah" accompaniment resumes at the beginning of stanza 2; then the close of stanza 2 is marked by the same change to a purely chordal texture as is the end of stanza 1.

Stanza 3 is distinguished from the previous stanzas in several ways: it goes more slowly, has a new melody and another kind of accompaniment. The lower part of the piano accompaniment now moves in chords, while the upper part of the accompaniment moves much faster (and faster than the voice) in a pattern that is neither line nor chord (see Ex. 3-5). Such a pattern is often called a *figure*—a term that is useful largely because it can be applied to a wide variety of nondescript patterns.

The figure here persists throughout stanza 3. As a figure, considered as part of the texture, it does not change—although it is obvious that the exact pitches that make up the figure do change; for example, the first changes in pitch come at the word "*Lie*-(be)."

The lower part of the accompaniment changes in texture as stanza 3 proceeds. Toward the end, there are fewer notes sounding at once in the lower part (sometimes only one at a time) and these notes move faster. Indeed, under "Ein Wörtchen um und um"

Ich   fra —   ge kei —   ne Blu — me,   ich   fra —   ge kei —   nen Stern

Melody (voice)

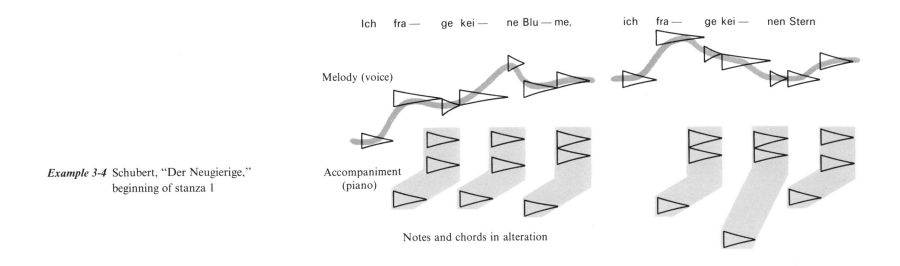

Example 3-4 Schubert, "Der Neugierige,"
beginning of stanza 1

Accompaniment
(piano)

Notes and chords in alteration

sie   können mir al —   le nicht sa — gen,   was   ich   er —   führ´   so gern.

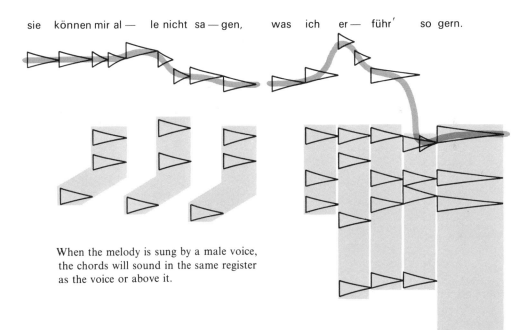

When the melody is sung by a male voice,
the chords will sound in the same register
as the voice or above it.

Chords (merging with melody at end)

(the first time), the lower part of the accompaniment takes on the form of a line—a bass line, going on simultaneously with the melody line in the voice part. This happens in such a way as to prepare for the repetition of the text "Ein Wörtchen . . . ." In other words, the change in texture is made at this point, not arbitrarily, but for the express purpose of shaping the whole stanza as the composer wishes.

CHANGES IN TEXTURE IN STANZA 4. A much more striking change in texture marks the beginning of stanza 4 ("Ja, heisst das eine Wörtchen"—"'Yes' is that little word"). The figure in the accompaniment ceases abruptly, the piano now playing a simple sustained chord (Ex. 3-6). Against this chord, the voice seems to declaim its text rather than sing it. The sense of melody seems to disappear temporarily from the voice part. (This is especially noticeable over the second chord and the text "Das andre heisset Nein.")

The change in either melody or accompaniment by itself would be much less striking than both together, for together the changes bring about a new texture in this song. The whole songlike character is disturbed; something different has happened, clearly something else different is going to follow.

At the word "Nein" ("no"), indeed, something else does happen—a striking change, produced by a number of factors (Ex. 3-7). Here again, texture is not the only factor or even the most important one; but a change in texture does take place, and it reinforces the other concomitant changes.

For the text lines "Die beiden Wörtchen schliessen/ Die ganze Welt mir ein" ("In these two words the whole world is bound up for me"), and their repetition, voice and piano are related in a way new to this song. We can no longer call it melody and accompaniment, for even though the piano plays chords, the top profile of these chords is almost identical to the voice part. Actually it sounds as though the melody is in

the piano part, the voice merely chiming in. And the melody moves in a way so closely related to the chords as to be virtually indistinguishable from them. The texture is chordal throughout: the term "homophonic" applies very well to such a passage, for there is little to distinguish one line from another—except the timbre of the voice part and the fact that it has words to sing. (In the repetition of the text, however, the voice part has slight ornaments that give it a slight measure of independence.)

RETURN AT THE END. After the distinctive setting of this particular line of text—selected by the composer as the dramatic climax of the song—the texture returns to what it was for stanza 3. In fact, the music for stanza 5 ("O Bächlein") largely repeats the music for stanza 3. The song ends with the piano postlude, in which the piano plays both the accompaniment it has been playing and a melody over it.

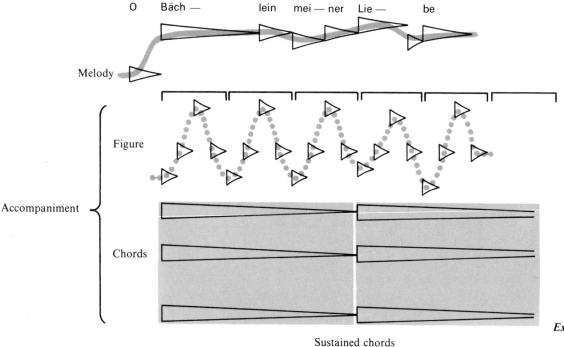

O Bäch —   lein mei — ner Lie —   be

Melody

Accompaniment {

Figure

Chords

Sustained chords

Shows repetition of the figure in the upper part of the accompaniment. When the melody is sung by a male voice, this figure will sound *above* it.

Example 3-5 Schubert, "Der Neugierige," beginning of stanza 3

40

After you have located the individual changes in texture and studied each kind of texture with the help of Exs. 3-3 through 3-7, listen to the whole song several times while following the German text and the summary next to it (page 37). The changes in texture help block out the song into its stanzas and into its high-level shape, which can be expressed schematically as *A A B C B*.

The texture changes also highlight the dramatic progress of the text, which contains the perennial question by the boy, "Does she love me?" He asks it, not of a flower, but rather of his companion the brook, in which he places a strange confidence (as we will discuss later in connection with the whole cycle).

Claudio Monteverdi (1567–1643)
"SI CH'IO VORREI MORIRE" (MADRIGAL)

Schubert's song "Der Neugierige" showed how the simple texture of melody and accompaniment could be varied so as to set off one section of the song from another. Also, the textural distinction between the melody and the accompaniment was reinforced by a corresponding distinction in timbre between voice and piano. This timbre distinction made the difference between the melody and the accompaniment easier to hear but at the same time may have made it harder to concentrate on texture by itself. In order to study

the functioning of texture in a purer state, we need to go to a piece with relatively low degrees of timbre difference.

Monteverdi's madrigal "Si ch'io vorrei morire" (from his Book IV of madrigals) is for five vocal parts—soprano, alto, two tenors, and bass. It has no instrumental accompaniment. The five vocal lines are combined in a variety of textures, and the changes from one texture to another provide one of the most important kinds of sectional division in the piece.

"Si ch'io vorrei morire" is performed swiftly and passionately; your first impression may be one of breathless confusion. The changes in texture come in quick succession; and, since each texture in itself is

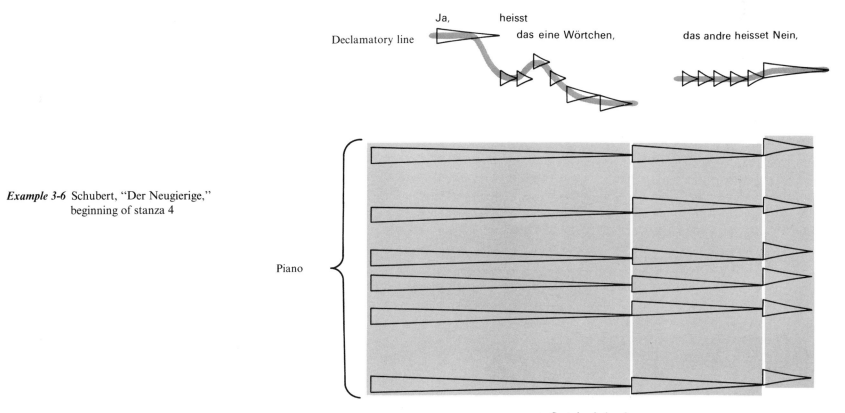

Example 3-6 Schubert, "Der Neugierige," beginning of stanza 4

tightly woven, there is little opportunity to pull the textures apart with your ears as the piece is going by. The diagrams, in other words, will show more than you can actually hear during a performance (at least, until you are reasonably familiar with the piece). Still, "Si ch'io vorrei morire" is valuable as a study in sudden identification of textures—like a pack of flash cards.

Listen to the madrigal several times straight through to gain an idea of the whole, no matter how indistinct your impression may be. As you can perhaps infer from the text, the idea of the whole in this case overrides niceties of image or a finely balanced phrase structure. Match up the Italian text with the piece as you listen to it, so that you can identify text lines with musical sections.

The text of the actual poem (by Giambattista Marini, 1569–1625) is printed here in italics; the text in regular type shows the repetitions made by Monteverdi in setting the poem to music. Only some of the repetitions are printed here complete, however; further repetitions of all or part of a line are indicated by the word "repeated."

As you come to know the piece, you will see in what respects Monteverdi has used music to support the poem's form and in what respects he has adapted the text to his own idea of musical form. At the triple alternating statements of "Deh stringetemi fin ch'io venga meno" and "A questo bianco seno," the music prevails most upon the text. We will find that these statements make important use of changes in texture.

CHORDAL AND STAGGERED TEXTURE. First we will take up the different textures as they appear in order in the piece; then we will consider briefly the effect of the whole succession.

The madrigal begins in a purely chordal texture (Ex. 3-8). As the five voices sing the first line of text, "Si ch'io vorrei morire," they sing the syllables of the text at exactly the same time, so that their pitches blend together in successive blocks of sound. The five voices are not singing the same pitch: the texture is not monophonic but polyphonic. Yet the voices are so tightly woven into chords that it is practically impossible to follow any single voice as a line—except the top line (the soprano) and possibly the bass. Note that the texture is not melody and accompaniment, for there is nothing to set the soprano off from any other line. The texture is chordal, homophonic.

Toward the end of Ex. 3-8, as "ch'io vorrei" is being sung for the third time, a subtle change takes place in the texture. The five voices no longer sing their syllables at exactly the same time but instead become staggered with respect to each other. If we tried to draw vertical lines in this part of Ex. 3-8, the lines would cut through notes in one or another voice, instead of neatly separating one block of notes—one chord—from the next, as before.

The staggering of voices makes the texture less chordal. Simultaneously, the staggering encourages the listener to hear individual lines slightly more than before. These two changes are really a single change described from opposite extremes: at one extreme, several voices or parts blend into chords; at the other extreme, they stand alone as independent lines; between these extremes are many varied textures. The texture at the end of Ex. 3-8 is only one step from chordal texture in the direction of independent lines. The texture of the next two lines, "Hora ch'io bacio amore/La bella bocca del mio amato core," similarly fluctuates between chords and a slight staggering of voices.

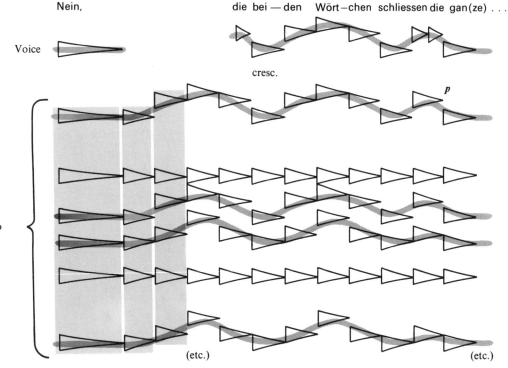

Homophonic texture: Heard as a succession of chords, only top and bottom lines audible as lines. Note that the voice line is almost identical to the top line of piano.

Example 3-7 Schubert, "Der Neugierige," from stanza 4

COUNTERPOINT AND IMITATION. Texture in which two or more relatively independent lines are combined is called *counterpoint*, or *contrapuntal texture*. There is no sharp division between contrapuntal and chordal texture: instead, "chordal" and "contrapuntal" represent opposite tendencies on a continuum or even merely different ways of hearing the same passage (for some listeners, the staggering of the syllables in the passage just discussed might be sufficient to make it sound contrapuntal).

Contrapuntal, chordal, and melody-and-accompaniment textures are all polyphonic; the difference is that in chordal texture there is no independent line, in melody and accompaniment there is one, and in counterpoint there are at least two. Lines are usually made independent by being given some interesting contour—by being made more like the melody of a melody-and-accompaniment texture.

1   *Si ch'io vorrei morire* (ch'io vorrei morire,
      ch'io vorrei morire)
2   *Hora ch'io bacio amore*
3   *La bella bocca del mio amato core*
4   *Ahi car'e dolce lingua* (repeated)
5   *Datemi tant'humore* (repeated)
6   *Che di dolcezz'in questo sen m'estingua.*
7   *Ahi vita mia* (repeated)
8   *A questo bianco seno* (repeated)
9   *Deh stringetemi fin ch'io venga meno.*
      A questo bianco seno (repeated)
      Deh stringetemi fin ch'io venga meno.
      A questo bianco seno (repeated)
      Deh stringetemi fin ch'io venga meno.
10 *Ahi bocca, ahi baci,*
11 *Ahi lingua torn'a dire*
12 *Si ch'io vorrei morire* (ch'io vorrei morire,
      ch'io vorrei morire.)

Now would I die,

   Love, as I kiss
The lovely mouth of my heart's desire.
Dear tongue, sweet tongue, feed me such humors
Drawn of that breast that I shall be
Extinguished quite.
My love, my love,
Unto that white breast
Crush me to compass my dwindling.

O mouth, O kisses,
Let my own tongue return to me
That I may say: now would I die.

English translation © 1956 by Chester Kallman. Used by permission.

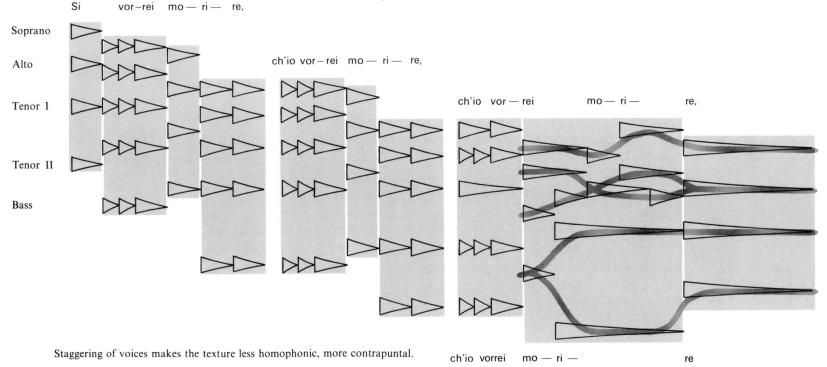

Staggering of voices makes the texture less homophonic, more contrapuntal.

Example 3-8 Monteverdi, "Si ch'io vorrei morire," line 1

One particular way of creating a sense of independence among two or more lines is to give each line the same melodic figure but to stagger them so that no two lines have the figure at exactly the same time. Each line *imitates* the distinctive melodic figure presented by the preceding line; this is called *imitation*, or *imitative texture*. The several textures described so far are shown schematically in Ex. 3-9a and b.

Example 3-9 Kinds of texture

As "Si ch'io vorrei morire" proceeds, it makes increasing use of contrapuntal textures, especially imitation. The first example of imitation is not, perhaps, the clearest: at "Ahi car'e dolce lingua" the voices overlap in vehement impatience, no one voice seeming to care what friction it will create by its entrance. Words are difficult to make out; all alignment of the syllables is gone. Example 3-10 shows that the texture is imitative, but so close and dense is the

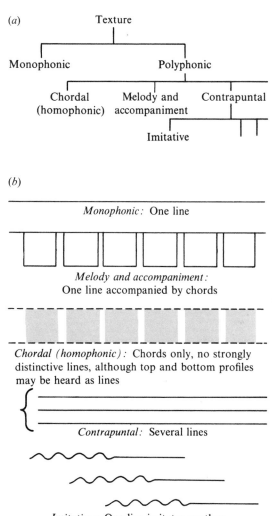

imitation that individual lines can be heard here scarcely more than in the chordal section.

In Ex. 3-10, the beginning of this imitative section is written out twice, the second time (*b*) with the voices separated vertically from each other more than they are in actual pitch, in order to show more clearly the imitative pattern and the way the bottom voice starts in again on top. This pattern is not carried out strictly; nevertheless, until the next line of text appears ("Datemi tant'humore"), the texture is for only three voices instead of five as before. In other words, the texture of this passage is different from that of the preceding passage by being both imitative and thinner.

The text line "Datemi tant'humore" enters in imitation too, but may go unnoticed since there is no clear break to mark the first entrance. Example 3-11 shows the imitative entrances, but not the whole texture; other voices are still singing "Ahi car'e dolce lingua" as Ex. 3-11 starts. After the first entrance of "Datemi," the voices sometimes enter in pairs, as shown in the example. All voices continue to sing after they enter, so that by the end of Ex. 3-11 the texture has become five-voiced again.

The full five-voiced texture continues until the end of line 6. Once the voices have entered on "Datemi tant'humore," the texture sounds merely staggered: as shown in Ex. 3-12, vertical lines drawn so as to mark the beginnings of notes in some voices would cut across the middle of notes in other voices. The end of this passage is similar in texture (as well as in some other respects) to the end of the opening passage on "ch'io vorrei morire."

The next line of text, "Ahi vita mia," brings more intricate imitation (see Ex. 3-13). The top two voices work closely together, forming, in effect, one thick line instead of two separate independent lines. The entrance of the top two voices is quickly followed by the bass, then the tenor, in imitation (these imitative entrances are numbered 1, 2, 3). The same order of imitative entrances is immediately repeated twice; the beginning of the first repetition is shown in Ex. 3-13.

Another set of imitative entrances follows immediately ("A questo bianco seno"). Now the voices are grouped together, two in one group, three

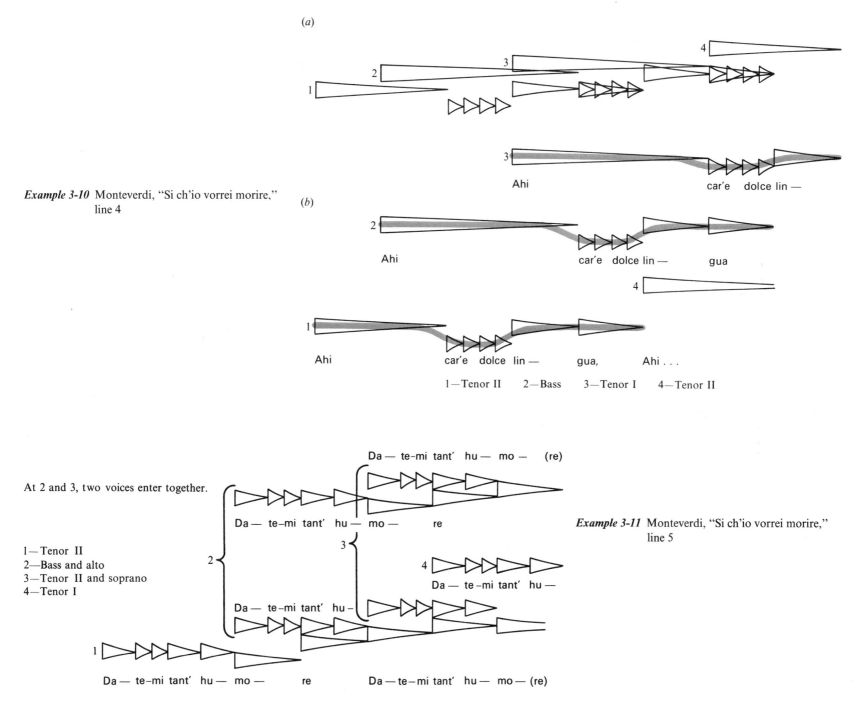

(a)

Ahi   car'e dolce lin —

Example 3-10 Monteverdi, "Si ch'io vorrei morire,"
line 4

(b)

Ahi   car'e dolce lin —   gua

Ahi   car'e dolce lin —   gua,   Ahi . . .

1—Tenor II   2—Bass   3—Tenor I   4—Tenor II

At 2 and 3, two voices enter together.

Da — te-mi tant' hu — mo — (re)

Da — te-mi tant' hu — mo —   re

Example 3-11 Monteverdi, "Si ch'io vorrei morire,"
line 5

1—Tenor II
2—Bass and alto
3—Tenor II and soprano
4—Tenor I

Da — te-mi tant' hu —

Da — te-mi tant' hu —

Da — te-mi tant' hu — mo —   re   Da — te-mi tant' hu — mo — (re)

Example 3-12 Monteverdi, "Si ch'io vorrei morire," line 6

Che   di . . .   dol —   cez —

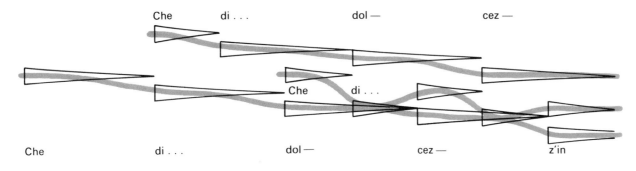

Che   di . . .   dol —   cez —   z'in

Che   di . . .   dol —   cez —   z'in   que —   sto   sen   in

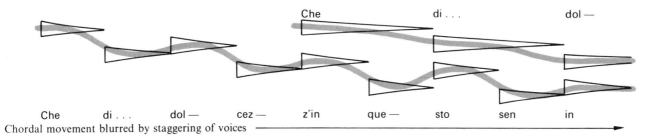

Che   di . . .   dol —

Che   di . . .   dol —   cez —   z'in   que —   sto   sen   in
Chordal movement blurred by staggering of voices ⟶

z'in   que —   sto   sen

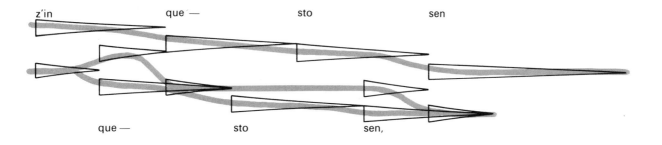

que —   sto   sen,

cez —   z'in   que —

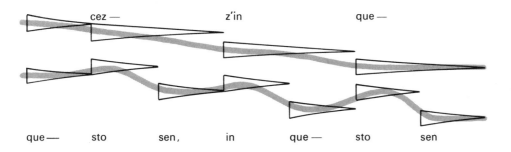

que —   sto   sen,   in   que —   sto   sen

Example 3-13 Monteverdi, "Si ch'io vorrei morire," line 7

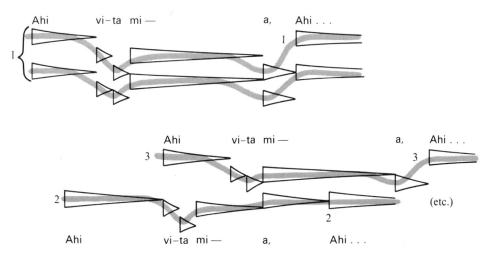

in the other (Ex. 3-14; the groups are numbered 1, 2). So quickly does the alternation take place that it is hard to hear the qualities of the texture; but, as you can see in Ex. 3-14, the two voices in group 1 are close together, while the three voices of group 2 are further apart; the top lines of the two groups are the same, but the top line of group 2 is an octave higher than that of group 1.

In these imitative passages, the five participating voices often produce a texture in which only three or four voices are actually sounding at a given moment, since each voice frequently pauses to let the entrance of another be heard. The pauses are not especially noticeable, for the same reason that all the voices seldom sound at once—the overlapping characteristic of imitative texture. The complexity and intensity of imitative texture make up for the fact that all five voices are not sounding continuously, so that such a passage may actually sound thicker than the purely chordal five-voiced passage at the beginning of the madrigal.

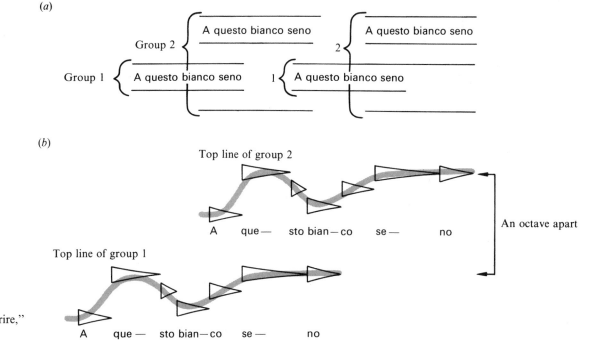

Example 3-14 Monteverdi, "Si ch'io vorrei morire,"
line 8

(*a*)

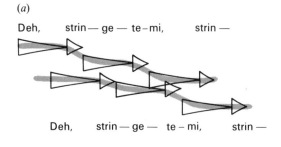

Deh,   strin — ge — te – mi,   strin —

Deh,   strin — ge — te – mi,   strin —

Example 3-15 Monteverdi, "Si ch'io
vorrei morire," line 9

(*b*)

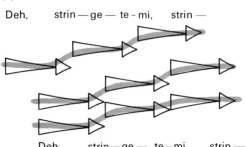

Deh,   strin — ge — te – mi,   strin —

Deh,   strin — ge — te – mi,   strin —

(*c*)

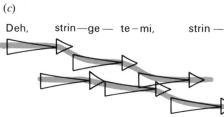

Deh,   strin — ge — te – mi,   strin —

Deh,   strin — ge — te – mi,   strin —

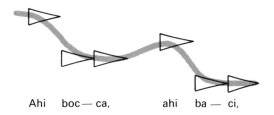

Ahi   boc — ca,   ahi   ba — ci,

In any case, the reduction to two voices at the start of the next line of text is a striking change of texture ("Deh stringetemi fin ch'io venga meno"). This is the first of three statements of "Deh stringe-temi . . ."—statements that become progressively more intricate in texture (Ex. 3-15). The first "Deh stringetemi" is imitative, the two voices chasing each other down in a very tight pattern (Ex. 3-15*a*). In the second statement of "Deh stringetemi" (Ex. 3-15*b*), the bottom two voices are paired and set against the third, uppermost, voice in the same kind of tight pattern. The third statement resembles the first, but now a third voice is added with a different kind of line and a different text—"Ahi bocca, ahi baci,/Ahi lingua" (Ex. 3-15*c*).

This relatively extended portion of the madrigal, then, is made of alternating repetitions of the same or similar blocks of material—one block for "A questo bianco seno," one for "Deh stringetemi fin ch'io venga meno." Changes in texture are one of the principal ways in which the repetitions are varied.

A contrapuntal texture frequently allows a transition more flexible or gradual than is possible with blocklike chordal sounds, since in a contrapuntal texture different lines can do different things at the same time. The new text and line added under the third "Deh stringetemi" lead easily to the following passage, which is simply the line already added ("Ahi bocca, ahi baci,/Ahi lingua")—now in a full five-voiced texture. Here four voices are grouped together

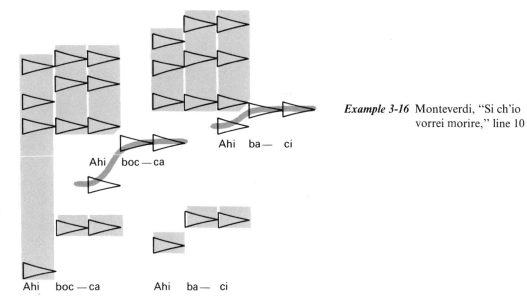

Ahi ba— ci

Ahi boc —ca

Ahi boc — ca   Ahi ba— ci

Example 3-16 Monteverdi, "Si ch'io
vorrei morire," line 10

into chords and set in opposition to the fifth voice in yet another imitative pattern (Ex. 3-16). The pattern is again very dense, and the initial impression may be one of merely staggered chords; but closer understanding with the help of the diagram will bring sensitivity to the way a composer uses imitation to quicken the motion of a piece. The last line of text, a repetition of the first line, is set to the same music.

OVERALL PLAN OF TEXTURES. In "Si ch'io vorrei morire," changes in texture are among the most prominent events of the piece. The lines or threads of sound have but little substance of their own; they gain substance by being woven into a fabric, and the texture of the fabric is one of the most important aspects of the form it assumes.

In grasping the form of a piece it often helps to represent the changes in one of the piece's aspects abstractly, visualizing these changes by means of some kind of diagram. As diagrams become abstract, they tend to mean less and less to everyone except the person who made them. The most useful diagrams

will be those you make for yourself—and you should not hesitate to make a profusion of diagrams to clarify for yourself aspects of musical form. Remember that a diagram can never be an adequate representation of a whole piece, but may often be a useful representation of one aspect of that piece.

Example 3-17 is the kind of abstract diagram that, while an inadequate representation of the madrigal as a whole, may be a useful representation of the varieties of texture in the piece. Example 3-17a tries to show only the general kind of texture in each section, as already described. Vertical lines in the diagram represent predominantly chordal texture; horizontal lines, texture that makes some use of imitation. The number of horizontal lines indicates the prevailing number of voices active at that point. No attempt has been made to show the long upward or downward progression in pitch so obvious in certain sections (as at "Ahi car'e dolce lingua") or to show repetition within a section, as at "Ahi vita mia," where the texture of only the first set of imitative entrances is shown. In the first section, the diagram shows the

gradual staggering of the voices. At "Che di dolcezz'in . . ." the diagram shows the persistent staggering that cuts across the suggestion of a chordal texture. At "Ahi bocca" in the next-to-last section, the diagram shows one voice giving an imitative dimension to the chordal movement of the other four.

The purpose of the diagram, however, is not to represent individual sections (which require the more detailed kind of description provided earlier) but rather to give a sense of texture changes throughout the madrigal. Example 3-17b reminds us that the madrigal ends with the same texture in which it began and that this full five-voiced texture asserts itself decisively at only one other spot in the piece—at "Che di dolcezz'in . . . ." These three spots act as textural pillars for the piece as a whole; thinner imitative textures are strung out in succession between these pillars. The greatest variety of textures occurs during the repetitions of the two lines "A questo bianco seno" and "Deh stringetemi."

Because "Si ch'io vorrei morire" is short, the texture plan can be held in mind while listening to the

(a)

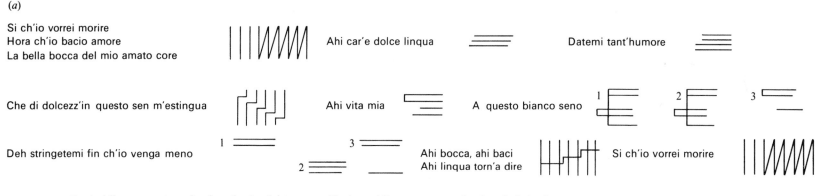

Si ch'io vorrei morire
Hora ch'io bacio amore
La bella bocca del mio amato core

Che di dolcezz'in questo sen m'estingua

Deh stringetemi fin ch'io venga meno

Ahi car'e dolce linqua

Ahi vita mia

Ahi bocca, ahi baci
Ahi linqua torn'a dire

Datemi tant'humore

A questo bianco seno

Si ch'io vorrei morire

Vertical lines suggest predominantly chordal texture.   Horizontal lines suggest predominantly imitative texture.

(b)

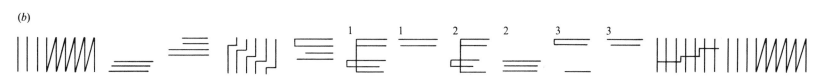

Example 3-17 Monteverdi, "Si ch'io vorrei morire": Plan of textures

whole piece. In listening to longer pieces, it may be difficult to sustain the sense of the large plan; we tend to become absorbed in the moment, hence miss the relationship of the moment to the whole. Yet in many larger pieces, an overall plan of texture changes may be an essential feature of their structure.

Ludwig van Beethoven (1770–1827)
SYMPHONY NO. 7
ALLEGRETTO (SECOND MOVEMENT)

In the Allegretto of Beethoven's Seventh Symphony, a wide variety of textures is integrated into an overall progression: the movement begins with simple textures, then rises to a high point of intensity and complexity, finally dying away to something reminiscent of the beginning. The form of the movement is expressed in several other ways, too; dynamics and timbre are especially important and will be mentioned during the discussion of the texture changes.

Listen to the movement all the way through to gain a rough idea of its arclike form. Also on first hearing you should notice two interludes—sections that are distinctly different in feeling from the primary character of the movement. The interludes are more serene, sunnier, smoother. (Their distinctive effect is due in large part to something we will study later as harmonic color.) The interludes, which are very similar to each other, break up the movement in an obvious way (Ex. 3-18). The other sections are more complex than the interludes, and their interrelationships are more various.

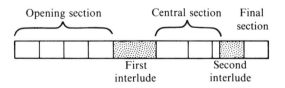

Example 3-18 Beethoven, Allegretto: Section plan

THE SHAPE OF THE FIRST SECTION. The very first chord, for winds, stands in a curious relationship to the rest of the movement—one not immediately clear. This chord is omitted from the following discussion and from Exs. 3-19, 3-20, 3-21, and 3-22.

The first section (that is, everything after the first chord up to the first interlude) gives an overall impression of an increase in dynamics from very soft to very loud, dropping back to very soft just at the end of the section. Actually, the dynamic curve is slightly more complex than that, as shown in Ex. 3-19: the crescendo to fortissimo takes place relatively quickly, during subsection 3; and before that the dynamic level remains piano or pianissimo.

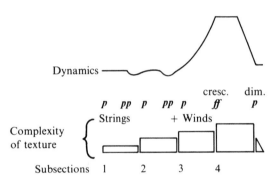

Example 3-19 Beethoven, Allegretto, first section: Plan of opening section

Similarly, this first section seems to involve a steady increase in instrumental resources; yet here, too, the only major change in timbre is the addition of winds—again in subsection 3. There are more subtle changes in timbre as the strings move up to successively higher registers in subsections 2, 3, and 4.

One of the most important factors in the sense of continuing buildup throughout the first section is the periodic change of texture, always in the direction of greater thickness or complexity (until the very end). These changes are represented in Ex. 3-19 by the heights of the successive blocks for subsections 1 through 4; the exact nature of each textural change will be discussed soon. Closely associated with the use of successively higher registers in each sub-

section, the changes in texture are important indications of where each subsection begins.

At the beginning of subsection 1, the strings play very softly in a purely chordal texture. It is difficult to hear individual lines in this opening passage; one hears the top line, and perhaps the bass. The strings are exactly synchronized in their movement, as if they were singing the same words at exactly the same time: the texture is homophonic.

There is little to distinguish the top line from the others, except the fact that it is on top. Still, it is melodious enough for us to remember as a tune and identify when we hear it again. It will become one of the basic melodies of the movement.

The first change of texture involves adding a much more distinctive line to the chordal texture—as if a stroke of bold, bright color had been drawn over a neutral background. The texture resulting from the change is contrapuntal rather than chordal. There is the new, distinctive line; there is the old top line, now sounding in a register higher than before; and the old bass line, now separated from its original chordal context and given greater rhythmic animation, is more independent (Ex. 3-20). Homophony has given way to counterpoint.

The new line in subsection 2 can be called a *countermelody*—a melody in counterpoint to the first one. If the first melody is called the *theme*, or *subject*, (terms we will use more precisely later) the new line is called *countertheme*, or *countersubject*.

One might argue that what we have called a

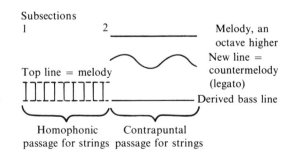

Example 3-20 Beethoven, Allegretto, first section (first half)

countermelody was really the principal melody, and that what we heard in subsection 1 was only the accompaniment to the principal melody, played once just as introduction before the principal melody was heard. But even though subsection 1 is soft in dynamic level and homophonic in texture and even though its top line is not strongly projected, still it is strong enough to be heard as an independent line when, in subsection 2, it is played off against the countermelody. At any rate, during subsection 2 there is more than just melody and accompaniment; the tension and excitement of counterpoint are clearly present.

Contrapuntal lines should have some kind of push and pull against each other if they are to maintain their independence. This melodic independence is heard most clearly in subsection 2 at those places where the first melody stops for breath. If you go back to subsection 1, these breathing places will be very clear; they divide subsection 1 into three phrases (Ex. 3-21a).

If you listen now to subsection 2, you will hear that the melody in the top line retains these three phrases exactly. The countermelody is especially active in the breathing place between phrases 2 and 3; it does not stop for breath but provides a link, a little surge of energy lifting from the end of one phrase to the beginning of the next (Ex. 3-21b).

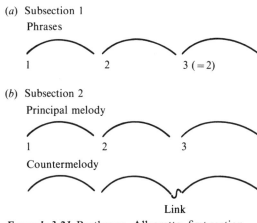

(a) Subsection 1
    Phrases

    1   2   3 (=2)

(b) Subsection 2
    Principal melody

    1   2   3

    Countermelody

                           Link

Example 3-21 Beethoven, Allegretto, first section, subsections 1 and 2: Phrase structure

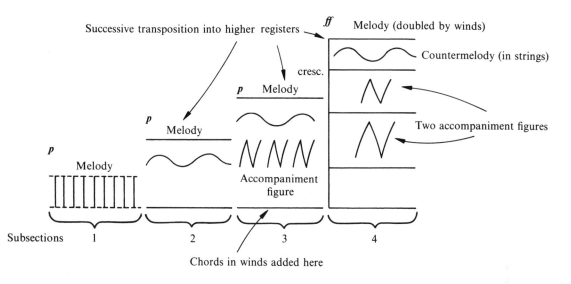

Example 3-22 Beethoven, Allegretto, first section: Plan of texture

Subsection 3 has very much the same shape as subsections 1 and 2: it consists of the same three phrases in both principal melody and countermelody. These two lines are now played in a still higher register by the violins (Ex. 3-22).

Underneath the lines—in the space left vacant by their transposition upward—is added a new accompaniment figure (Ex. 3-22). Roughly the same kind of figure as that we encountered in the second section of Schubert's "Der Neugierige" (see page 38), it provides a richer, more animated background for the lines above it. During this subsection, a crescendo to forte gains momentum rapidly; Beethoven has been careful to correlate the crescendo (which merely involves the instruments playing louder) with the expansion of the texture, lest we ask, "What are they shouting for?" The expanded texture seems actually to call for a crescendo—or at any rate makes the crescendo seem perfectly natural.

The climax of the crescendo is at the start of subsection 4. The principal melody and countermelody are still the same, but both have been shifted once more to a still higher register (Ex. 3-22). The principal melody is now played by the winds, doubling the line in resonant sonorities, spread over four octaves. The

countermelody soars high in the violins. The previous accompaniment figure is insufficient to fill the space left by this new transposition of the melodies upward. Another accompaniment figure has been added—one that does not exactly fit the first figure; together they create a continuous buzz of sound in the middle and bottom of the texture. From the simple homophonic beginning in the strings, the texture—now for full orchestra—has been periodically expanded to include first counterpoint and then an elaborate accompaniment.

THE FIRST INTERLUDE. After a relaxation of texture at the very end of the first section, the interlude brings a fresh texture. The interlude is not simple in its texture—indeed, it may be difficult to tell by ear exactly what is happening. Yet there is only one principal melody rather than two. The texture is melody and accompaniment, rather than contrapuntal.

The melody of the interlude, which is not as distinctive a line as either of the melodies in the first section, is played by winds (at the outset by clarinets and bassoons) in a rich, sonorous combination. The way the winds are combined recalls the doubling observed, for example, in subsection 4 of the first section: that is, the winds seem to be playing more or less the same line in different registers (Ex. 3-23).

The lower strings are playing along with the winds; in fact, you probably will not hear the lower strings as such. The upper strings (first violins), on the other hand, are clearly audible because they have a distinctive accompaniment figure, moving faster than the winds. The accompaniment figure is hung from the melody, so to speak: it frequently plays one of the melody notes, dropping from the melody and returning to it in several different ways. The texture is completed by a bass that repeats the rhythm of the beginning of the movement in pizzicato notes—as if to remind us that the interlude is part of the same piece.

The texture at the beginning of the interlude is characteristic of the interlude as a whole. Sometimes the upper winds become thicker, through addition of other winds (flutes, oboes, and horns); at other times they become thinner, with an occasional shift to imitation between two solo winds (for example, clarinet and horn). Behind these relatively subtle changes in texture, the violins keep up their accompaniment figure uninterrupted.

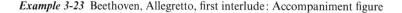
Accompaniment figure for first violins (legato) shown in dark notes and marked by brackets

Example 3-23 Beethoven, Allegretto, first interlude: Accompaniment figure

The texture of the interlude represents a carefully reckoned compromise. On the one hand, this texture must be simpler, less intense, than the preceding section if the interlude is to sound like an interlude. A more complex texture would obscure the overall shape at this point. On the other hand, too simple a texture would be out of line with the first section. If the level of complexity reached during the first section should be allowed to drop too far, the articulation at the beginning of the interlude would be too great—which could, paradoxically, make the interlude more important than an interlude should be. A completely homophonic texture, for example, might produce a very solemn effect. Beethoven's solution—a simple melody, richly doubled and given an intricate accompaniment—is a relief to the many-layered texture of the first section while still maintaining a sufficient level of intensity.

BETWEEN THE TWO INTERLUDES. The warm, relaxed atmosphere of the interlude is swept away by a brief loud pounding over several different registers in quick succession (Ex. 3-24). What follows is derived from the first section and strongly recalls it, so that

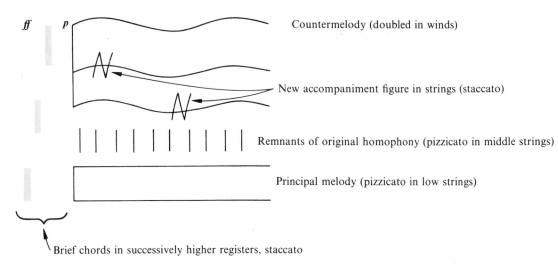

Example 3-24 Beethoven, Allegretto, beginning of middle section

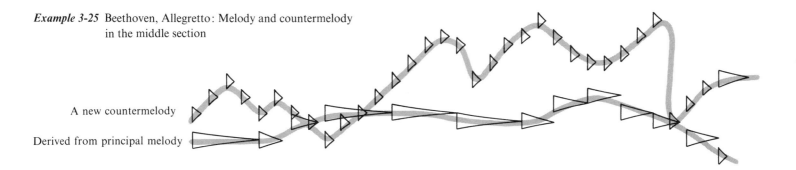

Example 3-25 Beethoven, Allegretto: Melody and countermelody
    in the middle section

A new countermelody

Derived from principal melody

the sectional shape of the first three sections is *A B A*. The material from the first section now appears in a new arrangement, however, so that a more precise representation of the sectional shape is A_1 *B* A_2.

The countermelody is now the uppermost line (Ex. 3-24). It appears in three octaves in winds (flute, oboe, and bassoon). The principal melody is now in the bass, with some of the homophony from subsection 1 scattered about in the middle strings, *above* the principal melody. Much more prominent in the middle strings, however, is a new accompaniment figure, faster than any heard in the movement so far. The texture as a whole is less massive but more intricate than that of the first section; it represents a still more complex arrangement of the original materials. Melody and phrase shapes remain as before, with three phrases clearly apparent in both principal

melody and countermelody. This complex texture persists about as long as one subsection of the first section (with an extra phrase added at the end as a prolongation).

The next section brings an imitative texture—probably the most intricate texture of the whole movement. The intricacy develops slowly; in fact, the beginning sounds like a simplification of texture, a reduction to only two lines. One of these, played by the first violins, is derived from the principal melody; and this line will be imitated throughout the passage. Against it—in fact usually higher in pitch (even though played by second violins)—is a new countermelody, unlike anything heard so far in the movement. The new countermelody moves relatively fast and in a manner more suggestive of an accompaniment figure than a melody (Ex. 3-25). Yet the whole

effect is one of counterpoint rather than melody and accompaniment. Something urges the ear to pay more attention to the differences between the lines than to their similarities.

The two lines of Ex. 3-25 are represented schematically at 1 in Ex. 3-26. At 2 in Ex. 3-26, the two lines are exchanged, so that the new countermelody is below instead of above; this exchange has the effect of introducing the main subject of imitation in a new register, providing the first imitative entrance. This same subject enters a third time in the lower strings (at 3, Ex. 3-26), first with the countermelody above, then (at 4) exchanged so that the countermelody is below. From here on, the principal subject reappears several times, accompanied by the countermelody, amid extensions and variations in each line. Later we will study more closely the kinds of melodic

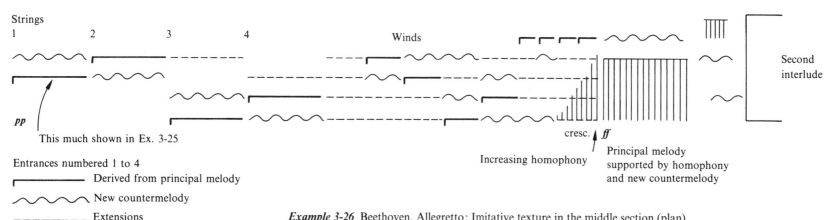

Strings

1   2   3   4   Winds

Second
interlude

pp

This much shown in Ex. 3-25

Entrances numbered 1 to 4

———————— Derived from principal melody

〜〜〜〜〜 New countermelody

— — — — — — Extensions

cresc. *ff*

Increasing homophony

Principal melody
supported by homophony
and new countermelody

Example 3-26 Beethoven, Allegretto: Imitative texture in the middle section (plan)

processes involved in imitative passages such as this; here, be aware of the novel effect this texture has in the movement as a whole.

The four independent lines pursue their divergent paths for about the length of subsection 1, until finally they are swept up in a crescendo and are dissipated in a return to a basically homophonic texture (Ex. 3-26). That is, the larger part of the orchestra pounds out the principal melody fortissimo in pure homophony, while the woodwinds play the new countermelody introduced in the imitative section. In other words, the oldest element and the newest, each in its most forceful form, are now combined.

ROLE OF THE IMITATIVE SECTION. The intricate imitative texture of the section just discussed is clearly different from the rest of the movement, which is often contrapuntal but not imitative. This difference in texture affects the overall shape of the movement. Looking back at Ex. 3-18, the movement appears to consist of a number of subsections grouped by the interludes: there are four subsections before the first interlude and three between the two interludes, the passage in imitation being represented there by the second of these three. But even a few listenings indicate that the overall shape is not that simple.

A thorough discussion of the various ways in which the subsections can be grouped into larger sections would not be appropriate here. Furthermore, the movement is not unambiguous in this respect: different observers will interpret its overall shape differently. One of the crucial factors in any interpretation, however, is the imitative section. In terms of texture, this section is basically *different* from its surroundings and could even be considered as a separate, contrasting element in the movement as a whole. In terms of melody, on the other hand, the imitative section is basically *similar* to its surroundings in that it is built upon the same theme. Often the listener must balance one factor against another (here, texture against melody) in determining shape.

FROM THE SECOND INTERLUDE TO THE END. Whatever the interpretation of the stretch between the interludes, the appearance of the second interlude is a clear return to the melody, mood, and texture of

the first interlude. All is as it was, except that the second interlude is much shorter than the first. The suave, sonorous melody and the smooth accompaniment figure dispel the intricacies of imitation.

The final section brings a partial return to the homophony of the beginning; yet not without complexity, because here—for the first time—the integrity of the lines themselves is brought into question, whereas before, the lines were intact no matter how complex the texture. At the end of the second interlude, after a very soft transition, the texture becomes abruptly chordal (at the fortissimo). This spot is marked by strong, abrupt contrasts of dynamics and timbre. From here to the end, the musical material is derived from the opening subsection—but the derivation may not be immediately clear because of the way the material is distributed around the orchestra.

Starting with the highest notes, pianissimo in the flutes and oboes (see Ex. 3-27), the principal melody appears with four successive timbres, all within phrase 1. The basic texture is homophonic, as in the opening subsection (with a soft pizzicato chordal accompaniment in the strings). But the differences in timbre every five notes and the concomitant differences in register break up the line. The descent through four timbres and registers is repeated for the

next phrase of the melody; then, as the movement comes to a close, the dissolution of the line goes even further. A final chord in the winds matches the opening chord of the movement—and here, at last, that isolated opening chord shows its relationship to the rest of the movement.

TEXTURE AND THE SHAPE OF THE MOVEMENT. After you can follow the characteristic textures of each section, listen to the whole movement with perhaps nothing in front of you except Ex. 3-18, which merely outlines the subsections. Aside from the interludes, each of these subsections contains the principal melody; each treats it in a different texture. The procession of textures begins with very simple homophony, going on to an elaborate countermelody and a thickly figured accompaniment before the first interlude. After this interlude, the texture continues to become more intense, reaching a peak in the imitative section. Thereafter, a reduction in intensity takes place, with the texture itself becoming homophonic in the last section. But just as the interludes could not be made overly simple in texture, so the last section must maintain something of the accumulated tension of the movement to be effective in context. Effectiveness is achieved by breaking up the simple texture with changes of timbre and register.

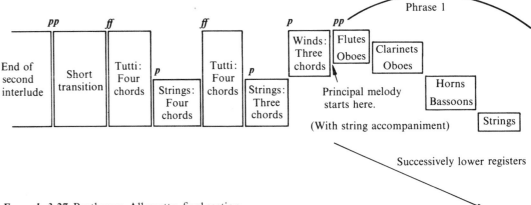

Example 3-27 Beethoven, Allegretto, final section

Exercises for further listening

I. SCHUBERT: "DER MULLER UND DER BACH" (DIE SCHONE MULLERIN, SONG 19)

Listen to the song as you follow the text given here. Concentrate on the textures in the piano accompaniment as you listen again.

PART I

Der Müller:
Wo ein treues Herze in Liebe vergeht,
Da welken die Lilien auf jedem Beet.
Da muss in die Wolken der Vollmond gehn,
Damit seine Tränen die Menschen nicht sehn.
Da halten die Englein die Augen sich zu,
Und schluchzen und singen die Seele zur Ruh'.

The miller lad:
Where a faithful heart dies of love,
there the lilies wither in every bed.
Then into the clouds the full moon must ride,
so that his tears shall not be seen by men.
Then the angels close their eyes,
and sob and sing the soul to rest.

PART II

Der Bach:
Und wenn sich die Liebe dem Schmerz entringt,
Ein Sternlein, ein neues, am Himmel erblinkt.
Da springen drei Rosen, halb rot und halb weiss,
Die welken nicht wieder, aus Dornenreis.
Und die Engelein schneiden die Flügel sich ab,
Und gehn alle Morgen zur Erde herab.

The brook:
And when love is released from sorrow,
a star, a new one twinkles in the heavens.
There spring up three roses, half red, half white,
never to wither, from the prickly stems.
And the angels cut their wings off,
and come every morning down to the earth.

PART III

Der Müller:
Ach Bächlein, liebes Bächlein, du meinst es so gut:
Ach, Bächlein, aber weisst du, wie Liebe tut?
Ach, unten, da unten, die kühle Ruh'!
Ach, Bächlein, liebes Bächlein, so singe nur zu.

The miller lad:
Dear brooklet, you mean it so well,
but brooklet, do you know what it is to be in love?
Ah down, down there, the cooling rest!
Ah brooklet, dear brooklet, just sing me to sleep.

German text selected and translated by Philip L. Miller. Reprinted from *The Ring of Words*, © by Doubleday and Company, Inc., by permission.

1. How many different textures do you hear in the piano accompaniment?   **1.** a
____ **a.** Two
____ **b.** Three
____ **c.** More than three

2. These two textures are arranged in the pattern   **2.** b
____ **a.** *A B A*   ____ **c.** *A B B A*
____ **b.** *A B*   ____ **d.** *A B A B*

3. The change from the first to the second texture takes place   3. b
___ **a.** In the middle of part I
___ **b.** At the beginning of part II
___ **c.** In the middle of part II
___ **d.** At the beginning of part III

4. The first texture could be described as   4. c
___ **a.** Contrapuntal   ___ **b.** Continuous figuration
___ **c.** Chordal   ___ **d.** Monophonic

5. The second texture could be described as   5. a
___ **a.** Continuous figuration
___ **b.** Chordal
___ **c.** Monophonic
___ **d.** Contrapuntal

QUESTIONS FOR DISCUSSION

A. What event in the poem is symbolized by the change in texture at the beginning of part II?
B. When the miller lad sings again (part III), why does the accompaniment continue with the figuration of part II instead of returning to the chords of part I?

II. SCHUBERT: ''AM FEIERABEND'' (DIE SCHONE MULLERIN, SONG 5)

On your first listening follow the text, given here. (An English translation is given in Chapter 11.) Answer questions 1 through 5. For convenience, the piano interludes as well as the text lines are numbered here. The signs 〚: :〛 indicate a repeat of the text.

1 __ __ (*Piano*)	13 __ __ 〚:Jeder Knappe tut mir's nach. :〛	25 __ __ Könnt' ich brausend die Räder führen!
2 __ __ (*Piano*)	14 __ __ (*Piano*)	26 __ __ Könnt' ich wehen durch alle Haine!
3 __ __ Hätt' ich tausend Arme zu rühren!	15 __ __ Und da sitz' ich in der grossen Runde	27 __ __ Könnt' ich drehen alle Steine!
4 __ __ Könnt' ich brausend die Räder führen!	16 __ __ (*Piano*)	28 __ __ 〚:Dass die schöne Müllerin
5 __ __ Könnt' ich wehen durch alle Haine!	17 __ __ In der stillen, kühlen Feierstunde,	29 __ __ Merkte meinen meinen treuen Sinn! :〛
6 __ __ Könnt' ich drehen alle Steine!	18 __ __ (*Piano*)	30 __ __ (*Piano*)
7 __ __ 〚:Dass die schöne Müllerin	19 __ __ Und der Meister spricht zu Allen:	31 __ __ Dass die schöne Müllerin
8 __ __ Merkte meinen treuen Sinn! :〛	20 __ __ 〚:Euer Werk hat mir gefallen. :〛	32 __ __ (*Piano*)
9 __ __ (*Piano*)	21 __ __ Und das liebe Mädchen sagt	33 __ __ Merkte meinen treuen Sinn!
10 __ __ Ach, wie ist mein Arm so schwach!	22 __ __ 〚:Allen eine gute Nacht. :〛	34 __ __ (*Piano*)
11 __ __ Was ich hebe, was ich trage,	23 __ __ (*Piano*)	35 __ __ (*Piano: end*)
12 __ __ Was ich schneide, was ich schlage,	24 __ __ Hatt' ich tausend Arme zu rühren!	

"Texture" refers to the piano accompaniment only.

1. Determine where there are significant contrasts in texture. Indicate each change of texture by placing a check in the left-hand blank beside the text line.

1. There are texture changes at numbers 2, 3, 10, 14, 19, 23, 31, 32, 33, 34, 35

2. Indicate each appearance of chordal texture (chords, not broken chords) by placing a check in the right-hand blank beside the text line.

2. Chordal texture appears at numbers 1, 10 through 13, 19 through 22, 31, 33, 35

3. The texture that begins at number 3 consists of
___ **a.** Broken chords
___ **b.** Counterpoint
___ **c.** Both *a* and *b*
___ **d.** Neither *a* nor *b*

3. a

4. Does the figuration that begins at number 3 return anywhere in the song?
___ Yes ___ No

4. Yes

5. Where?

5. At 23 through 30 and briefly at 32

QUESTIONS FOR DISCUSSION

A. Does the texture at 3 through 8 (and again at 23 through 29) relate to the poem in any way? If so, how?

B. Does the contrasting texture at 10 through 13 relate to the poem in any way? If so, how?

C. What is the effect of the texture at 19 through 22, in relation to the texture that precedes it? To the texture that follows it? What relation, if any, has the texture at 19 through 22 to the meaning of the poem?

D. What is the function of the rapid changes of texture at the end of the song (at 31 through 35)? What is their effect? Do they have any relation to the meaning of the poem?

III. BARTOK: STRING QUARTET NO. 6. MESTO I, II, III, IV

Listen to Mesto I. Answer questions 1 and 2.

1. The texture of Mesto I consists of
___ **a.** Chords only
___ **b.** Two melodies combined
___ **c.** A single melody with accompaniment
___ **d.** A single melody without accompaniment

1. d

2. This type of texture is called

_____ **a.** Polyphonic

_____ **b.** Monophonic

_____ **c.** Homophonic

_____ **d.** Contrapuntal

2. b

Listen to Mesto II. Answer questions 3 through 6.

3. In Mesto II, the melody from Mesto I is in

_____ **a.** The highest register, on the top of the texture

_____ **b.** The middle register, in the center of the texture

_____ **c.** The lowest register, at the bottom of the texture

3. c (in the cello)

4. The other instruments play

_____ **a.** A single independent melody, each instrument in the same register

_____ **b.** A single independent melody, doubled in several registers

_____ **c.** A chordal accompaniment

_____ **d.** Three-part counterpoint, a separate line for each instrument

4. a

5. How many independent lines (not instruments) are heard simultaneously in Mesto II?

_____ **a.** One _____ **b.** Two _____ **c.** Three _____ **d.** Four

5. b

6. In Mesto II,

_____ **a.** Imitation occurs between voices

_____ **b.** Imitation does not occur

6. b

Listen to Mesto III. Answer questions 7 through 14.

7. In Mesto III, how many instruments (not lines) do you hear at the beginning?

_____ **a.** One _____ **b.** Two _____ **c.** Three _____ **d.** All four

7. c (first and second violins, and cello in a high register)

8. How many instruments (not lines) do you hear at the end of Mesto III?

_____ **a.** One _____ **b.** Two _____ **c.** Three _____ **d.** All four

8. d

9. The texture of Mesto III could be described as

_____ **a.** Chordal (homophonic)

_____ **b.** Contrapuntal

_____ **c.** Melody with accompaniment

9. b

58

10. How many separate lines (not instruments) are there throughout Mesto III?   **10.** c

___ **a.** One   ___ **b.** Two   ___ **c.** Three   ___ **d.** Four

11. At the beginning of Mesto III, the original melody is heard in the   **11.** a (first violin)

___ **a.** Top voice   ___ **b.** Middle voice

___ **c.** Bottom voice

12. As Mesto III continues, parts of the original melody are heard in   **12.** b

___ **a.** The highest and lowest voices, but not in the middle voice

___ **b.** The highest and middle voices, but not in the lowest voice

___ **c.** All three voices

13. In Mesto III,   **13.** a

___ **a.** Imitation occurs between some of the voices

___ **b.** Imitation does not occur

14. The imitative voice always enters   **14.** b

___ **a.** After the first voice has finished

___ **b.** Before the first voice has finished, so that an overlap occurs

Listen to the beginning of Mesto IV through the first crescendo to *f*, ending just before the *pp* section. Answer questions 15, 16, and 17.

15. The texture of this section is   **15.** c

___ **a.** Homophonic

___ **b.** Melody with accompaniment

___ **c.** Contrapuntal

___ **d.** Monophonic

16. In this section of Mesto IV, how many independent contrapuntal lines are present?   **16.** c

___ **a.** Two

___ **b.** Three

___ **c.** Four

17. In this section, the original melody or a recognizable variant of it   **17.** c

___ **a.** Is heard in the top voice only

___ **b.** Is heard in the bottom voice only

___ **c.** Is heard in imitation between the two outer voices

___ **d.** Is not heard at all

Listen to the remainder of the movement. Answer questions 18 through 21.

18. The texture of the remainder of Mesto IV   18. b
___ **a.** Remains unchanged throughout
___ **b.** Varies from section to section

19. The prevailing texture is   19. b
___ **a.** Melody and accompaniment
___ **b.** Counterpoint
___ **c.** Homophony
___ **d.** Monophony

20. Which one of the following textures is not present?   20. c
___ **a.** Imitative counterpoint
___ **b.** Nonimitative counterpoint
___ **c.** Monophony
___ **d.** Melody and accompaniment
___ **e.** Chords

21. When the original melody, from Mesto I, returns just before the end, it is   21. a
___ **a.** Accompanied by one other line
___ **b.** Accompanied by chords
___ **c.** Unaccompanied

PATTERNS IN TIME may be as simple as the ticking of a clock or so complex as to resist the most subtle analysis. They may be standardized patterns formed over and over again in many pieces, or they may be unique to a particular piece. The patterns may leap out of the music, as when played by a drum solo; or they may be hidden behind dense timbres and textures. In all cases, however, the shapes a piece assumes as it unfolds in time will be an essential aspect of the piece.

Speaking generally, the temporal aspect of a piece —the way it unfolds in time—is referred to by the term *rhythm*. This term is difficult to define and to use; many people would not want to use it in the very general sense just indicated, preferring to restrict the definition of "rhythm" one way or another. In fact, any answer to the question "What is rhythm?" would probably turn out to be argumentative. We might say, "Rhythm is motion in time." That definition seems to fit much of the music that is familiar to us; but, then, our culture lays great stress upon motion, especially motion toward a goal. Music from other historical periods and from other places (as well as some of our own recent music) may not be so concerned with getting somewhere. Its rhythms may not even seem to involve motion; still, they are rhythms.

We can understand rhythm more easily if we think of it, not as an entity to be defined, but rather as an aspect—the temporal aspect—of a piece of music. We considered other aspects of music (such as timbre or texture) individually, and we can do the same for rhythm. A direct way to isolate the rhythmic aspect of a piece is to clap in time to its rhythm as you hear it. (This will be easy or difficult to do according to whether the rhythm of the piece is simple or complex.) The clapping extracts the rhythm—or at least some important factors of the rhythm—from other aspects of the piece, such as its timbre or texture. But even though it may be simple to isolate the rhythm of a particular piece in this way, it would be difficult, as well as risky, for us to try to discuss rhythm in general apart from actual pieces. Our immediate goal is to develop sensitivity to whatever rhythms, whatever temporal patterns, we find in specific pieces.

There is, however, one component of temporal

CHAPTER 4 RHYTHM AND METER

organization that can be studied in the abstract. Patterns in time, unlike patterns of timbre or texture, can be heard in terms of a simple, obvious set of coordinates: time can be measured in equal units, and these units can be arranged in regular multiples and systems as coordinates for both regular and irregular patterns—a process like that of projecting a gracefully irregular curve upon a piece of graph paper in order to become more acutely aware of its shape.

Almost anyone can imagine a pulse that occurs at equal intervals of time (as long as the pulse does not go too fast or too slow—limitations we will explore later). This kind of regular pulse provides the primary coordinate for studying rhythms. Tapping your foot at equal intervals in time to a piece of music is a bodily manifestation of such a pulse. Musicians sometimes use a device called a *metronome*, which produces equidistant ticks or flashes of light to help them compare their playing with a pulse.

Even though no piece of music consists exclusively of simple pulses, a great many pieces include such pulsation in their rhythmic patterns. When you tap your foot to the rhythm of a piece, you are marking a pulse that corresponds to some element of regularity in the rhythm. The coordinate has not been selected at random, in other words; instead, you have selected a coordinate, or pulse, that is commensurate with the rhythm.

Clearly, there is an intimate relationship between rhythm as it appears in actual pieces of music and the equidistant pulses we can supply as a coordinate.

While keeping that relationship in mind, you should be aware of the difference between the pulse, which is perfectly regular, and the rhythm of the music, which may be regular or irregular but is almost always more complex or more detailed than the pulse.

RHYTHM AND METER. *Meter* in its simplest form is a pulse of the kind just described—a pulse occurring at equal intervals of time, against which one can measure musical rhythms. Meter usually takes more complex forms through various groupings of the pulses into systems, as we will describe soon. Even in its simplest form as a pulse, however, it is possible to define meter and to compare it to rhythm. We should say that meter and rhythm are often compared and the results are expressed in almost as many different ways as there are people to make the comparison. In this book we will treat meter and rhythm as quite distinct phenomena, then proceed to study their close relationship.

We will use "meter" to refer to equidistant pulses that the listener infers from the music and that he expects to continue beyond the present into the immediate future. In Ex. 4-1, the rhythm of an imaginary piece is represented by the jagged line; the rhythm is complex but shows sharp peaks of intensity that happen to come at equal intervals. The listener detects these equal intervals, then abstracts them from their rhythmic context as the basis for an equidistant pulse or meter, against which he hears the whole rhythm of the piece. The listener does not know what the

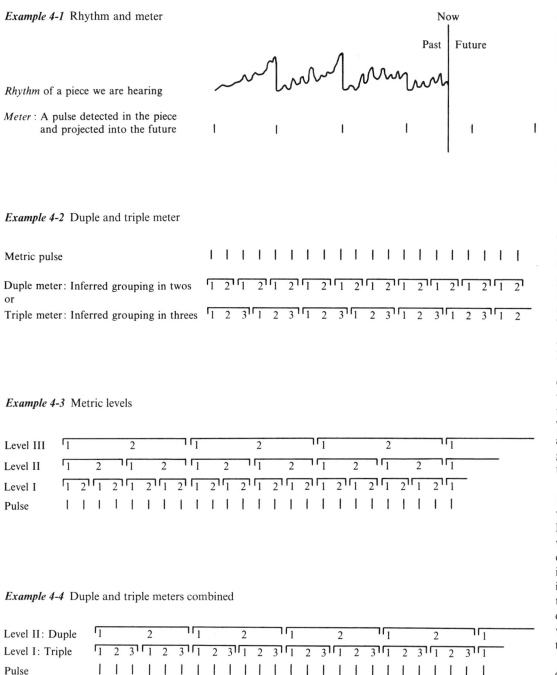

Example 4-1 Rhythm and meter

Now

Past | Future

Rhythm of a piece we are hearing

Meter: A pulse detected in the piece
and projected into the future

Example 4-2 Duple and triple meter

Metric pulse

Duple meter: Inferred grouping in twos

or

Triple meter: Inferred grouping in threes

Example 4-3 Metric levels

Level III

Level II

Level I

Pulse

Example 4-4 Duple and triple meters combined

Level II: Duple

Level I: Triple

Pulse

rhythm will do next, but he projects the meter into the future as the most likely prediction. All of this happens as an almost automatic reaction on the part of the listener.

Meter is absolutely regular, since its function is to provide a steady background clock against which to hear varying rhythmic shapes. A metronome that ticked irregularly would be of little use. The word "meter" means "measure" (note that a clock is a time-meter); meter measures musical rhythm. When rhythms are very regular (at the composer's option), then we often describe them as *metrical rhythms*, which means roughly the same as *regular rhythms*.

METRIC GROUPINGS. Confronted with regularly recurring events, such as the ticks of a clock or metronome, most people organize these events by grouping them. If you attempt to count such a regular pulse, you probably do not count ONE ONE ONE . . . but rather ONE TWO ONE TWO ONE TWO . . . or ONE TWO THREE ONE TWO THREE ONE TWO THREE . . . or perhaps some other short grouping over and over. This regular grouping of pulses is one of the most important aspects of meter.

When pulses seem to be organized into regularly recurring patterns of two (ONE TWO ONE TWO . . .) we speak of *duple meter*. We call a pattern containing three pulses (ONE TWO THREE ONE TWO THREE . . .) *triple meter* (Ex. 4-2). In the absence of any influences to the contrary, most people seem to group a perfectly regular pulse into twos rather than threes, into duple rather than triple meter.

METER AT DIFFERENT LEVELS. As we group pulses, we seem automatically to try to group the groups. If we group a series of pulses into twos, for example, we may also group these twos into larger twos. This can be described as a grouping on different *levels*; indeed, the grouping of groups provides a specific idea of what is meant by level of organization. The three different groupings in Ex. 4-3 represent three different levels of metrical organization. The level with the largest group (in this case, level III) is said to be the highest level.

Different people are aware of levels to varying degrees. Some people are sensitive to several superimposed levels. That is, they hear many pulses—say, thirty-two—as forming a single large group at a high level; they hear the thirty-third pulse as marking the beginning of another clear group. Other people might group the same series of pulses only in twos or fours, that is, only at one or two low levels.

Most listeners can hear at least two metric levels clearly. In Ex. 4-3, for instance, we can hear the pulses grouped in twos at level I, and the twos grouped into larger twos at level II.

Pulses can be grouped in twos at one level, in threes at another. In certain combinations of this type, it is very obvious that two different groupings operate simultaneously. A clear example is a grouping of threes at level I, twos at level II, as in Ex. 4-4.

RELATION OF METER AND RHYTHM ON A LOW LEVEL. To illustrate metric groupings as they apply to the rhythm of a piece, we will trace the rhythmic construction of a Schubert song, studying first the system of pulses at the lower levels.

Franz Schubert (1797–1828)

DIE SCHONE MULLERIN
"DAS WANDERN" (SONG 1)

When we infer a meter from the music, we construct whatever metric system corresponds most closely to the rhythmic structure of the music. The metric groupings on each level and the number of levels will depend on how the music sounds.

Listen to the beginning of "Das Wandern" several times. The notes of the piano accompaniment move at a rapid pace in an unvarying pattern. Example 4-5 represents the successive sounds of this accompaniment—the fastest notes—with wedges. At this very low level, the music seems to suggest a metric grouping in twos.

If you try to count along with the music at this pace, however, you will soon become breathless. As you listen again, count on the next higher metric level, as in Ex. 4-6; you will find that the grouping is still duple. The pyramid can easily be continued to higher levels. The next metric level, shown in Ex 4-7, is also duple. In order to satisfy yourself that duple

Example 4-5 Schubert, "Das Wandern": Lowest metric level

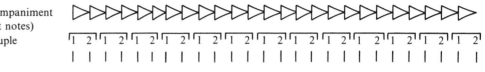

Piano accompaniment (fastest notes)

Level I: Duple

Example 4-6 Schubert, "Das Wandern": Second metric level

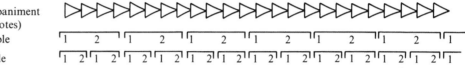

Piano accompaniment (fastest notes)

Level II: Duple

Level I: Duple

Example 4-7 Schubert, "Das Wandern": Third metric level

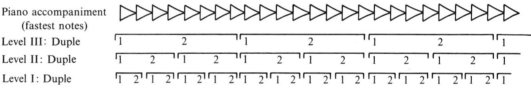

Piano accompaniment (fastest notes)

Level III: Duple

Level II: Duple

Level I: Duple

grouping is the most appropriate, you can try grouping pulses in threes at any of these levels. While you may be able to count threes, you will soon realize you are counting against the rhythm of the music instead of with it.

So far you have been counting meter. What about the rhythm? Listen to the first line of the vocal part several times, so that you can sing it to yourself (or at least say the words in time to the music). Now try tapping the pulses at level II, as you follow along in Ex. 4-8. It may be difficult to sing and tap at the same time, but try it at least long enough to sense the difference between singing and tapping that soon develops.

Although the voice part starts out with each of its

notes corresponding to a pulse at level II, it does not continue as regularly. At "Müllers," for example, there are two vocal notes for each pulse on level II, and the second "Wan-" is longer than a single pulse.

The notes of the vocal part and of the accompaniment are the rhythm; the pulses you tapped represent the meter. The rhythms of this piece happen to be very simple; they coincide with the meter, for the most part. Or to put it differently, it is easy to find a meter that corresponds closely to the rhythm. Such regular rhythms (as mentioned) are often called metrical rhythms. In the case of "Das Wandern," the rhythm allows us to trace a metric pulse throughout the piece at levels I, II, and III—and at higher levels too, as we will see.

Example 4-8 Schubert, "Das Wandern": Rhythm of the vocal part

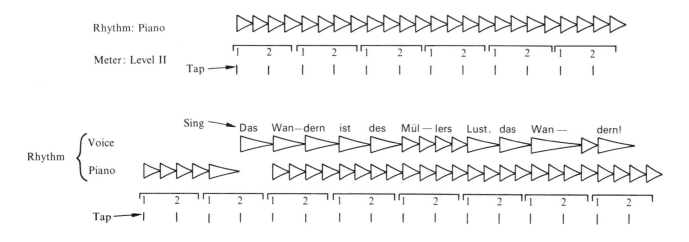

Example 4-9 Principal metric level

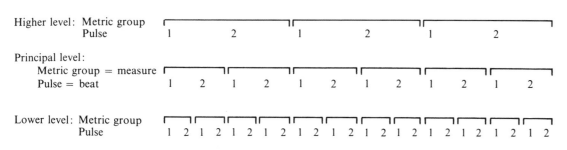

PRINCIPAL LEVEL. Sometimes you need to keep track of several metric levels at once. Usually, however, you will decide which of several levels is the most useful or most meaningful or most convenient for counting. Indeed many pieces can be counted easily on only one level.

To keep track of rhythmic detail in performance, musicians habitually count at a fairly low level, although by no means always at the lowest level, for notes on that level often go by so fast as to render counting them impractical (as with the fastest notes in "Das Wandern"). Musicians find that counting faster than two or three times per second is inconvenient, while counting slower than once every two seconds is difficult to do accurately without also keeping track of the subdivisions. Counting, in other words, is usually done at a rate ranging between half a second and two seconds for each count.

A piece may have an extensive hierarchy of rhythmic levels and may suggest a corresponding hierarchy of metric levels; but one of these levels—one of the lower ones—will have a pulse falling between the limits just discussed. This is most likely to be taken as the principal one by trained as well as untrained listeners. In some cases, the determination of the

Example 4-10 Schubert, "Das Wandern": Principal metric level

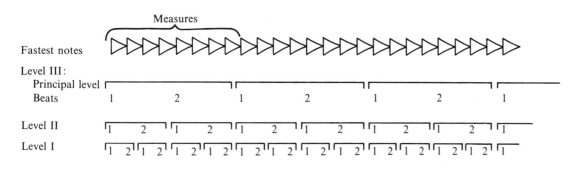

principal metric level may be a matter of choice, for there may be two levels whose rates of pulse falls within the acceptable limits.

BEAT AND MEASURE. Having identified the principal levels, we can use it to define two important terms, *beat* and *measure*.

The term "beat" is used in a variety of contexts. In a purely physical sense, it refers to the motion of the conductor's right hand as it keeps track of the meter; that motion (to which we will return in a moment) is the conductor's beat. In another sense, "beat" is used to describe a vital rhythmic quality of music; we say certain music has a strong rhythmic beat. This rhythmic meaning of the word may be very hard to define.

In speaking of beat in a metric sense, however, we are dealing with something more definable. We can say that beat is the metric pulse at the principal level. Pulses on levels below the principal level may be called *subdivisions of the beat*. Pulses on higher levels are sometimes colloquially called *big beats* (Ex. 4-9).

Similarly, the term "measure" refers to the metric group at the principal level. As a metric group, a measure can be duple or triple; that is, it can include either two or three pulses. If the music demanded it, the measure could include five pulses, or seven. Groups of four pulses would mean that two levels were involved, with the pulses grouped in twos at the lower level, then the twos grouped in twos at the next higher level. (See Appendix C for a discussion of the measures used in notation.)

For any given piece, you must decide first, whether the rhythm allows you to infer from it a metric pulse; then, at what *levels* you can hear a metric pulse, and, what the *grouping* is at each of these levels; finally, which level is the *principal level*. Having decided on a principal level, stick with the beat and the measure at that level until the rhythm of the music changes drastically enough to force you to change your metric framework.

The term "measure" also refers, in musical notation, to the length of the unit used by the composer to notate the principal metric group of the piece. A composer decides what he thinks is the principal metric level of his piece, then writes the piece down in that basic meter or measure. The measures are marked

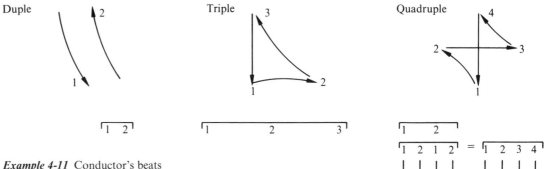

Example 4-11 Conductor's beats

off on the page by clear vertical lines, called *bar lines*; hence a measure (or space between adjacent bar lines), is also called a *bar*. (See Appendix C for a brief description of the notation of meter and rhythm.)

Since in this book we are working from what we hear and not from what we see in the musical score, we will use the term "measure" to refer to the metric groups at the level we decide (by listening) is the principal level. Our choice may or may not be the same level and the same metric group selected by the composer for his notation. In most cases, however, the difference will not be crucial: you might, for example, hear a slow beat with a strong subdivision in a piece that the composer notated in fast beats.

In "Das Wandern," we determined by listening that the rhythms suggest regular recurring pulses at three different levels; each level turned out to be duple, not triple. Either level II or level III could serve as the principal level for the piece; Schubert's notation uses level III. If we choose level III as the principal level, we can refer to each of its pulses as a beat and to each of its metric groups as a measure. There are two beats in each of these measures (Ex. 4-10).

PRINCIPAL LEVEL AND THE CONDUCTOR. One of the most important things a conductor does is to indicate the beat. The conductor actually keeps up a perpetual count with his right hand, so that the performers can keep track of the meter at the principal level. There are many ways of indicating the count, but the ways most commonly encountered are shown in Ex. 4-11. These are views from the conductor's back, as you

would see him from the audience. In addition to these patterns—or sometimes in place of them—the conductor may indicate something about the pulse at higher levels. Watching a conductor's beat closely can give a valuable insight into the way he conceives the meter of a piece.

The conductor's indications for rhythm are much less formalized than those for meter, being as varied as the rhythm itself. The conductor's rhythmic gestures are sometimes very apparent but more often are very subtle and visible only to the players.

UPBEAT AND DOWNBEAT. From the conductor's beat, common usage has adopted the terms *upbeat* and *downbeat*. Speaking in terms of meter, the count of ONE is called the downbeat, for on that count the conductor brings his hand downward.

The term "upbeat" is used to describe a beat that immediately precedes a downbeat and is very closely linked to it, for instance, by being the first note in a piece or section. A piece that starts THREE ONE TWO THREE ONE TWO THREE ONE . . . is said to start on the upbeat. Upbeats can be linked to their following downbeats in more subtle ways, too. Of the various terms associated with beat, "upbeat" is the least susceptible of a strict definition. (Sometimes a term borrowed from Greek poetry, *anacrusis*, is used as a synonym for "upbeat.")

In Ex. 4-8, it is clear that the vocal part starts in the middle of a metric group: the syllable "Das," the first word of the song, comes on count TWO of level II. At level II, then, the vocal part does not start on a downbeat but on an upbeat. This is an excellent example of how a count of TWO that begins a piece or a section can be closely linked with a following downbeat: the syllable "Das" and its count of TWO obviously go with the following word "Wandern," which begins on the downbeat, ONE.

The upbeat beginning, which can be found at the beginning of the other vocal phrases of the song as well, is an instance of how rhythm differs from meter. Metric groups begin, by definition, on ONE; but the composer can begin his music on any count he pleases. We will see many times a significant difference between the rhythmic grouping—the way the notes of the music go together—and the metric grouping that we infer as a regular background to the rhythm.

Sometimes the terms "upbeat" and "downbeat" are used in a purely rhythmic context, without reference to a metric count. Their application is then more intuitive and more difficult. In many kinds of music, we speak of a downbeat in a certain place because we *feel* a downbeat there; such a downbeat may or may not fall on a count of ONE, and we may or may not be able to show how or why it is a downbeat. This is a transferred use of the term: it borrows the concept of downbeat (and also upbeat) from a clear metrical context for application in a more ambiguous rhythmic context. We will encounter an example of this later, in Chapter 5.

TEMPO. Music whose beat is near the upper limit of the range discussed—one beat every half second or faster—is said to have a relatively fast pace, or *tempo*. Music whose beat falls near the lower limit—once every 2 seconds—moves at a slow tempo. Tempo, in itself, does not affect the meter or the rhythmic patterns of a piece of music: any given piece can be played at a number of slightly different tempos, slower or faster.

A large difference in the tempo of a particular piece, however, could mean that the beat on what was the principal level now goes too slow or too fast to be perceived as a beat. Another level will become the principal level, the pulses on that level falling into the range appropriate to a beat. The difference in tempo, then, can bring about a reinterpretation of the metric and rhythmic structure.

The Italian tempo terms used as titles of movements—such as the Presto of Beethoven's Symphony No. 7—refer to the speed of the beats. Not all the notes in the Presto, for example, are fast; but the beat is fast. Similarly, not all the notes in a slow movement are necessarily slow, but the beat is slow.

CAUSES OF METRIC GROUPINGS. So far we have avoided the question, "What causes us to hear a certain pulse or to choose a certain metric grouping?" We have merely observed that one or the other kind of grouping was suggested by the music. In general, anything in the music that creates or suggests a regular grouping can be the clue to determining the appropriate meter. To take a very simple example, if the timbre of a piece changed regularly every three pulses, this timbre change could set up a very clear grouping and could suggest a certain meter. An abrupt change of register every three pulses could also suggest a certain meter (Ex. 4-12).

Example 4-12 Timbre and register as causes of metric grouping

(*a*)

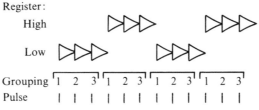

(*b*)

These are crude examples—crude because they involve only one musical element in a very obvious way. Ordinarily, in real music we find much more subtle combinations of several elements operating together. Often a sense of grouping is built of just such a combination of elements. In such cases, we may not be able to separate the effects of the individual elements;

we may be aware only of the resultant grouping.

When clear, regular pulses can be heard on two or more levels at once, the way these pulses coincide and reinforce each other will have a strong effect on their grouping. In "Das Wandern," for example, the way the pulses on levels I and II fit together is one of the strongest determinants of the duple meter that prevails at the upper levels. The pulses on level II, by their mere presence, require a grouping in twos of the pulses on level I. In a piece whose rhythms are as clear and regular as this, the metric groups could not be construed in any other way. In many pieces, however, rhythms are not so clear and simple, and the metric groupings produced through coincidence of patterns on different levels are frequently an important factor.

ACCENT. One of the thorniest problems in rhythm is presented by *accent*, a term that refers to something real—but something that is perceived differently by different observers.

Speaking functionally, an accent is something that protrudes, sticks out, draws attention to itself and away from its neighbors. A significant change in any musical element could cause an accent. If we hear a note as accented, upon analysis we could find associated with that note some change or contrast that made it stick out. The note might be longer or louder or higher or lower or different in some other way from those around it.

Accents are frequently associated with the beginnings of metric groups, with the count of ONE. To put it another way, if accents appear regularly in a series of pulses, they will suggest—if not demand—a metric grouping and with it a meter, as in Ex. 4-13.

The matter is complicated, however, by the fact that we seem to attribute accents to the beginnings of metric groups whether or not the beginning of the group protrudes or is accented in any perceptible way. When we count out meters or discuss them or even think about them, we tend to project or to emphasize the metric grouping by supplying an accent in the form of a stress or emphasis on the beginning of each group: ONE TWO THREE ONE TWO THREE. Old-fashioned piano teachers rapped their students' knuckles on every ONE, thereby instilling a badly exaggerated sense of stress into the notion of meter. Throughout the greater part of music's history, however, the sense of stress associated with metric groups has undoubtedly been far more supple and subtle.

In general, accent is a more restricted phenomenon than grouping. To put it another way, the factors that produce *groupings* are more varied and are present in a broader variety of circumstances than are those that produce *accents*. We can find groupings of some kind in virtually all music, whereas there might be many kinds of music in which we would be reluctant to point out accents. Not all accents produce metric groups: an isolated accent has little or no metric significance. Only when accents recur often enough and regularly enough to suggest a grouping—or when they occur in conjunction with a regular grouping produced by other means—are they definitely associated with meter.

In "Das Wandern," for example, you may sense a very subtle accent at the beginning of every metric group on level II, at least in the piano introduction (see Ex. 4-14). However, the accent is sensed rather than heard: you may be convinced that the accent is there, yet if you listen to a performance very carefully and objectively you probably will not detect any increase in loudness on each ONE of level II.

Another kind of accent operates at level III in the voice part. The words of the song carry their own poetic accents or stresses; these have been integrated into the rhythm of the song—to some extent into its musical meter (Ex. 4-15). The relative strength of the accent can be shown roughly by the height of the peak at the beginning of each note. The strength of accent will vary a good deal from one performance to another, depending on how heavily accented the performers feel the piece should be.

THE RELATION OF METER AND RHYTHM ON A HIGHER LEVEL. An awareness of metric groups becomes dim at levels above those we have discussed; rhythms, however, frequently extend their influence to very high levels. Often the ear senses an approximate regularity in high-level rhythms, but is unable to determine if the regularity is exact because of the difficulty of maintaining a high-level meter as a basis for measurement. You can develop sensitivity to

Example 4-13 Accents as a cause of metric grouping

Example 4-14 Schubert, "Das Wandern": Accents in the piano introduction

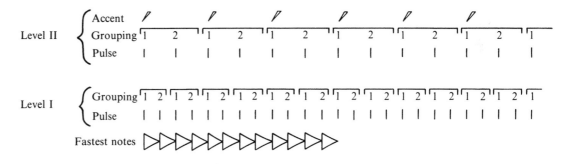

Example 4-15 Schubert, "Das Wandern": Text accents

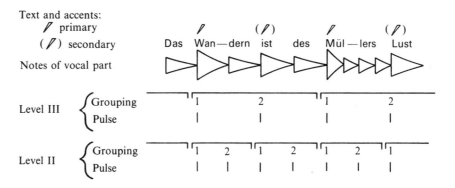

high-level regularity by counting measures in a piece (such as "Das Wandern") whose phrases are regular.

The phrases of the vocal part in "Das Wandern" are clearly set off by the short interludes for piano while the voice pauses. These interludes appear between vocal phrases 1 and 2 and between 2 and 3. Listen to the song with special attention to the way these vocal phrases follow one another in time. Rely on the pauses in the vocal part to mark off phrases. Phrases 1 and 2 are clearly more or less the same length, while phrase 3 is just as clearly longer.

(Piano introduction)
Phrase 1:
Das Wandern ist des Müllers Lust, das Wandern.
(Short interlude)
Phrase 2:
Das Wandern ist des Müllers Lust, das Wandern.
(Short interlude)
Phrase 3:
Das muss ein schlechter Müller sein,
Dem niemals fiel das Wandern ein.
Das Wandern, das Wandern, das Wandern, das
  Wandern.
(Piano introduction to next stanza)

In spite of the fact that the third phrase is longer, there is a strong feeling of regularity about the song. By counting out the measures in each phrase, you can discover just how regular the rhythm is, just how much longer the third phrase is.

Example 4-16 shows beats per measure at level III. These beats go by too fast to be useful in counting out the length of phrases. On the other hand, the pulses at level IV are already too slow to be conveniently grouped into yet higher levels that would reach up to the phrase level. A convenient way of measuring phrase lengths is simply to count measures, as found at the principal level. In other words, in Ex. 4-16 we are merely counting pulses at level IV to see how many pulses (or measures) are in each phrase.

The piano introduction takes up four measures. That is, the voice starts its first phrase on the fifth measure; or, more precisely, the voice begins with an upbeat on the syllable "Das," just before the fifth measure. Similarly, vocal phrase 1 and the short piano interlude together take up four measures. Vocal

phrase 2, beginning on the upbeat at the end of the fourth measure, also takes up four measures, counting the interlude. In other words, the piano introduction, the first vocal phrase, and the second are all the same length. There is a regular rhythm operating at the phrase level. The piece does not merely *seem* regular; its rhythmic shapes are regular at the higher levels. The regularity contributes to the naïve folk-song character that Schubert intended.

From the words "Das muss" to where the piano starts its introduction again, the phrase structure is less obvious. With the four-measure groups firmly in mind, you can hear that from "Das muss" on, the vocal phrase is eight measures long; you may hear it as two four-measure phrases run together without an interlude, as shown in Ex. 4-16. Once you start hearing four-measure groups in a piece whose rhythm has a prevailing regularity, you will be inclined to project the four-measure grouping into areas where it may not be explicit, as long as the rhythm of the music does not actually contradict such a grouping.

On the other hand, since there is no very strong division into 2 four-measure phrases after "Das muss," the music might seem to form one long eight-measure phrase, going from "Das muss" all the way to the end of the stanza, "das Wandern."

In either case, it is clear that the rhythm of this passage is different from the rhythm of the first two vocal phrases, for there is no piano interlude nor any decisive pause at the end of four measures in the vocal part; the effect is much more continuous. The phrase structure (in the vocal part) of two shorter phrases plus a longer one is an example of rhythm as opposed to meter, the meter being represented by our count of the four-measure groups at level IV. The rhythm gives the song its distinctive shape—its musical shape, for the meter is simply a mechanical way of measuring the rhythm, at the higher levels of phrase just as at the lower levels of detail.

The largest rhythm in "Das Wandern" is formed by the repetition of all the music of the first stanza for the following stanzas. This very simple rhythm, involving a literal return, is easily perceptible at the beginning of each new stanza. The rhythm is emphasized by the return of the piano introduction between each pair of stanzas. Practice listening to this example of high-level

rhythm; try to feel the regular length of the stanzas and the very slow pulse that marks the beginning of each new stanza.

(Piano introduction)
Voice—stanza 1:
Das Wandern ist des Müllers Lust,
  Das Wandern!
Das muss ein schlechter Müller sein,
Dem niemals fiel das Wandern ein,
  Das Wandern.
(Piano introduction)
Voice—stanza 2:
Vom Wasser haben wir's gelernt,
  Vom Wasser!
Das hat nicht Rast bei Tag und Nacht,
Ist stets auf Wanderschaft bedacht,
  Das Wasser.
(Piano introduction)
Voice—stanza 3:
Das sehn wir auch den Rädern ab,
  Den Rädern!
Die gar nicht gerne stille stehn,
Die sich mein Tag nicht müde drehn,
  Die Räder.
(Piano introduction)
Voice—stanza 4:
Die Steine selbst, so schwer sie sind,
  Die Steine!
Sie tanzen mit den muntern Reihn
Und wollen gar noch schneller sein,
  Die Steine.
(Piano introduction)
Voice—stanza 5:
O Wandern, Wandern, meine Lust,
  O Wandern!
Herr Meister und Frau Meisterin,
Lasst mich in Frieden weiter ziehn
  Und wandern.
(Piano epilog: same as introduction)

By analogy with the kind of pulse felt clearly at lower levels, it is possible to feel a pulse at very high levels— such as the stanza level in "Das Wandern." Difficult to cultivate, this sense of a very slow pulse is valuable for hearing many pieces in which the composer has set in motion very large rhythms.

Example 4-16 Schubert, "Das Wandern," stanza 1

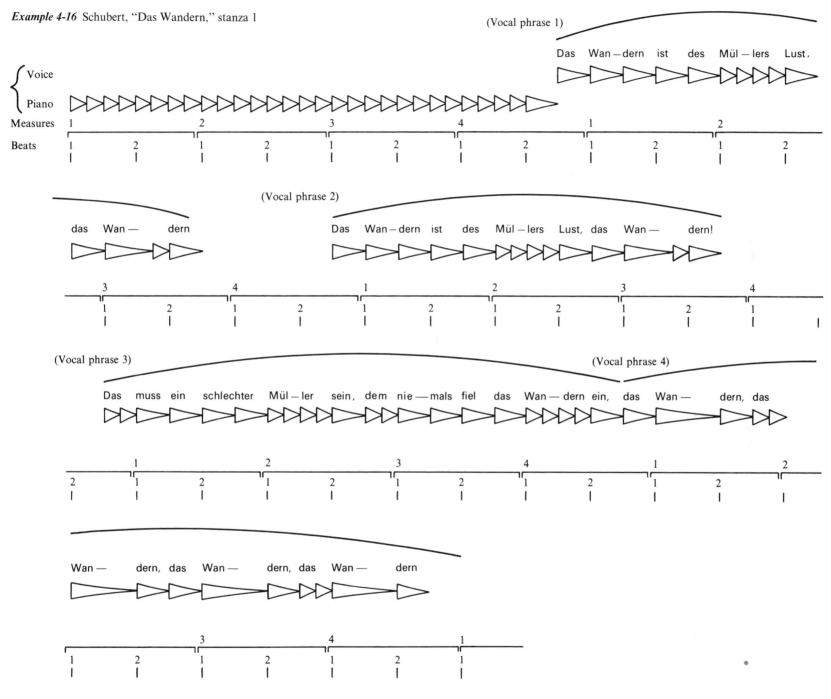

Exercises for further listening

SCHUBERT: "DIE LIEBE FARBE" (DIE SCHONE MULLERIN, SONG 16)

A complete text and translation will be found in Chapter 11. Listen first to the entire song, noting that the music of stanza 1 is exactly repeated for stanzas 2 and 3.

Beat, meter, and levels. Listen to the first two lines of stanza 1. Answer questions 1 through 10.

Text: In Grün will ich mich kleiden,/In grüne Tränenweiden

1. The lowest metric level (level I) is that of
   ___ a. The fastest notes in the piano accompaniment
   ___ b. The slowest notes in the piano accompaniment
   ___ c. The notes sung to the text, "In Grün will ich mich"

      1. a

2. The pulses at level I are grouped
   ___ a. In threes   ___ b. In twos

      2. b

3. Indicate the pulses at the next higher level (level II) by drawing them above the pulses of level I:
   Level II
   Level I ′ (etc.)

      3. II ′ ′ ′ ′ ′
   I ′ ′ ′ ′ ′ ′ ′ ′ ′ (etc.)

4. The level II pulses correspond to
   ___ a. The slowest notes in the piano accompaniment
   ___ b. The notes sung to the text, "In Grün will ich mich"
   ___ c. The notes sung to the syllables, "*klei*-(den); *wei*-(den)"

      4. b

5. The pulses at level II are grouped in
   ___ a. Twos   ___ b. Threes

      5. a

6. Which scheme below illustrates the pulses at level III?
   ___ a. In Grün will ich mich klei - den
         ′   ′   ′   ′   ′   ′   ′

   ___ b. In Grün will ich mich klei - den
         ′   ′   ′   ′

   ___ c. In Grün will ich mich klei - den
         ′   ′   ′   ′

      6. c

7. The vocal part begins

____ **a.** On a downbeat

____ **b.** On an upbeat

7. b (In Grün will ich mich)
    ↑   ↓

8. The pulses at level III are grouped

____ **a.** In twos

____ **b.** In threes

8. a

9. The principal metric level (at which it is most convenient to beat or count)

____ **a.** Can only be level III

____ **b.** Can only be level II

____ **c.** Can only be level I

____ **d.** Could be either level II or III (depending on performance)

____ **e.** Could be either level I or II (depending on performance)

9. d (Schubert has written this song so that level III is notated as the principal level)

10. The tempo of the song—the speed at which the beats at the principal level move—is

____ **a.** Very fast to moderately fast

____ **b.** Moderate to somewhat slow

____ **c.** Slow to very slow

10. b

Rhythmic groups. Listen to stanza 1, following the text given here. Answer questions 11 through 13.

Text of stanza 1:

1 In Grün will ich mich kleiden,
2 In grüne Tränenweiden,
3 Mein Schatz hat's Grün so gern,
4 Mein Schatz hat's Grün so gern.
5 Will suchen einen Zypressenhain,
6 Eine Heide voll grünem Rosmarein.
7 Mein Schatz hat's Grün so gern,
8 Mein Schatz hat's Grün so gern.

11. The most complete stopping point occurs at the end of

____ **a.** Line 1

____ **b.** Line 4

____ **c.** Line 6

____ **d.** Line 8

11. d (at the end of line 8)

12. A slightly weaker stopping point occurs at the end of

____ **a.** Line 1

____ **b.** Line 3

____ **c.** Line 4

____ **d.** Line 6

12. c (at the end of line 4)

13. Which of the following diagrams best expresses the rhythmic groupings within stanza 1? (Numbers refer to the lines of the text)

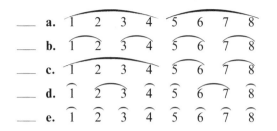

___ **a.** 1 2 3 4 5 6 7 8

___ **b.** 1 2 3 4 5 6 7 8

___ **c.** 1 2 3 4 5 6 7 8

___ **d.** 1 2 3 4 5 6 7 8

___ **e.** 1 2 3 4 5 6 7 8

13. c (b is also a possible answer; compare, however, the degree of separation between lines 2 and 3 with that between lines 6 and 7)

Phrase lengths. Listen to stanza 1 again. Determine how many measures there are in each vocal phrase. Answer questions 14 through 19.

14. Each phrase within stanza 1 comprises
___ **a.** One line of text (1, 2, 3, etc.)
___ **b.** Two lines of text (1 and 2, 3 and 4, etc.)
___ **c.** Three lines of text (1, 2, and 3; 4, 5, and 6; etc.)
___ **d.** Four lines of text (1, 2, 3, and 4; 5, 6, 7, and 8)

14. b

	Text:					
	In Grün will ich mich	klei-	den, in	grüne	Tränen- (etc.)	
Count measures:	1		2		3	
Principal level (III)	1	2	1	2	1	2

15. Phrase 1 (lines 1 and 2) consists of _____ measures.
16. Phrase 2 (lines 3 and 4) consists of _____ measures.
17. Phrase 3 (lines 5 and 6) consists of _____ measures.
18. Phrase 4 (lines 7 and 8) consists of _____ measures.
19. Phrase 4 is an exact repeat of phrase _____ .

15. Four
16. Four
17. Five!
18. Four
19. 2

Listen to the opening and closing piano phrases. Answer questions 20, 21, and 22.

20. From the first downbeat (on the first note) through the downbeat before the voice enters, the opening piano phrase comprises _____ measures.

20. Five

21. The piano phrase at the end of the song (beginning on the voice's last word, "gern") comprises _____ measures.

21. Five

22. These two piano phrases
___ **a.** Are identical
___ **b.** Are not identical

22. a

72

Regular and irregular rhythms. Answer questions 23, 24, and 25.

23. The rhythm of "Die liebe Farbe" is
___ **a.** Completely regular at all levels
___ **b.** Irregular at one or two levels, regular otherwise
___ **c.** Irregular at all levels

23. b

24. Irregularity occurs at
___ **a.** The stanza level
___ **b.** The phrase level
___ **c.** Metric level III
___ **d.** Metric level II

24. b

25. In what way are the phrases irregular?

25. Some are four measures long, some are five.

QUESTIONS FOR DISCUSSION

A. What is the longest note sung by the voice within (not at the end of) a phrase? What is the rhythmic effect of this extended note?

B. Consider the relationship of the rhythm and tempo of "Die liebe Farbe" to the meaning of the text. Compare, in this regard, the settings of "Die liebe Farbe" and "Das Wandern."

CHAPTER 5   REGULAR AND IRREGULAR RHYTHMS

IN SCHUBERT'S "DAS WANDERN," the rhythmic structure was so regular that we had no difficulty determining its metric grouping at all levels, from the fastest notes in the accompaniment up to the level of the stanza. Most music is more complex, incorporating irregular rhythms at one or more levels. The irregularity of rhythm may go so far as to obliterate any perceptible meter. We will study next a piece that provides an easy transition from clear, regular rhythms to rhythms that are partially, and temporarily, irregular.

Joseph Haydn (1732–1809)

SYMPHONY NO. 100
MENUETTO AND TRIO (THIRD MOVEMENT)

The third movement of Haydn's Symphony No. 100 consists of three large sections—Menuetto, Trio, and Menuetto (repeated). Within the Menuetto, we will be most concerned with rhythm in terms of phrases; the phrase structure begins with very clear, regular shapes, goes on to become less clear and regular, then returns to relative clarity at the end.

In addition, the Menuetto, as well as the Trio, give a good illustration of the way a detail of rhythm at the lowest level can create a sense of rhythmic movement that permeates a whole section and of how a change in rhythmic detail—under the right conditions—can produce a change in the sense of rhythmic movement. Such a change in rhythmic detail is one of the main factors setting off the Trio from the Menuetto.

Finally, we will find that the same rhythmic detail

that gives the Menuetto its distinctive sense of movement is intimately related to its phrases and to the way they gain and lose clarity. Here is a place to study the *integration* of different rhythmic levels.

OVERALL FORM OF THE MOVEMENT. On first hearing, the larger plan of Haydn's Menuetto and Trio will be clear to you. The whole movement consists of Menuetto, Trio, and a shortened repetition of the Menuetto. It may require several hearings to determine the Menuetto's internal structure, which can be represented like this:

$$A_1 \quad A_2 \quad B \quad A_3 \quad B \quad A_3$$

The Trio has a similar structure.

$$C_1 \quad C_1 \quad D \quad C_2 \quad D \quad C_2$$

When the Menuetto is repeated after the Trio, it is slightly abbreviated.

$$A_1 \quad A_2 \quad B \quad A_3$$

The sense of return within the Menuetto and within the Trio, as well as the very broad sense of return produced by the repeat of the Menuetto after the Trio, are important aspects of the larger rhythm of the piece. Our immediate concern, however, is at the lower levels of phrase and beat.

PHRASE STRUCTURE OF THE MOVEMENT. Within the Menuetto, a first or second hearing will readily reveal the A_1 A_2 shape. Section A_1 is made up of two phrases: the first is like a question, the second like an answer. We will encounter this question-and-answer shape often and will study at another time the melodic inflection that makes it sound like a question and answer, also called *antecedent-consequent*. For our study of rhythm, we need only notice the clear break at the end of each phrase and the fact that the phrases seem about equal in length. The music provides us an opportunity to hear this pair of phrases again, in the A_2 section, which has substantially the same music but played more softly and emphasizing winds rather than tutti (Ex. 5-1).

BEAT. The Menuetto has a very strong beat and a very clear grouping of beats. The beat is clear from the outset—natural enough in a type of piece derived from dance music (Ex. 5-2).

METER. From listening, you will find that the beats are grouped in threes, that is, the meter at the principal level is triple. An attempt to count the beats ONE TWO ONE TWO . . . simply fails to correspond to the rhythm of the piece as we actually hear it. The metric grouping in threes persists throughout the Menuetto and Trio—but with some interesting disturbances, as we will see.

In Ex. 5-2 the first beat of the piece (which falls on a group of four fast notes) is counted THREE. In other

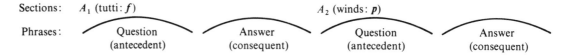

Sections: A_1 (tutti: **f**) A_2 (winds: **p**)

Phrases: Question (antecedent)   Answer (consequent)   Question (antecedent)   Answer (consequent)

Example 5-1 Haydn, Menuetto, section A_1: Antecedent-consequent phrases

words, as the example shows, the piece starts on an upbeat, just as does the vocal part in Schubert's "Das Wandern." You can try counting the Menuetto beginning with ONE (for the group of four fast notes), and you may be able to continue with regular groups of three beats for some time; but you will probably sense something peculiar about the accentuation—as if it were ONE TWO THREE, ONE TWO THREE. Beginning with an upbeat, THREE ONE TWO conforms more readily to the rhythmic sense of the music.

Remember how a conductor makes clear the nature of triple meter by the way he beats it. His hand goes down for the downbeat on ONE, sideways for TWO, and up for the upbeat on THREE (Ex. 4-11). Practice moving your right hand in this pattern, then try beating out the threes for the first section of the Menuetto.

RHYTHMIC GROUPING. At the beginning of the Menuetto, the first rhythmic group (formed by the upbeat and the following two beats) is repeated. That is, the rhythmic pattern of four short and two long notes is repeated, falling on the same counts as before; naturally, you hear these notes in the same rhythmic grouping as the first time. In Ex. 5-3 a slur is used to mark each rhythmic group that begins with the upbeat.

After two such groups, the four fast notes appear a third time; here, however, the note pattern changes. Your sense of rhythmic grouping will respond immediately to the change in note pattern: since there is no obvious place to subdivide the six notes following, the third group appears longer—as shown by the third slur.

In this case, the rhythmic groupings are clear and easy to hear. Many times, however, the rhythmic grouping is intentionally unclear, and different people may hear very different groupings in the same music. Your goal should be to hear whatever grouping there is when the grouping is obvious, and also to recognize places where the grouping is not obvious, places where the composer asks you to be in doubt for a while, to suspend judgment.

LOWER METRIC LEVELS. One of the factors contributing to the rhythmic grouping just discussed is the reappearance of the four fast notes on beat THREE. These four fast notes are like the fastest notes in "Das Wandern," which constituted the lowest level of that song. These fast notes appear only intermittently in Haydn's Menuetto, not continuously as they did in "Das Wandern." The intermittent use makes the faster notes more prominent; they are not background murmur, as in Schubert's song, but instead play a more prominent role. As the Menuetto unfolds, Haydn does more and more with these fast notes.

Between the level of these fast notes and the principal level there is a third level frequently represented by the notes in the piece (Ex. 5-4). The notes at this level do not make such a distinctive impression as the four fast notes—perhaps because notes at this intermediate level (II) are soon used for the accompaniment, in section A_2. Still, the notes at this level do have an important role to play: they are found at the end of the first antecedent phrase, again at the end of the first consequent phrase. Like the four fast notes, the notes at level II will gain importance later in the piece.

RHYTHMIC FIGURE IN MENUETTO AND TRIO. A recognizable pattern of notes, especially of faster notes that are subdivisions of a beat, is often called a rhythmic *figure*; more generally, such patterns are called rhythmic *figuration*. The pattern of four fast notes is a prominent rhythmic figure of this Menuetto. Rhythmic figure plays an important role in producing the sense of movement characteristic of a piece.

The effect of rhythmic figuration can best be appreciated at the moment when the figure changes. Such a moment comes at the beginning of the Trio; in fact, the Trio as a whole is set off from the Menuetto

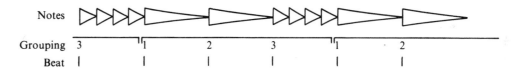

Example 5-2 Haydn, Menuetto (beginning): Beat

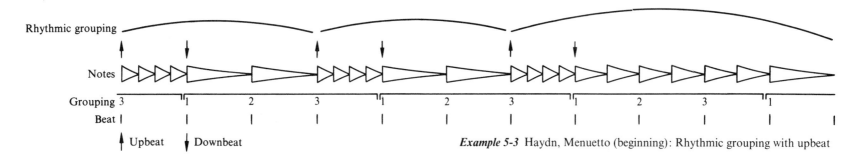

Example 5-3 Haydn, Menuetto (beginning): Rhythmic grouping with upbeat

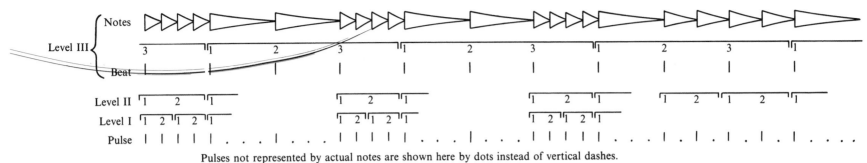

Pulses not represented by actual notes are shown here by dots instead of vertical dashes.

Example 5-4 Haydn, Menuetto (beginning): Metric levels

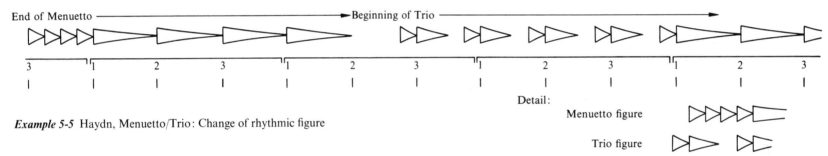

Example 5-5 Haydn, Menuetto/Trio: Change of rhythmic figure

by a decisive change to a new figure. This new figure fits within the same basic beat. You can, and should, continue counting at the principal level straight through from Menuetto into Trio. The change lies in the way the fastest notes are arranged within the beat (Ex. 5-5).

When a piece has only one distinctive rhythmic figure, used throughout the piece, that figure may be a decisive factor in establishing the character of the piece. If you listen to the songs in Schubert's cycle *Die schöne Müllerin*, for example, you will find that many of the songs owe their individuality to the special accompaniment figure peculiar to each song.

COUNTING OUT THE PHRASES OF THE MENUETTO. The rhythmic nature of the Menuetto makes it

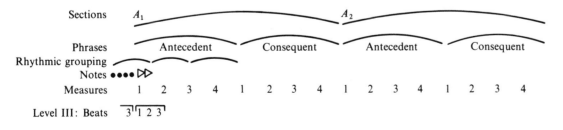

Example 5-6 Haydn, Menuetto, sections A_1 and A_2: Phrase structure

necessary to follow rhythmic events on several levels at once—on the lowest levels (I and II), on the principal level (III), and on the level of phrase length (IV). Ultimately, you need to be aware of how events on these levels work together to shape the piece at its highest level.

Even on first hearing, the opening phrases *seemed* regular in length; if now you count them out, you will discover that indeed they are exactly so (Ex. 5-6). The first antecedent, first consequent, second antecedent, and second consequent are each four measures long (counting three beats in each measure). As we already saw, during sections A_1 and A_2 the figure of four fast notes appears only on beat THREE, never on beat ONE or beat TWO. At the end of the first antecedent and of the first consequent, there is a rest, or silence, on count TWO. (In Ex. 5-6, the four fast notes are shown by black dots in place of wedges, because of the small scale of the diagram.)

IRREGULAR RHYTHMS AND PHRASES. This section of regular rhythm serves as a reference point for the charming irregularities that are to follow immediately. In order to be as conscious as possible of these irregularities, you should count through the next section, B. Try first to count beats per measure at the principal level: count ONE TWO THREE doggedly through thick and thin. This may be difficult. Try to hear as much of the *rhythm* of the piece as you can, that is, let the rhythm of the sounds push or pull against the beat that you are trying to maintain.

At this level, you will encounter two different kinds of irregularity. Most noticeable is the shift in placement of the figure of four fast notes: at first it appears as usual on THREE, but further into the B section it appears on ONE as well, and soon after also on TWO, as shown in Ex. 5-7. These appearances take place in different layers of the orchestral texture, sometimes in the upper parts, sometimes in the bass, sometimes between. The total rhythmic effect, however, is that the motion of the fastest notes becomes for a short time continuous, obliterating the previously clear relationship between meter and figure at the lower levels.

The second kind of irregularity appears just before a return to the opening theme takes place. Much of the B section is in a full, strong tutti sound. Just as it gets softer (right before the A_3 section), the rhythmic figure changes to something quite unlike the rhythmic motion up to that point (Ex. 5-8). There are now *three* equal subdivisions per beat, rather than four. The subdivision into threes has a striking effect at this point in the piece—an effect it would not have had elsewhere. The motion in threes gracefully, expressively, dissolves the complexity that has been

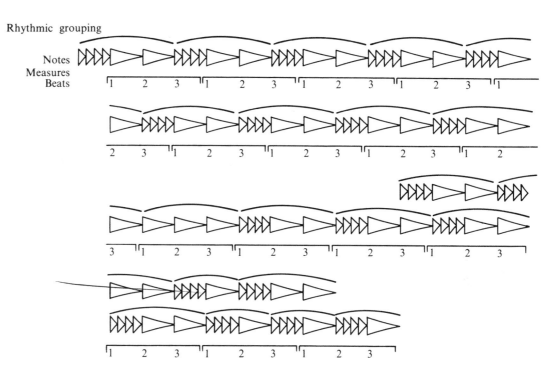

Rhythmic grouping

Notes
Measures
Beats

Example 5-7 Haydn, Menuetto, section B (first part): Meter and rhythmic figure

Example 5-8 Haydn, Menuetto, section B (end): A new rhythmic figure

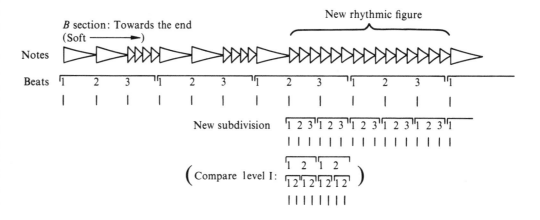

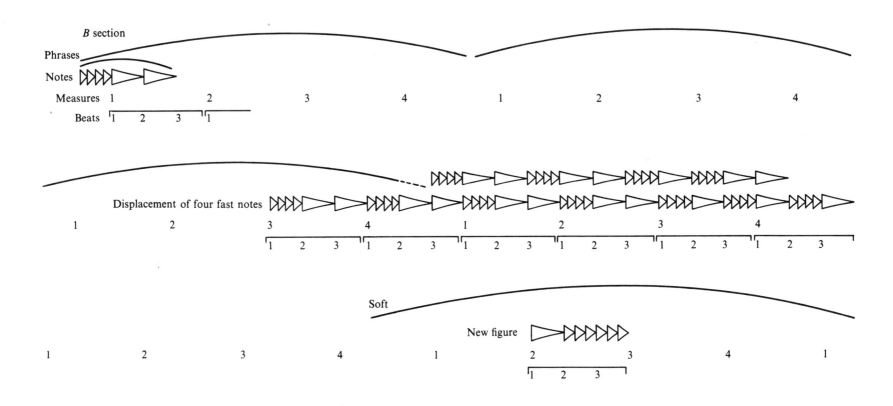

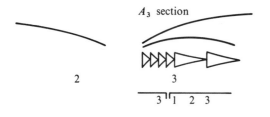

Example 5-9 Haydn, Menuetto, section *B*: Plan

built up in the preceding measures by the displacement of the group of four fast notes. The way is cleared for the return to the regularity of the opening rhythm.

The *B* section shows irregular rhythms at higher levels as well. To be fully aware of the progression from the clarity of A_1 and A_2 through an area of lesser clarity in *B*, count measures in groups of four from the beginning of the Menuetto, continuing into *B*. There are no rests in *B* to mark off four-measure groups; nevertheless, you will be able to hear up to three regular phrases, as shown by the slurs in Ex. 5-9. But at the point where you encountered the displacement of the rhythmic detail, the phrasing will no longer correspond to the four-measure groups. The clear, regular phrasing of sections A_1 and A_2 has been replaced by phrasing that is less clear or

less regular—or both, at least for a short time. The loss of clarity on the phrase level is directly associated with the displacement of rhythmic figure on the beat level. Indeed, the shift of the rhythmic figure seems an important factor in obliterating the clear phrasing with which the piece began.

In this piece, as in many others, there is an inner connection between rhythmic changes occurring on different levels. That is to say, the piece is one piece, not several pieces going along simultaneously on the several levels. The idea of *level* is simply an analytic tool that helps clarify the workings of the piece. The piece itself exists on all levels at once. Therefore, even though you may react more strongly to one level than to another, you should be alert for rhythmic events on other levels that support or relate to the event you happen to notice.

Example 5-10 Haydn, Menuetto, section A_3: Elision

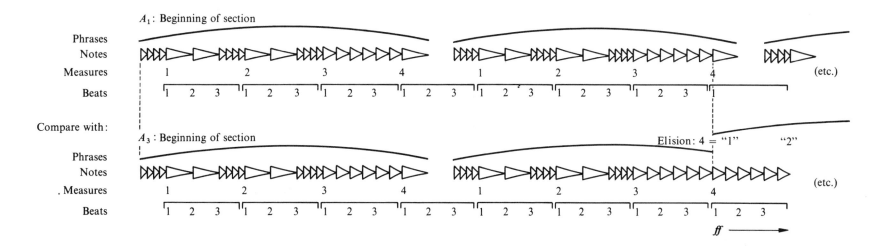

ELISION. The end of the Menuetto provides an important example of a complex phrase structure frequently encountered. The A_3 section begins exactly like the A_1 section and proceeds through four measures of antecedent, then four measures of consequent. In the fourth measure of the consequent, however, just where a phrase ending is expected, a new vigorous start is made. The rhythm acts as if it were beginning a phrase instead of ending one; this measure feels like a ONE rather than a FOUR (Ex. 5-10). Notice that the feeling of a fresh start is reinforced by the energetic entrance of a rhythmic figure, drawn from the end of the first phrase of the Menuetto. Here again the handling of phrase structure and of rhythmic figure are related.

The particularly forceful effect at the point where a FOUR turns into a ONE is called *elision*. The ex-

pected end of one phrase has been *elided* into the beginning of the next. Instead of ending with the pause we might expect here, the rhythm leaps ahead to begin something new. Phrase elisions are common in music that has frequent four-measure phrases, for elision is one of the most important ways of achieving excitement and continuity as a relief to metrical rhythm.

OVERALL RHYTHM OF THE MENUETTO. Awareness of the shift in the Menuetto from a clearly phrased beginning through a more continuous middle, to a restoration of clarity at the end should lead to an understanding of the overall rhythm of the Menuetto. We can also express this as a long-range accumulation of tension toward the middle of the Menuetto, then a release of the tension with the return of the opening

clarity of phrase structure—a partial release, for there is still the elision at the end to be reckoned with.

Béla Bartók (1881–1945)
STRING QUARTET NO. 6
BURLETTA (THIRD MOVEMENT)

A listener hears and reacts to a sense of rhythmic movement even without understanding how the rhythm works. You may feel that a piece has a strong beat, yet be unable to count its meter; you may feel that the piece has a sense of phrasing, yet find no clear points of articulation. Often, however, rhythms that seem at first incomprehensible may turn out to embody some of the regularity heard in "Das Wandern." Your first experience with the rhythms of

Example 5-11 Bartók, Third Movement: Plan

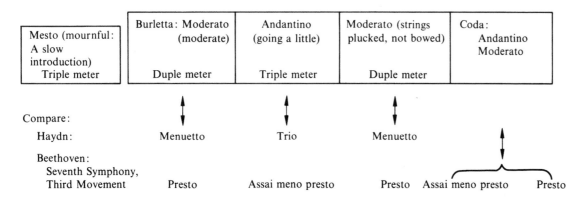

Example 5-12 Bartók, Burletta, Moderato: Section plan

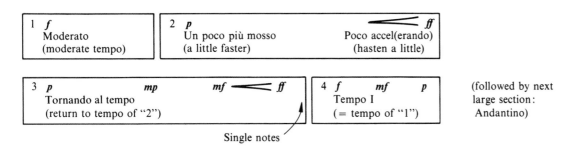

the next piece to be studied may be one of frustrating confusion. With a little practice, however, you will find that its rhythms share to some extent the regular pulsation of "Das Wandern," and its overall shape resembles that of Haydn's Menuetto.

SECTIONAL STRUCTURE OF THE THIRD MOVEMENT.
The third movement of Bartók's quartet consists of five large sections, each clearly separated from the others not only by rhythmic figuration, as in Haydn's Menuetto, but also by changes in meter and tempo. So important, in fact, are the meter and tempo changes that we can use them to map out the largest sections of the third movement (Ex. 5-11).

The movement begins with a slow section that Bartók labels Mesto.* The underlying meter is triple, although in this as in the other sections the meter may not be easy to determine, for reasons we will study. The slow Mesto section stands apart from the rest of the movement; it will make more sense when we consider the quartet as a whole (Chapter 15).

The second part of the movement is labeled *Burletta* ("burlesque"); here begins the main body of the movement, consisting of two basic tempos in sectional alternation. One of these tempos is *Moderato* ("mod-

*"Sad." (This section is similar to the Mesto at the beginning of the quartet, studied in Chapter 3.)

erate"); the other, *Andantino* ("going along a little"). The Moderato section is in a duple meter, the Andantino in a triple meter.

After the Andantino, the Moderato returns—same tempo, same meter, basically the same music, but with a striking change in timbre. After the Moderato we hear a little of the Andantino, then a little of the Moderato a third time for a conclusion.

Tempo is intimately bound up with beat and rhythmic motion; often we must be clear about the beat before we can be sure of the tempo. In this third movement, however, the tempo contrasts are clear in themselves and also are clearly supported by such factors as contrasts of meter and of timbre.

SECTIONS WITHIN THE MODERATO.
Just as tempo is an important factor articulating the structure of the whole movement, so it is important in defining sections within the first Moderato. Here, however, the changes of tempo are more subtle.

Shortly after the start of the Moderato, Bartók indicates *Un poco più mosso*—"a little faster." This marks a new section. Then, soon after, Bartók indicates *Poco accel(erando)*—"hasten a little"—and very soon after that, *Tornando al tempo*—"return to the tempo (you were just playing)." The accelerando is a momentary hastening at the end of this second section; the return to the immediately preceding tempo marks the start of a third section. Both tempo changes are clearly audible. In addition, the accelerando ends with a crescendo to a strong fortissimo, and the return to the preceding tempo immediately thereafter begins softly.

At the end of the third section, the music again becomes loud; the end of the section is marked by a series of strong repeated notes—a single pitch hammered out by all four instruments together. This striking transition is followed immediately by a return to the opening Moderato tempo and to the opening music as well (Ex. 5-12).

Having these sections of the Moderato clearly in mind should help you keep track of the complex rhythmic motion contained in them. The rhythms tend to become most complex in the middle of each of these four sections. The beginning of each section is relatively clear in its rhythmic effect; but, by the time you are part way through a section you may be completely disoriented, so intricate do Bartók's rhythms become.

REGULAR RHYTHMS AT THE BEGINNING OF THE MODERATO.

As you listen to the Moderato section, you may notice how strikingly its rhythms are accented. Many people would characterize this music as strongly rhythmic, meaning that the rhythm calls attention to itself, to the point of being the most noticeable element in the music.

At first, indeed, you may find Bartók's strongly accented rhythm so compelling that you are relatively unaware of, or not interested in, the metric structure. At the beginning of Haydn's Menuetto, on the other hand, the basic triple meter catches your attention right away—as much as the rhythmic patterns that produce it. Yet there are only a few kinds of rhythm in Bartók's Burletta not already encountered in Haydn's Menuetto. Bartók's rhythms differ from Haydn's in degree: they are more irregular, more violently accented, more subversive of meter.

If you can listen through some of the distracting accents at the very beginning of the Moderato, you may soon perceive a rhythmic regularity: the intense detail seems to be coming in groups of equal length, and sometimes these groups seem to add up to larger groups. If we turn our attention to the strong, clear pulse—the fastest pulse—of the opening notes, we find that we can count that pulse right through the rhythmic groups. The groups turn out to be regular; each contains eight pulses, as shown in Ex. 5-13.

These particular groupings are made clear in the music by changes of dynamics (f to ff) and changes of texture (especially from the first group of eight pulses to the second group).

Only at one point (marked * in Ex. 5-13) does the beginning of the Moderato present a possible confusion: the last pulse in the third group of eight seems to start something new. This slight irregularity, however, is easily understood as an upbeat to the next group of eight.

In spite of certain rhythmic distractions to be discussed soon, from the groups of eight pulses, it is possible to infer metric groups at the lower levels. The pulses are clearly grouped in twos at the lowest

Example 5-13 Bartók, Moderato (beginning): Rhythmic groups

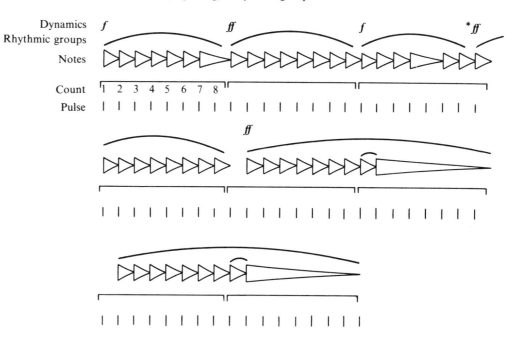

Example 5-14 Bartók, Moderato (beginning): Metric levels

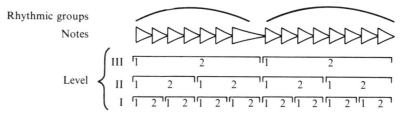

level, and we can continue to pyramid them in twos up to level III, as in Ex. 5-14. Furthermore, it is possible—at least at the beginning of the Moderato—to regard level III as the principal level. As is clear from Ex. 5-14, each measure at level III contains a group of eight pulses.

Counting measures at level III leads the listener to the realization that the higher-level groupings are also regular at the beginning of the Moderato, as shown in Ex. 5-15. Just as in Schubert's "Das Wandern" and in the more regular sections of Haydn's Menuetto, the regular rhythms at the lower level tend to

Example 5-15 Bartók, Moderato (beginning): Higher rhythmic groupings

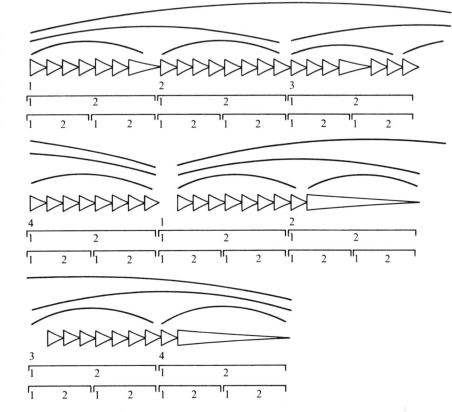

Phrase groups
Rhythmic groups
Measures
Level III
Level II

There is no doubt that the ONEs are ONEs; yet there is a very strong accent on the TWOs that seems hard to reconcile with their position in the metric scheme (see Ex. 5-16). The kind of strong accent that would seem appropriate on ONE has been shifted to TWO. This kind of rhythmic displacement is sometimes called an *offbeat rhythm*, or an *accented offbeat*, because at the next higher level (level II), the accents fall off the beat, rather than on it.

ONE ′ TWO ′ ONE ′ TWO

A stronger kind of rhythmic displacement occurs in measure 3. Find the long note in measure 3 of Ex. 5-15, then look at it in detail in Ex. 5-17. This strongly accented note starts on count TWO of level I and continues through the following count ONE. As a result, no new note appears on this ONE, and the effect of rhythmic displacement is greater than with offbeat rhythms, where the count of ONE has a note, even if less strongly accented than the TWO. On level II, the accented note starts off the beat and continues through the following downbeats. Displacement of this kind is called *syncopation*.

In spite of the rhythmic displacements just studied, the beginning eight measures of Bartók's Burletta are metrically regular in their basic outline. From measure 9, however, the displacements become so severe and so sustained that the original meter can be

organize themselves into larger regular patterns at the phrase level. To repeat an earlier caution: Bartók's detail is so intense that you may at first not hear any phrasing that corresponds to Ex. 5-15. But if you can step back from the detail as you listen, you should be able to hear the large groupings of measures almost as clearly as those at the beginning of Haydn's Menuetto. There is even a hint of question and answer in Bartók's rhythmic grouping.

You would not be able to hear regular rhythms much beyond the end of Ex. 5-15, for various kinds of rhythmic displacement at the lower levels—present from the beginning of the Moderato—begin to inter-

fere seriously with the regularity of the rhythms. Throughout much of the Moderato, rhythmic displacement is in the foreground, and consequently calls for more detailed comment here.

RHYTHMIC DISPLACEMENT. On listening to detail, the ear may well be confused by the strong emphasis on the TWO counts at level I in the opening measure. If we counted the first measure so as to reflect the accents as well as the meter, we might well count (at level I)

ONE TWO ONE TWO ONE TWO ONE (TWO)

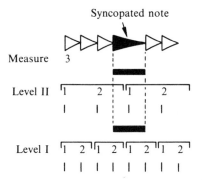

Syncopated note

Measure 3

Level II

Level I

Example 5-17 Bartók, Moderato: Syncopation

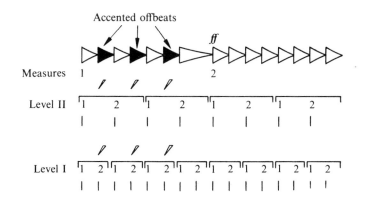

Accented offbeats

Example 5-16 Bartók, Moderato: Offbeat rhythm

Example 5-18 Bartók, Moderato: Metric placement of slide figure

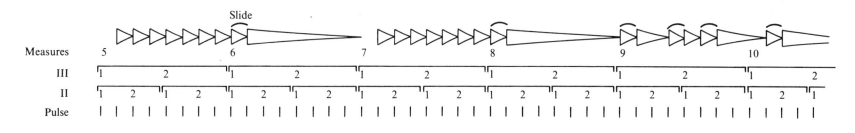

felt only with great difficulty, if at all. There are no standard terms (such as "syncopation") for the kinds of rhythmic displacement Bartók uses from measure 9 on.

In measures 6 and 8, you heard one of Bartók's distinctive devices of timbre—a prominent glissando between the first two pulses in the measure. The crudity of this particular slide is part of the burlesque effect of the movement. More interesting, however, is the rhythmic displacement of the slide in measures 9 and 10 (Ex. 5-18).

When you first hear the slide, it is clearly associated with the downbeat, count ONE of the measure (measures 6 and 8); in measures 9 and 10, the slide's metric position has become ambiguous, through rhythmic displacement. The meter, but not the

rhythm, is destroyed in the process. After you have listened to the passage a few times, you will probably find yourself easily pulled along by the rhythmic movement; but if you try to count twos at level II, you may have considerable difficulty—and even if you succeed, the count will not seem to have much significance for the rhythm you hear. Example 5-18 shows how the slide figure is related to the previous but now inaudible meter.

Throughout the rhythmic displacement, the pulse at the lowest level continues in the accompaniment. We sometimes use the term *unit pulse* to describe a pulse at the lowest level when that pulse cannot be grouped metrically. The term "unit pulse" will be increasingly applicable throughout the following sections of the Moderato.

SECOND SECTION OF THE MODERATO. The unit pulse continues from the end of the first section into the second section, now going a little faster in accordance with the tempo designation *Un poco più mosso* (see Ex. 5-12). In this section, severe rhythmic displacements occur almost immediately, making a metric understanding of the section difficult. Eventually Bartók's persuasive rhythm provides us with its own frame of reference; but, for the purpose of learning to respond to his more irregular rhythms, we can continue to make use of a count. The unit pulse continues on the lowest level throughout this second section; we can count it in groups of eight—the grouping established at the beginning of the Burletta —even though this grouping is heard only once or twice at the beginning of the second section.

Example 5-19 Bartók, Moderato, second section: Nonmetric downbeats

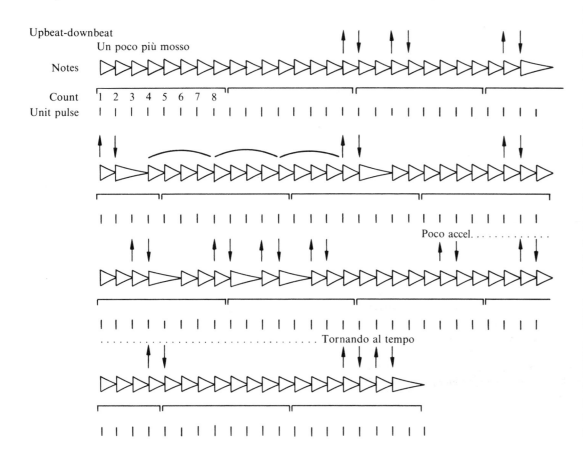

Following Ex. 5-19, count the indicated groups of eight through the second section. Ignore for the moment all except the continuity of the pulse. The pulse may be hard to hear in the accelerando—and, indeed, you may not be able to follow it in one of the more hectic performances.

Once you can follow the unit pulse, listen to the push and pull of the rhythms against the arbitrary count of eight. The important thing is to sense the progression into a nonmetric realm of rhythm. Yet at the same time that you notice how irregular are the actual rhythms, you will also become increasingly aware of their own distinctive force.

The chief feature that organizes these irregular rhythms is the strong accent that recurs, with more and more insistence, throughout the section. The accented notes are indicated in Ex. 5-19 by downward-pointing arrows; these accented notes, which are sometimes twice as long as the unit pulse, very soon acquire the feeling of a downbeat (especially since purely metric downbeats are scarce).

These downbeat accents are usually preceded by a clear upbeat; the upbeats are marked in Ex. 5-19 by upward-pointing arrows. You can tell from the diagram that the downbeats have less and less to do with the count of eight as the section goes on. During the

accelerando even these downbeats are obliterated—as if Bartók wanted to be quite sure we were lost by the end of the section. At any rate, the end of the section is marked by a sudden, but unmistakable, reappearance of the upbeat-downbeat figure. This small rhythmic detail has been given the job of organizing the rhythmic flow of the section.

THIRD SECTION OF THE MODERATO. Still another kind of rhythmic displacement occurs at the beginning of the third section—an insistent rhythmic repetition that seems dancelike and regular, yet eludes any attempt to find a regular grouping.

Underlying the insistent rhythm is a unit pulse—the same pulse heard in the two preceding sections. You could count out the pulse in groups of eight, as before; but here it would be even harder—and strangely so, for the rhythmic effect of this third section is on the whole less erratic, more contained than the unstable second section.

Superimposed on the unit pulse, you can hear the upbeat-downbeat figure from the second section, now less prominent but paradoxically more persuasive. You can hear it in the accompaniment, repeated over and over, but prevented from becoming regular by the occasional insertion of an extra note or two, as in Ex. 5-20a. In the upper parts the upbeat-downbeat figure appears in a more complex pattern, whose most frequent form is shown in Ex. 5-20b. This pattern, too, is frequently upset by the insertion of other rhythmic values.

The patterns in the upper parts and in the accompaniment are, as it were, set in motion at the same time and allowed to proceed simultaneously—a procedure sometimes called *polyrhythm*. They are linked together by the unit pulse, and both use the upbeat-downbeat figure; but they seem at first to have little else in common. The result is a very special blend of rhythmic irregularity with persuasive, even hypnotic, continuity.

The third section does not get much more complex as it goes on; its complexity is present from the beginning of the section—unlike the first and second sections, which began with relatively regular rhythms before becoming irregular. The third section ends with a very striking insistence on one repeated pitch.

The repetition (a concentrated expression of the unit pulse) seems to erase all the previous rhythms in preparation for the closing section.

The closing section begins with a recall of the opening tempo and some of the opening rhythms. The upbeat-downbeat figure from section 2 is suggested; its repetitions lead quickly to a dissolution of the rhythmic pulse. The Andantino section that follows brings with it a contrasting set of rhythms.

AN OVERVIEW OF THE MODERATO. The Moderato moves through a series of intense rhythmic details with frequent, severe displacement or disruption of a metric pulse. At the level of detail, the piece seems uncompromising: whether you are excited by the detail or merely irritated, you will find that these low-level rhythms absorb most of your attention. They tend, at first, to stand in the way of a perception of the larger shape. But if you can listen over the detail to hear the larger rhythms at the section level, the detail itself quickly starts to make more sense.

Listening at the section level, you can hear in each section an increase in complexity—or at least, rhythmic intensity—as the section proceeds. The change to a new section is marked by at least some sense of clarification (even in the case of the third section, which, as we saw, has the most complex beginning of all the sections). In this way the rhythm of the detail is linked to the larger rhythm, to the ebb and flow at the section level. If you respond to this larger rhythm, you have understood the most important rhythmic aspect of the piece, even though the workings of the detail remain obscure or go by too fast to grasp. And the larger rhythm is just as clear, in spite of all the irregular detail, as in Haydn's Menuetto, with its consistently metrical structure. Rhythmic clarity, in other words, does not depend upon the presence of meter.

Richard Wagner (1813–1883)
TRISTAN UND ISOLDE (A MUSIC DRAMA)
PRELUDE (VORSPIEL)

RHYTHMS AT A VERY HIGH LEVEL. Meter and rhythm at lower levels are relatively easy to grasp—for

Example 5-20 Bartók, Moderato, third section: Unit pulse with upbeat-downbeat figure

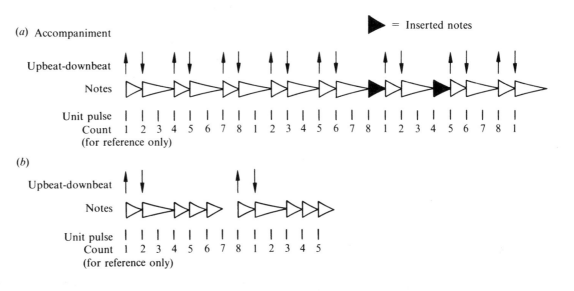

musicians and listeners alike. Rhythms at higher levels, however, seem much more difficult to grasp, in spite of the fact that such larger rhythms play an important part in the listener's instinctive response to a piece. The Prelude (also called *Vorspiel*) to Wagner's music drama, *Tristan und Isolde*, offers a very convincing example of a high-level rhythm that emerges as one of the most important features shaping the piece.

Being a Prelude, this piece is not a complete, independent entity. When performed as part of the music drama it leads directly into the first act. When performed separately as a concert piece, sometimes the Prelude is provided with an alternate ending (one composed by Wagner himself) to make it sound like an independent piece; and sometimes it is left in its original open-ended form but followed by an orchestral version of the end of the work—a scene called Isolde's *Liebestod* (Love death).

As you listen to the Prelude for the first time, much of the rhythmic detail will probably seem clear and meaningful in terms of the discussion in this chapter

and the one before, although certain details may be at first difficult to place in the prevailing pulse. The tempo at first is *langsam und schmachtend* (German, "slow and yearning") later *belebend* ("becoming animated"). The pulse is not only very slow, but also fluctuates on occasion; for both of these reasons your attention will probably be absorbed in the rhythmic detail. In order to be aware of the large rhythm you will have to direct your attention consciously to the higher levels. As soon as you do become aware of the large rhythm you will realize how strong a pull it exerts. Remember that large rhythms do not make their presence felt all at once; they require time in which to unfold.

FIRST PHRASE GROUP. At the very beginning of the Prelude, the groups of sounds are defined by long pauses between each group. When we study the Prelude in detail (Chapter 10), we will discuss the ingredients of these groups. For now it is sufficient to distinguish the timbres of strings and winds, with their characteristic rhythms.

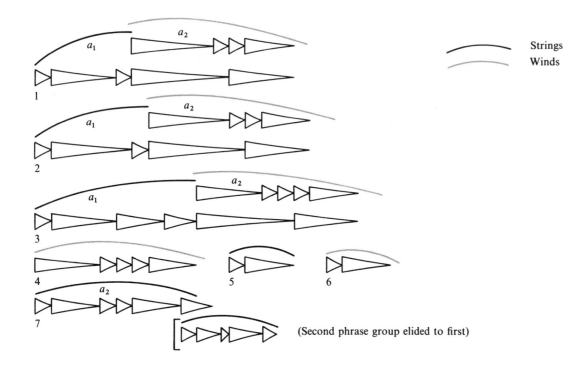

4

5

6

7

(Second phrase group elided to first)

Example 5-21 Wagner, Prelude, first phrase group

Example 5-22 Wagner, Prelude, second phrase group

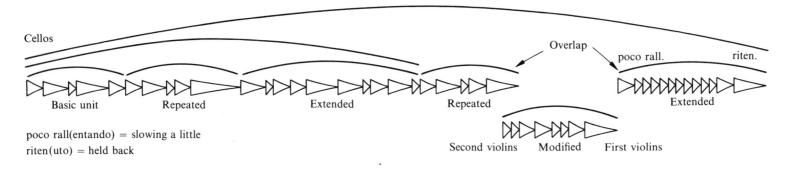

poco rall(entando) = slowing a little
riten(uto) = held back

The way smaller rhythms accumulate into larger ones becomes apparent during the first minute of the Prelude. Group 1 (in Ex. 5-21) is long enough to be considered a phrase; so are groups 2 and 3, both similar to group 1 in their rhythmic detail (as well as in other respects). Groups 4 through 6 are shorter, too short to be considered phrases. But as groups 4 through 6 are being played, a larger rhythm can be felt in the form of a phrase group that includes all of Ex. 5-21—group 1 through group 7, the culmination of the first phrase group.

The momentum of this larger rhythm seems to override detail. For example, pauses are important at the beginning as divisions between phrases; but it does not seem to matter that no pause marks the end of the larger rhythm after group 7. The next phrase (starting at the end of Ex. 5-21) is elided to group 7, not separated by a pause, yet it is perfectly clear that groups 1 through 7 constitute one rhythmic unit, and that another starts directly afterward.

Such larger rhythms are produced in a variety of ways throughout the Prelude. Sometimes the persistence of a single leading timbre (for example, cellos) fuses a series of basic rhythmic units into a larger rhythm. Sometimes alternations between winds and strings set off the rhythmic units from each other; but even then something pulls these units together. One of the most important factors marking the beginning of some new phrase groups is the use of a different rhythmic motive. Yet here, too, individual rhythmic

motives tend to evolve from one shape into another; they tend to grow toward each other in such a way that the growth process itself produces a sense of rhythmic momentum, while the resulting similarity of motives contributes to the sense of unity.

SECOND PHRASE GROUP. The second phrase group, which starts at the end of Ex. 5-21, has its own distinctive rhythmic pattern. This pattern appears at the beginning of the phrase group, as shown in Ex. 5-22; while it is not long enough or complete enough to be called a phrase, it does provide a basic rhythmic unit for the whole phrase group in much the same way as phrase 1. We have placed a slur over each rhythmic pattern in Ex. 5-22 to show how these patterns provide the units for the phrase group.

Fix the basic rhythmic pattern in your ear, then try to hear the meaning of the shortest slurs, those on the lowest level. The rhythm is more continuous here than at the beginning of the Prelude, where pauses clearly separated the groups. Yet it should be possible to hear the rhythmic shapes represented by the slurs. Instead of units marked off from each other, you may hear recurrent surges of rhythmic energy, or you may sense the rhythm as a very slow pulse—a pulse without a sharp attack or release.

By running the groups into one another Wagner encourages the perception of a larger phrase group. As shown in Ex. 5-22, the basic unit is repeated, then extended; this much fuses together into the phrase

group represented by the slur at the second level. The basic unit appears twice again, the second time in a more intense modification. These statements overlap, as does the extension that follows. All the details function together to push the rhythmic motion forward to the end of the extension, fusing everything in Ex. 5-22 together into the large rhythms shown by the longest arch.

Here, as throughout the Prelude, dynamics help make the shape clear. In general each phrase group starts softly, then progresses by a carefully controlled manner to a louder dynamic level. The ensuing reduction to a softer level at the start of the next phrase group is often a clear guide to the phrase structure.

THIRD PHRASE GROUP. A third phrase group, shown in Ex. 5-23, starts with the last detailed rhythmic pattern we need consider in the Prelude. A syncopation occurs on the first note of the pattern; this note in the melody bridges over a metric downbeat, but the downbeat can be heard clearly in the accompaniment. For convenience, the metric downbeats are marked with arrows throughout Ex. 5-23, since there are a number of syncopations. You should, however, be listening at a level high enough so that the syncopations do not seriously obscure the rhythmic structure.

This third phrase group is more regular than the preceding two. The opening rhythmic pattern is literally repeated, these two statements falling together into a larger rhythm. Then a modification of

Example 5-23 Wagner, Prelude, third phrase group

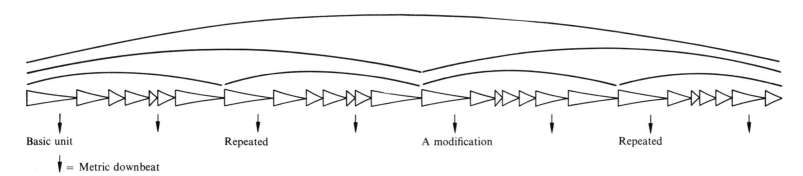

Basic unit   Repeated   A modification   Repeated

↓ = Metric downbeat

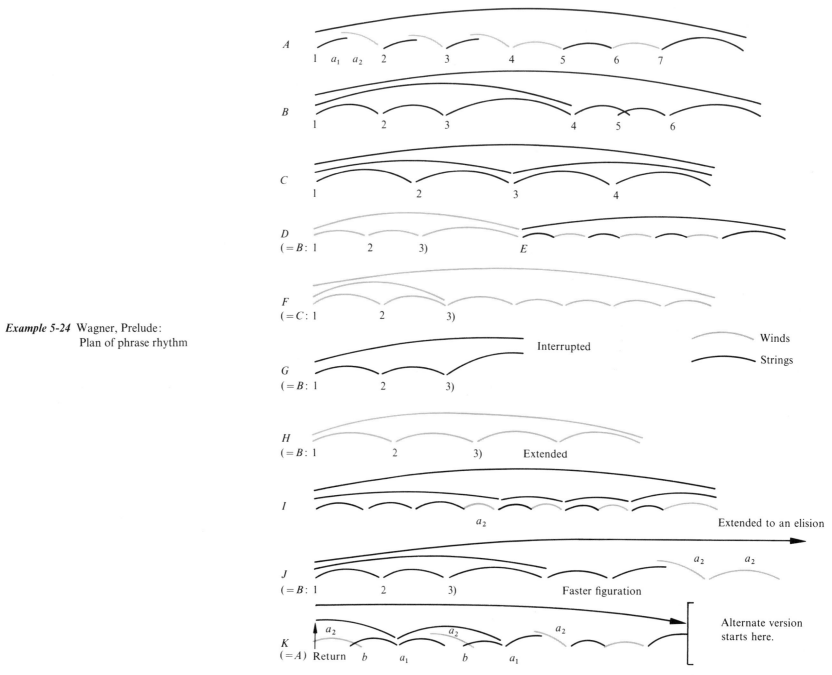

Example 5-24 Wagner, Prelude:
Plan of phrase rhythm

88

the pattern is stated and repeated, forming another larger rhythm. A crescendo helps make the last two statements of Ex. 5-23 form the logical extension of the first two.

OVERALL PLAN. With rhythms the size of those in Exs. 5-21, 5-22, and 5-23 in mind, you can follow the overall rhythm of the Prelude. In Ex. 5-24 you will find the three phrase groups already discussed, along with the remaining phrase groups of the Prelude, all shown in less detail. Each phrase group is labeled with letters from A to K; the three we have studied are A (Ex. 5-21), B (Ex. 5-22), and C (Ex. 5-23). In general, the remaining phrase groups begin with the rhythmic pattern of either B or C: D, G, H, and J begin almost exactly like B; I begins with a rhythmic modification (its melody, however, is different from that of B). Phrase group F begins like C. The winds' rhythmic pattern in A (that is, a_2) also reappears in phrase group I. At the point marked "return" (phrase group K) the opening music of A returns more or less intact, with its pauses filled in by the rhythmic pattern from B.

The details of the rhythm, as just described, serve here only for orientation. Indications of timbre are also useful for keeping track of where you are, even though the timbre combinations tend to be flexible and often not sharply contrasted. As shown in Ex. 5-24, strings predominate in phrase groups B and C, winds in D and F. In E, strings and winds alternate in clear antiphony, although as the Prelude approaches its high point the richer orchestration obscures individual timbres. (This passage may sound very different in various performances, depending on which contrapuntal strand or strands the conductor wishes to emphasize.) Finally, in J, only the brass can cut through. Clear opposition of timbres, however, is restored with the return to the original material in K.

Phrase groups B and C never appear in a completely simple form; but in their reappearances at D and F they are clearly more complex than they were at first: D is, in effect, extended by E, and F similarly is extended into repetitions of a fragment of the original rhythmic unit. As in the latter part of phrase group A, the repetition of fragments in E and at the end of F has two results: it diminishes a sense of phrasing at *lower* levels, while helping to create the sense of a much longer phrase at *higher* levels. This same process is at the work in the Prelude as a whole.

Starting at phrase group I, a rapid rhythmic figure is added in the violins, leading into a modified presentation of the rhythmic pattern from B. By this time the tempo has quickened, and now the rhythmic units seem shorter, more insistent. After three statements of the modified B figure (each time with the rapid lead-in), the winds answer with their a_2 figure; this alternation, too, tends to quicken the high-level rhythm. During phrase group J, the rhythmic units run together so much that clear demarcations are probably not audible; the feeling of rhythmic pulse, however, is distinctly stronger, as surges in strings and brass alternately lead forward to the high point. The buildup of rhythmic momentum subsides at the return of the material from phrase group A—but

only partially: the addition of the rhythmic unit from B, in what were originally the pauses of phrase group A, tends to keep the motion going.

The alternate endings for the Prelude begin at the point in K corresponding roughly to the end of phrase group A. At that point the large rhythm of the Prelude, the rhythmic shape we are concerned with here, has run its course.

If the phrases and phrase groups at the beginning are like waves, the large rhythm can be compared to the motion of a tide; the rhythm of the whole Prelude is like a rising flood tide followed by an ebb. The purpose of the wave-tide comparison is only to call attention to the large rhythm that governs the whole Prelude. We do not need to conclude from this analogy that the Prelude is about the sea. Musical rhythms have their own meanings, which we may—but need not—associate with nonmusical events. But whatever the terms we use to describe the rhythm of the Prelude, its long accelerated buildup, cresting at the high point, then immediately subsiding, seems to be an essential part of the shape.

A study of meter and of low-level metrical rhythms could easily suggest that rhythm was entirely a matter of a regular pulsation occurring in regular, clearly articulated groups. But rhythm is much more than those things, and can be found in their absence. Rhythms—especially large rhythms—do not depend on clearly perceptible points of articulation or on regular systems of beats to exert their pull. Considered in its broadest sense, rhythm is not merely a matter of the temporal detail of a piece, but instead is practically synonymous with shape itself.

Exercises for further listening

I. BEETHOVEN: SYMPHONY NO. 7, ALLEGRETTO (SECOND MOVEMENT), SECTION 1

Listen to the first subsection of section 1. Answer questions 1 through 17.

1. After the initial chord, the low-level rhythm of this subsection is   **1.** a
   ____ **a.** Regular, with a clear meter
   ____ **b.** Irregular, with a clear meter
   ____ **c.** Irregular, without a clear meter

2. The first subsection is built of   **2.** b
   ____ **a.** A variety of simultaneous rhythmic figures
   ____ **b.** A single rhythmic figure repeated many times
   ____ **c.** A succession of many rhythmic figures and patterns

3. Which of the following letter diagrams best represents the figure from which the rhythm   **3.** c
   of the subsection is built? (*L*: long; *S*: short)
   ____ **a.** *L S S*
   ____ **b.** *L S S L S S*
   ____ **c.** *L S S L L*
   ____ **d.** *L S L S L S*

4. The longer notes of the figure are   **4.** a
   ____ **a.** Twice as long as the shorter ones
   ____ **b.** Three times as long as the shorter ones
   ____ **c.** Only slightly longer than the shorter ones

5. Pulses at the lowest metric level in this subsection (level I) coincide with   **5.** a
   ____ **a.** The short notes of the rhythmic figure:

   ▷▷▷▷▷
   | | | | | | | |

   ____ **b.** The long notes of the rhythmic figure:

   ▷▷▷▷
   | | | |

   ____ **c.** Neither of these

90

6. Pulses at the next higher metric level (level II) are equivalent to

_____ **a.** One long note of the rhythmic figure:

_____ **b.** Two long notes of the rhythmic figure:

_____ **c.** Neither of these

7. Level II pulses are grouped in

_____ **a.** Threes
_____ **b.** Twos
_____ **c.** Neither threes nor twos

8. Indicate the next higher metric level (level III) by drawing its pulses below those of level II.

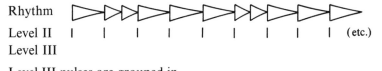

Rhythm

Level II | | | | | | | | (etc.)

Level III

9. Level III pulses are grouped in

_____ **a.** Twos
_____ **b.** Threes
_____ **c.** Neither twos nor threes

10. Which seems to be the principal metric level (the level at which it is most convenient to beat or count)?

_____ **a.** Level I   _____ **b.** Level II
_____ **c.** Level III   _____ **d.** None of these

11. If level II is the principal level, each measure corresponds to a single pulse at

_____ **a.** Level II
_____ **b.** Level III
_____ **c.** Neither of these levels

12. Throughout subsection 1, the rhythmic figuration

_____ **a.** Is continuous, without large internal groupings
_____ **b.** Falls clearly into several large phrase groups

6. a

7. b

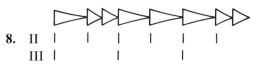

8. II | | | | | |

III | | | |

9. a

10. b

11. b

12. b

13. How many phrase groups do you hear in subsection 1?   **13.** b
_____ **a.** Two _____ **b.** Three _____ **c.** Four _____ **d.** Five

14. Is each phrase group the same length?   **14.** Yes

15. How many measures are there in each phrase group? (Count at metric level III, one count   **15.** b
per measure.)
_____ **a.** Four measures
_____ **b.** Eight measures
_____ **c.** Sixteen measures

16. Within each phrase group, how many complete or almost complete statements of the   **16.** c
rhythmic figure are there?
_____ **a.** Two _____ **b.** Three _____ **c.** Four _____ **d.** Five

17. Within each phrase group, which statement of the rhythmic figure has been shortened?   **17.** d
_____ **a.** The first _____ **b.** The second
_____ **c.** The third _____ **d.** The fourth

Listen again to subsection 1, following the diagram that is given below. Note the regularity of the rhythm at various levels.

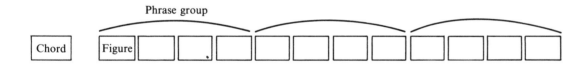

Listen to subsection 2. Answer questions 18 through 25.

18. Throughout this subsection   **18.** b
_____ **a.** Only one rhythmic pattern occurs at a time
_____ **b.** There are two simultaneous rhythmic patterns
_____ **c.** There are three or more simultaneous rhythmic patterns

19. Of the two rhythmic patterns,   **19.** a
_____ **a.** One is the same as that from subsection 1
_____ **b.** Neither is the same as that from subsection 1
_____ **c.** Both are the same as that from subsection 1

20. The rhythmic pattern from subsection 1 is the one heard here in the   **20.** b
____ **a.** Woodwinds
____ **b.** Highest and lowest strings
____ **c.** Middle strings

21. The second rhythmic pattern—or *counter rhythm*—   **21.** b
____ **a.** Is very similar to the original rhythmic pattern
____ **b.** Contrasts strongly with the original rhythmic pattern

22. In the new counter rhythm,   **22.** b
____ **a.** There are no new note values: all the long and short notes are the same duration as those in the original pattern
____ **b.** There are new note values, longer and/or shorter than those in the original pattern

23. The rhythm of the new pattern (that is, of the counter rhythm)   **23.** b
____ **a.** Is as regular as the first rhythmic pattern
____ **b.** Is less regular than the first rhythmic pattern

24. The large rhythmic groupings established in subsection 1 (8 + 8 + 8 measures)   **24.** a
____ **a.** Are again present in subsection 2
____ **b.** Are not present in subsection 2

25. In the first rhythmic group (first eight measures) of subsection 2, syncopation occurs twice in the counterrhythm. Follow the diagram given here as you listen to these measures. Which two letters in the diagram occur at the points of syncopation?   **25.** c and e

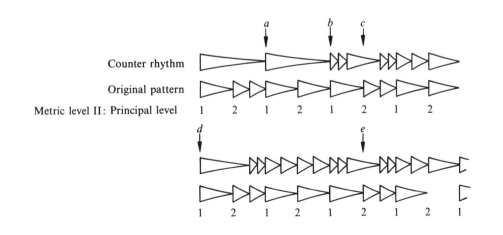

26. In subsection 3,   **26.** c
___ **a.** Only the original rhythmic figure is present
___ **b.** Only the counter rhythm is present
___ **c.** Both the original figure and the counter rhythm are present
___ **d.** Neither the original figure nor the counter rhythm is present

27. In addition to these two simultaneous rhythmic patterns,   **27.** a
___ **a.** There is a new, regular rhythmic figure in the accompaniment
___ **b.** There is a new, irregular rhythmic figure in the accompaniment
___ **c.** There are no further rhythmic patterns

28. The previous eight-measure rhythmic groupings   **28.** b
___ **a.** Are not present in subsection 3
___ **b.** Are again present in subsection 3

29. Listen carefully to the various rhythmic layers in subsection 4. Indicate which of the follow-   **29.** a, b, c, d are present.
ing rhythmic events you think are present.
___ **a.** The original rhythmic figure
___ **b.** The counter rhythm
___ **c.** The regular accompaniment figure (from subsection 3)
___ **d.** A new, regular accompaniment figure
___ **e.** A new, irregular accompaniment figure

30. The previous eight-measure rhythmic grouping   **30.** b
___ **a.** Is not present in this subsection   ___ **b.** Is again present in this subsection

31. At a high level, the entire first section of the Allegretto   **31.** a
___ **a.** Is rhythmically regular   ___ **b.** Is rhythmically irregular

32. One important source of rhythmic irregularity at lower levels is   **32.** b
___ **a.** The original rhythmic figure
___ **b.** The counter rhythm
___ **c.** The various accompaniment figures

33. The overall effect of the rhythmic structure of section 1 is that of   **33.** b
____ **a.** A sudden dramatic change from one type of rhythm to another
____ **b.** A steady increase in the number of different rhythms occurring simultaneously
____ **c.** A gradual increase from a single, relatively inactive rhythm at the beginning, to a single, very active rhythm at the end

QUESTIONS FOR DISCUSSION

A. Listen to the two remaining principal sections of the Allegretto. Does the original rhythmic grouping of section 1 (8 + 8 + 8 measures) recur at any point? Can this rhythmic figure be heard? Where is the counter rhythm present? At what point does the rhythmic activity seem most intense? What elements of rhythmic regularity obtain? Of rhythmic irregularity? Which finally prevails—regularity or irregularity?

B. Discuss the rhythmic structure and detail of the two interludes. Do any rhythmic figures from the *A* sections occur? How does the rhythm of the interludes differ in effect from that of the principal sections?

C. Listen to the entire movement. In what way—if at all—can the large sectional structure be heard in terms of rhythm?

II. STRAVINSKY: LES NOCES, SECOND TABLEAU

Listen to the entire Tableau, following the text in Chapter 13. Answer questions 1, 2, and 3.

1. Tap or beat as you listen. Which of these statements is true?   **1.** c
____ **a.** You can continue the regular beat that you set up at the beginning throughout the entire Tableau.
____ **b.** You can continue the regular beat that you set up at the beginning throughout some sections only.
____ **c.** It is difficult to continue beating or tapping regularly for long.

2. The tempo   **2.** b
____ **a.** Does not change throughout the Tableau
____ **b.** Changes several times in the course of the Tableau

3. A sudden change of tempo occurs at number   **3.** b
____ **a.** 43
____ **b.** 50
____ **c.** 62

Listen from 50 up to 53, following the transliteration given here. Answer questions 4, 5, and 6.

50 (*Two basses, p*)
   1 Boslovite otech, s materyu svago tsadu,
   2 ko stolnu gradu pristupit kamennu stenu razbit.
51 (*Tutti, mf*)
   3 Gde sidit tam Khvetis gosudar,
   (*Two basses, p*)
   4 Svoyu suzhenuyu ponyat.
52 (*Tutti, mf*)
   5 Tak svechey svetik naydet.
   (*Two basses, p*)
   6 V sobor, cherkov skhodit,
   7 Serebryan krest potselovat.
   (*Tutti, mf*)
   8 Bozhiya milost Bogorodicha!

4. The most striking type of rhythmic contrast in this passage is that of   **4.** b
___ **a.** Regular versus irregular rhythm
___ **b.** Slow versus fast tempo
___ **c.** Duple versus triple meter

5. Indicate which lines of the text are sung in a slow tempo (S) and which are sung in a fast   **5.** 1: S
tempo (F).   2: S
___ 1   3: F
___ 2   4: S
___ 3   5: F
___ 4   6: S
___ 5   7: S
___ 6   8: F
___ 7
___ 8

6. The contrasts in tempo   **6.** a
___ **a.** Correspond to the contrasts in timbre
___ **b.** Do not correspond to the contrasts in timbre

Listen to the beginning of the second Tableau, from 27 up to 29, following the text on the facing page as you listen. Answer questions 7 through 10.

7. How are the beats grouped? After careful listening, indicate the groupings on the text diagram by drawing vertical lines to separate each group.

Text: Pre-   chi-   sta-   ya   Mat
Beats: ʼ   ʼ   ʼ   ʼ   ʼ   ʼ
        kho-   di,   kho- di   k nam u
        ʼ   ʼ   ʼ   ʼ   ʼ
        khat, sva-   khe   po- mo-   gat
        ʼ   ʼ   ʼ   ʼ   ʼ   ʼ
               kud-   ri   ras- che- sat,
        ʼ   ʼ   ʼ   ʼ   ʼ
        Khve- tis-   ie-   vy   kud- ri,
        ʼ   ʼ   ʼ   ʼ   ʼ
        kud-   ri   ras- che- sat, Pam-
        ʼ   ʼ   ʼ   ʼ   ʼ
        fil-   yi-   cha   ru- sy.   Kho-
        ʼ   ʼ   ʼ   ʼ   ʼ
        di,   kho-   di   k nam u   khat
        ʼ   ʼ   ʼ   ʼ   ʼ
        kho-   di   k nam u   khat kud-
        ʼ   ʼ   ʼ   ʼ   ʼ
        ri   ras-   che- sat.
        ʼ   ʼ   ʼ   ʼ

8. Indicate the number of beats that each group contains.

___ Group 1
___ Group 2
___ Group 3
___ Group 4
___ Group 5
___ Group 6
___ Group 7
___ Group 8
___ Group 9
___ Group 10

9. Each rhythmic group contains
___ **a.** Six beats   ___ **b.** Either 4, 5, or 6 beats
___ **c.** Either 5, 6, or 7 beats   ___ **d.** Seven beats

10. As you listen again, count the beats within each rhythmic group aloud in time to the music: "1 2 3 4 5 6, 1 2 3 4 5 6 7, 1 2 3 4 5 6, . . ." You are counting
___ **a.** High-level meter   ___ **b.** Low-level meter
___ **c.** Unit pulses   ___ **d.** Tempo

---

7. Pre-   chi-   sta-   ya   Mat |
        ʼ   ʼ   ʼ   ʼ   ʼ   ʼ
        kho-   di,   kho-   di   k nam u
        ʼ   ʼ   ʼ   ʼ   ʼ
        khat, |sva-   khe   po- mo-   gat
        ʼ |ʼ   ʼ   ʼ   ʼ   ʼ
              |kud-   ri   ras- che- sat, |
        ʼ |ʼ   ʼ   ʼ   ʼ |
        Khve- tis-   ie-   vy   kud- ri, |
        ʼ   ʼ   ʼ   ʼ   ʼ
        kud-   ri   ras-   che- sat, | Pam-
        ʼ   ʼ   ʼ   ʼ   ʼ
        fil-   yi-   cha   ru- sy.| Kho-
        ʼ   ʼ   ʼ   ʼ |
        di,   kho-   di   k nam u   khat |
        ʼ   ʼ   ʼ   ʼ   ʼ
        kho-   di   k nam u   khat |kud-
        ʼ   ʼ   ʼ   ʼ   ʼ |ʼ
        ri   ras-   che-   sat. |
        ʼ   ʼ   ʼ   ʼ |

8. Group 1: 6
        Group 2: 7
        Group 3: 6
        Group 4: 5
        Group 5: 6
        Group 6: 5
        Group 7: 6
        Group 8: 7
        Group 9: 5
        Group 10: 5

9. c

10. c

97

Listen to the section at 30, following the text given here. Answer questions 11, 12, and 13.

```
Text:  Kho-  di,    kho-  di    k nam u
Beats:  ,     ,     ,     ,     ,     ,
        khat, kho-  di    k nam u     khat,
        ,     ,     ,     ,     ,     ,
        sva-  khe-  po-   mo-   gat
        ,     ,     ,     ,     ,     ,
        kud-  ri    ras-  che-  sat.
        ,     ,     ,     ,     ,
```

11. The beats shown below the text

    ___ **a.** Are organized regularly in twos

    ___ **b.** Are organized regularly in threes

    ___ **c.** Are organized regularly in fives

    ___ **d.** Are not organized into regular groups

11. d

12. Indicate the rhythmic groupings by drawing vertical lines on the text diagram to separate each group.

12.
```
   Kho-  di,    kho-  di    k nam u
   khat, | kho-  di    k nam u    khat, |
   ,       ,     ,     ,     ,     ,
   sva-    khe-  po-   mo-   gat        |
   ,       ,     ,     ,     ,     ,
   kud-    ri    ras-  che-  sat. |
   ,       ,     ,     ,     ,
```

13. Indicate the number of unit pulses in each group.

    Group 1 ___

    Group 2 ___

    Group 3 ___

    Group 4 ___

13. Group 1: 7

    Group 2: 5

    Group 3: 6

    Group 4: 5

Listen to the section at 33, following the text. Answer questions 14 through 17.

```
Text:  Pre-  chi-  sta-  ya    Mat,  kho-
Beats:  ,     ,     ,     ,     ,     ,
        di,   kho-  di    k nam u     khat,
        ,     ,     ,     ,     ,     ,
        sva-  khe   po-   mo-   gat   kud-
        ,     ,     ,     ,     ,     ,
        ri    ras-  che-  sat.
        ,     ,     ,     ,
```

14. At 33, the rhythmic groupings

____ **a.** Are regular

____ **b.** Are irregular

15. These irregular groups

____ **a.** Are not the same as those at 30

____ **b.** Are the same as those at 30

16. Mark off the groupings on the text, as before.

17. How many unit pulses are in each group?

Group 1 ____

Group 2 ____

Group 3 ____

Group 4 ____

Listen to the entire Tableau again, noting how the placement of the three excerpts (at 27, 30, and 33) affects the overall rhythmic shape of the Tableau.

14. b

15. a

16.

Pre-	chi-	sta-	ya	Mat,	kho-
´	´	´	´	´	´
di,	kho-	di	k nam	u	khat,
´	´	´	´	´	
sva-	khe	po-	mo-	gat	kud-
´	´	´	´	´	´
ri	ras-	che-	sat.		
´	´	´	´		

17. Group 1: 5

Group 2: 7

Group 3: 5

Group 4: 5

99

CHAPTER 6 LINEAR ORGANIZATION OF PITCH

SO FAR, WE HAVE REFERRED to the musical factor of pitch only in gross ways. We distinguished between higher and lower voice types (such as soprano and alto), as well as higher and lower registers within a single range. In discussing texture we assumed a perception of pitch sufficient to follow individual lines in a contrapuntal texture.

In this chapter, we will start concentrating on pitches and relationships among pitches, setting aside for the moment consideration of timbre and texture. To some extent, pitch relationships can be understood apart from rhythm, but not entirely; we will need to discuss some of the rhythmic features of the pieces to be studied in order to clarify the pitch relationships. In general, all pitch relationships must be referred to the context of the piece in which they occur.

Pitch relationships function along several different dimensions, at many different levels. Perhaps the best way to begin is with monophony—with a single line—because here individual pitches are easy to hear, their relationships and function in the overall design relatively easy to grasp. Our first specific discussion of pitch, then, will concern pitch relationships in the linear or melodic dimension.

Béla Bartók (1881–1945)
STRING QUARTET NO. 6
MESTO (FIRST MOVEMENT, INTRODUCTION)

Bartók's String Quartet No. 6 opens with an expressive melody for solo viola, which we already met as an example of monophonic texture (Chapter 3). As a slow introduction to the first movement, the melody becomes important for the structure of the whole quartet, which we will study later (in Chapter 15). Our concern at this point is to hear the Mesto as an isolated line.

Only one pitch is heard at any one time in the introduction. The only pitch relationships there are to hear in this line are the relationships formed by the pitches as they occur in succession. The texture of the introduction provides no chords, no counterpoint, nothing beside the single line. A verbal or analytical understanding seems at first irrelevant to an isolated melody as beautiful as this one: there seems, at first, to be so little to say, so much just to hear. Yet as you listen more closely, to perceive more fully what is going on in this introduction, you can become sensitive to several aspects of both its larger design and its detail.

MELODIC DIRECTION. One of the most obvious aspects of the line is that it goes up or down to form a perceptible shape. Our diagrams have often represented this aspect of musical line by a gray line drawn through the wedges used for individual notes. As observed before, there is no line actually there in the music, which consists of discrete bits of sound. Sometimes, to be sure, we hear only the bits of sound, the isolated notes; but often (as in Bartók's Mesto) we hear a melodic curve, a smooth rise and fall of motion that links the bits of sound together into a line. The line may even seem more real than the individual pitches—one of the mysteries of the musical experience.

The gray line in Ex. 6-1, representing all of the Mesto, goes through most of the individual notes, hence traces most of the twists and turns of the melody. However, the direction of the melody can be perceived at several different levels. Your impression of the melodic shape of the Mesto might simply be of a gradual rise to a high point, then a descent to the end; you could represent this shape by drawing a simple arc, which would reflect the shape of the melody just as truly as the line in Ex. 6-1, but at a higher level.

Such an arc, in fact, might show something about the overall design of the melody not immediately apparent from Ex. 6-1, even though the arc—with its long, smooth shape—might miss most of the individual wedges. Similarly, lines could be drawn through half, say, or two-thirds of the notes in such a way as to show the general contour of the line more precisely than the arc but with more sense of overall direction than Ex. 6-1. Different listeners might have various opinions as to what directions such a line should take.

Compared to the simple rise and fall of the arc, the actual line in Ex. 6-1 has many twists and turns. These detailed changes of direction are sometimes called *inflections* (as when we say that a line is inflected or "bent"). Inflection is a very important feature of many melodies; indeed, such details may be as important as the overall direction in making a melody interesting or expressive. In listening to melody, you should be aware of both details of inflection and overall direction—and of the relationship between them.

At the end of Ex. 6-1, the line falls expressively to a conclusion or *cadence*. The term "cadence," used in music or poetry in several senses, means "falling." In music it is used mainly for the sense of repose at the end of a phrase or section. The sense of falling can be conveyed through pitch by a literal falling of the line from higher to lower, as here, or by more subtle kinds of falling motion expressed in complex combination of pitches, to be discussed further on.

RHYTHM OF THE LINE. With its overall rise and fall firmly in mind, we can consider the melody in more detail. For this purpose, it will be helpful to refer to the rhythm of the Mesto, according to the procedures worked out in Chapter 4. There is a slow, steady pulse, at the lowest level, grouped in threes at level I (Ex. 6-2). The rhythmic grouping at higher levels is not obviously metric: at first it seems as though there were a metric grouping in threes at level II; this does not, however, correspond to the rhythm throughout the Mesto. A grouping in twos at level II, however, can be followed throughout the Mesto, even though it may seem less convincing at the start.

A clear sense of rhythmic grouping will emerge after only a few hearings. The grouping will be most apparent at the lower levels, as indicated by the slurs in Ex. 6-2. Groups 1, 2, and 3, even though short, are clearly set off from each other. Group 4 leads strongly onto group 5, giving the effect of an elision: the last note of group 4 is also the first note of group 5. In group 7 the motion starts to slacken; the notes lengthen in preparation for the cadence of the section.

The rhythmic detail contributes still more to the overall shape. Rhythmically, group 1 is like group 3, group 2 like group 4 (Ex. 6-3). These four groups go together in antecedent-consequent pairs. After the elision that connects groups 4 and 5, group 5 begins as if it were the antecedent of a third pair. (Its rhythm is the same as that of groups 1 and 3, only the first note is lengthened.) This time, however, the antecedent is followed, not by a consequent, but by a rhythmic repetition of the antecedent.

Groups 1 and 2 can be regarded as the first phrase

Example 6-1 Bartók, Mesto

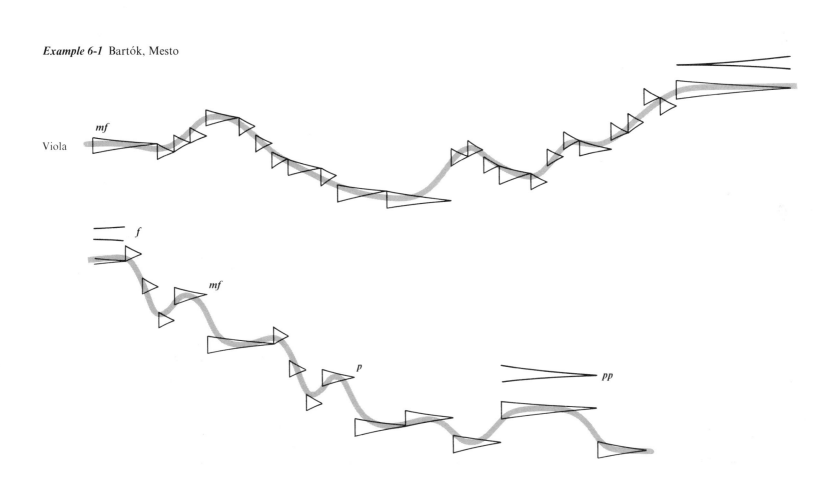

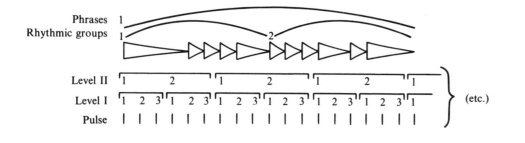

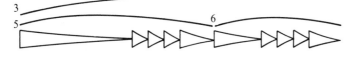

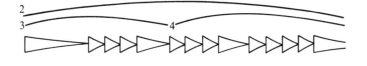

Example 6-2 Bartók, Mesto: Rhythm and meter

Example 6-3 Bartók, Mesto: Antecedent-consequent phrases

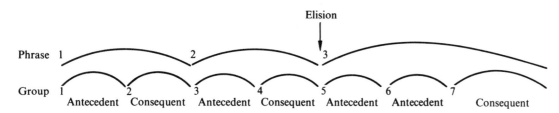

of the Mesto, groups 3 and 4 as the second phrase, and groups 5, 6, and 7 as the third phrase (Ex. 6-3).

SEQUENCE. The details in the rise and fall of the melody work closely with the rhythmic phrasing to shape the line. This is heard most easily, perhaps, in groups 5 and 6, where group 6 repeats the rhythm of 5 instead of answering it. The two groups also have the *same melodic shape*, even though the actual pitches are different. This important distinction is sometimes difficult to grasp. If we diagram the melody with as much detail as we use for the rhythm, the similarity of shape between groups 5 and 6 will perhaps be more clear (Ex. 6-4).

A melodic pattern such as group 5 could, of course, be repeated at the same pitch level, using all the same pitches; such literal repetition is a frequent and important aspect of melodic design. Or a pattern can be repeated at a different pitch level, higher or lower (in this case, lower), using different pitches but exactly the same melodic shape. Or the repetition might involve only a rough similarity of shape. The relationship between groups 5 and 6, involving the same shape and different pitches, is called a *sequence*. The repetition can occur at successively higher pitch levels, or at successively lower ones. There can be as many repetitions in a sequence as the composer wishes. The unit of repetition can be as short as a few notes or as long as a phrase group. (Since the point of a sequence is *literal* repetition of shape at a new pitch level, any variation in shape is an exception that must be dealt with separately.)

Now consider groups 1 through 4. As we saw, groups 3 and 4 repeat the rhythm of 1 and 2; but here the melodic shape is not repeated, either at the original pitch level or at any other level. There is not even a rough melodic similarity between group 1 and group 3 or between group 2 and group 4—no matter how much the strong sense of rhythmic repetition may suggest melodic similarity. In overall direction as well as detail, phrase 2 proceeds differently from phrase 1.

MELODIC INVERSION. Considered as a whole, group 1 ascends, even though it begins with a descent; as a whole, group 3 descends even though it begins with an ascent. Similarly, group 2 descends, while group 4 ascends (Ex. 6-5). Phrase 2 is, in a very rough melodic sense, an upside-down version of phrase 1; this kind of melodic relationship, called an *inversion*, is sometimes carried out very strictly, so that there may be no doubt that two phrases have the same melodic shape even though one is an inversion of the other. Here, however, the inversion is only approximate.

MELODIC INTERVALS. When we say that two phrases have the same melodic shape or that they have different shapes, we have so far spoken only in terms of the shape as represented by a line drawing. Such an approximation of a series of points or pitches is not a precise description of the similarity or difference in melodic shape. A sharper sensitivity to melody requires still another kind of awareness.

In most music, melodic line moves from one distinct pitch to the next, rather than sliding from one pitch to another like a siren. There are distinct *intervals* between lower and higher pitches—intervals that appear in our diagrams as vertical distance on the page. Sometimes the intervals may be very small, as between the first and second pitches of Bartók's Mesto or between the second and third pitches or between the third and fourth (Ex. 6-6).

Sometimes the intervals are larger, as between the first and second pitches of phrase 2. This interval is of moderate size; some melodic intervals are very much larger.

Many intervals in the melody of the Mesto are very small—so small that it is difficult to imagine any other pitch that would fit between the two pitches actually sounding. The first two pitches of the melody seem this close. Since the melody moves away from and back to the opening pitch, the interval between the first and second notes is the same as the interval between the second and third. The *direction* of the first interval is descending, that of the second is ascending; but the *size* of the two intervals is the same.

Between the third and fourth notes the same interval appears again. If you can fix the size of this interval in your ear, you should, with a little practice, be able to hear that between the fourth and fifth notes is a larger interval—still relatively small, but larger than the interval between preceding notes (Ex. 6-6).

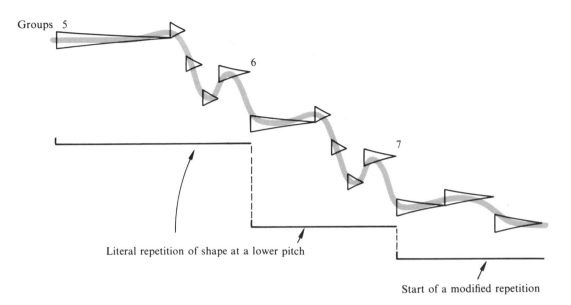

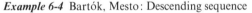

Literal repetition of shape at a lower pitch

Start of a modified repetition

Example 6-4 Bartók, Mesto: Descending sequence

Example 6-5 Bartók, Mesto: Inversion

Phrase 1
Group 1

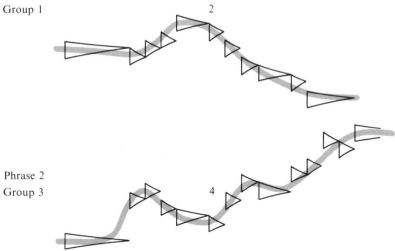

Phrase 2
Group 3

103

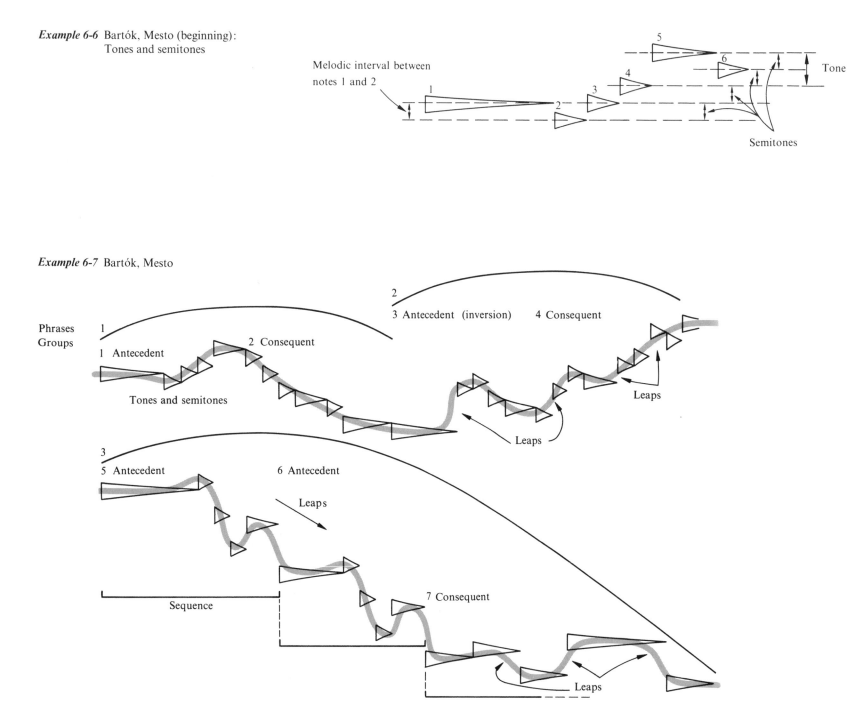

Example 6-6 Bartók, Mesto (beginning):
Tones and semitones

Melodic interval between
notes 1 and 2

Tone

Semitones

Example 6-7 Bartók, Mesto

Phrases
Groups

1

1 Antecedent

2 Consequent

Tones and semitones

2

3 Antecedent (inversion)   4 Consequent

Leaps

Leaps

3

5 Antecedent   6 Antecedent

Leaps

Sequence

7 Consequent

Leaps

With a little more practice and experimentation, you might be able to hum a pitch lying between the fourth and fifth notes. If you cannot find such a pitch, the music itself will provide it in the very next note—the sixth—of the Mesto. In Ex. 6-6, we can see that this sixth note has the effect of dividing the larger interval into two smaller intervals, each the size of the smallest interval used among the beginning notes.

The melody, as it unfolds, seems to seek out pitches that do not reinforce or repeat preceding pitches but rather fall in the intervals between them. The melody has a searching, restless quality directly related to its way of locating new pitches.

TONE AND SEMITONE. Musicians have names for the sizes of the various intervals commonly found in music. For example, the size of the first interval is called a *semitone*, meaning "half a tone." Semitones appear between notes 1 and 2, 2 and 3, 3 and 4, and 5 and 6 (see Ex. 6-6).

The larger interval between notes 4 and 5 is called a *tone* (or a *whole tone*). It is the interval of which the semitone is said to be a half. As in Ex. 6-6, this tone can be divided into two semitones. A semitone is often called a *half step*; and a tone, a *whole step*. Our concern here, however, is not with individual intervals and their sizes, but rather with their use in compositions, where the perceived size and the effect of an interval depend a great deal on context. In the beginning of Bartók's Mesto, the semitones prevail over the tones, and so seem to be a basic unit, while the whole tones seem in contrast to be relatively large. In many other pieces, semitones are not so prevalent and often appear to be subdivisions of tones—as their name implies.

STEP AND LEAP. Throughout phrase 1, there are no intervals other than tones and semitones. At the beginning of phrase 2, between notes 1 and 2, we meet a larger interval. This larger kind of interval is called a *leap*, to distinguish it from a whole or half *step*. Motion by leap is also called *disjunct motion*, to distinguish it from the *conjunct motion* of a line that uses only whole steps and half steps. The line of the introduction begins in conjunct motion, then gradually includes more and more leaps until its motion is predominantly disjunct. The change from conjunct to disjunct motion is an important factor in the shape of the line (Ex. 6-7).

PITCH REPETITION. In some pieces, the composer, wishing to emphasize a certain pitch level, will call attention to it by repeating the pitch in some obvious fashion. Later we will study some music in which pitch repetition is used in this way.

In the Mesto, however, Bartók seems intent on minimizing the short-term effect of pitch repetition: relatively few pitch repetitions occur, and those that do are often placed in rhythmically less prominent positions—on counts TWO or THREE instead of ONE, for example. Avoidance of obvious pitch repetition is an important factor in the strangely expressive quality of this introduction. Such an avoidance also has the effect of forcing the ear to hear each pitch and interval as it comes along, for there is little to encourage us to refer all the pitches and intervals to an obvious reference point or framework of pitch.

THE MESTO AS A WHOLE. The continuity of the Mesto is provided by the direction of the melody, that is, by the shape of the line, as well as by the clarity of the phrasing. The overall shape represented in Ex. 6-1 pulls together all the details we have been discussing and is always perceptible in and through them, once the relationship of line and detail has been grasped.

Another kind of continuity is provided by the very carefully controlled growth of complexity in the melody as it unfolds and also in the gradual increase in the size of the intervals used. The first half of phrase 1, using nothing but tones and semitones, rises simply and easily to form the first question; the answer follows in descending motion just as simply, the only element of complexity being the strong tendency to avoid, in the consequent, pitches used in the antecedent.

Phrase 2, the second question-and-answer pair, begins more decisively with a leap instead of a step; then the line falls back, seeming to lose its way for a moment in semitone motion. The consequent starts to move definitely upward, by step and leap combined. At the end of the consequent, the motion continues through the elision until it reaches the long high note at the climax of the melody. This note serves as the beginning of the third, most urgent antecedent; something about the shape of the third antecedent is at once more complex and more memorable than its predecessors. In any case, the antecedent is reiterated in sequence, extending the phrase and leading the overall curve downward—more by leap than by step now, as the intervals, as well as the overall range, gradually become larger. The end of this third phrase becomes, in context, broadly emphatic, all in longer notes with one very solemn descending leap at the end (see Ex. 6-7).

The more familiar one becomes with this melody, naturally, the clearer its shape seems. Yet some aspects of its pitch organization may not become clearer: for most listeners, perhaps, there will be little sense of any repeated pitch throughout the whole melody, no matter how familiar the melody becomes —although a few listeners may sense a return at the end to a pitch closely related to the very beginning. But that is not essential to an understanding of the melody in terms of direction and intervalic motion, its dominant melodic features.

REFERENCE POINTS AND AREAS OF PITCH. In Bartók's Mesto, pitches derive their significance largely from their participation in the unfolding line: they are higher or lower than the pitches immediately preceding and help create patterns of up and down, of smaller and larger intervals. In many other pieces, pitches derive their significance more through a sense of distance from a reference point supplied by the context of the pitches themselves. The sense of motion of each new pitch is heard as motion toward or away from the point of reference. Such pieces may still have a sense of linear direction, of melodic shape; but the direction will be referred to one or two predominant pitches, so that the line unfolds in a closed area (as it were) instead of an open one.

Reference points for pitch can be supplied in many different ways. All such ways, however, have to do with the context within an individual piece. Often a point of reference is provided by one of the pitches actually sounding in the piece; but more than one pitch can be brought into play. Sometimes several different pitches form a hierarchy of some kind that sets up coordinates of pitch location against which melodic distance and direction within the piece are projected. The possibilities are many. We will study a few of them in a piece of Gregorian chant.

Gregorian Chant

"RESURREXI" (INTROIT)

Gregorian chant is ancient monophony used traditionally in the Roman Catholic Mass of Holy Communion service. "Resurrexi" ("I am risen") is a chant for Easter Sunday; it is called an *introit* ("entrance song") because it was composed to be sung during the procession into church in preparation for Mass.

Like Bartók's Mesto, then, the chant presents only one pitch at a time; but unlike the Mesto, the chant presents its pitches in such a way that you can easily hear contrasting groups of pitches—a lower group and a higher one—instead of a continuous ascent or descent. The entire chant is divided into five easily perceptible sections, alternately lower and higher in pitch (Ex. 6-8). The *A* sections are all identical; sections B_1 and B_2 are very similar to each other in melody, but they have a different text. (In some performances the sectional shape may be $A\ B_1\ B_2\ A$; but the contrast of higher and lower sections will still be clear.)

Example 6-8 "Resurrexi": Sections

Section	1	2	3*	4	5
Register	Low	High	Low	High	Low
Sectional form	A	B_1	A	B_2	A

*Omitted in some performances

RHYTHM. As you study "Resurrexi" in more detail, you will become aware soon (if you are not already) that its rhythm is not metric. We noticed that the absence of meter is most obvious at the lower levels. At the level of phrase, the chant "Resurrexi" has very clear rhythms; merely by listening for the places where the melody pauses briefly, you can gain a clear idea of the phrase structure of the first section, while in the second section the phrase structure is even more obvious (Ex. 6-9).

Section *A*
Phrase 1  Resurrexi, et adhuc tecum sum, alleluia;

2  posuisti super me manum tuam, alleluia;

3 mirabilis facta est scientia tua, alleluia, alleluia.

Section B_1

1 Domine probasti me, et cognovisti me:

2 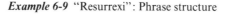 tu cognovisti sessionem meam et resurrectionem meam.

Section B_2

1 Gloria patri, et filio, et spiritui sancto;

2  sicut erat in principio, et nunc, et semper;

3 et in secula seculorum. Amen.

Example 6-9 "Resurrexi": Phrase structure

Example 6-10 "Resurrexi" (section B_1): Repeated pitches

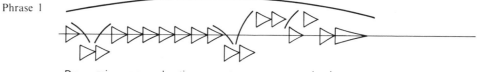

Phrase 1

Do — mi — ne probasti me, et co — gno —vi-sti me:

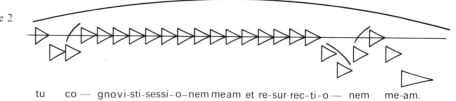

Phrase 2

tu   co — gnovi-sti-sessi-o-nem meam et re-sur-rec-ti-o — nem   me-am.

There is a pulse, of the kind we called unit pulse, running throughout the piece. The pulse here is somewhat more flexible than the unit pulse we encountered in Bartók's Burletta, being subject to slight expressive variations in tempo.

CENTRAL PITCHES. The difference between sections A and B can be roughly described as one of register. More specifically, in section B it is obvious that pitches are being repeated—one pitch in particular—in a way that was not found in Bartók's Mesto. The manifold repetitions of this one pitch create all by themselves the image of a straight horizontal line, so that it should not be difficult to understand such a line in a pitch diagram of section B (Ex. 6-10).

Listen to all of section B_1, then continue through the intervening section A (if it is present) to B_2, noticing how the repeated pitch seems familiar on its return in B_2. Mere repetition of pitches can create stable guidelines in pitch organization that thereafter maintain themselves in the ear for surprisingly long stretches of time.

In the second section, most of the other pitches are also repeated; one such pitch appears above the most frequent pitch, another one below. At the end of the section, two more pitches appear with much less repetition—one of them only once.

PITCH FUNCTION. The fact that some pitches appear more frequently than others is only a rough indication of the relationships among them. We can go on to refine these relationships by discussing the functions that different pitches play in their respective sections. In the second section (B_1), as you already heard, one pitch is very frequent: it is the vehicle for much of the text. The most frequent pitch, in this particular kind of chant, is called a *reciting note* because so much of the text is recited on it. The pitches immediately above and below it function as ornaments, relieving the sameness of the reciting note. The lower pitches of this set appear only at the end of the section; their function is to bring the section to a close. It is interesting that this should be done by the least frequent pitches, rather than by the most frequent.

The relative functions of pitches in the first section

are less obvious. After a few hearings, however, it should become clear that one of the pitches is predominant over the others because it acts as a point of reference for them—especially in the first phrase. The pitch on the horizontal line in Ex. 6-11 is one of the most frequent pitches, but more than that, it seems to be a point of return for the melody after a rise or fall. Other pitches may be momentarily more expressive or emphatic, but the pitch on the horizontal line sounds central to the set. At any rate, it represents the average pitch level: other pitches are higher or lower in relationship to this one.

Another important pitch is the very first pitch of the chant (Ex. 6-12). This pitch is far less frequent than the central one, but in a subtle way it, too, serves as a reference point; together with the central one it establishes a frame for the whole first section.

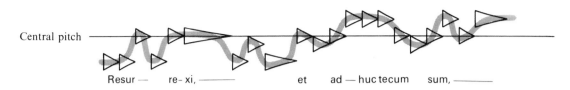

Central pitch

Resur — re- xi, ——— et ad — huc tecum sum, ———

Example 6-11 "Resurrexi" (beginning): Central pitch

Example 6-12 "Resurrexi" (beginning): Frame

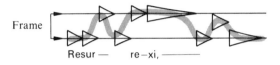

Frame

Resur — re-xi, ———

UPPER AND LOWER NEIGHBORS. Other pitches in the first section tend to refer themselves to this frame. The pitch immediately above the central one (it first appears on "adhuc," Ex. 6-13a) is used frequently thereafter—more frequently in fact than the lower pitch of the frame. The function of this pitch frequently is to alternate with the central one, providing the opportunity for movement away from the central one and back to it. This less stable pitch

Example 6-13 "Resurrexi": Upper and lower neighbors

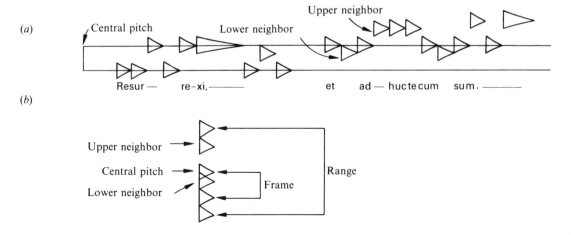

(a) Central pitch Lower neighbor Upper neighbor

Resur — re-xi, ——— et ad — huc te cum sum, ———

(b)

Upper neighbor →
Central pitch →   Frame   Range
Lower neighbor →

Example 6-14 "Resurrexi" (section *A*): Motion around the frame

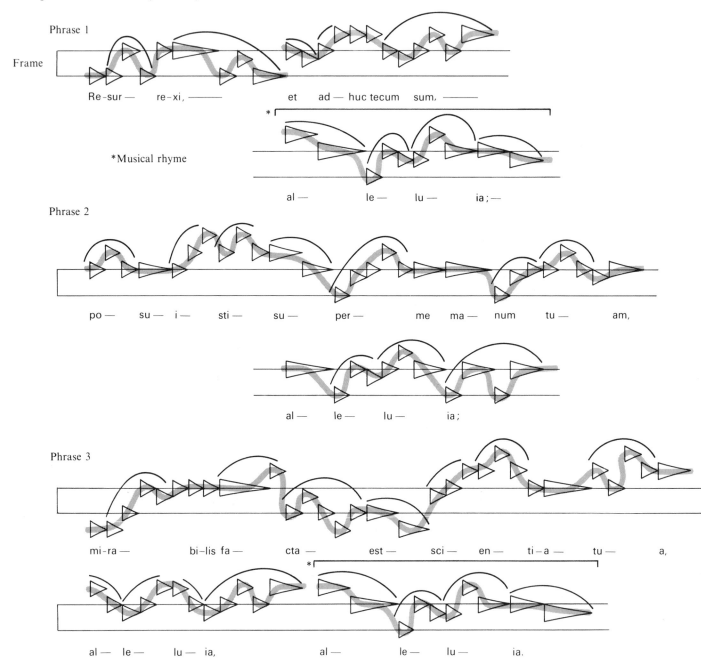

has no independent position in the piece; its position is defined by reference to the central one—it is "the pitch next above the central one." In this text we shall call such a pitch a *neighbor*, or more specifically an *upper neighbor*.

We noticed how the melody of the second section (B_1) did not end on one of the more frequent pitches but instead on a pitch that appeared nowhere else. A similar thing takes place in the first section, although in a less extreme form: the melody does not end on the central pitch, but on its *lower* neighbor— a pitch that has been only moderately frequent and not very prominent (Ex. 6-13*a*). The lower neighbor, like the upper one, is less stable than the central pitch. All in all, it is a curious pitch for an ending; its choice as the end of the first phrase, of the section, and of the whole chant gives a distinct, peculiar color to the chant.

MELODIC MOTION AROUND THE FRAME. There are only two other pitches in the first section. One lies below the frame, the other above the upper neighbor. These are the top and bottom pitches of the range. Example 6-13*b* gives an abstract representation of all the pitches used in section *A*.

With the relationships among these pitches established in your ear, you can perceive more clearly the melodic movement *within* the first section. Throughout section *A*, there is a gradual expansion outward from the frame: the pitches above and below the two pitches of the frame are stressed more and more, until the chant seems to fill the whole range. The expansion sometimes takes place below the frame, sometimes above it. The fact that the melodic movement can be heard as above, within, or below the frame gives a specific sense of distance and direction to the melody.

Follow Ex. 6-14 as you listen to section *A*, hearing how the melodic movement goes above and below the frame. Phrase 1 sets out the frame, emphasizes the central pitch, and goes one step above it, to the upper neighbor. Phrase 2, which begins on the central pitch, emphasizes that pitch even more than did phrase 1. In addition, phrase 2 rises two steps above the frame to the highest pitch of the first section. The rise takes place early in phrase 2; afterward the

melody returns to the central pitch, with its upper and lower neighbors, and occasionally touches the lower pitch of the frame. Phrase 3 explores below the frame: the low pitch that starts phrase 3 is not really very low, but in context it adds a sense of depth to the pitch content of the piece. After this low pitch is confirmed, the line rises quickly to the top of the range, thus traversing the whole range of the section within a relatively short time; then it falls gradually to the conclusion of the section, ending on the lower neighbor.

MUSICAL RHYME. The frequent repetition of pitches makes possible identification of the individual pitches and perception of their relationships to each other. There is relatively little repetition, however, of melodic figures or patterns. Even after several hearings, there is little of melodic shape that sticks in the memory, and as you listen you may be bewildered by the way the melody finds new configurations for the same pitches.

As a result, you are perhaps mildly surprised when you notice an internal repeat of melodic material. The end of the first phrase (" . . . tecum sum, alleluia") turns up at the end of the third phrase as the second of the two "Alleluias" (see Ex. 6-14). All by itself, this one repeat does not seem to have the structural force it would have in a piece that made extensive use of such repetitions. A repeat of the end of a phrase is sometimes called a *musical rhyme*, because of its similarity in function to a poetic rhyme.

TONES AND SEMITONES. The melodic movement in "Resurrexi" is mainly conjunct—that is, in tones and semitones. Once you hear which intervals are tones and which are semitones, you will soon discover that the tones and semitones always occur in certain places relative to the two pitches that provide the frame for the first section. More precisely, the semitone occurs only between the central pitch and its lower neighbor (Ex. 6-15). Conjunct motion descending from the top of the frame—or ascending to it—is always by semitone; all other conjunct motion in the piece is by tone, not semitone.

The location of the semitone is one of the reasons the top of the frame is such a prominent pitch in the

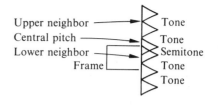

Example 6-15 "Resurrexi": Tones and semitones

section. It is not the only reason, of course, for the pitch next below it also borders on the semitone, but is much less prominent. And the upper neighbor is almost as prominent as the central pitch, even though it does not border on the semitone. But the location of the semitone helps identify the location of the pitches in the frame to each other and to the rest of the pitches in the section. Pitch frequency, function in the piece, and differentiation through the place of the semitone all work together to give a clear sense of location in the piece. In general, a sense of "where we are" in the pitch structure of a piece will depend upon a network of pitch factors that often (but not always) come to a sharp focus in a reference point or a frame.

MELODIC CHARACTERISTICS. Much of the expressiveness of "Resurrexi" depends upon the clear relationship of each pitch to the frame and through the frame implicitly to all the other pitches of the section. Once you realize that "Resurrexi" moves within a carefully circumscribed set of pitches, then you can better appreciate its grace and solemnity, the leisurely way its line moves up and down through the set. Paradoxically, the melodic motion can be more free to move in unexpected directions because of the firm sense of pitch set. As you develop a sense of where each pitch is, relative to the others in the piece, you will depend less upon following the direction of the melody, knowing that there are only certain places it can go. Indeed, the melody of "Resurrexi" twists and turns on almost every syllable in such an ornamental fashion that an overall shape to the line is hard to perceive. Ascending and descending motions of very short duration are balanced against one another with great sensitivity.

"Resurrexi" makes it clear that the one kind of motion not to expect here is a steady, sustained ascent or descent. If you listened to "Resurrexi" expecting to hear the broad curves of Bartók's Mesto, you would be disappointed with the relatively narrow range, the continued use of the same intervals and pitches, and the lack of clear phrase shapes such as question and answer or sequence. Appreciation of "Resurrexi," as

of any melody, depends upon finding the aspects of pitch organization that are most significant for that melody; in the case of "Resurrexi," one of the most important aspects is an easily perceptible pitch set through which the melody can move in a freely ornamental manner.

In this respect, "Resurrexi" is very different from Bartók's Mesto. These are not the only two types of melody, of course, and neither is completely lacking in the qualities of the other; yet they serve to show two

very different aspects of melody. If you expected to find in Bartók's Mesto the kind of pitch set in which each pitch could readily be referred to a frame, you would again be disappointed, this time by the wide range, the avoidance of clear pitch repetition, and the lack of one clear central pitch or frame. An appreciation of Bartók's Mesto depends upon a willingness to hear melodic direction and follow it, trusting in the direction itself, as it unfolds, to provide continuity to the piece.

Exercises for further listening

GREGORIAN CHANT: "ALLELUIA PASCHA NOSTRUM" AND "VICTIMAE PASCHALI LAUDES" (PROSE) FROM THE EASTER MASS

Listen to both chants, following the texts below. Answer questions 1 and 2.

ALLELUIA

Alleluia, alleluia!
Pascha nostrum immolatus est Christus.

PROSE

1 Victimae paschali lau*des* _____
   immolent Christi*ani* _____
2a Agnus redemit o*ves* _____
   Christus innocens Pa*tri* _____
   reconciliavit peccato*res* _____
2b Mors et vita duel*lo* _____
   conflixere miran*do* _____
   dux vitae mortuus, regnat viv*us*. _____
3a Dic nobis Mari*a*, _____
   quid vidisti in v*ia*? _____

4a Sepulchrum Christi viven*tis* _____
   et gloriam vidi resurgen*tis* _____
3b Angelicos tes*tes*, _____
   sudarium, et ves*tes*. _____
4b Surrexit Christus spes me*a*: _____
   praecedit suos in Galilae*am*. _____
5a* Credendum est magis sol*i* _____
   Maria vera*ci* _____
   quam Judeo*rum* _____
   turbae fala*ci*. _____
5b Scimus Christum surrexis*se* _____
   a mortuis ve*re*: _____
   tu nobis, victor *Rex*, _____
   miser*ere*. _____
6 Am*en*. _____
   Allelu*ia*. _____

*5a is usually omitted in performance.

1. In the "Alleluia," the manner in which the text is set is primarily   1. b
   ___ a. One note per syllable (syllabic)
   ___ b. Many notes per syllable (melismatic)
   ___ c. Several (2 to 4) notes per syllable

2. In the prose, the manner in which the text is set is primarily   2. a
   ___ a. One note per syllable (syllabic)
   ___ b. Many notes per syllable (melismatic)
   ___ c. Several (2 to 4) notes per syllable

Listen to "Victimae paschali laudes," following the text. (A translation is given in Chapter 10.) Answer questions 3 through 9.

3. The melody moves into a register markedly higher than that of line 1 in   3. c
   ___ a. Lines 2*ab* and 3*ab*
   ___ b. Lines 3*ab* and 4*ab*
   ___ c. Lines 2*ab* and 5*ab*
   ___ d. Line 6

4. The melody begins in a register markedly lower than that of line 1 in   4. a
   ___ a. Line 3*ab*
   ___ b. Line 4*ab*
   ___ c. Line 6

5. In the text above, each cadential syllable is in italic type. Whenever you hear a cadence at the same pitch as the first one (lau*des*), check the blank that follows the cadential syllable.

    5. Each blank should be checked *except* the following:
    2*a* oves
    2*b* duel*lo*
    5*a* so*li*, Judeor*um*
    5*b* surrexis*se*, *Rex*

6. This recurrent cadential pitch forms the bottom pitch of a *frame*. The upper pitch of the frame is which of those in italic here?   6. c
       Vic-*ti*-mae pas-*cha*-li laudes, / *im*-molent Christiani
   ___ a. That sung to "-*ti*-"
   ___ b. That sung to "-*cha*-"
   ___ c. That sung to "*im*-"

7. All of the cadences that were not on the lower frame pitch fall on the upper frame pitch.   7. a
   ___ a. True   ___ b. False

111

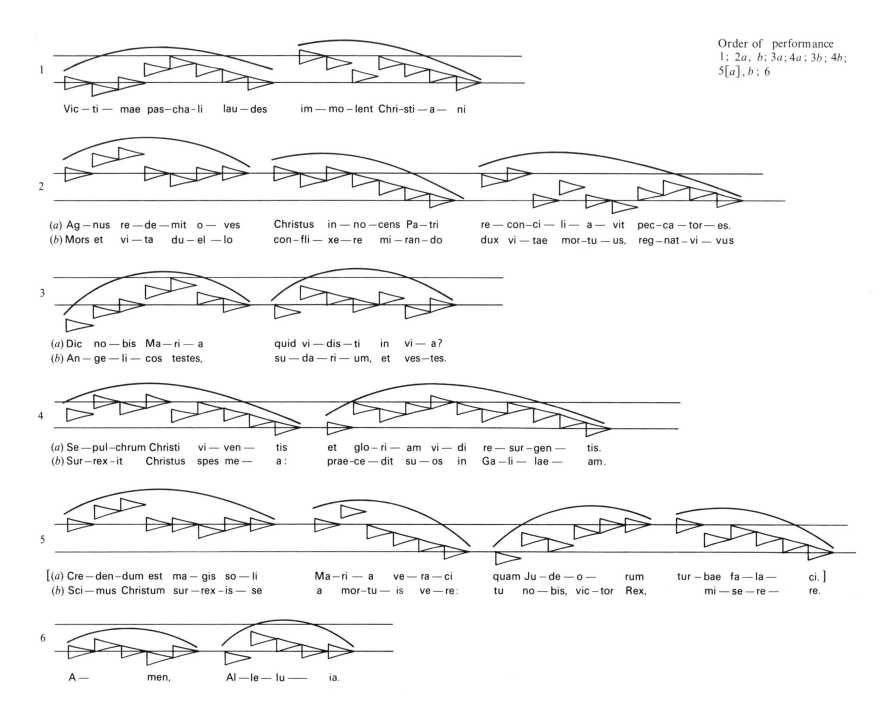

Order of performance
1; 2a, b; 3a; 4a; 3b; 4b;
5[a], b; 6

1

Vic — ti — mae pas—cha-li lau—des im — mo—lent Chri-sti—a— ni

2

(a) Ag—nus re—de—mit o— ves Christus in — no—cens Pa—tri re — con—ci— li— a— vit pec-ca—tor—es.
(b) Mors et vi—ta du — el —lo con—fli— xe—re mi—ran-do dux vi — tae mor-tu—us, reg-nat—vi— vus

3

(a) Dic no—bis Ma—ri—a quid vi—dis—ti in vi—a?
(b) An — ge—li— cos testes, su—da—ri—um, et ves—tes.

4

(a) Se—pul—chrum Christi vi—ven— tis et glo—ri—am vi—di re—sur—gen— tis.
(b) Sur—rex-it Christus spes me— a: prae—ce—dit su—os in Ga—li—lae— am.

5

[(a) Cre—den—dum est ma—gis so—li Ma—ri—a ve—ra—ci quam Ju—de—o— rum tur—bae fa—la— ci.]
(b) Sci—mus Christum sur—rex-is—se a mor-tu— is ve—re: tu no—bis, vic—tor Rex, mi—se—re— re.

6

A— men, Al—le—lu— ia.

8. The beginning of line 5*ab*

_____ **a.** Is like the beginning of line 1*ab*

_____ **b.** Is like the beginning of line 2*ab*

_____ **c.** Is like the beginning of line 3*ab*

_____ **d.** Is like the beginning of line 4*ab*

9. Make a simple letter diagram illustrating the overall melodic shape of "Victimae." Show significant repeats by repeated letters (. . . F F . . .)

8. b

9. A B B C D C D (E) E F

or

A B B C D C D (B′) B′ E

Listen again to the entire prose, following the pitch diagram. Can you hear the upper and lower frame pitches clearly as reference points?

Listen to the "Alleluia," following the diagram given here. Answer questions 10 through 13.

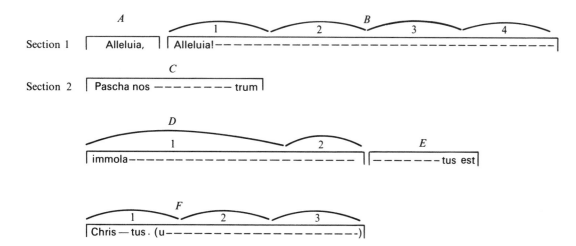

The letters refer to phrase groups, the slurs to phrases or subphrases. (No distinction is made here between phrases and subphrases.)

10. The first phrase group to move into a register distinctly different from that of *A* and *B* is

_____ **a.** Group *C*　　_____ **b.** Group *D*　　_____ **c.** Group *E*　　_____ **d.** Group *F*

10. b (group *D*)

11. The register of phrase group *D* is notably

_____ **a.** Higher than that of *A*, *B*, and *C*

_____ **b.** Lower than that of *A*, *B*, and *C*

11. a

113

12. Phrase groups *E* and *F*

_____ **a.** Stay in this higher register

_____ **b.** Move back to the original register

_____ **c.** Move to a very low register

12. b

The lower frame pitch of this chant is that sung on "Al-le-lu- (u—)-ia." The upper frame pitch is that sung on "Allelu-(u—)-ia."

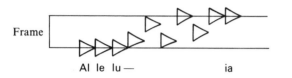

Frame

Al le lu —   ia

13. Indicate each phrase group that ends on the lower frame pitch by "L," each phrase group that ends on the higher frame pitch by "H."

_____ Group *B*

_____ Group *C*

_____ Group *D*

_____ Group *E*

_____ Group *F*

13. Group *B*: L

Group *C*: neither L nor H

Group *D*: L

Group *E*: L

Group *F*: L

Listen to each phrase group separately. Answer questions 14 through 24.

14. Phrase B_1

_____ **a.** Circles around the lower frame pitch

_____ **b.** Circles around the upper frame pitch

_____ **c.** Moves from the upper to the lower frame pitch

_____ **d.** Moves from the lower to the upper frame pitch

14. d

15. Phrase B_2

_____ **a.** Circles around the lower frame pitch

_____ **b.** Circles around the upper frame pitch

_____ **c.** Moves from the upper to the lower frame pitch

_____ **d.** Moves from the lower to the upper frame pitch

15. c

16. Phrase B_3

_____ **a.** Circles around the lower frame pitch

_____ **b.** Circles around the upper frame pitch

_____ **c.** Moves from the upper to the lower frame pitch

_____ **d.** Moves from the lower to the upper frame pitch

16. c

17. Phrase B_4
___ **a.** Circles around the lower frame pitch
___ **b.** Circles around the upper frame pitch
___ **c.** Moves from the upper to the lower frame pitch
___ **d.** Moves from the lower to the upper frame pitch

17. d

18. Phrase group C
___ **a.** Circles around the lower frame pitch
___ **b.** Circles around the upper frame pitch
___ **c.** Moves from the upper to the lower frame pitch
___ **d.** Moves from the lower to the upper frame pitch

18. b

19. Phrase D_1
___ **a.** Circles around the lower frame pitch
___ **b.** Circles around the upper frame pitch
___ **c.** Moves from the upper to the lower frame pitch
___ **d.** Moves from the lower to the upper frame pitch

19. b

20. Phrase D_2
___ **a.** Circles around the lower frame pitch
___ **b.** Circles around the upper frame pitch
___ **c.** Moves from the upper to the lower frame pitch
___ **d.** Moves from the lower to the upper frame pitch

20. c

21. Phrase group E
___ **a.** Circles around the lower frame pitch
___ **b.** Circles around the upper frame pitch
___ **c.** Moves from the upper to the lower frame pitch
___ **d.** Moves from the lower to the upper frame pitch

21. c

22. Phrase F_1
___ **a.** Circles around the lower frame pitch
___ **b.** Circles around the upper frame pitch
___ **c.** Moves from the upper to the lower frame pitch
___ **d.** Moves from the lower to the upper frame pitch

22. d (the final note is the lower frame pitch)

23. Phrase F_2

_____ **a.** Circles around the lower frame pitch
_____ **b.** Circles around the upper frame pitch
_____ **c.** Moves from the upper to the lower frame pitch
_____ **d.** Moves from the lower to the upper frame pitch

23. c

24. Phrase F_3

_____ **a.** Circles around the lower frame pitch
_____ **b.** Circles around the upper frame pitch
_____ **c.** Moves from the upper to the lower frame pitch
_____ **d.** Moves from the lower to the upper frame pitch

24. c

Listen to the entire chant. Answer questions 25 and 26.

25. There is a clear relation between the melody to which the first "Alleluia" is set (phrase A) and phrases _____ and _____ .

25. B_1 and F_1

26. The concluding phrase (F_3) most resembles phrase

_____ **a.** B_2
_____ **b.** B_4
_____ **c.** D_2
_____ **d.** E

26. b (B_4, the end of the first section)

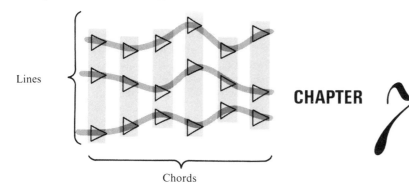

Example 7-1 Lines and chords

Lines

Chords

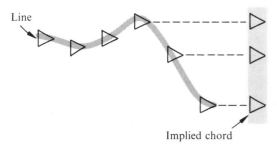

Example 7-2 Chord implied in a line

Line

Implied chord

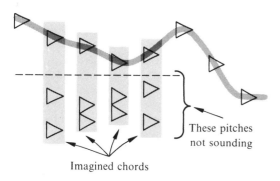

Example 7-3 Chords imagined to go with a line

These pitches not sounding

Imagined chords

CHAPTER **7** HARMONIC ORGANIZATION OF PITCH

SO FAR, WE HAVE CONSIDERED pitch organization only in music whose texture was monophonic. Much of the music we encounter, however, is not monophonic but instead has some thicker texture—chordal, melody with accompaniment, contrapuntal, or some other kind. These textures regularly present more than one pitch at a time. The pitches sound in simultaneous combinations, which may take a great variety of specific shapes but which have in common the simultaneous sounding of two or more pitches. For the sake of simplicity in the discussion immediately following, we will use the term "chord" or "chordal" to refer to the simultaneous sounding of several pitches.

CHORDS AND HARMONY. As we discussed in studying Bartók's Mesto and the chant "Resurrexi," melody has to do with a succession of single pitches. Not every imaginable succession of pitches is a melody; nor did we try to lay down the conditions under which melody must exist. There is enough mystery in melody to make that attempt futile, and anyway the attempt would not be appropriate to this book.

Similarly, in music with a chordal texture there is another mysterious quality, *harmony*; it has to do with a succession of chords. Not every imaginable succession of chords is harmony; nor will we try to lay down the conditions under which harmony must exist. We will limit outselves to the study of a few pieces in which different kinds of harmony are to be

found, hearing in which respects the pitch organization of these pieces depends on harmony and, in each case, how the aspect of harmony affects the shape of the piece.

As we saw in Chapter 3, a chord is a phenomenon of texture—more than one pitch sounding at once in such a way (that is, in such a texture) as to draw attention at least as much to the block of simultaneous sounds as to the motion of individual lines (Ex. 7-1). When we studied chords in the chapter on texture, we did so without keeping close track of the pitch content. Now we need to consider the pitch content of chords much more specifically (as we did in moving from line to melody), analyzing and naming some of the simpler, more fundamental aspects of harmony.

Harmony is found most readily in chords, where the simultaneity of pitches is most obvious; but you should be aware of harmony in other situations where simultaneity is *implied* by the content of the piece. Harmony can be found in music that is not very chordal in texture. You can even hear harmony in a melody alone, if you consider two or three successive (usually disjunct) pitches *as if* they were sounding at once (Ex. 7-2).

Another way of hearing harmony in melody is to imagine chords that could go with individual pitches of the melody (Ex. 7-3). The application of these more subtle considerations depends upon context (they are not applicable, for example, to the two melodies discussed in the preceding chapter); we mention them to show that harmony is only partially dependent upon a chordal texture. To put it differently, a chordal texture is only one way the composer has of encouraging us to hear together the pitches he wishes to blend into harmonies.

SINGLE HARMONIES AND HARMONIC PROGRESSIONS.
Pitches that are blended into harmonies are apt to be difficult to hear singly—especially when the harmonies are presented in a chordal texture. It takes a great deal of training to identify the constituent pitches of a four- or five-note chord played on the piano, even when only a single chord is played and held; identifying individual pitches in a rhythmic succession of chords is not usually practical within the context of this book. We cannot, in other words, take you inside the chord to study how it is built.

Consequently, our attention must be directed to the succession, or progression, of several chords, with each chord treated as a unit. This is not entirely a bad thing; in fact, in many ways it is a good thing, mainly because it encourages an approach to harmony that has much the same spirit—and uses much the same tools—as our earlier approach to melody. It is not possible to hear melody in a single pitch; and in a certain sense it is not possible to hear harmony in a single chord. At least, in a single chord you cannot hear the direction of harmonic movement or the location within a harmonic area—qualities important for harmony as well as for melody. This is not to say that important things cannot be learned from the study of a single chord, particularly about the ways in which pitches blend together to make a harmony. But this book is not concerned with such things, nor will the absence of them hinder you much in the perception of overall shape.

LINEAR CLUES TO HARMONIC SHAPE.
The step from perception of melody to perception of harmony is difficult, because the perception of a single pitch seems so immediate, the perception of a harmony so elusive. In following a succession of harmonies, a listener naturally tries to fix on some feature of melody or line as a guide. Given a melody with chordal accompaniment, for example, the ear naturally follows the melody, even though the real shaping force may come from the chords in the accompaniment.

Ludwig van Beethoven (1770–1827)

SYMPHONY NO. 7
POCO SOSTENUTO (INTRODUCTION TO THE FIRST MOVEMENT)

By way of making a transition from melody to harmony, we will study the Poco sostenuto ("somewhat sustained") from Beethoven's Seventh Symphony, a piece that makes important use of melodic or linear clues to help the ear follow complex harmonic progressions and to clarify the overall shape. Considered at the very highest level, this introduction has one main function—to introduce the symphony, more particularly the first movement. Beethoven chose to make the introduction massive, cloudy, seemingly out of focus, so that when the fast section of the first movement begins, the symphony seems suddenly to come into focus. There are other ways of making an introduction (for example, the Mesto from Bartók's Quartet No. 6), but this is the way Beethoven chose here. One of the important steps in understanding a large work is to perceive and interpret the functions of the various sections, so as to be able to say, "This is an introduction, that is an interlude," and so on for whatever functional parts the work may have.

THE TWO INTERLUDES.
The introduction, then, is deliberately not clear—or, at any rate, it is cloudy; nonetheless, you can make out a sectional shape. Two distinct interludes are perceptible. Surrounding these interludes are stretches of mighty orchestral sonorities that may at first make little sense. Your first understanding of the introduction could perhaps be represented as in Ex. 7-4.

Example 7-4 Beethoven, Poco sostenuto, interludes

Interlude   Interlude

These interludes are—first of all—interludes, not main events. No matter how indistinct in detail the intervening stretches may seem, these stretches are clearly the bulk of the introduction, the most weighty part. It is as if you had understood only two parenthetical remarks in a short speech while missing the main argument. One of the reasons the interludes are parenthetical has to do with the pitch relationships in the introduction as a whole; and, even though you may not yet be able to hear those relationships precisely, it is worthwhile to know abstractly that pitch relationships can cause this parenthetical effect.

The reasons the interludes are immediately grasped have to do with timbre, texture, and melody. Probably elements of timbre and texture come to your attention first; the changes of timbre and texture in the interludes are clear—not so hard to grasp as the pitch relationships. Equally obvious is the fact that the interludes have a distinctive melody; this is the kind of clue referred to earlier, a melodic clue to a harmonic shape. You may, in fact, feel that the melody of the interludes is the only melody worth talking about in the whole introduction. In any case, the melody is what makes the interludes most clear, while the absence of as tuneful a melody in the surrounding sections is one of the factors that make them at first so confusing. Furthermore, since the two interludes have basically the same melody, the fact that it reappears in the second interlude strengthens and clarifies the impression it makes, especially in contrast to the seeming lack of clear return in the other sections.

A problem posed by these interludes is one commonly encountered in larger works. Tuneful melodies, such as this one, often seem to be but passing moments in a much longer discourse that is much less melodious. If the composer can write such beautiful melodies (we might ask), why does he bother to do anything else? But we should rather ask, since he knew his art well enough to write such melodies, he obviously must have had a good reason for doing something else; what was it? There must be much more to pitch organization than melody in the sense of lyric tune. We must deal with the fact that the melody in the interludes is only a clue to a grander design.

HARMONY IN THE INTERLUDES. In comparing the interludes with the rest of the introduction, it is apparent that the interludes are more stable than the rest—like islands of calm in a turbulent sea. The reason that the interludes seem more stable is that their *harmonies* are more stable: a relatively small number of different harmonies are used in the interludes, and these harmonies are used in a repetitive, stable shape. In most of the rest of the introduction, by contrast, there are a greater number of harmonies, arranged in more unstable shapes. All this will take some further explanation; and to all this the melody is only a clue.

Listen to the first interlude, following along with the melody in Ex. 7-5 but listening as much as possible to the whole context of the interlude. The problem is to hear the harmonies; you can do this best by listening for the *changes* in harmony, indicated in Ex. 7-5 by the boxes. We are not concerned with melodic change for its own sake (nor with rhythmic change for its own sake—although the changes in the harmony have a definite rhythm); timbre and texture are changing subtly, too, but for the moment we are not concerned with them. The changes to listen for now are changes in the sound of the relationships among all the pitches heard at any one time, including the melody.

The first harmony in the interlude is soon replaced by another, labeled in Ex. 7-5 as the second harmony. There are new pitches in the melody too, as well as in the accompaniment; but some of the accompanying pitches do not change, being instead held over from the first harmony into the second. The change in harmony includes and encompasses the changes, or lack of change, in individual lines; it is qualitatively different from a mere summation of individual lines. Even if most of the pitches did not change, with only one line making a slight change in pitch, it is still conceivable that a profound change in harmony could result.

After the second harmony, the first returns (Ex. 7-5). The beginning of the melody returns too, but again we are concerned with the melody, not for its own sake, but only as a part of the overall change at that point. It is conceivable that the first harmony could return without a return of the melody.

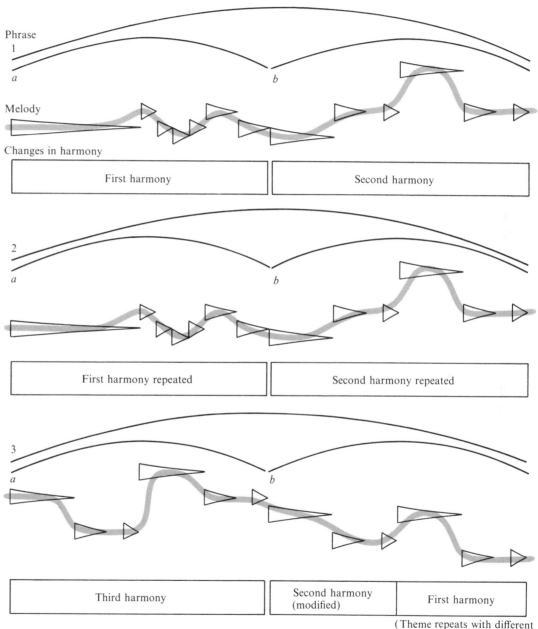

Example 7-5 Beethoven, Poco sostenuto, first interlude

Phrase 1

a   *b*

Melody

Changes in harmony

First harmony	Second harmony

2

a   *b*

First harmony repeated	Second harmony repeated

3

a   *b*

Third harmony	Second harmony (modified)	First harmony

(Theme repeats with different timbres and registers.)

119

The second harmony also returns; then there is a new harmony, the third. Here the melody does nothing really new: it repeats the rhythmic figure it just had. The pitches are different, and they are an expression of the changing harmony. The third harmony is clearly different from either of the other two.

After the third harmony comes a harmony that sounds something like the second one but is not identical to it: the individual pitches are the same, but their distribution—hence the relationship among them—is different. The next change, however, brings a clear return to the first harmony, and this return can easily be verified by comparing the end of phrase 3 with the repeat of the whole phrase group that follows immediately. There is no change of harmony as we go from the end of phrase 3 to the beginning of phrase 1 of the repeat. In other words, the first harmony returns before the return of the first phrase of the melody.

HARMONIC CHANGE AND MOTION. Consider again the first two harmonies: in context, the second seems to fulfill and to complete the first. After only a few hearings, the ear expects that the second will follow the first or, to put it differently, we expect that the first will lead to the second; if it did not, the harmonic motion would seem incomplete. You can verify this by listening closely to the harmony at the end of the first phrase group and again at the end of the second, where the interlude ends (see Ex. 7-5). Has it ended with a sense of completion? Clearly not; it has broken off incomplete, giving way to a resumption of the loud tutti that preceded the interlude.

We can represent the motion of these harmonies in Ex. 7-6. Each block represents a harmony; the arrow leading from the first block to the second represents the expectation that the first harmony will lead to the second. The relative vertical placement of the blocks on the diagram brings up the very difficult matter of harmonic distance, which may become clear only after concentrated listening. For now, bear in mind that distance up and down in the harmony diagrams has *nothing whatsoever* to do with distance up and down in pitch; if it were practical to express harmonic distance in some other graphic way (say, by changing

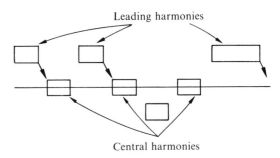

Example 7-6 Beethoven, Poco sostenuto: Harmonic direction in the interlude

colors), we would do it, in order to avoid confusion with melodic distance and movement. Understanding harmonic distance involves first listening closely to many harmonic progressions to develop a sense of what harmonic motion is. An abstract definition will be meaningful only after you learn to follow movement in the realm of harmony.

In this book we will call the first harmony of Ex. 7-6—and all harmonies that have its specific function —the *leading harmony*, or *leading chord*. We will call the second harmony—and all harmonies which have its specific function—the *central harmony*. Musicians customarily call the leading chord the *dominant* (or under certain conditions the *dominant seventh*) and the central harmony the *tonic*, but those terms are not so useful for our purposes because they do not immediately suggest the functions of these harmonies.

From this interlude, you can at least gain a sense of the back-and-forth motion of the harmonies, from the first to the second, then to the third and back to the second, and finally back to the first. It is the sense of motion we are most concerned with, not the characteristics of the individual harmony. Look at the horizontal line drawn through the second harmony in Ex. 7-7, and compare it to the horizontal line drawn through the predominant pitch in "Resurrexi" (Ex. 6-11). In both cases, the motion (melodic in one case, harmonic in the other) is around this horizontal line, departing from it and returning. The motion may not end on the line if the composer does not wish it to, but the harmony on the line will retain a feeling of centralness. The interlude keeps turning in on its harmonic center, producing a harmonically stable

area. The use of only three closely related harmonies in the interlude produces a sense of closure and stability that is in sharp contrast to the surrounding sections.

Example 7-7 Beethoven, Poco sostenuto: Harmonic center in the interlude

Leading harmonies

Central harmonies

HARMONIC MOTION AT THE START OF THE POCO SOSTENUTO. With these characteristics of the interludes in mind, we can begin to make some sense of the other sections. They are more diffuse in timbre and texture. At the very beginning, there are loud, short chords, separated by what might be the beginning of a line in the solo oboe. However, this line moves so slowly and with such wide leaps that it is hard to follow, and anyway it soon disappears as it passes from one wind instrument to another amid the gathering obscurity of the full orchestra.

The harmonies change slowly enough to be perceived one by one; they are changing, in fact, at about the same rate as in the interludes. However, since we hear a succession of different harmonies with no immediate sense of return or repetition, it is difficult to perceive any grouping of harmonies such as we heard in the interludes. No harmony emerges clearly as central. The succession of harmonies seems to lead off at a tangent; their relationship to the original harmony becomes less and less clear. Eventually, after fourteen measures (each group of two measures at the beginning is marked off by a tutti chord) the harmonic progression returns to its point of origin.

BASS LINE AS LINEAR CLUE. There is no tuneful melody to guide the listener, as in the interludes; but amid all the harmonic obscurities, a melodic element —a line—leads through this and subsequent passages. Instead of trying to follow the harmonies, follow the bass line; you will find that from the beginning of the Poco sostenuto it descends steadily with a clear, purposeful sense of direction, giving direction as it goes to the inchoate harmonies above it (Ex. 7-8).

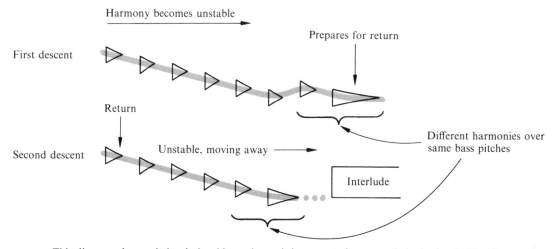

This diagram shows pitch relationships only, omitting repeated notes and rhythmic relationships.

Example 7-9 Beethoven, Poco sostenuto: Bass line

Example 7-8 Beethoven, Poco sostenuto (beginning): Bass line as linear clue

In following the bass line, we have reverted back from harmony to melody; the purpose of this example is to help clarify what harmony is and what it is not. Harmony is sometimes very difficult to follow; when the ear cannot find its way through an unstable progression of harmonies, it grasps anything that presents itself, such as a prominent line. Sometimes it seems as though the composer compensated for his difficult harmonies by leaving a clear guideline—as Beethoven has done. At other times it seems as though the composer wanted us to get lost in unstable har-

monies. That is a different kind of listening problem, which we will deal with later.

If you follow the bass line on its first descent, you will find that it eventually reaches bottom (as it were) and remains stationary. During the descent, the harmonies have produced an unstable effect; when the bass line becomes stationary, the harmony becomes more stable. (You might be able to hear that the harmony over the stationary pitch of the bass line has a leading relationship to the one that follows over the new bass note, but this is not particularly obvious, especially since you have been following line, not harmony.)

As the bass line starts to move again, it does so by returning to its first pitch and resuming the descent (Ex. 7-9). Again the harmonies are unstable, and again the bass line provides the only clear guide. But this time, while the bass line descends much as it did before, the harmonic situation above it has changed considerably. In particular, the lowest pitch itself is the same; but, since the harmony is different, the pitch behaves differently. At any rate, this pitch and its harmony lead in a different direction, into the first interlude.

While the bass line has been making its second descent, your attention may well have been distracted by the incessant hammering that has broken out above. Fortissimo figures in the strings are flung repeatedly upwards. So great is the contrast to the music over the first bass descent that you may scarcely perceive the repetition. But try to hear the repeat that is begun, in order to be more aware of the difference when it comes, toward the end of the second descent.

The difference is harmonic and results in a move to a new harmonic *area*—a concept we will consider more closely later. For now, try only to hear a difference (no matter how vague) between the harmonies over the first and second bass-line descents, and how the harmonies over the second descent lead away to some unpredictable goal (Ex. 7-9). These qualities distinguish the opening section from the interlude that follows.

HARMONIC MOTION THROUGHOUT THE POCO SOS-TENUTO. Between the two interludes, the harmony is again unstable; again the guide is the bass line. Here it ascends instead of descends, which gives a new sense of direction. The ascent urges the introduction into new harmonic areas, maintaining and increasing the sense of distance from the beginning and of tension relative to it. Here, too, the harmonies themselves as they appear over each new bass note seem more and more distant as they proceed, leading further away in some indeterminate direction. Stability and a goal to the ascent are provided by the return of the clear harmonies and closed harmonic shape in the second interlude.

After the second interlude, rhythmic motion dissipates; and little continuity is provided by any element except the bass, which for its part can hardly be said to have a line. Still, the prolonged bass pitch that emerges from the second interlude and the bass pitch that succeeds it a semitone lower do provide a linear movement. What is interesting about these two pitches is the great harmonic distance between them in spite of the small linear interval. The two pitches are burdened with enough harmonic import (even though little harmony is actually sounding in the thin texture) so that moving from one to the other is like crossing a boundary between two very different areas. Not only that, but the arrival at the last bass pitch seems to resolve the accumulated tension somewhat in the manner of a central harmony following a leading harmony.

The harmony over the last bass pitch is *not* a central harmony, however, for it, too, has a leading quality that demands resolution. Something has to follow; that something is a harmony that will complete and fulfill the expectations raised by the prolonged bass note. The fulfillment comes in the next section of the symphony.

With the aid of melody and line, it is possible to understand a good deal about harmonic shape even before you can single out individual harmonies. You should be able to hear in the Poco sostenuto the alternation of stable with unstable sections, the alternation of movement confined to a stable harmonic area with movement directed toward some unknown goal. The sectional plan summarized in Ex. 7-10 is largely dependent upon harmonic factors; if you can follow the plan, you are probably hearing a good deal of the harmony.

One other feature of the harmonic organization may possibly be clarified with the help of the plan.

Section	A_1	A_2	B_1	A_3	B_2	C
Texture	loud tutti chords solo line (fragments)	+ ascending figures	melody and accompaniment	ascending figures	melody and accompaniment	
Harmony	unstable	unstable, moving away	stable	unstable	stable	leading
Bass line	descending	descending			ascending	prolonged note

B_1 and B_2 are the interludes.

Example 7-10 Beethoven, Poco sostenuto: Plan

The two interludes have a fresh sound that we have seen to be the product of many factors—melody, timbre, texture, harmony. Harmony is the most subtle of these, but it is also the most important. The harmonies of the first interlude seem to be in a different part of the forest, a remote location. Curiously, the remoteness is felt in both interludes, not just the first, while at the same time the two interludes are not very far harmonically from each other. If you can hold the melody of the first interlude in your ear until the second interlude (or can skip from one to the other on the record), you may be able to hear how close they are and how distant is the intervening section with its strong harmonic motion over the ascending bass line. Compare the structure of "Resurrexi," which depends upon the alternation of sections with different registers. There, the distance between the first and second section is in terms of pitch level; here in the Poco sostenuto it is in terms of *harmonic area*. If we diagram groups of harmonies as we diagramed groups of

Example 7-11 Beethoven, Poco sostenuto: Harmonic areas

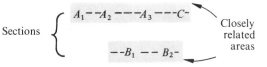

The areas in the top line are remote from those in the bottom line.

pitches, we can represent the harmonic movement of the Poco sostenuto as in Ex. 7-11. Sections A_1, A_2, A_3, and C, even though cloudy and unstable, all constitute one large harmonic area relative to sections B_1 and B_2, which constitute a different harmonic area.

A STUDY OF HARMONIC DETAIL. The following discussion of a Schubert song is designed to provide more specific, detailed information about harmony; but it may well leave you with the feeling that so much detailed explanation is out of keeping with the way you actually hear music. In Beethoven's Poco sostenuto, we concentrated on broader aspects of harmonic movement, as suggested by linear clues. Be prepared for the amount of detail we will point out in Schubert's song; regard it as a special study to develop certain harmonic concepts. Remember that our study of Beethoven's Poco sostenuto, concerned with broader aspects, was closer to the reality of the experience of listening.

Franz Schubert (1797–1828)

DIE SCHONE MULLERIN "DER MULLER UND DER BACH" (SONG 19)

"Der Müller und der Bach," is the next-to-last song in Schubert's cycle *Die schöne Müllerin*. There are three clear stanzas in the text: the first stanza is the lament of the lovelorn miller lad, the second stanza is imagined to be sung by the brook, the third is the response of the lad. After we discuss the harmonic shape of the song, we can return to the text and its relationship with the song. (A translation appears in Chapter 11.)

(First stanza—the miller lad)
Wo ein treues Herze in Liebe vergeht,
Da welken die Lilien auf jedem Beet.
Da muss in die Wolken der Vollmond gehn,
Damit seine Tränen die Menschen nicht sehn.
Da halten die Englein die Augen sich zu,
Und schluchzen und singen die Seele zur Ruh'.

(Second stanza—the brook)
Und wenn sich die Liebe dem Schmerz entringt,
Ein Sternlein, ein neues, am Himmel erblinkt.
Da springen drei Rosen, halb rot und halb weiss,
Die welken nicht wieder, aus Dornenreis.
Und die Engelein schneiden die Flügel sich ab
Und gehn alle Morgen zur Erde herab.

(Third stanza—the miller lad)
Ach, Bächlein, liebes Bächlein, du meinst es so gut:
Ach, Bächlein, aber weisst du, wie Liebe tut?
Ach, unten, da unten die kühle Ruh'!
Ach, Bächlein, liebes Bächlein, so singe nur zu.

Listen first to the whole song, noting the fact that these three stanzas of text are clearly reflected in the music. Even without a text, the musical sections would be clear on the basis of factors we have already studied, such as rhythm and texture.

The meter throughout the song is in slow groups of three, represented by the beginning chords in the accompaniment, which fall on ONE and TWO: ONE TWO (THREE) ONE TWO (THREE). Rhythms at lower levels occur in the vocal part but not in the piano accompaniment during the first section. Throughout the second and third sections, however, the piano accompaniment includes a continuous pulse at level I (Ex. 7-12). The rhythmic character of the vocal part remains remarkably uniform throughout the song.

HARMONIC COLOR: MAJOR AND MINOR. The three sections of the song are also distinguished from each other by changes that affect the whole set of pitches used in each section. The effect of the changes is immediately perceptible on first hearing, even before you make any effort to isolate or understand in-

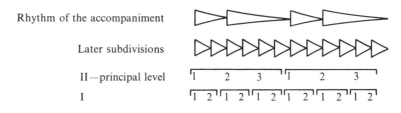

Example 7-12 Schubert, "Der Müller und der Bach": Metric levels

dividual chords or harmonies. There is something about the harmonic quality that changes abruptly at the beginning of the second section and again at the beginning of the third. This particular kind of harmonic change is called a change in harmonic *color* (or a change of harmonic *mode*).

At first the change in harmonic color may be perceived simply as a change in mood or atmosphere; soon, however, it should become apparent that the change is intimately associated with the choice of pitches used throughout the different sections. The new harmonic color introduced at the beginning of the second section lasts throughout this section and makes the section as a whole contrast with the whole first section.

The changes in harmonic color are clear enough to shape the song as a whole (Ex. 7-13); not only do they set off sections one from another, but also the color of the third section is obviously similar to that of the first, making a clear return, or *A B A*. It should be added that the third section is not as homogeneous in color as the first and second sections, for toward its conclusion the third section changes so as to end with the color of the second section. This means—as far

Example 7-13 Schubert, "Der Müller und der Bach": Plan of sections and harmonic color

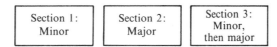

as harmonic color is concerned—that the overall shape is not really *A B A* but rather *A, B, AB*.

The two kinds of harmonic color found in sections *A* and *B*, respectively, are met very frequently; their technical names are so current that they should be included here. The first section is characterized by *minor* harmonies, the second by *major* harmonies; or the first section is said to be "in minor," the second "in major" (which are short for "in a minor key" and "in a major key"—there will be more about keys further on). It is possible to show the exact difference in pitch relationships that goes with the terms "major" and "minor," but we will not do that here, for two reasons. First, we are describing harmony as chords, rather than as individual pitches. Second, we must continue to stress the pitch organization at the highest possible level—no matter how vague or ill-defined that organization may seem at first. The ear can learn about relationships among pitches only by listening to them; the relationships cannot be made much clearer *to the ear* merely by using more technical language to describe them. Relationships such as those in "Der Müller und der Bach" may seem ill-defined at first, but they will become clearer with repeated hearings, as long as you listen persistently at the highest level you can. If you grasp the sense of the overall pitch organization, even though indistinctly, then and only then will a discussion of the functions of small units—chords, intervals, and pitches—be meaningful.

Turning now to the first section (*A*), fix its phrase structure in your ear. Text and music are divided into three large phrase groups, of two phrases each.

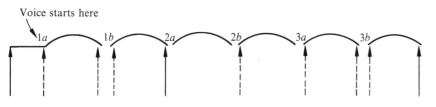

Solid arrow = very similar harmony
Dashed arrow = roughly similar harmony

1a Wo ein treues Herze in Liebe vergeht,

1b da welken die Lilien auf jedem Beet.

2a Da muss in die Wolken der Vollmond gehn,

2b damit seine Tränen die Menschen nicht sehn.

3a Da halten die Englein die Augen sich zu,

3b und schluchzen und singen die Seele zur Ruh'!

Example 7-14 Schubert, "Der Müller und der Bach": Similar harmonies in the first section

Example 7-15 Schubert, "Der Müller und der Bach": Similar harmonies shown in another way

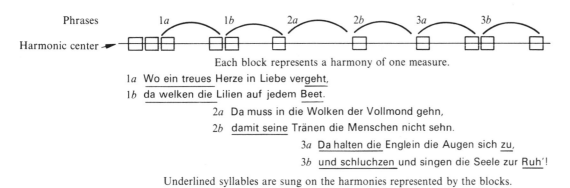

Each block represents a harmony of one measure.

1a Wo ein treues Herze in Liebe vergeht,

1b da welken die Lilien auf jedem Beet.

2a Da muss in die Wolken der Vollmond gehn,

2b damit seine Tränen die Menschen nicht sehn.

3a Da halten die Englein die Augen sich zu,

3b und schluchzen und singen die Seele zur Ruh'!

Underlined syllables are sung on the harmonies represented by the blocks.

Musical phrases in the first section

1a Wo ein treues Herze in Liebe vergeht,

1b Da welken die Lilien auf jedem Beet.

2a Da muss in die Wolken der Vollmond gehn,

2b Damit seine Tränen die Menschen nicht sehn.

3a Da halten die Englein die Augen sich zu,
   (same as 1a)

3b Und schluchzen und singen die Seele zur Ruh'.
   (same as 1b)

The music for lines 1a and b is repeated for lines 3a and b. The music for lines 2a and b is different in some respects; but, as we already noticed, the texture and rhythmic pattern remain the same throughout the entire section.

The most obvious part of the texture—the vocal line—is perhaps the least useful guide to understanding the harmony of the first section. The melody moves from the top to the bottom of its range relatively quickly, telling us little just by its profile or direction. The melody of Bartók's Mesto, by comparison, is very much easier to follow *as a line*, that is, in its profile of ascent and descent.

The piano accompaniment, however, moves more deliberately and with a greater sense of focus. The pitches in the accompaniment are grouped into chords by the texture. Listen for the sense of the harmonic motion in the accompaniment by considering the relationship of one chord to the next.

HARMONIC RHYTHM. Begin by listening only for sameness or difference among the chords of the first section. As a preliminary step, note that there are two chords in each measure; the two chords come on counts ONE and TWO. They are so closely related, however, and blend so well together that they should be counted as a single harmony. In each measure, then, there is really only one harmony. To put it differently, changes in harmony create a rhythm of their own. This rhythm—*harmonic rhythm*, it is called—is often an important and distinctive aspect of the pitch organization of a piece.

Sameness among *harmonies* in this section is perhaps easiest to perceive if you concentrate upon the harmony at the very beginning, the harmony at the end of phrase 1b, and the harmony at the end of 3b (that is, at the end of the section). You will find these harmonies pointed out in Ex. 7-14. The harmony at the very beginning is played by the piano alone, while the other two include the voice; but this difference in timbre does not obscure the basic identity of the harmonies considered *as harmonies*. This is an important distinction, one that we will have to make in several different ways.

Listen now (with the help of Ex. 7-14) for a less exact kind of similarity among the harmonies already singled out and those that occur at the beginning of the vocal part, at the end of phrase 1*a*, at the beginning of 1*b* and of 2*b*, at the beginning and end of 3*a*, and at the beginning of 3*b*. In Ex. 7-14, the only difference that distinguishes the harmonies at the dotted arrows from those at the solid arrows is the pitch in the voice part; the accompaniment is identical in all the places indicated. This is an example of how melody can inflect harmony by choice of individual pitches. The melody's pitches at the beginning and end of phrase 1*a*, for example, make the harmony sound different— but only a little different—from the harmony in the piano introduction. As you come to grasp the function of this particular harmony in this piece, you will understand more clearly the inflection produced by the melody.

HARMONIC CENTER. The sameness shown in Ex. 7-14 can be represented by the same kind of diagram we used for harmonies in Beethoven's Poco sostenuto (Ex. 7-7). In Ex. 7-15 the sameness of the chords is represented by the horizontal line; each block represents the harmony of one measure.

Compared to the harmony found at all the points indicated, all the other harmonies in the section are different—some more, some less. Even more important, all the other harmonies are less stable in their context than the harmony we have singled out. To put it another way, none of the other harmonies could stand at the end of the section and produce the same degree of finality. The harmony we have singled out can be said to be at the *harmonic center* of the section. As we have seen in discussing melody, "center" is a spatial term (as is "area"), and the phenomena we are dealing with are not spatial but musical. It should be intuitively clear, however, that in an important sense

the harmonies of this section revolve around the one we have called harmonic center, returning to it in order to end.

Furthermore, the center is not a melodic center (any more than it is, say, a rhythmic center); the harmonic center is in no sense midway in pitch level between high and low pitches. Its centralness has nothing to do with range or register. It is, however, analogous to the centralness of the central pitch in "Resurrexi" in that there we recognized a component of centralness beyond mere frequency or register, a centralness in function more than in position. In the concept of harmonic center, we again encounter the elusive dimensions of harmonic distance and direction— dimensions that are really different from melodic distance (interval) and direction. As a reminder: distance up and down on our harmonic diagrams represents *harmonic* distance, or distance away from the harmonic center, not *melodic* distance up and down in pitch level. It may be helpful, in trying to see why harmonic distance is not well represented in diagrams, to remember that spherical distance is not well represented on a flat piece of paper. Take the diagrams as suggesting only relative harmonic distance.

HARMONIC PROGRESSION. To gain a more specific understanding of harmonic distance and direction,

consider the harmony that is perhaps most closely related to the harmonic center. Listen to the harmony that precedes the central harmony at the end of phrases 1*b* (at "jedem Beet") and 3*b* (at "Seele zur Ruh'."). Or better, listen to the *progression* formed by these two harmonies—for just as melody is found only in a progression from one pitch to another, so the real meaning of harmony is found only in the progression from one harmony to another.

The progression of these two harmonies is the same as that heard between the first and second harmonies of the first interlude in Beethoven's Poco sostenuto (Ex. 7-7). That is to say, the two harmonies in each case bear the same relationship to each other, even though many other things about them—including the specific pitches—are different. We have already identified the *central harmony* in Schubert's song; the harmony that precedes it (at the places indicated in Ex. 7-16) is the *leading harmony*.

In Ex. 7-16 (as in Ex. 7-7 for Beethoven's Poco sostenuto), the leading harmony is represented by a block above the line; an arrow connects this block to the one on the center line. The harmony represented by the upper block seems to pull toward the following harmony; you can almost hear the latter coming. This is the meaning of the arrow, which points out a harmonic direction.

Example 7-16 Schubert, "Der Müller und der Bach": Central and leading harmonies

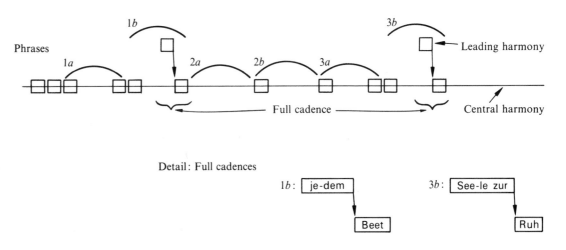

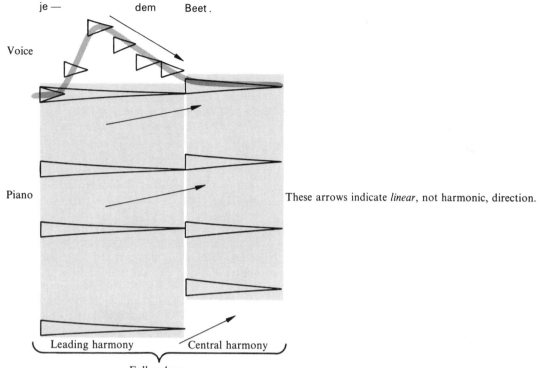

je — dem Beet .

Voice

Piano

These arrows indicate *linear*, not harmonic, direction.

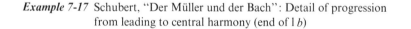

Leading harmony   Central harmony

Full cadence

Example 7-17 Schubert, "Der Müller und der Bach": Detail of progression
from leading to central harmony (end of 1*b*)

HARMONIC CADENCE. The first of the two blocks is placed above the line, higher than the second block, because the harmonic motion seems to "fall" from the first harmony to the second. These two harmonies taken together constitute one type of harmonic cadence; as we saw in connection with melody and rhythm, "cadence" means a falling and is used for stopping the musical flow. Frequently a cadence seems to be the goal of the preceding harmonic motion, the arrival point of the phrase.

We have already studied cadences produced by a falling motion in rhythm and melody; here is a cadence produced by a "falling" motion in the harmony. There are several kinds of harmonic cadences; this particular kind is often called a *perfect cadence*, or *full cadence*, because its motion has such a final effect, suitable for the end of a section or of a piece.

Note that the first of the two chords of the cadence is not necessarily higher than the second in pitch level. In a diagram of all of the pitches of this particular progression (at the end of phrase 1*b*), the actual note-to-note motions of the lines of this harmonic progression are both descending and ascending (Ex. 7-17).

Aside from the fact that Ex. 7-17 represents more detail than we want to go into here, the kind of direction represented by the arrows is melodic direction, not harmonic direction. The "up and down" of the harmonic motion is in another dimension.

Note also that direction is intimately associated with groups of harmonies, not with single harmonies —even if we can sense the direction in the first chord of the cadence. These same chords, placed individually into a different context, could move in different directions.

Similarly, the direction characteristic of the full cadence can be found among other harmonies in this same piece, in fact in this very section. Listen closely to the first section up through phrase 2*a*. With practice, you should hear the motion of the full cadence at the *beginning* of phrase 2*a*, twice in succession, both times at new pitch levels (Ex. 7-18).

In the first of this pair of cadences, the first harmony is similar to the central harmony (last chord of 1*b*) but not similar enough to be called the same. The central harmony is stable, sitting firmly at the end of its phrase; but the first harmony in phrase 2*a* seems about to fall from its position. Indeed, it does fall to the next harmony, producing the motion of a full cadence, even though the cadence does not lead to the harmonic center of the piece or to the end of a phrase or section.

The next two harmonies in phrase 2*a* also have the motion of a full cadence. These two cadences in succession form a sequence—a *harmonic* sequence, not a melodic one. (There are melodic sequences present here, too.) The effect of these two cadences in sequence is to give a certain limited finality and stability to the end of 2*a*; but (and most important) the stability is in a place clearly different from the harmonic center of the piece so far. In other words, phrase *2a* involves a departure from the harmonic center; the direction of the harmonic motion is *away*, and the resulting distance (though not great) is farther away from the center than are the other phrases.

The central and leading harmonies, and the relationship between them, do more than provide endings; together they furnish a frame of reference for the rest of the harmonies. They provide a much stronger reference than does the central harmony by itself—indeed, the progression of the two harmonies is very important in making the central harmony sound central. We can indicate this frame by drawing another horizontal line through the harmonies that lead or pull toward the central harmony (Ex. 7-19).

Some of the other harmonies in this section sound very similar to the leading harmony—so similar that they can be identified with it. At the end of phrase *2b*, the last harmony (which is prolonged for an extra measure) is the leading harmony; yet at first its effect may seem slightly different. This is because of several subtle factors, some of them rhythmic. The leading harmony at the end of *2b* occurs in a rhythmic position where we expect to hear an ending harmony, which makes it sound slightly less leading than it might; the end of a phrase is reached (and passed, because of the prolongation) and no resolution to the central harmony has yet occurred. It is clear, however, that the piece cannot end there; and, indeed, the next phrase (*3a*) brings the resolution to the central harmony—but only as the beginning of a phrase, not as the end of one.

OPEN ENDINGS. The ending of *2b* is called an *open ending* because harmonically it sounds as if it is not a complete stopping place. Ending on the leading harmony is one way of making an open ending (but not the only way). A cadence that ends on the leading harmony is called a *half cadence.*

There is an important difference between the ending of phrase *2a* and that of *2b*. Phrase *2a* ends with a full cadence, but on a central harmony that is not the center of the section. Phrase *2b* ends much nearer the harmonic center, on the leading harmony. Neither ending can be the ending of the piece, but for different reasons.

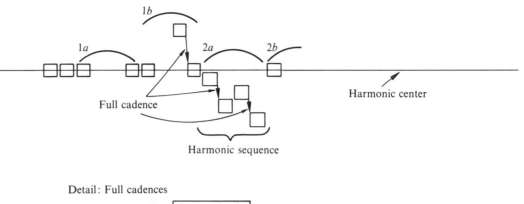

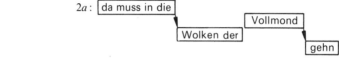

Example 7-18 Schubert, "Der Müller und der Bach": Full cadences in nonfinal positions

Example 7-19 Schubert, "Der Müller und der Bach": Open/closed endings and harmonic motion around a frame

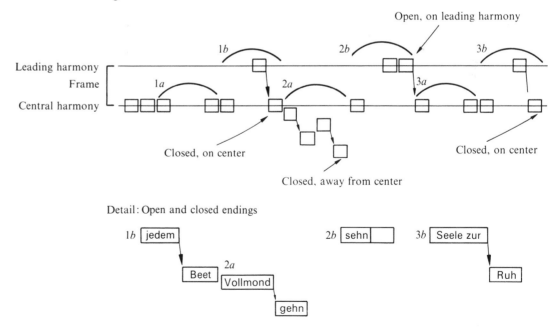

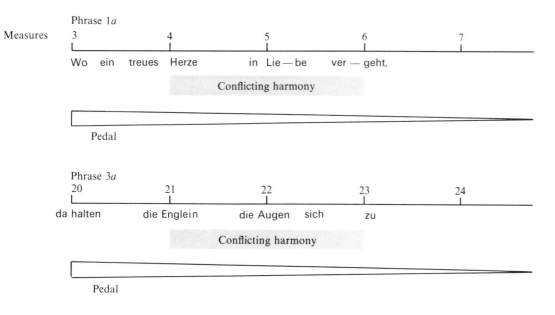

Example 7-20 Schubert, "Der Müller und der Bach": Location of pedal notes

PEDAL NOTES. The leading harmony is also used, although not in a penultimate position, near the beginning of phrase 1a and its repeat, phrase 3a (Ex. 7-20). These places may well seem confusing once you start listening closely to the harmony, for in the two measures 4 and 5 (and in 21 and 22 in the repeat) there are parts of two different harmonies sounding at once. The most obvious pitch is in the bass, where the bass note of the central chord (which has been sounding since the start of the piece) con-

tinues through these two measures. This bass note is such an important part of the central harmony that it could almost represent the harmonic center all by itself. As long as it continues to sound, it refers to the harmonic center. On the other hand, the pitches above the bass note are clearly not those of the central harmony; rather, they belong to the leading harmony.

A note that is prolonged through changing harmonies is called a *pedal note*, a *pedal point*, or sometimes just a *pedal*. (Such notes gained currency on the

organ, where they are conveniently played by the organist's feet on the pedals.)

Different listeners hear such combined harmonies differently. For some, these two measures at the beginning of phrases 1a and 3a are a clouded expression of a continuing central harmony; for others, an equally clouded expression of a move to the leading harmony. Even if it is not clear which of the two harmonies prevails in these two measures, it is clear that both are present. These measures help establish the two harmonies as the frame of the section.

HARMONIC AREA. In the first section as a whole, we find that the bulk of the harmony is involved directly in the frame (Ex. 7-21). Of the harmonies singled out so far, only those of phrase 2a are off the frame; that is, of the harmonies in the section, some are so closely related to the center as to constitute a *harmonic area* around it. A harmonic area is characteristically anchored firmly on a central harmony established with the help of a full cadence.

Not all the harmonies in a piece or section need necessarily be in the harmonic area established around the central harmony. Some harmonies may be on the fringes of the area—that is, they may not be closely related to the harmonies grouped around the central one; other harmonies may be outside the area altogether. In "Der Müller und der Bach," the harmonic area consists almost entirely of the leading chord and the central chord; but in other pieces there could be several other closely related chords in the area. Musicians use the technical term *key* for what we call here harmonic area. (See Ex. 7-22.)

Example 7-21 Schubert, "Der Müller und der Bach": Harmonic area

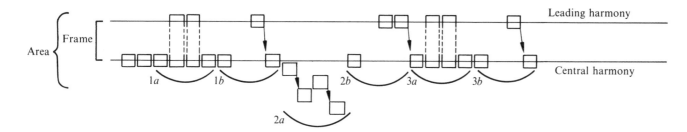

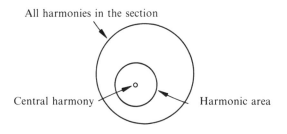

Example 7-22 Harmonies and harmonic area

A full cadence on a different harmony will tend to make that harmony central and to result in a change of harmonic area. Such is the nature of the harmonic motion in phrase 2a; we could indicate this harmonic motion by making a bulge extending the circle of the harmonic area and by showing the suggestion of a new harmonic center with appropriate representations of the full cadence at the end of this phrase (Ex. 7-23). Harmonic motion takes place into the bulge and out again. The area represented by the bulge is not established very firmly. The original area remains primary in the section, and the area of the bulge can be called a *secondary harmonic area*. Many pieces use a cluster of harmonic areas, one of them being primary.

Example 7-23 Motion to a secondary harmonic area

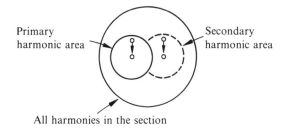

A SPECIAL HARMONY. We have now accounted for most of the harmonies in the first section; one more calls for special mention. In phrases 1b, 2b, and 3b, we notice, probably even on first hearing, a very expressive harmony (Ex. 7-24). In phrase 1b it occurs on the word "Lilien." We have placed it way off from

the frame in Ex. 7-24 to suggest how remote it is harmonically from the harmonic area of this section. The remoteness has much to do with the expressive effect of the harmony. If we heard this particular chord in another context, there might not seem to be anything expressive about it. In this case, context alone causes the harmonic intensity of this chord.

Expressive as it is, this single harmony does not result in even a temporary move to another harmonic center. The harmonic motion involved in phrase 1b as a whole is less than the motion in phrase 2a (see Ex. 7-19).

Listeners may tend to identify the concept of harmony with intense harmonic effects such as the chord in phrase 1b. That is, they may tend to notice the harmony more when it is intense and to ignore it the rest of the time. Actually each of two aspects needs to be emphasized: intense harmonies such as this are among the most important resources of harmony; but they would not have the effect they do unless projected against the stream of leading and central harmonies that make up most of the piece and establish its principal harmonic area.

Attempts such as Ex. 7-24 to represent harmonic movement reveal the limitations of a two-dimensional diagram. The motion from the expressive chord *back* to the leading chord will soon seem reasonably smooth; it is the motion *to* the expressive chord that is so striking. In other words, the distance to this chord should be much greater in the diagram than the distance returning from it—which cannot be done on this type of diagram. If the diagram were on a cylinder or tube so that return routes were available around the back side of the tube, the representation could be more accurate (Ex. 7-25). All that, however, becomes unduly complicated; the purely musical expression of the motion is much more clear.

MELODY IN THE FIRST SECTION. Melody plays a different role in "Der Müller und der Bach" than in Bartók's Mesto, or in the chant "Resurrexi." Even though the melody is strongly projected by a solo voice over a simple accompaniment, as in "Der Müller und der Bach," still the harmonies in the accompaniment are often decisive in shaping the piece.

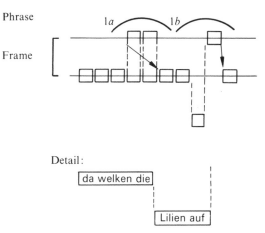

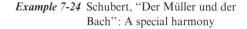

Example 7-24 Schubert, "Der Müller und der Bach": A special harmony

Example 7-25 Another way of showing harmonic distance

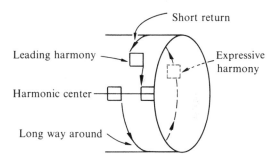

In "Der Müller und der Bach," the melody of the vocal line has the important function of inflecting the harmonic shape, of giving it an interesting, expressive, finely wrought profile. If the piano accompaniment of the first section were played by itself, the harmonic shape of the section would be remarkably clear—but not very interesting. The vocal line furnishes increased rhythmic animation—although that could perfectly well be supplied by the accompaniment (and is, in the second and third sections). More important, the pitches of the vocal line furnish melodic animation that enlivens the harmonic shape.

The relationships between melodic and harmonic aspects constitute one of the most variable relationships in music. In this particular song, the melody is on the one hand relatively active, moving up and down, frequently by leap rather than by step; it seems more active than that of either Bartók's Mesto or "Resurrexi." On the other hand, Schubert's melody often spells out one by one the pitches that are stated as a chord in the accompaniment, and in this respect the melody seems less active than Bartók's.

The harmonic aspect of melody is so important in this piece that it should be studied closely in one example, even if the relationship of melody and harmony is too complex to follow consistently. What you need to hear is that in any one measure almost all the pitches of the melody participate in the harmony, as active partners in producing that harmony. Such pitches are called *chord tones*, as distinct from *non-chord tones*, or pitches that are not part of a given harmony. We can represent chord tones and non-

chord tones in our diagram by shading the latter and leaving the former white. For the sake of simplicity, consider only phrase 1*b* (Ex. 7-26).

The non-chord tones here are not at all prominent, mainly because they are approached and left by step; the ear accepts them as part of the line, not noticing their discrepancy with the harmony. Schubert's melody sounds very smooth and easygoing, but its simplicity is deceiving—as you can discover by trying to sing it. The melodic motion actually is complex and full of skips; its apparent smoothness is largely due to the fact that the skips are from one chord tone to another (as in measures 8 and 9 in Ex. 7-26); hence they derive continuity from the harmony of which they are a part.

We noticed before that the vocal part tended to repeat its rhythmic pattern throughout the song. Phrases 1*a* and 1*b*, for example, have much the same rhythm (Ex. 7-27). In some respects, the similarity of rhythmic figure entails a similarity of melodic detail as well; an important instance occurs in measures 4 and 8. In both measures, an abrupt leap upwards occurs on the first two notes of the measure. In measure 4, the leap has the effect of returning momentarily to touch upon the place that the line just left— that is, the first note of the vocal part (Ex. 7-28).

In measure 8, the effect is different, even though the melodic shape is the same, for measure 8 includes the remote chord (on "Lilien"), and the melody outlines this chord. Since the chord is remote and strange-sounding in this context, the pitch at the top of the leap in the vocal part does not confirm something already present in the measure before but instead contributes to the special effect of this particular measure.

Something wonderfully dark and broadening occurs here in measure 8, something that strains our diagram. Note that the pitches of the melody in measure 8 are only a very little bit lower or higher than the pitches of measure 4; but mere intervallic distance up or down does not seem to have much bearing on the way the notes sound in harmonic context, for these pitches in measure 8 seem to sound far away.

We have studied the harmony of the first section of "Der Müller und der Bach" in considerable detail—

Example 7-26 Schubert, "Der Müller und der Bach": Melody and harmony

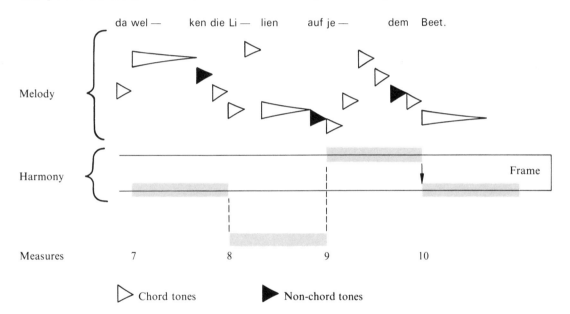

Example 7-27 Schubert, "Der Müller und der Bach": Rhythm of phrases 1*a*, 1*b*

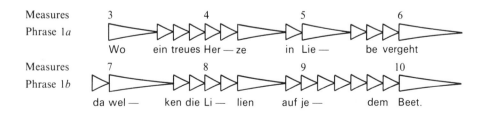

more than would come to our conscious attention while listening to the song under normal circumstances. Harmonic factors such as those we have studied have a strong, sometimes decisive, effect upon the appreciation of a piece, even while conscious attention is directed to other aspects such as rhythm or melody or the words of the song.

FIGURATED CHORDS. A distinctive feature of the second section (compared to the first) is the texture of the piano accompaniment. Instead of a chord (or a note) on ONE, followed by a chord on TWO, as in the first section, the accompaniment to the second section includes a continuous figure of flowing rhythm. Against this figure are sometimes heard chords or notes on ONE and TWO, as before; sometimes there is the related rhythm shown in Ex. 7-29.

The flowing rhythmic figure changes the texture in a subtle way. It is important to hear this difference; but it is just as important to hear that it is no more than a difference in rhythmic figure and texture, for the pitches of the figure continue to form a single harmony in each measure. The harmonic rhythm is much the same as in the first section: the harmonies change at the beginning of each measure, even though each harmony is now expressed one pitch at a time in the piano figure instead of simultaneously in a chord. (Compare the way the *vocal* part in the first section sometimes spells out melodically the chord sounding in the accompaniment.)

Example 7-30 shows the pattern you hear in the second section (in measure 29, for example, the very beginning of the second section). The six notes spread out over three beats (one measure) sound out three pitches, which if played all at once would be a chord. The timbre of the piano causes the notes to blend together so that the effect of a chord is produced: the first notes of the figure continue to sound long enough to overlap the notes at the end of the figure. By the end of each measure, in fact, the pitches of the chord are all sounding just as if they had all been struck at once. (This effect is intensified by a special device on the piano called a *damper pedal*, because it releases the dampers that normally keep the piano strings from continuing to sound after being played. Much of the sustaining effect produced by use of the

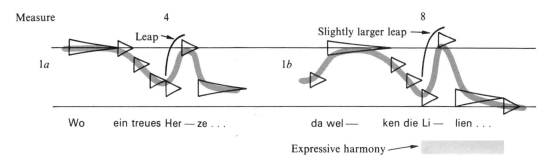

Wo   ein treues Her — ze . . .   da wel — ken die Li — lien . . .

Expressive harmony ——→

Example 7-28 Schubert, "Der Müller und der Bach": Melody and harmony in phrases 1a, 1b

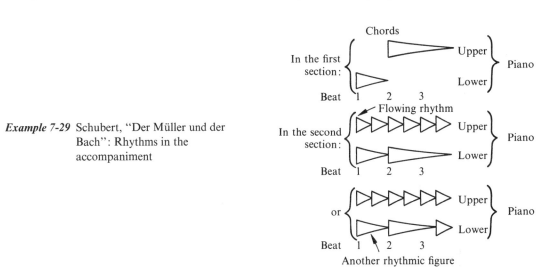

Example 7-29 Schubert, "Der Müller und der Bach": Rhythms in the accompaniment

Example 7-30 Schubert, "Der Müller und der Bach": A figurated chord

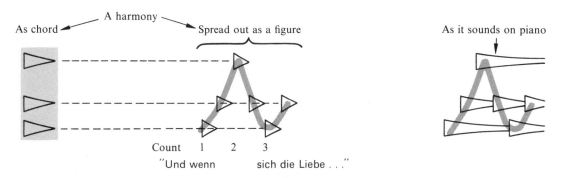

Count 1   2   3

"Und wenn   sich die Liebe . . ."

Beginning of second section = measure 29; upper part of accompaniment only.

131

damper pedal is lost in recording; in any case, the effect is much more noticeable in "live" performance.)

The texture of the accompaniment of sections 2 and 3 is sometimes said to be in *figurated* chords, that is, chords expressed in a figure. Sometimes chords in such a figure are called *broken* or *arpeggiated*, that is, played in the manner of a harp (from the Italian word *arpeggio*). Whenever such an effect is present, try to hear the whole harmony that is sounding (rather than just the individual pitches as they are spelled out) in order to hear how harmonies—not just pitches—are grouped.

PLAN OF THE SECOND SECTION. Fix in mind the phrase plan of the second section, which in many respects is very similar to the plan of the first.

Musical phrases in the second section

4a   Und wenn sich die Liebe dem Schmerz entringt,
4b   Ein Sternlein, ein neues, am Himmel erblinkt,
4c   Ein Sternlein, ein neues, am Himmel erblinkt.
5a   Da springen drei Rosen, halb rot und halb weiss,
5b   Die welken nicht wieder, aus Dornenreis.
6a   Und die Engelein schneiden die Flügel sich ab,
    (Same as 4a)
6b   Und gehn alle Morgen zur Erde herab,
    (Same as 4b)
6c   Und gehn all Morgen zur Erde herab.
    (Same as 4c)

The most obvious feature of this phrase plan is the literal repeat of phrases 4a, b, and c as 6a, b, and c. The literal repeat brings with it a repeat of the

harmony—the harmonic center, the harmonic area, everything. The intervening phrase group, 5a and b, is different in harmony from 4a, b, and c and 6a, b, and c; and this difference turns out to be very important simply because so much else about phrase group 5a and b is the same or very similar to 4a, b, and c and 6a, b, and c. Our chief concern with the second section will be to hear and to understand the harmonic shift that affects phrases 5a and b.

Consider the shape of the first phrase group, 4a, b, and c. The diagram in Ex. 7-31 includes a block for each harmony, as in the diagrams for the first section. Do not, however, concentrate on each block (or the harmony it represents), but rather on the overall shapes produced. Each phrase of this first group has a different harmonic function. The first phrase, 4a

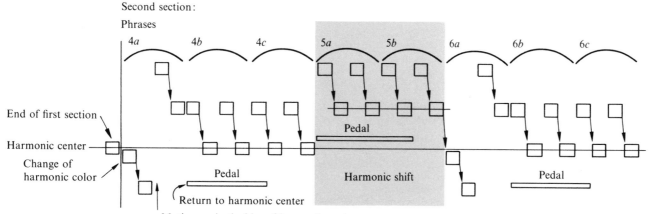

Example 7-31 Schubert, "Der Müller und der Bach," second section

4a Und wenn sich die Liebe dem Schmerz entringt,
4b ein Sternlein, ein neues, am Himmel erblinkt,
4c ein Sternlein, ein neues, am Himmel erblinkt.
5a Da springen drei Rosen, halb rot und halb weiss,
5b die welken nicht wieder, aus Dornenreis.
6a Und die Engelein schneiden die Flügel sich ab,
6b und gehn alle Morgen zur Erde herab,
6c und gehn alle Morgen zur Erde herab.

("Und wenn . . ."), functions mainly as a contrast to the preceding section: it brings the new harmonic color that will characterize the coming section but does not clearly define a harmonic area (it moves around too much for that). The second phrase, 4b ("Ein Sternlein . . ."), does establish a harmonic area, mainly through the pedal note and the alternation of central harmony and leading harmony.

The third phrase, 4c, is very closely linked to the second; in fact, it merely repeats the text ("Ein Sternlein . . .") to a varied repetition of the melody, over the continuing pedal note in the accompaniment. The third phrase confirms the harmonic area and provides a satisfying end to the phrase group.

A HARMONIC SHIFT. The material of the second phrase group, 5a and b, is familiar, for this group is built entirely upon the melodic figure introduced in phrase 4b in the bass of the piano accompaniment. This means that the second phrase group wastes no time establishing its harmonic area, for from the beginning the pedal note makes its presence felt, as do the leading and central harmonies alternating over it (Ex. 7-31).

The harmonic area established, however, is different from the area immediately preceding; a harmonic shift to a secondary area has taken place. The music does not move gradually away from one place to another (as in the middle of the first section), but rather steps decisively to the new location at the beginning of the phrase, remains there until the end, then slides gracefully back to the original area as the new phrase begins.

Musicians use the word *modulation* to refer to shifts such as this. There is much difference of opinion, however, as to exactly what constitutes a modulation in precise, technical terms. Some musicians would call this particular shift a modulation, some would not.

This harmonic shift gives the middle of the section a fresh sound; without it, the section would sound dull and repetitious. (A musician could demonstrate this to you by playing the section with the second phrase group *transposed*, or moved back, to the same harmonic area as the first phrase group so that no shift takes place.) Harmonic shifts of this type can be

of the greatest importance for the way a piece sounds. Sensitivity to such shifts in harmonic location helps make clear the point of many extended repetitions of rhythmic and melodic detail.

A listener's first awareness of a harmonic shift is merely that a shift has occurred; only after much practice can the ear identify the relationship of the new area to the old one. Hearing changes of harmonic area is much like hearing changes from one chord to another: first you hear sameness or difference; then, and only gradually, do you hear the relationships between different chords. Example 7-32 shows the shift in phrases 5a and b in terms of mere difference between the old area and the new one. The largest circle includes all the harmonies in the second section. The lower of the two circles inside the large circle represents the harmonic area established in phrases 4a, b, and c and 6a, b, and c. The upper of the two circles represents the new harmonic area of phrases 5a and b.

Example 7-32 Shift of harmonic area

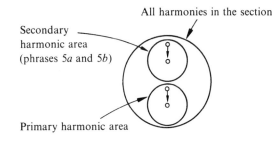

Secondary harmonic area (phrases 5a and 5b)

All harmonies in the section

Primary harmonic area

It is evident from listening to this phrase group that the modulation is not to a remote key but to one nearby. That a listener can gauge the nearness or remoteness of one key to another might be called a second stage of awareness, coming after the perception of mere difference. For much of our listening experience, this is as far as we need go. In this one case, however, it is worthwhile to note the exact relationship between keys, so as to see what makes one key close to another. Example 7-33 expresses Ex. 7-32 more precisely: the leading harmony of the old area becomes the central harmony of the new area;

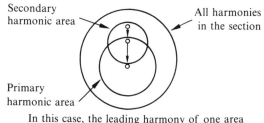

Secondary harmonic area

All harmonies in the section

Primary harmonic area

In this case, the leading harmony of one area is the central harmony of the other area.

Example 7-33 Shift of harmonic area: A special case

thus, at the end of phrase 5b, the return to the old area is accomplished merely by interpreting the new central harmony as a leading harmony. The closeness of the relationship accounts for the ease and grace of the transition to phrase 6a.

In addition to making the familiar material in phrases 5a and b sound fresh and interesting, the harmonic shift gives the following phrase group (6a, b, and c) a feeling of warmth. Much more than a mere symmetrical repetition, the return of the first phrase group at 6a, b, and c shows the great expressive power that lies within the sense of harmonic movement— often difficult to grasp at first, but capable of being heard, and well worth the effort.

CHANGE FROM SECTION 2 TO SECTION 3. All aspects of musical shape seem to become clearer at important sectional divisions; at the end of a section and the beginning of a contrasting one, the outlines of the section just ended seem thrown into relief by the contrast. The transition from the second section of "Der Müller und der Bach" to the third (from phrase 6c to phrase 7a) contains in compact form the relationship of harmonic color between the second section, which is in major, and the first and third sections, which are in minor.

Listen carefully to the figured chord in the accompaniment, during the last note the voice sings in the second section (end of phrase 6c) and during the next measure (before 7a). Everything about these two measures is the same, except for one pitch, which is lowered in the second measure (Ex. 7-34). Seemingly a small change—but what a profound effect it has

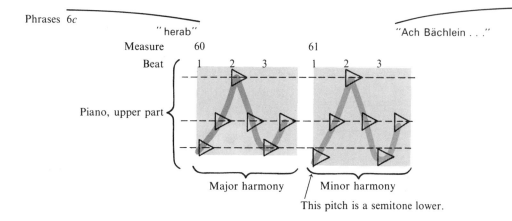

Phrases 6c

"herab"   "Ach Bächlein . . ."

Measure   60   61

Beat   1   2   3   1   2   3

Piano, upper part {

Major harmony   Minor harmony

This pitch is a semitone lower.

Example 7-34 Schubert, "Der Müller und der Bach": Transition from major to minor

upon the harmonic color! With the lowering of that single pitch we are transported abruptly from the bright world of the second section back to the darker world of the first one. There is no obvious shift in harmonic area, such as that heard at the second phrase group of the second section (where the melodic figure of phrase 5*a* was repeated in 5*b* at a different pitch level). Here, at the end of the second section, the harmonic area remains constant; only one inner pitch slides downward by the interval of a semitone. And yet the resulting change in harmonic color may seem much more striking—and certainly easier to hear—than the change of area in the course of the second section.

We can express the relationship of major and minor roughly with the same kind of diagram used for the harmonic shift in the second section. The two inner circles in Ex. 7-35 represent the major and minor areas found in the second and third sections. As shown in the diagram, these two areas share the same leading harmony, and their central harmonies are almost identical. (A major key can have a more remote relationship to a minor one if the two keys do not share the same central tone: in this particular case the two areas are in one of the most easily recognized relationships.)

Example 7-35 Schubert, "Der Müller und der Bach": Major and minor areas

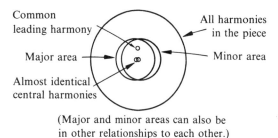

Common leading harmony

All harmonies in the piece

Major area

Minor area

Almost identical central harmonies

(Major and minor areas can also be in other relationships to each other.)

The important thing here is to connect the two harmonies shown in Ex. 7-34 to the two sections with which they are identified. The major harmony characterizes the kind of sound heard throughout the second section and especially the two central harmonies. Similarly, the minor harmony characterizes the first section.

PHRASING AND HARMONIC STRUCTURE IN THE THIRD SECTION. The third section is built mostly of material from the first; but the material is rearranged, and the ending is strikingly different (Ex. 7-36).

Phrases in the third section	Equivalent phrase in the first section
7*a* Ach, Bächlein, liebes Bächlein . . .	1*a*
7*b* Ach, Bächlein, aber weisst du . . .	2*b* (and 4*c*, end)
7*c* Ach, unten, da unten . . .	2*a*
7*d* Ach, Bächlein, liebes Bächlein . . .	3*b* (modified)

7*e* (*Same as 7d with a closed ending*)
Piano epilog

There are five phrases (not counting the epilog) instead of six as in the first section, and they are not arranged in pairs. The phrases of the first section have been rearranged so that each ends slightly more open than the preceding one. Phrase 7*a* is closed, as was 1*a*; phrase 7*b* has the decisively open quality of the leading harmony as in 2*b*. Phrase 7*c* moves away from the harmonic center in the fashion of 2*a*. The strong closed ending originally provided by phrase 1*b* has been omitted altogether.

In other words, the phrase endings in the third section lead with mounting intensity away from the center, without any larger articulation such as would come at the end of a phrase group. The move cul-

134

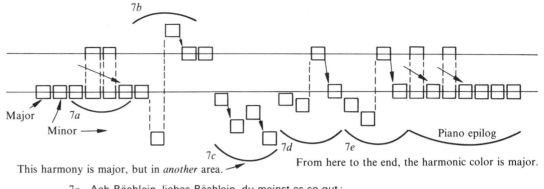

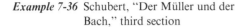

Example 7-36 Schubert, "Der Müller und der Bach," third section

Major 7a

Minor ⟶

7b

7c

7d

7e

Piano epilog

This harmony is major, but in *another* area.

From here to the end, the harmonic color is major.

7a Ach Bächlein, liebes Bächlein, du meinst es so gut;

7b Ach Bächlein, aber weisst du, wie Liebe tut?

7c Ach unten, da unten, die kühle Ruh'!

7d Ach Bächlein, liebes Bächlein, so singe nur zu!

7e Ach Bächlein, liebes Bächlein, so singe nur zu!

minates in a shift of harmonic color from minor to major in the course of phrase 7d, without benefit of an articulation of any kind. The shift transfigures the end of the song, making the third section far more than a mere return of the first section.

Clearly, the inner harmonic structure of this third section would have far less effect if it did not function as a reconciliation of the two contrasting sections in major and minor that came before. The change in harmonic color within the third section reaches out beyond the section to bind the whole song together.

The song makes sense on purely musical grounds; we do not need to go to the text for an explanation of the shape of the music. Still, the text is there; and we should take note of the relationship between the meaning of the text and the music, for a very simple but effective relationship exists.

This particular song plays a pivotal role in the song cycle as a whole: the miller lad abandoning all hope of winning the girl he loves, sings to his old companion, the brook, expressing in folklike, legendary images the reaction of Nature and the angels to love's despair (section 1). The brook adds another set of images—but they are images of apotheosis instead of defeat (section 2). In the lad's reply (section 3), he sings of suicide; but in his last lines indicates that he welcomes the brook's interpretation of it. It is this sense of acceptance, of peaceful resignation, that Schubert has chosen to illuminate with the last, conclusive change from minor to major.

Exercises for further listening

I. SCHUBERT: "DIE LIEBE FARBE" (DIE SCHONE MULLERIN, SONG 16)

Listen to stanza 1, following the text given here. (A complete translation will be found at the end of Chapter 11, and a diagram on page 139.)

Text lines	Musical phrases	Text lines	Musical phrases
1a In Grün will ich mich kleiden,	1	3a Will suchen einen Zypressenhain,	3
1b In grüne Tränenweiden,		3b Eine Heide voll grünem Rosmarein,	
2a Mein Schatz hat's Grün so gern,	2	4a Mein Schatz hat's Grün so gern,	4
2b Mein Schatz hat's Grün so gern.		4b Mein Schatz hat's Grün so gern.	

1. The overall melodic shape of the vocal phrases is
 —— **a.** *A A B C* —— **b.** *A B B C*
 —— **c.** *A B A C* —— **d.** *A B C B*

                   1. d

2. The piano introduction consists of
 —— **a.** One phrase —— **b.** Two phrases —— **c.** Three phrases

                   2. a

3. The cadence that concludes the piano introduction creates
 —— **a.** An open ending —— **b.** A closed ending

                   3. b

4. The cadence that concludes the first vocal phrase creates
 —— **a.** An open ending —— **b.** A closed ending

                   4. a

5. The cadence that concludes the second vocal phrase creates
 —— **a.** An open ending —— **b.** A closed ending

                   5. b

6. The cadence that concludes the third vocal phrase creates
 —— **a.** An open ending —— **b.** A closed ending

                   6. a

7. The cadence that concludes the last vocal phrase creates
 —— **a.** An open ending —— **b.** A closed ending

                   7. b

8. You would expect the final cadence of the song to provide
 —— **a.** An open ending —— **b.** A closed ending

                   8. b

9. Is this in fact what happens? (Listen to the end of the last piano passage, after stanza 3.)
 —— Yes
 —— No

                   9. Yes

10. The open ending which occurs at the ends of phrases 1 and 3 is caused by
 —— **a.** A half cadence (ending on the leading harmony)
 —— **b.** A deceptive cadence (moving from the leading harmony to a harmony other than the central one)
 —— **c.** Neither *a* nor *b*

                  10. a

11. In a full cadence, such as those at the ends of phrases 2 and 4
 —— **a.** The leading harmony is preceded by the central harmony
 —— **b.** The central harmony is preceded by the leading harmony
 —— **c.** A harmony other than the central one is preceded by the leading harmony

                  11. b

12. The central pitch of the vocal melody (the pitch that seems most conclusive as an ending) occurs at the end of

_____ **a.** Line 1*b* ("wei-*den*")   _____ **b.** Line 2*b* ("*gern*")   _____ **c.** Line 3*b* ("Rosma-*rein*")

12. b

13. Place a check mark above each italicized word or syllable that is sung on the central pitch, as is done for "gern" at the end of line 2*b*.

13. Line 1*a*: "Grün," "-den"
(Line 2*b*: "gern")
Line 4*b*: "gern"

1*a*   *In Grün* will *ich* mich *klei-den*,
1*b*   In grüne Tränenwei-*den*,
2*a*   Mein *Schatz* hat's Grün so *gern*,
2*b*   Mein *Schatz* hat's Grün so *gĕrn*.

3*a*   Will suchen einen Zypressen-*hain*,
3*b*   Eine *Hei*-de voll grünem *Ros*-ma-*rein*,
4*a*   Mein *Schatz* hat's Grün so *gern*,
4*b*   Mein *Schatz* hat's Grün so *gern*.

14. After the cadence in the piano introduction, there is a single repeated note heard in the

_____ **a.**   Upper part of the piano accompaniment
_____ **b.**   Lower part of the piano accompaniment

14. a

15. This repeated note continues at the same pitch

_____ **a.**   Through phrase 1, then changes pitch at phrase 2
_____ **b.**   Through phrases 1 and 2, then changes pitch at phrase 3
_____ **c.**   Through phrases 1, 2, and 3, then changes pitch at phrase 4
_____ **d.**   Through all four vocal phrases

15. d

16. Fix this pitch firmly in your memory. Sing it as you listen to the piano introduction.

_____ **a.**   The pitch is always present in the piano introduction
_____ **b.**   The pitch is not always present in the piano introduction

16. a

17. The pitch of the repeated piano note first occurs in the voice part in phrase 1 ("*In Grün* will ich mich *klei*den"), with the word or syllable

_____ **a.**   "In"   _____ **b.**   "Grün"   _____ **c.**   "klei-"

17. a

18. A pitch that is sustained or repeated (like this one) through several changing harmonies is called a

_____ **a.**   Central pitch, or tonic
_____ **b.**   Pedal, or pedal tone
_____ **c.**   Harmonic area, or key

18. b

19. The pitch of the repeated pedal note

_____ **a.**   Is the same as the central pitch
_____ **b.**   Is not the same as the central pitch

19. b

20. The leading harmony in phrases 2 and 4 occurs in the piano accompaniment, in conjunction with the words

Mein Schatz hat's Grün so gern, mein Schatz hat's Grün so gern.

___ **a.** "gern, mein"   ___ **b.** "Schatz hat's"
___ **c.** "Grün so"   ___ **d.** "gern"

20. c

21. The central pitch is most closely associated with the
___ **a.** Leading harmony   ___ **b.** Central harmony   ___ **c.** Neither *a* nor *b*

21. b (hear this at the cadences of phrases 2 and 4)

22. The repeated pedal tone is most closely associated with the
___ **a.** Leading harmony   ___ **b.** Central harmony   ___ **c.** Neither *a* nor *b*

22. a (hear this at the ends of lines 2*a* and 4*a*)

23. In lines 2 and 4, which words or syllables are sung at the same pitch as the repeated pedal tone?

23. c

Line 2a: Mein Schatz hat's Grün so gern,
Line 2b: Mein Schatz hat's Grün so gern.

___ **a.** "Schatz hat's" (from line 2*a*)
___ **b.** "Grün so" (from line 2*a*)
___ **c.** "Mein Schatz hat's Grün" (from line 2*b*)
___ **d.** "gern" (from line 2*b*)

24. In general, the melodic motion is a mixture of step and leap (conjunct and disjunct motion). However, some sections of the melody are striking in their use of one of these kinds of motion. Check each subphrase that is predominantly conjunct.
___ **a.** 1*a*   ___ **b.** 1*b*   ___ **c.** 2*a*   ___ **d.** 2*b*
___ **e.** 3*a*   ___ **f.** 3*b*   ___ **g.** 4*a*   ___ **h.** 4*b*

24. d (2*b*)
e (3*a*)
h (4*b*)

25. The largest leap (from the upper limit of the range to the lower limit) occurs within which subphrase?
___ **a.** 1*a*   ___ **b.** 1*b*   ___ **c.** 2*a*   ___ **d.** 2*b*
___ **e.** 3*a*   ___ **f.** 3*b*   ___ **g.** 4*a*   ___ **h.** 4*b*

25. f (3*b*)

26. The two subphrases, 2*a* and 2*b* (also 4*a* and 4*b*) are contrasted in
___ **a.** Harmonic area   ___ **b.** Harmonic color   ___ **c.** Central harmony

26. b

27. The first of these subphrases is in
___ **a.** Major
___ **b.** Minor

27. a

Schubert, "Die liebe Farbe" (Die schöne Müllerin, song 16)

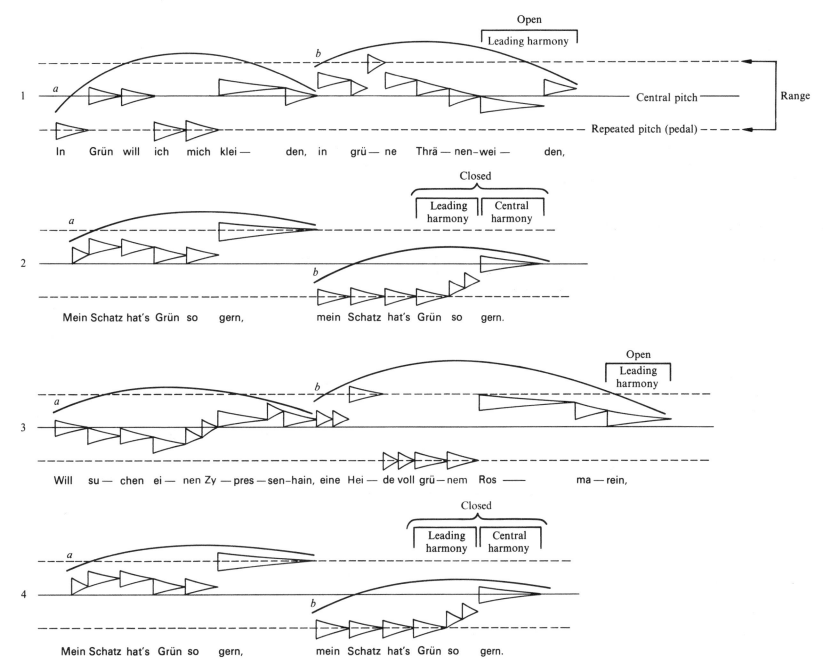

28. The second is in

____ **a.** Major   ____ **b.** Minor

28. b

29. The song as a whole is in

____ **a.** Major   ____ **b.** Minor

29. b

QUESTION FOR DISCUSSION

Explain the relationship between the words "Mein Schatz hat's Grün so gern" and the change in harmonic color from major to minor that accompanies their repetition. What larger meaning does this pair of lines have within the story of the song cycle? What larger implications might the change of harmonic color suggest? (See the diagram on page 139.)

II. SCHUBERT: "DER NEUGIERIGE" (DIE SCHONE MULLERIN, SONG 6)

Sectional shape. This song is divided into several clear sections, numbered here 1 through 5 (the piano interludes are not included in the numbering). Listen to the entire song as you follow the sectional divisions in the text. (A translation can be found in Chapter 11.) Answer questions 1 through 14.

Text lines		*Musical sections*	*Text lines*		*Musical sections*	*Text lines*		*Musical sections*
	(*Piano*)		5a	O Bächlein meiner Liebe,	3	8b	Die ganze Welt mir ein.	
1a	Ich frage keine Blume,	1	5b	Wie bist du heut' so stumm!		9a	Die beiden Wörtchen schliessen	
1b	Ich frage keinen Stern,		6a	Will ja nur Eines wissen,		9b	Die ganze Welt mir ein.	
2a	Sie können mir alle nicht sagen,		6b	Ein Wörtchen um und um,			(*Piano*)	
2b	Was ich erführ' so gern.		6c	Ein Wörtchen um und um.		10a	O Bächlein meiner Liebe,	5
						10b	Was bist du wunderlich!	
3a	Ich bin ja auch kein Gärtner,	2		(*Piano*)		11a	Will's ja nicht weiter sagen,	
3b	Die Sterne steh'n zu hoch;		7a	Ja, heisst das eine Wörtchen,	4	11b	Sag', Bächlein, liebt sie mich?	
4a	Mein Bächlein will ich fragen,		7b	Das andre heisset Nein,		11c	Sag', Bächlein, liebt sie mich?	
4b	Ob ich mein Herz belog.		8a	Die beiden Wörtchen schliessen			(*Piano*)	
	(*Piano*)							

1. Sections 1 and 2

____ **a.** Are exactly alike (in rhythm, tempo, meter, melody, harmony, etc.)

____ **b.** Are almost the same

____ **c.** Are strongly contrasting

1. b

2. Sections 2 and 3

____ **a.** Are exactly alike   ____ **b.** Are almost the same

____ **c.** Are strongly contrasting

2. c

3. Which type of contrast is *not* present between sections 2 and 3? **3.** c
___ **a.** A change of accompaniment pattern
___ **b.** A change of meter
___ **c.** A change of timbre
___ **d.** A change of harmonic color
___ **e.** A change of tempo

4. In sections 1 and 2, the accompaniment consists of **4.** a
___ **a.** Chords
___ **b.** Two or more independent melodies (counterpoint)
___ **c.** Broken chords

5. In section 3, the accompaniment changes to **5.** b
___ **a.** Two or more independent melodies
___ **b.** Broken chords
___ **c.** Thicker chords than in sections 1 and 2

6. Sections 3 and 4 **6.** c
___ **a.** Are exactly alike   ___ **b.** Are almost the same
___ **c.** Are completely contrasting

7. In section 4, the accompaniment changes to **7.** d
___ **a.** Two or more independent melodies
___ **b.** Broken chords
___ **c.** Chords, as in sections 1 and 2
___ **d.** Thicker chords than in sections 1 and 2

8. Do the meter and tempo change between sections 3 and 4 as they did between sections 2 **8.** No
and 3?
___ Yes   ___ No

9. In section 3 the accompaniment was relatively independent of the vocal melody. Is this also **9.** No
true of section 4?
___ Yes   ___ No

10. Section 5 **10.** c
___ **a.** Is completely different from any of the previous sections
___ **b.** Slightly resembles a previous section
___ **c.** Strongly resembles a previous section

11. Section 5 resembles section   11. c
    ___ **a.** 1   ___ **b.** 2   ___ **c.** 3   ___ **d.** 4

12. Which letter diagram most closely resembles the sectional shape of the song?   12. c
    ___ **a.** $A\ B_1\ C\ D\ B_2$ ___ **b.** $A_1\ A_2\ B\ C\ D$
    ___ **c.** $A_1\ A_2\ B_1\ C\ B_2$ ___ **d.** $A_1\ B_1\ A_2\ C\ B_2$

13. These five sections seem to divide more simply into   13. a
    ___ **a.** Two large sections   ___ **b.** Three large sections

14. The two large sections are   14. b
    ___ **a.** $A_1\ A_2\ B_1\ C,\ B_1$ ___ **b.** $A_1\ A_2,\ B_1\ C\ B_2$
    ___ **c.** $A_1\ A_2\ B_1,\ C\ B_2$

Overall harmonic shape. Answer questions 15 through 29.

15. In the accompaniment of line 1*a* ("*Ich fra*-ge kei-ne *Blu*-me"), the central harmony occurs   15. b
    with which syllable of the text?
    ___ **a.** "Ich"   ___ **b.** "fra-"   ___ **c.** "Blu-"

16. In the accompaniment of line 1*a* ("*Ich* fra-ge *kei*-ne Blu-me"), the leading harmony occurs   16. a
    with which syllable of the text?
    ___ **a.** "Ich"   ___ **b.** "kei-"

17. The first phrase (the piano introduction) ends with   17. b
    ___ **a.** An open ending   ___ **b.** A closed ending

18. The piano introduction establishes the principal harmonic area. Does the first vocal phrase   18. a
    (lines 1*a* and *b*)
    ___ **a.** Stay within this area?
    ___ **b.** Move away to another area?

19. The next vocal phrase (lines 2*a* and *b*)   19. b
    ___ **a.** Stays within the original area
    ___ **b.** Moves to another area

20. The ending of this phrase (at "erführ' so gern") is   20. b
    ___ **a.** Open (in the new harmonic area)
    ___ **b.** Closed (in the new harmonic area)

142

21. Section 2 (the next two phrases, lines 3*a* and *b*, and 4*a* and *b*)
_____ **a.** Moves through the same harmonic areas as the first section
_____ **b.** Moves through different harmonic areas than the first section

21. a

22. Section 3 (lines 5*a* and *b*, 6*a*, *b*, and *c*) ends
_____ **a.** In the original harmonic area
_____ **b.** Away from the original harmonic area

22. a

23. The ending of line 6*c* is
_____ **a.** Open   _____ **b.** Closed

23. b

24. Section 4 (lines 7, 8, and 9) ends
_____ **a.** In the original harmonic area   _____ **b.** Away from the original harmonic area

24. b

25. The ending of this section is
_____ **a.** Open (in the new area)   _____ **b.** Closed (in the new area)

25. b

26. At what point does the original harmonic area return?
_____ **a.** Not until the end of section 5 (line 11*c*)
_____ **b.** Not until the middle of section 5 (line 11*a*)
_____ **c.** At the beginning of section 5 (line 10*a*)

26. c

27. Section 5 ends
_____ **a.** In the original harmonic area   _____ **b.** Away from the original harmonic area

27. a

28. The final vocal cadence (at "liebt sie mich," in line 11*c*) is
_____ **a.** An open ending   _____ **b.** A closed ending

28. b

29. On the diagram, indicate the three important harmonic areas, by marking the boxes "C" for central harmonic area, "S" for the second harmonic area, "T" for the third harmonic area. Mark one letter per box.

29.

Line   1 2   3   4   5   6   7 8 9 10 11
| C | S | C | S | C | ∿ T | C |

Section | 1 | 2 | 3 | 4 | 5 |

Line   1 2   3   4   5   6   7   8   9   10   11

| | | | | | ∿ | |
Unstable

143

Some harmonic details. Answer questions 30 and 31.

30. In sections 3 and 5, an expressive harmony occurs which does not appear anywhere else in the song. In the following diagram,

Section 3: O B̲ä̲c̲h̲l̲e̲i̲n̲ ̲m̲e̲i̲n̲e̲r̲ Lie be, wie b̲i̲s̲t̲ ̲d̲u̲ ̲h̲e̲u̲t̲'̲ ̲s̲o̲ s t u m m !
Section 5: O B̲ä̲c̲h̲l̲e̲i̲n̲ ̲m̲e̲i̲n̲e̲r̲ Lie be, was b̲i̲s̲t̲ ̲d̲u̲ ̲w̲u̲n̲d̲e̲r̲-̲ lic h !

____ **a.** _____ indicates the
    1. Central harmony   2. Expressive harmony   3. Leading harmony
____ **b.** ---------- indicates the
    1. Central harmony   2. Expressive harmony   3. Leading harmony
____ **c.** ═════ indicates the
    1. Central harmony   2. Expressive harmony   3. Leading harmony

30. a. 1
       b. 3
       c. 2

31. The new, expressive harmony is surprising because
____ **a.** It effects a change of harmonic color   ____ **b.** It effects a change of harmonic area
____ **c.** It is the leading harmony in an unexpected place

31. a

QUESTIONS FOR DISCUSSION

A. Explain the figuration of sections 3 and 5 in relation to the text.
B. Explain the striking shift in harmonic area in section 4, in relation to the text of that section.

III. BEETHOVEN: SYMPHONY NO. 7, ALLEGRETTO (SECOND MOVEMENT)

Overall harmonic shape. Listen to each of the five large sections of the Allegretto, noting the type and degree of harmonic contrast between each pair of sections.

Listen to section 1. Answer questions 1, 2, and 3.

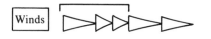

1. From the opening wind chord to the measure immediately following,
____ **a.** There is a change of register but not of harmony
____ **b.** There is a change of harmony but not of register
____ **c.** There is a change both of harmony and of register

1. a

2. Section 1 as a whole   **2.** a
____ **a.** Stays within a single harmonic area
____ **b.** Moves from one harmonic area to a second harmonic area

3. The harmony of the opening wind chord   **3.** a
____ **a.** Is the central harmony of section 1 as a whole
____ **b.** Is the leading harmony of section 1 as a whole
____ **c.** Is neither the central nor the leading harmony

Listen to the end of section 1 and to all of the first interlude. Answer questions 4, 5, and 6.

4. The first interlude as a whole is   **4.** c
____ **a.** As stable harmonically as section 1
____ **b.** More stable harmonically than section 1
____ **c.** Less stable harmonically than section 1

5. Compare the end of section 1 and the beginning of the first interlude.   **5.** b
____ **a.** The beginning of the first interlude has a different harmonic center than that of section 1
____ **b.** The beginning of the first interlude has the same harmonic center as section 1 but a different harmonic color
____ **c.** The beginning of the first interlude has the same harmonic center and the same harmonic color as section 1

6. The contrast in harmonic color occurs because   **6.** a
____ **a.** The end of section 1 is in minor, the beginning of the first interlude in major
____ **b.** The end of section 1 is in major, the beginning of the first interlude in minor

Listen to the beginning of the middle section. Answer questions 7 and 8.

7. Does the beginning of the middle section return to the same harmonic area as that of section 1?   **7.** Yes
____ Yes   ____ No

8. Section 1 was primarily in minor. The first interlude was primarily in major. The middle   **8.** b
section begins in
____ **a.** Major
____ **b.** Minor

Listen to the end of the middle section and the beginning of the second interlude. Answer questions 9 and 10.

145

9. Does the second interlude return to the same harmonic area as the beginning of the first interlude?

___ Yes ___ No

9. Yes

10. Is there a minor/major contrast between the middle section and the second interlude?

___ Yes ___ No

10. Yes

Listen to the final section. Answer questions 11 and 12.

11. The last section as a whole is harmonically

___ **a.** Unstable ___ **b.** Stable

11. b

12. The last section

___ **a.** Returns to the same harmonic area as that of the first and middle sections
___ **b.** Moves to a different harmonic area than that of the first and middle sections

12. a

Listen to the two wind chords that open and close the Allegretto. Answer question 13.

13. These two chords

___ **a.** Contain the same harmony but at different registers
___ **b.** Are at the same register but contain different harmonies
___ **c.** Are identical in harmony and register

13. c

Harmonic detail in the first subsection. Listen to the first subsection of section 1, following the diagram given here. Answer questions 14 through 23.

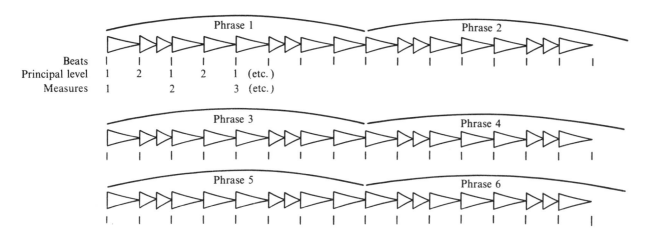

146

14. The six phrases of this subsection have the following melodic shape: **14.** c
___ **a.** *A B C D E F*
___ **b.** *A B A B C D*
___ **c.** *A B C D C D*
___ **d.** *A B A B A B*

15. The ending of phrase 1 is   **15.** b
___ **a.** Open
___ **b.** Closed

16. Phrase 2   **16.** b
___ **a.** Stays in the same harmonic area as phrase 1
___ **b.** Moves to a new harmonic area

17. The ending of phrase 2, within the new harmonic area, is   **17.** b
___ **a.** Open
___ **b.** Closed

18. Phrases 3 and 5   **18.** b
___ **a.** Stay within a single harmonic area (are stable)
___ **b.** Do not stay within a single harmonic area (are unstable)

19. The type of melodic organization found in phrases 3 and 5 is called   **19.** b
___ **a.** Repetition
___ **b.** Sequence
___ **c.** Figuration

20. Phrases 4 and 6   **20.** a
___ **a.** Return to the original harmonic area
___ **b.** Do not return to the original harmonic area

21. Phrases 4 and 6 end   **21.** b
___ **a.** Open
___ **b.** Closed

22. The harmony of phrase 4 most closely resembles that of   **22.** a
___ **a.** Phrase 1
___ **b.** Phrase 2
___ **c.** Phrase 3

23. On the diagram below, indicate the harmony by marking each box with one of the following letters: "C" for central harmony, "L" for leading harmony, "U" for unstable harmonies, and "S" for stable harmonies in an area other than the principal harmonic area. Mark only one letter per box.

23.

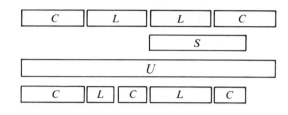

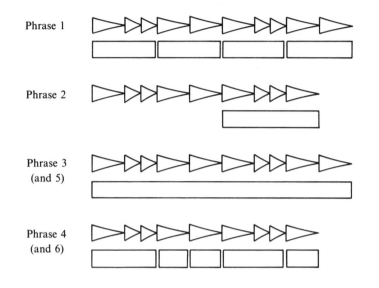

Procedure:

1. Follow the scheme of the canzonetta below as you listen the first time.
2. Read the description of the instrumental sections (preceding question 1) and questions 1 through 8. Listen one or two times, concentrating on the instrumental sections, then answer these questions.
3. Read questions 9 through 20, concentrating on the vocal stanzas. Try to answer as many questions as possible on one listening.
4. Read questions 21 through 25 on rhythm. One listening, or perhaps memory alone, should suffice for answering these questions.
5. Question 26, on cadential patterns, is to be answered in the blanks opposite the text below.
6. Questions 27 through 33 concern the bass line and require some difficult listening. Try them, but do not be discouraged if you find it hard to hear the bass well.
7. Answers to the quiz will be found following question 33.

(*Instrumental section 1, repeated; instrumental section 2, repeated; instrumental section 3*)

Stanza 1 (phrases):

1	Amor che deggio far/se non mi giova amar/con pura *fede*?	—	1	O love, what must I do since I do not enjoy loving by faith alone?	
2	Servir non vo' così/piangendo notte e dì/per chi nol *crede*.	—	2	Nor do I wish to serve sorrowfully night and day a disbeliever.	
3	E non si può veder/l'amoroso pensier/da l'occhio hu*mano*,	—	3	And since none may discern another's thoughts of love relying on human sight,	
4	Dunque un fido amator/dovrà nel suo dolor/languir in*vano*.	—	4	Therefore the man who loves faithfully, in his grief must suffer vainly.	

(*Instrumental interlude*)

Stanza 2 (phrases):

5	Intesi pur tal hor/che nella fronte il cor/si porta *scritto*;	—	5	Her understanding is that a man's heart is writ plainly upon his face;	
6	Hor come a me non val/scoprir l'interno mal/nel volto *afflitto*.	—	6	But none may read the pain within me if he look for looks afflicted.	
7	Ingiustissimo Re,/perchè la vera fè/nota non *fai*?	—	7	Why, unjust ruler, Love, do you allow true faith to go unmanifest?	
8	Perchè lasci perir/voci, sguardi e sospir/se'l vedi e'l *sai*?	—	8	Why do you let voice, glance and sigh that you know well and serve you, perish?	

(*Instrumental interlude*)

Stanza 3 (phrases):

9	O come saria pur/Amor dolce e sicur/se'l cor s'apr*isse*;	—	9	How sweet and how serene could love be if the heart might open; love would then	
10	Non soffrirebbe già,/Donna senza pietà,/ch'altrui mor*isse*.	—	10	No longer suffer that pitiless woman should kill him who loves her.	

(*Instrumental interlude*)

Stanza 4 (phrases):

11	E dunque sotto il Ciel/non v'è d'alma fedel/segno ve*race*?	—	11	But may, upon this Earth no truly faithful soul make true signs of his love?	
12	Ahi fato, ahi pena, ahi duol,/hor credami chi vol/ch'io mi do *pace*.	—	12	O fate, O pain, O grief! Believe me when I say I would be peaceful.	

English translation © 1956 by Chester Kallman. Used by permission.

I. INSTRUMENTAL SECTIONS

Instrumental sections introduce the canzonetta and return between the vocal stanzas. The first three instrumental sections are played without pauses between them: section 1 is repeated; section 2, which starts with a rising sequence and ends with a descending line, is also repeated; section 3, which begins with a rising line, is not repeated.

Listen to all of the instrumental sections, following the scheme above; answer questions 1 through 8.

1. The instrumental ensemble consists of an accompaniment of cello and harpsichord, plus
____ a. One high melody instrument
____ b. Two high melody instruments
____ c. Three high melody instruments

2. The two melody instruments are
____ a. Two woodwinds
____ b. Two strings
____ c. One woodwind, one stringed instrument

3. The repeat of the first instrumental section
____ a. Is played by the same instruments as the original statement
____ b. Is not played by the same instruments as the original statement

4. The repeat of the second instrumental section
____ a. Is played by the same instruments as the original statement of section 2
____ b. Is not played by the same instruments as the original statement of section 2

5. Which instrument is absent in the first statement of section 2 and present in the repeat?
____ a. The woodwind melody instrument (recorder)
____ b. The high stringed instrument (violin)
____ c. The cello   ____ d. The harpsichord

6. The instrumental interlude between stanzas 1 and 2 is the same as
____ a. Instrumental section 1 (without repeat)
____ b. Instrumental section 2 (without repeat)
____ c. Instrumental section 3

7. The instrumental interlude between stanzas 2 and 3 is the same as
____ a. Section 1 (without repeat)   ____ b. Section 2 (without repeat)
____ c. Section 3

8. The instrumental interlude between stanzas 3 and 4 is the same as

_____ **a.** Section 1 (without repeat)

_____ **b.** Section 2 (without repeat)

_____ **c.** Section 3

II. NUMBER AND TYPES OF VOICES

Listen to the vocal stanzas, following the text. Answer questions 9 through 20.

9. Stanza 1 is sung by

_____ **a.** One voice at a time

_____ **b.** Two voices at the same time

_____ **c.** Three voices at the same time

_____ **d.** Four voices at the same time

10. In stanza 1

_____ **a.** The same voice sings throughout

_____ **b.** One voice sings phrases 1 and 3, a second voice sings phrases 2 and 4

_____ **c.** One voice sings phrases 1 and 2, a second voice sings phrases 3 and 4

11. These voices are

_____ **a.** Both female voices

_____ **b.** Both male voices

_____ **c.** One male voice, one female voice

12. Stanza 2 is sung by

_____ **a.** One voice at a time

_____ **b.** Two voices at the same time

_____ **c.** Three voices at the same time

_____ **d.** Four voices at the same time

13. In stanza 2

_____ **a.** The same pair of voices sings throughout

_____ **b.** One pair sings phrases 5 and 6, a second pair sings phrases 7 and 8

14. The first pair of voices in stanza 2 consists of

_____ **a.** Two male voices   _____ **b.** Two female voices

_____ **c.** One male voice, one female voice

15. The second pair of voices in stanza 2 consists of
___ **a.** Two male voices
___ **b.** Two female voices
___ **c.** One male voice, one female voice

16. Stanza 3 is sung by
___ **a.** One voice at a time
___ **b.** Two voices at the same time
___ **c.** Three voices at the same time
___ **d.** Four voices at the same time

17. These voices are
___ **a.** Three female voices
___ **b.** Three male voices
___ **c.** Two female voices, one male voice
___ **d.** Two male voices, one female voice

18. The male voice is relatively
___ **a.** High (tenor)   ___ **b.** Low (bass)

19. Stanza 4 begins with one voice, a solo
___ **a.** Soprano   ___ **b.** Tenor   ___ **c.** Bass

20. The rest of stanza 4 is sung by
___ **a.** Two voices   ___ **b.** Three voices   ___ **c.** Four voices

III. RHYTHM

Answer questions 21 through 25.

21. The meter is
___ **a.** Duple throughout   ___ **b.** Triple throughout
___ **c.** Alternately duple and triple in successive sections

22. The rhythm of the vocal part(s)
___ **a.** Varies greatly from phrase to phrase
___ **b.** Repeats, with some variations, for each phrase throughout the canzonetta
___ **c.** Sometimes repeats, sometimes is completely different

23. The rhythm of the vocal part(s)
___ **a.** Has no relation to that of the poem
___ **b.** Is closely related to, or derives from, the rhythm of the poem
___ **c.** Follows the rhythm of the poem only occasionally

24. The rhythm of each phrase
___ **a.** Begins on an upbeat   ___ **b.** Begins on a downbeat

25. How are the beats grouped in each phrase?
___ **a.** 6 + 6   ___ **b.** 8 + 16   ___ **c.** 4 + 8

IV. CADENCES

Listen to the cadence patterns of the vocal phrases. Answer question 26.

26. In the text above indicate whether each cadence (italic in the text) is open ("O") or closed ("C"). (Use the blanks provided opposite the text.)

V. BASS LINE

As you listen, concentrate only on the bass line, played by the cello and/or the harpsichord. Answer questions 27 through 33.

27. The bass line of instrumental section 1
___ **a.** Ascends   ___ **b.** Descends
___ **c.** Jumps around, then descends
___ **d.** Jumps around, then ascends

28. The bass line of instrumental section 2 is
___ **a.** Completely different than that of section 1
___ **b.** Exactly the same as section 1
___ **c.** Similar to that of section 1 only at the beginning

29. The bass line of instrumental section 3 is
___ **a.** Completely different than that of sections 1 and 2
___ **b.** Exactly the same as that of sections 1 and 2
___ **c.** Similar to that of sections 1 and 2 only at the beginning

153

30. The bass line of phrases 1 and 2 of stanza 1 is
___ **a.** Completely different than the bass line of the three instrumental sections
___ **b.** Exactly the same as that of the three instrumental sections
___ **c.** Similar to that of the three instrumental sections

31. The general direction of the bass line in phrase 1 is
___ **a.** Ascending
___ **b.** Descending
___ **c.** First ascending, then descending
___ **d.** First descending, then ascending

32. The bass line of phrases 3 and 4 of stanza 1
___ **a.** Is like the bass of the instrumental sections
___ **b.** Is like the bass of phrases 1 and 2
___ **c.** Resembles neither of these

33. Fill in the blanks in the table given here, indicating whether the bass line of stanzas 2, 3, and 4 is the same as the bass line of the instrumental sections (mark the blanks "A"); the same as the bass line of stanza 1 (mark the blanks "B"); or different from either of these (mark the blanks "C").

Section	Bass line
Instrumental section 1	A
1	A
2	A
2	A
3	A
Stanza 1, phrases 1 and 2	B
phrases 3 and 4	B
Instrumental section 1	A
Stanza 2, phrases 5 and 6	___
phrases 7 and 8	___
Instrumental section 2	A
Stanza 3	___
Instrumental section 3	A
Stanza 4	___

1. b		**18.** b		**28.** b	
2. c		**19.** a		**29.** c	
3. a		**20.** c		**30.** **a**	
4. b		**21.** a		**31.** c	
5. d		**22.** b		**32.** b	
6. a		**23.** b			
7. b					

24. a (Ámor che deggio far)
(with ↑ ↓ arrows above)

8. c

9. a

25. c
A-mor	che	deggio	far		se
1	2	3	4		

non	mi giova	amar con	pura
1	2	3	4

	fe-		de	
	5	6	7	8

10. c

11. a

12. b

13. b

26.
fede	C	fai	C
crede	O	sai	O
humano	C	aprisse	C
invano	O	morisse	O
scritto	C	verace	C
afflitto	O	pace	C

14. b

15. a

16. c

17. c

27. c

33. Stanza 2, phrases 5–6: B
phrases 7–8: B
Stanza 3, B
Stanza 4, B
(The instrumental sections all have bass line A;
the vocal sections all have bass line B.)

CHAPTER 8   THEME AND MOTIVE IN THE PRESTO OF HAYDN'S SYMPHONY NO. 100

THE ASPECT of pitch organization that is most difficult for the listener is the perception of larger design. You might well be frustrated in trying to apply the sense of harmonic location and direction learned in the relatively small dimensions of a Schubert song to a much larger work. Relationships that seemed clear in the progress from chord to chord or from phrase to phrase would no longer be clear, or even perceptible, amid larger dimensions. The clear melodic lines of the song would be absent, or at best intermittent, separated by long stretches where only harmonic direction was present—and that hard to follow.

Under these conditions the ear must be satisfied with partial or tentative indications of shape. The ear must accept a gap between detail and large design, a gap that will be filled in only by greater familiarity with the work, and then only if the composer has wished to fill in the gap in constructing the work.

WIDE-ANGLE LISTENING. It is, however, this first rough approximation of the shape of a work, that you do most often. Cultivate this kind of listening, and learn not to be discouraged by it, for only if you get something out of a difficult work on first hearing will you be motivated to hear it again. One of the most important listening skills is that of hearing pitch organization with wide-open ears—like taking a picture with a wide-angle lens—so that you grasp something of the whole even while missing most of the parts.

Wide-angle listening is essential in listening to any aspect of music—timbre, texture, rhythm, pitch, or any other; indeed, wide-angle listening logically implies taking in *all* aspects at once, rather than only one. Wide-angle listening needs to be especially emphasized, however, after we have made such a close study of certain specific kinds of pitch relationships in a relatively clear, closed context. Usually pitch relationships are less clear, more complex, and they extend over broader dimensions than those of Schubert's "Der Müller und der Bach"; usually our perception of them will be rougher and more open.

THEME AS LINEAR CLUE. In dealing with Beethoven's Poco sostenuto we found linear factors—a brief melody, a bass line—to be of great assistance in understanding an extended difficult work. The bass line guided the ear through passages that were unstable in harmony. The brief melody set off an interlude from its surroundings and called attention to the stable harmonies and closed harmonic area.

As an additional shaping factor, the brief melody returned in the second interlude. By its return the melody did more than highlight just one stretch of the piece; the return of the melody gave the piece a sense of continuity. In this particular case, the melody was associated with an interlude, while the principal sections had no clear melody. Just as often (and in the example we will study), a clear melody occurs in a principal section as a means of identifying it when it returns. When a melody is used in this or in some

other way to shape a piece, it is called a *theme*—much as the "theme" of an essay is a recurrent idea around which the essay is organized.

A musical theme (speaking roughly) is a group or pattern of pitches with a strong, distinctive identity—strong enough to be recognizable when it returns later in the piece. There are many different kinds of themes —long and short, simple and complex, obvious and obscure. Often a theme is melodic, but a melody is not a theme unless it functions as a theme in a piece.

A line does not have to have a clear, closed shape to be used as a theme; often only a fragment of a clear linear shape, the beginning, say, makes a good theme. Furthermore, not all themes are linear. Some themes are identified by their harmonies, or by their texture, or by their rhythm. Even a distinctive timbre could function as a theme.

The nature of a theme, however, is far less important than its function, its role in the piece. A melody that appears only once is just a melody; a melody that returns at various times during the piece, giving it a larger shape, is a theme. A very simple example is the shape *A B A C A D A*, where *A* is the theme.

A theme is often so short that it cannot, by itself, be a whole section. As mentioned, a theme is often a fragment of a melody, not a whole melody; for that reason the example of a sectional shape *A B A C A D A* is too simple to give an adequate idea of how a theme shapes a larger work. Perhaps one important feature of a theme is that it permits a kind of organization more complex than a simple sectional one.

MOTIVE AND THEME. We will consider themes together with related elements called *motives*—although motives can and frequently do operate quite independently of themes. We have already met rhythmic motives in the Menuetto from Haydn's Symphony No. 100 (Chapter 5); now we will consider melodic or linear motives. The important components of a melodic motive are the direction of its linear shape and the intervals between its pitches. The direction and the intervals always come in some rhythmic shape, of course; but just as we could discuss rhythmic motives somewhat apart from their melodic shape, so we can discuss melodic motives apart from their rhythmic shape.

Indeed, one of the important features of a motive is its aptitude for being dissolved into its components. A theme (speaking roughly again) seems by nature to have the possibility of developing a strong identity; a motive, on the other hand, seems to be destined to lose its identity by breaking down into its constituent rhythms and intervals.

Associated with this difference between themes and motives is the difference in their characteristic roles in the larger design: a theme returns intermittently, providing one kind of strong division in a form; a motive typically appears throughout a shorter or longer passage (or even an entire section or piece), providing the continuity, if not the whole substance, of the music during that passage. These are only general tendencies, of course; a specific example will give a better idea of how themes and motives are used.

Joseph Haydn (1732–1809)
SYMPHONY NO. 100
PRESTO (FINALE)

A good example of themes and motives shaping an overall design is provided by the Finale (last movement) of Haydn's Symphony No. 100. This Finale has a principal theme that returns intact to mark off the largest sections of the movement. The same theme is also a source for the melodic and rhythmic motives that account for much of the content of these sections.

THEMATIC RETURNS. Listen to the Finale two or three times before trying to make up your mind about its overall shape. Start to become familiar with the dimensions of the movement and the variety of things contained in it. You will soon be aware that the theme heard at the very beginning of the movement makes several clear returns.

For a first approximation of the form of the whole movement, take into account only the *exact* returns of the opening theme. These returns are always played softly by the strings, as at the beginning. Near the beginning of the movement, an optional repeat is indicated in the score; and performances differ because of the conductor's choice at that point. The overall pattern of returns of the theme is given in Ex. 8-1 in two versions, one with the optional repeat,

the other without. In the complete version there are five returns, that is, six statements of the theme. We will refer to the six statements as numbered in the complete version.

As shown in Ex. 8-1a, the theme is repeated immediately after it is first stated. This repeat merely emphasizes the theme; it does not shape the movement significantly. Statements 3 and 4, on the other hand, come after intervening, contrasting material played by the tutti; in these statements, the theme starts to emerge as the principal organizing factor in the movement. The theme brings with it a sense of return, of closure, of completion. In statements 3 and 4, the theme starts to function as a theme, instead of just a lighthearted dance tune.

The tutti between statements 2 and 3 (and the identical music between 3 and 4) is longer than the theme; also it is more complex and varied in timbre and structure—as if the composer were telling us not to be misled by the short, simple melody at the beginning, for the movement was going to be much more substantial than that. The promise of substance is made good in the long stretch between statements 4 and 5, a stretch that is disproportionately long compared either to the theme or to the stretch between statements 2 and 3. We will find this very long section in the center of the movement to be the scene of the most intense use of motives derived from the theme.

After a long delay, the theme returns at statement 5 (Ex. 8-1), with the effect of a return to the beginning

after a long digression. Here the theme has a structural function much more weighty than its lighthearted character suggests; certainly the theme could not have the effect it does in statement 5 if it had never appeared in the movement before or had not been so thoroughly prepared. Its appearance at 5 seems to set off everything following statement 4 as a separate entity—what is called the second section in Ex. 8-1.

On first hearing, you probably could not grasp everything between 4 and 5 as a section, for that stretch of the piece is far too varied and complex. Yet even on first hearing, you can grasp something of the effect of the exact returns that frame the section and, through those exact returns, can begin to perceive the larger outlines of the piece. The composer is using the theme as a clue. Later, you may find out some of the more subtle ways in which the theme is related to the rest of the piece. You might even—after close familiarity—decide that there were important aspects of the shape of the piece not suggested by the theme. Nonetheless, in this particular piece, the theme is a primary shaping factor and an obvious one. Since statements 5 and 6 are *exact* repeats, everything else is—to some degree—*different*, and as we have suggested, the perception of this difference should be the first, most basic, perception of the shape of the piece.

Notice how the pitch level of the theme remains the same on each return; the theme is neither higher nor lower when it returns but is at exactly the same

Example 8-1 Haydn, Finale: Return of the theme

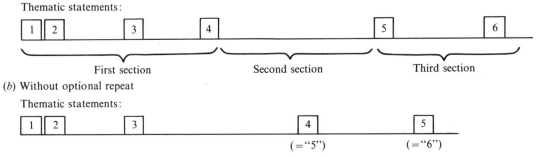

(a) With optional repeat
Thematic statements:

(b) Without optional repeat
Thematic statements:

pitch level. This is easily perceptible through statement 4. Most listeners cannot be sure that a theme returns at the same pitch level when the return occurs after a long interval of time. The returns of the theme at the end of this Finale (statements 5 and 6) are too far removed from the beginning for most people to remember the original pitch level. Subtle shifts in the level of the return could be made without many listeners being aware of it. A listener is most aware of sameness or difference in pitch level in connection with themes or sections that follow one right after another. Where a theme or section returns after intervening material, you may be only vaguely aware of approximate sameness or of difference. The material intervening between statements 2 and 3, and between 3 and 4 is short enough so that the identity of pitch level among these statements can easily be perceived.

PITCH LEVEL OF RETURN. The thematic returns just discussed will seem simple and straightforward; one reason for emphasizing them is to establish a clear idea of what is meant by "exact return" and "same pitch level." When the theme returns in the places just discussed, it is *exactly* the same in all respects, and at *exactly* the same pitch level. There are many possible kinds of return, ranging from exact returns (such as these) through modified returns; inexact, fragmentary, or disguised returns; down to the barest hints of similarity to a theme already heard.

STRUCTURE OF THE THEME. In order to hear more clearly the contrast between the theme and the material that intervenes between its statements, study more closely the inner structure of the theme itself, as you find it at the very beginning of the Finale.

The theme provides a remarkably clear example of alternate open and closed endings. To perceive the open or closed effect of these phrase endings no special analysis is required; the ear reacts to them immediately (Ex. 8-2).

While the effect of open and closed endings will probably be clear, you may have difficulty at first understanding these pitch relationships in terms of the discussion of "Der Müller und der Bach." The principles are the same, but melody and harmony go together in Haydn's theme in a way we have not yet encountered. The basic harmony at the end of phrase 1 (the antecedent) is the leading harmony, even though its sound is covered for a moment by the melody (Ex. 8-3). Similarly, the basic harmony at the end of phrase 2 (consequent) is the central harmony, even though the sound is covered by the melody here, too.

Example 8-4 shows how the melody covers the harmony at the phrase endings; it is a diagram of the linear motion of the melody around its central pitch. This central pitch is the one that emerges most strongly from the central harmony; it sounds in the bass of the central harmony.

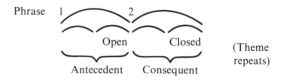

Example 8-2 Haydn, Finale: Open and closed phrases in the theme

APPOGGIATURAS. The long note in the melody at the end of phrase 1 (Ex. 8-4) is the central pitch, and as such it conflicts with the leading harmony sounding below it. The conflict is a graceful one but a conflict nevertheless. In this particular kind of clash, where an accented non-chord tone sounds against a harmony that it does not belong to, the maverick tone is called an *appoggiatura*, an Italian word that means a *leaning* note (from *appoggiare*, "to lean"). Another appoggiatura appears at the end of phrase 2. Both times, the appoggiatura, which is rhythmically long and accented, *resolves* to the pitch below, which is a chord tone in the underlying harmony. The melodic pitch in both cases—the appoggiatura—is unstable relative to the harmony. At the phrase level, the leading harmony at the end of phrase 1 is unstable relative to the central harmony at the end of phrase 2; it is this harmonic relationship that makes the first phrase open, the second closed.

Example 8-3 Haydn, Finale: Harmony in the theme

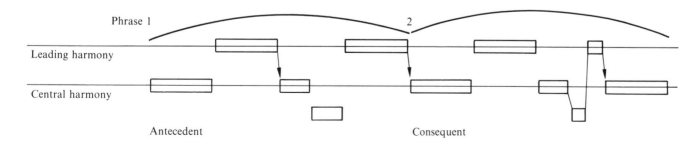

Example 8-4 Haydn, Finale: Melody and harmony in the theme

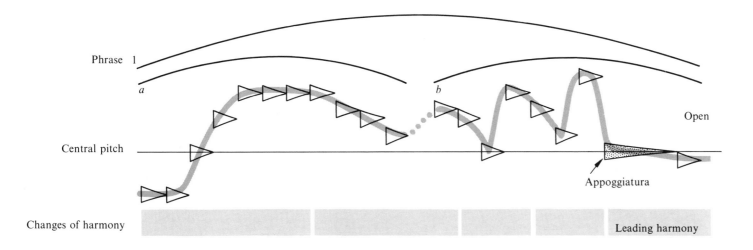

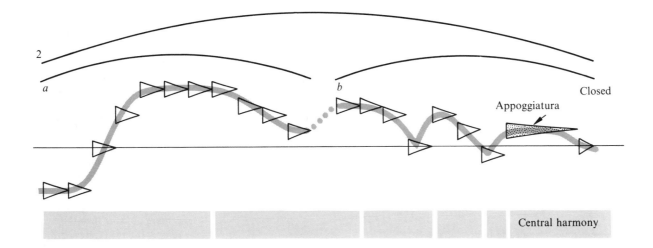

Example 8-5 Haydn, Finale: Meter of the theme

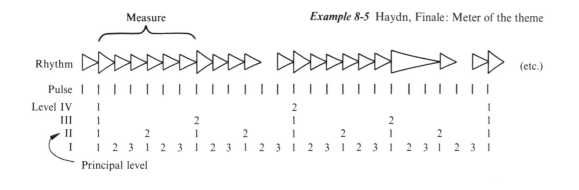

RHYTHM OF THE THEME. The predominant character of the theme is that of a dance tune: its tuneful melodic motion is supported by a lilting rhythm. The rhythm itself is quite regular, corresponding closely to a metric scheme. The fastest pulse is grouped in threes, the threes into twos, which form measures; and the measures make up two-, four-, and eight-measure groups (Ex. 8-5). The rhythmic detail is closely coordinated with the regular phrase structure, as can be seen in a comparison of phrases 1 and 2 (Ex. 8-6). The rests in measures 2 and 6 and the long notes at the beginnings of measures 4 and 8 make it clear that we are dealing with a four-measure phrase whose rhythm is immediately repeated. Then both

Example 8-6 Haydn, Finale: Rhythm in the theme

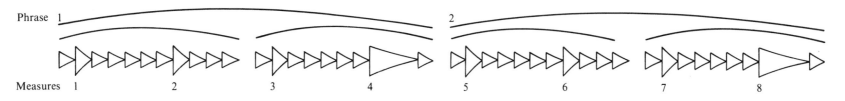

four-measure phrases are repeated again; that is, the music represented in Ex. 8-6 is heard twice in succession.

RELATIONSHIP OF THEME AND FIRST TUTTI. The first tutti, which comes between theme statements 2 and 3 (see Ex. 8-1), contrasts with these surrounding theme statements in many ways. The theme has a very clear harmonic structure (a small set of harmonies, open and closed endings, clear harmonic centers), and an easily recognized melodic shape; hence (as we heard) its return is immediately perceived. The first tutti, on the other hand, does not have such a clear structure, either in melody or in harmony. It is longer than the theme, as well as being more complex and diffuse. The tutti's rhythmic movement, however, is very similar to that of the theme; the differences between theme and tutti, in other words, have more to do with pitch than with rhythm.

The result is that the return of the theme at 3 and 4 is more obvious than the return of the tutti (with the repeat, the tutti between 3 and 4 is the same as the

Example 8-7 Haydn, Finale: Motives in the theme

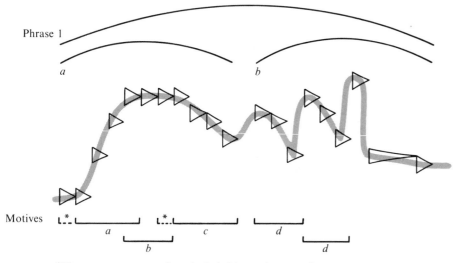

*These notes are sometimes included in motives *a* and *c*.

tutti between 2 and 3). You may not even notice that the second tutti (if performed) exactly repeats the first. The sense of return is attached to the theme: it is the theme that returns to frame the tutti, not the other way around. The predominance of the theme, established at the beginning of the Finale, will be essential to its overall design. This predominance arises in part from the fact that the theme has a clear identity, a closed melodic and harmonic shape. The character of the theme may seem too lighthearted (trivial, even) to assume such importance in a movement. But themes are important not just for what they are, but rather for how they are used.

MOTIVIC DEVELOPMENT IN THE FIRST TUTTI. Even though the first few notes of the tutti recall the theme and even though the tutti continues to remind us of the theme, the material of the theme is transformed by a process called *motivic development*—development that takes place at the motivic level and involves a progressive modification of motives. We will study motivic development in this tutti and in the second section of the Finale (between theme statements 4 and 5). In order to understand a passage of motivic development, you must know where the motives come from and how they are used. Usually, you determine these two things in the reverse order: first, you notice the passage of motivic development; then, on further study, you go back to discover the sources of the motives.

Listen several times from the beginning of the Finale through thematic statement 4, noticing the details of the tutti that recall the theme. As soon as you are convinced that there is some kind of melodic relationship between theme and tutti, it will make sense to study the theme more closely—or from a different point of view—than you did before. At first, the theme sounds so tuneful, so clear and closed, that there is no reason to single out its constituent melodic elements. However, when the tutti starts to single out these elements by the way it uses the theme, we need to pay even more attention to the theme's inner structure. Example 8-7 shows all the pitches of the first phrase of the theme (measures 1 through 4), and labels four groups of pitches as *a*, *b*, *c*, and *d*; these four groups are the source of the melodic material

used in the tutti. Each group can be called a motive.

You could not reliably have picked out these motives before hearing the tutti. Even after hearing the tutti, picking out the motives seems to tear the theme apart in an unreasonable way. Yet this is the way the melodic material for many pieces is derived.

The important thing is that having broken apart the original melodic mold, the composer must get the motives back together into some larger design.

Once you have located motives *a*, *b*, *c*, and *d* in the theme, turn to Ex. 8-8, which is designed to facilitate reference to specific places in the first tutti.

Example 8-8 Haydn, Finale: Motives and clues in the first tutti

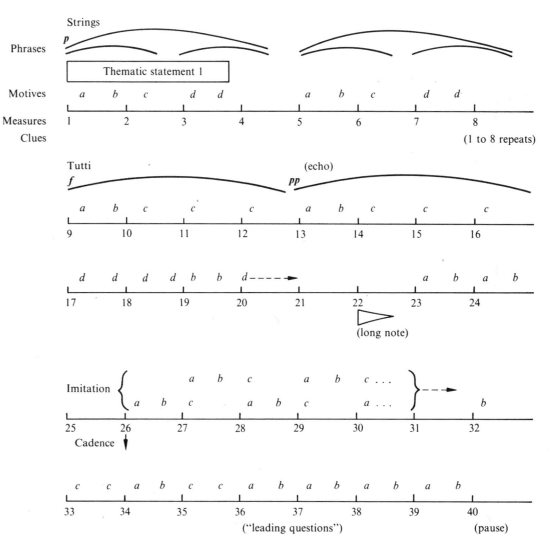

The numbers on the horizontal lines represent measures in the tutti. The theme is given first in order to show how the rhythm is divided into measures. The theme also includes indication of the motives, for reference to Ex. 8-7.

Listen from the beginning of the Finale (going back to the beginning after measure 8 for the repeat of the theme), then continue through the first tutti, following the rhythm measure by measure. The first time through, merely keep track of measures; on subsequent hearings, after you have the rhythm in mind, you will be able to note which motives are sounding in each measure, as indicated in Ex. 8-8 by the letters *a*, *b*, *c*, and *d*.

Your first impression may well be that the resemblance of material in the tutti to motives from the theme is primarily a rhythmic resemblance rather than a melodic one. There is, indeed, one strong rhythmic motion that runs throughout the Finale, and is responsible for many of the similarities between individual motives.

The beginning of the tutti falls into two very clear phrases; the first starts forte, the second—an echo—pianissimo (it is in the strings only). In the forte phrase, motives *a*, *b*, and *c* are joined together as in the theme; then motive *c* is played twice more, extending the phrase. The whole pattern is repeated for the echo. The result is a phrase whose inner structure is very different from the first phrase of the theme. Such *motivic extension* is an important process that sometimes accounts for long stretches of larger works.

After the echo, the tutti resumes with motive *d*. By the process of extension, *d* now appears much further away from *a* than in the theme; but, so far at least, the composer is using the melodic material of the theme, in the order in which it appeared in the theme.

The dotted line ending in an arrowhead in Ex. 8-8 indicates further motivic extension and development. The motivic development here in measures 20 through 23 is minimal; there will be ample opportunity later to study further motivic development in this and other pieces.

When the process begun with *d* has run its course and reached a cadence in measure 26, the music returns to motives *a*, *b*, and *c* (taken together), now treating them in imitation. The lower instruments begin; the upper ones follow. More repetition and extension take place during measures 30, 31, and 32; and, although the motives are not drastically transformed, still the shape of motives *a* and *b* is manipulated so that it serves nicely as a questioning, leading connection ("What happened then?") instead of a beginning.

Following the process of motivic development is often absorbing; but the composer did not intend his piece to be nothing but a treasure hunt for motives. After you have understood the motivic workings of a developmental passage, it is important to free your ear from the level of motivic detail in order to grasp the musical sense of the passage. One good way of doing this is to concentrate on the harmonic context.

HARMONIC MOTION IN THE FIRST TUTTI. The tutti does not move far harmonically from the harmonic area of the theme. In fact, you are not likely to notice the harmonic direction of the tutti as direction but only as a sense of slightly increased tension or excitement. The harmonic movement of the tutti serves the purpose of introducing subtly fresh sound into the Finale and of broadening the harmonic area

Example 8-9 Haydn, Finale, first tutti

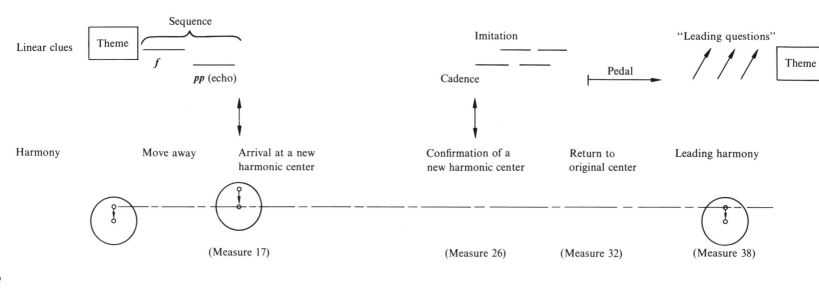

around the theme but not of providing a striking harmonic contrast to it. (Such striking contrasts will come later in the movement.) The main function of the tutti is fulfilled if it helps fix in the ear the harmonic area of the returning theme.

In Ex. 8-9, at the bottom, is represented the harmonic motion from the theme at statement 1 through the tutti to the return of the theme at statement 3. The motion is from one harmonic area to another. We are concerned now, not with motion between individual harmonies, but with motion between *areas*. The areas are represented by circles, each indicating the leading and central harmonies. Technically speaking, a modulation takes place from one area to another and back.

The motion in the first tutti is the same kind encountered in the middle of Schubert's "Der Müller und der Bach": the leading harmony of the first area becomes the central harmony of the second (as shown by the dotted line in Ex. 8-9). You will not hear this relationship, however, except at the moment of transition back to the original area; at that point, the central harmony of the second area is perceptibly transformed into the leading harmony for the return of the theme. The transformation is accomplished through a pedal note that emerges from the second harmonic area, as indicated in Ex. 8-9.

The upper part of Ex. 8-9 shows some of the *linear* clues to the harmonic movement that is indicated abstractly at the bottom. After the theme, the tutti steps away from the original key by means of two phrases in sequence—the opening phrase and its echo. The new key is reached immediately thereafter and is confirmed by the cadence in measure 26.

The imitation on motives *a*, *b*, and *c* begins in the new key, right after the cadence; but motion away from that key follows immediately. The arrival at the leading harmony of the first key (soon to return with the theme) is marked by the use of motives *a* and *b* in what were earlier called "leading questions."

Do not try at first, however, to relate the harmonic motion shown in Ex. 8-9 to the motivic detail of Ex. 8-8. The clues provided in Ex. 8-9 should be sufficient to orient you to the harmonic motion— which is the hardest aspect to follow. After you can tell from the clues where the harmonic changes take place, do not follow even the clues but look only at the representation of harmonic movement at the bottom of Ex. 8-9, in order to fix its sense in your ears.

On your next listening, do not look at the diagram at all but instead try to follow the long curve of the harmonic motion just by ear. You should be able to hear the temporary instability as the music moves away from the theme's harmonic area at the start of the tutti, then the arrival at a new stable area and its confirmation, and finally a smooth return to the area of the theme. This most general sense of the harmonic motion pulls together the changing motivic detail into a coherent musical flow.

SUBDIVISIONS OF THE SECOND SECTION. Between theme statements 4 and 5 comes the longest part of the piece, called "second section" in Ex. 8-1; we need to divide it into shorter, more manageable sections. Several subdivisions present themselves—indeed, one of the problems with the second section is its large number of subsections in a seemingly whimsical

order. Even if we look only for subsections marked off by the theme or by a motive related to the theme, we will still find no one simple solution, for motives from the theme turn up in a number of different contexts throughout the section.

Bearing in mind, then, that the principal features of the second section are a complex structure and an equally complex relationship to the melodic material of the first section, it is expedient to divide the second section into halves, so that the first half ends right after the sudden fortissimo blast from the timpani and the second half begins with the several false starts on the theme immediately following (Ex. 8-10). These false starts are perhaps the most prominent use of the theme (that is, of motives *a*, *b*, and *c*) within the second section; they mark the place where we might most expect to hear a complete return of the theme. We do not get such a return here, of course, for instead the false starts initiate yet another train of events.

MOTIVIC DEVELOPMENT IN THE SECOND SECTION. The following discussion of the second section is concerned with motivic development and uses the same procedures as does the discussion of the first tutti. The second section does not go far before the process of motivic development results in some basically new motives. Here we enter a realm of analysis subject—more than usual—to personal interpretation and disagreement. The intent of the following discussion is to show the most obvious aspects of motivic development in this piece, the aspects that probably guide the ear on the first few hearings; and then to suggest ways in which your own under-

Example 8-10 Haydn, Finale, second section

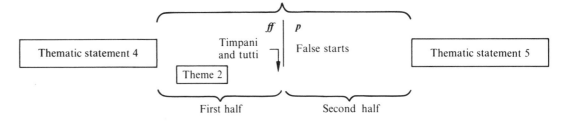

Example 8-11 Haydn, Finale: Development of motives in the second section

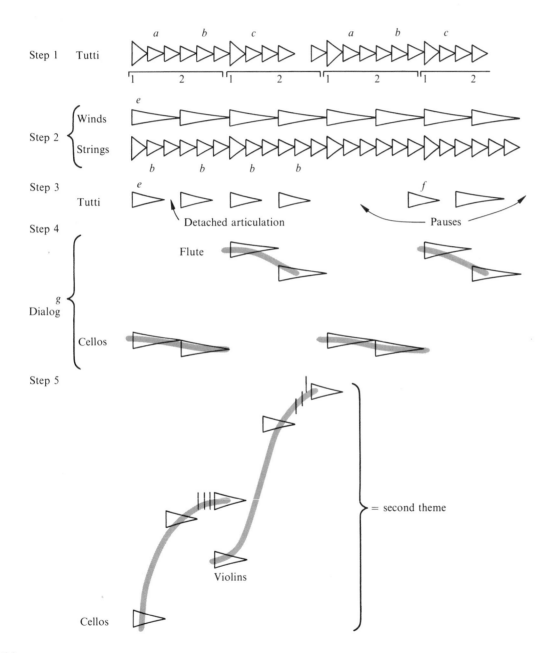

standing of this piece (or a similar piece) might proceed.

In Ex. 8-11, you will find the main steps in motivic development that go on in the first half of the second section. There are five steps indicated here. (Other analyses could result in more or fewer; the continuity between steps is far more important than the number of steps decided upon for discussion.) As in the first tutti, rhythm plays a large part in the motivic development, larger here than before. Read through the following discussion with reference to Ex. 8-11 before you try to find these steps in the music.

Step 1 is just the opening set of motives from the theme. In step 2, the strings extend motive *b* by itself and simultaneously the winds accompany with longer notes. The change is a subtle one and would go unnoticed, if it were not for what happens next. In step 3, the whole tutti plays these longer notes fortissimo; the fastest notes have ceased. Soon even these longer notes are interrupted by pauses, as shown in Ex. 8-11.

If you compare step 3 (with the pauses) directly with step 1 (from the theme), there is no similarity. Yet the music of step 3 grows almost unnoticed from step 1; it would be hard to find any clear sectional division or point of thematic contrast between the passages representing steps 1 and 3. We should, therefore, relate the new motive in step 3 (the longer notes separated by the pauses) to the theme through the process of motivic development; at the same time, we should make clear that the motive did not appear in the original theme. The longer notes are labeled *e* in step 2, *f* in step 3, to show that they are motives derived from the theme, like *a*, *b*, *c*, and *d*.

Step 4 of Ex. 8-11 shows the motive *f* in a new context and sufficiently different to be called *g*: instead of being interrupted by pauses, the motive is played in dialog between flute in a high register and cellos (with basses) in a low register, with accompanying strings between. Motive *g* is far from the original melodic content of the motives; rhythm alone provides the continuity, yet the continuity is strong enough to persuade the ear that all these motives arise from one linear process.

In step 5, the dialog between high and low instruments continues, but another change has taken place. The change is manifest in several ways—in the direc-

164

tion of the melodic motion, which now rises instead of falling as in the measures immediately preceding; in the new animation of the melodic figures with their grace notes; and in the more closed, songlike shape of the resulting melodic line. (This line is the hardest aspect to grasp, for in order to follow it the ear has to hear both parts of the dialog, played now by cellos and violins.)

The melodic material heard in step 5 is sufficiently different from what came before to be designated as a new *theme*, not just a new motive derived from the first theme. It certainly is derived, following upon the previous material as logically as night follows day; but such a result can be called different no matter how logical the connection.

It should be emphasized that we are dealing with only the linear aspect of the whole musical flow. If you hear but little difference between what we call the second theme and the preceding motives, remember that many basic aspects of the music provide a persuasive sense of continuity throughout this whole

section. The rhythm in particular—especially at the lowest level—sweeps along in a way that obscures the kind of subdivision just described. The harmony, too, is moving smoothly, without any changes striking enough to call attention to subdivisions. The changes going on in the melodic structure of the work have the quality of subtle inflections of a basically continuous musical flow.

Look now at Ex. 8-12, which traces the steps in motivic development as they occur in the flow of the music. Follow along the measure numbers in Ex. 8-12 (as in Ex. 8-8), merely to pinpoint the steps in motivic development as indicated. Example 8-12 takes you through the first half of the second section, as you can see from Ex. 8-10.

Motivic development is a remarkable way of organizing a piece or a section of music. The compelling continuity of motivic development (brought about by making many small changes instead of a few large ones) gives a feeling of sameness, of homogeneity, to the section. At the same time, the successive small

changes keep the continuity from becoming uniformity; they allow interesting, expressive inflection to occur in the line anywhere the composer wishes.

Then, too, the successive small changes do eventually result in large differences that form long-range contrasts between the end products of development and the original motives. Finally, motivic development permits these same end products—the result of breaking down an original theme into its smallest particles—to be instantly and convincingly reconstituted into the original theme. Such reconstitution is an effective way of handling a return: it makes the return of the theme, when it eventually comes, seem like the natural outgrowth of the intervening material.

HARMONIC CHANGE IN THE SECOND SECTION. During the second half of the second section (see Ex. 8-10), harmonic changes are much more striking than motivic ones. Very little new motivic material is produced; instead, the motives from the first half of the section appear in an order that sometimes seems

Example 8-12 Haydn, Finale: Development of motives in the second section

Step 1 · Step 2 · Step 3

Measures 49 50 51 52 53 54 55 56 57 58 59 60 61
Fastest notes ▷▷▷▷▷▷▷▷▷ ▷▷▷▷▷▷▷▷▷▷

62 63 64 65 66 67 68 69 70 71 72 73 74
Pause (65) Pause (67) Pause (69) Step 4 · Step 5 = theme 2

75 76 77 78 79 80 81 82 83 84 85 86 87
Theme 2 starts to repeat · Further development of motives *a, b, c*

88 89 90 91 92 93 94 95 96 97 98 99 100

101 102 103 104 105 106 107 108 109 110 111 112 113
Step 3 again, with pauses · Timpani blast · Pause · Second half starts

114 115 116 117 118 119 120 121 122 123 124

capricious, compared to their original order of development. The motives (including one new one—*h*) together with themes, dynamics, and some other indications, are shown in Ex. 8-13; we will refer to this example in tracing the harmonic context—which seems to offer the best approach to the sense of the second half. The principal harmonic shifts are laid out in Ex. 8-14, which you can follow with the music after reading the discussion.

The first false start is in minor; no change of harmonic center takes place, only a color change from major to minor—very noticeable, because the line is that of theme 1, which suddenly loses its lighthearted character for a moment. We hear motives *a*, *b*, and *c* as a question, then repeated as an answer (Ex. 8-13, detail).

Immediately, there is a second question and answer of *a*, *b*, and *c*, now in a major key; but this time a clear shift in harmonic center has taken place. You need not be concerned about where the new harmonic center is; but note that the shift has taken place midway in the second section, in connection with the first reconstitution of theme 1 since the section began. Here, as elsewhere in this piece, important harmonic shifts do not occur arbitrarily or in isolation but are always closely connected to other factors of line or sectional shape.

The answer to the second false start (see Ex. 8-13, detail) leads to a seemingly whimsical return of motive *f*, extended by *a* and *b*; after a single longer note in the strings, theme 2 makes its abrupt, and unexpected, appearance. This statement of theme 2 is especially important because of its remote harmonic location. The shift takes place very abruptly, with a falling melodic motion in the strings. Indeed the harmonic effect, too, is a falling one, as if we had stepped off one level to a lower one. The fall is shown graphically at measure 145 in Ex. 8-14.

The fall to a remote harmonic area is an important feature of the second section and of the whole movement. It contributes a richness of pitch resources without which the movement would incline more toward the trivial nature latent in theme 1. You can compare the effect of this remote key to the effect of that expressive chord in Schubert's "Der Müller und der Bach": there a single chord moved outside the

harmonic area; here a whole group of chords, with its own center, moves outside the group of harmonic areas used in this movement so far. The move takes place at a very high level of harmonic organization—one of the highest you will ordinarily be asked to consider, relating as it does to sections within a movement.

When you listen for this remote area, you should not of course merely listen to the passage containing theme 2 in isolation, for that passage contains only a small group of chords that move around their own clear harmonic center. The point of the shift is the relationship of this center to the preceding centers, and this relationship you can hear only by listening through the whole second section.

When you do this, use theme 2 as a point of comparison; that is what it is there for. In the first half of the second section, theme 2 is a clear expression of the harmonic center established early in the second section. On its return in the second half, theme 2 brings the new remote harmonic center. Try to hold as much of the feeling of the first appearance in your ear as you can, in order to heighten your sense of the remoteness of the return. (If you do this by direct comparison on a recording, you may be surprised at how distant, harmonically, the two statements of theme 2 are from each other.)

The next harmonic shift indicated in Ex. 8-14 (measure 156) merely makes the central harmony into a leading one; coming as it does soon after the previous shift, it may scarcely be noticed. Note, however, that motive *f* has now been given an ascending direction and should be considered another motive, *h* (Ex. 8-13).

After a pause, *h* returns in imitation and in minor instead of major. This change of harmonic color is indicated at measure 166 in Ex. 8-14. Remember that a change in color need not—in this case, does not—involve a change in harmonic area.

There is a mood of uncertainty and expectancy about the music at this pause. The capricious order of things, together with the turn to a distant harmonic area for theme 2, have produced a situation in which we expect something decisive to be done. It is the sort of situation in which a simple return of theme 1 could have a stabilizing effect, but perhaps that would be

too simple under the circumstances. In any case, theme 1 would have a strong closing effect (as we will hear later), and the composer apparently felt the movement should go on longer.

Haydn's solution is bold, yet perfectly logical. By putting motive *h* into minor (without changing the harmonic area) and by using it as the subject of imitation, he creates a mood much more serious than anything in the movement so far. The motivic development assures continuity with what has gone before. The shifts of harmonic area and color give a sense of difference, of remoteness; and the texture of imitation, even though simple, adds a tone of solemnity.

The rest of the second section follows easily, for the most important moment has passed. There is a turn to major, in another harmonic area (measure 174). This shift sounds very easy and natural; unfortunately, it does not seem that way on the diagram, simply because it involves another of those harmonic routes not easily diagrammed in two dimensions. The dotted ascending line in Ex. 8-14 does not mean that a harmonic ascent of striking magnitude has occurred, but only that the harmonic motion would better be pictured going around the back side of a cylinder (as in Ex. 7-25).

From here to the end of the section, the harmonic movement drops by easy stages, through the dialog for flute and cellos, to reach the "leading questions" (borrowed from the first tutti) and with them the leading harmony of the original harmonic area. The second section ends with an open cadence; in other words, it ends not just preparing for but demanding the return of the original area along with the return of theme 1.

In its large design, the second section has made an economical use of motivic development and harmonic shifts. The motivic development of the first half has produced several new motives and a new theme. Harmonic shifts, kept to a minimum during this development, have been used to throw themes and motives into sharper relief in the second half. Drastic harmonic shifts have been concentrated in a relatively small area right after the beginning of the second half, where they satisfy the need for fresh sound and establish a point of maximum departure

Example 8-13 Haydn, Finale, second half
of the second section

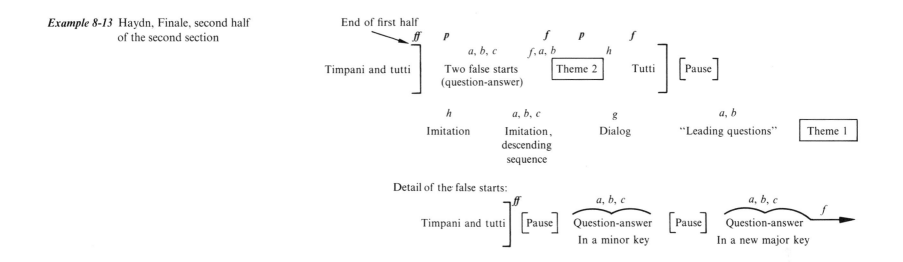

Detail of the false starts:

Example 8-14 Haydn, Finale: Harmonic motion in the second half of the second section

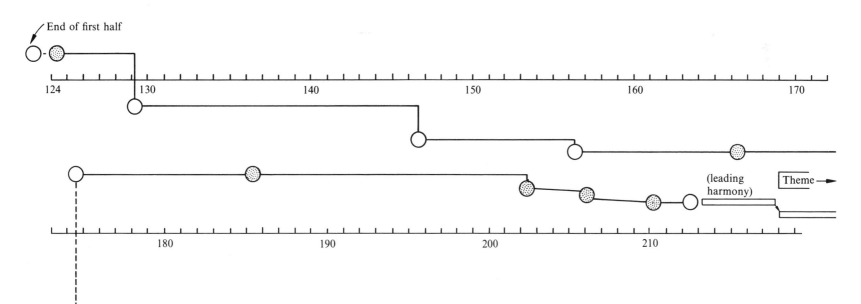

in preparation for the long slide back to the harmonic center of the movement.

THE THIRD SECTION. Since the third section serves to conclude the movement, it is structured differently than the second section. Framed by two exact returns of theme 1, the third section has no motivic development of importance; it does, however, have one more striking harmonic departure (Ex. 8-15).

After the return of theme 1 comes a tutti. At least, a tutti is started, but soon it becomes soft and dark. The usual rhythmic figuration disappears, its place taken by a new rhythm involving relatively long notes. There seems to be little or no motivic relation to anything preceding (though possibly this is a further development of *e*). The effect is strangely like the solemn moment of imitation in the second section—strangely, because of the lack of explicit melodic similarity. Underlying the effect is a move to a remote harmonic area, confirmed by the loud tutti (*a* and *b* in imitation) that follows.

A gradual return to the original key is accomplished, using an extension of the "leading questions" motive. The reestablishment of the original harmonic center is celebrated by the return of theme 2. Eventually the last exact return of theme 1 appears, and the movement soon ends.

The third section can be used as another exercise in hearing departures into remote harmonic areas and may be easier to follow in this respect than the second section. Starting with the exact return of theme 1 (Ex. 8-15), listen through to theme 2; in this section, themes 1 and 2 are in the same key, while almost everything between is a harmonic digression. You should hear clearly the entry into the remote harmonic area and the gradual emergence from it, culminating in theme 2.

With that much firmly in mind, do not neglect to listen to the whole movement, remembering on one hand the identity of theme 1 in its six exact appearances and on the other the appearances of theme 2 in three different harmonic locations (Ex. 8-16).

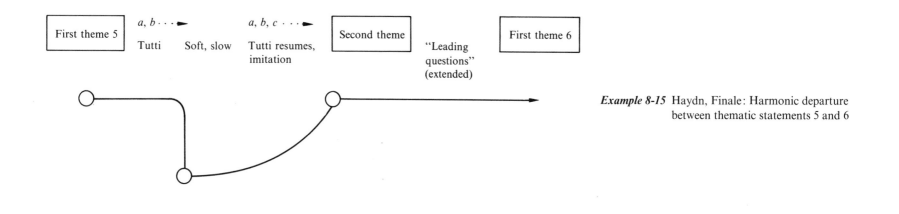

Example 8-15 Haydn, Finale: Harmonic departure between thematic statements 5 and 6

Example 8-16 Haydn, Finale: Harmonic positions of first and second themes

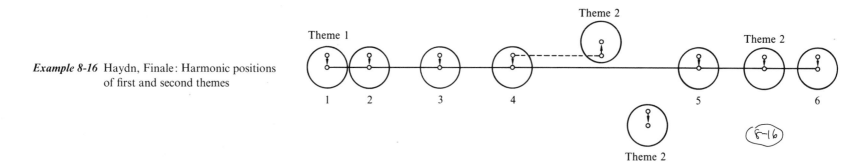

168

Exercises for further listening

BEETHOVEN: SYMPHONY NO. 7, ALLEGRO CON BRIO (LAST MOVEMENT)

Listen to the entire movement, following the diagram of sections given here, in order to locate the various statements of the opening motive.

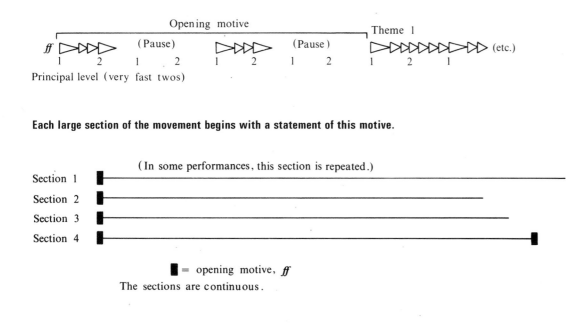

Each large section of the movement begins with a statement of this motive.

The first theme, which immediately follows the opening motive, contains four phrases. Listen to the first statement of this theme. Answer questions 1 through 13.

1. The melodic shape of phrase 2
___ **a.** Is essentially the same as that of phrase 1
___ **b.** Differs considerably from that of phrase 1

  1. a

2. The melodic shape of phrase 3
___ **a.** Is essentially the same as that of phrase 1 (and 2)
___ **b.** Differs considerably from that of phrase 1 (and 2)

  2. b

169

3. The melodic shape of phrase 4
_____ **a.** Is essentially the same as that of phrase 3
_____ **b.** Differs considerably from that of phrase 3

4. The rhythmic detail of the theme
_____ **a.** Varies considerably from phrase to phrase
_____ **b.** Is similar in each phrase

5. The rhythm of the opening motive
_____ **a.** Is related to the rhythm of theme 1
_____ **b.** Is not related to the rhythm of theme 1

6. As you listen to theme 1, tap two fast beats per measure; count the number of measures in each phrase of the theme. Phrases 1 and 2 have _____ measures each; phrases 3 and 4 have _____ measures each.

7. In the middle of the first phrase of theme 1, the melody (in the violins)
_____ **a.** Leaps downward   _____ **b.** Leaps upward
_____ **c.** Does not contain a leap

8. Phrases 1 and 2 each end
_____ **a.** Harmonically open   _____ **b.** Harmonically closed

9. Phrases 3 and 4 each end
_____ **a.** Harmonically open   _____ **b.** Harmonically closed

10. Listen carefully to the bass line of theme 1. Throughout phrases 1 and 2, until the cadence, the bass line
_____ **a.** Leaps around   _____ **b.** Doubles the violin melody
_____ **c.** Repeats a single note

11. This repeated bass note (pedal) is most closely related to
_____ **a.** The central harmony, with a feeling of harmonic closure
_____ **b.** The leading harmony, with a feeling of harmonic incompleteness

12. In the bass line of phrases 3 and 4
_____ **a.** The same pedal note is heard as that in phrases 1 and 2
_____ **b.** Another pedal note is heard
_____ **c.** There is no pedal note

3. a (the melodic shape of the theme is therefore _a a b b_)

4. b

5. a

6. Eight, eight (each of the four phrases contains 8 measures)

7. b

8. b

9. b

10. c

11. b

12. c

13. Throughout theme 1, the rhythm of the bass line 13. a
___ **a.** Emphasizes the accented offbeats (1 *2* 1 *2*)
___ **b.** Emphasizes the metrical downbeats (*1* 2 *1* 2)
___ **c.** Is the same as the rhythm of the melody (violin line)

Listen in turn to each section of the movement, concentrating on identifiable appearances of theme 1, rather than on motivic fragments of the theme. Answer questions 14 through 23.

14. Is there a further statement of theme 1 in section 1? 14. No
___ Yes ___ No

15. Is there a complete statement of theme 1 anywhere in section 2? 15. Yes
___ Yes ___ No

16. In section 2, the complete statement of theme 1 occurs 16. b
___ **a.** Immediately after the opening motive
___ **b.** Somewhere in the course of the section (other than at the beginning or the end)
___ **c.** At the end of the section

17. This complete statement of the theme 17. b
___ **a.** Is in the same harmonic area as the statement in section 1
___ **b.** Is in a different harmonic area than the statement in section 1

18. At the outset of section 2, an incomplete appearance of theme 1 occurs just after the opening 18. a
motive. It consists of various statements of
___ **a.** The first half of phrase 1 ___ **b.** The last half of phrase 1
___ **c.** The first half of phrase 3 ___ **d.** The last half of phrase 3

19. In section 3, immediately after the opening motive, 19. b
___ **a.** There is a complete statement of theme 1
___ **b.** There is a partial statement of theme 1
___ **c.** There is a theme other than theme 1

20. This partial statement of theme 1 consists of 20. a
___ **a.** Phrases 1 and 2 only (*a a*) ___ **b.** Phrases 1 and 3 only (*a b*)
___ **c.** Phrases 3 and 4 only (*b b*)

21. The harmonic area of this statement 21. a
___ **a.** Is the same as that of theme 1 in section 1
___ **b.** Is the same as that of the complete statement of theme 1 in section 2
___ **c.** Is different from either of these

171

22. Is there another recognizable statement of theme 1 in section 3?   **22.** No
___ Yes
___ No

23. Is there a complete statement of theme 1 in section 4?   **23.** No
___ Yes
___ No

Listen to the entire movement, section by section, following the appearances of the various themes. On the sectional diagram above indicate the approximate placement of each of the statements of theme 1. Answer questions 24, 25, and 26.

24. In section 2 the order in which the various themes appear   **24.** b
___ **a.** Is essentially the same as that in section 1
___ **b.** Differs considerably from that in section 1

25. In section 3, the order in which the various themes appear   **25.** a
___ **a.** Closely resembles that of section 1
___ **b.** Closely resembles that of section 2
___ **c.** Differs considerably from that of sections 1 and 2

26. In section 4, the order in which the various themes appear   **26.** d
___ **a.** Closely resembles that of section 1
___ **b.** Closely resembles that of section 2
___ **c.** Closely resembles that of section 3
___ **d.** Differs considerably from that of sections 1, 2, and 3

QUESTIONS FOR DISCUSSION

A. How many distinct themes are there? Which sections or parts of sections are dominated by the material from a single theme?

B. Which seem more stable harmonically, the thematic passages or the motivic passages?

C. Where do you hear motivic material derived from the first measure of theme 1? From the upward leap in the first phrase of theme 1? From the bass line of theme 1 (and from its rhythmic shape)?

D. Is the fourth section of the Allegro con brio essentially thematic or motivic in character? Is it relatively stable or unstable harmonically? What part does the leading-harmony pedal play?

E. How does the motivic treatment contribute to the sense of rhythmic excitement?

IN WORKING with Haydn's Finale, we were guided to a great extent by linear aspects—themes, motives, and their development. We followed the direction of the harmonic motion, taking note of the harmonic areas, as well as some of the relationships among them. The Vivace (first movement) from Bartók's Quartet No. 6 makes use of harmonic areas and centers, but they are established in ways different from those used in Haydn's Finale. The Vivace also has a well-developed system of themes and motives to guide us through its shape. This system has its starting point in the Mesto and Pesante that were discussed in the chapters on texture and line.

CHAPTER 9 THEME AND MOTIVE IN THE VIVACE OF BARTOK'S STRING QUARTET NO. 6

HARMONIC CONTEXT. Bartók's harmonic context is different from Haydn's or from Schubert's in that Bartók's individual harmonies seem more complex; indeed, they often are more complex: if we were to study their internal construction we could discover the factors that make them so. Compared to Haydn's harmony, Bartók's will sometimes seem ambivalent. You will not often hear in Bartók the same clear sense of harmonic direction found in Haydn. For example, you will not often hear the particular kind of harmony we called a leading harmony. A sense of direction is by no means absent from Bartók's harmony, but it is a kind of direction much more apparent to hindsight than foresight. Often you will arrive at a point in Bartók's music with the feeling that everything before has led cogently to that point; yet each harmony along the way could have led in several directions equally well.

SECTIONS IN THE FIRST MOVEMENT. As for its overall shape, the Vivace with its Mesto introduction is a complex, challenging piece; but it moves in an easily understood rhythm that drives us or swings us over the initial obscurities. The low-level meter is the same—in pulse and grouping—as that of Haydn's Finale, although with more irregularities and changes of tempo.

Listen straight through the Mesto and Vivace a few times with the help of Ex. 9-1, noting some purely rhythmic breaks that divide the movement into its longest sections. As already mentioned, the

Pesante and the beginning of the Vivace are marked by stop-and-go phrasing, with several short melodic groups set off from each other by pauses (see Chapter 3). Once the swift forward motion of the Vivace is established, it sometimes fluctuates but rarely stops, and usually a stop marks an important division. These divisions are indicated schematically in Ex. 9-1. The divisions, however, are less clear than they might be because one break tends to be followed immediately by another; two or three

breaks in relatively quick succession, instead of just one, are used to mark off one section from another.

The indentations two-thirds of the way along the diagram of section 1 of the Vivace (Ex. 9-1) indicate slightly longer notes that you may take to be the end of the section. Continue past them until you hear the forward motion slacken noticeably, then listen for a high, held note in the violins, with a relaxed chord touched lightly below in the viola and cello; a long pause follows. This marks the end of the first section.

Example 9-1 Bartók, Vivace

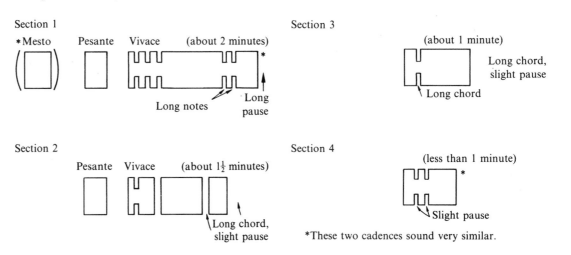

(As an aid in identification of this point, you can listen first to the very end of the movement, where similar texture, rhythm, and harmony appear.)

The break at the end of this first long section is the clearest in the movement; the breaks that follow are less clear, partly because the pauses are not so long. The second section begins much like the first, with stop-and-go phrases beginning *pesante* ("heavily").

A high, long, soft chord followed by a pause is the first of two breaks that mark the end of the second section; in the next break following soon after, the chord has low as well as high pitches. After the third section is under way, there is a third pause, less pronounced.

The end of the third section and the beginning of the fourth are marked by another high chord, this time forte. From here to the end of the movement, the rhythm is less continuous: there are at least two clear pauses, and you may feel there are more, depending upon the performance. The rhythmic motion slackens in preparation for a quiet, leisurely conclusion.

THEMES AND MOTIVES. Themes and motives play important roles in the shape of the movement. The themes, on the one hand, may seem less easy to hear and identify—on first as well as on subsequent appearances—in comparison with those in Haydn's Finale. Motives, on the other hand, are even more in evidence than in Haydn's Finale; you may find the motivic development to be the most absorbing, persuasive aspect of the work, the aspect that gives you the easiest access to its essentially lyric flow.

Not all the motives have their source in the themes of the Vivace, incidentally; ahead of the Vivace stands the Mesto, the beautiful melody we studied in Chapter 6, and the origin of much of the motivic material of the movement is found in the Mesto.

FIRST AND SECOND THEMES. Two principal themes guide us through the Vivace. The first of these is heard in its most complete form at the beginning of the Vivace, played by the solo violin. It becomes apparent during the first few hearings that this theme consists of the same pitches as the melody of the first violin in the Pesante, only played faster. That melody in turn has grown out of the Mesto. In fact, the linear continuity at the motivic level is so prominent here that it may at first prevent you from identifying the theme as a distinct entity. The stop-and-go phrasing at the start of the Vivace helps set off statements of the theme.

As shown in Ex. 9-2, the theme is stated here three times; the second time it is slightly altered, the third time *inverted*. After the third statement and a pause, the rhythm surges forward; from here on, the theme tends to get lost in the thicker texture. It is still there, however, lending homogeneity by its presence and occasionally coming to the surface, either in its original form or inverted.

Not quite halfway through section 1, the tempo slows for a moment; and, without a real pause or break, a second theme appears, played by the first violin over a more sustained accompaniment (including a pedal). This second theme has a distinctive rhythm and melody—more songlike but with a

Phrase 1

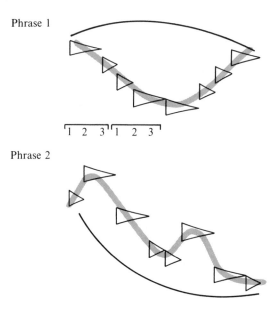

Phrase 2

Example 9-3 Bartók, Vivace, second theme

curious rhythmic twist (Ex. 9-3). The rhythm is characterized by long and short notes in an alternating order—long-short, short-long; then in phrase 2, short-long, long-short. The linear shape of phrase 1 is a simple descent plus ascent, returning to the point of origin. Phrase 2 has a melodic sequence, with a shape reminiscent of the sequence in the Mesto (see Ex. 6-4). After phrase 2, as the pedal continues, the theme's graceful lilt can still be felt; but the melody is harder to follow. The beginning of the theme remains its most distinctive part.

Example 9-2 Bartók, Vivace, first theme

(*a*) First statement   (*b*) Second statement—altered   (*c*) Third statement—inverted

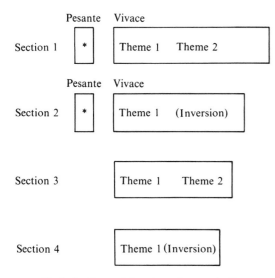

*Includes theme 1 in a tense harmonization

Example 9-4 Bartók, Vivace: Thematic statements

The second theme, like the first, is relatively compact. It, too, exercises a latent influence that extends all the way to the pause at the end of the first section.

Once introduced in the first section, these two themes reappear at decisive points in sections 2, 3, and 4, guiding the musical discourse (Ex. 9-4). To summarize briefly these reappearances, theme 1 is stated at the beginning of section 2 and is developed thereafter, in both normal and inverted forms. Theme 2 is not stated in section 2 (although a fragment of its second phrase is used, in a new context). In section 3, both themes appear, in the same order and relative position as in section 1; but there is less space between them. Section 4 has two clear statements of theme 1 (one being inverted) and only hints of theme 2. These hints, as well as many other references to the themes occurring throughout the movement, are not shown in Ex. 9-4, which shows only the clearest thematic statements.

Thematic statements are more prominent in sections 1 and 3. Especially in these sections, the thematic statements function as relatively stable areas amid the flux and rhythmic surge characteristic of the movement generally. That is to say, the composer arranges a stable area as an effective presentation of his theme, to make sure the theme is clearly established as a point of departure—and eventually as a point of return.

If a theme is presented in an unstable area, it may not catch your attention right away. For example, you notice the first theme when played by the first violin alone at the beginning of the Vivace (Ex. 9-4); but, as pointed out, this same line is played by the first violin in the Pesante just before—there, however, over a series of increasingly tense, unstable harmonies. You probably do not notice this line in the Pesante until it is pointed out, and even then the statement in the Pesante never has the sense of clear, bright focus found at the beginning of the Vivace. The Vivace statement seems to be at once the point of arrival of everything before and the point of departure for what follows.

Listen through from the first theme to the second theme, in order to hear how the second theme, too, seems relatively stable. Even after its clear, songlike phrases cease, the pedal continues underneath, maintaining the harmonic stability. As long as the pedal lasts, the music seems to stay in one place—even though that place may be expressed in relatively complex or ambivalent harmonies.

BETWEEN THE TWO THEMES. If you can hear that theme 2 is relatively stable, you have also sensed the relative instability of the music between theme 2 and theme 1. The new melody can be regarded as the outward sign of the inner change in harmonic movement—a change from unstable to stable, in a new harmonic area. These changes are sketched in Ex. 9-5.

With themes 1 and 2 as reference points, you can follow the movement between in terms of ascending and descending pitch, using linear clues as you did in following the movement through the unstable portions of Beethoven's Poco sostenuto (Ex. 7-9). Example 9-6 shows detailed indications of the three statements of theme 1 at the beginning of the Vivace—the first clear and stable, the second moving away, the third inverted.

A rhythmic surge follows the inversion of the

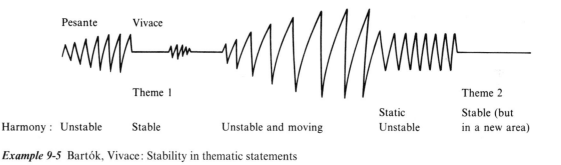

Example 9-5 Bartók, Vivace: Stability in thematic statements

Example 9-6 Bartók, Vivace, from theme 1 to theme 2

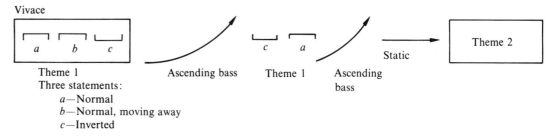

theme; the bass line can be heard working its way slowly but methodically upward. The upward motion is the main component—and the most obvious one—in the direction of this passage. Once you have grasped the basic thrust of a passage such as this, you will be able to follow many parts of Bartók's quartet that may at first have seemed hopelessly complex in their harmonies.

The end of the first ascent in the bass line is marked by an inversion of the theme in the first violin. The effect of this and other thematic references that follow the ascent is obscured by the fact that they are not made in prominent solos, but amid thick textures with competing lines. The inverted statement is followed immediately by a normal one (*c*, then *a* in Ex. 9-6). During the normal statement, the bass has already started another ascent; this ascent moves faster and is over sooner.

After the second ascent comes a kind of passage often found in this quartet: the linear motion becomes static; the cello keeps returning to the same pitch with the effect of an intermittent pedal; the upper parts also seem to reiterate pitches or circle around the same pitch. (The rhythm, too, is repetitive and insistent.) Lacking a sense of linear ascent or descent, the passage does not, on the other hand, contain a clear thematic statement such as that at the beginning of the Vivace or as in theme 2, which follows. The passage has instead a sense of anticipation; it is preparing, in fact, for theme 2.

ASCENTS AND DESCENTS AFTER THEME 2. The passage after theme 2 to the end of section 1, like the passage between the two themes, can best be understood by following its linear clues—especially those that indicate ascending or descending motion. Such motion here is very clear, since it is expressed, not just in one line, but often in all four lines at once. As shown in Ex. 9-7, the ascents and descents come in pairs: the overall motion is up, then down; up, then down, with a brief ascent at the end.

Theme 2 ends fortissimo (a few moments after the end of the pedal note); a soft, very fast, agitated passage starts the first ascent in Ex. 9-7. This ascent moves upward by very small stages, with semitone motion predominating in all lines. Soon all reach a

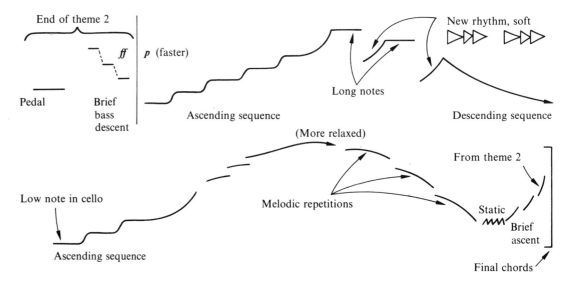

Example 9-7 Bartók, Vivace, first section after theme 2

single long high note—the note you might earlier have taken as the conclusion of section 1 (see Ex. 9-1). This high note is followed by a clear long-short-long rhythm in all parts, and the whole group of several measures is repeated sequentially at a lower pitch. The descent continues in a more complex texture, reaching finally the very bottom of the cello's range.

The second ascent is less straightforward, more involute. Its climax is perhaps not so strikingly marked; but it is clear enough, since it is followed by a general broadening and relaxation of rhythm and loosening of texture during the subsequent descent. As the texture thins out, the lines increase their tendency to go their several ways: the descent is finally evident only in the bass line, while the upper parts begin to seek a central pitch upon which to rest, their linear motion becoming more static. The section ends with a brief ascent to the last high chord.

Throughout the first section there are three kinds of passages—clear thematic statements, passages marked by strong linear ascents or descents, and static passages. These three kinds seem to show a clear sense of function relative to one another. The

ascents and descents are often used to extend a thematic statement; a static passage often introduces one. Even without grasping the harmonies, you can approximate their functional significance and follow the sense of the movement by interpreting carefully these linear clues.

CLIMAX IN THE SECOND SECTION. In the second section, theme 2 does not make an appearance in the clear, distinct way it did in the first section. Theme 1, however, is almost continually present one way or another. Superimposed upon static or moving passages, various forms of theme 1 shape the section and with it the movement as a whole. Section 2 leads up to a climax, then recedes from it; this climax has a force that extends all the way to the end of the movement.

The second section is set off at its beginning by a pesante passage similar to the one near the beginning of the movement. Next comes a statement of theme 1 by the cello and viola together, but now in a thicker texture. After the long chord and pause, there begins a static passage far more extended than any in the first section (Ex. 9-8). Cello and violin repeat short figures over and over again, with no ascent or descent or any kind of long-range pitch change. Such repetition is often called *ostinato* (Italian, "obstinate"); that is, a figure so repeated is an ostinato figure.

Against the ostinato, the other instruments play fragments from theme 1, not as clear thematic statements, but rather as part of a process of motivic development to be discussed later. Even though the fragments show linear motion, they do not interfere seriously with the overall static nature of the passage.

When the ostinato ceases—or, better, gives way to a pizzicato accompaniment figure—long ascents and descents resume their function as guides to the linear progress of the section. Successive statements of theme 1 are extended up, then down, by individual instruments, as shown in Ex. 9-8.

After four complete ascents and descents (and one abortive start), the music rises to a peak of intensity, achieving a climax by a clarification of what has taken place. At first, it seems as though theme 1 is merely being extended to form a descent; but, as the violins frenetically repeat the descent by itself, it becomes clear that the descent is actually the inversion of the theme. The climactic repetition of the descent is a modified statement of that inversion, so that again a thematic statement functions as a point of arrival. The climax is followed immediately by a short, harsh passage dominated by slides in the violin and viola, serving as the dissolution of what came before and clearing the way for a new start.

The rest of the second section is static; what motion there is does not lead decisively anywhere, and the linear directions in individual instruments do not seem strong enough to override the repetitions in the accompanying instruments. Only at the end of the section is there a brief rise, and that soon reaches the long, held chord that closes the section.

The prevailing motion of the first section was one of ascent (in spite of the descents used in preparation for the end of the first section). The second section, too, after its initial static passage, is dominated by the long rise to the climax. So strong is the climax that it seems to be a watershed in the movement as a whole: no more impressive ascent can be imagined to follow it. Instead, it seems only natural that from here on the movement should descend—in its overall gradient— to its conclusion.

THE THIRD AND FOURTH SECTIONS. With this in mind, it is easier to understand the changes made in the third section that differentiate it from the first (Ex. 9-9). Static passages replace the ascents that characterized the first section. The new static passage interpolated before theme 2 is a striking example of the kind of movement that now dominates the third section; the static passage replaces an ascent of the first section. The statements of theme 1 are less clear, less decisive (the inversion is absent completely). On the other hand, the statement of theme 2 emphasizes —far more than the previous statement—the tendencies of this theme to close in on itself. The openness and ascending thrust of the first half of the movement are replaced throughout the third section by closed or static shapes.

An even more specific example of the change in movement is provided by the passage that follows theme 2: originally an ascent, this passage is now a descent, the material simply being inverted (Ex. 9-9). The ascending material that occurred subsequently in the first section is reduced to a minimum. Curiously, the descending material is also eliminated—partly to condense the ending, partly to facilitate a reiteration of the high, long note (Ex. 9-9) that acts as the close of the section.

In terms of linear clues, the fourth, final, section is diffuse and indeterminate. A clear thematic statement of the inversion of theme 1 is the most identifiable event. The long-range thrust of the Vivace has come to rest during the third section; what follows in the fourth seems to be reflection and afterglow.

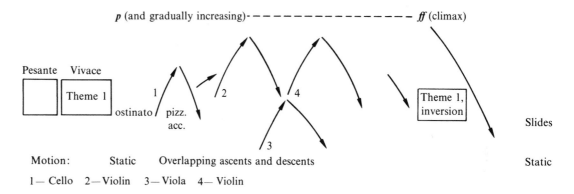

Example 9-8 Bartók, Vivace: Linear clues in section 2 (through climax)

Example 9-9 Bartók, Vivace: Sections 1 and 3 compared

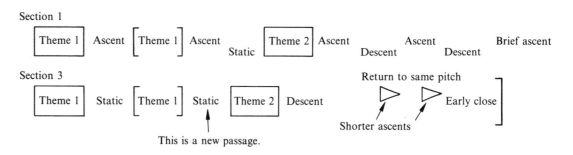

Example 9-10 Bartók, Vivace: Steps in the development of the first theme

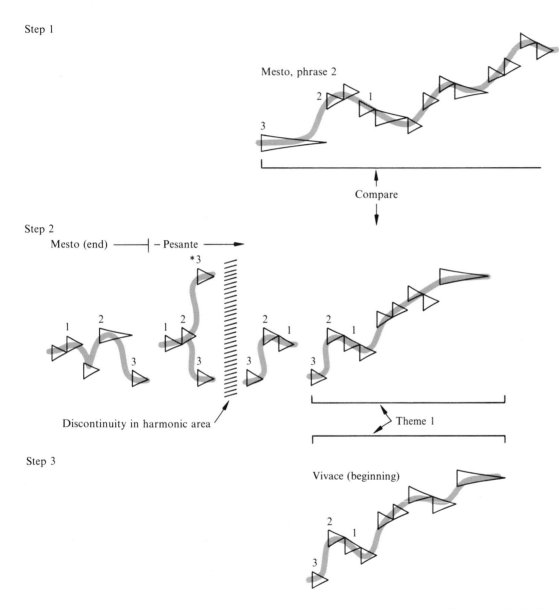

Step 1

Mesto, phrase 2

Compare

Step 2

Mesto (end) ——————|— Pesante —————→

Discontinuity in harmonic area

Theme 1

Step 3

Vivace (beginning)

*The two simultaneous 3's are an octave apart. Other changes of register have been eliminated and rhythmic values simplified in order to show similar shapes of theme and motive.

MOTIVES IN THE FIRST MOVEMENT. Bartók's quartet is rich in motivic development. Derivation of motives from themes and interrelationships among motives and systems of motives can be traced from one end of the quartet to the other. We will not follow the motivic processes throughout the first movement but will concentrate on only a few passages in order to identify the principal motives in some of their characteristic roles.

The first theme of the Vivace is itself a product of motivic development. This process starts in the Mesto. When we discussed the Mesto as melody, we took no account of its motivic possibilities, since these become apparent only later, within the rest of the movement; now that we are concerned with the rest of the movement, we need to return to the Mesto as the source of some important material.

Example 9-10 shows steps in the formation of the first theme. Step 1 is the beginning of the second phrase of the Mesto (see Ex. 6-7). Step 2 includes the last notes of the Mesto, and all of the Pesante that follows. Step 3 is theme 1, in its first statement.

As far as the theme is concerned, Ex. 9-10 shows nothing that cannot be heard fairly easily. As shown at the end of step 2 and in step 3, theme 1 is played heavily (Pesante) just before it is played quickly and lightly (Vivace). The harmonization of the theme in the Pesante may obscure it at first but not after the theme has once been heard clearly. With these two statements of the theme in mind, you can hear the similarity to the second phrase of the Mesto (step 1), which has more pitches but the same basic shape.

The motivic relationships shown at the beginning of step 2 are only slightly more difficult to follow. The last two pitches of the Mesto (rhythmically very prominent) are repeated as the second and third pitches of the Pesante; these pitches are labeled 2 and 3 in Ex. 9-10. They are preceded in the Pesante by the pitch labeled 1, which is also prominent in the end of the Mesto, as indicated. In effect, the Pesante begins with a more concise repetition of the last group of the Mesto.

Two pitches labeled 3 are given at the beginning of the Pesante. The lower of these follows the melodic shape—the falling leap—found in the Mesto;

the upper 3 is the same pitch in the next higher octave (played by violins). In providing a transition from the monophonic Mesto, the Pesante begins with all instruments in unison pitch, then gradually spreads into parts and a chordal texture. The two 3's an octave apart are the first split in the monophonic texture. The line may seem to have a different shape at that point.

Next, a sharp pitch discontinuity occurs, due to a radical shift in harmonic area. We have not discussed harmonic areas in this piece (except to imply their ambiguity in the Mesto), and you are not likely to hear the shift as such. You should, however, be aware of the sharp discontinuity at the point indicated; and eventually you should hear how the first three pitches in the Pesante belong with the end of the Mesto, while the fourth and following pitches belong with the rest of the Pesante—especially since the pitches on each side of the discontinuity are heard more than once.

On the other hand, the shape—as opposed to the pitch content—of the fourth, fifth, and sixth notes clearly has something to do with that of the first three notes. As indicated by the numbers, the three pitches after the discontinuity reproduce the interval structure of the three pitches before the discontinuity, only in reversed, or *retrograde*, order. The second motive is said to be the retrograde of the first (taking the lower 3 as the important one; if we took the upper 3, the retrograde would be partly inverted). Retrogrades are not inherently audible, but this one is so short and simple that you can sense a motivic kinship even if you do not hear the literal retrograde.

Theme 1, then, is related to the Mesto in two separate ways. As a theme it is a modified form of phrase 2 of the Mesto (step 1); it is also the product of motivic development from the end of the Mesto (step 2). One could go on to derive the last interval of the Mesto from the first interval of phrase 2, thus joining the two relationships together.

Theme 1 is the immediate source for much of the motivic material of the first movement. So pervasive is this material—especially the first three notes of the theme (numbered 3, 2, 1 in Ex. 9-10)—that pointing out all their appearances would be far too lengthy to do here.

An idea of the way motives from the first theme are used can be gained from the passage between themes 1 and 2. Almost all the material in fast notes in this passage is directly derived from theme 1. At the end of the passage (in the static place just before theme 2; see Ex. 9-6), the head motive of theme 1 appears in longer notes too, accented and very prominent. Motivic extension, then, provides a strong sense of continuity throughout the beginning of the Vivace (up to the second theme). If you can hear both the motivic extension and the accented motivic statement, you will have a good grasp of the passage in spite of its harmonic complexities.

The soft, agitated passage immediately following the second theme is one of those derived from the introductory Mesto; Ex. 9-11 shows this motivic relationship. The motive shown in Ex. 9-11 dominates much of the music up to the end of the first section, appearing in several forms. The use of this motive makes the closing subsection sound different from the preceding portions of the Vivace, which have included only theme 1 and its extension and theme 2.

However, toward the end of the closing subsection (during the last descent—see Ex. 9-7), a more lyrical motive is heard several times in descending sequence. It moves in a long-short, long-short rhythm; and,

Example 9-11 Bartók, Vivace: A motive derived from the Mesto

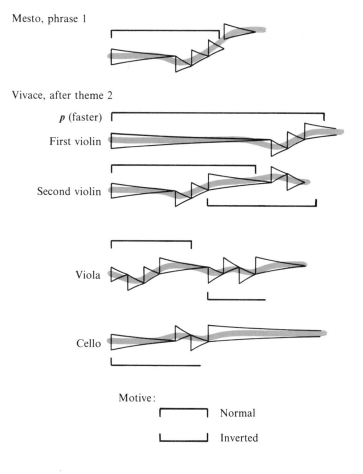

although it seems very familiar, its source is not immediately obvious. Is it a rhythmic smoothing out of the second theme, whose rhythm was a distinctive long-short, short-long? Or is it something else? One of the most fascinating resources of motivic development is the possibility of hidden (or even indeterminate) relationships among motives. Everything about a piece need not be clear, in fact a certain amount of mystery often makes an important contribution to the shape of a piece. Sometimes an unexpected clarification is even better, as when a clear quotation from theme 2 leads up to the long high note at the end of section 1.

One more feature of motivic development should be pointed out, simply because it poses a question that leads into the inner recesses of the piece. As mentioned before (Ex. 9-9), in the third section the first and second themes are separated, not by ascents, as before, but by a new, static passage. This passage is built on the reiteration of a very simple motive—two notes a small leap apart. The leap is sometimes descending, more often ascending (even though the passage as a whole is static).

Where does the motive come from? In context, it springs from theme 1, as an appendage to the last note of the theme, which is usually prolonged. The two-note motive was not *always* there; it must have been added somewhere in the course of the movement. But where? By attentive listening you may find where the two-note motive first rises to the surface. Even if you do not—or especially if you do not—you will sense how the static passage is both new and well prepared.

Themes and motives, when used, may provide one of the easiest kinds of access to a piece. You should not, however, allow that fact to cause you to rely on themes and motives completely, neglecting other aspects of design. As already pointed out, even where motivic development goes on almost continuously (as in the first movement of Bartók's quartet), it may not give a complete picture of the piece; and usually motivic development is less continuous than in Bartók's Vivace. It is usually more fruitful to gain a rough sense of overall motion first (if that is possible), relying later on motives to individualize the broad outlines. There would be a

danger in hearing only the themes, as there would in seeing only the principal subject of a painting; there would be a danger in hearing only the motives, as in seeing only the brushwork rather than the design it filled.

HARMONIC RELATIONSHIPS IN THE FIRST MOVEMENT.
Such caution must be extended in another direction as well. We have used themes and motives, together with other linear clues such as ascents or descents, as clues, thereby implying that they are clues *to* something. That something is the complete form of the piece, which we intuit directly but approach analytically only in stages. Concepts of harmony provide a closer stage than theme or motive, simply because concepts of harmony require us to consider all the lines sounding at any one time, not just the line (or lines) that happen to carry significant themes or motives. Themes (when they are linear) and motives take their place in the harmonic context, along with nonthematic or nonmotivic lines.

The complexity and ambivalence of Bartók's harmony makes it impractical to discuss it in detail here. Much of the difficulty of Bartók's harmony, however, lies in discussing it as opposed to hearing it. Trained and untrained listeners alike probably hear much clearer harmonic relationships in Bartók's music than they can conceptualize.

Some aspects of the first movement that are properly harmonic have already been discussed, at least roughly. We noted the stable effect of themes, and the unstable effect of the passages intervening; a very large component of these effects is their harmonic context. We noticed a difference between stable thematic statements and static passages that were often anticipatory—that is, unstable—in effect; here, too, the harmonic component is very important.

In the harmonic relationships of sameness and difference you may encounter the greatest difficulty with Bartók's music. Discussion of a few of the most obvious of such relationships will pinpoint the problem. As Ex. 9-10 shows, there is a sharp discontinuity in pitch content after the first three notes of the Pesante. If you were to hear only the last five notes of the Mesto and the first three of the Pesante, you would be aware of an area with a central pitch—the

next-to-last note of the Mesto. (This happens also to be the first pitch of the Mesto, and may, as already mentioned, be heard by some listeners as a center for the entire Mesto.)

The pitches after the discontinuity belong to a different harmonic area; but this is not immediately clear because first they are stated singly, then in a very tense harmonic context. Only gradually does the sense of harmonic area make itself felt, beginning with the first statement of the theme in the Vivace. The last, long note of this statement, while not a central pitch, is as good a pitch as any to fix in mind; but a rough intuition of the whole first theme may be more fruitful.

With some practice you should be able to hear that the second statement of the theme (Ex. 9-12) begins like the first, but moves off toward some other harmonic area. Similarly, the inversion starts in the same harmonic area as the theme but also moves somewhere else. The first long note of the inversion is another useful point of reference.

From this point, relationships become more difficult. The next statements of the theme, inverted as well as normal, are in the same harmonic area as the opening statements but are shifted to a lower octave. Because of the intervening passage, these basic identities may be difficult to hear (also, different listeners react to them in different ways). However, try listening from the beginning of the Vivace up to the second theme while looking at Ex. 9-12; subsequent statements of the first theme—normal or inverted—are in the same harmonic area as that shown for the first statements. You may not relate the later statements to the earlier ones in any way except as the repetition of a melodic shape. Or you may sense a vague similarity in harmonic location, a vague sameness in the actual pitches—perhaps just the absence of any significant pitch *difference*. With practice and concentration, you may be able to hear that the statements are indeed the same harmonically and that the linear activity of the bass line has resulted in a return to the original harmonic area.

The return of the head motive in longer notes in the static passage following (Ex. 9-13) is also in the same harmonic area as in the Pesante, with a change in octave. These similarities tie everything occurring

Example 9-12 Bartók, Vivace: Pitch relations in the first theme

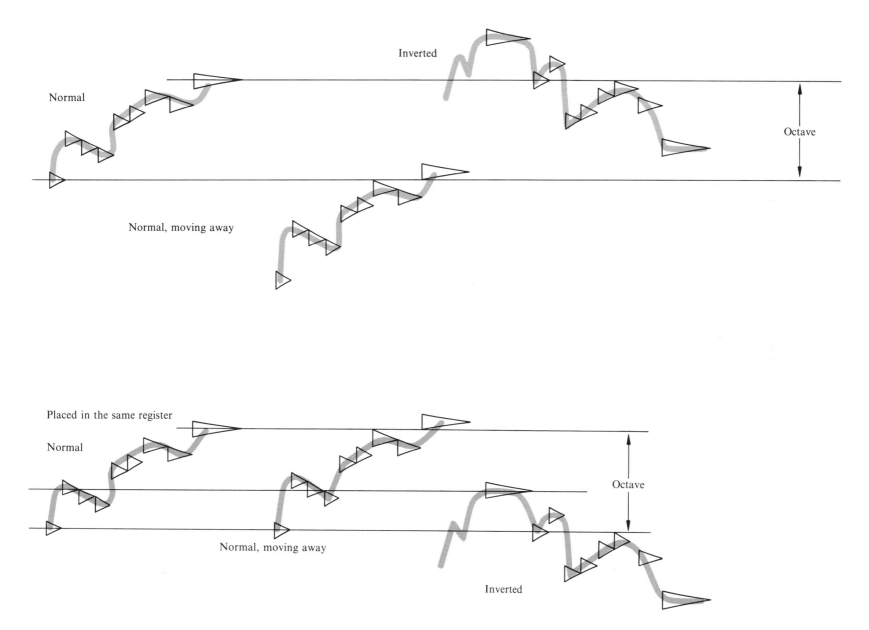

Vivace, beginning

In the static passage before theme 2

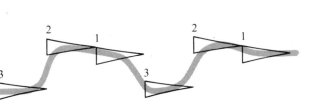

Theme 1, normal position

Head motive of theme 1, repeated several times

Example 9-13 Bartók, Vivace: Theme 1 and subsequent motive

before the second theme very closely to the Pesante—except, that is, for the first three notes of the Pesante, which belong to a different harmonic area. The sameness prevailing throughout the Vivace up to the second theme is an important factor in the fresh, evocative sound of the second theme, which moves decisively to a new area.

After the second theme, harmonic relationships are still less accessible; also the distances between reference points approach or exceed the limits of sensitivity of most listeners. Yet relationships of sameness persist: the brief quotation from theme 2 that ends the section is at the same pitch level as its first appearance, and the last chord of the section, introduced by this brief quotation, is built on the top and bottom pitches of theme 2.

This, as well as many other relationships, is shown in Ex. 9-14, which gives three harmonic areas for the movement. Immediately after section 1, for example, the following Pesante begins and sustains the har-

monic area of the first three notes of the first Pesante—rather than the area of the first theme. If you can hear pitch relationships in broad enough scope, you can hear a tension running through the movement, a tension expressed in compact form between the two discontinuous areas in the first Pesante.

The movement finally ends in the area of theme 1. This is made clear by the long held chord at the end of section 3 and at the end of the movement, as well as by the thematic inversion in section 4.

Such identities of pitch relationships exist in this and many other pieces and can be easily demonstrated at the piano. It would be wrong to ignore their existence; at the same time, it would be misleading and discouraging to suggest that most listeners are aware of hearing them. Pitch relationships, even more than rhythmic relationships, can exert their force all the way up to very high levels of musical organization. When operative at high levels, pitch relationships challenge the sensitivities of the most

acute and experienced listener. We all hear as much as we can—some more, some less; we should look upon the expanding universe of pitch as an opportunity to hear more.

Yet it is characteristic of the context of Bartók's quartet that clear reference points for pitch relationships occur at widely separated times—usually at sectional divisions. These intermittent points of comparison would be ineffectual and not worth noticing if they were as unrelated to the intervening music as they may seem on first acquaintance. There must be—and is—more continuity to the harmonic organization than that provided us by intermittent, infrequent reference points. *How* the harmony gets where it is going is as important, if not more important, than the fact of sameness between two widely separated chords. This "how" is much more accessible than are the pitch identities; they are the natural products of the motion that runs throughout the whole piece.

Example 9-14 Bartók, Vivace: Some pitch relationships in the whole first movement

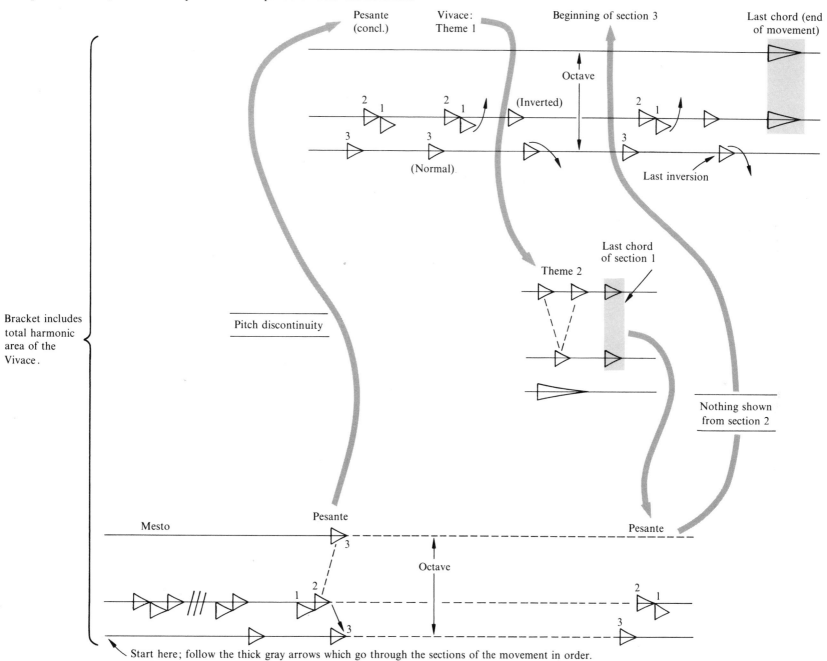

183

Exercises for further listening

Sectional shape of the Tableau. Listen to the entire Tableau, following the text in Chapter 13. Answer questions 1, 2, and 3.

1. Considered as a whole, the First Tableau is grouped into   **1.** b
   ____ **a.** Two large sections
   ____ **b.** Three large sections
   ____ **c.** Four large sections

2. Section 1 continues as far as rehearsal number   **2.** b
   ____ **a.** 7   ____ **b.** 9   ____ **c.** 12

3. Section 2 continues from 9 up to number   **3.** b
   ____ **a.** 18   ____ **b.** 21   ____ **c.** 24

Theme and pitch relations in section 1. Listen to the first section of the First Tableau, up to 9, following the text in Chapter 13. Answer questions 4 through 15.

4. The first section is built on two contrasting themes : the bride's lament (the opening theme)   **4.** b
   and a second theme which enters
   ____ **a.** At 1   ____ **b.** At 2   ____ **c.** At 3

5. The bride's lament is usually sung by   **5.** a
   ____ **a.** Solo soprano
   ____ **b.** Women's chorus
   ____ **c.** Men's chorus

6. The contrasting theme at 2 is usually sung by   **6.** b
   ____ **a.** Solo soprano
   ____ **b.** Women's chorus
   ____ **c.** Men's chorus

7. The contrasting theme is   **7.** b
____ **a.** At a higher pitch level than the bride's lament
____ **b.** At a lower pitch level than the bride's lament
____ **c.** At the same pitch level as the bride's lament

8. The material sung by the solo soprano at 1 is   **8.** b
____ **a.** Exactly the same as that at the beginning
____ **b.** A variant of that at the beginning
____ **c.** New material

9. How has the bride's lament been changed?   **9.** a
____ **a.** It is faster at 1
____ **b.** It is slower at 1
____ **c.** It has a different set of pitches at 1

10. Are all of the statements of the bride's lament (up to 9) at the same pitch?   **10.** Yes
____ Yes   ____ No

11. The melody of the bride's lament (at the beginning and at 1) contains   **11.** b
____ **a.** Two different pitches (excluding the grace notes)
____ **b.** Three different pitches (excluding the grace notes)
____ **c.** Many (five to ten) different pitches

12. The central pitch of the bride's lament   **12.** a
____ **a.** Is the highest of the three main pitches (sung to "*Ko-*")
____ **b.** Is the middle pitch (sung to "Ko-*sal* mo-*ya*")
____ **c.** Is the lowest of the three main pitches (sung to "*mo*-ya")

13. The central pitch of the theme at 2 is   **13.** b
____ **a.** One of the accented pitches ("*Che*-su pochesu")
____ **b.** The repeated pitch ("Che-*su pochesu . . .*")
____ **c.** A pitch other than *a* or *b*

14. What is the relation of the central pitch of the bride's lament to the central pitch of the   **14.** b
theme at 2?
____ **a.** They are the same pitch
____ **b.** They are an octave apart
____ **c.** They have no clear relation

15. As a whole, the first section of the First Tableau is

    ___ **a.** Extremely stable harmonically, with no contrast in pitch center

    ___ **b.** Somewhat unstable, with several contrasting pitch centers

    ___ **c.** Extremely unstable, with many contrasting pitch centers

15. a

Theme and pitch relations in the First Tableau. Listen to all of the First Tableau, following the text in Chapter 13. Answer questions 16 through 27.

16. At what point do you first hear a real contrast in central pitch?

    ___ **a.** At 9   ___ **b.** At 12   ___ **c.** At 16

16. a

17. Thematic material that clearly contrasts with the opening themes begins

    ___ **a.** At 8   ___ **b.** At 9   ___ **c.** At 16   ___ **d.** At 21

17. b

18. At what point do you hear an exact return of any of the themes from section 1?

    ___ **a.** At 14   ___ **b.** At 21   ___ **c.** At 24

18. c

19. The theme at 24 is

    ___ **a.** The same as the bride's lament that opens the Tableau

    ___ **b.** The same as the bride's lament at 1

    ___ **c.** The same as the theme at 2

19. c

20. The theme at 24

    ___ **a.** Returns at its original pitch

    ___ **b.** Returns at a different pitch

20. a

21. How long after its entry at 24 does the theme continue?

    ___ **a.** To 25

    ___ **b.** To 26

    ___ **c.** To the end of the First Tableau

21. c

22. Beginning at 26, the central pitch of this theme

    ___ **a.** Remains constant until the end of the First Tableau

    ___ **b.** Moves downward

    ___ **c.** Moves upward

22. b

23. The central pitch of this theme descends to a pitch that

    ___ **a.** Is higher than the new central pitch at the beginning of the Second Tableau

    ___ **b.** Is lower than the new central pitch at the beginning of the Second Tableau

    ___ **c.** Is the same as the new central pitch at the beginning of the Second Tableau

23. c

24. The opening bride's lament   **24.** a

 ____ **a.** Never returns in its original form after section 1

 ____ **b.** Returns in its original form somewhere in section 3

25. The same set of pitches associated with the bride's lament   **25.** a

 ____ **a.** Returns between 21 and 24 in the solo soprano

 ____ **b.** Returns between 16 and 19 in all parts

 ____ **c.** Does not return in the First Tableau

26. In reference to its central pitches, section 2 as a whole (9 up to 21) **26.** b

 ____ **a.** Is somewhat less stable than section 1 (there are two or three contrasting central pitches)

 ____ **b.** Is much less stable than section 1 (there are many changing central pitches)

 ____ **c.** Is as stable as section 1 (there is a single central pitch)

27. Except for its ending (just before the Second Tableau), section 3   **27.** b

 ____ **a.** Is less stable than section 2

 ____ **b.** Is more stable than section 2

187

PART TWO

Overall musical shape

UP TO THIS POINT in the book, we have been concentrating on one aspect at a time—aspects such as timbre, texture, rhythm, and pitch. Study of any one aspect has often led to an approximate understanding of the shape of a whole piece or of a section. In any case, we have tried to relate the study of each aspect to the whole shape of the piece in which we found it. However, sometimes (especially in the case of themes) the single aspect only helped orient us in the piece, without accounting for enough of its bulk to provide a comprehensive understanding.

From this point on, we will be concerned with all aspects of a piece and the way they work together. This does not mean that we will no longer discuss the specific aspects already studied or, on the other hand, that we will discuss all these aspects in each piece. It *does* mean that we will take up whichever aspects seem important at the moment and will try to relate aspects to each other in terms of their function within the piece.

In dealing with pieces as wholes, we should consider ever more intensively their shape at the highest level. At that level, it is difficult to maintain a proper balance among conflicting demands of the listening experience. Full awareness demands a grasp of the overall plan of a piece at its highest level *and* of the relationship of all its details to that plan. The "and" is the difficult part. On the one hand, the whole piece means the whole as we hear it—the succession, in order, of all the sounds of the piece. The whole is the set of relationships among all the elements or features of the piece, as those relationships come into existence during a performance of the piece.

On the other hand, the whole has a meaning beyond the totality of all the details. Sometimes, indeed, a selection of details gives better access to the whole than the totality—just as the recollection of a key sentence may bring back the whole point of a speech much better than an impression of every word that was said.

In an effort to grasp a piece at its highest level, we will continue to describe its shape in general terms, such as "*A B A*." There is a tendency to think that generalities are, "in general," vague and superficial, that only in detail do you get at profound truth. But truth can be found in generalities, and they are vague

CHAPTER 10   SOME APPROACHES TO OVERALL SHAPE

or not depending on how you treat them. The shape of a piece at its highest level may be its most significant aspect; dealing with that shape by means of general concepts may be the best way of understanding the idea that burned in the composer's mind until he expressed it in the form of a piece.

Actually the procedure from here on will not be radically different from what it has been. The new task is to decide for each piece which aspect (or combination of aspects) is most important and which aspects are less important or even irrelevant to the shape of the piece. This must be decided on the basis of the piece itself: we must let the piece tell us what is important and what is not. Sometimes a piece may tell us very drastic things (if we let it); for example, a piece may tell us that shape itself is unimportant— at least in that piece. Some pieces even try to tell us that they are not pieces at all, in which case we have to grope around to discover what the approach should be.

The point is, no single approach (no matter how comprehensive) works automatically for all pieces; and nothing is more injurious to creative listening than the attempt to go systematically through a prearranged set of categories (such as timbre, texture, rhythm, and pitch) for each piece, checking off isolated features. The authors hope very much that this book is not used exclusively in such a fashion. However, if you have difficulty finding a way to begin with a piece—if nothing seems to offer itself as an approach, then it is useful to run through the various

aspects quickly in your mind, asking yourself whether any is relevant to the piece at hand; this procedure often helps to get conscious perception started down a fruitful path. In dealing with larger, multimovement forms, we will employ this procedure occasionally in order to show how it may help in approaching unfamiliar or bewildering material.

Of the pieces now to be discussed, many have already been studied, at least in part. We will refer back to any previous discussion and will assume an understanding of it. We will begin with some shorter pieces, then go on to some longer pieces with texts, and finally to some longer, multimovement pieces without text. In each of these pieces—as in every piece—there is some special problem of approach.

Gregorian Chant
"VICTIMAE PASCHALI LAUDES" (PROSE)

In beginning with a piece of chant, we do not mean to imply that chant is on the whole easier than other kinds of music. Because it is chant, however, it requires the listener to make an obvious selection among the aspects to be considered—and so illustrates one of the most important steps in approaching any piece.

"Victimae paschali laudes," like the introit "Resurrexi," is a chant from the Mass for Easter Sunday. It is a kind of chant known as a *prose*, or sometimes a *sequence* (this is a completely different usage of the word "sequence," unrelated to the more common usage described in Chapter 6). "Victimae paschali laudes" differs from "Resurrexi" in kind of text, relationship of text to music, kind of melody, and overall design—as will become clear from a study of the piece itself.

RELEVANT ASPECTS. Listen to "Victimae paschali laudes" two or three times just to gain an idea of what it contains, as well as what it does not contain. It is sung by a choir of men, singing in unison. The quality of sound is richly sonorous, but it is uniform throughout. There is no *contrast* in timbres. You should be aware of the timbre as a feature of the whole piece, but you need not deal with it as a factor of internal differentiation.

In some performances, a smaller group of singers (sometimes even a solo singer) sings every other phrase. When that happens, the difference in timbre would, of course, be a factor to be considered.

"Victimae paschali laudes" is sung completely in unison. There are no chords; there is no counterpoint; the texture is monophonic and uniform throughout. The piece has a texture, in other words, but a minimum kind of texture that shows no change.

If you try to determine a meter for the piece, you soon run into difficulties: there is, in fact, no meter, no regular grouping of pulses. However, it would of course be wrong to conclude that there is no rhythm or that the rhythm is irregular in all respects. Actually, rhythm is one of the aspects that should be considered most carefully. There is a unit pulse; and, at higher rhythmic levels, there is a clear phrase structure, as is apparent from first or second hearing.

Line is obviously important in "Victimae paschali laudes"; it may seem, in fact, that the piece is all line, no other aspect of pitch being apparent. As we discovered with "Resurrexi," however, in a line there may be aspects of pitch organization besides the direction of the line itself. Just what these other aspects are may not be immediately clear; you should be prepared to listen closely for any kind of pitch relationships that may be operative.

You might have made the foregoing assessment quickly—almost unconsciously—during your first listening; or you might have listened several times

without being able to decide how to proceed. We have spelled out the initial assessment to show that in this case not all aspects are relevant. We will concentrate on the most prominent ones, which are rhythm, at the level of phrase, and line.

And text: in every piece with a text, that text may provide the most important access to the music. As with musical aspects, we do not know in advance which aspect of the text will be significant. It may be the poetic shape (meter and rhyme) or the grammatical shape (phrases and sentences) or the poetic imagery or the overall meaning. We should pay close attention to the meaning in any case, because it is part of the piece, even if it does not affect the purely musical factors. If the text is in a foreign language, we need a translation. Text and translation are given here in lines that correspond to the phrase shapes at the highest level.

RHYTHM AND MELODY. The notes of "Victimae paschali laudes" seem to flow in a steady unit pulse, without much differentiation by accent or length; it is not immediately apparent which notes are structurally important. The individual pitches that stick in the ear most easily, however, are those that come at brief pauses in the rhythmic motion. These pitches are a little longer than the rest and are sometimes

followed by a short break, giving the ear time to absorb them. If we indicate these longer notes in the text, we find that they break up the text into phrases and subphrases, as shown here for the beginning.

1 Victimae paschali lau*des* immolent Christia*ni*
2a Agnus redemit o*ves*: Christus innocens Pa*tri* reconcilia*vit* peccato*res*.
2b Mors et vita duel*lo* conflixere miran*do*: dux vitae mort*uus*, regnat vi*vus*.

Perhaps you are first aware of the shortest units (". . . lau*des*" and ". . . a*ni*"), which turn out to be subphrases. As you hear the line more clearly in terms of these subphrases, you will become increasingly aware of the musical phrases corresponding to the text phrases numbered 1, 2a, 2b . . . . Then it becomes clear (if it was not already) that the melody for 2b is identical with the melody for 2a. Going on, 3a and 3b have the same music, as do 4a and 4b; these are harder to hear because phrases 3 and 4 interlock in the scheme 3a 4a 3b 4b. Phrases 5a and 5b have new music—although even in the first few hearings you may notice a motivic reference at the beginning of these phrases to phrases 2a and 2b. Such motivic references, often noticed early in your experience with a piece, should be carefully noted but set aside until phrase structure and sectional structure, as well

1 Victimae paschali laudes immolent Christiani.
2a Agnus redemit oves: Christus innocens Patri reconciliavit peccatores.
2b Mors et vita duello conflixere mirando: dux vitae mortuus, regnat vivus.
3a Dic nobis, Maria, quid vidisti in via?
4a Sepulcrum Christi viventis, et gloriam vidi resurgentis;
3b Angelicos testes, sudarium, et vestes.
4b Surrexit Christus spes mea: praecedet suos in Galileam.
*5a Credendum est magis soli Maria veraci, quam Judeorum turbae falaci.
5b Scimus Christum surrexisse a mortuis vere: tu nobis, victor Rex, miserere! Amen. Alleluia.

*Line 5a is usually omitted in performance.

1 To the Paschal Victim let Christians offer praises.
2a A lamb has redeemed the sheep: Christ, the innocent, to the Father has reconciled sinners.
2b Death and life have fought an awesome battle: the prince of life, who died, lives and reigns.
3a Tell us, Mary, what did you see on the way?
4a "The tomb of Christ, who lives; and I saw the glory of Him rising;
3b Angelic witnesses, the shroud, and vestments.
4b Christ, my hope, has risen: He goes on before His friends to Galilee."
*5a More to be believed is Mary, only truthful, than the unbelieving crowd of Jews.
5b We know indeed that Christ has risen from the dead: Have mercy upon us, conqueror and king! Amen. Alleluia.

as overall pitch organization, have become clear or until you decide that these factors are not operative in the piece, in which event you must rely to a much larger extent on motivic processes.

You may have had either or both of two difficulties with pitch organization of "Victimae paschali laudes": the pitch content may have seemed too uniform, making it difficult to sense any significant motion; or the line may have seemed to wander without enough clear reference points to define its shape. For every piece you must discover anew the dimensions of pitch within which it moves. In the present case, you can do this most easily by trying to retain in your ear the pitches that mark the ends of phrases and subphrases. This turns out to be a fruitful procedure.

All phrases (as numbered 1, 2a, 2b, . . .) end on the same pitch; and only two other pitches appear at the ends of subphrases, as shown in Ex. 10-1. Thus, the rhythm at higher levels singles out a pitch that may serve as a reference point for the others. Exactly what set of relationships exists between this pitch and the others remains to be seen. Moreover, the rhythmic structure also gives us the other two pitches that are used for subphrases (2a: "oves," "reconciliavit"); since their rhythmic function is subsidiary, their pitch function may be too. With the aid of these pitches, we can begin to develop a sense of hierarchy among all the pitches in the piece. Rhythmically prominent pitches often—but not always—help clarify the pitch relationships in a piece. Using prominent pitches in this way is largely a matter of trial and error, but it is worth a serious trial.

Within the framework of pitches shown in Ex. 10-2, the movement of the line takes on more signi-

ficance as it moves above or below the final pitch, as it steps out away from the final pitch or slides easily back down to it. In phrase 1, the line rises and falls twice, each time approaching the final the same way. The whole phrase is solidly rooted on its final note. In phrase 2a, on the other hand, the line begins high and goes higher, centering on the upper subsidiary note and ending its first subphrase there. It is not just that the line moves differently; it moves in a different area relative to the final. You can sense the transition from this higher area, centered on the upper subsidiary note, back down to the area around the final note during the second subphrase ("Christus innocens Patri"), which again ends solidly on the final. Then, as if to balance the high beginning of phrase 2a, the end circles around and below the final note ("reconciliavit peccatores"). Phrase 2a, then, has a different line, a different sense of melodic motion through different areas of pitch. This motion is intimately bound up with its different subphrase structure—so intimately that the two can hardly be separated.

Rhythm and melody here seem to be two not very different ways of looking at the same thing. The pause in the middle of phrase 1 at "paschali laudes" has much greater rhythmic significance because the pitches involved in the pause are similar to those at the end of the line on "Christiani." In phrase 2a, the rhythm reinforces the melody: the pause on "oves" confirms the subsidiary pitch in its function and clarifies the more elaborate melodic motion taking place. The rhythm of the successive subphrases is felt through their melodic grouping, as each drops to a lower pitch level.

At the higher levels, much the same interaction

between rhythm and melody can be found. Phrases 2a and 2b are heard as two distinct phrases because of the pause at the ending of each. Each phrase gains a sense of integrity through the direction of the line within it. At a higher level, the identity of phrases 2a and 2b in melody creates another kind of rhythm at a level above that of phrase.

In phrases 3a, 4a, 3b, and 4b, the rhythm at this higher level is affected as much by register as by the repetition of melody. Phrase 3a starts low and does not ascend very high; phrase 4a is relatively static in its melodic motion, moving back and forth in an area between the final pitch and the upper subsidiary one. Thus phrases 3a and 4a are distinctly different in register and line, making their alternation clear. As phrases 3b and 4b continue, this alternation brings an increased breadth to the rhythm operating at the phrase level.

As you may have heard earlier, phrases 5a and 5b bring a motivic reference to 2a and 2b in the high register, which has been avoided by the intervening phrases. Even though the reference involves only a few notes, its effect is unmistakable: it closes the form of the piece with a sense of return. The more complex subphrase structure and the different melodic line do not diminish the effect of return but merely slow the motion for an ending. The brief motivic reference also produces a sense of stress or accent at that particular point in the phrase—not just because it is a motivic reference but because it is so placed as to assume importance in the rhythm of the higher levels. The stress on the start of 5b is used to project the central meaning of the text—"We know indeed that Christ has risen from the dead." This, too, refers back to the thought of phrase 2b, the inter-

Example 10-1 "Victimae paschali laudes": Ends of phrases and subphrases

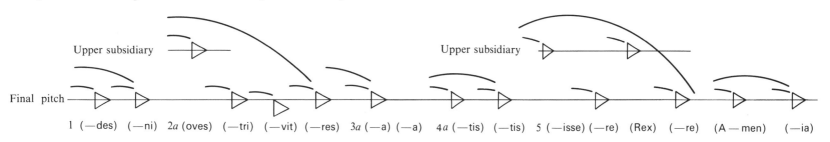

Example 10-2 "Victimae paschali laudes": Melodic motion around the frame

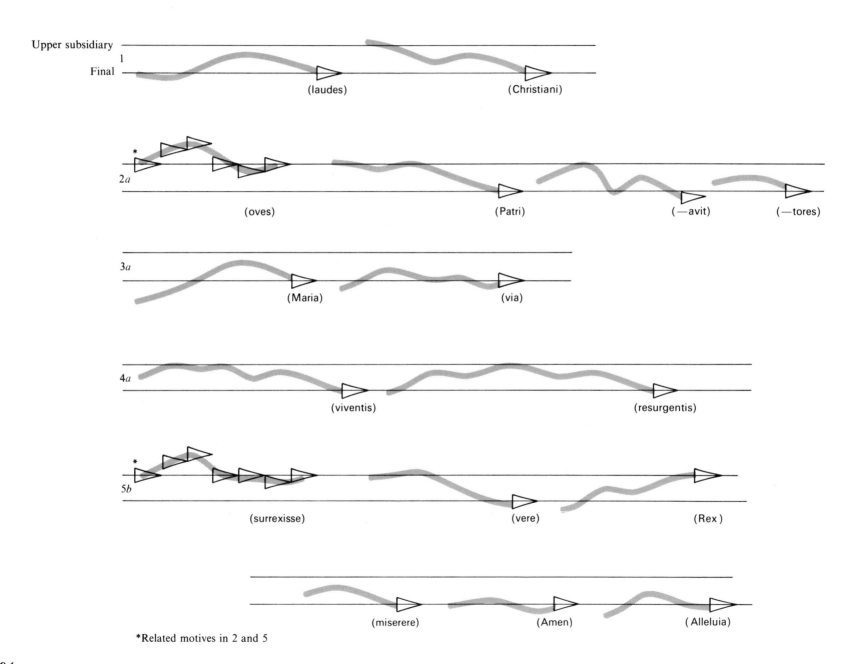

Upper subsidiary

Final

1

(laudes)   (Christiani)

*
2a
(oves)   (Patri)   (—avit)   (—tores)

3a
(Maria)   (via)

4a
(viventis)   (resurgentis)

*
5b
(surrexisse)   (vere)   (Rex)

(miserere)   (Amen)   (Alleluia)

*Related motives in 2 and 5

vening phrases being used for the dialog with Mary.

There are many other details of line that could be discovered, particularly the use of rhymes or near-rhymes to help mold the subphrase structure, for example, "viventis . . . resurgentis" in phrase 4a. Most important, however, is to understand the way rhythm and line, neither very striking by itself, combine to create a clear form. Because the piece is short, with no complexities of timbre or texture, you can easily experience the interplay among different levels and among different aspects. The same sense of interplay is found in far more elaborate pieces, but there you will need to concentrate harder to hear it.

Gregorian Chant
"HAEC DIES" (GRADUAL)

It would be wrong to give the impression that music whose resources are simple always has a form as clear as that of "Victimae paschali laudes." Another chant from the Easter Mass, "Haec dies," uses the same resources with very different results. "Haec dies" has its own kind of text-music relationship, of line, and of overall shape. The two chants make an interesting contrast—a significant one, since in the traditional liturgy "Haec dies" was sung immediately before "Victimae paschali laudes." "Haec dies" is a type of chant called a *gradual*, a traditional and enigmatic term.

Listen to "Haec dies" several times, following the text as given here. (Some recordings do not repeat the section "Haec dies . . . in ea" at the end.) Some aspects of this chant are similar to "Victimae paschali laudes": the texture is monophonic; the timbre is that of a men's choir. In "Haec dies," however, there will definitely be a slight change of timbre in certain places. A smaller group of singers sings the words, "Haec dies," and also "Confitemini Domino, quoniam bonus: quoniam in saeculum misericordia." These changes of timbre, even though subtle, will be noticeable simply because they are the only such change in the quality of sound throughout the piece.

So far, "Haec dies" is similar to "Victimae paschali laudes"; and, if the two pieces are sung by the

same choir in the same general manner (as they are on recordings of the Easter Mass), their effects will be superficially alike. However, as we noted in dealing with "Victimae paschali laudes," aspects that remain unchanged throughout the piece are not relevant to its inner construction. The same is true when we compare two pieces: we can set aside factors that are the same in the two pieces and can concentrate on those that are different.

On that basis, the differences between the two pieces turn out to be considerable. One of the first you might notice is in the relationship of text syllables to notes. In "Victimae paschali laudes," the relationship was syllabic: almost every syllable had only one note. In "Haec dies," on the other hand, many syllables have several notes; and some syllables are set to melismas, for example, "Dominus, exultemus, et laete-mur in e-a."

Because of the melismatic setting of "Haec dies," the ratio of text to music is drastically different, as you can tell by comparing the texts of the two chants, comparing at the same time the lengths of their musical settings. "Haec dies," with much less text, is considerably longer.

As another consequence, "Haec dies" has a different relationship between phrases of text and phrases of music. In "Victimae paschali laudes," the musical phrasing corresponds closely to the way the text is laid out in phrases, but in "Haec dies" what sounds like a whole phrase seems to fall in some cases over two or three syllables. (Such matters are difficult to see for yourself when the text is in a foreign language; but in the present case you can get a rough idea from the sentence structure of the English translation.)

At the level of rhythmic detail, the unit pulse is more evident in "Haec dies" than in "Victimae paschali laudes," where the strictly syllabic setting and the strong phrase structure give the rhythmic motion clear shapes. In "Haec dies," because of its melismas and their unpredictable placement, the ear relies more on the rhythmic detail, hence is more aware of the lack of a regular grouping at that level. In fact, *any* grouping of individual pulses, regular or irregular, is hard to perceive. Some notes are longer than others, but the longer and shorter notes do not

seem to form any clear or repetitive pattern. The pulse of the faster notes, however, is roughly equidistant; this pulse, in the absence of any other metric element, provides the only feature of regularity in the rhythm.

The melismatic setting of "Haec dies" contributes directly to the difficulty of trying to perceive the phrase structure. There are, however, breaks and pauses in the flow of the unit pulse; these breaks divide the text into the following phrases:

1	Haec dies	This is the day
2	quam fecit Dominus:	that the Lord hath made;
3	exultemus,	let us rejoice
4	et laetemur in ea.	and be glad in it.
5	Confitemini Domino,	We will trust in the Lord,
6	quoniam bonus:	for he is good:
7	quoniam in saeculum	and everlasting
8	misericordia eius.	is his mercy.
	(Haec dies . . . in ea.)	

The striking aspect of this phrase structure, when compared with that of "Victimae paschali laudes," is the absence of a hierarchy of phrase and subphrase. "Haec dies" seems to proceed in a series of phrases roughly equal in length and importance; it is very difficult to perceive a larger grouping of these phrases; nor, on the other hand, is there any consistent subdivision of these phrases into subphrases—the melismas seem to preclude it.

If we project the pitches at the ends of phrases onto horizontal lines, as we did for "Victimae paschali laudes," we find a very different situation. To begin with, the final notes of the several phrases reinforce each other much less than do those of "Victimae paschali laudes." Of twelve final notes (counting those in the repeat) in "Haec dies," six are the same, including the one at the very end; and these six are spaced out more or less evenly. Your ear, however, may not be convinced that this final note is really functioning as a central one. The greater freedom of rhythmic detail and especially of the melismas makes it hard to hear a relationship between one appearance of this final note and the next.

Together with the note above it in Ex. 10-3 (used at the ends of phrase 2), the final note forms a framework that runs throughout the chant. Example 10-4 shows this framework as found in phrases 1 and 2.

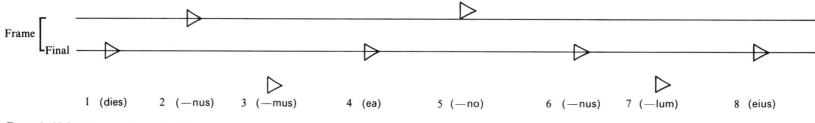

Example 10-3 "Haec dies": Ends of phrases

Example 10-4 "Haec dies": Line in phrases 1 and 2

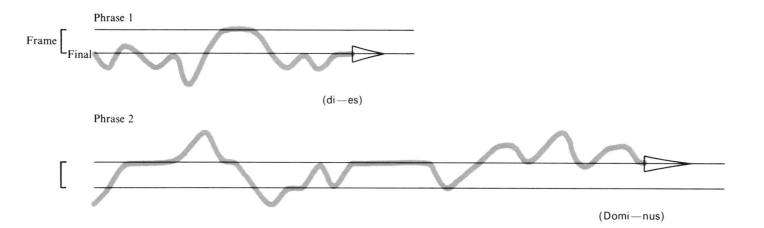

Relative to this framework, the first line of "Haec dies" has an unpredictable, rhapsodic quality of motion: it dwells on the framework for relatively long stretches, decorating it in subtle ways, then surges off elsewhere, quickly traversing a wide range—as when it drops to the end of phrase 3 or when it rises for the melisma at the end of phrase 4 on "e-a" or most of all on the word "quoniam" of phrase 6. The actual range here is no greater than in "Victimae paschali laudes," but it seems greater because of the kind of melodic motion.

At the higher levels, "Haec dies" has still more curious differences. There are two substantial returns of melodic material. Phrase 7, "quoniam in saeculum," is almost the same as phrase 3, "exultemus";

and the repeat of "Haec dies . . . in ea" (phrases 1 through 4) after phrase 8, when performed, is exact. The curious thing is that these returns have so little impact. On first hearing, they may escape notice; through repeated hearings, it is possible to learn that they are there, yet somehow they never seem to become an important event in the shape of the piece. In this respect, perhaps more than any other, the deep-seated difference. between "Haec dies" and "Victimae paschali laudes" becomes clear.

In listening to "Victimae paschali laudes," the ear is encouraged to grasp larger dimensions, higher levels. The detail is less absorbing, the overall shape more so. Just the reverse is true of "Haec dies": frustrated in a search for a clear overall shape, the

ear focuses on the lower levels and finds at that level a wealth of absorbing, intricate detail. The reason this happens has to do with the way the two pieces are built. There is no reason to try to hear both pieces the same way; the thoughtful listener will try to match his approach to the nature of the piece, relying on intuition as well as on a careful survey of the aspects of the piece to guide him.

To what does "Haec dies" owe its musical sense, if not to any of the more obvious aspects discussed? This is really a different question, one that would lead us further than we can go in this book. By weighing carefully the factors that entered into very low-level choices (for example, "Why does this note come after that note?"), it might be possible to trace the musical sensibilities that guided the composer through a long succession of choices. There are many pieces (both monophonic and polyphonic) in which the large design can only be intuited out of a consideration of detail.

Krzysztof Penderecki (1933–   )
TO THE VICTIMS OF HIROSHIMA, THRENODY

Threnody means "song of lament." The piece has a specified extramusical meaning, in other words, beyond its purely musical meaning. We probably first ask, "What does the piece tell us about the extramusical subject? How does it communicate the lament?" Eventually we might want to ask, "What does the subject tell us about the piece?" Another way of asking the same question is "Would the piece have a different effect if it had a different title?"

The Threnody is an exceptionally intense piece; you may find it difficult to listen to for very long at one time. One of the first important functions of the title is to channel the listener's initial reaction to the piece into an understanding of it as a lament. The extreme intensity is more easily appreciated as an expression of grief than it would be if left undefined.

You may find that the piece speaks directly to you, or you may find that it does not; in either case, the problem is the same as with every piece discussed in this book—how to bring to consciousness the aspects of the piece so that it can be better understood. The Threnody, in spirit as well as technique, is the kind of uncompromising piece that forces the listener back to a consideration of basic facts of listening. For this reason, it is a fruitful piece to consider at this point in the book, even though we cannot provide adequate answers to the questions the piece raises.

TIMBRE, PITCH, AND RHYTHM. What will strike you, perhaps, as most intense about the Threnody (at least during first hearings) is the quality of the sound. Timbre may seem to be the most prominent factor—perhaps even the only factor. The timbre is, indeed, very intense; but while the piece as a whole contains several different timbres, upon reflection they are not so many nor so different as they seem at

first. (All the sounds in the piece are produced by an orchestra of fifty-two strings.)

The quality of sound is so intense that perhaps the ear does not at first pick up components other than timbre. While you should try to maintain your awareness of the impact of the sound, you should try at the same time to take stock of its components, for only through them can you become conscious of more subtle shaping factors in the piece. As you give these other components attention, they will become increasingly important.

One such component is pitch. Your first impression, especially of the first minute or so, may be that pitch is not a significant factor in the Threnody. You may not, at first, distinguish individual pitches. In fact, when a single, clear, distinct pitch is eventually sounded, it is something of an event. Listen for this first unmistakably clear pitch at a point about 1 min 50 sec after the start of the piece, noticing how its "pitchness" seems to be a new quality of sound.

As you listen up to this "first pitch" a few times, however, you should gradually become aware that the sounds preceding it also have pitch; the difference is not the presence or absence of pitch but rather simple, clear pitch as opposed to complex pitch. You may first become aware of the pitch content of the beginning only as a gradual drift downwards from a very high register. But if "higher" and "lower" are qualities of the sound, then pitch must be an operative factor.

What is happening in the first minute of the Threnody is that several pitches are sounding at any one time, in very close proximity to each other—an effect sometimes called a *cluster*. At the beginning of the Threnody the clusters produce a rough, shrill quality; they also mask the familiar violin sound.

Combinations of pitches, in other words, have produced a sound whose most prominent quality is timbre rather than pitch. Yet pitch is there, operating in some of its usual ways: changes of pitch combinations may assume a linear direction or may eventually indicate some more complex kind of motion.

Low-level rhythm, like pitch, may at first seem absent from the Threnody; but in this connection the piece requires a consideration of basic matters.

There is enough differentiation of sound in the Threnody—the piercing attacks on new layers of sound at the beginning, for example—to provide an awareness of discrete events. There is *succession*: the events are perceived as occurring one after another. There are intervals of time between successive events; in other words, there are *durations*. All the materials of rhythm are there.

SECTIONS. Rather than waiting for sharp breaks to mark off sections, it is easier to listen for a stretch of prevailing sameness in quality of sound or in overall sense of movement, then compare that to a succeeding stretch, without worrying too much where one ends and the other begins. Listening on this basis, try to follow the whole piece with the aid of Ex. 10-5 (and, if necessary, a watch). The example shows six sections, each dominated by a particular kind of sound or movement.

During the first section, changes of any kind are slight and subtle. The sense of very slow, sustained rhythmic movement pervades everything. There are changes of dynamic level from the initial forte to piano, then back to mezzo-forte, the changes occurring at relatively long intervals (see Ex. 10-5). From about 0 min 50 sec, very subtle changes gradually occur in the timbre: what starts out as a mere tremor in the quality of a sustained cluster becomes a sustained fibrillation involving very rapid, very soft decorative figures that surround and eventually displace the sustained pitches. A remarkable sense of growth and development accompanies this passage, which extends from about 0 min 49 sec to the appearance of that "first pitch" at 1 min 49 sec. Yet the original slow pace continues uninterrupted.

Soon after you become aware of the distinct pitch at 1 min 49 sec, you will hear an unusual kind of pitch movement—a glissando, but a strangely deliberate one through a wide interval. At first, the slides are relatively inconspicuous, but more striking ones soon follow. Section 2 is dominated by very prominent glissandos. Sometimes two simultaneous pitches slide in opposite directions; when they converge on a single pitch, a sense of progression is apparent: the single pitch functions as a resolution of what came before (Ex. 10-6). This is not a matter of timbre, but of pitch

Example 10-5 Penderecki, Threnody: Sectional plan

Section 1

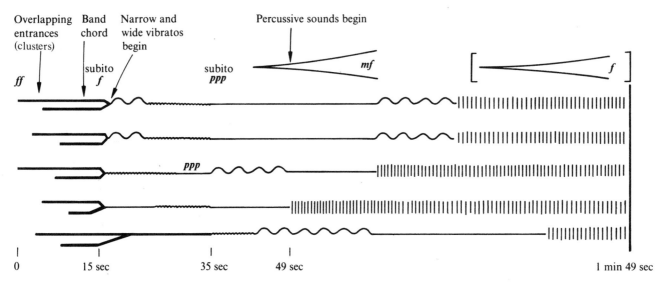

Overlapping entrances (clusters)

Band chord

Narrow and wide vibratos begin

Percussive sounds begin

ff

subito *f*

subito *ppp*

mf

f

ppp

| 0 | 15 sec | 35 sec | 49 sec | 1 min 49 sec |

Section 2

Section 3

Sustained single pitches, widening to clusters and returning to single pitches

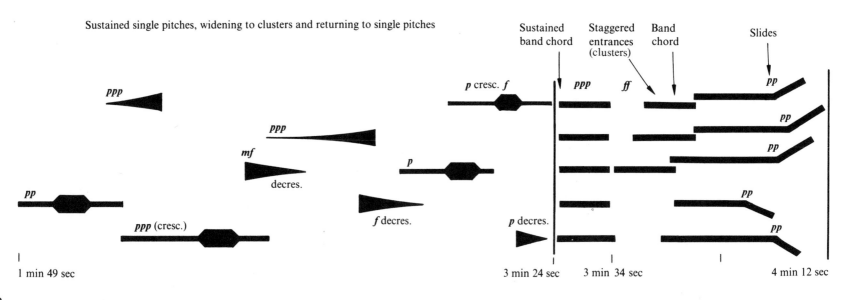

ppp

ppp

mf

decres.

p

f decres.

pp

ppp (cresc.)

Sustained band chord

Staggered entrances (clusters)

Band chord

Slides

p cresc. *f*

ppp

ff

pp

pp

pp

p decres.

pp

pp

| 1 min 49 sec | | 3 min 24 sec | 3 min 34 sec | | 4 min 12 sec |

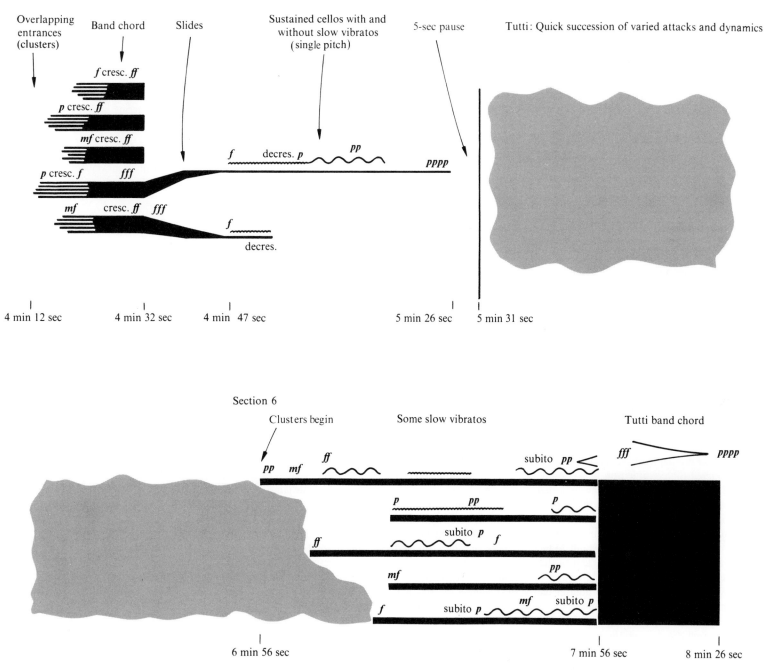

Section 4

Overlapping entrances (clusters) Band chord Slides Sustained cellos with and without slow vibratos (single pitch) 5-sec pause

Section 5

Tutti: Quick succession of varied attacks and dynamics

f cresc. ***ff***

p cresc. ***ff***

mf cresc. ***ff***

p cresc. *f* ***fff***

mf cresc. ***ff*** ***fff***

f decres. *p* *pp* ***pppp***

f

decres.

4 min 12 sec   4 min 32 sec   4 min 47 sec   5 min 26 sec   5 min 31 sec

Section 6

Clusters begin   Some slow vibratos   Tutti band chord

pp *mf* ***ff***   subito *pp* ***fff***   ***pppp***

p   *pp*   *p*

ff   subito *p* *f*

mf   *pp*

f   subito *p*   *mf*   subito *p*

6 min 56 sec   7 min 56 sec   8 min 26 sec

199

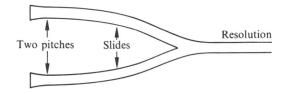

Example 10-6 Penderecki, Threnody: Glissandos
resolving to a single pitch

movement, felt here—of all places in the Threnody—most keenly.

Section 3 is dominated by a kind of sound that had already appeared briefly at the beginning—a combination of pitches, sounding simultaneously, that seems to spread over a wide range or band of pitches. The combination is similar to a chord, in that individual pitches sounding together form a new entity. We can call it a *band chord* (this is not a standard term), referring to the way the chord seems to extend evenly through a whole band or spectrum of pitches.

At the start of section 3, the first band chord is piano and not so different from the one at the beginning of the piece. But soon another band chord starts forte; additional layers of sound build this chord into an unusually intense blast of sound. The section as a whole consists of band chords in various arrangements. Your first impression, again, will be one of a new timbre; but then you will hear more precisely that it is the kind of pitch combination that is new, while the timbre is much the same as it was.

Section 4 is also dominated by band chords and might be considered the continuation of section 3; yet at the end of section 3 there seems to be a real break, as the whole sound slides through the extreme upper registers and disappears. Then there is a series of entrances of single pitches that culminates in yet another band chord, which gives way abruptly to the bitterest chord of all, strongly accented. Out of this last chord emerges the long cello note (Ex. 10-5).

The end of section 4 is marked by a note in the cellos that goes on for so long that time itself seems to have stopped. Eventually, the mere continuation of this note is in itself a source of intensity: anything seems more likely than the continuation. When some-

thing else does happen, it comes as more of a relief than a surprise.

The new event is a strong pizzicato note—a new timbre that remains characteristic of the next section. Here again, the ear reacts first to the raw quality of sound, only gradually resolving it into its components, rhythm and pitch. There are now audible many clear, distinct, sustained pitches, often in recognizable solo timbres. There are also scratchy tones, produced by rapid articulations of a single pitch. There are percussive effects, sometimes isolated blips but later multiple, complex repercussions; and finally some very high, very brief squeaking figures.

The pitches involved in these various sounds are often widely separated—very high ones, alternating in quick succession with very low ones. Instead of a successive linking of events, there seems to be instantaneous movement from one register to another far away.

The temporal component of section 5 is a focus on low-level rhythm, more or less lacking up to this point. Events now succeed one another rapidly enough to make possible the idea of a pulse. You may or may not hear a pulse—certainly not a metrical one; yet a sense of rhythmic movement can be perceived.

Section 5 begins abruptly; you can pinpoint its first note. Section 6, with its sustained sounds and extremely slow rhythms, is a different matter. There is no sharp dividing line between sections 5 and 6; instead there is a gradual transition. At about 7 min 0 sec, you will become aware of a sustained combination of pitches that sounds subtly different from the materials of section 5, more like those of sections 1 or 3. The animation characteristic of section 5 continues for a while underneath the high sustained pitches, being phased out little by little.

TEXTURE. We can profitably use the concept of texture to describe the various effects found in the Threnody. If the frontal impact of the sounds in sections 3 and 4 can be called chords, then perhaps the texture of the first minute of section 1 can be termed "line" and can be compared to a "contrapuntal" texture in the contrasting section 5. Such terms must be used carefully, because they were developed within specific stylistic contexts—they were applied originally not to

any kind of line or chord but only to certain kinds. In using them to describe effects in Penderecki's Threnody, we are extending their application. The important point is that the Threnody uses various textures that can be readily distinguished one from another.

The more you can distinguish the various intense sounds of the Threnody, the more you can react to their succession in terms of larger rhythmic movement and pitch organization. You probably will not get far in following a specific pitch organization in the Threnody, but you should be able to hear the different kinds of pitch movement; and the sense of rhythmic movement—of pacing—should be relatively clear.

TITLE AND CONTENT. How is the shape of the piece related to its title and intent? We can approach this question only indirectly. On an intuitive basis, we can say that the piece uses sound in a dark, heavy manner rather than a light, bright one; if the same piece, under another title, had been intended as a divertimento or a joke, it would have been a very bad joke. The sound of the piece is certainly *appropriate* to its subject—which is not quite the same as saying that the piece unequivocally expresses the subject. In any case, we would have to conclude that the subject of the piece, strictly speaking, is restricted to that of a lament; specific circumstances of Hiroshima seem to be involved only in the dedication, not in the structure of the piece. At least, the piece seems far too serious, its anguish reaches far too deep, to permit us to see in the music any pictorial references to Hiroshima or any other purely external allusions such as mushroom-shaped clouds or the sound of airplanes.

Another way of approaching the problem is to ask, "Does the piece suggest, or require, a context outside the purely musical one?" It certainly suggests one: the initial intensity is difficult to absorb on its own terms, and (as we noticed before) the title gives the intensity focus and artistic limit. Perhaps no matter how familiar the piece becomes, its intensity still spills over the edges of the purely musical form.

TITLES AND PROGRAM MUSIC. You will frequently encounter orchestral pieces that have titles referring to extramusical contexts. In addition to titles, some orchestral pieces (called, generally, *program music*) have been provided by their composers with *programs* —literary (or even pictorial) descriptions, clues, or analogs for the content of the piece. If the composer of such a piece merely intends to depict in his music a story or a set of images—and if he succeeds—then of course the piece is straightaway comprehensible without requiring any specially musical understanding. Generally speaking, however, examples of program music you are likely to encounter are more challenging than that: their content will be as much musical as it is literary or pictorial, the program being merely a clue to the less accessible but more profound meanings inherent in the music. A program, then, is comparable to the text of a song cycle or opera, a factor that has to be understood with reference to the musical factors. In this respect, program music is no different from any other kind of music; in all cases, you must come to grips with the musical shape of a piece in order properly to appreciate whatever context the piece may have.

Richard Wagner (1813–1883)

TRISTAN UND ISOLDE
PRELUDE (VORSPIEL)

The Prelude was discussed in Chapter 5 as an example of a piece controlled very clearly by a single long-range rhythmic impulse. As you refine your perception of this large rhythmic shape by relating to it other factors, try not to let these other factors obscure your perception of the shape. The details of the Prelude are rich and attractive; the tempo is slow enough to allow ample opportunity to become lost in them.

As we said in Chapter 5, the high-level rhythm can be understood by analogy with wave-motion underrun by a flooding, then ebbing tide. The purpose of the analogy was to point out the long dimensions of rhythmic movement in the Prelude. Compared with this high-level rhythm, the rhythmic detail is relatively unimportant. The Prelude is metrical at its three lowest levels, with only a few rhythmic patterns being used throughout (as discussed before).

The low-level rhythm, in other words, provides continuous movement but not the means for shaping

this movement. The shaping is done at the level of the phrase group. These phrase groups, as sketched in Chapter 5, are clearly audible just as rhythms; but now, by taking into account aspects of line and harmony, we can fill in the phrase groups, making their relationships to each other more specific.

Example 10-7 Wagner, Prelude: Motives

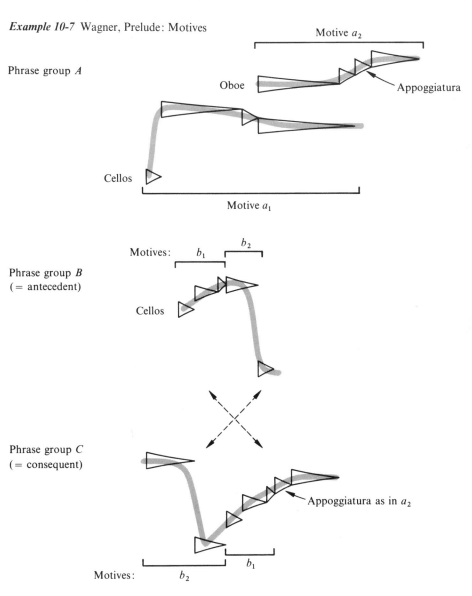

You are immediately aware, on first hearing, that the Prelude is melodious, but you are perhaps less aware of the specific lines with their clear beginnings and endings. One reason it is easy to confuse the various lines one with another is that they have melodic motives in common. Example 10-7 shows the principal motives of the Prelude, as found at the beginnings of the three main phrase groups we identified in Chapter 5 (see Exs. 5-21, 5-22, 5-23).

In phrase group A, from the very beginning of the Prelude, the cellos have a motive (a_1) distinguished by a large leap upward. The oboe's motive (a_2) consists entirely of movement by half steps. The third note of a_2 is an appoggiatura of a kind that reappears elsewhere in the Prelude, in phrase group C as well as in phrase group A.

The line at the beginning of phrase group B has two distinct motives labeled b_1 and b_2; b_1 ascends by step, b_2 drops through a wide leap. These same motives reappear at the beginning of phrase group C but in reverse order (b_2, then b_1) and are followed by the appoggiatura from motive a_2.

This relatively small group of motives provides material for most of the Prelude, giving a sense of

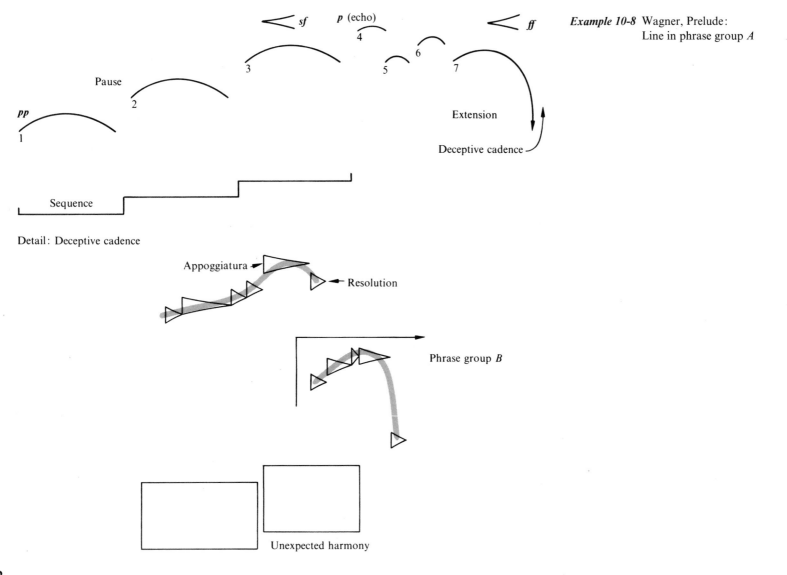

Example 10-8 Wagner, Prelude: Line in phrase group A

continuity, of homogeneity, to the whole. In this respect, the motives are closely related to the metric uniformity of the Prelude, for the motives are the very substance of the low-level rhythm, which is basically metric. Insofar as motives contribute to the sense of flowing sameness of the Prelude, however, they do not shape its larger rhythms.

PHRASE GROUP A. The best way to differentiate the lines of the various phrase groups and to gain a sense of their interrelationships is to consider the whole shape of the line of each phrase group. The most obvious feature of the line of phrase group *A* is its three-stage ascending sequence (shown in Ex. 10-8). The three opening statements, separated by pauses, repeat the same material at progressively higher pitches. The sequence, a linear factor, transforms the rhythmic repetitions into a shape that rises to a high point. In addition, the fragments of line at 4, 5, and 6 are heard as melodic echoes of what came before and of each other. Finally (even though it concerns har-

mony rather than line), the striking effect at the end of phrase group *A* needs to be mentioned here: the line ends on a deceptive cadence. The line itself comes to rest on an expected pitch; but the harmony beneath the line is unexpected and leads off into another harmonic area. The deceptive cadence has a profound effect upon the sense of phrase group *A*; it also opens the door to the rest of the Prelude.

PHRASE GROUP B. Simultaneously with the resolution of the appoggiatura over the unexpected harmony (see the detail, Ex. 10-8), phrase group *B* starts in the cellos. In Ex. 10-9, the line of phrase group *B* is shown in conjunction with the rhythmic shape from Ex. 5-22. The repetition of the basic rhythmic unit takes the form of an ascending sequence. Even though both rhythm and line are soon modified, the sequence can be heard at the beginning of the third rhythmic arch, pulling the rhythmic units together into a line characterized by an overall ascent.

The extensions of phrase group *B* are relatively

simple in line and rhythm but complex in harmony. Two harmonic shifts take place in succession, as marked in Ex. 10-9; each seems to escape momentarily in a different direction from the expected harmonic area; yet somehow both are brought back into the longer line that governs the whole phrase group. The line ends with more rising motion and a sense of openness.

One of the most difficult, most important, steps in understanding the shape of the Prelude is hearing the phrase relationship that exists between phrase groups *B* and *C*. These two phrase groups stand in the relationship of antecedent and consequent. Hearing this relationship involves, first of all, hearing phrase groups *B* and *C* as units—in itself no easy task. To pinpoint the problem, you must be able to hear through the extensions and repetitions with their harmonic twists in the second half of phrase group *B*, for if the first half of *B* were followed directly by *C*, the antecedent-consequent relationship would be clearer.

Example 10-9 Wagner, Prelude, phrase group *B*

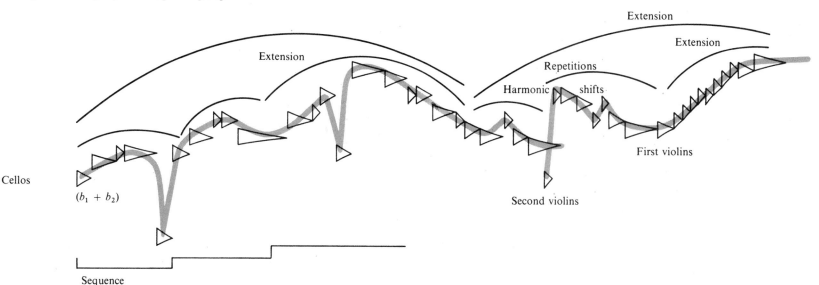

PHRASE GROUP C. The consequent is opposed to the antecedent in line and harmony and also is simpler in rhythm. The consequent opens with a descending sequence (see Ex. 10-10). The two extensions are at the same basic pitch level, in spite of the raising of one prominent pitch in the second extension. The harmonies under the sequence fall by easy, regular motion to a half cadence, without the surge and drive heard in the harmonies of the antecedent. Even in the extensions, the harmonies, while more intense, are still more regular than those of the antecedent—as you can hear by comparing them directly with the antecedent when it follows in phrase group D.

Everything about phrase group B, the antecedent, is less stable, more driven, than phrase group C, the consequent. These two phrase groups belong together in a large rhythm of tension and relaxation. Similar relationships can be found in many places at the lower levels of the Prelude; there are many smaller antecedents and consequents. But for the purposes of a discussion of high-level shape, we can call phrase group B *the* antecedent phrase of the Prelude and phrase group C *the* consequent.

OVERALL PLAN. You can follow the phrase structure of the Prelude at its highest level with the aid of Ex. 10-11. The effect of the linear antecedent-consequent relationship of phrase groups B and C is to create a higher grouping than is apparent from a consideration of rhythmic detail alone; the difference is symbolized in the braces around B and C, and around D, E, and F, in Ex. 10-11.

The consequent, C, does not appear in the Prelude after phrase F. The effect of eliminating it is to accelerate the phrase rhythm at the highest level, producing much the same kind of insistence as is found at lower levels within, say, phrase group F, toward the end. From G on, only the antecedent appears; variety is accomplished by changing the pitch level of the antecedent (as at G) or by alternating the antecedent with a modified form (as at I)—which also happens to incorporate insistent, accelerated repetitions.

HARMONIC MOTION. It is a paradox of the Prelude that its harmonies, in seemingly constant motion as if agitated by profound restlessness, are clustered

around lines that return again and again at the same pitch. The return of phrase group A at the same pitch in K is easily understandable: this return marks the completion of the rhythmic cycle. It is not so easy to understand the return of the antecedent B, at the same pitch in every case except G. Even at J, where the Prelude is being wrought up to its most intense point, the antecedent line is at its original pitch. Even more curious, just before (in I), the oboe's motive, a_2, returns at its original pitch. Here, the return of a_2 brings no sense of the closure felt strongly in K; yet not only line but also the harmonization of a_2 in I is close to the beginning of the Prelude. The reason for the lack of closure here must have something to do with the rhythmic motion, strong enough to override a suggestion of pitch.

The reiteration of the pitch level of the antecedent seems to contribute to the insistent feeling of the Prelude. The consequent, too, returns at its original pitch. If you could compare the beginning of the antecedent with the consequent, you would find a significant difference in harmonic area. This is not immediately apparent in the Prelude as you hear it,

Example 10-10 Wagner, Prelude, phrase group C

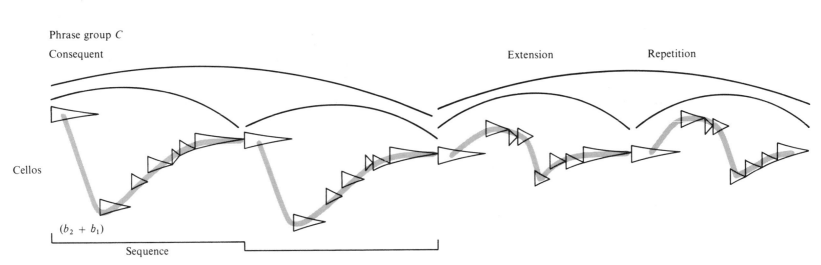

because the extensions and repetitions that end the antecedent, with their harmonic twists, make the transition from the one harmonic area to the other. Yet somewhere in the experience of the piece is a basic opposition between antecedent and consequent. Their alternation in the first half of the Prelude is what makes that half broader, slower, than the second half.

The use of the same pitch levels again and again would not be possible without intense variety at the lower levels of harmonic structure. The flux and surge of individual harmonies is immediately apparent—indeed, it has seemed to many observers to be the most prominent aspect of the Prelude. You can get a more specific idea of harmonic variety by listening very carefully to successive statements of the antecedent, hearing how it is subtly reharmonized each time. The intense harmonies have the very important function of attracting attention to momentary effects, so that the larger shape—which, considered abstractly, is very simple—will not seem obvious.

END OF THE PRELUDE. As explained in Chapter 5, there are alternate endings to the Prelude, depending on whether it is to be played in a concert or as an introduction to the music drama. From a structural point of view, the dramatic version is the most interesting. In this version, the end of Ex. 10-11 is followed by yet another statement of the antecedent, incomplete but still at the same pitch; it is reharmonized, not to urge it on this time but rather to turn it in a new direction. As a result, the end of the Prelude is left wide open, preparing for the stage action and singing that follow immediately.

Considered either by itself or as an introduction to the drama, the Prelude is a remarkable example of how the form of a piece sometimes seems to be identical with its highest-level rhythm, or at least to be best expressed by that rhythm.

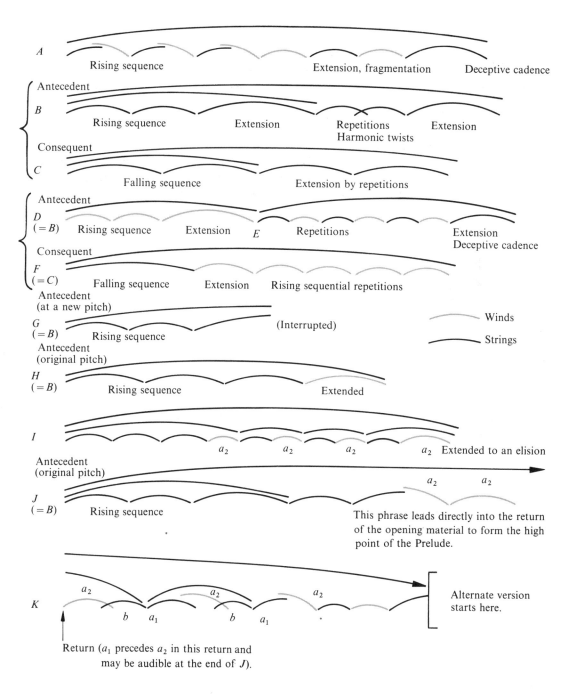

Example 10-11 Wagner, Prelude:
Plan of phrase groups

Exercises for further listening

I. SCHUBERT: "PAUSE" (DIE SCHONE MULLERIN, SONG 12)

A first look at the overall shape. Listen to the entire song, following the text given here. You may wish to look at the discussion questions (following question 28) now, and keep them in mind as you listen in detail and answer questions 1 through 4. To answer these questions, listen again to the piano introduction, keeping in mind the overall shape of the song. Relate the details of the piano accompaniment to the larger shape.

Text of "Pause" (A complete translation will be found at the end of Chapter 11.)

Section 1:

A (*Piano introduction*)

1 Meine Laute hab' ich gehängt an die Wand,
2 Hab' sie umschlungen mit einem grünen Band,
3 Ich kann nicht mehr singen, mein Herz ist zu voll,
4 Weiss nicht, wie ich's in Reime zwingen soll.

Section 2:

B (*Piano*)

5 Meiner Sehnsucht allerheissesten Schmerz
6 Durft' ich aushauchen in Liederscherz,
7 Und wie ich klagte so süss und fein,
8 Glaubt' ich doch, mein Leiden wär' nicht klein.

C (*Piano cadence*)

Section 3:

9 Ei, wie gross ist wohl meines Glückes Last,
10 Dass kein Klang auf Erden es in sich fasst,
11 Dass kein Klang auf Erden es in sich fasst?

D (*Piano cadence*)

Section 4:

E (*Piano*)

12 Nun, liebe Laute, ruh' an dem Nagel hier!
13 Und weht ein Lüftchen über die Saiten dir,
14 Und streift eine Biene mit ihren Flügeln dich,
15 Da wird mir so bange, und es durchschauert mich.

Section 5:

F (*Piano*)

16 Warum liess ich das Band auch hängen so lang'?
17 Oft fliegt's um die Saiten mit seufzendem Klang.

G (*Piano*)

18 Ist es der Nachklang meiner Liebespein?
19 Soll es das Vorspiel neuer Lieder sein?

H (*Piano*)

20 Ist es der Nachklang meiner Liebespein?
21 Soll es das Vorspiel neuer Lieder sein?

I (*Piano conclusion*)

1. The piano introduction consists of

___ **a.** One phrase
___ **b.** Two phrases
___ **c.** Three phrases
___ **d.** Four phrases

1. b

2. The melodic shape of the introduction is

    ____ **a.** $a\,a\,b\,b$ ____ **b.** $a\,b\,a\,b$ ____ **c.** $a\,a_1\,b\,b_1$ ____ **d.** $a\,b\,a\,b_1$

              2. d

3. The first phrase $(a\,b)$ ends

    ____ **a.** With a full cadence (closed)

    ____ **b.** With a half cadence (open)

              3. b

4. The second phrase $(a\,b_1)$ ends

    ____ **a.** With a full cadence (closed)

    ____ **b.** With a half cadence (open)

              4. a

Listen to the entire song, concentrating on the material from the piano introduction. Follow the text given above as you listen. Answer questions 5 through 9.

5. Which of the piano passages contain material from the introduction?

    ____ B   ____ C   ____ D   ____ E   ____ F   ____ G   ____ H   ____ I

              5. E, F, G, H, I

6. Which one of the piano passages is like the first phrase of the piano introduction?

    ____ E   ____ F   ____ G   ____ H   ____ I

              6. E

7. Which one of the piano passages is similar to the last phrase of the piano introduction?

    ____ F   ____ G   ____ H   ____ I

              7. I

8. In which sections of the song does material from the piano introduction occur in the accompaniment to the voice part? Mark each one.

    ____ **a.** In section 1   ____ **b.** In section 2

    ____ **c.** In section 3   ____ **d.** In section 4

    ____ **e.** In section 5

              8. a, d, e

9. Does material from the piano introduction ever appear in the vocal line?

    ____ Yes

    ____ No

              9. No

Harmonic relationships. Listen to the entire song, section by section as directed, following the text. Keep the overall shape in mind as you work with the harmonic detail. Answer questions 10 through 28.

10. The piano introduction

    ____ **a.** Stays within a single harmonic area

    ____ **b.** Moves from one harmonic area to another

              10. a

11. The music of lines 1 through 4　　　　　　　　　　　　　　　**11.** a
____ **a.** Begins and ends in the same harmonic area
____ **b.** Begins in one harmonic area and ends in another

12. The music of lines 1 through 4　　　　　　　　　　　　　　　**12.** a
____ **a.** Is in the same harmonic area as the piano introduction
____ **b.** Is in a different harmonic area than the piano introduction

13. Section 1 ends (at the end of line 4)　　　　　　　　　　　　　**13.** b
____ **a.** With a half cadence　　____ **b.** With a full cadence

14. At what point in the song does the harmonic area of section 1 next appear?　**14.** c
____ **a.** At the beginning of section 2
____ **b.** At the beginning of section 3
____ **c.** At the beginning of section 4
____ **d.** At the beginning of section 5

15. The song ends (piano conclusion, I)　　　　　　　　　　　　　**15.** a
____ **a.** In the original harmonic area
____ **b.** In another harmonic area

16. At the beginning of section 2　　　　　　　　　　　　　　　　**16.** c
____ **a.** There is a change of harmonic color but not of harmonic area
____ **b.** There is a change of harmonic area but not of harmonic color
____ **c.** Both the harmonic color and the harmonic area change
____ **d.** Neither the harmonic color nor the harmonic area changes

17. From the end of section 1 to the beginning of section 2, the harmony has changed from　**17.** b
____ **a.** Minor to major
____ **b.** Major to minor

18. Section 2 as a whole　　　　　　　　　　　　　　　　　　　**18.** c
____ **a.** Is entirely in minor
____ **b.** Is entirely in major
____ **c.** Fluctuates back and forth between major and minor

19. Section 2 ends　　　　　　　　　　　　　　　　　　　　　**19.** b
____ **a.** With a full cadence in the original harmonic area
____ **b.** With a full cadence in another harmonic area

20. Section 3 as a whole   **20.** b
___ **a.** Stays within a single harmonic area
___ **b.** Moves through more than one harmonic area

21. Section 3 ends   **21.** c
___ **a.** With a full cadence in the original harmonic area
___ **b.** With a full cadence in another harmonic area
___ **c.** With a half cadence in the original harmonic area

22. Section 4, which begins in the original harmonic area,   **22.** b
___ **a.** Ends in the original harmonic area   ___ **b.** Ends in another harmonic area

23. Section 5 begins   **23.** c
___ **a.** In minor
___ **b.** In the original harmonic area
___ **c.** In a distant harmonic area

24. Section 5 as a whole   **24.** b
___ **a.** Stays within a single harmonic area
___ **b.** Moves through several harmonic areas

25. At what point does the original harmonic area return?   **25.** c
___ **a.** In line 17, on "*Klang*"
___ **b.** In line 18, on "Liebes*pein*"
___ **c.** In line 19, on "*sein*"

26. The music of lines 20 and 21 repeats the harmonies of   **26.** c
___ **a.** Lines 16 and 17
___ **b.** Lines 17 and 18
___ **c.** Lines 18 and 19

27. In the final piano phrase (I), the harmony changes from   **27.** d
___ **a.** Minor to major
___ **b.** Major to minor
___ **c.** Minor to major, back to minor
___ **d.** Major to minor, back to major

28. The most distant harmonic excursions occur in sections   **28.** b
___ **a.** 1 and 2   ___ **b.** 3 and 5   ___ **c.** 4 and 5

209

QUESTIONS FOR DISCUSSION

A. What is the overall shape of "Pause"? Is its sectional shape as clear as that of "Die liebe Farbe"? As that of "Der Neugierige"? Would a relative lack of clarity of shape be significant in terms of the poem?

B. How is the accompaniment related to the vocal line? Is the accompaniment or the vocal melody more important in shaping the song? How is the material from the first measure of the piano introduction used in the song: as figure? as motive? as theme? Does the role played by the accompaniment in "Pause" differ from that of the accompaniment in other songs from *Die schöne Müllerin* that you have studied?

C. Of what significance is the change of harmonic color in the concluding piano phrase? Is it related to the harmonic shape of the song? To the meaning of the poem?

D. "Pause" has the same harmonic center as that of the song which follows it, "Mit dem grünen Lautenbande." Compare the two songs: To what extent can they be thought of as a pair? Which is more stable harmonically? Which has a clearer, more straightforward sectional shape? How does the harmonic and sectional shape of each song relate to the meaning of the poem in each case?

E. Return to question A. Would you answer it differently, now that you have done some detailed harmonic listening? To what extent does harmony shape the song at a high level? Are other elements—melody, rhythm, texture, motivic detail—as important? More important?

II. DAVIDOVSKY: SYNCHRONISMS NO. 3 FOR CELLO AND ELECTRONIC SOUNDS

Listen to the entire work; you may wish to consider the discussion questions (following question 24) before answering questions 1 through 3.

1. The work opens with
___ **a.** Cello alone
___ **b.** Cello and electronic sounds
___ **c.** Electronic sounds alone

1. a

2. At the very beginning of the cello part
___ **a.** There is a high sustained tone followed by a generally descending line
___ **b.** There is a low sustained tone followed by an ascending line
___ **c.** The cello plays entirely disjunct, pizzicato pitches

2. b

3. The material at the very beginning of the piece
___ **a.** Never returns again   ___ **b.** Returns somewhere in the middle
___ **c.** Returns just before the end

3. c

4. The return of the sustained note from the opening of the piece   **4.** a
____ **a.** Is at the same pitch as the original note
____ **b.** Is not at the same pitch as the original note

5. The return of the opening material   **5.** b
____ **a.** Is exactly the same as the original statement
____ **b.** Is shorter than the original statement
____ **c.** Is longer than the original statement

6. In this work   **6.** c
____ **a.** Both the cello and the electronic sounds play continuously throughout
____ **b.** The electronic sounds play continuously; the cello is present only part of the time
____ **c.** The cello plays continuously; the electronic sounds are present only part of the time

7. In their timbre, rhythmic shape, and melodic gesture, the electronic sounds and the cello   **7.** b
____ **a.** Are completely differentiated; there is no similarity between them
____ **b.** Are somewhat similar, each imitating the other's gestures
____ **c.** Are exactly alike, the electronic sounds imitating the cello sounds

8. The texture consists principally (but not entirely) of   **8.** b
____ **a.** Chords ____ **b.** A single line ____ **c.** Counterpoint

9. The melodic line   **9.** b
____ **a.** Contains few leaps (is conjunct) ____ **b.** Contains many leaps (is disjunct)

10. The cello   **10.** c
____ **a.** Remains mainly in a high register
____ **b.** Remains mainly in a low register
____ **c.** Moves rapidly through various registers

11. In this section, the cello most often plays   **11.** a
____ **a.** Arco (with the bow) ____ **b.** Pizzicato (plucking the strings)

12. The tempo of this section is
_____ a. Basically slow to medium, with some fast rhythmic details
_____ b. Basically fast to very fast, with some slow notes

12. a

13. The rhythm is
_____ a. Metrically organized
_____ b. Not metrically organized

13. b

14. Within the basic, moderately slow tempo,
_____ a. There is a clearly perceptible unit pulse
_____ b. The rhythm moves in flexible groupings without a clear pulse
_____ c. Neither unit pulse nor rhythmic groupings are perceptible

14. b

15. The rhythm shapes the melodic lines so that
_____ a. All of the pitches have equal importance
_____ b. Some pitches are syncopated
_____ c. Some pitches are stressed and serve as important points of arrival

15. c

Listen from the first entrance of the electronic sounds as far as the long pause following a very high pitch in the cello. (The electronic sounds stop, reenter, and stop again during this section.) Answer questions 16 through 19.

16. The electronic part enters
_____ a. With a single sustained pitch
_____ b. With a flurry of rapid sounds
_____ c. With chords

16. a

17. In their first appearance, the electronic sounds
_____ a. Continue the general linear and rhythmic character of the previous cello section
_____ b. Contrast greatly with the rhythmic and linear character of the previous cello section

17. a

18. The texture of this section, until the cello again plays alone, might be described as
_____ a. Chordal
_____ b. Counterpoint between two distinct lines
_____ c. A single line
(Do not let the changing timbre of the electronic sounds distract you!)

18. b

19. From the point at which the electronic sounds first drop out until the cello's high cadential note, the cello plays mainly
_____ a. Arco (with the bow)
_____ b. Pizzicato (plucked strings)

19. a

Listen to the section following the cello's cadence and subsequent pause, until the end of the piece. (This section begins with solo cello, arco.) Answer questions 20 through 24.

20. Between the entrance of the electronic sounds and the return of the opening material, the cello plays

    ___ **a.** Arco

    ___ **b.** Pizzicato

    20. b

21. The electronic sounds

    ___ **a.** Resemble the cello's pizzicato sounds

    ___ **b.** Are much more legato than the cello's pizzicato sounds

    21. a

22. The passage with pizzicato cello and electronic sounds

    ___ **a.** Is as linear as the preceding part of the piece

    ___ **b.** Is less linear, more discontinuous than the preceding part of the piece

    22. b

23. Immediately before the return of the opening passage, the register of the cello and of most of the electronic sounds becomes

    ___ **a.** Very high

    ___ **b.** Very low

    23. b

24. The moment of return is marked by

    ___ **a.** The cello's change from pizzicato to arco

    ___ **b.** The disappearance of the electronic sounds

    ___ **c.** Both *a* and *b*

    ___ **d.** Neither *a* nor *b*

    24. c

QUESTIONS FOR DISCUSSION

A. Does the return give an *A B A* shape to the work? In answering this question, consider the overall proportions of the piece. How important is the return in shaping the piece?

B. Are the cello part and the electronic part equal in importance? Or does one provide an accompaniment to the other?

C. The beginning of the piece is marked *Espressivo assai*—that is, "very expressive." How has the composer used melodic and rhythmic shape, register, and various types of contrast to achieve intensity of expression?

D. How could you describe the overall shape of *Synchronisms No. 3*? To what extent is the piece shaped by rhythmic and melodic detail? By contrasts in timbre and texture? By high-level repetition? (Review questions A and B before answering this question.)

Review quiz 2

I. SHAPE, THEME, AND MOTIVE

Listen to the entire movement. Answer questions 1 through 7.

1. The first large contrast during the Allegretto involves a sudden change from
   ___ **a.** Duple to triple meter
   ___ **b.** Triple to duple meter
   ___ **c.** Major to minor harmonic color
   ___ **d.** A moderate tempo to a very slow tempo

2. Immediately following the contrasting section in minor
   ___ **a.** The opening theme (in major) returns
   ___ **b.** New material (in major) appears
   ___ **c.** There is a change to triple meter

3. The return of the opening theme is
   ___ **a.** Exactly the same as the original statement
   ___ **b.** Longer than the original statement
   ___ **c.** Shorter than the original statement

4. After this return,
   ___ **a.** The opening theme is not heard again in the movement, in a recognizable form
   ___ **b.** The opening theme is heard again in the movement, in a recognizable form

5. In its final return, the opening theme
   ___ **a.** Is exactly the same as at the beginning
   ___ **b.** Is exactly the same as in its second, shortened appearance
   ___ **c.** Is shorter than in its second appearance

6. In the movement as a whole
   ___ **a.** There are two distinct and contrasting themes
   ___ **b.** There is only one distinct theme
   ___ **c.** There are at least three distinct and contrasting themes

7. The sections in which the theme does not appear are built principally upon

___ **a.** Motives not derived from the theme

___ **b.** Figuration

___ **c.** Motives derived from the theme

II. TIMBRE

Listen to the movement as a whole, following the sectional diagram given here. Answer questions 8 through 15.

1 — Theme (major, *p*)

2 — Contrasting section (minor, begins *f*)	3 — Theme (shortened)

4 — Motivic section	5 — Theme (short)	6— Motivic section Tutti *ff*	7— Motivic section (Begins *p*)

8. Section 1 is played by

___ **a.** Tutti (strings, winds, brass, and percussion)

___ **b.** Groups of woodwinds and strings

___ **c.** Strings only

___ **d.** Woodwinds only

9. Section 2 begins with

___ **a.** Tutti

___ **b.** Woodwinds and strings

___ **c.** Strings only

___ **d.** Woodwinds only

10. The beginning of section 3 is played by

___ **a.** Tutti

___ **b.** Woodwinds and pizzicato strings

___ **c.** Woodwinds and bowed strings

___ **d.** Strings only

11. Section 3 ends with

___ **a.** Tutti

___ **b.** Groups of woodwinds and strings

___ **c.** Strings only

___ **d.** Woodwinds only

12. Section 4 is played by

____ **a.** Tutti   ____ **b.** Woodwinds and bowed strings

____ **c.** Woodwinds and pizzicato strings   ____ **d.** Woodwinds only

13. Section 5 is played by

____ **a.** Tutti   ____ **b.** Groups of woodwinds and strings

____ **c.** Strings only   ____ **d.** Woodwinds only

14. Immediately preceding the *ff* tutti in section 6, there is a striking passage played by

____ **a.** Strings and woodwinds

____ **b.** Brass and percussion

____ **c.** Strings and percussion

15. In the last section

____ **a.** There is a contrast between strings and woodwinds

____ **b.** There is a contrast between small groups and tutti

____ **c.** Both *a* and *b* are true

____ **d.** Neither *a* nor *b* is true

III. STRUCTURE OF THE THEME

Listen to section 1 (the theme), following the phrase diagram given here. Answer questions 16 through 25.

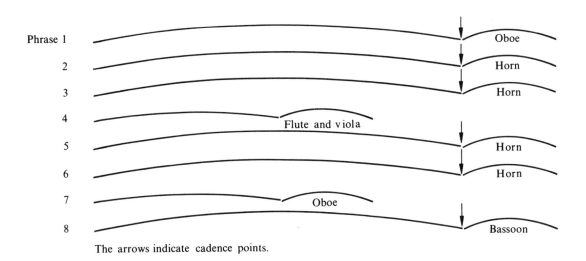

The arrows indicate cadence points.

16. Phrase 1 (strings and solo flute) ends with

___ **a.** A full cadence ___ **b.** A half cadence ___ **c.** Neither *a* nor *b*

17. Phrase 2

___ **a.** Has exactly the same melodic shape as phrase 1

___ **b.** Has a melodic shape somewhat related to that of phrase 1

___ **c.** Has a melodic shape completely different than that of phrase 1

18. Phrase 2 is played by

___ **a.** Strings only

___ **b.** Strings and woodwinds

___ **c.** Woodwinds only

19. Phrase 3 is played by

___ **a.** All the woodwinds and strings

___ **b.** Flute and strings

___ **c.** All the woodwinds and brass

20. Phrase 3

___ **a.** Stays within the original harmonic area

___ **b.** Moves to a closely related harmonic area

21. Phrase 4 (a short phrase) consists essentially of

___ **a.** The central harmony (in the original harmonic area)

___ **b.** The leading harmony (in the original harmonic area)

22. Phrase 5 ends

___ **a.** Open, in the original harmonic area

___ **b.** Closed, in the original harmonic area

___ **c.** In a harmonic area other than the original one

23. Phrases 6, 7, and 8 are played by

___ **a.** Woodwinds only

___ **b.** Strings only

___ **c.** Woodwinds and strings

24. Phrases 6, 7, and 8 as a group

___ **a.** Are like phrases 2, 3, 4 ___ **b.** Are like phrases 3, 4, 5

___ **c.** Resemble no previous phrases

25. Indicate by means of letters (*a*, *b*, etc.) the phrase shape of the entire theme.

IV. HARMONIC AND THEMATIC RELATIONS IN THE ALLEGRETTO

Listen to the entire movement, keeping the shape and harmonic area of the theme in mind. Answer questions 26 through 31.

26. The phrase shape of the shortened version of the theme in section 3 is
___ **a.** $a_1 \, a_1 \, b \, a_2$
___ **b.** $a_1 \, b \, a_2$
___ **c.** $a_1 \, b \, b \, a_2$

27. The return of the theme in section 3
___ **a.** Is in the original harmonic area
___ **b.** Is not in the original harmonic area

28. In section 5, the only part of the theme that remains is phrase
___ **a.** a_1
___ **b.** b
___ **c.** a_2

29. The return of the theme in section 5
___ **a.** Is in the original harmonic area
___ **b.** Is not in the original harmonic area

30. From what part of the theme does most of the motivic material in the Allegretto derive?

31. At what point in the movement is there a striking change of harmonic center?
___ **a.** At the beginning of section 2
___ **b.** At the beginning of section 4
___ **c.** At the *ff* tutti passage in section 6
___ **d.** At the end of section 7

ANSWERS TO REVIEW QUIZ 2

1. c
2. a
3. c
4. b
5. c
6. b
7. c
8. b
9. a
10. b
11. a
12. d
13. a
14. b (trumpet and timpani)
15. c
16. b
17. a
18. c
19. b
20. b
21. b
22. b
23. a
24. b
25. $a_1\ a_1\ b\ a_2\ b\ a_2$
26. b
27. a
28. c
29. a
30. From the beginning (first 6 notes) of the theme
31. c

CHAPTER 11

SCHUBERT'S SONG CYCLE DIE SCHONE MULLERIN

WE CAN BEGIN a study of multimovement pieces with Schubert's song cycle *Die schöne Müllerin*. So far, we have studied several songs from the cycle: "Der Neugierige," "Das Wandern," "Am Feierabend," "Die liebe Farbe," and "Der Müller und der Bach." Each of these songs had a clear, complete shape. In dealing with each song individually, we had no strong feeling that it was a fragment—except, possibly, a feeling that the text of the song was somehow incomplete, as if there was more to the story that we should know.

The problem of larger form in *Die schöne Müllerin* is to a great extent a problem of the relationship of music and text. A sense of purely musical form is strongest in the individual song; it is weaker in the cycle as a whole. Musically speaking, the cycle consists of a long succession of units, each clearly formed in itself, placed together in a relatively loose overall form.

THE TEXT OF THE CYCLE. Schubert made a selection of texts from a somewhat longer cycle of poems with the same title by Wilhelm Müller (1794–1827). Müller provided his cycle with a preface, making very clear his intention. He thought of his cycle as a rustic, folklike work to be read by sophisticated city dwellers in the winter; he hoped to bring to them an atmosphere of naïve yet poignant drama. However, he deliberately used a nondramatic, essentially lyric format—a succession of songlike poems whose dramatic continuity is implicit rather than explicit. Each poem embodies an intense moment in the story;

the story itself is often only hinted at, sometimes left completely to inference or imagination. By omitting some of the poems, Schubert made the details of the story even less explicit.

This kind of text tends to lay stress on fleeting allusions in individual poems, in the manner of a folk ballad that only alludes to the tragic circumstances of a story well known to the ballad's audience. In the case of Müller's cycle of poems, the technique of allusion is used consciously and deliberately, as is also the naïve, rustic tone. The frequent use of strophic form (as in the texts of the songs we have already studied) is also a deliberate use of a simple, folklike device.

The story itself is simple and perennial: the footloose lad falls in love with the miller's daughter, apprentices himself to the miller to be near her. She does not return his love or at least is not faithful; in despair he casts himself into the millstream. A more detailed idea of the story can best be gained by reading through the complete text and translation, which follow at the end of the chapter.

THE TEXT AS DRAMA. Considered as a drama, the cycle is clearly a monolog. That is, only the miller lad speaks; we hear the miller's daughter only as she speaks in his memory and the brook only as it speaks in his imagination. We know nothing of her inner feelings, only of his. Out of his lyric musings and passionate outcries, we must reconstruct the events of the story; and the story, in its external aspects, seems far less important than the miller lad's inner

life of fantasy, love, desperate decision, and final renunciation. We get to know the brook, for example, better than the miller's daughter herself, for the brook is the lad's constant companion in fantasy and his true friend at the last. If the story is a drama, it is almost completely an inner one; for all we know, the boy and the girl may never have actually exchanged more than the most casual remarks.

TEXT AND MUSIC. The idea of the poem cycle, then, presents the composer with some delicate problems. Heavy-handed dramatic expression is out of the question; the poem will not allow it. An obvious sense of continuity, too, is inappropriate. Schubert's musical design faithfully reflects Müller's poetic one. Schubert provides an independent musical setting for each poem. The musical connection between songs is implicit and allusive (as we will hear)—seldom explicit. The song is the stronger unit; the cycle is relatively weaker. Still, the cycle has a continuity, just as the poems have a story.

The poetic cycle is strong enough to stand by itself without music; that is the way it was originally intended. One way of setting the cycle to music would be to provide only the simplest kind of music, in strictly strophic form, for each poem—as a folk singer might sing it. Schubert's setting is far more ambitious than that: the music undertakes to convey a deeper expression on its own, rather than merely serving as a vehicle for the text. Moreover, the music, by its deviation from strophic form or by some other formal complexity not expected in a simple song, diverts attention from the surface meaning of the poem to deeper realms of meaning as much musical as they are poetic.

The strong tendency toward discontinuity manifests itself not only in outward format of the music, but in inner substance as well. It is difficult to hear the cycle as a musical whole—or at least, it is difficult to become aware of the factors that shape it into a whole. Here is a case in which it is helpful to consider the basic aspects of music in turn, to see which might possibly contribute significantly to the overall shape.

TIMBRE. The timbre of the cycle is constant throughout: all the songs are sung by solo voice and are accompanied by piano. There is no provision for different voices to sing the words spoken by different characters (for example, the girl or the brook)—as there would be in a truly dramatic setting. The only concession, as it were, to dramatic verisimilitude is that the singer is a man (tenor or baritone), although sometimes the whole cycle and often individual songs are sung by a woman.

The piano accompaniment, too, provides a uniform timbre. More varied accompanimental timbres could be provided, for example, by an ensemble of winds and strings. It would not be fair, however, to say that the piano's quality of sound is completely uniform throughout, for the piano has many resources and in the hands of a skilled performer can produce—within its basic timbre—a wide variety of sounds. However, as far as the composer is concerned, changes in the quality of sound are produced by changes in the texture of the accompaniment, in still more subtle changes in the spacing of notes in harmonies, and in the kinds of rhythmic figure.

ARTICULATION. The articulation, while extremely important at the level of detail, does not change in ways that are significant for the overall design of the cycle. The most important aspect of the articulation is the smooth legato (for the sake of the melody) combined with a clear enunciation of the words—a combination diligently striven for by the most famous performers of this work. Like the uniform timbre of voice and piano, the prevailing legato is related to the songlike quality of the work; it is appropriate that songs (especially songs that so often sound like folk songs) should be sung in this manner. Timbre and articulation, being uniform, help establish a sense of continuity in the cycle.

DYNAMICS. Changes in dynamics are frequent throughout *Die schöne Müllerin*. Many such changes are expressly directed by the composer, many more are added by individual singers and accompanists. There is, of course, no way to tell just by listening which are which; however, it is always in order to try to decide whether the dynamics you hear in a performance are appropriate to the piece as a whole and to determine what the dynamics have to do with other

aspects of construction. Generally speaking, in *Die schöne Müllerin* the dynamics have structural significance only at the lower levels: they serve to throw a phrase into relief or to provide variety from one phrase to the next. Sometimes dynamics have a special dramatic function. In "Der Neugierige," for example, the climactic statement, " . . . Nein, die beiden Wörtchen schliessen die ganze Welt mir ein," is provided with a crescendo that reverts abruptly to a pianissimo, which is the dynamic level prevailing throughout the song. Indirectly, then, dynamics are related to the larger design through lines of text that happened to be dramatically intense as well as significant for the story.

While articulation is generally uniform and dynamics are primarily of low-level importance, accents on the level of detail sometimes have surprisingly long-range significance in *Die schöne Müllerin*. Many of the songs have an especially accented note, usually toward the end of the song and usually in the voice part. In "Das Wandern," for example, prominent accents occur at the end of each stanza on the words "Das *Wan*dern, das *Wan*dern, das *Wan*dern, das *Wan*dern." Accents such as these can become the focal point of a song; standing out above the rest of the song, they sometimes seem to enter into relationships with other accents in other songs.

It is remarkable—and characteristic of *Die schöne Müllerin*—that such low-level events as single accented notes could participate directly in high-level structure. A similar thing happens with details of the story (the green ribbon, for example) that take on importance all out of proportion to their intrinsic nature. All this happens easily in the allusive language of the folk ballad.

We cannot, however, begin with a study of the accents but must instead gain a more comprehensive idea of the succession of songs; later we can discuss how some of the accents and other details help shape the succession.

TEXTURE. In "Der Neugierige" changes in texture helped divide the song into sections. The texture prevailing in this song (and throughout the cycle) is melody and accompaniment, but several subtle varieties of this prevailing texture made their appear-

ance. In some sections, the accompaniment was strictly chordal; in others, it moved rhythmically in the "um-pah" manner; in still others, the rhythmic movement took the form of figuration. In "Der Müller und der Bach," such figures could be so closely related to harmonies as to be inseparable, such as the combination of rhythmic figure and harmony in a figurated chord. The accompaniment to "Das Wandern" consists of figurated or broken chords throughout. Finally, you need to be alert everywhere in *Die schöne Müllerin* to sudden, brief appearances of special textures for special purposes. In "Der Neugierige," a climactic line of text (" . . . Nein, die beiden Wörtchen schliessen die ganze Welt mir ein") calls forth a texture new to that song. The new texture is a very simple one (it is homophonic); it is the change that is decisive.

The texture of broken chords is particularly important at the higher levels of *Die schöne Müllerin*—so important that its presence or absence can be used to make a rough preliminary map of the cycle. You could profitably listen to the beginning of each song, in order to gain an idea of the distribution of textures.

"Das Wandern" has an accompaniment consisting completely of broken chords. The same kind of accompaniment is heard throughout the second song, "Wohin?" The figuration of the third song ("Halt!") is also in broken chords, although here the kind of figure used in connection with the broken chords is different; even so, the insistent rustling of the accompaniment texture seems to group the third song with the first two.

The fourth song, "Danksagung an den Bach," is noticeably slower than the preceding ones, and the accompaniment often suggests melodic lines rather than broken chords. Perhaps if there were only these four songs to consider, the textural differences among them would be significant. Considered in the context of the whole cycle, however, the first four songs can be grouped together by their common use of broken-chord accompaniment. This grouping becomes apparent during the fifth song, "Am Feierabend," which begins abruptly with a change to a chordal texture in the piano part, in brusque rhythms strongly articulated by silences; this is a new texture, a new sound in the cycle. At first, the new texture sounds for only a moment; then before the voice enters, the piano accompaniment returns to arpeggiated chords. But as the song proceeds, the chordal texture returns in several forms. The textural continuity of the first four songs has been clearly interrupted.

From this point on, broken-chord accompaniment—when it appears—is likely to be noticed as an event of greater or less significance. In a moment, we will try to see more precisely what that significance might be; but first, looking ahead briefly, the next song is "Der Neugierige," which begins with a chordal accompaniment. A broken-chord figure follows later in the song, interrupted by the special homophonic passage on "Nein, die beiden Wörtchen schliessen die ganze Welt mir ein." The seventh song, "Ungeduld," has an agitated accompaniment, but not because its chords are broken; rather, the chords are rapidly repeated. Much of the accompaniment is closer to the "um-pah" type. Song 8, "Morgengruss," is entirely chordal in its beginning, becoming mildly broken as it goes along but never with the insistence found in the first four songs.

Song 9, "Des Müllers Blumen," can be said to have a broken-chord accompaniment; but the next song, "Tränenregen"—even while having much in common with "Des Müllers Blumen"—is substantially more linear in the texture of its accompaniment. Song 11 ("Mein!") makes obvious use of broken chords throughout; with "Mein!" we seem to have returned decisively to the kind of texture established at the beginning of the cycle. Several aspects of this song seem to mark a division in the cycle—the song seems like the end of a major section. One of these aspects is the reappearance of broken-chord accompaniment.

1	"Das Wandern"	
2	"Wohin?"	broken-chord
3	"Halt!"	accompaniment
4	"Danksagung an den Bach"	
5	"Am Feierabend"	mixed
6	"Der Neugierige"	
7	"Ungeduld"	repeated chords
8	"Morgengruss"	mixed
9	"Des Müllers Blumen"	broken chords
10	"Tränenregen"	linear
11	"Mein!"	broken chords

TEMPO. We noticed that the fourth song, "Danksagung an den Bach," was slower than the first three: changes of tempo are another shaping factor in the cycle. Tempo changes occur with much greater regularity than the changes in texture just described. In fact, during much of the cycle, slower and faster tempos alternate in a manner that indicates the composer used tempo changes as a basic means of variety. Listed here are the tempos for the first eleven songs: the original directions to the performers (in German, not Italian) do not always give an unequivocal indication in the absence of the music and so are placed in parentheses, with their translations. The last column in the table reflects the sense of the tempos in context.

1	"Das Wandern"	(*Mässig geschwind*—moderately fast)	moderately fast
2	"Wohin?"	(*Mässig*—moderate)	moderate
3	"Halt!"	(*Nicht zu geschwind*—not too fast)	faster
4	"Danksagung an den Bach"	(*Etwas langsam*—somewhat slow)	slower
5	"Am Feierabend"	(*Ziemlich geschwind*—rather fast)	faster
6	"Der Neugierige"	(*Langsam*—slow)	slower
7	"Ungeduld"	(*Etwas geschwind*—somewhat fast)	faster
8	"Morgengruss"	(*Mässig*—moderate)	a little slower
9	"Des Müllers Blumen"	(*Mässig*—moderate)	moderate (a little faster)
10	"Tränenregen"	(*Ziemlich langsam*—rather slow)	slow
11	"Mein!"	(*Mässig geschwind*—moderately fast)	fast

For the most part, faster and slower tempos alternate song by song. Songs 8 and 9 ("Morgengruss" and "Des Müllers Blumen") are both moderate in tempo, hence carry out the alternation less clearly; still, song 9 is more lilting than song 8. The most obvious effect of the alternation is greater variety in the whole succession of songs: two slow songs in succession might sound too sustained, while the second of two fast ones in succession might lose its effectiveness. But (as we will see later) the strict alternation is not carried out through the whole cycle.

One would think that the text of each song dictated the tempo through its mood—and, indeed, some of the texts clearly demand and receive certain tempos. "Ungeduld" ("Impatience") must be fast; "Tränenregen" ("Rain of Tears") probably has to be slow. Many of the others are not so definite, however; their tempos seem often to be at the composer's option, and the composer's choice seems to have been

influenced to a large extent by the need for variety of pacing.

The more interesting aspect of the matter is that the shape arising from the tempo changes has little or no correspondence with the shape arising from the changes in texture. If we combine the list of textures with the list of tempos, in other words, no correlation appears. Songs with broken-chord accompaniment can be either faster or slower. There is no inherent reason why these two aspects *should* correlate in any particular way. The point is, if they *did* correlate the result would be a very regular structure with much stronger contrasts. We have encountered instances where several aspects were correlated to produce a clear, strong shape (for example, Beethoven's Presto).

In comparison, the shape of *Die schöne Müllerin*—at the highest level—is more diffuse.

We should not, however, conclude that *Die schöne Müllerin* is unstructured—that is, uncontrolled; it is merely irregular, which should be taken neither as a defect of the piece nor as a deficiency on the part of the composer. Here is one of the underlying conditions of musical composition, a condition often encountered whenever we try to relate all the aspects of a piece to each other. A piece in which every section that was fast was also loud, in major, and scored for brass, while all other sections were slow, soft, in minor, and scored for muted strings would run the risk of being inartistic, that is, crudely obvious. It is not regularity that makes a piece artistic; rather, it is the skill and sensitivity (and sense of purpose) with which various regular aspects are balanced against one another. In some pieces, the result is more regular than in other pieces—at the composer's option.

ACCOMPANIMENT FIGURES AS A SHAPING FACTOR. In a work that is but loosely correlated, a relatively casual association of elements can become meaningful. We noticed before that the most prominent changes in texture were associated with broken-chord figures in the accompaniment. Pursuing this aspect more closely (and making allowances for the prevailing irregularities of overall design as just discussed), it is possible to hear in a specific set of broken-chord figures an association with an element of the story.

The broken-chord figures are especially prominent at the beginning, in the first four songs. In the first song, the text itself (especially stanza 2) suggests the motion of the brook as the meaning of the perpetual motion in the accompaniment. When a similar figure pervades the second song too, our attention may well be drawn to this aspect of the music (especially because the second song is *not* strophic, and the persistence of the figure is that much more noticeable).

The second song first describes, then addresses, the brook. The text confirms the relatively simple connection between the poetic image (the brook) and the insistent musical figure. Whether you think of the connection in a purely pictorial way (imagining the running figure to represent the motion of the brook) or at some deeper level of meaning is less important than the fact that the connection is easily made.

Having made it, we eventually might find our way to other less obvious connections. Both the first and second songs reflect the inner thoughts of the miller lad. Does his urge to wander (song 1) surface in his own consciousness in the image of the brook (song 2), which clearly has a fundamental importance in his personality? And is it this function of the image that is made musically apparent by the similarity of the broken-chord figures in the first and second songs? The connection is suggested rather than indicated. But when related figures appear in song 3 ("Halt!") and song 4 ("Danksagung an den Bach") as the lad continues to address the brook, the connection is strengthened. The slower tempo of song 4 might even help, not hinder, the connection, for it shows the persistent conjunction of musical figure and poetic image under varying conditions.

Song 5 ("Am Feierabend") brings, in part, a change of figure. Here the identity of broken-chord figure and brook is weakened, for the figure is present but not the brook. In song 6 ("Der Neugierige"), however, the connection is made more explicitly than before: the figure reappears precisely at the miller lad's address to the brook ("Bächlein meiner Liebe").

From here through the middle of the cycle the connection remains less confirmed, possibly even weakened. A suggestion has been made; it is in the nature of this work to allude, not to press forward to certain conclusion.

STROPHIC FORM. Other shaping factors appear throughout the cycle, some of them correlated with those already studied, some not. There are two principal alternatives to the inner construction of each song—strophic or not strophic. "Das Wandern," the first song, is strophic. "Wohin?" (the second) is not strophic; it does have a clear, repetitive plan, however, which we could represent at the highest level as *A B A*. Each of the other songs that are not strophic has its own plan, sometimes as simple as this, sometimes more complex. ("Der Neugierige" is *A B C B*.) Our interest here is not in the internal structure for its own sake (which would require detailed study of each song) but rather in the arrangement of strophic and nonstrophic songs throughout the cycle —for this distinction is easily heard and is an important factor in the shape of the cycle.

1	"Das Wandern"	5 strophes
2	"Wohin?"	*A B A*
3	"Halt!"	(no sections)
4	"Danksagung an den Bach"	*A B A*
5	"Am Feierabend"	*A B A*
6	"Der Neugierige"	*A B C B*
7	"Ungeduld"	4 strophes
8	"Morgengruss"	4 strophes
9	"Des Müllers Blumen"	4 strophes
10	"Tränenregen"	3 strophes and epilog
11	"Mein!"	*A B A*

It is clear from a listing of the plans of songs 1 through 11 that all of the strophic songs except the first are grouped together. It should be pointed out that this grouping is emphatically not a function of the poetry: all the *poems* from 1 through 11, except 5 and 11, are strophic; Schubert chose nonstrophic plans for 2, 3, 4, and 6. A connection to the grouping by texture immediately suggests itself—with the proviso, as before, that in this work connections are not carried through strictly. It does seem, however, that the association of the broken-chord figure and the brook in songs 2, 4, and 6 might have some inner affinity with the more irregular plans used in those songs. Another more tenuous correlation is this: the strophic plans tend to increase as the lad becomes more involved with the miller's daughter.

HARMONIC AREAS IN SONGS 1 THROUGH 11. A different, more specific, grouping appears between songs 9 and 10. Song 9 ("Des Müllers Blumen") describes the lad's act of devotion—his most explicit acts toward the maiden; song 10 ("Tränenregen") relates what might have been their first intimate encounter (although it is very difficult to decide whether the encounter is anywhere as significant to her as to him). Schubert has chosen to link the two songs closely, as if song 10 were the sequel to song 9. He does this by choice of harmonic area and by the continuity of rhythm and melody. The piano introduction to song 10 could just as well be considered as a thoughtful epilog to song 9 (which has no epilog of its own). The rhythmic connection is obvious enough, even though "Tränenregen" (song 10) is slower. The melodic connection is harder to pin down: there is no obvious thematic or motivic identity between "Des Müllers Blumen" and "Tränenregen." Yet, in the world of *Die schöne Müllerin*, such a connection need only be hinted at for us to think it possible.

The identity of harmonic area is perhaps the most important link between "Des Müllers Blumen" and "Tränenregen"; and, with the factor of harmonic area, the link becomes significant for the entire first half of the cycle. Both songs are strophic; neither is very fast; together they take up a sizable stretch of time. Their common key becomes one of relative importance in the first half of the cycle. Furthermore, it confirms harmonic relationships increasingly in evidence for some time. The same key appeared already in song 7 ("Ungeduld") and—in minor instead of major—in song 5 ("Am Feierabend").

Other harmonic relationships, too complex to be discussed in this book, have an effect that may be perceptible to an attentive ear: from the second song on, the harmonic areas seem to fluctuate, then to converge on the area established in songs 9 and 10 (Ex. 11-1). This area in turn leads to song 11.

Before going any further, it should be said that the harmonic areas just mentioned (Ex. 11-1) are by no means as cogent in their succession as the areas in, say, Haydn's Finale (Chapter 8). Only occasionally in *Die schöne Müllerin* can you hear a close relationship between the keys of adjacent songs (as between songs 9 and 10 or 10 and 11). More often you hear only a refreshing change of key, as between songs 1 and 2 or between 7 and 8 and again between 8 and 9. In such progressions, you will not be aware of any sameness or of a direction of change but only of the fact that there is a change.

Furthermore, you are probably not aware of a return to the harmonic area of a previous song. Through close attention, you may perceive that song

Example 11-1 Schubert, *Die schöne Müllerin:*
Harmonic areas
in songs 1 through 11

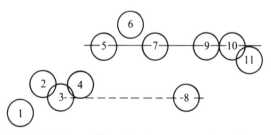

Songs 5, 7, 9, and 10 are in the same area but with changes of color (major/minor). The central harmony of songs 2 and 10 becomes the leading harmony of songs 3 and 11, for example:

9 returns to the area of song 7. The effect of this sequence of songs is that after "Ungeduld" (song 7), "Morgengruss" (song 8) appears as a bright, fresh sound, while "Des Müllers Blumen" (song 9) resumes something of the idea and the sound of song 7. However, the harmonic return in song 9 is not likely to be uppermost; for that matter, neither is the sameness of area found in songs 9 and 10. It is the quality of change that becomes eventually the most significant aspect of harmonic organization.

Song 11 ("Mein!") seems definitely to be an arrival of some kind. The text, by itself, indicates that some sort of understanding has been reached between the lad and the girl—if not in reality, then at least in his imagination. He is sure: "She is mine!" Again, it is very hard to tell what basis his conviction has, what the real feelings of the girl are. She remains a shadowy figure; the facts that reach us are the facts of the lad's inner thought and feeling. And the music tells us that he is convinced. This song "Mein!" resumes the buoyant mood first encountered at the beginning in the songs that used the broken-chord figures; and the harmonic area of "Mein!" has a quality of resolution, of arrival, heard in no other song so far.

Example 11-1 may help you to understand the reasons for this sense of arrival. Although some of the harmonic progressions from song to song are remote (as from song 1 to song 2), others are not so remote. Song 2, for example, is very close to the key of song 3; the central harmony of song 2 is the leading harmony of song 3. Since song 4 is in the same key as song 2, the reverse relationship holds between songs 3 and 4 as between songs 2 and 3: the leading harmony of 3 becomes the central one of 4. The relationships between the following songs are less close, until we reach songs 9, 10, 11. As we saw, songs 9 and 10 are in the same key. The central harmony of this key becomes the leading harmony of song 11 ("Mein!"), which is why this song sounds like an arrival at a harmonic goal. The arrival is intensified by that fact (which we have already observed) that the key of songs 9 and 10 has been established in songs 5 and 7.

Throughout the cycle, key relationships continue to be difficult to follow; yet certain other kinds of harmonic relationships come into sharper focus as the story itself moves more surely to its conclusion.

MAJOR AND MINOR. Perhaps the most obvious harmonic feature of the second half (if not of the whole cycle) is the striking juxtaposition of major and minor and the exploitation of these contrasting colors for expressive effect. These changes are summarized here.

1	"Das Wandern"	major
2	"Wohin?"	major
3	"Halt!"	major
4	"Danksagung an den Bach"	major/minor in middle
5	"Am Feierabend"	minor/major in middle
6	"Der Neugierige"	major/minor for the brook
7	"Ungeduld"	major
8	"Morgengruss"	major
9	"Des Müllers Blumen"	major
10	"Tränenregen"	major/minor in the epilog
11	"Mein!"	major
12	"Pause"	major/minor in middle
13	"Mit dem grünen Lautenbande"	major
14	"Der Jäger"	minor
15	"Eifersucht und Stolz"	minor/major in last half
16	"Die liebe Farbe"	minor/major for accent
17	"Die böse Farbe"	major/minor— ambivalent
18	"Trockne Blumen"	minor/major/minor
19	"Der Müller und der Bach"	minor/major/ minor/major
20	"Des Baches Wiegenlied"	major

Contrasts of major and minor appeared relatively early in the cycle but there only occasionally. The middle section of song 4 ("Danksagung an den Bach") starts abruptly in a contrasting minor. Song 5 ("Am Feierabend") uses a contrasting major color in several ways. "Der Neugierige," as we heard, uses major and minor interchangeably when the lad addresses the brook. The most prominent such use in the first half is the epilog to "Tränenregen" (song 10), where the minor color provides the musical point to the whole song. The first six stanzas describe what appears to the miller lad as a tender moment of togetherness; then the seventh stanza, beginning in minor, tells of the girl's curt departure.

Similarly striking use of major-minor contrasts appear more regularly with song 15, "Eifersucht und Stolz." The first half of the song, in a mood of jealous fury, is in minor. Then, as the lad strikes a devil-may-care pose, the music turns to major. The effect is irony, of course; and the irony is carried out in the brook's figure, which continues uninterrupted through the harmonic change.

"Die liebe Farbe" and "Die böse Farbe" (songs 16 and 17) are in the same harmonic area. Both contain contrasts of major and minor but in opposite ways. "Die liebe Farbe," basically in minor, turns twice in each stanza to major at "Mein Schatz hat's Grün so gern" ("My sweetheart is so fond of green"). This striking harmonic effect, reinforced by a long high note on "gern," becomes the focal point of the song; yet the song is in minor.

"Die böse Farbe" is more ambivalent: it tends to start phrases or sections in major, then finish them in minor. The piano introduction as well as the voice both start firmly in major; the voice sings in major, "I would like to go out into the world, out into the wide world," then continues in minor, " . . . if only it weren't so green out in the woods and the fields!" Similarly, when the text mentions the hunting horn, the accompaniment imitates it, the first time in major, then again—as the lad goes on to his complaint—in minor.

The first section of "Trockne Blumen" is basically in minor. (This and many other pieces in minor move to major *in another key*, but in such a way that the effect of changing *key* is much more prominent than the associated change of *color*. The changes between major and minor we have been discussing in *Die schöne Müllerin* are primarily changes in color within the same key.) In its second section, "Trockne Blumen" changes to major as the lad turns from lament to thoughts of spring. This is a problematic transition in the text; the lad's more positive thoughts seem to come too soon or to lack adequate preparation. More than a change from minor to major is required to make the transition convincing—and, indeed, Schubert's solution is relatively complex, as we will see. At the end of the song, as if to admit that

the time for overcoming despair was not yet, the music turns abruptly back to minor.

"Der Müller und der Bach," song 19, has an even more complex plan of major and minor (which we have already studied). The lad's lament continues in the first section, in minor; the brook answers in major. The lad, in turn, answers in minor but changes to major as if in response to what the brook had to tell him. This is the last, decisive change of harmonic color; the concluding song has only the slightest touch of minor.

HARMONIC AREAS IN SONGS 12 THROUGH 20. The harmonic areas of the second half of the cycle are shown in Ex. 11-2. There is, if anything, less sense here of overall harmonic direction than there was in the first half. Granting the looseness of connection, however, it is still possible to see—and eventually to hear—a plan vaguely similar to that of the first half of the cycle. There are two songs (16 and 17) in the same key; the central harmony of this key becomes the leading harmony of the next. Songs 16, 17, and 18, then, correspond to songs 9, 10, and 11—but the effect is much weaker in the second half, with no strong arrival at song 18 as there was at song 11, "Mein!"

Example 11-2 Schubert, *Die schöne Müllerin*: Harmonic areas in songs 12 through 20

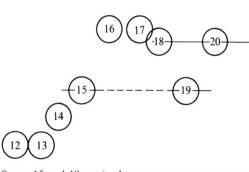

Songs 15 and 19 are in the same area, as are songs 12 and 13, 16 and 17, 18 and 20 but with variations in color (major/minor). The central harmony of song 17 becomes the leading harmony for song 18.

Much more prominent in the second half are the striking key changes—seemingly unexplained by text or musical plan and therefore evocative of some hidden meaning—at the beginning of each new song. Such changes are especially strong between "Eifersucht und Stolz" and "Die liebe Farbe" (songs 15 and 16), between "Trockne Blumen" and "Der Müller und der Bach" (songs 18 and 19), and between "Der Müller und der Bach" and "Des Baches Wiegenlied" (songs 19 and 20). These evocative changes seem to represent the chief function of harmony in this part of the cycle—along with the major-minor changes that we found in almost every one of these same songs. It is true that harmonic organization within each individual song often provides the sameness of key that helps give each song its identity; but we scarcely notice the sameness, so intense seem the changes. Each new change seems to open a fresh possibility in a story that is (considered purely as a story) slow-moving and to a large degree predictable.

LINEAR RELATIONSHIPS. As the threads of the story tighten toward the close, certain details of linear construction become important. On first acquaintance with *Die schöne Müllerin*, you probably hear little or nothing in the way of motivic or thematic return. Each song seems to have its own melody, not specifically related to any other in the cycle. Schubert always seems to have a new tune—and a good one—for each new piece. Yet you are probably also aware of a feeling, as the cycle unfolds, that you have heard some of these melodies before in the cycle, if only you could remember where. Motivic or thematic recall is implicit, rarely explicit, in *Die schöne Müllerin*. But precisely because it is implicit, it has the greater effect —and greater propriety.

We would not pursue the matter further without at least some explicit motivic connections. One such connection (as explicit as this allusive work allows) can be heard between the second section of "Eifersucht und Stolz" (song 15—the first melody in major) and the beginning of "Die böse Farbe." The bold, rising lines in these two places are similar enough (though not identical) to suggest a connection (Ex. 11-3). The texts help out: in "Eifersucht und Stolz," the lad instructs the brook to run to the girl to tell her how he is playing with the children, unconcerned about her attention to the hunter. In "Die böse Farbe," the lad begins with a strong impulse to go back to wandering, with no further thought to the girl. Neither show of bravado lasts for long; in both cases the bright melody soon becomes darker.

Once you notice one such relatively clear linear connection between songs, you are apt to hear many more. Often such connections turn out to be imaginary. Connections need not, however, be explicit in order to be real; and some connections legitimately occupy a middle ground between those that are really there and those we only think we hear.

Consider, for example, the words connected with some strongly accented notes, beginning in song 6, "Der Neugierige" (Ex. 11-4). In the middle of a phrase in the *B* section, the word "ein" is twice sung out on a high, accented note. Later, "Nein" also appears on an expressive note. Then in the next song, "Ungeduld,"
the word "dein" dominates the refrain by appearing in it twice on long, high, climactic notes. Thus the syllable begins to rhyme in song 9 ("Des Müllers Blumen") and song 10 ("Tränenregen"). Finally in song 11 ("Mein!"), the key word, "mein," occurs forcefully at the climaxes of the song—with emotional as well as structural significance. The accented rhyme binds the first half of the cycle together, making stronger the feeling of arrival and closure apparent in "Mein!"

Example 11-3 Schubert, *Die schöne Müllerin:* Linear relationships in songs 15 and 17

"Eifersucht und Stolz" (song 15)

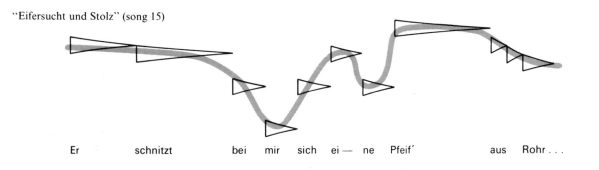

Er   schnitzt   bei   mir   sich   ei — ne   Pfeif'   aus   Rohr . . .

"Die böse Farbe" (song 17)

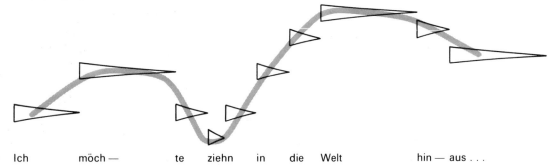

Ich   möch —   te   ziehn   in   die   Welt   hin — aus . . .

Example 11-4 Schubert, *Die schöne Müllerin:*
Rhyming notes in songs 6, 7, and 11

"Der Neugierige" (song 6)

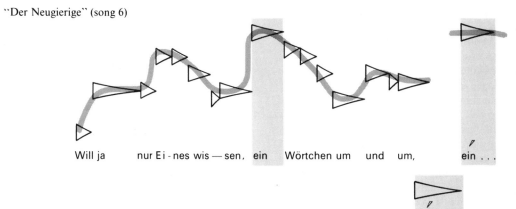

Will ja   nur E i - nes wis — sen, ein Wörtchen um   und   um,   ein . . .

Ja, heisst das eine Wörtchen, das andre heisset Nein,

"Ungeduld" (song 7)

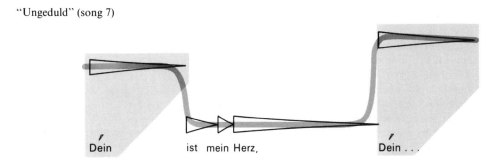

Dein   ist mein Herz,   Dein . . .

"Mein!" (song 11)

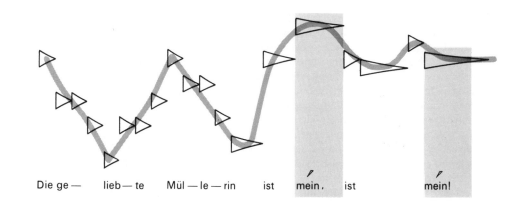

Die ge —   lieb — te   Mül — le — rin   ist   mein,   ist   mein!

227

In "Die liebe Farbe" (song 16), the main accented note is a high one on "gern"—"is so *fond* of" (Ex. 11-5). This occurs six times in the song, always in connection with the abrupt, evocative turn to major; it is clearly the focal point of the song. Then in "Die böse Farbe," a similar line leads to the very same note, now with a different syllable, "bleich" (blanched). The "anti-rhyme" is full of programmatic significance: it is white against green, as song 17 makes clear. Earlier in the cycle, it was a text rhyme ("-ein") that reached out across songs; here it is a "musical rhyme," a repeated pitch. And whereas the high note in "Die liebe Farbe" is full of warmth and lift, the high note in "Die böse Farbe" is an agonized reaching, followed by a higher, even more strongly accented note (and a striking harmony, similar to that intense chord in "Der Müller und der Bach").

If you can persuade your ears to hear connections between prominent notes in different songs (which is not easy), perhaps you can find significance in even less explicit connections. We already noticed that the lad's positive thoughts of spring toward the end of song 18 ("Trockne Blumen") are problematic; possibly their place in the story is better understood by focusing attention on the remarkable music to which they are set (Ex. 11-6). Strong accents are written over "Blüm(-lein)" and "al(-le)" by the indication *fp*, or "forte followed immediately by piano." The harmony rocks back and forth on two chords several times before it moves to a strong, sure cadence on "aus." The harmony is rich and memorable; the top line in the accompaniment is distinctive (the vocal line is less important here).

Example 11-6 compares this passage to another at the end of song 20, "Das Baches Wiegenlied." This, the musical conclusion of the whole cycle, is set in similar rocking harmonies, with the same top line *in the accompaniment* (the vocal line, while very expressive, is again less important for the sake of the connection to song 18; but the vocal line does participate intermittently in the rocking motion). The distinctive melodic motion goes on longer this time and is not interrupted by the expressive upward surge heard before in the accompaniment under "Mai ist kommen." Yet "Bächlein aus" moves to the same sure cadence as "Winter ist aus." By this less-than-

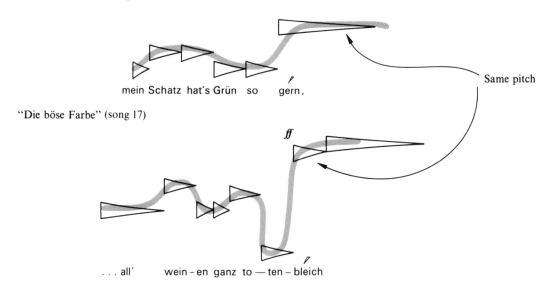

"Die liebe Farbe" (song 16)

mein Schatz hat's Grün so gern,

"Die böse Farbe" (song 17)

ff

Same pitch

. . . all' wein-en ganz to — ten – bleich

Example 11-5 Schubert, *Die schöne Müllerin:* Linear relationships in songs 16 and 17

obvious connection, the seemingly premature thoughts of spring in song 18 are shown to be a real prefiguration of the outcome of the story, as reached in song 20.

There are even weaker connections, however, that could be suggested to anyone who cared to listen for them. The beginning of "Des Baches Wiegenlied," for example, could recall the poignant line "War es also gemeint?" ("Was this what was intended?") at the beginning of "Danksagung an den Bach," song 4—heard more distinctly in the line at the end of the song (Ex. 11-7). These two songs are in different keys; you need to hear them in the same key in order to catch the admittedly faint echo. Also, if one is in the properly suggestive frame of mind, perhaps the conclusion of "Des Baches Wiegenlied" (the passage shown in Ex. 11-6) has some hidden connection with the conclusion of "Das Wandern" way back at the beginning of the cycle; but such a connection is too fragile to commit to a diagram.

It can be argued that any similarity present in such examples is accidental, not intentional, and therefore should be ignored. It is, however, hard to ignore something that is there. There is a third alternative between intentional and accidental—the composer may have built in the connection without being explicitly aware of it, simply as part of a continuous act of composing the piece. Most important is not how such a connection got there, but rather how we react to it. The more tenuous the connection, the less strongly it should be depended upon for conclusions about the work. Of course such connections can be far more reliably understood with the help of a text; it is in pieces without text that excessive reliance on hidden motivic connections can distort understanding of a piece.

Fascinating as such details may be, the large design of the cycle, expressed in relatively gross features such as tempo and figure, will continue to be the most reliable guides in the second half.

"Trockne Blumen" (song 18)

(Piano)

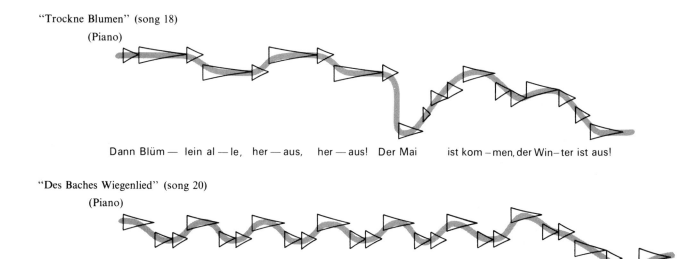

Dann Blüm— lein al —le, her —aus, her —aus! Der Mai   ist kom –men, der Win–ter ist aus!

"Des Baches Wiegenlied" (song 20)

(Piano)

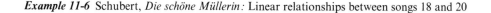

Bis das Meer   will trin— ken die Bäch —lein aus,   bis das Meer   will trin— ken die Bächlein   aus .

Example 11-6 Schubert, *Die schöne Müllerin:* Linear relationships between songs 18 and 20

Example 11-7 Schubert, *Die schöne Müllerin:* Linear relationships between songs 4 and 20

SHAPE OF THE SECOND HALF. The beginning of the second half is introduced by "Pause" (song 12), a poem clearly placed there for that very purpose (see the translation on page 236). In this poem, unlike all the others, the miller lad seems to speak to an audience, or at any rate in a self-conscious way that suggests an art form rather than a lover's fantasy.

Almost everything about this song seems to mark a break in the cycle. Texture and figure are new. The harmonic area is the same as in the first song ("Das Wandern")—an area untouched since the beginning of the cycle. As the song goes on, it almost seems to lose its way—or at any rate it becomes hard to follow —as it employs new melodic idioms and moves into new harmonic areas. Parts of the song may be "echoes" of previous material; other parts certainly suggest a "prelude to new songs."

After "Pause," faster and slower tempos alternate less regularly.

"Danksagung an der Bach" (song 4)

War es al — so gemeint? . . .

"Des Baches Wiegenlied" (song 20)

Gute Ruh', gute Ruh'!

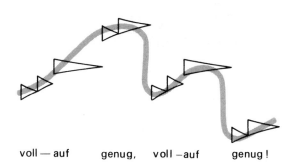

voll — auf   genug, voll –auf   genug !

229

12	"Pause"	Ziemlich geschwind	Rather fast
13	"Mit dem grünen Lautenbande"	Mässig	Moderate
14	"Der Jäger"	Geschwind	Fast
15	"Eifersucht und Stolz"	Geschwind	Fast
16	"Die liebe Farbe"	Etwas langsam	Somewhat slow
17	"Die böse Farbe"	Ziemlich geschwind	Rather fast
18	"Trockne Blumen"	Ziemlich langsam	Rather slow
19	"Der Müller und der Bach"	Mässig	Moderate
20	"Des Baches Wiegenlied"	Mässig	Moderate

Two fast songs (14 and 15) come in succession. "Der Jäger" (song 14) has a character and sense of movement different from all other songs in the cycle; it is an alien intrusion—as is, of course, the hunter himself. "Eifersucht und Stolz" (song 15) is also fast, but its character represents a clear return to the miller lad's inner world. The most obvious indication of this return is the running figure associated with the brook; the identity of the figure seems much more certain now, after the equally fast, equally persistent but contrasting, figure in the hunter's song. (The brook's figure returns here after a relatively long absence.) In fact, the similarity of tempo between "Der Jäger" and "Eifersucht und Stolz" seems insignificant in comparison to the difference in figure.

"Die liebe Farbe" and "Die böse Farbe" (songs 16 and 17) are obviously a pair of songs designed for high contrast. Difference of tempo (slow—fast) is one important ingredient in the contrast. Since slower and faster tempos are not alternating so regularly in the second half of the cycle, a change of tempo here can make a particular poetic point. The way figure is used may support this point: "Die liebe Farbe" has no trace of a broken-chord figure; it uses instead a repeated-note figure throughout. "Die böse Farbe" is less sure of itself, as far as use of figure goes (and in other respects, as we will see). The piano introduction to "Die böse Farbe," however, makes clear reference to the broken-chord figure—which then reappears at important points in the song.

The absence of the broken-chord figure in "Die liebe Farbe" and its presence in "Die böse Farbe" clearly reflect the content of the texts. In "Die liebe Farbe," the lad's thoughts are given over completely to the girl. The song is bitter and has an undercurrent of irony; but it does seem to express his continuing devotion to her and his despair at losing her. She is his treasure; she likes green—it is "her favorite color." She is so fond of hunting, he would go hunting—but for death. He would disappear forever in a green grave. In "Die böse Farbe," however, the lad shows a forceful—if still ambivalent—return to his own identity. He is angry; he would go out (to wander!) in the "wide world," if only the world were not so green. So, too, his musical identity, which was completely obliterated in "Die liebe Farbe," returns in "Die böse Farbe," if only sporadically. And somehow he manages to encompass the clear reference to the hunter's horn (the new figure in the accompaniment two-thirds of the way through the song) into his own world. The hunter defeats him; but the greater danger lies with the girl.

That danger is not yet passed. "Trockne Blumen" (song 18) initiates the group of three songs—all relatively slow—that bring the inner drama to a resolution. The lad is still subject to empty despair, as the first half of "Trockne Blumen" shows. There are few figures of any kind here, only detached, funereal chords. The second half of the song, however, brings a new tone, embodied in a new figure. It might be something we heard before (it has the sense of movement characteristic of the brook's figure); still, it is different. The song looks forward rather than back. "May is here! Winter is past!" It is not clear yet what the change of season, or of figure, means.

In "Der Müller und der Bach" (song 19), the meaning becomes clearer. The first part of the song is, again, empty and desperate. Then again a more lively figure enters; and this time it is obviously identified as the brook's figure, for the brook is speaking. As we already saw (Chapter 7), the brook places the lad's defeat into a new context. Tempo remains slower rather than faster; the end is at hand. But some part, at least, of the miller lad—the part identified with the brook—exists beyond the circumstances of this personal tragedy. And we know it is indeed a part of the miller lad, for when the brook itself *really* speaks in "Des Baches Wiegenlied" (as opposed to what we now see to be the lad's own brooklike thoughts in the preceding song), it does so in quite new figures that are not broken chords.

There might be several possible interpretations of the cycle besides the one just offered. The most basic nature of the work—a story presented in intermittent moments of lyricism—opens the door to uncertainty and ambiguity in trying to discern meaning. Indeed, if all were clear, it would be a poorer work. What we have tried to show is that it may be possible to arrive at an interpretation of inner meanings from such simple, objective facts about the music as texture, tempo, and figure, taken in conjunction with the specific meanings provided in the texts themselves. The external shape of a work can be relied on to tell us at least something about its inner meaning or at any rate something about how the composer understood that meaning.

Obviously, an interpretation based only upon the relatively gross facts pertaining to whole songs and their succession in the cycle cannot exhaust the meaning of a work such as this. Such facts, however, are as reliable in their guidance to meaning as they are to overall design: we start with such facts to grasp the shape of the work; we should start with them also to work toward an interpretation. To start with details is to invite a one-sided, arbitrary reading of a work. Details must be considered, of course, if the interpretation is to gain depth and substance; but the details can be reliably understood only in the framework of the whole.

Franz Schubert
DIE SCHONE MULLERIN
(SONG CYCLE)

---

1. DAS WANDERN (ROVING)

Das Wandern ist des Müllers Lust,
    Das Wandern!
Das muss ein schlechter Müller sein,
Dem niemals fiel das Wandern ein,
    Das Wandern.
    Vom Wasser haben wir's gelernt,
    Vom Wasser!
Das hat nicht Rast bei Tag und Nacht,
Ist stets auf Wanderschaft bedacht,
    Das Wasser.
    Das sehn wir auch den Rädern ab,
    Den Rädern!
Die gar nicht gerne stille stehn,
Die sich mein Tag nicht müde drehn,
    Die Räder.
    Die Steine selbst, so schwer sie sind,
    Die Steine!
Sie tanzen mit den muntern Reihn
Und wollen gar noch schneller sein,
    Die Steine.
    O Wandern, Wandern, meine Lust,
    O Wandern!
Herr Meister und Frau Meisterin,
Lasst mich in Frieden weiter ziehn
    Und wandern.

Roving is the miller's delight,
    roving!
It is indeed a very poor miller
who never felt the urge to rove—
    roving!
    From the water we learned this,
    from the water!
It does not rest by day or night,
but is always bent on roving,
    the water!
    We see it too in the mill-wheels,
    the mill-wheels!
They never want to stop
and never they nor I get tired of the turning,
    the mill-wheels!
    Even the mill-stones, heavy as they are,
    the stones!
They join in the merry dance
and want ever to go faster,
    the stones!
    O roving, roving, my delight,
    O roving!
O master and mistress,
let me go my way in peace,
    and rove!

2. WOHIN? (WHITHER?)

Ich hört' ein Bächlein rauschen
Wohl aus dem Felsenquell,
Hinab zum Tale rauschen
So frisch und wunderhell.
    Ich weiss nicht, wie mir wurde,
Nicht wer den Rat mir gab,
Ich musste auch hinunter
Mit meinem Wanderstab.
    Hinunter und immer weiter,

I heard a brooklet gushing
from a spring among the rocks,
gushing down into the valley,
so fresh and wonderfully clear.
    I don't know how it happened,
or who gave me the idea,
but I too couldn't resist following it down
with my walking stick.
    Down, always farther,

German text selected and translated by Philip L. Miller. Reprinted from *The ring of words*, © 1963 by Doubleday and Company, Inc., by permission.

Und immer dem Bache nach,
Und immer frischer rauschte,
Und immer heller der Bach.
  Ist das denn meine Strasse?
O Bächlein, sprich, wohin?
Du hast mit deinem Rauschen
Mir ganz berauscht den Sinn.
  Was sag' ich denn vom Rauschen?
Das kann kein Rauschen sein!
Es singen wohl die Nixen
Tief unten ihren Reihn.
  Lass singen, Gesell, lass rauschen,
Und wandre fröhlich nach!
Es gehn ja Mühlenräder
In jedem klaren Bach.

and always along the bank,
and always brisker
and clearer the brook gushed.
  Is this the way I am to go,
Tell me, brooklet, whither?
You have, with your gushing,
enchanted my very soul.
  What am I saying about the gushing?
Gushing it cannot be!
The nixies are singing
and dancing far below.
  Sing on, comrade, gush on,
and go your happy way!
There are mill-wheels turning
in every clear stream.

3. HALT! (HALT!)

Eine Mühle seh' ich blinken
Aus den Erlen heraus,
Durch Rauschen und Singen
Bricht Rädergebraus.
  Ei willkommen, ei willkommen,
Süsser Mühlengesang!
Und das Haus, wie so traulich!
Und die Fenster, wie blank!
  Und die Sonne, wie helle
Vom Himmel sie scheint!
Ei, Bächlein, liebes Bächlein,
War es also gemeint?

I see a mill showing
through the alders;
through the gushing and singing of the water
breaks the noise of the wheel.
  Welcome, welcome,
sweet song of the mill!
And the house, how comfortable it looks!
And the windows, how they glitter!
  And the sun, how brightly
it shines from heaven!
O brooklet, dear brooklet,
was this what was intended?

4. DANKSAGUNG AN DEN BACH
(THANKS TO THE BROOK)

War es also gemeint,
Mein rauschender Freund,
Dein Singen, dein Klingen,
War es also gemeint?
  Zur Müllerin hin!
So lautet der Sinn.
Gelt, hab' ich's verstanden?
Zur Müllerin hin!
  Hat sie dich geschickt?
Oder hast mich berückt?
Das möcht' ich noch wissen.
Ob sie dich geschickt.
  Nun wie's auch mag sein,
Ich gebe mich drein:
Was ich such', hab' ich funden,
Wie's immer mag sein.
  Nach Arbeit ich frug,

Was this what was intended,
my gushing friend,
your singing and your sounding,
was this what was intended?
  To the maid of the mill!
So the meaning resounds.
Isn't that it? Have I understood it?
To the maid of the mill!
  Did she send you,
or have you beguiled me?
That I want to know—
Did she send you?
  Now whatever happens,
I'm yielding;
what I am seeking I have found,
whatever may happen.
  I applied for work;

Nun hab' ich genug,
Für die Hände, für's Herze
Vollauf genug!

now I have enough
for my hands and for my heart,
Enough and to spare!

5. AM FEIERABEND (AFTER WORK)

Hätt' ich tausend
Arme zu rühren!
Könnt' ich brausend
Die Räder führen!
Könnt' ich wehen
Durch alle Haine!
Könnt' ich drehen
Alle Steine!
Dass die schöne Müllerin
Merkte meinen treuen Sinn!
　Ach, wie ist mein Arm so schwach!
Was ich hebe, was ich trage,
Was ich schneide, was ich schlage,
Jeder Knappe tut mir's nach.
Und da sitz' ich in der grossen Runde,
In der stillen kühlen Feierstunde,
Und der Meister spricht zu Allen:
Euer Werk hat mir gefallen;
Und das liebe Mädchen sagt
Allen eine gute Nacht.

If I had a thousand
arms to move!
If I could keep
the mill-wheels roaring!
If I could blow
through all the groves!
If I could turn
all the mill-stones!
So that the beautiful maid of the mill
might notice my faithful nature!
　Ah, how feeble is my arm!
What I can lift, what I can carry,
what I can chop, what I can strike,
any apprentice can do as well as I.
And there I sit in the great circle
in the quiet cool leisure hours,
and the master says to all:
"Your work has pleased me."
And the dear girl says
to all a good-night.

6. DER NEUGIERIGE (THE QUESTION)

Ich frage keine Blume,
Ich frage keinen Stern,
Sie können mir alle nicht sagen,
Was ich erführ' so gern.
　Ich bin ja auch kein Gärtner,
Die Sterne steh'n zu hoch;
Mein Bächlein will ich fragen,
Ob mich mein Herz belog.
　O Bächlein meiner Liebe,
Wie bist du heut' so stumm!
Will ja nur Eines wissen,
Ein Wörtchen um und um.
　Ja, heisst das eine Wörtchen,
Das andre heisset Nein,
Die beiden Wörtchen schliessen
Die ganze Welt mir ein.
　O Bächlein meiner Liebe,
Was bist du wunderlich!
Will's ja nicht weiter sagen,
Sag', Bächlein, liebt sie mich?

I do not ask a flower,
I do not ask a star;
none of them could tell me
what I want so much to know.
　Anyway, I'm no gardener;
the stars are too high.
I will ask the brooklet
if my heart was deceiving me.
　O dear brooklet,
how quiet you are today!
I want to know only one thing,
one little word, over and over.
　"Yes" is that little word—
the other one is "No."
In these two words
the whole world is bound up for me.
　O dear brooklet,
how strangely you behave!
I will not repeat what you say—
tell me, brooklet, does she love me?

233

7. UNGEDULD (IMPATIENCE)

Ich schnitt' es gern in alle Rinden ein,
Ich grüb' es gern in jeden Kieselstein,
Ich möcht' es sä'n auf jedes frische Beet
Mit Kressensamen, der es schnell verrät,

Auf jeden weissen Zettel möcht' ich's schreiben:
Dein ist mein Herz, und soll es ewig bleiben.
    Ich möcht mir ziehen einen jungen Star,
Bis dass er spräch' die Worte rein und klar,
Bis er sie spräch' mit meines Mundes Klang,
Mit meines Herzens vollem, heissen Drang;
Dann säng' er hell durch ihre Fensterscheiben:
Dein ist mein Herz, und soll es ewig bleiben.
    Den Morgenwinden möcht' ich's hauchen ein,
Ich möcht' es säuseln durch den regen Hain;
O, leuchtet' es aus jedem Blumenstern!
Trüg' es der Duft zu ihr von nah und fern!
Ihr Wogen, könnt ihr nichts als Räder treiben?
Dein ist mein Herz, und soll es ewig bleiben.
    Ich meint', es müsst' in meinen Augen stehn,
Auf meinen Wangen müsst' man's brennen sehn,
Zu lesen wär's auf meinem stummen Mund,
Ein jeder Atemzug gäb's laut ihr kund;
Und sie merkt nichts von all' dem bangen Treiben:
Dein ist mein Herz, und soll es ewig bleiben!

I would carve it on the bark of every tree;
I would chisel it in every stone;
I would sow it in every flower bed
with watercress, which, growing quickly, would
        give it away;
on every white scrap of paper I would write it;
Thine is my heart, and shall be thine forever!
    I would like to teach a young starling
until it would speak the words clearly,
until it would speak with the sound of my voice,
with the full fervent longing of my heart;
then it would sing clearly through her window;
Thine is my heart, and shall be thine forever!
    To the morning wind I would breathe it;
I would whisper it to the quivering trees;
O let it shine from the heart of every flower!
Let its fragrance be borne to her from near and far!
O water, can you turn nothing but mill-wheels?
Thine is my heart, and shall be thine forever!
    I should think it must show plainly in my eyes,
on my cheeks anyone must see it burning;
it may be read upon my mute lips;
every breath I draw must proclaim it loudly,
and she notices nothing of all my anxious longing;
Thine is my heart, and shall be thine forever!

8. MORGENGRUSS (MORNING GREETING)

Guten Morgen, schöne Müllerin!
Wo steckst du gleich das Köpfchen hin,
Als wär' dir was geschehen?
Verdriesst dich denn mein Gruss so schwer?
Verstört dich denn mein Blick so sehr?
So muss ich wieder gehen.
    O lass mich nur von ferne stehn,
Nach deinem lieben Fenster sehn,
Von ferne, ganz von ferne!
Du blondes Köpfchen, komm hervor!
Hervor aus eurem runden Tor,
Ihr blauen Morgensterne!
    Ihr schlummertrunknen Äugelein,
Ihr taubetrübten Blümelein,
Was scheuet ihr die Sonne?
Hat es die Nacht so gut gemeint,
Dass ihr euch schliesst und bückt und weint
Nach ihrer stillen Wonne?
    Nun schüttelt ab der Träume Flor,
Und hebt euch frisch und frei empor

Good morning, beautiful maid of the mill!
Why do you look away
as though something had frightened you?
Does my greeting so sorely upset you?
Do I embarrass you so by looking at you?
Then I must go away.
    O let me only from a distance
look into your dear window,
only from a distance!
Come out, blond head,
come out from your arched gate,
blue morning stars!
    O sleepy eyes,
o little flowers heavy with dew,
why do you fear the sun?
Was the night so pleasant
that you now close up and droop and weep
for quiet happiness?
    Now throw off the veil of dreams
and look up fresh and free

In Gottes hellen Morgen!
Die Lerche wirbelt in der Luft,
Und aus dem tiefen Herzen ruft
Die Liebe Leid und Sorgen.

in God's bright morning?
The lark warbles in the air,
and out of the depths of the heart
love calls grief and suffering.

9. DES MULLERS BLUMEN (THE MILLER'S FLOWERS)

Am Bach viel kleine Blumen stehn,
Aus hellen blauen Augen sehn;
Der Bach der ist des Müllers Freund,
Und hellblau Liebchens Auge scheint,
Drum sind es meine Blumen.

Along the brook many little flowers grow;
out of their bright blue eyes they look;
the brook is the miller's friend,
and light blue are my sweetheart's eyes—
therefore they are my flowers.

Dicht unter ihrem Fensterlein
Da will ich pflanzen die Blumen ein,
Da ruft ihr zu, wenn Alles schweigt,
Wenn sich ihr Haupt zum Schlummer neigt,
Ihr wisst ja, was ich meine.

Close under her window,
there I plant my flowers;
call up to her when all is still,
when her head is nodding to sleep—
you know what I mean.

Und wenn sie tät die Äuglein zu,
Und schläft in süsser, süsser Ruh',
Dann lispelt als ein Traumgesicht
Ihr zu: Vergiss, vergiss mein nicht!
Das ist es, was ich meine.

And when she closes her eyes
and sleeps in sweet, sweet rest,
then whisper as in a dream
to her: Forget, forget me not!
That is what I mean.

Und schliesst sie früh die Laden auf,
Dann schaut mit Liebesblick hinauf:
Der Tau in euren Äugelein,
Das sollen meine Tränen sein,
Die will ich auf euch weinen.

And when in the morning she opens her shutters,
then look lovingly upward;
the dew in your eyes
will be the tears
that I will weep upon you.

10. TRANENREGEN (RAIN OF TEARS)

Wir sassen so traulich beisammen
Im kühlen Erlendach,
Wir schauten so traulich zusammen
Hinab in den rieselnden Bach.

We sat so intimately together
in the cool shade of the alders;
we gazed so intimately together
down into the rippling brook.

Der Mond war auch gekommen,
Die Sternlein hinterdrein,
Und schauten so traulich zusammen
In den silbernen Spiegel hinein.

The moon had risen
and then the stars;
and they looked so intimately together
down into the silver mirror.

Ich sah nach keinem Monde,
Nach keinem Sternenschein,
Ich schaute nach ihrem Bilde,
Nach ihren Augen allein.

I did not look at the moon,
nor at the starlight;
I only gazed at her image
only at her eyes.

Und sahe sie nicken und blicken
Berauf aus dem seligen Bach,
Die Blümlein am Ufer, die blauen,
Sie nickten und blickten ihr nach.

And I saw her nodding and glancing
up from the blessed brook;
the flowers on the bank, the blue ones,
were nodding and glancing up after her.

Und in den Bach versunken
Der ganze Himmel schien,
Und wollte mich mit hinunter
In seine Tiefe ziehn.

And sunken in the brook,
all the light of heaven shone,
and wanted to draw me down
into its depths.

Und über den Wolken und Sternen
Da rieselte munter der Bach,
Und rief mit Singen und Klingen:
Geselle, Geselle, mir nach!
    Da gingen die Augen mir über,
Da ward es im Spiegel so kraus;
Sie sprach: Es kommt ein Regen,
Ade, ich geh' nach Haus.

And over the clouds and the stars
the brook gurgled merrily,
and called out as it sang:
"Comrade, comrade!" after me.
    My eyes filled with tears;
the mirror of the stream was disturbed.
She said: "It is beginning to rain;
good-bye, I am going in."

11. MEIN! (MINE!)

Bächlein, lass dein Rauschen sein!
Räder, stellt eur Brausen ein!
All' ihr muntern Waldvögelein,
Gross und klein,
Endet eure Melodein!
Durch den Hain
Aus und ein
Schalle heut' ein Reim allein:
Die geliebte Müllerin ist mein!
Mein!
Frühling, sind das alle deine Blümelein?
Sonne, hast du keinen hellern Schein?
Ach, so muss ich ganz allein,
Mit dem seligen Worte mein,
Unverstanden in der weiten Schöpfung sein!

Brooklet, stop rippling!
Mill-wheels, stop roaring!
All you happy woodbirds,
large and small,
put an end to your songs!
Through the grove,
out and in,
let only one rhyme be heard:
The beloved maid of the mill is mine!
Mine!
Spring, have you no more flowers?
Sun, can't you shine more brightly?
Ah, so must I, all alone,
with my blessed word,
be understood by no one in all creation!

12. PAUSE (PAUSE)

    Meine Laute hab' ich gehängt an die Wand,
Hab' sie umschlungen mit einem grünen Band—
Ich kann nicht mehr singen, mein Herz ist zu voll,
Weiss nicht, wie ich's in Reime zwingen soll.
Meiner Sehnsucht allerheissesten Schmerz
Durft' ich aushauchen in Liederscherz,
Und wie ich klagte so süss und fein,
Glaubt' ich doch, mein Leiden wär' nicht klein.
Ei, wie gross ist wohl meines Glückes Last,
Dass kein Klang auf Erden es in sich fasst?
    Nun, liebe Laute, ruh' an dem Nagel hier!
Und weht ein Lüftchen über die Saiten dir,
Und streift eine Biene mit ihren Flügeln dich,
Da wird mir so bange und es durchschauert mich.
Warum liess ich das Band auch hängen so lang'?
Oft fliegt's um die Saiten mit seufzendem Klang.
Ist es der Nachklang meiner Liebespein?
Soll es das Vorspiel neuer Lieder sein?

    I have hung my lute on the wall,
and wound a green ribbon around it.
I can sing no more, my heart is too full.
I do not know how to force my feelings into rhymes.
The most intense pangs of longing
I ventured to breathe out in my little songs;
and when I lamented so sweetly and so beautifully,
I really thought that my suffering was not light.
But oh, how great is the burden of my happiness,
that no sound on earth can contain it?
    Now, my lute, rest here on your nail!
And if a breeze passes over your strings,
or if a bee touches them with his wings,
that will make me so anxious and shivery.
Why have I left the ribbon hanging there so long?
It often passes over the strings with a sighing sound.
Is it the echo of my love-sorrow?
Or can it be the prelude to new songs?

**13. MIT DEM GRUNEN LAUTENBANDE
(WITH THE GREEN LUTE-RIBBON)**

"Schad' um das schöne grüne Band,
Dass es verbleicht hier an der Wand,

"It is a shame that this beautiful green ribbon
is fading here on the wall,

Ich hab' das Grün so gern!"
So sprachst du, Liebchen, heut' zu mir;
Gleich knüpf' ich's ab und send' es dir;
Nun hab' das Grüne gern!

  Ist auch dein ganzer Liebster weiss,
Soll Grün doch haben seinen Preis,
Und ich auch hab' es gern.
Weil unsre Lieb ist immergrün,
Weil grün der Hoffnung Fernen blühn,
Drum haben wir es gern.

  Nun schlinge in die Locken dein
Das grüne Band gefällig ein,
Du hast ja's Grün so gern.
Dann weiss ich, wo die Hoffnung wohnt,
Dann weiss ich, wo die Liebe thront,
Dann hab' ich's Grün erst gern.

I am so fond of green!"
So you spoke to me today, dear.
At once I untie it and send it to you.
Now enjoy your green.

  Though your miller-lover may be all white,
green also has its value;
and I like green too.
Since our love is ever green,
since hope blooms green in the distance,
therefore we are fond of it.

  Now wind in your hair
nicely the green ribbon—
you are so fond of green.
Then I know where my hope lies,
then I know where love is enthroned—
then green is my favorite color.

14. DER JAGER (THE HUNTER)

Was sucht denn der Jäger am Mühlbach hier?

Bleib', trotziger Jäger, in deinem Revier!
Hier giebt es kein Wild zu jagen für dich,
Hier wohnt nur ein Rehlein, ein zahmes, für mich.
Und willst du das zärtliche Rehlein sehn,
So lass deine Büchsen im Walde stehn,
So lass deine klaffenden Hunde zu Haus,
Und lass auf dem Horne den Saus und Braus,
Und schere vom Kinne das struppige Haar,
Sonst scheut sich im Garten das Rehlein fürwahr.

  Doch besser, du bliebest im Walde dazu,
Und liessest die Mühlen und Müller in Ruh'.
Was taugen die Fischlein im grünen Gezweig?
Was will denn das Eichhorn im bläulichen Teich?
Drum bleibe, du trotziger Jäger, im Hain,
Und lass mich mit meinen drei Rädern allein;
Und willst meinem Schätzchen dich machen beliebt,
So wisse, mein Freund, was ihr Herzchen betrübt:
Die Eber, die kommen zu Nacht aus dem Hain,
Und brechen in ihren Kohlgarten ein,
Und treten und wühlen herum in dem Feld:
Die Eber die schiesse, du Jägerheld!

  What then does the hunter want here by the
    mill-stream?
Stay in your own country, impudent hunter!
Here is no game for you to hunt;
only one doe lives here, a tame one, for me.
And if you want to see my gentle young deer,
leave your gun in the woods,
and leave your barking dogs at home,
and leave off sounding your noisy horn;
shave the unkempt beard from your chin
lest indeed you frighten the doe in her garden.

  Yet it would be better for you to stay in the woods,
and leave the mill and the miller in peace.
What would a fish be doing in the green branches?
Or a squirrel in a blue pond?
So stay in the grove, impudent hunter,
and leave me alone with my three mill-wheels.
And if you would win the love of my sweetheart,
then know, my friend, what is troubling her heart:
It is the boars that come from the woods at night,
and break into her cabbage patch,
and tramp around and upset things in the field;
shoot the boar, hunter, if you want to be a hero!

15. EIFERSUCHT UND STOLZ (JEALOUSY AND PRIDE)

Wohin so schnell, so kraus und wild, mein lieber
    Bach?
Eilst du voll Zorn dem frechen Bruder Jäger nach?

Kehr' um, kehr' um, und schilt erst deine Müllerin

Where are you bound, so fast, so roiled and wild,
    my beloved brook?
Are you rushing angrily after that insolent brother
    hunter?

Come back, come back, and first scold your maid of
    the mill

Für ihren leichten, losen, kleinen Flattersinn.
Sahst du sie gestern Abend nicht am Tore stehn,
Mit langem Halse nach der grossen Strasse sehn?
Wenn von dem Fang der Jäger lustig zieht nach Haus,
Da steckt kein sittsam Kind den Kopf zum Fenster
'naus.
Geh', Bächlein, hin und sag' ihr das, doch sag'
ihr nicht,
Hörst du, kein Wort, von meinem traurigen Gesicht;
Sag' ihr: Er schnitzt bei mir sich eine Pfeif' aus Rohr,
Und bläst den Kindern schöne Tänz' und Lieder vor.

for her easy, fickle, trifling inconstancy.
Didn't you see her last night, standing by the gate,
craning her neck down the wide road?
When the hunter goes gaily home from the hunt,
no well-behaved girl would put her head out of the
window.
Go tell her that, my brooklet, but don't tell her,

mind, a word about my mournful face.
Tell her: "He cuts a whistle from a reed near by,
and pipes pretty dances and songs for the children."

16. DIE LIEBE FARBE (THE FAVORITE COLOR)

In Grün will ich mich kleiden,
In grüne Tränenweiden,
Mein Schatz hat's Grün so gern.
Will suchen einen Zypressenhain,
Eine Heide voll grünem Rosmarein,
Mein Schatz hat's Grün so gern.
    Wohlauf zum fröhlichen Jagen!
Wohlauf durch Heid' und Hagen!
Mein Schatz hat's Jagen so gern.
Das Wild, das ich jage, das ist der Tod,
Die Heide, die heiss' ich die Liebesnot,
Mein Schatz hat's Jagen so gern.
    Grabt mir ein Grab im Wasen,
Deckt mich mit grünem Rasen,
Mein Schatz hat's Grün so gern.
Kein Kreuzlein schwarz, kein Blümlein bunt,
Grün, Alles grün so rings und rund!
Mein Schatz hat's Grün so gern.

    I will dress myself in green,
the green of the weeping willow;
my sweetheart is so fond of green,
I will look for a grove of cypress,
a heath full of green rosemary;
my sweetheart is so fond of green.
    Off to the jolly hunt!
Off through the meadows and hedges!
My sweetheart is so fond of hunting.
The game I am after is death,
the heath I call the sorrow of love;
my sweetheart is so fond of hunting.
    Dig me a grave in the turf;
cover me over with green grass.
My sweetheart is so fond of green.
No black cross, no gaudy flowers,
green, all green around and about!
My sweetheart is so fond of green.

17. DIE BOSE FARBE (THE EVIL COLOR)

Ich möchte ziehn in die Welt hinaus,
Hinaus in die weite Welt,
Wenn's nur so grün, so grün nicht wär'
Da draussen in Wald und Feld!
    Ich möchte die grünen Blätter all'
Pflücken von jedem Zweig,
Ich möchte die grünen Gräser all'
Weinen ganz totenbleich.
    Ach Grün, du böse Farbe du,
Was siehst mich immer an,
So stolz, so keck, so schadenfroh,
Mich armen weissen Mann?
    Ich möchte liegen vor ihrer Tür,
Im Sturm und Regen und Schnee,
Und singen ganz leise bei Tag und Nacht

    I would like to go out into the world,
out into the wide world,
if only it weren't so green
out in the woods and the fields!
    I wish I could pull down
all the green leaves from every branch;
I wish that all the green grass
could be bleached with my tears.
    O green, you evil color,
why must you always look
so proudly, so pertly, so maliciously
at me, poor white man?
    I would like to lie down before her door,
in the storm, the rain, and the snow,
and sing softly all day and all night

Das eine Wörtchen Ade!
  Horch, wenn im Wald ein Jagdhorn schallt,
Da klingt ihr Fensterlein,
Und schaut sie auch nach mir nicht aus,
Darf ich doch schauen hinein.
  O binde von der Stirn dir ab
Das grüne, grüne Band,
Ade, Ade! und reiche mir
Zum Abschied deine Hand!

just one word—good-bye!
  Listen, when a horn sounds in the woods,
I hear her at her window,
and though she doesn't see me
still I can look in at her.
  O untie from your forehead
the green, green ribbon!
Good-bye, good-bye! And give me
your hand in parting!

18. TROCKNE BLUMEN (WITHERED FLOWERS)

Ihr Blümlein alle,
Die sie mir gab,
Euch soll man legen
Mit mir in's Grab.
  Wie seht ihr alle
Mich an so weh,
Als ob ihr wüsstet,
Wie mir gescheh'?
  Ihr Blümlein alle,
Wie welk, wie blass?
Ihr Blümlein alle,
Wovon so nass?
  Ach, Tränen machen
Nicht maiengrün,
Machen tote Liebe
Nicht wieder blühn.
  Und Lenz wird kommen,
Und Winter wird gehn,
Und Blümlein werden
Im Grase stehn.
  Und Blümlein liegen
In meinem Grab,
Die Blümlein alle,
Die sie mir gab.
  Und wenn sie wandelt
Am Hügel vorbei,
Und denkt im Herzen:
Der meint' es treu!
  Dann Blümlein alle,
Heraus, heraus!
Der Mai ist kommen,
Der Winter ist aus.

All you flowers
that she gave me,
you shall lie buried
with me in the grave.
  How sadly you all
look at me,
as if you knew
how it happened to me?
  All you flowers,
how withered? How faded?
All you flowers,
what makes you so moist?
  Ah, tears do not make
the green of May,
nor cause dead love
to bloom again.
  And spring will come,
and winter will go,
and flowers will spring up
in the grass.
  And flowers will lie
on my grave,
all the flowers
she gave me.
  And if she should pass
by the mound,
and think in her heart:
He was faithful to me!
  Then all you flowers,
spring up, spring up!
May is here!
Winter is past!

**19. DER MULLER UND DER BACH
(THE MILLER AND THE BROOK)**

Der Müller:
  Wo ein treues Herze
In Liebe vergeht,

The Miller:
  Where a faithful heart
dies of love,

239

Da welken die Lilien
Auf jedem Beet.
　　Da muss in die Wolken
Der Vollmond gehn,
Damit seine Tränen
Die Menschen nicht sehn.
　　Da halten die Englein
Die Augen sich zu,
Und schluchzen und singen
Die Seele zur Ruh'.

Der Bach:
　　Und wenn sich die Liebe
Dem Schmerz entringt,
Ein Sternlein, ein neues,
Am Himmel erblinkt.
　　Da springen drei Rosen,
Halb rot und halb weiss,
Die welken nicht wieder,
Aus Dornenreis.
　　Und die Engelein schneiden
Die Flügel sich ab,
Und gehn alle Morgen
Zur Erde herab.

Der Müller:
　　Ach Bächlein, liebes Bächlein,
Du meinst es so gut:
Ach, Bächlein, aber weisst du,
Wie Liebe tut?
　　Ach, unten, da unten,
Die kühle Ruh'!
Ach, Bächlein, liebes Bächlein,
So singe nur zu.

**20. DES BACHES WIEGENLIED
(THE BROOK'S LULLABY)**

　　Gute Ruh', gute Ruh'!
Tu' die Augen zu!
Wandrer, du müder, du bist zu Haus.
Die Treu' ist hier,
Sollst liegen bei mir,
Bis das Meer will trinken die Bächlein aus.
　　Will betten dich kühl,
Auf weichem Pfühl,
In dem blauen krystallenen Kämmerlein.
Heran, heran,
Was wiegen kann,

there the lilies wither
in every bed.
　　Then into the clouds
the full moon must ride,
so that his tears
shall not be seen by men.
　　Then the angels
close their eyes,
and sob and sing
the soul to rest.

The Brook:
　　And when love
is released from sorrow,
a star, a new one
twinkles in the heavens.
　　There spring up three roses,
half red and half white,
never to wither,
from the prickly stems.
　　And the angels cut
their wings off,
and come every morning
down to the earth.

The Miller:
　　Dear brooklet,
you mean it so well,
but brooklet, do you know
what it is to be in love?
　　Ah, down, down there,
the cooling rest!
Ah brooklet, dear brooklet,
just sing me to sleep.

　　Sleep well, sleep well!
Close your eyes!
Wanderer, weary one, you have come home.
Here you will find faithfulness,
you shall lie down with me
until the sea drinks up the brooklets.
　　I will make you a fresh bed
on a soft pillow
in a little blue crystal room.
Come, come
whatever can cradle,

Woget und wieget den Knaben mir ein!
  Wenn ein Jagdhorn schallt
Aus dem grünen Wald,
Will ich sausen und brausen wohl um dich her.
Blickt nicht herein,
Blaue Blümelein!
Ihr macht meinem Schläfer die Träume so schwer.
  Hinweg, hinweg
Von dem Mühlensteg,
Böses Mägdelein, dass ihn dein Schatten nicht weckt!
Wirf mir herein
Dein Tüchlein fein,
Dass ich die Augen ihm halte bedeckt!
  Gute Nacht, gute Nacht!
Bis Alles wacht,
Schlaf' aus deine Freude, schlaf' aus dein Leid!
Der Vollmond steigt,
Der Nebel weicht,
Und der Himmel da oben, wie ist er so weit!

lull and rock the boy to sleep!
  If a hunting horn sounds
from the green wood,
I will bluster and storm around you.
Don't look in at him,
blue flowers,
you make bad dreams for my sleeper.
  Away, away
from the mill-bridge,
wicked girl, so that your shadow may not waken him!
Throw in to me
your dainty handkerchief
so that I may cover his eyes.
  Good-night, good-night!
Until the day of awakening,
forget your joys in sleep, forget your sorrows!
The full moon is rising,
The mists are retreating,
and the heaven above, how wide it is!

CHAPTER *12* THE FINALE FROM ACT II OF MOZART'S LE NOZZE DI FIGARO

SCHUBERT'S CYCLE *Die schöne Müllerin* had a dramatic interior and a lyric, or songlike, exterior. That is, the inner drama was not acted out on a stage but instead told as a story—and not just told, but sung in a series of songs, each musically complete in itself.

In contrast, Mozart's opera *Le Nozze di Figaro* ("The Marriage of Figaro") is explicitly dramatic in its outward form. It is acted on stage, with each character in the story represented by an actor. (In *Die schöne Müllerin*, one central character—the hunter—was not represented at all; and speeches of the girl as well as the brook were delivered by the singer, who was both narrator and protagonist.) In *Figaro*, the presence or absence of actors on stage and their interaction with each other physically as well as emotionally are important in shaping the music. Yet the music is profoundly lyric, in shape as well as spirit. The combination of dramatic and lyric elements in *Figaro* is a main source of its perennial fascination.

The combination is especially intense—one might say, volatile—in the Finale of Act II; at the end the Finale seems to catch fire, fusing drama and lyricism together. You can well begin to study this Finale simply by listening to the music alone; the dramatic text is, of course, essential, but its details will be much more meaningful if fitted into a hearing and an understanding of the musical shape of the whole.

Several observations about the overall shape of the Finale can be made even after one or two hearings. These observations concern long-range trends in the music, trends that hold good for the whole Finale,

even if they are subject to detours and backtracking.

The Finale is set for several solo voices and orchestra (woodwinds, brass, and strings). No significant long-range changes occur in the use of the orchestra throughout the Finale. The number of singers, however, increases from beginning to end, bringing about long-range changes in both timbre and texture. Each of these solo voices has a distinctive timbre, so that you are aware of the increase from two at the beginning to many (actually, seven) at the end. Since the singers sing all at once as well as alone or in various combinations of two or three, there is a gradual enrichment of texture. These are long-range trends in the Finale; at lower levels, there are frequent reductions of timbre and texture from rich, complex combinations back to a single voice, to a clear timbre in a simple texture.

Another long-range trend is perceptible in tempo: at its conclusion the Finale gives the impression of a long, sustained acceleration of tempo. Within this trend, however, the cutbacks are very prominent and very important. Indeed, a steady, unbroken increase in timbre, texture, and tempo throughout a piece lasting 25 minutes (the length of the Finale) would be very risky from an artistic point of view. The reduction of tempo that occurs several times in the Finale is essential to maintaining a fresh sense of rhythmic movement; this function of the slower sections is quite distinct from their dramatic function.

Dynamics and articulation are often extremely important as details but do not develop significant

long-range trends. Rhythmic changes (apart from tempo) and relationships of line and figure are important mainly at middle and lower levels. Changes in harmonic area, on the other hand, have an important long-range function; we will take them up later, since their function is not immediately apparent.

CHANGES IN TEMPO. It should be evident on first or second hearing that the Finale is clearly divided into sections; the divisions are most audible through changes in tempo. The musical shape—the dramatic shape, too—of the Finale is expressed in a series of sections, each section being relatively homogeneous and different from its neighbors. These sections are listed here by Mozart's tempo indications, roughly translated to indicate the tempo relationships as you hear them.

1	Allegro	fast
2	Molto andante	much slower, but still moving
3	Allegro	fast
4	Allegro con spirito	fast, spirited
5	Andante	slower
6	Allegro molto	very fast
7	Andante	slower
8	Allegro assai	very fast
9	Più allegro	still faster
10	Prestissimo	as fast as possible

We will devote more time to these sections of contrasting tempo and to the way they divide up the text and the drama. The first thing to notice about the sections (even before reading their texts) is that they give a particular kind of shape to the drama. The action of a dramatic plot does not *seem*, ordinarily, to fall into clearly defined sections but rather to proceed through gradual development. Mozart has apparently superimposed sectional contrasts upon the dramatic continuity; or perhaps he has revealed a sectional structure inherent in the dramatic action.

An important feature of the action that divides it into sections is the entrance (or exit) of a character. The action of the Finale can be mapped roughly according to the several entrances. One of the most prominent and important features of the action itself in the Finale is the steady increase in the number of characters on stage (this is the dramatic side of the increase in number of voices). Six characters enter in the course of the Finale; only one of them exits. Mozart has marked each entrance with a new section of music. And—as if to show that the lone exit is not an important feature of the shape—he has let it occur in the middle of a section.

Section 1:
Allegro   Count, Countess

Section 2:
Molto   Count, Countess;
   andante   *enter* Susanna

Section 3:
Allegro   Count, Countess, Susanna

Section 4:
Allegro con   Count, Countess, Susanna;
   spirito   *enter* Figaro

Section 5:
Andante   Count, Countess, Susanna,
                    Figaro

Section 6:
Allegro   Count, Countess, Susanna,
   molto   Figaro;
                 enter Antonio

Section 7:
Andante   Count, Countess, Susanna,
                    Figaro, Antonio;
                 exit Antonio

Section 8:
Allegro   Count, Countess, Susanna,
   assai   Figaro;
                         ⎧ Marcellina
                 enter ⎨ Bartolo
                         ⎩ Basilio

Section 9:
Più allegro   Count, Countess, Susanna,
                    Figaro, Marcellina,
                    Bartolo, Basilio

Section 10:
Prestissimo   Count, Countess, Susanna,
                    Figaro, Marcellina,
                    Bartolo, Basilio

Voice types (in order of appearance): Count, bari-

tone; Countess, soprano; Susanna, soprano; Figaro, bass; Antonio, bass; Marcellina, soprano; Basilio, tenor; and Bartolo, bass.

It is clear from this list that the entrances account for only some of the sections (entrances occur at the beginnings of sections 2, 4, 6, and 8). Some of the remaining sections are associated with developments in the action among the characters on stage.

Here we need to refer to the complete text of the Finale laid out at the end of this chapter. (The Italian version is by Lorenzo da Ponte, 1749–1838; the text of an opera is called a *libretto*—Italian, "little book.") This is a translation of all that is sung in the Finale, line by line the way it is sung, with the following special indications. When a line of text is immediately repeated (that is, sung twice in succession) it is surrounded by the musical signs for a repeat ⟦: :⟧. When different characters are singing *different* texts at the same time (which happens frequently) all the simultaneous texts are enclosed in brackets; sometimes in such cases one character will start his lines before another character. Repetitions of text in such simultaneous combinations (also frequent) are not indicated. Usually, there will be a well-defined subsection during which the several characters repeat their several texts simultaneously.

In section 1, the Count is threatening to break down a closet door in the Countess's room, since he is sure that in the closet he will find Cherubino, the page whom the Count suspects of flirting with the Countess. The Count is furious; the Countess is terrified, for Cherubino did indeed hide in her closet—for purely innocent reasons.

During an interval in which the Count and Countess have left the room (in the scene just preceding), the Countess's resourceful maid, Susanna, has got Cherubino out the window and has hidden herself in his stead in the same closet. At the end of section 1, then, the Count throws open the closet door, prepared to cut down a cowering pageboy, but finds instead—Susanna! She is cool, collected, and politely sarcastic. The exclamations of Count and Countess, "Susanna!" divide section 1 from section 2; Susanna's address "Signore!" marks the beginning of section 2. The suddenly slower tempo of section 2, formal and

restrained, is the musical embodiment of Susanna's exaggerated, sarcastic courtesy to the Count.

As we will see later, the whole structure of section 2 is built to reflect cool, subdued reactions (Susanna, formal; the Count, bewildered; the Countess, still holding her breath). Section 2 is relatively short. The Count steps into the closet to satisfy himself that Cherubino is indeed not there; and, during his temporary absence, the Countess conveys her terror and relief to Susanna. The Countess's speech ("Susanna, I'm finished") marks the beginning of section 3 and its return to a fast tempo. Strained formality gives way to a more relaxed animation as the characters converse more freely among themselves about the anticlimax. Section 3, which is the most complex of the Finale, moves through argument to temporary, fragile reconciliation.

The end of section 3 has a certain conclusiveness about it. Superficially, one could almost mistake it for an appropriate ending to the act, for the mood is warm and relaxed, the tension momentarily resolved. But neither Mozart nor the librettist, da Ponte, has any intention of ending the act that way; most of the Finale is yet to come. Once section 3 arrives at its end, it is made to end quickly—a shade too quickly for a solid conclusion. And before the audience can start applauding, in comes Figaro to the more lively music of section 4.

Figaro, the Count's valet, is to marry Susanna that very day. Their marriage (*the* "marriage of Figaro") is opposed by the Count because of his jealousy (he wants to make love to Susanna himself); the Count's lust for Susanna is the most disruptive factor in the situation and a basic motivation of the drama. In section 4, the Count tries yet another way to delay the marriage. Section 4 (like section 2) is relatively short; at first the Count cannot get through Figaro's ebullience. But then, with another gesture of exaggerated formality, the Count pulls out a letter written anonymously as a hoax by Figaro, advising the Count that the Countess will meet a lover that evening (Susanna is to impersonate the Countess and embarrass the Count). This is the letter mentioned in section 3, where the Countess and Susanna informed the Count of the true origin of the letter. Now the Count wishes to trap Figaro in his deceit; already knowing the answer, the Count asks Figaro who wrote the letter. The slower tempo of section 5 is the musical expression of the heavy formality with which the Count sets out to trap Figaro. This second reduction of tempo, like the first in section 2, springs naturally out of the dramatic action.

Unaware that the Count has been told, Figaro tries to brazen it out. To the Count's accusation, as well as to the urgings of the Countess and Susanna (at first covert, then open attempts to get signals straight with Figaro), he can only snarl "No! I don't know!"—although it is plain the denial is purely formal. Then he tries, with a desperate show of wit that falls flat, to return to his original purpose, the preparation for the ceremony itself. Susanna, Figaro, and the Countess entreat the Count to agree, while he worries (to himself) about the arrival of Marcellina—part of another scheme of delay.

Into this scene comes Antonio, the gardener, half drunk; this entrance marks section 6 and a very fast tempo. For a few moments all is confusion, as the Count tries to find out what happened (he welcomes the intrusion, of course), while the others try vainly to silence or to discredit Antonio—for they sense immediately that the person Antonio has seen "thrown" from the window was Cherubino escaping. Figaro, characteristically, tries to explain away the event by a series of lies which involve him ever more deeply in difficulties. This goes on at some length and at the furious tempo established for section 6. When it begins to look as though Figaro might actually put together a credible (if complicated) explanation, the drunk gardener, giving himself as much dignity as he can, produces his most damning evidence—papers dropped by whoever jumped out the window. "Then these must be your papers . . . ?"

The gardener's gesture of exaggerated courtesy marks section 7, the third reduction of tempo in the Finale. On stage at this point (as at the previous reduction) the papers themselves would be the focal point of attention and would serve as a dramatic accent to signal the new section. It is clear that in all three reductions of tempo (sections 2, 5, and 7) a dramatic event is closely associated with the change of tempo, even more specifically with the nature of the musical movement following the change. In all three

cases, the change functions to cut back the forward motion—dramatic as well as musical—thereby making possible a more effective acceleration later.

Thinking fast, the Countess sees that the document lacks the Count's seal. She passes this information along in whispers to Figaro, so that he may explain why the document should be in his possession rather than Cherubino's and thus extricate himself from the deepening contradictions of his pack of lies. No one is particularly satisfied with the outcome, however, and the section does not end strongly.

The beginning of section 8, with the entrance of Marcellina, Bartolo, and Basilio, is well marked by the new fast tempo. This is the last real section break of the Finale; sections 9 and 10 are merely stages in the sweeping acceleration toward the close. Marcellina, Bartolo, and Basilio inject a whole new complication, recounted very quickly, and virtually lost in the increasing pace and musical complexity. The aim of the composer and the librettist, at this point, is not to clarify but rather to confuse—to introduce more material than can be assimilated by the listener before the close of the act. Complications of plot and of music (especially in timbre and texture) work together to produce the dazzling rush to the finish. The task of making this section sound like a finish is carried by the phrase structure and especially by the treatment of harmonic areas, as we will see later. This is, after all, not the end of the opera, only the end of Act II; there is still time for things to be straightened out.

METRIC CHANGES. Sectional divisions throughout the Finale are marked by changes not only in tempo but also in meter. The changes in meter, however, do not contribute to the overall acceleration of the Finale; rather they help sharpen the contrast between sections. The meter tends to alternate between duple and triple. The triple meters are the exceptions; they appear on only one level (usually a very low level). Even when a triple meter is present, the other levels tend to be duple.

Example 12-1 shows the succession of meters, as heard in the beginnings of the various sections. The first change to triple is at the first Andante (section 2), when Susanna emerges from the closet. The triple

meter, which appears at the next-to-bottom level, lasts throughout the section. The Andante has several different rhythmic figures, one of which is triple at the lowest level; but that figure lasts only a short time and does not establish a meter.

The resumption of a faster pace in section 3 (Allegro) coincides with a return to duple meter. Here there are more rhythmic figures—and more varied ones than before. Only the first of these figures is shown in Ex. 12-1. Still, it is the basic shift to duple meter at all levels (along with the changes in tempo) that marks off the section as a whole from the preceding one.

The second appearance of triple meter comes with Figaro's high-spirited entrance in section 4. Here Figaro makes explicit reference to dancing, and the regular rhythms in triple meter seem to bear him out. The following Andante (section 5) returns to duple meter. The Finale shows no correlation, in other words, between triple meter and slower tempos—or triple meter and faster ones; triple meter is used simply as a factor of contrast, section by section.

In section 6, Antonio bursts in, and confusion follows. The section starts off in duple meter at all levels; as soon as Antonio starts his story ("From the balcony . . . ") the orchestra shifts to an accompaniment figure in a triple rhythm, which conflicts on the lowest level with the duple meter continuing in Antonio's part. This section is the most confused, most hectic, in dramatic context.

In the following Andante, the meter becomes triple at its lowest level. In this section, the rhythmic figuration is almost completely uniform throughout the section and coincides with the meter. The regularity of this Andante—a contrast to the confusion that prevails at lower levels in the preceding Allegro—helps to create the atmosphere of strained formality that has replaced the boisterous confusion of Antonio's entrance. The Andante—and with it Figaro's embarrassing predicament—continues in unbroken rhythm seemingly without end.

From section 8 on, the meter is consistently duple at all levels through to the end; sections 9 and 10 bring no contrast, only acceleration. In section 10, the tempo is so fast that sometimes the notes blur together, making perception of meter difficult.

Example 12-1 Mozart, Finale: Meters in the sections

Section 1: Allegro

(Count) E— sci_o-mai, garzon malna—to,

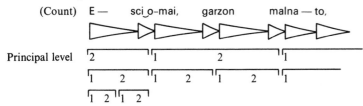

Principal level

Section 2: Molte andante

(Strings)

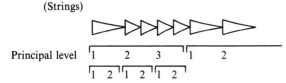

Principal level

Section 3: Allegro

(Strings)

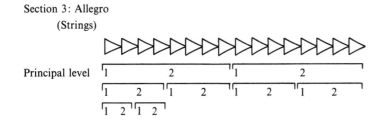

Principal level

Section 4: Allegro con spirito

(Tutti)

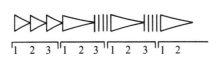

Section 5: Andante

(Count) Co— no-sce—te, si— gnor Fi-ga-ro,

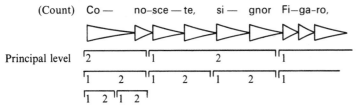

Principal level

Section 6: Allegro molto

(Tutti)

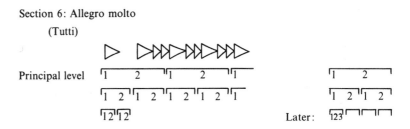

Principal level

Later:

Section 7: Andante

(Strings and winds)

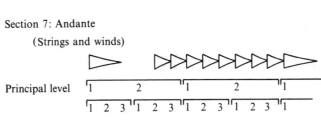

Principal level

Section 8: Allegro assai

(Tutti)

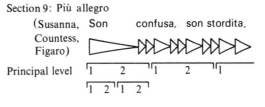

Principal level

Section 9: Più allegro

(Susanna, Son confusa, son stordita,
Countess,
Figaro)

Principal level

Section 10: Prestissimo

(Susanna, Cer— to_un dia – vol dell' in — fer — no
Figaro)

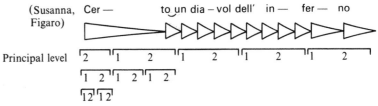

Principal level

245

HARMONIC PLAN. In succession of harmonic areas, Mozart's Finale is built differently than Schubert's *Die schöne Müllerin*. In the song cycle, contrast of harmonic area was most obvious in going from one song to the next; continuity of area between songs or clear return of the area used in a previous song after a contrasting one was so infrequent as to be especially noteworthy. In Mozart's Finale, changes in key in the succession of the sections are much less conspicuous. Only once, at section 4, does Mozart use that striking kind of harmonic change so frequent in Schubert's cycle. There, at section 4, a striking change is in order: Figaro's high-spirited entrance breaks abruptly into the relaxed mood of temporary reconciliation established among the Count, Countess, and Susanna, to initiate a new series of dramatic complexities. (The beginning of section 2 may also seem a striking change, but it is a change to a key close by.)

Just as Mozart wants to create a sense of long-range acceleration, so he creates a sense of direction to a harmonic goal. This sense of direction makes the Finale basically different in approach from *Die schöne Müllerin*, where indirect allusions and oblique references to the central line of development are normal. In Mozart's Finale, the key of one section seems to flow easily—if not imperceptibly—into the next. In fact, many of the relationships between sections are of the type in which the central harmony of one becomes the leading harmony of the next. The direction and overall shape apparent in Ex. 12-2 are strikingly different from the lack of direction and the complex shapes shown in Exs. 11-1 and 11-2 for *Die schöne Müllerin*. Admittedly, it is much easier to see the difference in the diagrams than to hear it in the music, for in the diagrams you see the pitch organization all at once, while in the music you hear it only little by little.

You might, however, be aware of something else in the harmonic organization of the Finale—the sense of return, of arrival, at the beginning of section 8. At first the arrival at this point will seem only like the arrival at the beginning of each of the preceding sections, 5, 6, and 7. After several listenings, however, you may hear the key at the beginning of section 8 as a return to the key of section 1. The harmonic return will become clearer as you become aware of other

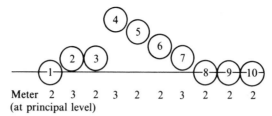

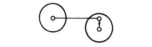

Meter 2 3 2 3 2 2 3 2 2 2
(at principal level)

From section 4 to 8, the central harmony of each section becomes the leading harmony of the next.

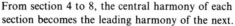

Example 12-2 Mozart, Finale: Harmonic areas

subtle similarities between these two sections, including similarities in pace as well as in rhythmic and melodic figuration.

Example 12-2 includes both harmonic area and meter. Listen for the change of area at the very beginning of each section, for that is where the change is most evident. After that, listen in each section for the meter, which will not be apparent until a phrase or two has gone by. For the purpose of hearing what has been discussed, keep your attention focused on the sections as units. Some of the sections change key significantly within the section; but each returns to its central harmony at its ending, much as each contains its varied rhythmic figuration within a single meter and tempo.

There is no doubt that the connections between sections of Mozart's Finale are generally smoother than the connections between songs in *Die schöne Müllerin*; the difference represents the differing intent of the two works. But underneath the compelling sense of continuity uppermost in Mozart's Finale, you can discover a surprising variety of structure in individual sections, for each section is designed to respond to the changing dramatic situation. Without attempting to discuss completely the structure of each section, we will describe the main structural point of each, as a basis for understanding the coordination of musical form and dramatic purpose.

SECTION 1—ALLEGRO. Section 1 is primarily concerned (as we saw) with the efforts of the Count to

open the closet door. He is enraged; he insists; the Countess attempts to explain but ends up yielding in terror. Imagine the Countess at first with her back to the door, then finally thrust, cowering, aside, while the Count bullies the key from her and advances on the door. In this particular section, you need to know not only what is going on in the plot but also how the action is being carried out on stage.

The pace of the section is hectic; yet for all its forward rush it allows clear divisions, as indicated in Ex. 12-3. (This and the following examples can be referred to the text at the end of this chapter.) Each subsection is started by the Count; the Countess merely responds.

Just before subsection *B*, the orchestra plays briefly without the singers—not a long break, but enough (in conjunction with some other factors, to be considered) to start a new subsection. Subsection *B* ends with the Count's flat contradiction to the Countess, "I'll say you are—to your face!" Mozart directs this line to be sung emphatically, interrupting the rhythmic momentum; the third subsection, *C*, is thus clearly prepared.

Within these three subsections, the use of texture in the voice parts is closely coordinated with the dialog. At first, in subsection *A*, Count and Countess make relatively long speeches; each sings a relatively clear, well-formed phrase. Their shorter, broken lines immediately following are of course reflected directly in the alternation of the singers. Now neither gets to sing a whole musical phrase, instead several speeches are subsumed under a single phrase. The alternation of longer and shorter speeches continues throughout to be an important factor in relation to the musical phrasing.

Toward the end of subsection *A*, Count and Countess sing together—a prominent change in texture. They sing different words, but somehow the effect of their singing at once seems a more important consideration than the need to hear them separately.

COUNT
Ah, I understand, worthless woman,
and I'll soon get my revenge.
COUNTESS
Your outrage wrongs me,
you insult me by doubting me.

Allegro, duple meter

Subsections:			Harmonic movement
A	Count	Esci omai . . . If you're coming out . . .	Establishes key
	Count	E d'opporvi ancor osate? And yet you dare oppose me?	Moves away
B	Count	Qua la chiave! Give me the key!	Returns
	Count	Va lontan dagli occhi miei! Get out of my sight!	Moves to a minor key
	Count	Vel leggo in volto! I'll say you are	Moves away briefly
C	Count	Mora, mora! Let him die!	Returns to original key

Example 12-3 Mozart, Finale: Subsections and harmonic movement in section 1

In addition to being dramatically true, their singing together (or *against* each other) brings the subsection to a strong close. At first they sing in imitation, then in homophony for the ending.

In subsection *B*, we hear them again singly. First come quick question-and-answer phrases, then a relatively long outburst by the Count ("Get out of my sight . . . "), then more quick alternation.

In subsection *C* they sing mostly together—or in such close alternation that you can barely hear them separately. The texture of subsection *C* as a whole brings section 1 to a close, just as a thicker texture closes subsection *A*.

Subsection *C* is made more conclusive by its repetition of melodies from the end of subsection *A*; these melodies—the ones specifically involved in the imitation—have the effect of a refrain. The sense of refrain is strengthened by the strong feeling of return to a central harmony, as you can hear by following the harmonic organization.

Each subsection begins on the same harmony. Subsection *A*, after establishing its key, moves firmly to a closely related key (as shown in Ex. 12-3); the orchestral link at the end of the section, however, just as firmly returns to the original key. The Count's insistent speech at the beginning of subsection *B*

("Give me the key!") hammers home this harmonic return.

In the middle of subsection B, the Count's longer speech is in minor. The shift is not a drastic one, but in context it is sufficient to make its point. At the end of *B*, another harmonic move occurs, but it is so short and quick that it merely has the effect of leaving the subsection open. Subsection *C* again reverts to the original key. Thus, while motion away from the center takes place in subsections *A* and *B*, the harmony insists—as does the Count—and the sense of return in subsection *C* is unmistakable.

SECTION 2—MOLTO ANDANTE. The pivotal event of sections 1 and 2 occurs between them: the Count opens the door, finding Susanna. Section 1 has led up to the event; section 2 is concerned completely with a reaction to it. No further action of importance takes place. Drama and music are static, reflective.

Nonetheless, section 2 contains two different responses to the pivotal event. These two responses are cast into a musical shape A_1 B A_2 (Ex. 12-4). Subsections A_1 and A_2, representing a polite, formal response, frame the section in a balanced manner. Subsection *B* represents a private, interior response on the part of each of the three characters—a musical and dramatic aside interrupting the formal one. Subsection A_1 is sung by Susanna alone; subsection *B* by all three—Count, Countess, Susanna—singing different words at once. Subsection A_2 has a duet for the Count and Susanna, singing at first separately, then together.

The formal response in subsection A_1 is cast in a triple meter, suggesting a court dance (a minuet); the effect is ironic, since it is clear from the drama that none of the characters *feels* polite. The strings begin, carrying the melody; Susanna starts to sing archly at a moment seemingly of her own choosing. The rhythms are very regular throughout A_1, the metric groups of three being grouped in twos and—at a still higher level—into fours. The harmonic organization is stable, in the sense that the several different harmonies employed are closely related to each other and to the central harmony. The subsection does not move to any other harmonic area; in fact, harmonic changes are so smooth that harmony scarcely seems a factor (the regular rhythms and balancing melodic phrases are more prominent).

Subsection A_2 seems to be an answer and continuation of A_1: the orchestra returns to the rhythms of

Example 12-4 Mozart, Finale: Subsections in section 2

Molto andante, triple meter

A_1	Susanna	Signore! Sir!	Solo. Stable harmonies. Regular rhythms and phrases.
B	Count	Che scola! A revelation!	Trio. Static harmony over a pedal. Ostinato figure in bassoon.
A_2	Count	Sei sola? Are you alone?	Duet. Resumes A_1. Stable harmonies. Regular rhythms and phrases.

A_1, in the same harmonic area and with some of the same melodies. Subsection A_2 does not literally repeat A_1, but is so neatly matched with it that the sense of return is obvious—especially in contrast to the intervening subsection B.

After Susanna's courteous sarcasm in subsection A_1, all three characters muse (in B) inwardly about the turn of events, each speaking to himself. To accompany this change in the dialog, a remarkable change takes place in the music—remarkable because the whole section is so homogeneous, the actual changes in musical structure so small and subtle. The harmony can be called static rather than stable: two harmonies (central and leading) alternate over an obvious pedal that lasts almost throughout the subsection. Clear melodic phrases disappear from the orchestra, and in their place the bassoon plays a descending ostinato scale passage. Over this soft, gracefully bemused accompaniment, the singers repeat their various lines as if in a momentary trance. The Count breaks the mood ("Are you alone?") in making the first direct address to Susanna. In other words, subsection B is a musical prolongation of the attitude of shocked surprise with which all react to Susanna's appearance.

SECTION 3—ALLEGRO. Section 3, Allegro, follows section 2 without a break. The section is concerned with a more extensive exploration of the characters' reactions to the discovery of Susanna—reactions beyond mere surprise (as found in section 2) and including adjustments and changes of attitude toward each other. They seek out the implications of the event and eventually find some kind of reconciliation in the light of it. This process of mutual adjustment we need to have clearly in mind.

The Count has perhaps the hardest time digesting what has happened; he returns several times to the details of the intrigue. Otherwise, he is busy entreating the Countess's pardon, for she, having regained her composure, is taking advantage of the situation to counterattack in force. In particular she throws his recent accusation ("I'm unfaithful . . .") back in his teeth.

Clearly a scene such as this requires music different from that of section 2 or even section 1. The dialog is complex, repetitive, yet developmental; there are no clear sectional divisions, but there is a gradual change—things are not the same at the end as they were at the beginning. The music, in its way, supports all these characteristics of the dialog.

In the previous sections, texture was often correlated with subsections, thicker texture (voices singing together) tending to come at the end of a subsection. In section 3 all voices sing together twice —once in the middle ("Confused, repentant"/"Cruel, cruel man!"), again at the end. The thicker texture in the middle, however, does not mark a very convincing section, as we will see. Generally speaking, the various factors of texture, harmony, and melody do not support one another in dividing the section clearly. Many times there is a change in one factor that does not produce a sectional division because of lack of support from other factors.

The easiest way to perceive the complex workings of section 3 is to try to keep track of the wealth of melodic material. There are six clear themes (some might better be called motives) that return to shape the section. That is, it is clear that they return; the shape they produce in returning is emphatically not clear.

Example 12-5 shows the six themes, as they first appear. Themes 1 through 4 appear mainly in the orchestra. Theme 3 accompanies the Count; theme 5 is the special property of the Countess and Susanna; theme 6 is sung by each of the three at one time or another. These six themes account for almost all the thematic material of the section; the vocal lines sometimes use other material that is melodious without being thematic.

The order of appearance of these six themes is indicated on the text at the end of this chapter. The only decisive feature of this succession of themes is the emergence of theme 2 as the dominant one at the end. This theme is usually associated with entreaty in this section, and its suave, insinuating character lends itself well to this purpose. We might expect that the sustained use of theme 2 toward the middle of the section (after Susanna: "My lady!") would produce a major section break after the three-voiced texture. What follows, however, is not a characteristic beginning (theme 3, Count: "But the page . . . ?"); this

rather gives the impression of picking up a line of thought broken off previously. Furthermore, the cadence at the end of the three-voiced texture is not in a harmonic area that lends itself to a sense of conclusion.

Similarly, when the Count seems to start a recapitulation ("Well, if you please,") with the first reference to theme 1, the harmonic area is not the original one and soon moves off in yet another direction. Such use of key is not obvious—in fact, will probably go unnoticed; but the sense of inconclusiveness resulting from the use of key is more noticeable and contributes significantly to the lack of strong internal subdivision, the continuing forward motion of the section.

SECTION 4—ALLEGRO CON SPIRITO. Section 3 is probably the most complex of the Finale; it is also the longest. Section 4, the shortest, is so clearly an accompaniment to action and dialog that it scarcely has an independent musical structure. It is loud, festive, and commonplace for Figaro's entrance and his mention of wedding festivities; then it becomes softer in response to the Count's "Calm down, less haste." It ends quickly and inconclusively, since the dialog leads directly to the next section. The main function of section 4 is felt at the higher levels of the Finale: this section makes the harmonic move to distant realms, setting up the possibility of a long slide back to the end (see Ex. 12-2).

SECTION 5—ANDANTE. Section 5 is the second of the slower sections in which a show of formality conceals (but only partly) the sarcastic animosity of one character toward another. In this case, the Count confronts Figaro with the letter Figaro wrote anonymously to the Count: "Do you know, my good Figaro . . . " In spite of the duple meter, the music recalls the dancelike music in triple meter at the previous Andante (section 2). Clear phrases, in clearly balanced pairs, appear throughout much of the melody. These phrases (as before in the other Andante) are often carried by the orchestra, the voices singing less connectedly. In this way, the monosyllabic responses of Figaro (almost snarled in some performances) to the questions of the other characters can all be set within a polite framework (Ex. 12-6).

Example 12-5 Mozart, Finale: Themes and motives in section 3

Allegro, duple meter

Themes (or motives)

1 Beginning of section 3

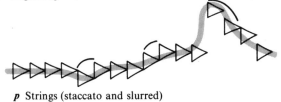

p Strings (staccato and slurred)

2 Just before Susanna's first speech, "Più lieta, . . . " ("Softly, don't worry")

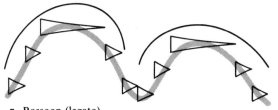

p Bassoon (legato)

3 Just before Count's final speech, " Che sbaglio mai presi! "

("What an error . . .")

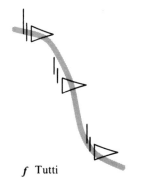

f Tutti

4 Count, " ma far burla simile " (". . . but playing jokes . . .")

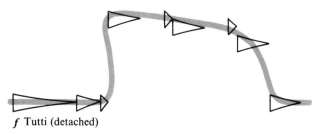

f Tutti (detached)

5 Susanna, Countess, ("Your foolish acts deserve no pity.")

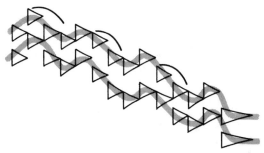

p Le vostre folli — e non mer — tan pietà

6 Susanna, ("Who could suspect . . .")

Co-sì   si con-dan—na chi può sos-pet-t ar

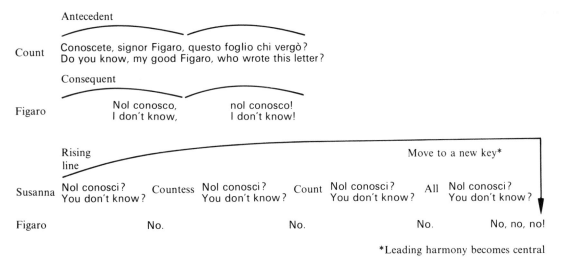

Count
> Antecedent
>
> Conoscete, signor Figaro, questo foglio chi vergò?
> Do you know, my good Figaro, who wrote this letter?

Figaro
> Consequent
>
> Nol conosco,   nol conosco!
> I don't know,   I don't know!

Rising line   Move to a new key*

Susanna Nol conosci? **Countess** Nol conosci? **Count** Nol conosci? **All** Nol conosci?
You don't know?   You don't know?   You don't know?   You don't know?

Figaro   No.   No.   No.   No, no, no!

*Leading harmony becomes central

Example 12-6 Mozart, Finale, section 5 (beginning)

Harmonically, the section is stable, but with a clear move to a closely related key. This is a good place to practice hearing the kind of move that makes the leading harmony the central one; the move is accomplished on Figaro's "No, no, no!"—the third "no" falling on the new central harmony. Some of the material of the first section is then immediately repeated in the new harmonic area (Ex. 12-6).

The air of formality is carried out at the highest level by a clear return to the original melody, in the original key, at Figaro's speech "To finish it gaily . . ." He is trying to pick up the mood of his entrance in the preceding section, but unfortunately things are far less gay now than they were then. His attempt at wit is forced, and the corresponding return in the music is heavy and overplayed. All the more genuine, then, appears the heartfelt petition in the following phrase ("Come, sir . . .") with its solid, expressive pedal note and rich harmonic superstructure. This phrase, C_2, incidentally, comes out of the middle of the section (Figaro: "My face may be lying"). There is no particular connection among the several texts for which C is used; rather, a musical form involving the return of A and C is unfolding as a counterpoint to a dramatic form. It is the musical form *as a whole*

that supports the dramatic point being made here (Ex. 12-7).

Just as sections 4 and 5 are linked together by Figaro's entrance, so are sections 6 and 7 linked by Antonio's. Sections 6 and 7, however, are in general more homogeneous and more continuous than any of the other sections so far. As the pace of the Finale picks up, the internal structure of the sections becomes simpler—or at least less clearly sectioned—than before.

SECTION 6—ALLEGRO MOLTO. One of the most important aspects of section 6 is the manner of delivery of the dialog—not what is being said, but *how* it is being said. The various inflections and the combinations of inflections crowded in on one another create a play of timbres that provides much of the intensity of the scene; harmony and melody are by contrast simple. There are various motives, as in section 3, but here in section 6 the motives have so little identity that the pattern of their return communicates little aside from boisterous confusion.

The quality of the dialog, then, is important. The half-drunk Antonio, clutching his broken pot of carnations, blurts out his story in the face of hectoring

by the Count and growing interference by the others as they realize the danger of Antonio's witness. As the number of characters on stage increases, so does the complexity of their conversation. The Count addresses now this one, now that. Figaro, Susanna, and the Countess often try to speak to each other without being heard by the Count. Antonio, something of an outsider to the whole intrigue, addresses everyone or sometimes no one as the others order him about or argue among themselves. The many different degrees of inflection are faithfully reflected in the musical setting, so that the unlikely proceedings take on an air of persuasive reality—as well as being an intricate interplay of word, timbre, and texture.

SECTION 7—ANDANTE. Section 7, which follows without a break, transforms the hectic triple rhythm sometimes appearing in section 6 into a basic metric pulse. This transformation, together with the slower pace of section 7, provides the musical foundation for the new dramatic mood. Here we have to picture the tableau on stage—outwardly formal and static, inwardly agitated. Presumably, the characters are standing in a half circle, the Count on one end with the Countess beside him, Susanna next to the Countess, Figaro on the other end. We have to imagine Antonio elaborately producing the papers (like the Count in section 5), the Count officiously (with both concealed relish and genuine interest) taking them over. The Countess surreptitiously peers over the Count's shoulder, eventually passing on information about the contents to Susanna, who in turn tells Figaro. The Countess, Susanna, and Figaro all try to seem unconcerned (except when they lash out at Antonio), yet all are nervous—especially Figaro, who makes a great show of producing other papers along with an unconvincing profusion of explanations in response to the relentless questions of the Count.

Like section 6, section 7 has no obvious subsections. There are two melodic motives in the orchestra, but the material is so uniform that no significant shaping results from their use. There is harmonic motion, but its use is relatively subtle. After they get rid of Antonio, the Count resumes his questions: "Well now?" This marks a repeat of the opening material in a new key (but the intervening material has not been a contrast, and the new key is very close to the old one). Here the intricacy of dialog, prominent in section 6, returns in the urgent asides of the Countess and Susanna ("Heavens! The page's commission!"). Then Figaro's pretended recall ("Oh, what a brain!") is set to a suddenly rich harmonic progression, emphasized by a quick crescendo to forte. Because of the prevailing uniformity this detail stands out, becoming a dramatic accent as well as a musical one. When Figaro finally puts together the whole fictitious explanation, it is time to "wind up this nonsense" (as the Count said earlier); and accordingly a return to the original key follows immediately, as the Count muses upon Figaro's perennial escapes ("This rascal drives me crazy"). As at other times, the characters retreat within themselves for a moment to collect their wits.

SECTIONS 8, 9, AND 10. Section 7 is the last reduction of dramatic and musical tempo. Thereafter, things speed on to a conclusion—at least, to a musical conclusion, for the entrance of Marcellina, Bartolo, and Basilio brings difficulties of plot far more severe than those encountered up to this point; as a final reaction the Countess, Susanna, and Figaro throw up their hands in despair of reaching a solution. In section 8, the Count attempts to bring about order with his "Silence, silence!"; but the others pay less and less attention to him as the two groups (Marcellina, Bartolo, Basilio, against Countess, Susanna, Figaro) alternately rail at each other and lament, or rejoice in, their own good or bad fortune. During sections 9 and 10 little emerges from the music except a strong sense of key, an ever-increasing animation of rhythm, and a crescendo of tumult. Even at the last moment, however, Mozart is careful to provide the briefest of effective reductions: Marcellina, Bartolo, and Basilio twice sing their words " . . . some propitious power . . . " to a soft, mock-pious invocation.

This Finale is not, of course, a complete work in itself or even one of the largest sections of a complete

Subsections:			Harmonic movement
A_1	Count	Conoscete, signor Figaro . . . Do you know, my good Figaro . . .	Establishes key
A_2	Susanna	E nol desti a Don Basilio . . . Didn't you give it to Don Basilio . . .	Moves, confirms new key
B	Count	Cerci invan difesa . . . In vain you look for defenses,	
C_1	Figaro	Mente il ceffo . . . My face may be lying . . .	Pedal on central note of new key
D	Count	Che rispondi ? What's your answer ?	
E	Susanna Countess }	E via, chetati . . . Go on, keep quiet . . .	Moves back
A_1	Figaro	Per finirla lietamente . . . To finish it gaily . . .	Original key
C_2	Figaro Susanna Countess }	Deh! signor, nol contrastate . . . Come, sir, don't be obstinate . . .	Pedal on central note of original key

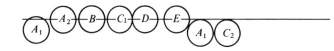

Example 12-7 Mozart, Finale: Subsections and harmonic movement in section 5

work. It is the conclusion of Act II, in an opera that has four acts. The greater part of each act consists of a series of *arias*, or songs, each of the dimensions (roughly) of one of the nonstrophic songs from *Die schöne Müllerin*. Many of the arias are for solo voice, others are *ensembles*—a *duet* for two voices, a *trio* for three; there are a few other ensembles that (like the Finale we studied) have more than three voices.

Between songs, separating them musically and connecting them dramatically, is a special kind of musical language called *recitative*, in which text is musically declaimed in relatively fast, speechlike rhythms but relatively slow-moving lines and harmonies.

An appreciation of the opera at the level of its acts would have to take account of the succession of songs throughout each act in musical terms similar to those we used for the sections of the Finale (or for the songs in *Die schöne Müllerin*); that is, differences in timbre, rhythm, melody, harmony, theme, and structure from one song to the next. In addition, account would have to be taken of the recitative links between the songs, which would make the shape of the whole different from the shape within the Finale.

Wolfgang Amadeus Mozart
LE NOZZE DI FIGARO
FINALE FROM ACT II

SECTION 1—ALLEGRO

Duple meter	CONTE	COUNT
Subsection A	Esci omai, garzon malnato,	If you're coming out, low-born brat,
	sciagurato, non tardar.	you wretch, don't be slow about it.
	CONTESSA	COUNTESS
	Ah, signore, quel furore	Ah, sir, your anger
	[[: per lui fammi il cor tremar. :]]	[[: makes my heart tremble for him. :]]
	CONTE	COUNT
Move to a closely related key	[[: E d'opporvi ancor osate? :]]	[[: And yet you dare oppose me? :]]
	CONTESSA	COUNTESS
	No, sentite . . .	No, listen . . .
	CONTE	COUNT
	Via, parlate!	Go on, speak!
	CONTESSA	COUNTESS
	No, sentite . . .	No, listen . . .
	CONTE	COUNT
	Parlate, parlate, parlate!	Speak, speak, speak!
	CONTESSA	COUNTESS (*trembling and terrified*)
	Giuro al ciel, ch'ogni sospetto, ch'ogni sospetto . . .	I swear by heaven, that every suspicion,
	e lo stato in che il trovate,	and that state in which you'll find him,
	sciolto il collo, nudo il petto . . .	his collar loosened, his chest bare . . .
	CONTE	COUNT
	Sciolto il collo! nudo il petto!	His collar loosened! his chest bare!
	Seguitate!	go on!
	CONTESSA	COUNTESS
	. . . per vestir femminee spoglie.	. . . was to dress him in girl's clothing.

	{ CONTE	{ COUNT
	[[: Ah, comprendo, indegna moglie,	[[: Ah, I understand, worthless woman,
	mi vo' tosto a vendicar.	and I'll soon get my revenge.
	CONTESSA	COUNTESS
	Mi fa torto quel trasporto,	Your outrage wrongs me,
	m'oltraggiate a dubitar. :]]	you insult me by doubting me. :]]
Subsection B	CONTE	COUNT (*turning back*)
Return to original key	[[: Qua la chiave!	[[: Give me the key!

A brace { indicates that two or more texts are being sung simultaneously.

	CONTESSA	COUNTESS
	Egli è innocente, :]] voi sapete . . .	He is innocent, :]] you know it . . .
	(*La Contessa gli da la chiave.*)	(*The countess gives him the key*)
	CONTE	COUNT
	Non so niente!	I know nothing!
	Va lontan dagli occhi miei,	Get far out of my sight,
	un' infida, un' empia sei,	You are unfaithful and impious,
	[[: e me cerchi d'infamar! :]]	[[: and you're trying to humiliate me! :]]
	CONTESSA	COUNTESS
	Vado, sì, ma . . .	I'll go, but . . .
	CONTE	COUNT
	Non ascolto!	I won't listen!
	CONTESSA	COUNTESS
	Ma . . .	But . . .
	CONTE	COUNT
	Non ascolto!	I won't listen!
	CONTESSA	COUNTESS
	Non son rea!	I am not guilty!
Brief harmonic move away	CONTE	COUNT
Subsection C	Vel leggo in volto!	I'll say you are, to your face!
Return to original key	[[: Mora, mora, e più non sia	[[: Let him die, and be no longer
	ria cagion, del mio penar.	the source of my troubles.
	CONTESSA	COUNTESS
	Ah, la cieca gelosia,	Ah, blind jealousy,
	qualche eccesso gli fa far! :]]	what excesses you bring about! :]]
	CONTE	COUNT
	[[: Ah, comprendo, indegna moglie,	[[: Ah, I understand, worthless woman,
	mi vò' tosto a vendicar.	and I'll soon get my revenge.
	CONTESSA	COUNTESS
	Mi fa torto quel trasporto,	Your outrage wrongs me,
	m'oltraggiate a dubitar. :]]	you insult me by doubting me. :]]
	CONTE	COUNT
	[[: Mora, mora, e più non sia	[[: Let him die, and be no longer
	ria cagion, del mio penar.	the source of my troubles.
	CONTESSA	COUNTESS
	Ah, la cieca gelosia,	Ah, blind jealousy.
	qualche eccesso gli fa far! :]]	What excesses you bring about! :]]
	(*Il Conte apre il gabinetto, e Susanna esce.*)	(*The count opens the closet, and Susanna comes out.*)
	CONTE	COUNT
SECTION 2—MOLTO ANDANTE	Susanna!	Susanna!
Triple meter	CONTESSA	COUNTESS
	Susanna!	Susanna!
Subsection A₁	SUSANNA	SUSANNA
Regular rhythms, stable harmonies	Signore!	Sir!

	Cos'è quel stupore?	What is this amazement?
	Il brando prendete,	Take your sword
	il paggio uccidete;	and kill the page;
	[:quel paggio malnato,	[:that low-born page
	vedetelo qua. :]	you see before you. :]

	CONTE	COUNT
Subsection B	Che scola! La testa	A revelation! I feel
Static harmonies over pedal; ostinato	girando mi va.	my head spinning.
	CONTESSA	COUNTESS
	Che storia è mai questa!	What a strange tale!
	Susanna v'è là.	Susanna was in there.
	SUSANNA	SUSANNA
	Confusa han la testa,	Their heads are muddled.
	non san come va.	They don't know what happened.

Subsection A₂	CONTE	COUNT
Return to rhythm of A₁	Sei sola?	Are you alone?
	SUSANNA	SUSANNA
	[:Guardate,	[:See yourself
	qui ascoso sarà.	whether anyone is in there.
	CONTE	COUNT
	Guardiamo, guardiamo,	We'll look, we'll look,
	qui ascoso sarà. :]	someone could be in there. :]

SECTION 3—ALLEGRO	(*Il Conte entra nel gabinetto.*)	(*The Count enters the closet.*)
Duple meter	CONTESSA	COUNTESS
Theme 1	Susanna, son morta,	Susanna, I'm finished,
	il fiato mi manca.	I cannot breathe.
	SUSANNA	SUSANNA
Theme 2	Più lieta, più franca,	Softly, don't worry,
	in salvo è di già.	he's already safe.
	(*Il Conte esce confuso dal gabinetto.*)	(*The Count comes confusedly out of the closet.*)
	CONTE	COUNT
Theme 3	[:Che sbaglio mai presi! :]	[:What an error I made! :]
	Appena lo credo;	I hardly believe it;
Theme 1	se a torto v'offesi	if I've done you wrong,
	[:perdono vi chiedo, :]	[:I beg your pardon, :]
Theme 4	ma far burla simile	but playing such jokes
	è poi crudeltà.	is cruel, after all.
	CONTESSA E SUSANNA	COUNTESS AND SUSANNA
Theme 5	[:Le vostre follie	[:Your foolish acts
	non mertan pietà. :]	deserve no pity. :]
	CONTE	COUNT
Theme 2	Io v'amo!	I love you!
	CONTESSA	COUNTESS
	Nol dite!	Don't say it!

254

		CONTE		COUNT

CONTE
Vel giuro!

CONTESSA
Mentite!

Theme 4 Son l'empia, l'infida
che ognora v'inganna.

CONTE
Theme 4 Quell'ira, Susanna,
m'aita a calmar.

SUSANNA
Theme 6 ⟦: Così si condanna
chi può sospettar? :⟧

CONTESSA
Adunque la fede
d'un anima amante,
sì fiera mercede
doveva sperar?

CONTE
Theme 4 Quell'ira, Susanna,
m'aita a calmar.

SUSANNA
Theme 6 ⟦: Così si condanna
chi può sospettar? :⟧
(*in atto di preghiera*)

Theme 2 Signora!

CONTE
Rosina!

CONTESSA
Crudele!
Più quella non sono,
ma il misero oggetto
del vostro abbandono,
che avete diletto
di far disperar.

Three-voiced texture
CONTE
Confuso, pentito,
⟦: son troppo punito; :⟧
⟦: abbiate pietà. :⟧
SUSANNA
Confuso, pentito,
⟦: è troppo punito; :⟧
⟦: abbiate pietà. :⟧
CONTESSA
Crudele, crudele!
Soffrir sì gran torto
An inconclusive section break ⟦: quest'alma non sa. :⟧

COUNT
I swear!

COUNTESS
You're lying!
I'm unfaithful and impious
and trying to humiliate you.

COUNT
Help me, Susanna,
to calm her anger.

SUSANNA
⟦: Who could suspect
one so vehement? :⟧

COUNTESS
Should then a faithful
lover's soul
expect in return
such harsh thanks?

COUNT
Help me, Susanna,
to calm her anger.

SUSANNA
⟦: Who could suspect
one so vehement? :⟧
(*entreating her*)

My lady!

COUNT
Rosina!

COUNTESS
Cruel man!
I am now no more
than the miserable object
of your desertion,
whom you delight
in driving to despair.

COUNT
Confused, repentant,
⟦: I've been punished enough; :⟧
⟦: have pity on me. :⟧
SUSANNA
Confused, repentant,
⟦: he's been punished enough; :⟧
⟦: have pity on him. :⟧
COUNTESS
Cruel, cruel man!
This soul cannot bear
⟦: to suffer such wrong. :⟧

255

	CONTE	COUNT
Theme 3	Ma il paggio rinchiuso?	But the page locked inside?
	CONTESSA	COUNTESS
Theme 2	Fù sol per provarvi.	Was only to test you.
	CONTE	COUNT
Theme 3	Ma i tremiti, i palpiti?	But the trembling, the excitement?
	CONTESSA	COUNTESS
Theme 2	Fù sol per burlarvi.	Was only to ridicule you.
	CONTE	COUNT
Theme 3	E un foglio sì barbaro?	And that wretched letter?
	CONTESSA E SUSANNA	COUNTESS AND SUSANNA
Theme 6	Di Figaro è il foglio,	The letter is from Figaro
	e a voi per Basilio.	and for you through Basilio.
	CONTE	COUNT
	Ah, perfidi! Io voglio . . . io voglio . . .	Ah, tricksters! If I could . . . if I could.
	CONTESSA E SUSANNA	COUNTESS AND SUSANNA
Theme 5	[: Perdono non merta	[: He deserves no pardon
	chi agli altri nol dà. :]	who withholds it from others. :]

	CONTE	COUNT
A false recapitulation		
Theme 1	Ebben, se vi piace,	Well, if you please,
	comune è la pace;	let us make peace;
Theme 2	Rosina inflessibile	Rosina will not be
	con me non sarà.	unforgiving with me.
	CONTESSA	COUNTESS
Theme 1	Ah, quanto, Susanna,	Ah, Susanna, how soft
	son dolce di core!	I am in the heart!
Theme 2	Di donne al furore	Who would believe again
	chi più crederà?	in a woman's anger?
	SUSANNA	SUSANNA
	Cogli uomin', signora,	With men, my lady,
Theme 6	[: girate, volgete,	[: we hesitate and falter;
	vedrete che ognora	you see how honor
	si cade poi là. :]	soon falls before them. :]
	CONTE	COUNT
Theme 2	[: Guardatemi!	[: Look at me!
	CONTESSA	COUNTESS
	Ingrato! :]	Ungrateful! :]
	CONTE	COUNT
	Guardatemi!	Look at me!
	Ho torto, e mi pento!	I was wrong and I repent!
	SUSANNA, CONTE E CONTESSA	SUSANNA, COUNT AND COUNTESS
	Da questo momento	From this moment on
	conoscerla	
	[: quest'alma a { conoscermi	[: we'll try to learn
	conoscervi	
	apprender potrà. :]	to understand each other. :]

SECTION 4—ALLEGRO CON SPIRITO
Triple meter
Change to distant key

FIGARO (*entrando*)
Signori, di fuori
son già i suonatori.
Le trombe sentite,
i pifferi udite.
Tra canti, tra balli
de' vostri vassalli . . .
[[:corriamo, voliamo,
le nozze a compir!:]]
CONTE
Pian piano, men fretta.
FIGARO
La turba m'aspetta.
CONTE
Pian piano, men fretta,
un dubbio toglietemi
[[:in pria di partir.:]]
FIGARO, SUSANNA E CONTESSA
[[:La cosa è scabrosa;
com' ha da finir?
CONTE
(Con arte le carte
convien qui scoprir.):]]

FIGARO (*entering*)
My lords, the musicians
are already outside.
Hear the trumpets,
and listen to the pipes.
With singing and dancing
for all the peasants . . .
[[:let's hurry out
to perform the wedding!:]]
COUNT
Calm down, less haste.
FIGARO
The crowd is waiting
COUNT
Calm down, less haste.
Relieve me of a doubt
[[:before we go.:]]
FIGARO, SUSANNA AND COUNTESS
[[:A nasty situation;
how will it all end?
COUNT
(Now I must play
my cards carefully.):]]

SECTION 5—ANDANTE
Duple meter
Subsection A₁

CONTE
Conoscete, signor Figaro,
questo foglio chi vergò?
FIGARO
[[:Nol conosco.:]]
SUSANNA
Nol conosci?
FIGARO
No!
CONTESSA
Nol conosci?
FIGARO
No!
CONTE
Nol conosci?
FIGARO
No!
SUSANNA, CONTESSA, CONTE
Nol conosci?
FIGARO
Change to new key No, no, no!

COUNT (*showing Figaro the letter*)
Do you know, my good Figaro,
who wrote this letter?
FIGARO (*pretending to examine it*)
[[:I don't know.:]]
SUSANNA
You don't know?
FIGARO
No!
COUNTESS
You don't know?
FIGARO
No!
COUNT
You don't know?
FIGARO
No!
SUSANNA, COUNTESS, COUNT
You don't know?
FIGARO
No, no, no!

257

Subsection A₂	SUSANNA	SUSANNA
	E nol desti a Don Basilio?	Didn't you give it to Don Basilio?
	CONTESSA	COUNTESS
	Per recarlo . . .	To take it . . .
	CONTE	COUNT
	Tu c'intendi?	Do you understand?
	FIGARO	FIGARO
	Oibò! oibò!	. . . oh God!
	SUSANNA	SUSANNA
	E non sai del damerino . . .	And don't you remember the young fop . . .
	CONTESSA	COUNTESS
	Che stasera nel giardino . . .	Who tonight in the garden . . .
	CONTE	COUNT
	Già capisci?	Now you understand?
	FIGARO	FIGARO
	Io non lo sò.	I don't know.
Subsection B	CONTE	COUNT
	Cerchi invan difesa e scusa,	In vain you look for defenses, excuses,
	il tuo ceffo già t'accusa;	your own face accuses you;
	vedo ben che vuoi mentir.	I see very well you're lying.
Subsection C	FIGARO	FIGARO
Pedal on central note of new key	[: Mente il ceffo, io già non mento. :]	[: My face may be lying, but not I. :]
	SUSANNA E CONTESSA	SUSANNA AND COUNTESS
	Il talento aguzzi invano;	You've sharpened your wits in vain;
	palesato abbiam l'arcano,	the whole secret is out,
	non v'è nulla da ridir.	and there's nothing to laugh at.
Subsection D	CONTE	COUNT
	Che rispondi?	What's your answer?
	FIGARO	FIGARO
	Niente, niente.	Nothing, nothing!
	CONTE	COUNT
	Dunque, accordi?	Then you admit it?
	FIGARO	FIGARO
	Non accordo!	I do not.
Subsection E	SUSANNA E CONTESSA	SUSANNA AND COUNTESS
	[: E via, chetati, balordo, :]	[: Go on, keep quiet, you fool, :]
	[: la burletta ha da finir. :]	[: the little game is over. :]
Subsection A₁	FIGARO	FIGARO
Return to original key of the section	Per finirla lietamente,	To finish it gaily
	e all'usanza teatrale,	as is usual in the theater,
	un'azion matrimoniale	we'll proceed now
	le faremo ora seguir.	to a matrimonial tableau.

<table>
<tr><td>Subsection C
Pedal on central note of original key</td><td>

FIGARO, SUSANNA E CONTESSA
〚:Deh! signor, nol constrastate;
consolate i { miei / lor } desir.

CONTE
(Marcellina, Marcellina,
quanto tardi a comparir!):〛

</td><td>

FIGARO, SUSANNA AND COUNTESS
〚:Come sir, don't be obstinate;
give in to { my / their } wishes.

COUNT
(Marcellina, Marcellina,
how long you delay in coming!):〛

</td></tr>

<tr><td>SECTION 6—ALLEGRO ASSAI
Duple meter</td><td>

(*Entra Antonio, il giardiniere, sbronzo,
con un vaso di garofani rotto.*)
ANTONIO
Ah! Signor, signor!
CONTE
Cosa è stato?
ANTONIO
Che insolenza! Chi'l fece? Chi fu?
FIGARO, SUSANNA, CONTE E CONTESSA
Cosa dici, cos'hai, cosa è nato?
ANTONIO
〚:Ascoltate!
FIGARO, SUSANNA, CONTE E CONTESSA
Via, parla, di' su.:〛

</td><td>

(*Enter Antonio, the gardener, half drunk,
and with a broken pot of carnations.*)
ANTONIO
Ah! Sir, sir!
COUNT
What has happened?
ANTONIO
What insolence! Who did it? Who?
FIGARO, SUSANNA, COUNT AND COUNTESS
What are you saying, what's this, what is it?
ANTONIO
〚:Listen to me!
FIGARO, SUSANNA, COUNT AND COUNTESS
Go ahead, speak up.:〛

</td></tr>

<tr><td>Triple meter at low level</td><td>

ANTONIO
Dal balcone che guarda in giardino
mille cose ogni dì gittar veggio;
e poc' anzi, può darsi di peggio?
Vidi un uom, signor mio, gittar giù!
CONTE
Dal balcone?
ANTONIO
Vedete i garofani?
CONTE
In giardino?
ANTONIO
Sì!
SUSANNA E CONTESSA (*a Figaro*)
Figaro, all'erta!
CONTE
Cosa sento!
SUSANNA, FIGARO E CONTESSA
Costui ci sconcerta;
quel briaco che viene a far qui?

</td><td>

ANTONIO
From the balcony that looks out on the garden
I've seen a thousand things thrown down;
but just now, what could be worse?
I saw a man, my lord, thrown out!
COUNT
From the balcony?
ANTONIO
See these carnations?
COUNT
Into the garden?
ANTONIO
Yes!
SUSANNA AND COUNTESS (*to Figaro*)
Figaro, get ready!
COUNT
What's this I hear!
SUSANNA, FIGARO AND COUNTESS (*aside*)
The fellow has upset everything;
what is that drunkard doing here?

</td></tr>
</table>

259

CONTE
Dunque un uom, ma dov'è gito?
ANTONIO
Ratto, ratto! il birbone è fuggito,
e ad un tratto di vista m'uscì.
SUSANNA (*a Figaro*)
Sai che il paggio . . .
FIGARO (*a Susanna*)
So tutto, lo vidi.
Ah, ah, ah, ah!
CONTE
Taci là!
FIGARO
Ah, ah, ah, ah!
ANTONIO
Cosa ridi?
FIGARO
Ah, ah, ah, ah!
CONTE
[: Taci là! :]
ANTONIO
[: Cosa ridi? :]
FIGARO
[: Tu sei cotto dal sorger del dì? :]
CONTE
[: Or ripetimi, :] un uom dal balcone?

ANTONIO
Dal balcone.
CONTE
In giardino?
ANTONIO
In giardino.
SUSANNA, FIGARO E CONTESSA
Ma, signore, se in lui parla il vino!
CONTE
[: Segui pure; :] nè in volto vedesti?

ANTONIO
No, nol vidi.
SUSANNA E CONTESSA
Olà, [: Figaro, ascolta! :]
CONTE
Sì?
ANTONIO
No, nol vidi.

COUNT
That man, where did he land?
ANTONIO
Rape, rape! the scoundrel fled
right away out of my sight.
SUSANNA (*to Figaro*)
You know, the page . . .
FIGARO (*to Susanna*)
I know everything, I saw him.
(*Aloud*) Ha, ha, ha, ha!
COUNT
Be quiet over there!
FIGARO
Ha, ha, ha, ha!
ANTONIO
Why are you laughing?
FIGARO
Ha, ha, ha, ha!
COUNT
[: Be quiet over there! :]
ANTONIO
[: Why are you laughing? :]
FIGARO
[: You're tipsy from break of day? :]
COUNT
[: Tell me again, :] a man from the
balcony?
ANTONIO
From the balcony.
COUNT
Into the garden?
ANTONIO
Into the garden.
SUSANNA, FIGARO AND COUNTESS
But sir, if he's been drinking!
COUNT
[: Go on anyway :] you didn't see his
face?
ANTONIO
No, I didn't.
SUSANNA AND COUNTESS (*to Figaro*)
Hey, [: Figaro, listen! :]
COUNT
Yes?
ANTONIO
No, I didn't.

FIGARO
Via, piangione, sta zitto una volta,
per tre soldi far tanto tumulto!
Giacche il fatto non può star occulto,
[: sono io stesso saltato di lì. :]

CONTE
[: Chi? Voi stesso? :]

SUSANNA E CONTESSA
Che testa! Che ingegno!

FIGARO
Che stupor! :]

ANTONIO
Chi? Voi stesso?

SUSANNA E CONTESSA
Che testa! Che ingegno!

FIGARO
Che stupor!

CONTE
Già creder nol posso.

ANTONIO
Come mai diventasti si grosso?

CONTE
Già creder nol posso, nol posso.

ANTONIO
Dopo il salto non fosti così.

FIGARO
A chi salta succede così.

ANTONIO
Ch'il direbbe?

SUSANNA E CONTESSA
Ed insiste quel pazzo?

CONTE (ad Antonio)
Tu che dici?

ANTONIO
A me parve il ragazzo.

CONTE
Cherubino!

SUSANNA E CONTESSA
[: Maledetto! :]

FIGARO
[: Esso appunto, :]
da Siviglia a cavallo quì giunto,
da Siviglia or ci forse sarà.

ANTONIO
Questo no, questo no, che il cavallo
io non vidi saltare di là.

FIGARO
Go on, old blubberer, be quiet for once,
making such a fuss for three cents!
Since the fact can't be kept quiet,
[: it was I who jumped from there. :]

COUNT
[: You? Yourself? :]

SUSANNA AND COUNTESS (aside)
What a brain! A genius!

FIGARO
What an upset! :]

ANTONIO
You? Yourself?

SUSANNA AND COUNTESS (aside)
What a brain! A genius!

FIGARO
What an upset!

COUNT
I cannot believe it.

ANTONIO
When did you grow so big?

COUNT
I cannot believe it.

ANTONIO
When you jumped you weren't like that.

FIGARO
That's how people look when they jump.

ANTONIO
Who says so?

SUSANNA AND COUNTESS (to Figaro)
Is the fool being stubborn?

COUNT (to Antonio)
What are you saying?

ANTONIO
To me it looked like the boy.

COUNT
Cherubino!

SUSANNA AND COUNTESS (aside)
[: Curses on you! :]

FIGARO (ironically)
[: At this moment :]
he must be on horseback,
arriving at Seville.

ANTONIO (naïvely)
No, that's not so; I saw no horse
when he jumped out of the window.

261

CONTE
Che pazienza! Finiam questo ballo!
SUSANNA E CONTESSA
Come mai, giusto ciel, finirà?

CONTE
Dunque tu . . .
FIGARO
Saltai giù.
CONTE
Ma perchè?
FIGARO
Il timor . . .
CONTE
Che timor?
FIGARO
Là rinchiuso
aspettando quel caro visetto,
tippe tappe, un sussurro fuor d'uso . . .
Voi gridaste . . . lo scritto biglietto
saltai giù dal terrore confuso,
e stravolto m'ho un nervo del piè!
(*tenendosi il piede, come se si fosse fatto del male*)

SECTION 7—ANDANTE

Triple meter

ANTONIO
Vostre dunque saran queste carte,
che perdeste?
CONTE
Olà, porgile a me.
FIGARO
[[: Sono in trappola. :]]
SUSANNA E CONTESSA
[[: Figaro, all'erta. :]]
CONTE
Dite un po', questo foglio cos'è?
FIGARO
Tosto, tosto . . . n'ho tanti, aspettate.
ANTONIO
Sarà forse il sommario dei debiti.
FIGARO
No, la lista degli osti.
CONTE
Parlate.
(*a Antonio*) E tu lascialo.
SUSANNA, CONTESSA E FIGARO
Lascialo,
Lasciami, e parti.

COUNT
Patience! Let's wind up this nonsense!
SUSANNA AND COUNTESS (*aside*)
How, in the name of Heaven, will it end?

COUNT (*to Figaro*)
So then you . . .
FIGARO
Jumped down.
COUNT
But why?
FIGARO
Out of fear.
COUNT
For what?
FIGARO
Here inside
I was waiting for that dear face,
when I heard an unusual noise . . .
You were shouting . . . I thought of the letter
and jumped out confused by fear,
and pulled the muscles in my foot!
(*holding his foot, as if it were injured*)

ANTONIO (*showing Figaro the page's commission*)
Then these papers must be yours,
and you lost them?
COUNT (*taking them*)
Here, give them to me.
FIGARO (*aside to Susanna and the Countess*)
[[: I am in a trap. :]]
SUSANNA AND COUNTESS
[[: Figaro, get ready! :]]
COUNT (*opening the letter, then closing it immediately*)
Tell me now, what letter is this?
FIGARO (*taking some more out of his pockets*)
Wait, I have so many . . . just a moment.
ANTONIO
Perhaps it is a list of your debts.
FIGARO
No, the list of innkeepers.
COUNT (*to Figaro*)
Speak.
(*to Antonio*) You leave him alone.
SUSANNA, COUNTESS AND FIGARO (*to Antonio*)
Leave him
me alone, and get out.

262

ANTONIO
Parto, sì, ma se torno a trovarti . . .

SUSANNA, CONTESSA, CONTE
Lascialo!

FIGARO
Vanne, vanne, non temo di te!

SUSANNA, CONTESSA, CONTE
Lascialo!

ANTONIO
Parto, sì, ma se torno a trovarti . . .

FIGARO
Vanne, vanne, non temo di te.
SUSANNA, CONTESSA, CONTE
Lascialo, e parti!

(*Antonio parte.*)

CONTE
Dunque? Dunque?
CONTESSA
(Oh, ciel! La patente del paggio!)
SUSANNA (*piano a Figaro*)
(Giusti dei! La patente!)
CONTE
Coraggio!

f   A change of harmony

FIGARO
[:Oh, che testa!:] Quest'è la patente,
che poc'anzi il fanciullo mi diè.

CONTE
Perchè fare?

FIGARO (*imbrogliato*)
Vi manca . . .

CONTE
Vi manca . . . ?

CONTESSA
(Il suggello!)

SUSANNA
(Il suggello!)

CONTE
Rispondi!

FIGARO
È l'usanza . . .

CONTE
Su via, ti confondi?

FIGARO
È l'usanza di porvi il suggello.

ANTONIO
I'm leaving, but if I catch you once
more . . .

SUSANNA, COUNTESS, COUNT
Leave him alone!

FIGARO
Go, go, I'm not afraid of you!

SUSANNA, COUNTESS, COUNT
Leave him alone!

ANTONIO
I'm going, but if I catch you
again . . .

FIGARO
Go on, I'm not afraid of you!
SUSANNA, COUNTESS, COUNT
Leave him alone!

(*Antonio leaves.*)

COUNT (*reopening the letter*)
Well now? Well now?
COUNTESS (*aside to Susanna*)
(Heavens! The page's commission!)
SUSANNA (*aside to Figaro*)
(Ye gods! The commission!)
COUNT
Courage!

FIGARO (*pretending to remember*)
[:Oh, what a brain!:] It's the commission
that the boy gave me a while ago.

COUNT
What for?

FIGARO (*confused*)
It needs . . .

COUNT
It needs . . . ?

COUNTESS (*aside to Susanna*)
(The seal!)

SUSANNA (*aside to Figaro*)
(The seal!)

COUNT
Your answer?

FIGARO (*pretending to think*)
It's the custom . . .

COUNT
Come on now, are you confused?

FIGARO
It's the custom to place a seal on it.

Return to original key of section	CONTE [[: Questo birbo mi toglie il cervello; tutto, tutto è un mistero per me. CONTESSA E SUSANNA Se mi salvo da questa tempesta, più non avvi naufragio per me. FIGARO Sbuffa invano, e la terra calpesta, poverino, ne sa men di me. :]]	COUNT (*aside, tearing up the letter*) [[: This rascal drives me crazy; the whole thing's a mystery to me. COUNTESS AND SUSANNA (*aside*) If I survive this tempest I won't be shipwrecked after all. FIGARO (*aside*) He pants and paws the ground in vain, poor man, and knows less than I do. :]]
SECTION 8—ALLEGRO ASSAI *Duple meter* *Return to original harmonic area of Finale*	(*Entrano Marcellina, Bartolo e Basilio.*) MARCELLINA, BARTOLO E BASILIO Voi, signor, che giusto siete, Ci dovete or ascoltar. CONTE Son venuti a vendicarmi. Io mi sento consolar. CONTESSA, SUSANNA E FIGARO Son venuti a sconcertarmi. [[: Qual rimedio ritrovar? :]] FIGARO Son tre stolidi, tre pazzi. [[: Cosa mai vengono a far? :]] CONTE Pian pianin, senza schiamazzi, [[: dica ognun quel che gli par. :]] MARCELLINA Un impegno nuzziale ha costui con me contratto; e pretendo che il contratto deva meco effettuar. FIGARO, SUSANNA E CONTESSA Come? Come? CONTE Olà, silenzio, silenzio, silenzio! Io son quì per giudicar. BARTOLO Io da lei scelto avvocato, vengo a far le sue difese, le legittime pretese io vi vengo a palesar. FIGARO, SUSANNA E CONTESSA [[: È un birbante! :]] CONTE Olà, silenzio, silenzio, silenzio! Io son quì per giudicar.	(*Enter Marcellina, Bartolo and Basilio.*) MARCELLINA, BARTOLO AND BASILIO (*to the Count*) You, sir, who are so just, you must listen to us now. COUNT (*aside*) They have come to avenge me. I'm beginning to feel better. COUNTESS, SUSANNA AND FIGARO (*aside*) They have come to ruin me. [[: What solution can I find? :]] FIGARO (*to the Count*) They are all three stupid fools. [[: Whatever have they come to do? :]] COUNT Softly now, without this clamor, [[: let everyone speak his mind. :]] MARCELLINA That man has signed a contract binding him to marry me, and I contend that the contract must be carried out. FIGARO, SUSANNA AND COUNTESS What? What? COUNT Hey, silence, silence, silence! I am here to render judgment. BARTOLO Appointed as her lawyer, I am here in her defense, to publish to the world her legitimate reasons. FIGARO, SUSANNA AND COUNTESS [[: He is a rogue! :]] COUNT Hey, silence, silence, silence! I am here to render judgment.

264

BASILIO
Io, come uom al mondo cognito,
vengo quì per testimonio
del promesso matrimonio,
con prestanza di danar.

FIGARO, SUSANNA E CONTESSA
〚: Son tre matti. :〛

CONTE
Olà, silenzio; lo vedremo.
Il contratto leggeremo,
tutto in ordin deve andar.

BASILIO
Known as a man of the world,
I come here as a witness
of his promise of marriage
when she loaned him some money.

FIGARO, SUSANNA AND COUNTESS
〚: They are all mad. :〛

COUNT
Hey, be silent; we'll see about that.
We will read the contract
and proceed in due order.

SECTION 9—PIU ALLEGRO
Duple meter

FIGARO, SUSANNA E CONTESSA
〚: { Son confusa, son stordita, / Son confuso, son stordito, }
{ disperata, sbalordita; / disperato, sbalordito; }
certo, un diavol dell'inferno
quì li ha fatti capitar.

CONTE, MARCELLINA, BARTOLO E BASILIO
Che bel colpo, che bel caso,
è cresciuto a tutti il naso;
qualche nume a noi propizio
quì { li / ci } ha fatti capitar. :〛

FIGARO, SUSANNA AND COUNTESS
〚: I'm confused, stupified,

hopeless and dismayed;

surely some devil from Hell
has brought those people here.

COUNT, MARCELLINA, BARTOLO AND BASILIO
A telling blow, a lucky chance,
victory is right before our noses;
some propitious power
has surely brought { them / us } here. :〛

SECTION 10—PRESTISSIMO
Duple meter

FIGARO, SUSANNA E CONTESSA
Certo un diavol dell'inferno
quì li ha fatta capitar.

CONTE, MARCELLINA, BARTOLO E BASILIO
Qualche nume quì ci ha fatta capitar.

FIGARO, SUSANNA AND COUNTESS
Surely some devil from Hell
has brought those people here.

COUNT, MARCELLINA, BARTOLO AND BASILIO
Some power has surely brought them here.

CHAPTER 13 STRAVINSKY'S LES NOCES

IGOR STRAVINSKY composed *Les Noces* ("The Wedding") originally with a Russian text, but the work was soon translated into French and has become generally known by its French title. We will be referring to the Russian version; perhaps we should have used the Russian title, *Svadyebka*.

TEXT. In dealing with *Les Noces*, we will have to rely heavily on the text for orientation within its 25-minute duration. A transliteration of the original Russian text, accompanied by a line-by-line literal translation into English, will be found at the end of the chapter. You may well wish to listen first once or twice without following the text, just to get an idea of the piece as a whole. Once you start following the text, you will find yourself fully engaged in the detail of the piece; it often requires full attention just to discover how the text matches up with the music.

The text provides a means of understanding many important aspects of the music of *Les Noces*. Stravinsky adapted and arranged the text from a volume of materials in the tradition of rural Russian festivities. In other words, the text of *Les Noces* exists in precisely the form it does because it was put in that form by the composer of the music. This situation is somewhat different from that in *Die schöne Müllerin*, where the text was written first to read just as poetry. Schubert's adaptation consisted in omitting certain poems; these omissions are of great importance, but still the rest of the cycle is more or less as he found it. In *Le Nozze di Figaro* the relationship of text and composer is closer, because da Ponte, the librettist,

arranged the text with Mozart's needs in mind; and Mozart himself had a hand in the arrangement.

A glance through the text of *Les Noces* should indicate the importance of the fact that the composer arranged it: he must have had a reason for wanting a text with such a discontinuous, nonconsecutive nature. In certain respects, however, the text is not so different from those we have already met. For example, *Les Noces* has many passages of lyric poetry, usually involving a clear image from Nature or rural life as a vehicle for thought or feeling. These sometimes seem enigmatic, like the lyric imagery of *Die schöne Müllerin*—and for precisely the same reason. In both cases, the most telling images occur in a certain isolation from their surroundings. In *Die schöne Müllerin* the images (such as the brook) were often not explicitly related to the story; aspects of relationship were left unsaid, to be supplied by our imagination. In *Les Noces*, particularly toward the end, the same process is carried much further. Elliptical allusions, implicit references, are used as a specific way of creating the folklike atmosphere of a static rural society, where the community of thought and feeling is so strong that the ordinary connectives can be left unsaid.

Another prominent aspect of *Les Noces* is the frequency with which more than one text is said or sung at the same time. There is a general atmosphere of boisterous confusion about the scene that we can soon relate more specifically to the subject matter. As an aspect of form, however, we should note that simultaneous texts were frequent in the Finale from

Act II of *Le Nozze di Figaro*—frequent and hard to follow. Mozart had good dramatic reasons for so doing; but dramatic reasons aside (and they could have been put aside if he had felt like it), the fact remains that the confusion in *Les Noces* is often no greater than that in *Le Nozze di Figaro*. What may make it seem at first greater is the less consecutive nature of *Les Noces* as drama.

Considered as drama, *Les Noces* poses some interesting problems. It is difficult to find the elements of a plot; character and motivation seem totally absent. Even in the externals usually associated with drama, we look in vain for a comprehensive plan. There are just enough stage directions (beginning with "curtain" at 1) to make us wish for more when we try to imagine the work performed on a stage. One of the most obvious anomalies is that solo singers do not match up with personages at the wedding: for example, the words of the bride are sung by the tenor soloist at the beginning of the Third Tableau. Nor is it at all clear what kind of acting should take place or whether the singers should do it or even whether there should be any at all.

All the existing stage directions are included in the text (in italics—those in parentheses have been added), so you can judge for yourself what the answers should be. The work is sometimes staged, usually as a ballet, with more or less elaborate pantomime against a minimal or symbolic set. More often, the work is performed without staging. If it is staged, then it seems that the staging must be created anew for each production out of the spirit and substance of music and text—as they appear to the producer.

The work is about a wedding. The wedding is long, elaborate, noisy; the whole village is there, with friends and relations from near and far. There is plenty to eat and drink—especially to drink. There are many things tradition requires the participants to do and say; everything seems to be a quotation. The pervading mood of ritual, of formalism, is one of the main factors that prevents the work from being realistic or naturalistic, giving it instead a tone of festal solemnity.

It does not matter exactly in what order these things are said or done. A sense of logical succession is often lacking. It seems sometimes that two separate rituals are being performed either simultaneously or in alternation, as if the composer had cut and spliced together bits of two separate text sequences.

The unit of succession seems to be the tableau. Each tableau (as we will see soon) has a set of events —some more, some less. Each tableau presents a scene, a moment from the wedding festivities frozen into a picture; but the moment selected is long enough to contain a variety of speeches, and these are arranged in an only approximately realistic order of succession; for within the tableau, dramatic time moves very slowly, at the composer's discretion.

As we already saw in Chapter 2, the First Tableau (the easiest to follow) presents the ritual preparation of the bride (Nastasia Timofeevna). Much of the text is given over to her lament—a ritual lament, not to be taken as motivation for a dramatic plot. A chorus of bridesmaids attends her, sometimes exercising their ritual office, sometimes echoing her lament, then eventually (at 9) singing a song of consolation. The text looks forward to future happiness, then abruptly (at 16) becomes a call to the wedding. Just as abruptly, it reverts (at 21) to the bride's lament, combined now with the first appearance of the litanies, or repeated prayers of intercession.

O Mary thou Virgin,
Come to us and aid us.

Litanies, the most obviously realistic element of all, will reverberate throughout much of the first half of *Les Noces*. At 21, the bride's mother speaks, but the part is sung by the tenor. The Tableau closes with bride and bridesmaids repeating some of their text from the beginning.

The Second Tableau presents an analogous scene at the home of the groom (Fetis Pamfilievitch). He, too, is having his hair prepared, and again the occasion provokes nostalgic but still ritualistic reminiscences. This time it is the parents who lament (at 35). Litanies are heard sporadically from the start of the Tableau, sometimes becoming inextricably mixed with the other elements. After the groom formally asks his parents' blessing (at 50), the party prepares to depart for the church; and the litanies become continuous enough to suggest a liturgical procession. Such intercessory acclamations, chanted in solemn procession, were so firmly rooted in Russian Orthodoxy as to be virtually equivalent to folk ritual—and in some ways indistinguishable from it.

The Third Tableau, like the second, is begun without dramatic transition or preparation (unless we imagine the procession to leave the groom's house, then to pass by the bride's house, to collect the rest of the wedding party; that amount of stage business, however, does not seem called for by the nature of the text). The bridesmaids pick up their previous mood of consolation and coming joy, and the bride (the tenor sings her words) asks her father's blessing. Then the litanies begin again, continuing until the wedding party is out of sight. From 80 on to the end, the stage directions are suddenly explicit: the mothers return to an empty stage to sing their ritual lament, then leave; the stage is empty once more, providing a break between the first and second parts of *Les Noces*.

The Fourth Tableau, which takes up the whole second half of the piece, is far more complex. The ritual continues; the sacred rites have been completed, but there are still many things to be said and done before the couple can properly be considered married. The Fourth Tableau takes place around a red table, presumably very large and covered with food and drink. Toward the end (just before 114), an usher shouts, "Poyte pesni!" ("Sing the songs!"). Actually that is what they have been doing since the beginning of the Tableau; we can most easily understand the abundance of disconnected imagery as representing the whole repertory of the songs that are sung at weddings. Certain songs emerge with relative clarity: there is the berry song at the start; the ring song with the young man, Palagy Spanovitch (at 91); the flying goose song, which becomes complex (starts at 93), eventually turning into the song of the beautiful swan (at 106). Mixed in with the songs are various ritual dialogs, such as the one concerning the duties of the wife (at 97), the (untold) story of Mary and Simon (at 101), and toward the end the several phases of getting the couple to bed—along with other "routines" too fleeting to identify with confidence. As at the end of the first half, the end of the second suddenly has some explicit staging: the door is closed on the couple in bed, the parents sit with backs to the door (and presumably arms folded), facing the company. One more song, a song of love, brings *Les Noces* to an end.

Clearly, the composer's intent is to catch and fix in a musical medium the mood of a Russian wedding: the noise and bustle, the color and gaiety, the age-old traditions both sacred and secular, and all the feelings attached to these—not the personal feelings of a particular Nastasia or her mother, but of all Nastasias and all their mothers as enshrined in folk ritual, together with the more deep-seated communal joy in the concelebration of matrimony.

At the same time, *Les Noces* is emphatically not just a folkloristic description; rather it uses a folkloristic situation for an artistic purpose. We should note in passing that *Les Noces* was not written in Russia for Russians. It is probably essential to the conception of the piece that it be sung in a language remote from the audience. At any rate, it would be excessively difficult to make a performing English translation that would be sure to have for modern urban listeners the required combination of naturalism and solemnity. We should note, too, that Stravinsky's personal interest in peasant weddings of his Mother Russia is only of passing concern to us; but his interest in a special artistic form (for which the wedding supplies the raw material) is of permanent importance. In *Les Noces*, he shows us a way in which apparent confusion can have real artistic significance. To this central idea of the work, folkloristic realism is purely tangential.

RHYTHM. Next to the abundance of richly percussive sounds, the most conspicuous aspect of *Les Noces* is certainly its rhythm. You will find yourself swept along by the rhythm long before you can make sense of the pitch organization—even before the organization of the rhythm itself is clear.

The rhythm is forceful, but irregular. That is, considering *Les Noces* as a whole, the rhythm gives an effect of great drive; but the regularity that would normally be expected to go along with such drive seems to remain veiled, just out of reach. Actually there are long stretches where the pulses are grouped regularly in twos, as shown in Ex. 13-1. Yet because of the way rhythm is handled in the piece as a whole, such passages have the curious effect of an exception,

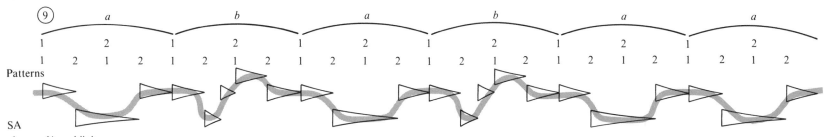

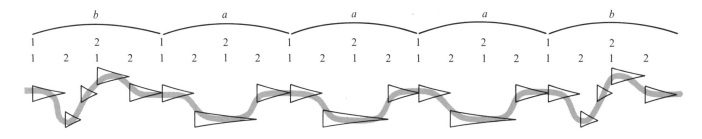

Patterns

SA

chorus Ne klich . . .

Example 13-1 Stravinsky, *Les Noces:* A rhythmic shape

rather than the rule: for a time, the pulses are grouped in twos—more we cannot say.

One kind of reason for the prevailing sense of irregularity can be seen in Ex. 13-1, if you consider it at a high enough level. Above the notes the rhythmic patterns are indicated under slurs. The first pattern of rhythm and line (as found in the first measure) is labeled *a*; that in the second measure, *b*. These two patterns alternate throughout the passage—but not regularly. As the letters and the larger slurs indicate, the rhythmic groupings at the high level gradually lengthen as more *a*'s are added between the *b*'s. The strongest unit seems to be the measure (not the fastest pulse), and the measures are grouped in irregular ways.

The process at work in Ex. 13-1 is repeated over and over throughout *Les Noces* in many different ways, at many different levels. The unit pulse seems to be everywhere (but going at different tempos), as the one common denominator among a wealth of rhythmic groupings. These groupings may be produced by any aspect of the piece—timbre, dynamics,

articulation, pauses, line, or harmony. They range in size from very small to very large.

One of the most remarkable features of *Les Noces* is the tendency of the rhythm to produce large groupings without going through a hierarchy of metric levels. You are likely to hear a forceful unit pulse, then gradually become aware that it is generating large groupings. A small but convenient example can be found in the First Tableau at 12, shortly after the passage just quoted in Ex. 13-1. At the lowest level, this passage (Ex. 13-2) shows how groupings in twos are often broken up by the insertion of an extra pulse to form a group of three. (That is, the *metric* grouping is "broken up"; the *rhythm* cannot be described as "broken up," for the extra pulses in this case bring about a fulfillment of the rhythmic shape.) The ear immediately perceives the return to the music of 12 that takes place soon after 13, to the words "Denyochek on svistit . . ." This is not merely a return of rhythmic and melodic detail, however; it has the feeling of a larger phrase, as indicated by the long slurs in Ex. 13-2. It would be difficult to decide

where shorter slurs should be placed in this passage. The long phrase seems to have grown directly out of the unit pulse and its irregular groupings, without the help of any clear shorter phrases.

As a result of prevailing metric irregularities (such as those in Ex. 13-2) and the failure of a metric system to develop in the middle levels, the rhythm of *Les Noces* does not encourage a feeling of movement toward a goal that is perceptible in advance—as easily happens, for example, in a piece whose rhythms show a consistent organization into four-measure groups. The unit pulse of *Les Noces* will often sweep you along but at the same time will leave you in a state of uncertainty about the outcome. Beginnings of rhythmic units (phrases or phrase groups) tend to assume a sense of weight and stability more than endings. Here we are discussing a possible reaction to rhythm, rather than an objective feature of the rhythm itself. Nevertheless, there seems to be an important difference between rhythms that are metric at higher levels and develop a sense of arrival, and the rhythms of *Les Noces*, which have instead a sense of departure;

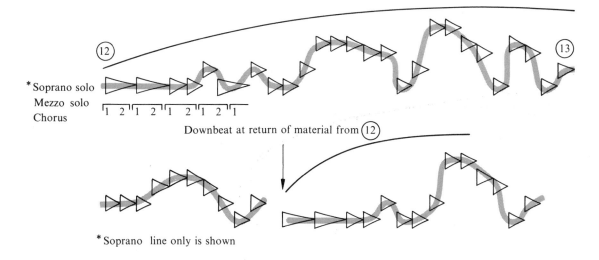

* Soprano solo
Mezzo solo
Chorus

Downbeat at return of material from ⑫

* Soprano line only is shown

Example 13-2 Stravinsky, *Les Noces:* Downbeat produced by a return

the difference is represented abstractly in Ex. 13-3. An instance from *Les Noces* can be found in Ex. 13-2, the strong initial downbeats occurring on the first note of the example and on the first note of the return ("De-nyochek").

Another kind of strong accent frequently encountered in *Les Noces* occurs, not at the beginning of a larger grouping as a point of departure, but instead toward the end of a grouping as a climax or as a termination, yet not a predictable one. The shouts of "Ray! Ray!" (at 16 and 17) in the First Tableau are this kind of accented punctuation. Other examples, often in the form of shouts or exclamations—and once as a clap—can be found throughout *Les Noces*. These unexpected accents are often followed by a brief silence and have the effect of closing off a large rhythmic group; they help shape the piece at relatively high levels.

Les Noces has a bewildering abundance of melodic and harmonic material; yet at the same time themes or motives often reappear. We might be tempted to trace thematic return and motivic development as the best ways to make sense of the piece as a whole. We will, indeed, identify the most literal returns and resemblances. Serious problems arise, however, in

trying to carry a linear analysis too far in this piece; we very soon would reach a stage in which the analysis would show only the background of sameness that provides the continuity of the whole piece. The most useful approach will be one that leads to a perception of the several *different* kinds of things that happen in *Les Noces*. As with *Die schöne Müllerin*, gross, obvious features offer a better starting point than more subtle melodic references among widely separated parts of the piece.

Example 13-3 Downbeats as arrivals and departures

A downbeat as a point of arrival in a regular rhythm

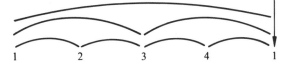

1   2   3   4   1

A downbeat as a point of departure in irregular rhythms

Only a very few things will be said here about the overall plan of the music. The piece comes to a very clear, very distinctive ending, for one thing. You might carry away from first hearing only an impression of this remarkable ending. Its construction and preparation will require some closer attention.

The division between the two halves of *Les Noces* is also clearly marked in the music. Here we meet one of the procedures most characteristic of the piece: the first half moves toward a climax in the Third Tableau,

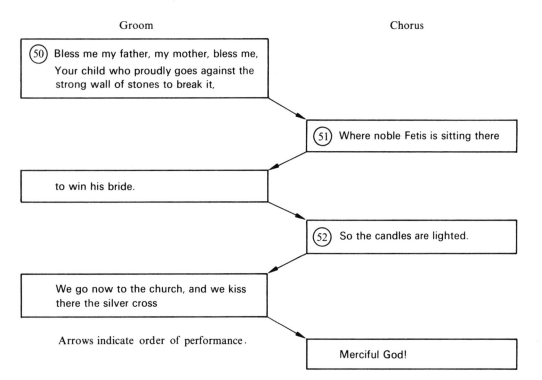

Groom   Chorus

50 Bless me my father, my mother, bless me,
Your child who proudly goes against the
strong wall of stones to break it,

51 Where noble Fetis is sitting there

to win his bride.

52 So the candles are lighted.

We go now to the church, and we kiss
there the silver cross

Arrows indicate order of performance.

Merciful God!

Example 13-4 Stravinsky, *Les Noces:* Two text sequences combined at 50

Example 13-5 Stravinsky, *Les Noces:* Return of bridesmaids' song

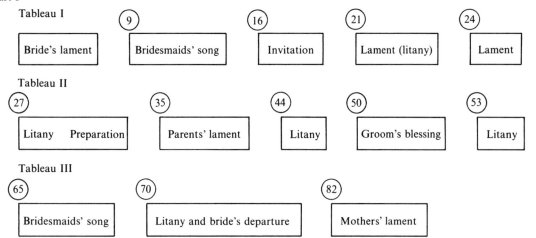

Part I

Tableau I

Bride's lament | 9 Bridesmaids' song | 16 Invitation | 21 Lament (litany) | 24 Lament

Tableau II

27 Litany   Preparation | 35 Parents' lament | 44 Litany | 50 Groom's blessing | 53 Litany

Tableau III

65 Bridesmaids' song | 70 Litany and bride's departure | 82 Mothers' lament

but the climax (at 77) is not followed by a clean break. Instead, the accumulated energy is smoothly and gradually dissipated (78 through 82), so that the climax is fully apparent only in retrospect. A transition is provided by the mother's lament (82 through 86). Although of a contrasting mood and harmonic color, this lament is still borne on the receding tide of the climax. Its main element of rhythmic contrast to the more energetic passages preceding is static motion, the lack of thrust and direction. Even if the stage is not emptied (in accordance with the stage directions), the music itself makes an emptiness here. The sound is continuous, but the shape is highly articulated—a combination of factors that returns again and again in *Les Noces*.

As you already heard (Chapter 2), the main musical sense of the First Tableau can be derived from external factors having to do with the qualities of the sound. Long, sustained solos, alternating with slightly faster choral passages, provide the setting for the bride's lament. In the context of the whole piece, you may be able now to hear how this lament functions as a slow introduction—an invocation. The brighter, faster choral passage that follows (at 9), culminating (at 16) in the shouts of "Ray, ray!" ("Come, come!"), is the real beginning of musical material to be heard frequently later. The First Tableau is rounded off by a return of the music for the bride's lament.

THE SECOND TABLEAU. In the Second Tableau you will soon notice two passages that are set off as contrasts. The first passage is another lament; this time the groom's parents lament the loss of their little boy (at 35). They sing a slower melody that rocks back and forth over a static harmony. The materials persist almost unchanged until 40.

The passage contrasting with this is the setting of the groom's request for his parents' blessing (at 50). The bass solo, supported by another bass from the chorus, sings a very sustained line that is suddenly, and surprisingly, songlike. In its simplicity, the groom's song is one of the most realistic in *Les Noces*.

The whole passage, however, is curiously distorted by the abrupt injections of loud, fast chorus; after each such injection the groom's song continues as before. Here two separate text sequences (song and

270

chorus) seem to have been spliced together (Ex. 13-4).

The parents' lament and the blessing of the groom stand out because they contrast with their surroundings. Like the interludes in Beethoven's Poco sostenuto (page 118), however, these two passages are not the main events in the section. They are more prominent but less important than the rest. Also, like Beethoven's interludes, these passages do help define the structure of the rest, as does the mothers' lament at the end of the Third Tableau. The two passages offer a relief from the choral chanting of the Second Tableau and thereby shape it into subsections.

The beginning of the Third Tableau (Ex. 13-5) is one instance of a clear thematic return that shapes the sectional plan. The scene reverts to the bride's house, and the bridesmaids make the change musically explicit by returning to the melody they sang in the First Tableau (at 9). The words are different, even though a similar mood of joy appears in both places. The melody reappears at exactly the same pitch level. Too much has happened between the two occurrences to identify the pitch as the same; the ear can, however, react to the pitch level along with the other aspects that are the same—timbre, especially—in hearing this as a strong return.

The first appearance of this theme was in the middle of the First Tableau, where it was evident but not obvious. Consequently, when the theme returns at the beginning of the Third Tableau, you may be sure you have heard the theme before but are not certain where. This effect is important for Les Noces, being another of the subtle aspects of its musical construction. You can search at length, but in vain, for the first appearances of what seem like thematic returns; and even when you do succeed in finding thematic antecedents, their position or function does not necessarily reveal the main outlines of the piece. Proper discussion of the use of theme in Les Noces requires that we approach it from other bases.

LITANIES. One such base—the most important in the first half of the work—is that of the litanies. These provide a musical continuity that stretches over the first three Tableaus; beginning inconspicuously, the litanies link these Tableaus together into a unity, emerging at the end as their most important feature.

Example 13-6 is an abstract of all the litany material from the first half of Les Noces. First, follow the explanation of Ex. 13-6, then listen to the first three Tableaus with the complete text, in which you will find indications corresponding to Ex. 13-6. Much intervening music has been left out of this example; we are dealing on a large scale with the same spliced

effect heard in the groom's blessing (see Ex. 13-4).

There are three distinct litany themes, whose returns can be followed easily once they have been isolated by means of the text from the intervening material. The first litany theme, called slow litany in Ex. 13-7, appears first right after the climax of the First Tableau (at 21); it is sung by tenor (doubled by

Example 13-6 Stravinsky, *Les Noces*, Part One: Litanies and related materials

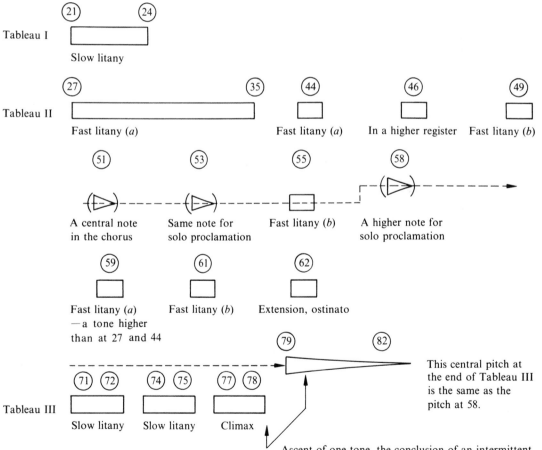

bass at 23), underneath the return of the bride's lament. As a melody, it is prominent and distinctive and is repeated several times.

The second litany theme, labeled fast litany (*a*) in Ex. 13-7, begins the Second Tableau. There is no connection with the first litany theme, except for the text. At the beginning of the Second Tableau (27 through 35), text and music of the litany alternate with texts having to do with Fetis and his curly hair; these texts have their own distinctive theme. The litany is generally soft, the rest loud, in sharp alternation.

After the parents' lament (35 through 40) and another, brighter passage (40 through 43), the fast litany (*a*) reappears intact, at its original pitch, and suddenly pianissimo. This return, a very clear one, shapes the Tableau, but at a relatively low structural level. This time the litany is uninterrupted by other material and continues much longer. At 46 the fast litany (*a*) appears an octave higher, fortissimo, with pianissimo passages that still belong to the litany.

At 49, the litany takes up a new musical theme, fast litany (*b*). Relatively brief, this passage terminates abruptly on a threefold statement of a very simple, regular pattern (Ex. 13-7)—"Pod na svadbu" ("Come to the wedding"). All of this line will return in important ways later on.

After 50 comes the groom's blessing. The material interjected by the chorus into the groom's song (see Ex. 13-4), which first appeared in alternation with litany (*a*) at the beginning of the Second Tableau, is now of interest for the sake of its first pitch. This pitch, represented by a single note at 50 in Ex. 13-6, is the same throughout the groom's blessing, then continues in the strong proclamation for solo bass at 53. The sequence of events just described is not properly a part of the litany, being a separate thematic system; but it soon becomes caught up in the litany, furnishing an important shaping factor. The fast litany theme (*b*) returns at its original pitch at 55, after a shout ("Oy!"). Here the text is not part of the litanies, instead it speaks of the groom's blessing and the "white feather"; yet the musical continuity is now strong enough to sweep this tangential reference up into the sense of the litany. In any case, the text soon returns to intercessions (after 57).

At 58, the litany texts are carried forward by the strong solo proclamations first heard (with secular texts) at 53. In an extremely brilliant entrance for

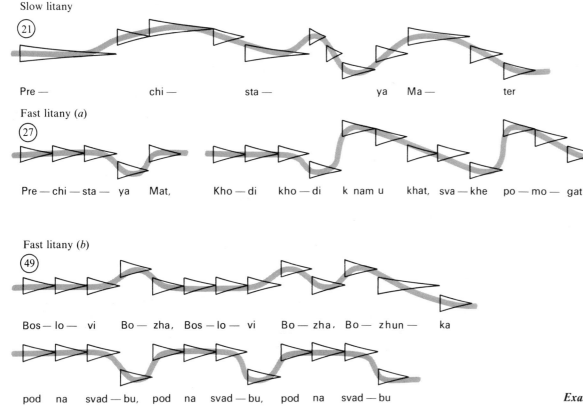

Example 13-7 Stravinsky, *Les Noces:* Litany themes

tenor solo, the melody from 53 reappears intact but higher in pitch. The effect of a higher terrace is very clear and is important for the pitch structure of the rest of the litany.

After another shout, a modified form of fast litany (*a*) returns at 59, a step higher than before so that it continues to carry the overall line upwards. Over a simple ostinato, the fast litany (*b*) returns at 61, still at its original pitch, and concludes with the same threefold repetition as earlier. The rest of the Tableau (from 62) presents litany texts addressed to Saint Luke, with new melodies placed over the continuing ostinato. The passage leads directly into the Third Tableau.

Having completely dominated the end of the Second Tableau, the litany gives way abruptly at the start of the Third Tableau to other material—the bridesmaids and their bright song from the First Tableau. But the litany is by now so firmly established that only a slight cue will be required to restore it to leadership. After the return of several melodic items in order from the First Tableau (65 through 70, derived from 9 through 16), the slow litany returns just before 71, with intercessions now addressed to Saints Cosmas and Damian; it comes soon again at 74, in a richer harmonic form but with melody intact. The litany having been reinstated, the bridesmaids' song leads the litany to its rhythmic climax at 77, with great éclat on the text

And with all the holy Apostles,
And with all the Angels.

The top pitch of the climax carries the overall line still higher. Soon a long sustained pitch that is passed around from one octave to another (from tenor solo to sopranos and altos, then to the whole chorus) brings the overall line to its conclusion.

This sustained pitch, the same as the one sung so brilliantly by the tenor solo at 58, serves as a central pitch for the ending of the first half of *Les Noces*. The arrival of the line at this note marks a strong resolution of harmonic forces that are operative throughout the first half, even if their effects are plainly audible only intermittently in the shape of the overall line.

In tracing the progress of the litany, we have followed only one sequence of related events. Other sequences are occurring at the same time, as is evident, for example, in the return of the bridesmaids' song (at 65 and 75). Still other musical events, such as the bride's opening lament, do not appear again after the First Tableau (at least not in easily recognizable form). Moreover, the litany sequence did not receive a clear, fresh start of its own but was discreetly phased in under the bride's lament. Little by little, the litany acquired form and momentum, eventually pulling other materials into its flow.

You can best perceive such forms, characteristic of *Les Noces*, when you give them ample opportunity to materialize of their own accord from the rich continuum of the whole piece. Ample opportunity means repeated listenings, as well as a relaxed, wide-open concentration. Attempts to make up your mind too early in the piece, or too early in your experience with it, about what is important or is going to become important will probably lead you astray; let the piece make up your mind for you. At the same time, attempts to account for every scrap of material you hear will be equally misleading. Much—but not all—of the melodic material of the piece participates in its long-range shapes.

We have traced the litanies in order to provide one access to the shape of the first half of *Les Noces*. As you gain familiarity with this half through following the litanies, you may well find your attention being drawn increasingly to other aspects, other sequences of related events; these may well assume greater importance than the litanies. To some degree, the piece does consist of several simultaneous orders; it is normal for perception of the piece to change as one or another of these orders becomes more meaningful. And if *Les Noces* should one day come to seem *too* orderly, you can restore the original sense of profusion by trying to follow all orders at once.

All of the foregoing is true of the second half of *Les Noces* as well. Here we will attempt an even less thoroughgoing account and will merely provide some approaches to this most complex part of a complex piece. We will trace in detail only the sequence of events that prepares the remarkable conclusion of the work.

The second half is all one Tableau—the Fourth; thus the Fourth Tableau is much longer than any of the preceding three. Lack of clear subdivisions within the Fourth Tableau makes its greater length especially noticeable. In a work that has a text, we would naturally look to the text first for a likely mode of division. In the last half of *Les Noces*, as we saw, there are many distinct subjects; on first hearing, the trouble is that there are too many, and they are not distinct enough. The fragmentary, disjunct, over-lapping bits of poetry and dialog should alert us to the fact that no clear subdivisions should be sought on the phrase level; and the text by itself does not seem to offer subdivisions at higher levels.

Similar gross features, such as timbre and texture, change too frequently to mark off clear subdivisions. Sometimes the use of chorus and solo seems to suggest an important subdivision; however, the suggestion is not carried through to a clear close, such as would mark off the subdivision from what follows. For example, at least twice, a solo is used to present a lyric line that contrasts with a preceding chorus and coincides with a new unit of poetry in a way that signals the start of a song. At 106, the soprano solo sings,

I have been on the blue sea, the sea and the lake.

The solo is soon replaced by more complex textures; but, both as theme and motive, the line continues to govern the music up to 110. Here the soprano solo sings another melody to the text

I have donned a golden belt,
plaited with pearls that hang down to the ground.

This song (the belt song) is immediately broken off; the theme, however, is used extensively later. Why was it not used extensively here? The answer is that the second half of *Les Noces* becomes complex before it becomes clear. Clarity emerges at the end, as a way of making an end—just as in the first half, where the gradual dominance of the litanies gave a shape to the whole.

One feature of the second half appears only a few times, generally at longer rather than shorter intervals, and seems intuitively apt for making usable divisions. From time to time, the singers abruptly switch to speaking, for one or two words or for several lines. The effect is always very prominent; it is interesting that ordinary speaking in a conversational tone can be such a special event in a piece of music. A composer can create a world that has its own ordinary procedures—such as singing; a deviation from the ordinary can be made to seem startling, no matter how familiar the deviation is under other circumstances. Considered purely as a change in the quality of sound, the spoken word brings a new kind of timbre and pitch and, to some degree, a new kind of rhythm, for even though the composer has indicated roughly the speed at which the speaking is to go, the words when spoken tend to assume their own rhythmic patterns.

On the first few hearings, the ear notes the intrusion of spoken words and lines, but does not yet pay attention to their location, except, perhaps, to note that the speaking tends to become more frequent as the Tableau goes on, as part of the general crescendo of festivity just before the ending. If we now excerpt all the spoken lines, we find that they are distributed around the second half in way that does offer a start toward a subdivision.

SPOKEN LINES

At 111 (tenor solo):
Now all you who are come to the feast, lead the bride
    in, the bridegroom is waiting lonely!

Just before 114:
Sing the songs!

Just before 125 (tenors):
Black are her brows!

At 125 (tenor solo):
Now, then, you old man, come and drink a little glass
    of wine.
Toast the young couple!
Our young ones need many things, they want to have
    a little house, to increase their home they will build
    a bath in the corner.

At 126:
Afterwards you will be heated:
So did our married pair begin their happy days
    together!
(bass solo):

Now then!
(men):
Ah, now then!
(women):
Ah, drink to their health.

After 129 (tenor solo):
Ah, don't you see that the girl no longer has it . . .
(women):
Who is calling there?
(bass solo):
From afar they are calling you! come to bed!

Right after 111, the tenor solo speaks the direction to lead in the bride; then, after addressing (with good-natured rudeness) the assembled company in a singing voice, he breaks out again in the shout "Sing the songs!" Here, as elsewhere, the spoken lines usually go on at the same time as some singing in other voices (and to other texts); the effect is that of speaking being added to the sung continuum. For special emphasis—as at "Sing the songs!"—the spoken words are heard alone and create a real break in the continuum.

The speaking between 111 and 114 introduces the new quality of sound into *Les Noces*. Once it is there as a possibility, its further appearances can function in more explicitly structural ways. (In general we can apply to such exceptional events the axiom "First time, accident; second time, coincidence; third time, regular occurrence.") After a relatively long interval of time, speaking reappears abruptly after 124: the tenor has been describing Nastasia, then (seconded by the tenors of the chorus) he exclaims about the beauty of her face.

> My Nastasia walks very quickly
> in her new coat lined with marten fur
> *Black are her brows!*

At the level of detail, the speaking conveys convivial enthusiasm; at higher levels it directly echoes "Sing the songs!" and can be taken as an equivalent break. It seems natural for a relatively complex combination of speaking and singing to continue for a while through the tenor's speech about gifts (125 and 126). Now the speaking, less of an event all by itself, leads

up to the ritual kiss between the bride and groom.

The stretch of speaking between 124 and 127 constitutes the second appearance of this quality of sound. A third and final appearance comes soon afterward, starting at 129. Here, too, the speaking goes on simultaneously with singing; and even though short, the passage produces a hectic effect. It has a function both dramatic and structural: at this point, the wedding couple is put to bed; and musically the work begins a closely knit final subsection that we will soon examine in greater detail.

We can use the spoken passages, then, to lay out the second half in the tentative manner shown in Ex. 13-8; that is, a first subsection through 113, a second subsection past 126, and a short preparation for the final subsection beginning in 130. As you organize the rest of the material within these divisions, do not hesitate to abandon them if they seem to be contradicted by more decisive factors.

Some of the other events of the second half are sketched into Ex. 13-8; they will be briefly summarized here. Relatively little material from the first half appears in the second, and the beginning of the second half introduces a great many new musical ideas. The mood is one of convivial uproar. At first, there is no long-range structuring in evidence, only a succession of items each relatively self-contained and self-explanatory. The opening choral theme, blared out fortissimo, acts as a refrain eventually; and the one isolated clap—a new timbre that does *not* ever return—serves as a focal point for a rough grouping of the materials between 87 and 106. The party is relatively boisterous throughout that passage, and the lyric songs at 106 (swan song) and 110 (belt song) are a distinctly new mood.

During the subsection from 114 through 126, a number of themes begin to return. The factor of reprise begins here to be important. The pattern of thematic return is not clear, however; you will be aware only that return of some kind is taking place.

In addition, a new theme is introduced at 114, sung by soprano and tenor solos as their part of the bed song dialog. As usual in this work, new themes are introduced casually and often go unnoticed. Also as usual, nothing ever turns out to be completely new: this theme is merely a rhythmic rearrangement of the

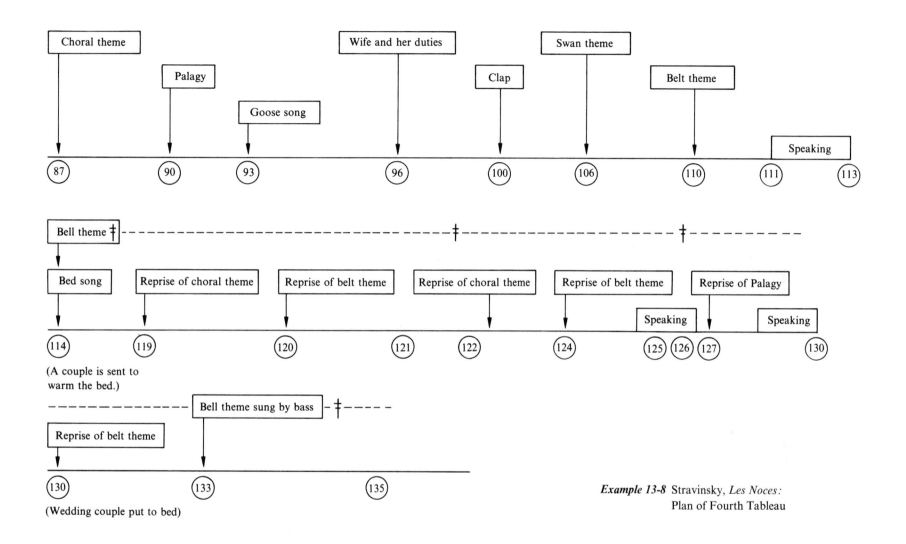

Example 13-8 Stravinsky, Les Noces:
Plan of Fourth Tableau

luminous song sung by bridesmaids in the First Tableau and again at the start of the Third Tableau. Notice that in its new form this bell theme (as it is labeled in Ex. 13-8) first appears right after the spoken line "Sing the songs!" (114), then soon after in the instruments (115), then in alternation with the belt theme after 120. When it reappears in the instruments, fortissimo, at 126, in the midst of the second spoken passage, it is already important.

The ending of Les Noces (as you have no doubt already noticed) is a musical miracle; no matter how often it is described or how thoroughly we take it apart, it always works on rehearing just as well as it did at first. The ending works because it has a very simple, solid foundation in the pitches involved and because it is so smoothly related to the rest of the work. It is distilled from the second half in much the same way as the litany conclusion of the first half;

and you should compare the ending of the first half to that of the second in order to hear something of an overall plan to the work.

We cannot trace the ending to its first antecedents, for they go all the way back to the beginning; we should, however, note the most explicit antecedents. This is the theme we have called (in anticipation) the bell theme in Ex. 13-8; as already noticed, behind this bell theme stands the bridesmaids' song from the

First Tableau. From the time of its first explicit appearance at 114, the bell theme is sung or played at several pitch levels but not at the level it assumes at the end. The level used for the instrumental appearance at 126 gives the theme an exceedingly bright sound, for the sake of the ritual kiss, but also so that the ending may have a slight sense of relaxation relative to this high point.

From the ritual kiss to 130, the musical material is all contrasting, in line as well as harmony; there is also the piling-up effect of the spoken lines. At 130, the belt theme returns as shown in Ex. 13-9, now set to the song about the bed ("My lovely little bed . . . "). The belt theme appears here alternately in two pitch positions, the second one a whole step lower. From both, however, the theme returns to the same final pitch, with noticeably more effort from position 2.

These two positions are shown in their pitch relation in Ex. 13-9; this example is abstract and contains only one statement in each position, in order to relate the belt theme clearly to its final pitch (and to the bell theme). The belt theme can ascend or descend to its final pitch, which resonates in several octaves throughout the ending. Example 13-9 shows the final pitch at two positions an octave apart.

You can listen to the ending, from 130 on, while looking at either Ex. 13-9 or Ex. 13-10. If you use Ex. 13-9, listen first for the belt theme each time it returns, trying to determine whether you hear it in position 1 (higher) or position 2 (lower). (Be aware of the brief excursion, into a harmonic area remote from the belt theme, that occurs between 131 and 132.) Notice the reiteration of the final pitch; when the bell theme is sung by the bass solo, try to hear how its pitches fit around the final pitch. This pitch, in octaves, is accompanied by another pitch, which you probably cannot hear when played with the final pitch as a chord (the bell chord) but which you can easily identify as an important note of the bell theme as sung by the bass. It is shown in Ex. 13-9 by the syllables in capital letters (-YA, -SA, -KA).

The bell chord, in other words, is not just a random sonority but is composed of two pitches from a theme that has become central to the second half. In composing Les Noces, Stravinsky possibly started with the bell chord, then worked out the progression of themes to lead up to it; but, in listening, you hear the themes first, the chord only at the end. The important aspect is that the chord seems to follow as the natural conclusion of the whole—in a way that a real bell (which might contain pitches not related to the preceding themes) would probably not achieve.

If you listen following Ex. 13-10, you will hear the bell note (the final pitch) at the end of most of the appearances of the belt theme, first in a lower octave, then in a higher one, with increasing force and finality. Usually, but not always, the bell note is accompanied by the bell chord.

From 133 on, the bell chord tolls repeatedly, but occurrences are carefully spaced out so far that no metric grouping develops; instead, the bell chord seems to give the last, most emphatic expression to the unit pulse that runs throughout. At first, the bell theme is sung by the bass, to the concluding song of love; then it is played by the instruments alone. Finally, nothing but the bell chord remains, casting its bright solemnity over the whole work. The sound continues, while the rhythm seems to cease; time comes to a stop.

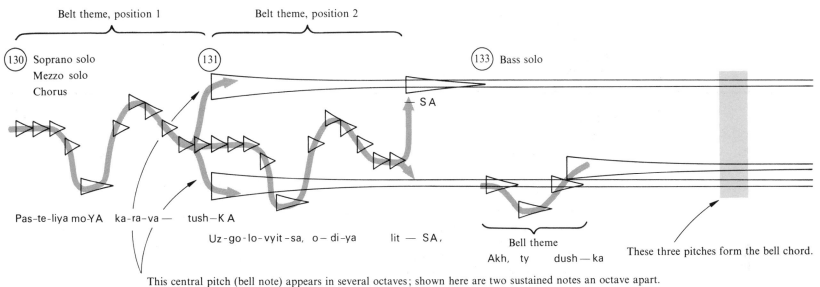

Belt theme, position 1   Belt theme, position 2

(130) Soprano solo
Mezzo solo
Chorus

(131)

(133) Bass solo

S A

Pas-te-liya mo-YA   ka-ra-va —   tush—K A

Uz-go-lo-vyit-sa,   o — di-ya   lit — SA,

Bell theme

Akh, ty   dush — ka

These three pitches form the bell chord.

This central pitch (bell note) appears in several octaves; shown here are two sustained notes an octave apart.
Belt theme ascends and descends to central pitch from both positions.
This diagram shows only the pitch relationships, not the succession of materials in the ending as a whole.

Example 13-9 Stravinsky, *Les Noces:* Themes and harmony at the end

Example 13-10 Stravinsky, *Les Noces:* Appearances
of belt theme, 130 through 133

Belt theme (positions 1 or 2) leading to the final pitch

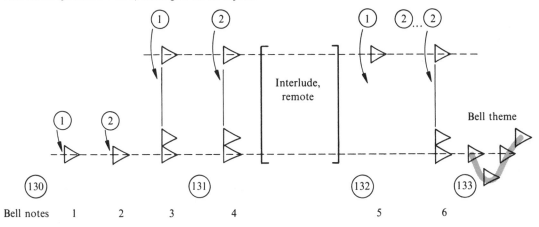

Interlude, remote

Bell theme

(130)   (131)   (132)   (133)

Bell notes   1   2   3   4   5   6

277

Igor Stravinsky

LES NOCES
SVADEBKA (THE WEDDING)

FIRST PART
FIRST TABLEAU: AT THE BRIDE'S

(Bride's lament)		Ss	Kosal moya ko . . . Kosa moya kosynka rusaya! . . .	Tress my tress, O thou fair tress of my hair, O my little tress.
Curtain	1		Vechor tebya kosynka matushka plyala,	My mother brushed thee, mother brushed thee at evening,
		SA	Matushka plyala!	Mother brushed thee!
		Ss	Sere bryanym kolechkom matushka vila,	My mother combed thee with a silver comb,
		SA	Matushka vila!	Mother combed thee!
Bride		Ss	O o kho kho! Yeshcho okhti mne!	O woe is me, O alas poor me.
Bridesmaids	2	SA	Chesu, pochesu Nastasyinu kosu,	I comb her tresses, Nastasia's fair tresses,
			Chesu, pochesu Timofeevny rusu,	I comb her hair, Timofeevna's bright hair.
			a yeshcho pochesu, a i kosu, zapletu,	I comb it and plait it,
		MSs	Alu lentu uplyatu.	with ribbon red I twine it.
	3	SA	Chesu, pochesu Nastasyinu kosu,	I comb her tresses, Nastasia's fair tresses,
			Chesu, pochesu Timofeevny rusu,	I comb her hair, Timofeevna's bright hair.
			Chesu pochesu, rusu kosu chesu	I bind her tresses, I comb them and plait them,
			Chastym grebnem raschesu.	With a fine comb I dress them.
Bride	4	Ss	Priekhala svashenka nemilostliva,	Cruel, heartless, came the matchmaker,
			chto ne milostliva, I ne zhalostliva!	Pitiless, pitiless cruel one,
	5		Nachala kosynku rvat i shchipat.	She tore my tresses, my bright golden hair, and pulled it.
		SA	Rvat i shchipat.	She tore it and pulled it.

SOLOISTS

Ss	*Soprano*
MSs	*Mezzo-soprano*
Ts	*Tenor*
Bs	*Bass*

CHORAL SINGERS

S	*Sopranos*
A	*Altos*
T	*Tenors*
B	*Basses*

A brace { indicates several singers singing different words at the same time.
A bracket [indicates several singers singing the same words at the same time.

English translation adapted by Oliver Ellsworth from that of D. Millar Craig, ⓒ for all countries 1957 by J. & W. Chester Ltd. Russian text by the composer, ⓒ 1922 by J. & W. Chester Ltd., transliterated by Oliver Ellsworth and David Brodsky. Text and translation used by permission of the publisher.

	6	**Ss**	I rvat i shchipat na dve zapletat,	She tore it to plait it in two plaits,
		SA	Na dve zapletat . . .	To plait it in two plaits.
		Ss	O o kho kho! Yeshcho ohkti mne!	O woe is me, O alas, poor me.
Bridesmaids	**7**	**SA**	Chesu, pochesu Nastasyinu kosu,	I comb her tresses, Nastasia's fair tresses,
			Chesu pochesu Timofeevny rusu,	I comb her hair, Timofeevna's bright hair.
			a yeshcho pochesu, a i kosu, zapletu,	I comb it and plait it,
		MSs	Alu lentu uplyatu.	with ribbon red I twine it.
	8	**MSs**	Goluboyu perevyu!	Twine it with a ribbon blue.
		SA		
Bride			Kosal moya, kosynka rusaya.	Golden tresses bright, O my tresses fair.
(Bridesmaids' song)	**9**	**SA**	Ne klich, ne klich lebedushka,	Weep not, O dear one, weep not,
			Ne klich v pole belaya	Let no grief afflict thee,
			Ne plach ne tuzhi, Nastasyushka,	Weep no more, Nastasia,
			Ne plach ne grusti dusha Timofeevna.	O weep no longer, my heart, my Timofeevna.
	10	**Ts**	Po batyushke,	Of your father think,
		Ts	po matushke,	your mother's care,
		Bs		
		SA	Po gromkom solovie vo sadu.	And of the nightingale in the garden.
	11	**Bs**	Kak svekor li batyushka k tebe budet milostliv,	Your father-in-law, he will welcome you,
			Kak svekor li matushka k tebe budet milostliva,	Your mother-in-law will bid you welcome
			k tebe budet zhalostliva.	And tenderly will love you as their own child.
		Ss	Uzh kak svekrov li matushka k tebe budet milostliva,	Your mother-in-law will bid you welcome
			k tebe budet zhalostliva.	And tenderly will love you as their own child.
	12	**Ss**	Khvetis, sudar Pamfilievich u tebya solovey vo sadu,	Noble Fetis Pamfilievitch, in your garden a
		MSs	Vo vysokom teremu,	nightingale is singing,
		SA		
	13		Vo vysokom Izukrashennom Denyochek on svistit	In the palace garden all day he whispers cooing
			i vsyu nochenku poyot.	notes, at nightfall hear him singing aloud his
				song of love.
	14	**Ss**	Tebya li, tebya li Nastasyushka	For you, Nastasia, his singing,
		MSs		
		SA		
		Ss	tebya li, svet Timofeevnu,	For you, Timofeevna, my dear one,
		MSs		
		SA		
		Ts		
		Bs		
	15		Zabavlyaet uteshaet	For your delight, your happiness,
			spat dolgo ne meshaet k obedne razbuzhaet.	He shall not disturb your sleeping, in time for Mass
				he'll wake you.
(Call to the wedding)	**16**		Ray ray! udaly skomoroshek s sela do sela,	Come, come, let us make merry from one village
				to another.
	17		Ray ray! Chtob nasha Nastasyushka,	Come, come, dear Nastasia shall be happy,
			chtob byla vesela.	She must be gay and joyful.
			Ray!	Come!
		Bs	Uzh chtob byla zavsegda.	She should always be of good cheer.

	18	Bs	S pod kamushka s pod belova,	Underneath the stones a brook flows,
		B		
		Ss	S pod kamushka, s pod belova rucheek bezhit,	Underneath the stones a brook flows making happy music,
		Ss	rucheek bezhit.	making happy music.
		MSs		
	19	Bs	S pod kamushka, s pod belova,	Underneath the stones a brook flows,
		Ss	S pod kamushka, s pod belova,	Underneath the stones a brook flows,
		Ss	tsimbalami byut, i pyut i pyut,	Like beating drums it sounds and sounds,
		MSs		
			V tarelki byut.	Like beating drums.
	20	S	Vot znat nashu Nastyuhku, znat nashu Timofeevnu	So our Nastasia, our Timofeevna,
		SA	k venchanyu vedut.	in marriage we give thee.
Bride and her mother (Slow litany)	21	Ss	Za . . . zapleti ko mne rusu kosu	Plait, plait my little tresses,
		Ts	Prechistaya Mater	O Mary thou Virgin,
			khodi k nam u khat svakhe pomogat.	Come to us and aid us.
	22	Ss	Uzh ty iz kornyu tugokhonko, Sredi kosy	Plait my hair and bind it with ribbon red, Bind it tightly
		Ts	Khodi, khodi k nam u khat svakhe pomogat, kosu raspletat.	Come, come to us and aid us, to plait her hair.
	23	Ss	Ne lyokhonko pod konets to alu lentochku.	O plait my hair and bind it with a ribbon red.
		Ts	Nastasyushki kosu Timofeevny rusu.	The hair of our Nastasia, our Timofeevna.
		Bs		
Bridesmaids	24	SA	Chesu, pochesu Nastasyinu kosu, Chesu pochesu Timofeevny rusu.	I comb her tresses, Nastasia's fair tresses. I comb her hair, Timofeevna's bright hair.
			Yeshcho pochesu Nastasyinu kosu,	I comb it, Nastasia, and plait it,
	25		Yeshcho pochesu Timofeevny rusu,	I comb it, Timofeevna, and plait it,
			A yeshcho pochesu, a i kosu zapletu,	I comb it and plait it,
			Alu lentu, upletu.	With ribbon red I twine it.
		Ss	Uzh ty lenta moya lentochka, Ala lenta buketova.	Blue, a ribbon blue, and ribbon red, like my lips,
	26	SA	Chesu, pochesu Nastasyinu kosu,	I comb her tresses, Nastasia's fair tresses,
			Chesu, pochesu Timofeevny rusu.	I comb her hair, Timofeevna's bright hair.
			Chesu, pochesu, rusu kosu chesu,	I bind her tresses, I comb and plait them,
			Chastym grebnem raschesu.	With a fine comb I dress them.
		Ss	Buketova, sfialetova.	A ribbon blue, like my eyes.

SECOND TABLEAU: AT THE BRIDEGROOM'S

(Fast litany (a))	27	TB	Prechistaya Mat, khodi, khodi k nam u khat, svakhe pomogat kudri raschesat,	Virgin Mother, come, come and aid our wedding, come hear our prayer,
		Ts	Khvetisievy kudri,	Comb the locks of Fetis,
		Bs		
		ATB		
	28	TB	kudri raschesat,	comb the fair locks,
		Ts	Pamfilyicha rusy.	the curls of Pamfilievitch.
		Bs		
		ATB		

	TB	Khodi, khodi k nam u khat,	Come, come and aid our wedding,
		khodi k nam u khat kudri raschesat.	Come aid our wedding and hear our prayer.
29	Ts	Chem chesat, chem maslit da Khvetisievy kudri?	Wherewith shall we brush and comb the fair locks of Fetis?
	Bs	Chem chesat, chem maslit da Pamfilyicha rusy?	Wherewith shall we brush and comb the curls of Pamfilievitch?
30	TB	Khodi, khodi k nam u khat, khodi k nam u khat	Come, come and aid our wedding, come and aid our wedding,
		svakhe pomogat kudri raschesat.	come hear our prayer.
31	Bs	Kinemsya, brosimsya, vo tri torga goroda;	Quickly let us take the three roads to town!
	Ts	Kupim my, kupim my paravanskago masla,	Let us buy, let us buy some pure oil,
32	Bs	rascheshem, razmaslim Khvetisovy kudri!	so that we can curl the locks of Fetis,
	Ts	rascheshem, razmaslim Pamfilyicha rusy!	so that we can curl the curls of Pamfilievitch.
33	TB	Prechistaya Mat, khodi, khodi k nam u khat, svakhe pomogat, kudri raschesat.	Virgin Mother, come, come and aid our wedding, come hear our prayer.
34	Ts	Khodi, khodi k nam u khat kudri raschesat!	Come, come aid our wedding and hear our prayer.
(Groom's parents' lament) 35	MSs	Vechor so vechoru sidel Khvetis vo teryomu.	Last night, last night Fetis sat within his house all the while.
Father	Ts	Sidel i Pamfilyich chesal rusy kudri.	Last night Pamfilievitch sat his fair locks brushing.
Both parents in turn 36	MSs	Vy komu to kudri dostanetes?	Now to whom will these curls belong?
		Oy, vy komu to rusy dostanetes?	Ah, to whom will these locks belong?
	Bs	Dostanetes, kudri krasnoy devitse.	Now they will belong to a rosy lipped maiden.
37	MSs	Vy komu to rusy dostanetes?	To whom will these locks belong?
		Uzh ty Nastyushka, poleley kudri!	Now Nastasia pour oil on them.
	Bs	Chto Nastasie Timofeevne,	Nastasia Timofeevna,
	Ss	Ty poleley rusy!	Pour oil on them!
38	Ss	Ty, Timofeevna, poleley rusy!	You, Timofeevna, pour oil on them.
	Bs	Kvas, chto malinoe desyatyu nalivan!	The comb is steeped in raspberry "kvas."
	MSs	Ty poleley rusy!	Pour oil on them!
39	Ss	Uzh vilis, povilis na Khvetisu kudri,	O the fair, the curly locks of Fetis,
	Bs	vilis, povilis na Pamfilyichu rusy.	the fair and curly locks of Pamfilievitch.
	MSs	Zavivala ikh matushka.	Thy mother curled them oft.
		Zavivala, da prigovarivala:	She curled them oft, saying as she curled them:
	Ts	Da prigovarivala:	Saying as she curled them:
40	SA	Bud ty moe dityatko belo rumyano,	Little son, be you white and rosy,
	Ts	Belo i rumyano!	White and rosy!
	SA	rumyano i neurochlivo!	and rosy-cheeked!
	Ts	Kalinoe parilo!	And another one will curl your locks,
	Bs	Malinoe stiralo!	And another one will love you.
	Ss	Na kom kudri, na kom rusiya?	Shining locks and curly whose are they?
		Na Khvetisu kudri rusiya,	The well-oiled and curled locks of Fetis,
		na Pamfilyichu poraschesaniya,	O Pamfilievitch lovely locks curly,
		poraschesaniya razbumazhenniya!	well-oiled and lovingly curled.
Friends 42	Bs	Spalat, spalat ottsu materi,	Glory to the father and to the mother,
		khorosho ditya vosporodili,	well have they brought up the child,
	MSs	umnago i razumnago,	wise and strong,

Groom		Ss	pokornago i poslovanago. Prilegayte, kudri rusiya k moemu litsu belomu k moemu umu razumu.	reasoning and obedient. Let my fair curls be in order upon my white face and grow used to my ways.
		Ts	Privykay, dusha Nastasyushka, k moemu umu razumu.	And grow used to my habits, dear Nastasia.
	43	MSs Bs B	A v Moskve, v Moskve to tem kudryam vzdivovalisya	Ah in Moscow, in the city
		Ss Ts SAT	da chto k obychyu molodetskomu.	dandy young habits are usual there.
(Fast litany (a))	44	ATB	Prechistaya Mat, khodi, khodi k nam u khat, svakhe pomogat kudri raschesat,	Virgin Mother, come, come and aid our wedding, come hear our prayer,
		Ts Bs ATB	Khvetisievy kudri,	Comb the locks of Fetis,
	45	ATB	kudri raschesat,	comb the locks,
		Ts Bs ATB	Pamfilyicha rusy.	the curls of Pamifilievitch.
		ATB	Khodi, khodi k nam u khat, Khodi k nam u khat kudri raschesat.	Come, come and aid our wedding, Come aid our wedding and hear our prayer.
(Fast litany (a) an octave higher)	46	Ss MSs Ts SAT	I ty Mater Bozhiya, sama Bogorodicha	And you, Mother of God, come Thyself,
		B	Pod na svadbu, pod na svadbu.	Come to the wedding, come to the wedding,
	47	Ss MSs Ts SAT	I so vsemi Postolami!	And with Thee all the holy Apostles.
		B	Pod na svadbu, pod na svadbu.	Come to the wedding, come to the wedding.
	48	Ss MSs Ts SAT	I so vsemi s angelyami.	And with Thee all the angels.
		B	Pod na svadbu, pod na svadbu.	Come to the wedding, come to the wedding.
(Fast litany (b))	49	Ss MSs Ts SAT	Boslovi Bozha, boslovi Bozha, Bozhunka. Pod na svadbu, pod na svadbu, pod na svadbu.	God bless us, God bless us, and His Son. Come to the wedding, come to the wedding, come to the wedding.
Bridegroom (—his request for parents' blessing)	50	Bs Bs	Boslovite otech, s materyu svago tsadu, ko stolnu gradu pristupit kamennu stenu razbit.	Bless me, my father, my mother, bless me, Your child who proudly goes against the strong wall of stones to break it.

	51	Ss MSs SA	Gde sidit tam Khvetis gosudar,	Where noble Fetis is sitting there,
		Bs Bs	Svoyu suzhenuyu ponyat.	to win his bride.
	52	Ss MSs SA	Tak svechey svetik naydet.	So the candles are lighted.
		Bs Bs	V sobor, cherkov skhodit, Serebryan krest potselovat.	We go now to the church and we kiss there the silver cross.
		Ss MSs SA	Bozhiya milost Bogorodicha!	Merciful God!
Best man	53	Bs	Smotrelshchiki, glyadelshchiki, zevaki i paloshny kolyubaki.	All you that come to see the bride passing by, did stay to see her taken away.
		Ss MSs SA	Boslovitetko vse knyazya novobrashnago!	All bless the prince upon his way.
	54	Bs	V put dorozhenku yekhati, suzheno ryazheno vzyat!	He has gone to wed his plighted bride.
		Ss MSs SA	Pod zolotoy venets stoyat!	On his brow to set a golden crown.
(*Fast litany* (*b*))	55	TB and tutti alter- nately	Oy! Lebedinoe pero upadalo!	Ah! There a white feather falls! The feather falls!
			Ivan palo! Pered teremom upadalo!	The feather falls! There now the flower fades!
	56		Ivan palo! upadal Khvetis pered rodnym batyushkoy: upadal Pamfilyich pered rodnoy matushkoy: prosit i mene	The feather falls! So did Fetis kneel down before his own father: So did Fetis kneel before his mother graciously, asking them
	57		i boslovi ko Bozhyu sudu yekhati, k svyatomu venchanyitsu. Kak privel Bog pod krestom i tak by pod ventsom.	to bless the son who goes to be married, he goes under your guard. May God keep him in His care and may the saints go with him too.
	58	Ts Bs	Boslovite vse ot starago do malago!	Lord bless us all from the oldest to the youngest.
		Ss MSs SA	Kuzmu Demiyanu sygrat!	Saint Damian bless us also.
		Ts Bs	Boslovi Bozha do dvukh porozhden	Bless them both O Lord

		Ss	Da stolko zhe nam svadbu sygrat!	bless the bride and the bridegroom!
		MSs		
		SA		
(*Fast litany* (*a*))	59	Ss	Oy!	Ah!
		MSs	Boslovi Bozha do dvukh porozhden,	Bless them both O Lord!
		Ts	Boslovi Bozha do dvukh posazhen,	Bless them both O Lord!
		Bs	Boslovi Bozha Mikita poputchik,	Bless the father Mikita O Lord!
		SATB	Mikhala Arkhanel	Michael the Archangel
	60		Boslovi Bozha Rozhdestvo Khristova,	Bless the mother Rozhdestvo Khristova,
			Boslovi Bozha khrestyn boslovlyati,	Bless all the faithful O Lord!
			k ventsu otpushchati.	All who fear and love Him.
(*Fast litany* (*b*)	61		Boslov Bozha, Bozhunka, Boslov Bozhunka!	Father and Son bless us!
Ostinato to end)			Pod na svadbu! Pod na svadbu! Pod na svadbu!	Come to the wedding! Come to the wedding! Come to the wedding!
	62	TB	Svyaty Luka, pod na svadbu, Svyaty Luka.	Saint Luke, come to the wedding, Saint Luke.
		SA	Svyaty Luka, pod na svadbu,	Saint Luke, come to the wedding,
	63	TB	Svyaty Luka slutsi svadbu,	Saint Luke bless our marriage rites,
		SA	Slutsi svadbu	bless our marriage rites,
		TB	Slutsi svadbu dvukh molodyonykh,	bless our marriage rites and the young couple,
			Slutsi svadbu.	Bless our marriage rites.
		SA	Dvukh posazhenykh.	Bless the young couple.
	64	Ss	Slutsi	Bless
		MSs		
		Ts		
		A		
		TB	dvukh posazhenykh.	the young couple.
		Ss	Slutsi svadbu dvukh suzhenykh.	Bless our marriage rites and the young couple.
		MSs		
		Ts		
		SATB		
		Ss	I pervy mladen!	And bless their children!
		MSs		
		Ts		
		Bs		
		SATB		

THIRD TABLEAU: THE BRIDE'S DEPARTURE

(*Bridesmaids' song*)	65	SA	Blagoslovlyalsya svetyol, mesyats	Brightly shines the moon on high,
			okolo yasnago solnushka blagoslovlyalas	beside the glowing sun,
	66		knyaginyushka u gosudarya	Even so the princess lived within the palace happily
			u batyushki, u gosudaryni	beside her aged father and her mother
			u gosudaryni matushki.	beside her dear Lord.
	67	Ts	Blagoslovi menya batyushka	O grant me your blessing, father,
		Ss	da na chuzhuyu storonushku.	for now I go to a foreign land.
		MSs		
		SA		

The father and mother	68	Bs	Pritapelas svetsa vosku yarago, Pered obrazom dolgo stoyutsi	See how bright the candles burn before the ikon, so I have stood before it long,
		Ss	Pristoyala knyaginya knyaginya skory nozhenki.	So the princess stood awhile and quickly then away she went.
Bridesmaids and ushers	69	MSs	Uzh kak boslovili oni devitsu	So they gave their blessing to their daughter fair,
		Ts	Pered batsuskoy gorko platsutsi	So she before her father stood weeping,
		Bs	Da chto na chetyre na storonushki,	And to every quarter of the world I go,
		Ts	Da chto na chetyre na storonushki.	And to every quarter of the world I go.
		Ss	Khlebom solyu Spasom obrazom.	Holding the ikon, bread, and salt.
Everyone	70	Ts	Svyaty Kuzma pod na svadbu, Svyaty Kuzma Dyemiyan pod na svadbu.	Saint Cosmas, come to the wedding, Saints Cosmas and Damian, come to the wedding.
		Ss	Vo gornitse, vo gornitse vo svyatlitse, Dva golubya na tyablitse.	In the little room, the happy room, Two doves are sitting.
	71	A	Svyaty Kuzma, pod na svadbu. Svyaty Kuzma skuy nam svadbu, Svyaty Kuzma, skuy nam krepku, krepku, tverdu, dolgovetnu, vekovetnu, s mladosti i do starosti.	Saint Cosmas, come to the wedding, Saint Cosmas, grant that the wedding, Saint Cosmas, grant that it may prosper, prosper, strong and enduring, from youth to old age.
(Slow litany)		B	Matushka Kuzma Demiyana po senyam khodila gvozdi sobirala.	The Mother and Saints Cosmas and Damian walked about the hall and came back.
	72	Ts	s mladosti i do starosti.	. . . from youth to old age.
		SATB	I do malykh detushek.	To the children, even unto them.
	73	Ss	Vo gornitse, vo gornitse, vo svetlitse	In the little room, the happy room,
		SA	Dva golubya na tyablitse.	Two doves are sitting.
		Ts	Oni pyut, oni pyut i lyut,	There is singing, dancing, drinking, too.
		Ss	V politiry byut, v tsimbali podygryvayut.	Tambourines sounding, cymbals are being played.
		MSs		
		S		
(Slow litany)	74	T	Svyaty Kuzma pod na svadbu.	Saint Cosmas, come to the wedding.
		A	Svyaty Kuzma slutsi svadbu, s mladosti i do starosti,	Saint Cosmas, bless the wedding, . . . from youth to old age.
		T	s mladosti i do starosti.	. . . from youth to old age.
		B	Kuzma Demiyan po senyam khodila,	Saints Cosmas and Damian walked about the hall,
			gvozdi sobirala,	they walked about the hall,
			svadebku kovala.	and then they came back.
		Ss	I do malykh detushek.	To our children, even unto them.
		MSs		
		Ts		
		Bs		
(Bridesmaids' song)	75	T	I ty, sama Mat Bozhiya,	And you, Mother of God,
		Ss	Ty, Mat Bozhiya, sama Bogorodicha,	You, Mother of God, the Savior,
		MSs		
		SA		
	76	T	Pod na svadbu, slutsi svadbu.	Come to the wedding, bless the wedding,

285

			Russian	English
	Ss		Slutsi svadbu, slutsi krepku.	Bless the wedding, bless the marriage.
	MSs			
	SA			
77	Ss		I so vsemi s Postolami	And with all the holy Apostles,
	MSs		I so vsemi s Angelyami.	And with all the Angels.
	Ts			
	Bs			
	SATB			
78	Ss		I, kak viyotsya khmel po tytsyu,	As the hops entwine together,
	MSs			
	T		I, kak viyotsya khmel po tytsyu,	As the hops entwine together,
79	Ss		tak by nashi moldye vilis drug kolo drugu,	so our newly married couple cling together.
	MSs			
	SA			
	Ts		. . . tsyu.	. . . entwine.
	Ts			
	Bs		tak by nashi molodye vilis drug kolo drugu.	so our newly married couple cling together.
	TB			
	Ss		. . . u-u-u.	. . . u-u-u.
	MSs			
	SA			
80	Ss		-u-u-u-u-u-u-u-u-u	-u-u-u-u-u-u-u-u-u
	MSs			
	Ts			
	Bs			
	SATB			
82	Ts		-u-u-u-u-u-u-u-u-u-u-u	-u-u-u-u-u-u-u-u-u-u-u
	Bs			
82	Ss		Rodimoe moyo dityatko, moyo miloye,	My own child, my dear one,
83	MSs		Rodimoe moyo dityatko, poila bylo ya kormila tebya.	My own child, Do not leave me, come again to me.
84	Ss		ne pokin menya goremychnuyu. Vorotis, vorotis moya dityatka, vorotis moya milaya,	Do not leave me lonely. Come back, come back my child, Come back my dear one,
	MSs		vorotis moya milaya. Zabyla ty, dityatko na stopke zoloty klyuchi.	Come back my dear one. You forgot, child, the golden keys
85	Ss		na shelkovom poyase.	which are hanging there.
86	Ss		Rodimoe dityatko.	My own child.
	MSs			

Bride's departure—everyone leaves with her (at measure 80)

The stage is empty (at measure 82)

Mothers of the bride and groom enter from each side (at measure 82)

Exit mothers. The stage is empty

SECOND PART
FOURTH TABLEAU: THE WEDDING FEAST

			Russian	English
(Choral theme: berry song)	87	SATB	Yagoda s yagodoy sokatilasya	The berries on a branch fell

		Yagoda yagode poklonilasya.	One berry bows to another.
	Ss	Ay lyuli, lyuli, lyuli! Lyushenki,	Ay lyuli, lyuli, lyuli! Lyushenki,
	Ss	ay lyuli!	ay lyuli!
	MSs		
	SAT		
88	Ts	Yagodka krasna,	A red berry,
	Ts	krasna!	a red one!
	TB		
	Ss	Ay lyuli!	Ay lyuli!
	MSs		
	SA		
	Ts	Zemlyanichka spela,	A strawberry did ripen,
	Ts	spela!	did ripen!
	BS		
	TB		
	Ss	Ay lyushenki, lyuli!	Ay lyushenki, lyuli!
	MSs		
	SA		
	Ts	Ay lyuli!	Ay lyuli!
	Bs		
	TB		
89	Ss	Yagoda yagode slovo molvila	One berry to another spoke sweetly
	MSs	Yagoda ot yagody ne vdali rosla,	Close one berry grew to another,
	Ts		
	Bs		
	SAT		
	Bs	Vesyol, vesyol khodit i Fyodor Tikhnavich.	So gaily gaily goes Theodor Tichnovitch.
	B		
	Ss	Odnato yagoda Khvetisushka sudar,	One berry represents the noble Fetis,
	MSs		
	Ts		
	SAT		
	B	Nashel, nashel zolot perstin,	I found, I found a golden ring,
90	Ss	A drugaya yagoda Nastasiyushka dusha.	And another berry sweet Nastasia.
	MSs		
	Ts		
	SAT		
	B	zolot s dorogim sy kamenem.	a ring set with precious stones.
(*Ring song*)	Bs	Yunyv, yunyv khodit.	A young man, a young man is coming.
	Ss	Palagey Spanovich.	Palagy Spanovitch.
	MSs		
	S		
	Bs	Poteryal zolot perstin.	I have lost a ring of gold.
	Ss	Palagey Spanovich.	Palagy Spanovitch.
	MSs		
	S		

287

91	Bs	Poteryal zolot perstin zolot s dorogim sy kamenyam.	I have lost a ring of gold set with precious stones.
92	SAT	Yunyv, yunyv, yunyv Palagey,	Young, young, young Palagy
		Yunyv Palagey khodit Spanych,	Young Palagy Spanovitch is coming,
		khodit Palagey, khodit Spanych.	Palagy is coming, Spanovitch is coming.
	B	Poteryal zolot perstin s dorogim sy kamenyam.	I have lost a ring of gold set with precious stones.

(*Flying goose song*)

93	Ss	Letala gusynya, letala!	A goose is flying, is flying!
	MSs		
	Ts		
	Bs		
	S	A yagoda yagode poklonilasya.	One berry bows to another.
	Ss	Letala syeraya, letala!	A grey one is flying, is flying!
	MSs		
	Ts		
	Bs		
	S	Yagoda yagode slovo molvila . . .	One berry to another spoke sweetly . . .
		u-lyu-lyu-lyu-lyu-lyu-lyu.	u-lyu-lyu-lyu-lyu-lyu-lyu.
	A	. . . letala! . . . letala!	. . . is flying! . . . is flying!
		. . . lyu-lyu-lyu-lyu-lyu-lyu-lyu.	. . . lyu-lyu-lyu-lyu-lyu-lyu-lyu.
	T	U-lyu-lyu-lyu-lyu-lyu, u-lyu-lyu, soboki!	U-lyu-lyu-lyu-lyu-lyu, u-lyu-lyu, soboki!
		U-lyu-lyu, borziya, u-lyu-lyu, kosiya,	U-lyu-lyu, borziya, u-lyu-lyu, kosiya,
		U-lyu-lyu-lyu-lyu-lyu . . .	U-lyu-lyu-lyu-lyu-lyu . . .
		U-lyu-lyu-lyu-lyu-lyu-lyu-lyu-lyu-lyu . . .	U-lyu-lyu-lyu-lyu-lyu-lyu-lyu-lyu-lyu . . .
	B	U-lyu-lyu-lyu-lyu-lyu . . . letala!	U-lyu-lyu-lyu-lyu-lyu . . . is flying!
		u-lyu-lyu-lyu-lyu-lyu . . . letala!	u-lyu-lyu-lyu-lyu-lyu . . . is flying!
		lyu-lyu-lyu-lyu-lyu-lyu-lyu-lyu . . .	lyu-lyu-lyu-lyu-lyu-lyu-lyu . . .
94	Ss	Oy, lyay!	Oy, lyay!
	MSs		
	Ts		
	Bs		
	SATB		
	Ts	Letala gusynya, letala.	A goose is flying, is flying.
	Ss	Oy!	Oy!
	MSs		
	Bs		
	SATB		
	Ts	Letala seraya, letala.	A grey one is flying, is flying.
	Ss	Oy! Oy!	Oy! Oy!
	MSs		
	Bs		
	SATB		
95	Ss	Kryliya primakhala.	Now its wings are beating.
	MSs		
	Ts	Mazoli potirala.	Its tiny feet are scratching.
	Ss	Oy! lyali, lyali, lyay!	Oy! lyali, lyali, lyay!
	MSs		
	Ts	Stolby skolykhala.	Clouds of dust rise.

	96	**Ss**	Oy, lyay!	Oy, lyay!
		MSs		
		Ts		
		Bs		
		SATB		
		Ts	Boyar probuzhdala.	Waking the nobles.
		Ts	Oy, lyay!	Oy, lyay!
		Bs		
		TB		
		Ss	Oy, lyay! Oy, lyali lyay!	Oy, lyay! Oy, lyali lyay!
		MSs		
		SA		
Groom's father		**Bs**	Vot tebya zhana!	Behold your wife!
		B	zhana!	wife!
		Ts	Ot Boga sazhdana.	She is given of God.
(Duties of the wife:)	**97**			
The men		**TB**	Sey lyon da kanapli.	She must sew the flax.
The women		**Ss**	Ay, my tebe Nastyushka govorili!	And what did we tell you dear Nastasia!
		MSs		
		SA		
The men		**TB**	Sprashivay s neyo rubashki da portki.	We told her she must keep the linen.
		Ts	. . . rubashki da portki!	. . . she must keep the linen!
The women		**Ss**	Oy, my tebe, milaya govorili!	Ah, we told you, dear one!
		MSs		
		SA		
Bride's mother leads her to her son-in-law	**98**	**MSs**	Zyatik moy lyubezny, vruchayu tebe docheryu lyubeznuyu.	To you my dear son-in-law, I entrust my daughter dear to you.
The best man, groom's mother, Svat, and marriage-broker in turn		**Ts**	Sey lyon da zamashki sprashivay s neyo rubashki.	We told her she must sew the flax and keep it.
	99	**Bs**	. . . poy, kormi da odevay!	. . . give her to eat and drink!
		Ss	poy, kormi da odevay da na rabotu otpravlyay.	give her to eat and drink and bid her work.
		MSs		
		Ts		
		SAT	Da na rabotu otpravlyay.	Set her to work.
		Ss	Rubi	Cut
		Bs	drova,	the wood,
		B		
		S	sprashivay.	ask again.
	100	**SATB**	*(Shchi.)*	*(Clap.)*
		Ts	Lyubi.	Love her.
		Ts	Lyubi, kak dushu,	Love her, like a dear one,
		Bs		
		Ts	tryasi, kak grushu.	shake her like a pear tree.
		Bs		
		TB		
(Story of Mary and Simon)	**101**	**SA**	Boyare vstavali v charki nalivali,	The nobles arose and filled the goblets,

	TB	v charki nalivali,	filled the goblets,
	SA	v charki nalivali,	filled the goblets,
		gostey obkhodili,	they went among the guests,
		Marie podnosili:	toasting Mary:
102	TB	Marie podnosili:	toasting Mary:
	Bs	"Vypey matushka, skushay Kharitonovna."	"Drink, little mother, eat, Kharitonovna."
103	Ss	"Ne pyu, ne kushayu, boyar ne slushayu."	"I do not drink, I do not eat, I do not listen to you nobles."
	Bs	"Ka by byl Simeon?"	"If Simon were here?"
	Ss	"Ya by spila, skushala, boyar poslushala."	"I would drink, I would eat, I would listen to you nobles."
104	SA	Oy, ty gusynya zvonkaya,	Oh, you noisy goose,
	Ts	kitayskaya.	chattering.
	Bs		
	B		
105	SA	Uzh ty gde gusynya zvonkaya,	Where have you been, noisy goose,
		gde pobyvala i chto videla?	where have you been, and what have you seen?
	B	. . . kitayskaya, pobyvala, i chto videla?	. . . chattering one, where have you been, and what have you seen?
	T	. . . pobyvala, i chto videla?	. . . have you been, and what have you seen?

(Swan song)

106	Ss	"I ya byla na sinem na mori, na mori na zere,	"I have been on the blue sea, the sea and the lake,
	A	Lyuli, lyuli!	Lyuli, lyuli!
	SA	Na mori, na zere.	On the sea, on the lake.
107	Ss	Na tom li na mori na zere lebyad belaya kupalasya,	There on the sea on the lake a little white swan was bathing.
	A	Lyuli,	Lyuli,
	SA	na belo polaskalasya."	washing her white dress."
	B	Oy!	Oy!
108	MSs	Byl li beloy lebyad na mori?	You saw a white one bathing on the sea?
		videl li ty, beloy lebyodku?	You saw a little white swan?
	Ts	"Da, i kak zhe mne da na mori,	"Yes, and how should I not have seen the sea,
		na mori ne byvat,	not have seen the sea,
	SA	da, i kak zhe mne lebyodushki ne vidat?"	yes, and how should I not have seen the little swan?"
109	Bs	U lebedya lebedushka pod krylom,	The swan has his mate beneath his wing,
		u lebedya kosataya pod krylom	the swan hides her beneath his wing
		u Khvetisa to Nastasyushka pod bochkom,	as Fetis Nastasia under his arm
		u Khvetisa Timofeevna pod krylom.	as Fetis Timofeevna under his wing.
	Ss	Dva lebedya, dva belykh plavali, na mori plavali,	Two swans, two white ones were swimming, were swimming on the sea.
	A	Oy, lyuli, oy lyuli	Oy, lyuli, oy lyuli
	SA	byelye plavali.	the white ones were swimming.

An usher, to the bride

110	Ts	Oy chem Nastasyushka udala?	Ah, Nastasia, what have you done?
	Bs	Ay, chem zhe ty . . .	Ah, what . . .

The bride (belt song)

	Ss	Ya po poyas vo zolote obvilas	I have donned a golden belt,
		zhemchuzhnye makhorchiki do zemli.	plaited with pearls that hang down to the ground.

Svat	**111**	**Bs**	Okh, poynik, propoynik Nastin batyushka.	O you merry old rogue, father of Nastasia.
An usher—spoken		**Ts**	Svatyushki, povorashivaytes, podavayte nevestu, zhenikh skuchaet!	Now all you who are come to the feast, lead the bride in, the bridegroom is waiting lonely!
		B	Propil svoyu chadu za vinnuyu charu.	He has sold his child for goblets of dear wine.
		Bs	Na vinnoy charochke, na medovoy stopochke!	Holding a goblet of rare old wine, a rare goblet!
The same usher	**112**	**Ts**	Krasny devitsy, pirozhniya masteritsy,	You fair maids, pastrycooks, and platewashers,
	113		zheny podkhiliya, malye rebyata,	you lazy wives, you foolish ones,
			gorokhovy tati, markovnye pagubniki!	you naughty ones among the wedding guests!
Spoken			poyte pesni!	sing the songs!
	114	**SA**	Khvetisushka skazhet:	Fetis says:
(Bell theme)		**Ss**	"spat khochu."	"I want to go to sleep."
An usher chooses a man and wife		**MSs**		
from among the guests, and sends		**Ts**		
them to warm the bed for the couple		**SA**	Nastasyushka molvit:	Nastasia replies:
		Ss	"i ya s toboy."	"and I with you."
		MSs		
		Ts		
		SA	Khvetisushka skazhet:	Fetis says:
		Ss	"korovat tesna."	"the bed is too narrow."
		SA	Nastasyushka molvit:	Nastasia replies:
		Ss	"budet s nas."	"that's fine for us."
		MSs		
		Ts		
		SA	Khvetisushka skazhet:	Fetis says:
		Ss	"deyalo kholodno."	"the blankets are cold."
		MSs		
		Ts		
		SA	Nastasyushka molvit:	Nastasia replies:
		Ss	"budet teplo."	"they will be warm."
		MSs		
		Ts		
	115	**S**	To Khvetisu pesenka, da chto yasnomu sokolu i so beloy lebyodushkoy, svet Nastasiey Timofeevnoy.	To thee, Fetis, we now sing this little song, and to the little white swan, dear Nastasia Timofeevna.
	116	**Ss**	Slyshish li Khvetis Gospodin?	Do you hear us, Master Fetis?
		MSs		
		SA		
			Slyshish li Pamfilievich?	Do you hear us, Pamfilievitch?
		SA	My vam pesnyu poyom, my vam chest vozdayom.	We are singing you a song, we are honoring you.
Svat and guests	**117**	**Bs**	Ne lezhi u . . .	Do not lie by . . .
		Bs	u krute berege.	by the steep river bank.
		B		
		Bs	Ne sidi, Savelyushka,	Do not sit down, Savelyushka,
	118		Vo besedushke,	In a summer house
		Bs	Sryazhay svadebku	a wedding prepare now
		B		

	Voice		English
	Bs	Khvetisavu.	for Fetis.
119	Bs	Okh!	Ah!
	SA		
Guests	SA	na izbe zeliya, uvyzbe veseliya.	in the farmhouse see how jolly a feast is held.
	Ts	Za stolom boyare oni med, vino pili,	Nobles sat at table drinking honey and wine,
	T		
	Ts	rechi govorili:	making speeches:
	Bs		
	TB		
120	Bs	u menya svadebka na divo suryazhena,	the good wife has prepared beer,
	Bs	devyati varov pivo vareno,	nine kinds of beer,
	B		
	Ts	A desyaty var zelena vina.	but the tenth is the best of all.
	Bs		
121	Ss	Vedut Nastasyushka na chuzku storonu	Our Nastasia goes away, to dwell afar-off,
	MSs	Na chuzhoy starone.	in a distant country.
	A		
	S	Umeuchi devke zhit, devke zhit!	Wisely shall she live there!
		da vse pokornoy devke byt!	and let her be submissive!
	Ss	Umeuchi devke, umeuchi zhit!	Wisely shall she live there.
	MSs		
	A		
	Ts	. . . devke zhit!	. . . wisely live!
	Bs		
	TB		
	Ss	Vse pokornoy devke, vsyo pokornoy byt!	and let her be submissive!
	MSs		
	A		
	Ts	. . . devke byt!	. . . be submissive!
	Bs		
	TB		
122	Ss	Pokornoy golovushke vezde lyubo khorosho.	She who is submissive is happy.
The guests in turn	Ss	I staromu i malomu vse nizky poklon.	Bow then courteously to the old and the young.
	Ts		
123	Ss	Molodym molodushkam ponizhe etogo.	To the youngest maidens you must bow lower.
	MSs		
	Ts		
	Bs	Po ulitse, yulitse da po shirokoy yulitse khodil,	He went down the street, down the narrow street,
		gulyal molodets.	the young man walked.
	B	Da po shirokoy yulitse . . .	Down the narrow street . . .
	Ss	Po zelenom sadu, po Nastinam sledam,	Upon the marks of Nastasia's feet in the green garden,
		glyadel smotrel Khvetisushka na Nastyushku svoyu:	Fetis stood and looked at the feet of his Nastasia:
	Ts	khodil, gulyal molodets molod molodoy.	the youngest of the youths went walking.
	T	molod molodoy . . . lentoy lilovoyu . . .	the youngest . . . on his head in winter . . .
	Bs	Svyazal svoyu golovu shlyapoy pukhovoyu.	On his head he wore a fine furry cap for winter.

		B	shlyapoy pukhovoyu.	a furry cap.
	124	Ts	U moey, u Nastyushki pokhodochka chastaya	My Nastasia walks very quickly
			shubochka novaya opushka bobrovaya	in her new coat lined with marten fur
Ushers—spoken		Ts	Nastya chernobrovaya!	Black are her brows!
		T		
An usher—spoken	125	Ts	Nuka, rodimy batyushka, ryumochku vypivay!	Now then, you old man, come and drink a little glass of wine!
The other ushers and bridesmaids		SAT	Ryumochku vypivay!	Drink a good glass of wine!
(Spoken)		Ts	Nashikh molodykh odaryay!	Toast the young couple!
		SAT	Molodykh odaryay!	Toast the young ones!
(Spoken)		Ts	Nashim molodym mnogo nado,	Our young ones need many things,
			oni khotyat domishkom zhit.	they want to have a little house,
		Ts	domishka pribavit,	to increase their home,
		Bs		
		Ts	na uglu banyu postavit.	they will build a bath in the corner.
(Sung)	126		Ty zaydyosh da poparishsya,	Come and have a bath,
(Spoken)			a posle togo pokhvalishsya:	afterwards you will be heated:
			vot kak stali nashi, molodye to zhit!	So did our married pair begin their happy days together!
Guests—spoken		Bs	Gorko!	Now then!
		Bs	Okh, gorko!	Ah, now then!
		TB		
		Ss	Okh, nelzya pit.	Ah, drink to their health.
		MSs		
		Ts		
		SA		
Bride and groom kiss		Bs	Nuzhe, nuzhe, nu;	Now, now, now;
		Ss	ryumochku vypivay,	drink to their health,
		MSs		
		A		
		Ts	a nashikh molodykh daryay,	toast our young couple,
		Ss	molodykh daryay.	toast the young couple.
		MSs		
		SA		
	127	Bs	Eta, eta, eta khot kuda, eto i taper stoit rublya,	This, this, this is good, and even now costs a ruble,
		Bs	a kak yey, yey boka nadut,	but if you squeeze it tightly in your hand,
		B		
	128	Bs	za etaku i dva,	then it is double,
		Bs	dva dadut.	it costs double.
		B		
		T	Khot by tak, khot by,	I don't care, I don't care,
			khot by tak, khot by rublikov	I don't care, I don't care how many rubles
		B	khot by tak . . . rublikov	I don't care . . . rubles
Ushers		Ts	Volga reka razlivaetsa,	The Volga overflows its banks,
		Bs		
		B		

Bridesmaids	SA	zyatik u vorot ubivaetsya:	I hear one calling before the gate:
	B	khot by pyat.	I don't care.
129	Ss	"Akh, tyoshsha moya, tyoshsha laskovaya!"	"Ah, my daughter, my naughty daughter?"
	MSs		
	Bs		
	SAT		
An usher—spoken	B	A kogda budet tvoya chest,	If your husband has the money,
	Ts	Ay, vy druzhki slepy, chto devka detinke boka protolkala,	Ah, don't you see that the girl no longer has it,
(Spoken)	B	khot by rublikov,	I don't care how many rubles,
	Ss	. . . u kletochku zvala?	. . . who is calling there?
	MSs		
	Ts		
	SA		
(Spoken)	Bs	A otdali nam devku, otdaytya postelku!	From far they are calling you! come to bed!
Svat, to the couple that is warming the bed.	B	khot by shest.	I don't care how much it costs.
The couple warming the bed comes out. Fetis and Nastasia are led in and put to bed, then left alone and the door is closed. The two fathers and two mothers station themselves before the door on a bench, everyone else facing them.			
130	Ss	Pasteliya moya, karavatushka!	My lovely little bed!
	MSs		
	ST		
(Belt theme)	AB	Na karavatushke perinushka,	On the bed there is a feather-quilt,
	Ss	na perinushke	on the feather-quilt
	MSs		
	ST		
	Ss	uzgolovyitsa,	there is a pillow,
	MSs		
	SAT		
	Ts	da	yes
	Ts	na perinushke	on the feather-quilt
	A		
	Ts	uzgolovyitsa.	there is a pillow.
	Bs		
	AB		
131	Ss	uzgolovyitsa odiya litsa,	I lay my head on the pillow,
	MSs		
	SAT		
	Ts	pod diyalitsom dobry molodets.	a handsome young man is under the covers.
	Bs	Dobry molodets	The handsome young

	Bs B	Khvetisushka,	Fetis,
	MSs A	Vorobey vorobku paruet,	The sparrow takes his mate with him,
	Ts Bs	posadivshi na karavat, Khvetis Pamfilievich.	having prepared his nest, Fetis Pamfilievitch.
132	Ss MSs SA	Khvetisushka Nastasyushku tseluit,	Fetis kisses Nastasia,
	Ts Bs TB	Yon tseluit miluit na ruchku kladyot,	He kisses her, caresses her, and holds her hand,
	Bs	na ruchku kladyo, ky serdechku zhmyo:	holds her hand and presses it upon his heart:
	Ss MSs SAT	na ruchku kladyo, ky serdechku	holds her hand and presses it
	Ss MSs Ts Bs SATB	zhmyo:	upon his heart:
(*Bell theme*) 133	Bs	"Akh, ty dushka zhyonushka, dannaya moya poglyadeniya, nochnaya moya zabava, pozhivyom my s toboy,	"Ah, you dear little wife, my own dearest treasure, my sweet, my honey, let us live in happiness,
134		khoroshenichka, chtoby lyudi nam zavidyvali."	dearest flower, so that the people will envy us."

Curtain falls slowly during the rest of the music.

AMONG BACH'S MANY PRELUDES and fugues for keyboard instruments (organ, harpsichord, and clavichord), those in the two collections known as *The Well-Tempered Clavier,* Books I and II, represent the most concentrated expression of musical shape. Each prelude is coupled with a fugue; prelude and fugue together form a unit, being in the same key and sometimes linked in other ways as well. The artistic unit is the individual pair—prelude and fugue—in a single major or minor key.

Each book has twenty-four preludes and fugues; each unit (prelude and fugue) is in a different key. In each book, twelve of the units are in major keys, twelve in minor keys. Since twelve major and twelve minor keys are all the major and minor keys there are and since a clavier ("keyboard") instrument must be specially tuned, or "tempered," to permit playing in all keys, Bach used the title "Well-Tempered Clavier" to indicate that a special kind of tuning would be required.

The unit—prelude and fugue—is not very tightly knit. There are only two parts, and each of the two parts is complete in itself (and can be played separately); consequently, no balance or symmetry takes place at the highest level. An *A B A* plan, for example, is not a possibility.

The fact that a prelude and its fugue are in the same harmonic area thus becomes of great importance; continuity of key is perhaps the most decisive aspect of continuity within the pair. You should by now be able to sense the sameness on your first hearing of a prelude and its fugue—even if you are aware of it only at the juncture between the prelude and the fugue.

PRELUDE AND FUGUE NO. 12 IN F MINOR. Begin by listening straight through the Prelude and Fugue several times. During the first or second hearing you will probably be far more aware of the differences between Prelude and Fugue. These differences will vary from one performance to another, because certain prominent aspects not specified by Bach are left open to varying interpretation by performers. Even though the basic timbre of performance (harpsichord, clavichord, or piano) is uniform throughout Prelude and Fugue, the quality of sound may vary considerably between Prelude and Fugue and from one performance to another. In one performance, the Fugue may be much brighter or louder than the Prelude; in another, Prelude and Fugue may have the same quality of sound. Bach left no directions on this point.

Neither did Bach specify the relative tempos of these preludes and fugues; here you will find great variation in different performances. In the F-minor Prelude and Fugue, however, the Fugue is usually played faster and in a livelier manner than the Prelude. Partly as a result of this tempo relationship, the Fugue will seem to be an accelerated finale to the longer, more reflective Prelude.

Whichever performance you hear, you can form, even on first hearing, some such idea of the relationship between Prelude and Fugue. One way to gain perspective on this kind of relationship is to imagine the same Prelude and Fugue in some different rela-

tionship. If the Fugue came before the Prelude, for example, or if the Prelude were repeated after the Fugue, or if some other piece came after the Fugue, the shape of the whole piece would clearly be different. Another way to gain perspective is to note carefully the effects of different performances.

You may also notice on first hearing (if not, soon thereafter) that the F-minor Prelude has fairly clear sections, with breaks at the highest levels. The Fugue, on the other hand, does not; it proceeds in one unbroken surge of rhythmic energy from beginning to end—a feature that works together with a faster tempo to produce the effect of an accelerated finale. While it is possible to hear a sectional plan in the Fugue, the sectional effect is relatively subtle, compared to the Fugue's obvious continuity.

TEXTURE AND MOTIVES IN THE F-MINOR PRELUDE. One of the most important aspects of the preludes and fugues in *The Well-Tempered Clavier* is texture. In the F-minor Prelude, you will soon sense that subtle changes in texture often take place. These are not obvious changes, such as from a monophonic to a polyphonic texture or from a homophonic to a contrapuntal texture. All the textures in the Prelude tend to be contrapuntal, that is, strongly linear, in one way or another; even a simple rhythmic figure is likely to have a suggestion of a melody. (Nowhere in this Prelude is the texture merely melody and accompaniment or simply chordal.)

Within the various contrapuntal textures, rhythmic and melodic motives are clearly audible. At the beginning of the Prelude, the motives have a strong identity and can often be easily identified on their return. Sometimes, however, different motives blend into one another or into some new motive. The process of change in and among the motives is the process of the piece itself.

At the beginning of the Prelude, each motive is associated with one of the distinctive contrapuntal textures, although later in the Prelude a motive may become detached from that texture. For convenience, we will show the motives as they are first heard as part of a distinctive texture (which can be regarded as a motivic group). In Ex. 14-1, motives a_1 and a_2 occur together as the elements of a distinctive texture, *a*.

Texture *a*

Texture *b*

Texture *c*

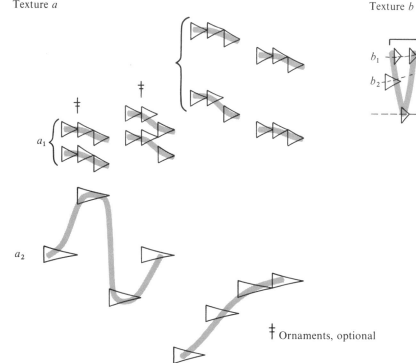

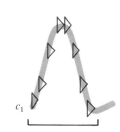

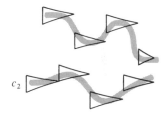

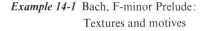

a_1

a_2

b_1 — Faster
b_2 — Slower

Motive

c_1

c_2

‡ Ornaments, optional

Example 14-1 Bach, F-minor Prelude:
Textures and motives

In texture *a*, heard at the very beginning of the Prelude, motive a_2 in the bass line has larger skips but moves through them slowly, firmly, and with legato articulation. Above the bass, the other two parts move together in motive a_1. Their motion is relatively faster, sometimes more stepwise. Pairs of notes are often slurred, and the line is interrupted by brief pauses. (At the beginning of each of the first two slurs, there is a grace note in some performances that momentarily blurs the pattern and strengthens the accent.) The pitch pattern changes subtly in the third and fourth groups of motive a_1, but the sense of the line—and of the texture—is maintained.

In texture *b* (Ex. 14-1), which follows immediately, there are again faster and slower motives, b_1 and b_2. The slower, b_2, is now articulated by brief pauses after each note, and is nowhere as firm or prominent as the motive a_2, although it is moving at the same rate. The faster motive, b_1—twice as fast as a_1—

moves above and below b_2. The *motivic* shape of b_1 is shown separately at the right in Ex. 14-1. But besides this motivic shape, the top notes of b_1 suggest a line, one that moves parallel to the line of b_2 as shown by the upper dotted line in Ex. 14-1. The leftover notes in b_1 (those below b_2) imply a pedal note.

We would not be concerned with these intricacies if there were an expressive vocal melody unfolding over this texture in a keyboard accompaniment, and such details would scarcely be heard in the pungent, percussive sonorities of *Les Noces*. However, in a piece for solo keyboard, details of texture are clearly audible—especially if the composer has made them important in the piece.

With a little reflection, for example, you can see that the shape of the inner line in *b* (motive b_2) is similar to the shape of the top line in *a* (motive a_1) and also to the shape of the bass line in *a* (motive a_2), even if there the intervals are much larger. The same shape

turns up again in texture *c*, in the bass line. Here, however, things are even more complex. A new, faster motive, c_1, assumes prominence in the upper line. Below, there are two lines, each moving slowly and overlapping rhythmically. Thus, a melodic shape (not a single line) runs through the three main textures, and it embodies a continuity that you may hear everywhere in the Prelude, yet may not always be able to locate.

SECTIONS AND RHYTHM. Considered as a whole, the Prelude has well-defined breaks within it. You will soon perceive that these breaks mark off sections that are repeated, in the following order: section *A*, section *A* repeated, section *B*, section *B* repeated. (Considered abstractly, this plan is called *binary*.) The *B* section is half again as long as the *A* section; furthermore, toward its close, the *B* section sounds briefly as though it was returning to the *A* section.

The effect is short-lived, however, and the *B* section soon ends. Still, this hint of a return is an important moment in the *B* section.

Within the large sectional plan, you will become gradually aware of a rhythmic regularity, perceptible first in changes of texture, then later just in changes of motive. These changes usually seem to come at equal intervals, creating a very slow pulse, which you may hear only as a lack of abrupt or unexpected change.

You can grasp this slow pulse by moving up to it from the pulses at the lower levels. The grouping is duple at all levels. The principal level (level III) is marked out by the bass line from texture *a* (Ex. 14-2). Levels II and III are represented by actual rhythmic values throughout the Prelude; level I (the fastest notes) first appears in texture *b*, then later on appears almost continuously. The few interruptions in level I become significant for the structure at higher levels. The regularity with which the rhythms coincide with the meter gives the Prelude its sense of quiet insistence.

Example 14-3 shows the whole Prelude laid out over the measures numbered consecutively from beginning to end. (The measures have not been numbered through the repeats of sections *A* and *B*, however; for the repeat of section *A*, return to the beginning of the diagram and starting counting 1, 2, 3 . . . ; for the repeat of section *B*, start counting 29, 30, 31 . . . .) After you have located the measures with the help of Ex. 14-2, listen to the whole Prelude with Ex. 14-3, noticing that at the beginning, changes of texture usually come every four measures, as shown in the diagram. The exceptions to the grouping in fours are important and tend to be some of the most interesting moments in the piece. The prevailing regularity, however, creates the sense of slow, tranquil movement.

SECTION A OF THE PRELUDE. The kinds of textures encountered are referred to on the right of Ex. 14-3. In section *A* (which is much easier to follow than section *B*), textures *a* and *b* alternate, the second appearance of texture *a* being extended to eight measures instead of four. Texture *c* appears first at measure 21. The only difficult aspect is the texture of the last group (25 through 28): at first, it sounds like a continuation of texture *c*—intensified, certainly,

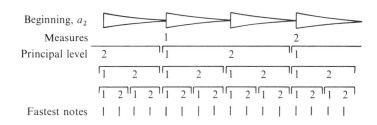

Example 14-2 Bach, F-minor Prelude: Meter

but not drastically different. Then the subtle acceleration of the patterns and the breaking up of the smooth motion prevailing in measures 21 through 24 will eventually call to mind texture *b*. To be more specific, a modified form of motive b_1 appears in the upper part, a modified form of c_2 in the lower part. The degree to which the texture has become more dense in the course of section *A* will become apparent with the repeat of the section and the return of texture *a*, bringing with it a feeling of openness and relaxation.

SECTION B OF THE PRELUDE. The same openness marks the beginning of section *B*, since there, too, we hear texture *a*. From that point on, however, the texture is subject to almost continuous change; the four-measure grouping occasionally gives way to other groupings.

In measures 33 through 36, motive b_1 is on the bottom, while new lines move slowly stepwise on top. Then, in measures 37 through 40, the top moves faster, and the bottom moves consistently without its brief pauses.

After measure 40, the texture moves in only two voices. The motives have now become far removed from their original form, even though the change has been gradual. In the lower part, a motive that is derived ultimately from b_1 alternates with a brief reference to motive c_1. The reference to initial motives, however, is perhaps not so important as the new, subtly different, qualities of line and rhythm emerging here in the middle of the *B* section. The movement seems somehow quicker, even though no rhythmic values faster than those of motive b_1 have

been introduced. The quickening shows up also in the more rapid changes of patterns over measures 45 and 46, then 47 and 48.

The resumption of a four-measure grouping (49 through 52) brings a sense of breadth—especially in connection with the clear reference in the upper part to texture *c*. This upper line is, to be sure, an inversion of texture *c*, and below it is something that sounds more like the top of *a*; but in spite of these intricacies, the sense of grouping in fours is clearer.

In measures 53 through 56, the motives change every two measures and now have but a tenuous relationship to the original motives. Because of this further departure, the return of texture *a* at measure 57, even though brief, is clearly identifiable. The sense of quickened motion is most apparent immediately after this return: something about the motion in measures 57 through 62—the way the lines twist and turn as if in a confined space, perhaps—makes this passage seem the most intense of the piece.

HARMONIC AREAS. Changes in texture and motive (especially rhythmic motive) have provided a sense of organization at a middle level—that of the four-measure grouping. At higher levels, the changes in harmonic area are very important in shaping the Prelude and in making it expressive, even though the areas are relatively close and the changes from one area to another smooth, not sudden. These changes, together with a few other features of harmonic organization to be discussed here, are summarized in Ex. 14-4.

Example 14-3 Bach, F-minor Prelude: Plan of textures, motives, phrases

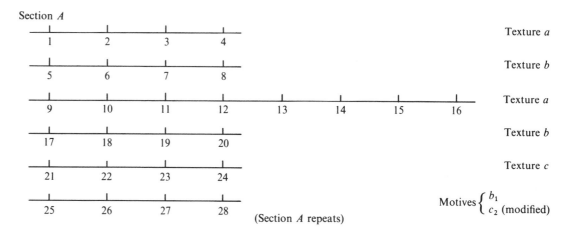

Section *A*

| 1 | 2 | 3 | 4 | | | | | Texture *a*
| 5 | 6 | 7 | 8 | | | | | Texture *b*
| 9 | 10 | 11 | 12 | 13 | 14 | 15 | 16 | Texture *a*
| 17 | 18 | 19 | 20 | | | | | Texture *b*
| 21 | 22 | 23 | 24 | | | | | Texture *c*
| 25 | 26 | 27 | 28 |

(Section *A* repeats)

Motives $\begin{cases} b_1 \\ c_2 \text{ (modified)} \end{cases}$

Section *B*

| 29 | 30 | 31 | 32 | Texture $a \begin{cases} a_1 \\ a_2 \end{cases}$
| 33 | 34 | 35 | 36 | $\{$ Motive b_1
| 37 | 38 | 39 | 40 | A new, two-voiced texture using b_1/c_1
| 41 | 42 | 43 | 44 | 45 | 46 | 47 | 48 |
| 49 | 50 | 51 | 52 | $\begin{cases} c_1 \\ a_1, \text{ modified} \end{cases}$
| 53 | 54 | 55 | 56 |

$\begin{Bmatrix} b_2 \\ b_1 \end{Bmatrix}$ modified, $\begin{cases} b_1 \\ \text{adapted from developments} \end{cases}$

Return

| 57 | 58 | 59 | 60 | 61 | 62 | Texture *a*, briefly
| 63 | 64 | 65 | 66 | Texture *c*
| 67 | 68 | 69 | 70 | $\begin{cases} b_1 \\ c_2 \end{cases}$

Section *B* repeats

Example 14-4 Bach, F-minor Prelude: Harmonic movement

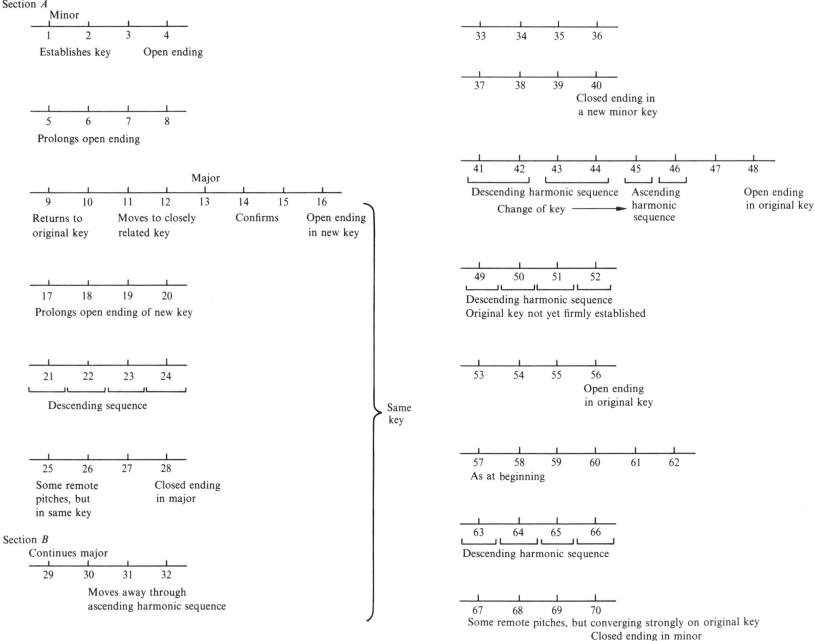

Section *A*

Minor

| 1 | 2 | 3 | 4 |

Establishes key   Open ending

| 5 | 6 | 7 | 8 |

Prolongs open ending

Major

| 9 | 10 | 11 | 12 | 13 | 14 | 15 | 16 |

Returns to   Moves to closely   Confirms   Open ending
original key   related key   in new key

| 17 | 18 | 19 | 20 |

Prolongs open ending of new key

| 21 | 22 | 23 | 24 |

Descending sequence

| 25 | 26 | 27 | 28 |

Some remote   Closed ending
pitches, but   in major
in same key

Section *B*

Continues major

| 29 | 30 | 31 | 32 |

Moves away through
ascending harmonic sequence

| 33 | 34 | 35 | 36 |

| 37 | 38 | 39 | 40 |

Closed ending in
a new minor key

| 41 | 42 | 43 | 44 | 45 | 46 | 47 | 48 |

Descending harmonic sequence   Ascending   Open ending
harmonic   in original key
Change of key ⟶   sequence

| 49 | 50 | 51 | 52 |

Descending harmonic sequence
Original key not yet firmly established

| 53 | 54 | 55 | 56 |

Open ending
in original key

| 57 | 58 | 59 | 60 | 61 | 62 |

As at beginning

| 63 | 64 | 65 | 66 |

Descending harmonic sequence

| 67 | 68 | 69 | 70 |

Some remote pitches, but converging strongly on original key
Closed ending in minor

Same key

The Prelude establishes a minor key at its very beginning in texture *a*; texture *b* serves to confirm the key while prolonging the sense of openness associated with the leading chord of the key. The pedal note implied at the bottom of texture *b* is an important factor in the leading harmony.

When texture *a* first returns (measures 9 and 10), it does so in the original minor key, then moves immediately to a closely related area in major (measures 11 and 12). From here to the end of section *A*, the music remains in this major area; furthermore, section *B* begins in the same area. If we take into account only the beginning and end of sections *A* and *B*, then, the original minor key and the subsequent major one are the most important keys of the Prelude: they are the poles of its harmonic movement (Ex. 14-5).

The relatively long harmonic and melodic sequence associated with texture *c* (measures 21 through 24) remains within the newly established major key. Even the expressive pitches introduced from outside this major area after the sequence (measures 25 through 28) seem to intensify rather than to weaken the area.

While the move to the major area is relatively clear and easy to hear, it is not very spectacular; more intense harmonic motion takes place in the *B* section —first through the sequence in the *a* texture (measures 31 and 32), then in the various extensions and developments that follow. The main point of arrival is the clear cadence in measure 40, in a new minor key. From here to the return of texture *a* in measure 57, the harmony finds its way gradually back to the original key. Generally speaking, the harmonic movement of the Prelude is leisurely—comparable to the slow pulse associated with the changes of texture and the grouping of downbeats in fours.

LINEAR RELATIONSHIPS. The greatest interest of the piece—and the chief source of its expressivity—lies, not in the larger rhythms with their relatively regular proportions, but rather in the way the details of line and rhythm fit into, or sometimes strain against, them. The development of motives (which we only began to trace) is a source of special interest.

For example, after a certain amount of reflection, one can find an origin for the seemingly long lines that

These two keys serve as poles of the harmonic movement in the Prelude.

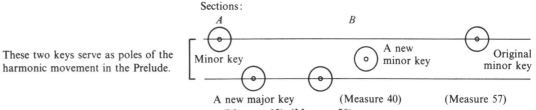

Example 14-5 Bach, F-minor Prelude: Poles of harmonic movement

soar over motive b_1 when it appears near the beginning of the *B* section (measures 33 through 36). They come from the line implied at one point in motive a_1 (measures 3 and 4, see Ex. 14-6). At that point, motive a_1 is not heard as a stepwise descending *line*, because in texture *a* the sense of line is so strongly represented in the bass, the upper parts being more concerned with rhythmic figure. In the passage from section *B*, the

sustained expressive lines are seemingly new, yet strangely reminiscent. Of such stuff are the intimate effects of the Prelude made.

Further familiarity with the Prelude would open up layer after layer of relationships. These would eventually become so subtle that one would not want to fix them in a diagram or description but would prefer to let them float freely in the sound of the

Example 14-6 Bach, F-minor Prelude: Derivation of lines at beginning of section *B*

Section *A*, beginning

Upper part only

Section *B*

Upper parts only

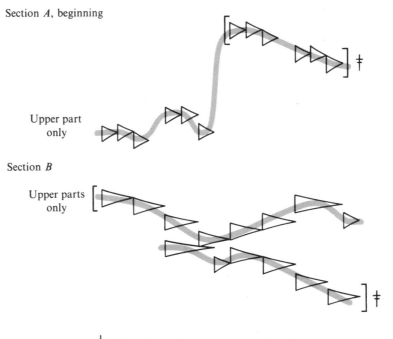

‡ These descending segments are related.

301

piece as performed, changing their meaning from one listening to another. If pieces such as this one have more profound layers of meaning, they are apt to involve the more fragile relationships among details—relationships that come to our attention only after we have become familiar with the more obvious, external features.

F-MINOR FUGUE. The Fugue is in the same harmonic area as the Prelude: you can hear the beginning of the Fugue grow right out of the chord at the end of the Prelude. The Fugue makes a move to the same major area that is found in the Prelude and in other, more subtle ways reproduces the Prelude's harmonic organization. If anything, the Fugue focuses on one harmonic area more than the Prelude does: the harmonic motion seems to circle ever more closely around the central harmony as the Fugue progresses.

IMITATIVE TEXTURE IN THE FUGUE. One of the important differences between Prelude and Fugue is in texture. Fugues in general tend to have an *imitative* contrapuntal texture, especially at their beginning. The initial use of imitation is one of the distinctive marks of a fugue. What happens after the beginning is more variable; the two fugues we will study proceed in two different ways. But (speaking generally again) fugues tend to be *contrapuntal* throughout; that is, they tend to have clear, distinct lines that can be followed separately, rather than blocklike chords or a texture of melody and accompaniment. So persistent is contrapuntal texture in fugues (including both of the fugues we will study) that we sometimes refer to the individual lines as "voices," just as if the F-minor

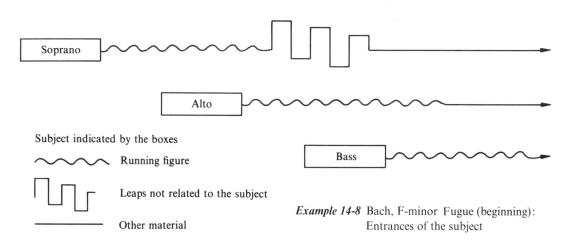

Subject indicated by the boxes

〜〜〜 Running figure

⎍⌐⎍ Leaps not related to the subject

———— Other material

Example 14-8 Bach, F-minor Fugue (beginning): Entrances of the subject

Fugue, for example, were sung by soprano, alto, and bass, instead of being played on a keyboard instrument. We will represent the three-voiced texture of the F-minor Fugue in our diagrams.

THE FUGUE SUBJECT AND ITS MOTIVES. The Fugue is begun by a solo "voice," the one that will turn out to be the "soprano." The line first heard at the beginning of the soprano part is the theme or *subject* of the Fugue: it will reappear throughout the Fugue in different voices and varying contexts, giving the Fugue a melodic identity. Perhaps the most ear-catching features of the subject are the leaps up and down, contrasted with the repeated notes (Ex. 14-7).

Once past these arresting leaps, the subject starts to run in stepwise motion with faster note values. At first, this faster part of the subject will seem mere

background noise. But it is characteristic of fugues that little or nothing is wasted; all of the subject usually reappears at least once in the fugue, often with a new function. For this reason, you should notice the motivic components of the running part of the subject as shown in Ex. 14-7. These components include an ascending motive (*a*), a turning motive (*b*), and another turning motive that starts with a little leap upward (*c*). We will not attempt to trace every appearance of these motives; but if they once come to your attention in the subject, you will hear and identify them at numerous places throughout the Fugue.

When the "alto" enters (Ex. 14-8), the soprano continues with the running motives *b*, *c*, and *a*, which now sound against the leaping part of the subject. The capacity of the subject for combination with itself is

Example 14-7 Bach, F-minor Fugue: Motives

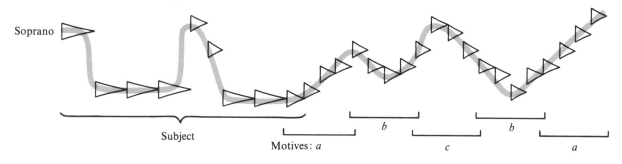

one of the sources of fascination found in fugues.

After the alto finishes the subject (both leaping and running parts), it continues as did the soprano when the alto entered. Meanwhile the soprano goes on to something else—slightly slower notes with big leaps one after another. These leaps are not so closely related to the subject; they do seem related to previous material, however, even if we cannot immediately identify the source.

Between the alto and bass entrances, there is a slightly longer time interval than between the soprano and alto entrances. These time intervals have definite rhythmic significance, for there is a slow pulse in the Fugue, just as there was in the Prelude. When the bass finally enters, soprano and alto go on to new material, only occasionally reminiscent of the subject's running motives.

ENTRANCES OF THE SUBJECT THROUGHOUT THE FUGUE. The first thing to listen for in the Fugue as a whole is the reappearance of the subject—the leaping part. Some of these reappearances are clear, some are partially hidden. Example 14-9 shows their approximate location in the Fugue and also the voice in which they appear. You could make such a diagram yourself, for this or any other fugue.

Example 14-9 includes a few other prominent features associated with the various entrances of the subject. Entrances 4 and 5 are in closely related major keys; that of entrance 4 is the same key into which section *A* of the Prelude moves and stays. As in the Prelude, the sound of the major is contrasted more sharply with the minor by using the same material (texture *a* in the case of the Prelude, the subject in the Fugue), first in minor then in major. In the Fugue, the leaping part of the subject particularly seems to take on a different character in major.

Entrance 6, in the bass, returns to the original minor key, as does also entrance 7. This alto entrance may be hard to hear; it not only is in the middle voice but also has a disguised beginning; furthermore, it occurs over a prominent pedal note in the bass, which seems to absorb the other voices temporarily into the harmonies built up over the pedal note.

In two places after entrance 7, you may think the pedal note is starting again, but each time it is merely

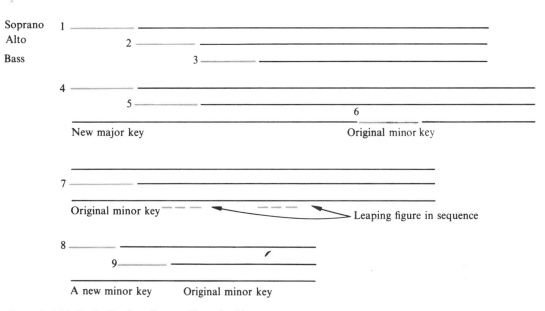

Example 14-9 Bach, F-minor Fugue: Plan of subject entrances

the repeated notes from the subject (and the leaping figure associated with them) sounding in ascending sequence in the bass. While these references to the subject are very clear, they do not count as full entrances.

Entrance 8 begins in a minor key other than the original one; furthermore, it is shorter than usual. Entrance 9, alto, follows entrance 8 at a time interval shorter than those at the beginning, and both entrances are broken off before they run through the normal form of the subject. This foreshortening will become more clear when we trace the high-level rhythm of the Fugue.

RHYTHM AT LOW AND HIGH LEVELS. The low-level rhythms of the Fugue, like those of the Prelude, are organized in duple meter throughout. The Fugue subject starts on an upbeat—a distinctive feature of this particular subject—but, aside from that, the rhythms align themselves easily into measures, as indicated in Ex. 14-10. We will use measure numbers for reference in the Fugue.

It is clear from Ex. 14-10 that the time interval between the first two entrances is four measures long: the subject begins with the upbeat before the first measure, and the upbeat of the next entrance comes at the very end of the fourth measure. This, at any

Example 14-10 F-minor Fugue: Rhythm of subject

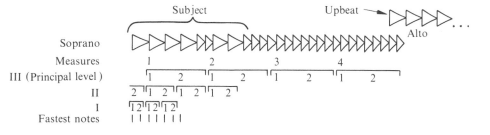

Example 14-11 Bach, F-minor Fugue: Plan

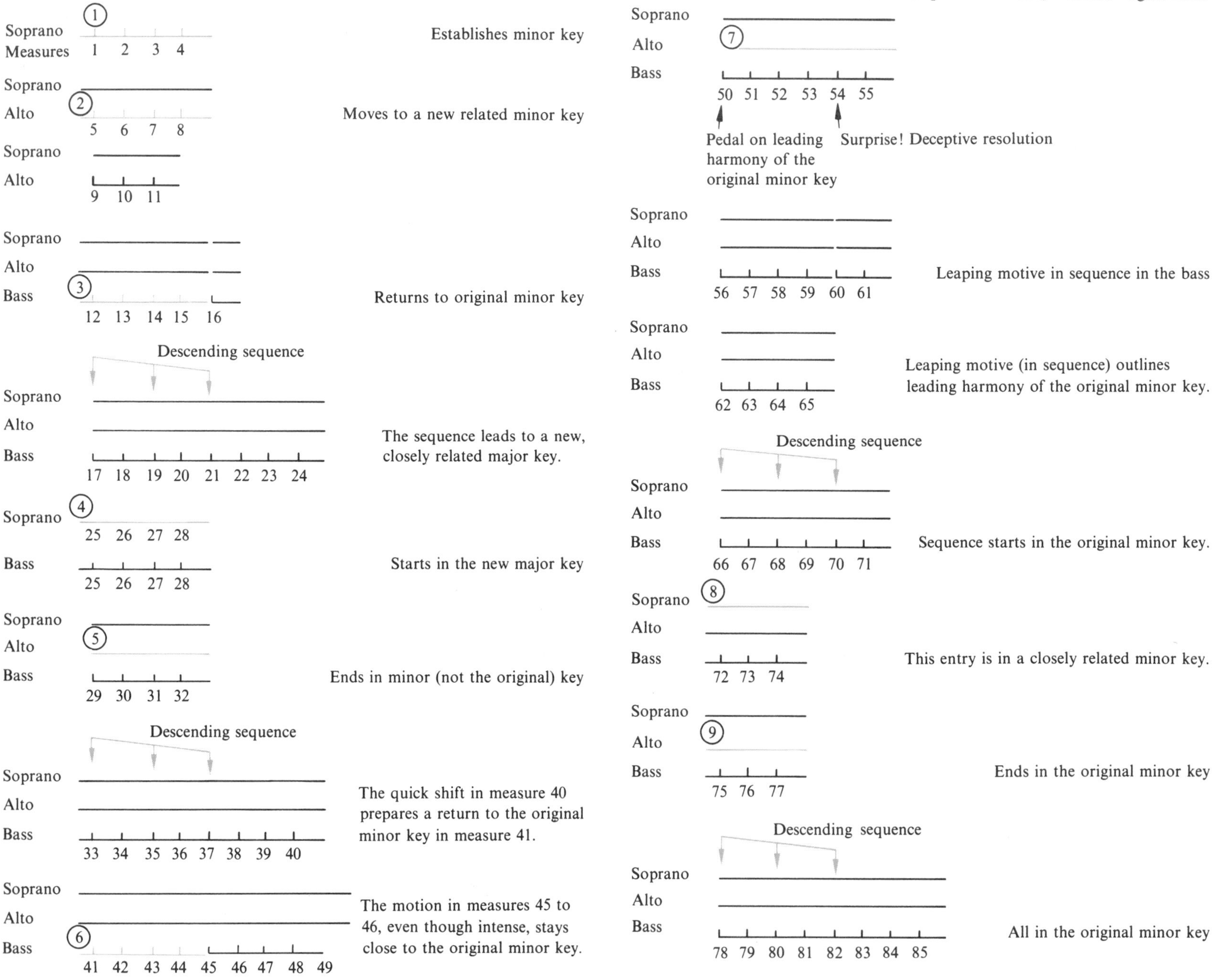

rate, is the arrangement at the beginning of the Fugue; we already noticed that toward the end of the Fugue the arrangement of entrances seems foreshortened. Between the beginning and the end, the four-measure grouping is increasingly sprung out of shape as the Fugue progresses.

Example 14-11 lays out the Fugue from beginning to end over consecutively numbered measures. Count two beats per measure (on level III) in Ex. 14-10, at first through the subject alone (for practice); then count through the whole Fugue with the help of Ex. 14-11. As you can see, Ex. 14-11 is merely Ex. 14-9 with measure numbers added and with rhythmic groupings made more clear by breaking up the diagram into distinct lines.

Begin to work with Ex. 14-11 by looking only at the lengths of the lines and the number of measures in each. The lines are set up to emphasize the four-measure grouping, which you should gradually begin to feel as a slow pulse.

The subject at the beginning, as we heard, is in four-measure groups. The interlude between entrances 2 and 3 is only three measures, but this does not interfere seriously with the impression of regularity created by the subject.

Measure 17 starts a broad descending sequence. It is really a harmonic sequence, reflected in all three voices. The music of this sequence comes four times in the Fugue, in slightly different arrangements and different keys; but each time, because of the clarity and regularity of its patterning, it brings with it a feeling of breadth and sweep that marks these places as among the loftiest in the Fugue. Usually, the descending sequence generates enough momentum to ride over one four-measure grouping on into another. Even though the sequence does not continue through the next four measures, its force continues to be felt for a group of eight measures. The third appearance of the sequence (measures 66 through 71) is broken off short by the return of entrance 8.

The irregularity of a single odd measure at measure 16 is probably not noticed or else is felt simply as an extension. Even though they may not be noticed, such extensions are important: complete regularity in a piece whose low-level rhythm is as insistent as this would soon have a dulling effect. An extension or abbreviation by even a single measure not only makes the rhythm more sprightly but also adds a sense of freshness to the whole sound of a piece.

After entrance 6 (bass) the irregularities in measure groupings are severe enough to dislocate our sense of high-level rhythm. Increased animation in measures 45 through 48 causes the rhythm to spill over the end of a four-measure group. Then the pedal starts at an odd spot in the deteriorating pattern. Finally the subject enters in the alto, preceded by a special melodic windup; but if we feel this entry in measure 51 as the start of a four-measure group, it is only with a wrench.

The fourth measure of entrance 7 (measure 54) has a striking harmonic effect. (At such moments, we need to consider the totality of what is happening, even if it means cutting across artificial divisions of melody, harmony, and rhythm.) Actually, the deceptive harmony in measure 54 does not move very far away; it merely substitutes a closely related harmony for the central one expected after the pedal on the leading harmony. This low-level harmonic change, however, is translated into an event of high potential by its position relative to the subject and to the process affecting rhythmic groups of measures at that point. A great surge is felt as a result of everything that has happened since measure 45.

Little by little, a sense of regularity is reestablished —partly by the insistent repetition of the leaping motive in the bass, partly by the strong resurgence of the descending sequence in measure 66. Even this regularity, however, is broken by entrance 8.

Entrances 8 and 9 are clearly in three-measure groups: the alto (entrance 9) enters too soon by one measure and in turn is broken off one measure early by the last appearance of the broad descending sequence. Such an acceleration of entries is apt to be the climactic event of a fugue; it has a special name, *stretto*, which means "tightening up" in Italian. And, indeed, a rhythmic tightening up is clearly apparent, once we can perceive the four-measure grouping as a norm.

HARMONIC MOTION. Example 14-11 includes, at the right, indications of the most prominent harmonic motion. The second entrance (alto) is obviously not identical in pitch to the first. It is at a different pitch level and even differs in some of its intervals. For our purposes, it is enough to note that it involves a slight shift of harmonic area—not far away, but still a shift, Entrance 3 brings a return to the original area, even though the subject is an octave lower in the bass than it was in the soprano.

We already mentioned the turn to a major key, an echo of the major key at the end of section *A* in the Prelude. The rest of the Fugue tends to stick more closely to the original key—or, at any rate, the moves to other minor keys are not as strongly established as in the Prelude. It is for this reason, perhaps, that the deceptive cadence in measure 54 comes as such a surprise.

PRELUDE AND FUGUE NO. 5 IN D MAJOR. The Prelude and Fugue in D major seem to have even less in common with each other than the Prelude and Fugue in F minor. In rhythm and figuration, the Prelude in D is drastically different from its Fugue. The difference in character may be greater or less in various performances but will never be eliminated completely in any reasonable interpretation. Performances of the Fugue in particular will vary considerably, with consequent changes in the balance of Fugue with Prelude. The Fugue may be a slow, reflective sequel to a lively Prelude or a slow, emphatic one; or it could be the Prelude that is slower (hence— given the nature of its figuration—heavily ornate) with the Fugue lighter and more animated. You will probably be able to decide which interpretation you prefer, but you may have difficulty deciding which interpretation best suits the composer's intention. There often seems to be no definitive way of resolving that question in the case of *The Well-Tempered Clavier*.

The D-major Prelude and Fugue do share the same key, and that may be their only explicit bond—aside from being played one after the other on the same instrument by the same performer. One might add, however, that in this case the Prelude is usually contrapuntal. No specific link is thereby established with the Fugue, but a certain continuity of texture does result.

The Prelude bristles with lively figuration that assumes thematic importance. On first hearing, you may be most aware of this figuration repeated incessantly, occupying the whole foreground with an almost oppressive luxuriance; the larger design may be completely hidden. Yet there is an important plan to the Prelude, at the level of phrase as well as of section. Our principal task will be to relate the luxuriant detail to this phrase and section plan.

PLAN OF THE PRELUDE. The section plan at the highest level can be easily described; it is the same plan (binary) as found in the F-minor Prelude. There are two sections, each to be repeated—but these repeats may be lacking in some performances. If the repeats are played, they establish by their mere presence the plan *A A B B*. There is a clear break at the end of section *A*. Section *B* is considerably longer than section *A*.

In the F-minor Prelude, we found a brief return of figure *a*, in the original key, toward the end of the *B* section. In the D-major Prelude, a substantial repeat of the *A* section takes place at the analogous point in the plan. Even though not exact, this repeat is similar enough to warrant expressing the section plan as A_1 A_1 B A_2 B A_2. (This plan is sometimes called *rounded binary*—"rounded" referring to the return of *A*—or sometimes *ternary*, because if the Prelude is played without repeats as A_1 B A_2, there are three successive sections.) The Menuetto of Haydn's Symphony No. 100 uses the same plan. The repeat at A_2 is not preceded by a break; but before it there is a prominent descending figure leading precipitously down to the low note that starts both sections A_1 and A_2.

THEME AND MOTIVES. The incessant repetition of the principal motives makes phrase structure extremely hard to hear in this Prelude. In order to detect phrases, we must start at the lowest metric levels, working our way up to rhythms that are expressed as groups of measures.

The theme, as heard at the very beginning, is shown in Ex. 14-12. Considered as a line, the theme is a straightforward ascent; the simple, regular turns downward do not obscure its direction. There are only two motives—the rapid stepwise motion of the first five notes (not counting the low bass note, which is an independent event) and the down-and-back

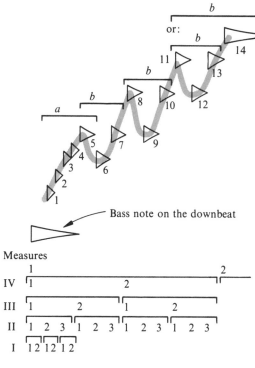

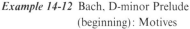

Example 14-12 Bach, D-minor Prelude (beginning): Motives

figure described by notes 5 through 7 (or 8 through 10 or 11 through 13). This three-note motive, labeled *b*, can be followed by a fourth note, for example, notes 11 through 14.

METER IN THE PRELUDE. The notes of motive *a* provide the fastest pulse; they are grouped in twos, at level I. The notes of motive *b* provide the pulse at the next higher level (II); this pulse is grouped in threes. If you decided that level II was the principal level (in other words, if you felt the piece had a fast beat), then the meter would be triple. However, you would discover that these triple measures were always grouped in twos (at level III) and the twos in twos (at level IV) regularly throughout the Prelude. The groupings at levels III and IV, then, are more than just tendencies toward regularity; they are metric.

We have not encountered, in this book, a piece whose structure was metric at so many levels—especially at levels above the principal level. Level II is likely to be felt as the principal level by many listeners, for the piece seems (intuitively) "fast," and the fast triple pulse at level II seems an appropriate beat. The pulse at level III, although metric, seems a little slow for a beat; the pulse at level IV is much too slow for a beat. Yet levels II and IV are metric levels—indeed, level IV provides a metric grouping essential to an understanding of the rhythm. To keep track of the highest level of the piece, we will have to count groups at level IV in the same way we have counted measures in other pieces.

You will need practice to hear the long-breathed rhythms of the Prelude. A convenient occasion is provided by the first four level-IV groups—or measures, as we will call them for convenience. Measures 1 and 3 contain the theme; measures 2 and 4 contain a contrasting motive found only here and at the beginning of sections *B* and A_2, always in alternation with the theme (Ex. 14-13). The contrasting motive descends easily in stepwise motion over a slowly leaping bass.

The contrasting motive is played differently in various performances, due to a presumed ambiguity in Bach's notation. The meter of this motive can either continue in its previously established pattern of three beats at level II for every beat at level III (Ex. 14-13, detail) or change to two beats at level II for every level-III beat. In the first case, the faster notes are uneven in length; in the second case, they are even.

However performed, measure 2 is a contrast to measure 1: taken together the two measures are a clear expression of "On the one hand . . . on the other . . . ." Measure 3 is like measure 1, except that the theme sounds an octave lower; measure 4 is like measure 2, with somewhat more rearrangement of pitches. The regular contrasts in these measures, placed in the context of a very stable harmonic area (with nothing but central and leading harmonies) contribute to the sense of a clear four-measure grouping.

Practice with Ex. 14-13 until you can confidently count the measures at their slow pace. Then listen to the whole Prelude while following Ex. 14-14; ignore

Example 14-13 Bach, D-major Prelude:
The contrasting motive

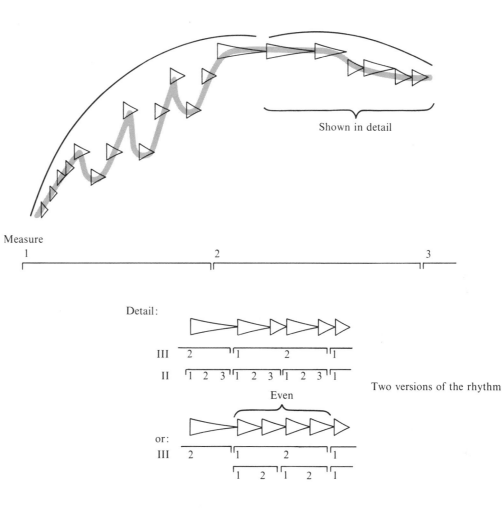

Measure

1   2   3

Shown in detail

Detail:

III   2   1   2   1

II   1   2   3   1   2   3   1   2   3   1   Two versions of the rhythm

Even

or:

III   2   1   2   1

1   2   1   2   1

all the indications in the diagram except the measure numbers, just following these through the bristling configurations of the theme during the first few hearings.

THEME AND MOTIVE IN SECTION A. As you follow through with Ex. 14-14, you will gradually sense the way the music falls easily into the four- or eight-measure groups represented by separate lines in the diagram. Many factors work together to produce these groupings; the first thing is to perceive their existence. The four-measure groups in Ex. 14-14 (that is, the shorter horizontal lines) tend to be clearly marked at their ends, but a division in the middle of the eight-measure groups is sometimes less clear and often is not present. Since the eight-measure groups do not contradict the four-measure groups and since these latter are so clearly set out at the beginning of both *A* and *B* sections, you should have no difficulty understanding the eight as doublings of the fours.

Once you can follow Ex. 14-14 through the whole Prelude, listen for the continuous use of the theme, whose linear direction is represented by the ascending and descending arrows. These arrows are placed roughly above or below the horizontal line, depending on whether the theme appears in a higher or lower register. Thus, in measure 1, the ascending arrow representing the ascending theme (compare Ex. 14-13) is placed above the line, while in measure 3 the same ascending line placed below the line represents the same theme an octave lower in pitch. The contrasting motive in measures 2 and 4 is not represented,

Example 14-14 Bach, D-major Prelude: Plan

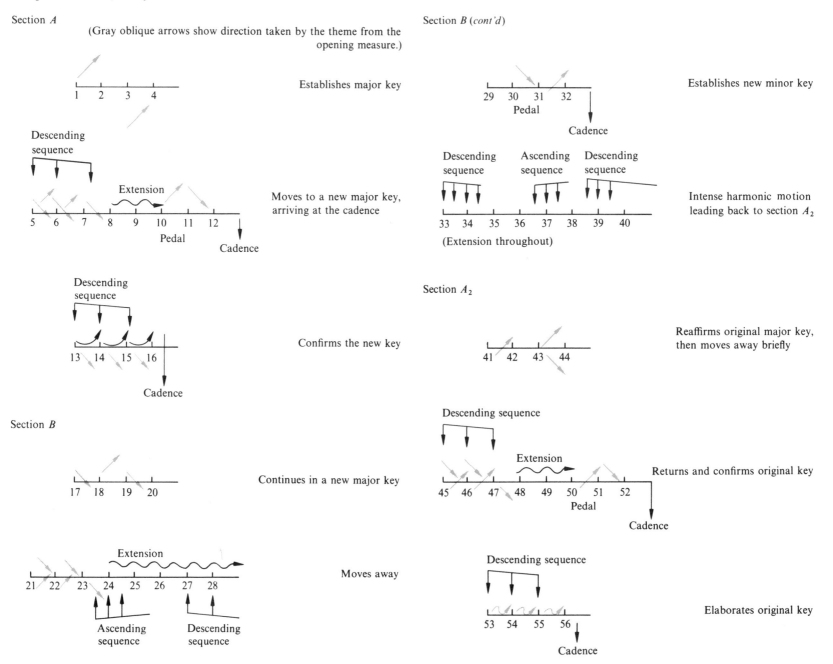

Section *A*

(Gray oblique arrows show direction taken by the theme from the opening measure.)

1 2 3 4   Establishes major key

Descending sequence

5 6 7 8 9 10 11 12   Moves to a new major key, arriving at the cadence
Extension
Pedal
Cadence

Descending sequence

13 14 15 16   Confirms the new key
Cadence

Section *B*

17 18 19 20   Continues in a new major key

21 22 23 24 25 26 27 28   Moves away
Extension
Ascending sequence   Descending sequence

Section *B* (*cont'd*)

29 30 31 32   Establishes new minor key
Pedal
Cadence

Descending sequence   Ascending sequence   Descending sequence

33 34 35 36 37 38 39 40   Intense harmonic motion leading back to section *A*₂

(Extension throughout)

Section *A*₂

41 42 43 44   Reaffirms original major key, then moves away briefly

Descending sequence

45 46 47 48 49 50 51 52   Returns and confirms original key
Extension
Pedal
Cadence

Descending sequence

53 54 55 56   Elaborates original key
Cadence

308

since it appears only here, then in measures 18 and 20, and finally in measures 42 and 44.

Almost all the other measures have some form of the theme itself or a motivic extension of the theme. Often the theme is combined with itself in imitation. Right away in measure 5, for example, the theme is heard descending at the beginning of the measure, then ascending at the middle of the measure. In these two appearances, the theme is shortened to half a measure. To complicate the texture even more, the rapid stepwise motive from the beginning of the theme is heard yet again at the end of the measure, descending. These appearances of the theme in measure 5 are shown in Ex. 14-15.

The pattern of measure 5 is repeated in measure 6, one step lower in pitch. Measures 5 and 6, in other words, constitute a descending sequence. The pattern is started a third time, another step lower, in measure 7; but the ascending statement of the theme is omitted, and the sequence peters out.

Example 14-15 Bach, D-major Prelude (measure 5): Motivic detail

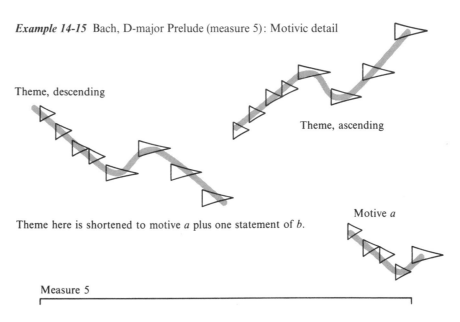

Theme, descending

Theme, ascending

Motive *a*

Theme here is shortened to motive *a* plus one statement of *b*.

Measure 5

Example 14-16 Bach, D-major Prelude (measures 8 and 9): Motivic detail

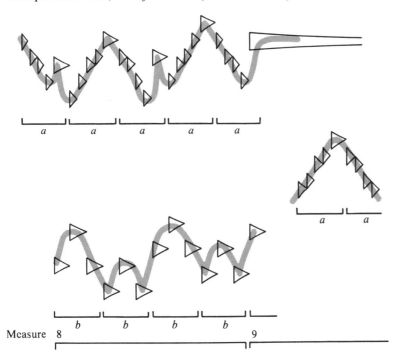

a *a* *a* *a* *a*

a *a*

b *b* *b* *b*

Measure 8 9

Motive *a* appears at the end of measure 7 up high instead of down low. Its rapid motion carries on through measure 8, by simple repetition of the motive. The whole measure can be regarded as a motivic extension. While motive *a* is being extended in the upper of the two lines, motive *b* is being extended in the lower line. Then, in measure 9, the whole pattern formed by the extension of motive *a* is repeated in a lower octave. This particular kind of extension, which accounts for much of the Prelude, is shown in Ex. 14-16.

Measure 10 brings back the theme in its original form—at least, as far as contour of line is concerned. A new harmonic context is provided by the choice of pitches, supported by a pedal in this measure and the next (where the theme appears again intact, descending). Further on, we will identify the harmonic function of these measures; here, note that measure 12, which resolves the harmonic motion into important cadence, has neither the theme nor its motives —being one of the few measures so lacking.

309

Measures 13 through 16 each contain the theme (descending) in imitation, with added complications (Ex. 14-17). Motive *a* appears twice in succession, followed by a modified form of *b*. The second entrance in each measure, imitating the first in a lower register, has time only for the two statements of motive *a*. Yet the effect is much closer to a statement of the theme than to motivic extension as found in measure 8.

Measures 14 and 15 repeat the pattern of measure 13 at successively lower steps, the three measures forming a descending sequence. The last measure of the section, measure 16, resembles measure 12: each lacks the theme or any other rhythmic motion on level I, each leads to a firm cadence.

HARMONIC MOVEMENT IN SECTION A₁. The two cadences in measures 12 and 16 are in the same harmonic area—an area different from the beginning of the Prelude—as you can easily hear at the moment the repetition of section A_1 begins. The whole A_1 section is shaped by a straightforward harmonic movement from the original area to a closely related one: the leading harmony of the original area becomes a central harmony at the end of the section. This, too, you can hear at the moment of repetition, when the last harmony of the section changes its function from a central harmony to the leading harmony of the beginning of the section.

You should be able to sense when this harmonic movement within section A_1 begins—the moment when the tide begins to run. The first four measures are stable; they move nowhere, as far as harmonic area is concerned. When the texture gets denser in measure 5, the harmonic movement begins. It continues steadily through the descending sequence in measures 6 and 7. The long pedal in measures 10, 11, and 12 provides the leading harmony for the new key, which is reached with the cadence in measure 12. The second descending sequence in measures 13 through 15 has the effect first of a digression, then of a roundabout confirmation of the new key, confirmed by the cadence in measure 16.

Thus the harmonic movement gives sense to the division of the section into groups of four, eight, and four measures. The first four measures establish the original area. The next eight measures make the move

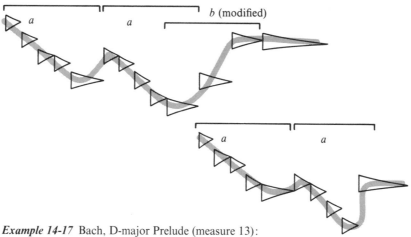

Example 14-17 Bach, D-major Prelude (measure 13): Motivic detail

to a new area. The last four confirm that area. This harmonic movement is summarized at the right of Ex. 14-14.

At the first encounter with the Prelude, you may well have found the repetitions of the theme too prominent, too insistent to permit a clear grasp of the larger design. They are prominent, there is no doubt. But by now you should begin to hear how different uses of the theme reinforce different phases of the form. Use of the theme in imitation coincides with harmonic movement, with opening up of the form to expansion. Motivic extension carries forward the expanding motion. Return of the theme in more integral shape tends to be associated with arrival or confirmation.

REFERENCE POINTS IN SECTIONS B AND A₂. As you already heard, the rest of the Prelude is repeated as a unit; but, on closer inspection, you will discover that a return of the *A* material at the end effectively subdivides the rest of the Prelude into sections $B\,A_2$. Furthermore, from Ex. 14-14 it can be seen that the *B* section (that is, measures 17 through 41, up to the return of the *A* material) is longer than A_1. You will find that the *B* section itself is divided into two still substantial subsections and that the latter part of the *B* section contains what might be regarded as the high point of the piece.

The imitations and extensions applied to the theme become more intense during the *B* section. We will discuss them in detail, but first try to grasp the outlines of this more difficult section. Follow through with the help of Ex. 14-14, listening for three particular moments—the beginning of section *B*, the cadence in measure 33, and the return of section A_2, in measure 41.

In spite of its initially amorphous impression, the *B* section can be regarded as an expanded, intensified version of A_1, as suggested in Ex. 14-18. The internal cadence at measure 33 is the reference point that permits the clear alignment with section A_1. Before the cadence (and the pedal), a length of four extra measures has been added. After the cadence, measure 33 sounds very much like 13; that measure in the A_1 section began a brief digression confirming the new key. In the *B* section, the same music begins the more extended digression that leads to the high point of the section.

The beginning of section *B* is similar to that of section A_1. There are differences: the theme is inverted—it descends instead of ascending; the contrasting motive in measures 18 and 20 (same as in measures 2 and 4) is buried under exuberant extensions of the theme, as is the second statement of the theme in measure 19 (same as in measure 3). Still, measures 17 through 20 have the solid, square shape

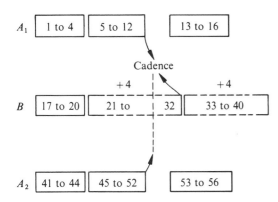

| A_1 | 1 to 4 | 5 to 12 | | 13 to 16 |

Cadence

| | | +4 | | +4 |
| B | 17 to 20 | 21 to | 32 | 33 to 40 |

| A_2 | 41 to 44 | 45 to 52 | | 53 to 56 |

Example 14-18 Bach, D-major Prelude: Comparison of sections A_1, B, and A_2

of measures 1 through 4; clearly, they make the beginning of section B sound like section A_1, in the new key confirmed at the end of section A_1.

After what will surely seem to be very dense texture with swirling lines and unstable harmonies, you will perceive a pedal note emerging in measure 30 (shown in Ex. 14-14). The music at this point will sound familiar—more familiar, that is, than what has immediately preceded it. Both the pedal and the use of the theme over it are very similar to the pedal in section A_1 (measures 30 through 32 are the same as measures 10 through 12). The pedal leads to the cadence, which falls on the beginning of measure 33 (same as measure 13). The main difference is in harmonic area: the area is minor now instead of major; and the center has shifted, being neither the original center nor the one established at the end of section A_1.

What follows is even more dense than before and even further from the theme in its original form. By the beginning of measure 40, the music seems to have tied itself up into a hard knot; but, on being wrenched, the knot suddenly comes apart, and the tension is abruptly released by the return of the theme in its original form, in the original harmonic area, and alternating with the contrasting motive—which now seems very calm and collected. (We could almost imagine Susanna stepping out of the closet; compare pages 243 and 247.)

MOTIVIC EXTENSION IN SECTION B. With these three reference points firmly fixed, we can plunge into the detail of section B without fear of losing our way. There is a tendency throughout the section for motive a to turn into a series of continuous rapid notes, losing thereby its thematic identity. This happens immediately, in measure 18, over the contrasting element (Ex. 14-19). The extension begun in measure 18 spills over into measure 19, obscuring the relationship between the contrasting element and the theme. Nor does the extension stop there: a trill in measure 19 passes the rapid motion on to further extension in measure 20, which covers up the second appearance of the contrasting element. This proliferation of motive a will characterize almost all of section B.

Example 14-19 Bach, D-major Prelude (measures 18 and 19): Motivic detail

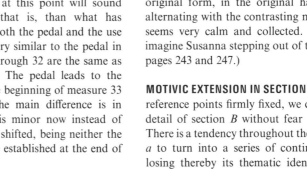

Measure
18

19

Motivic extension

a

Theme

b

a

Trill

Theme (descending)

Contrasting motive, in chords, ascending

311

Measures 21 through 32 assume the general shape of a long arch, subsuming much intense motivic detail. The imitative patterns in measures 21 and 22 are similar to those in measures 5 and 6, being merely compounded with the more insistent counterpoint of motive in the bass. In fact, to some degree the B section is following the order of events in section A_1 closely; but an expansive force is opening up the original shape.

An ascending sequence in measures 23 and 24 is formed in the soprano out of motive a. The ascending motion leads to a plateau in measures 25 and 26. A long descent starts in measure 27; here motive a has turned again into continuous rapid notes covering the next three measures (27, 28, and 29). A statement of the theme in measure 27, in the bass, is scarcely noticed. The descent is followed by the bass pedal note in measure 30, our previously established reference point for this first subsection of B.

The pedal note and the cadence provide a moment of relative relaxation. As soon as the cadence is reached, however, we are swept back into the surge of motivic extension and sequence, soon losing track of familiar materials. Motives a and b are combined in a particularly intense way in the descending sequence in measures 34 and 35 (Ex. 14-20).

An ascending sequence begins in measure 36, halfway through; soprano and bass answer back and forth in emphatic dialog, while the original theme seems forgotten in the heat of argument. At the peak of this ascending sequence (measure 38), harmonic stability deteriorates sharply, as foreign pitches are introduced into the area. The descent through measure 39 has an especially dark minor color, culminating in the tense, unstable chord at the beginning of measure 40. Motive a, present in ever-varying forms throughout these ascents and descents, finally unravels into the precipitous downward scale that leads to the low bass note and the return of section A_2.

SECTION A$_2$. The return of A_1—not just theme and key but section A_1 almost exactly the way it was in the beginning—raises the sense of the form to a new level. Section B engages us in its detail, specifically in motive a, and surprises us with events of more far-

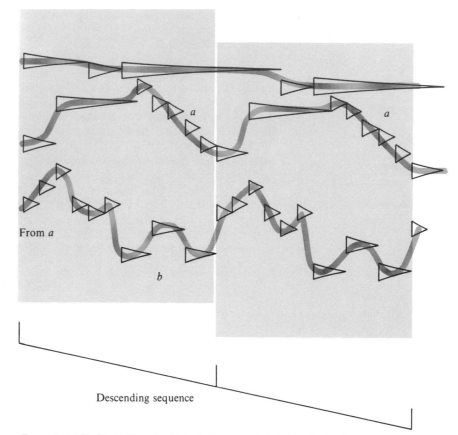

Example 14-20 Bach, D-major Prelude (measure 34): Motivic detail

reaching consequence. The return of A_1 seeks to draw our attention up from the level of detail to that of section: we are encouraged by the prevailing familiarity of events at lower levels to consider the larger design of the piece, something we were not encouraged to do previously.

The material as it appears in A_1 has a different effect from the same material in A_2. A_1 tells us many new things: A_2 brings back things we already know (that is, things we have learned during the performance of this piece) thereby bringing a sense of relaxation and balance after section B, which perhaps undid our familiarity with A_1—or at least confused it.

It is necessary to the identity of this piece that A_1 should return more or less intact. We could perhaps

imagine the piece consisting only of sections A_1 and B, or even of section B alone. There are pieces that have such a shape, but this one does not. The return of A_1 is not for the sake of the smaller things contained in it but rather for the sake of larger things of which it is a part; and when details are different in A_2 (as they occasionally are) we are surprised to be engaged again momentarily in detail.

THE D-MAJOR FUGUE. Of the four pieces from *The Well-Tempered Clavier* studied here (two preludes and two fugues), the Fugue in D major is certainly the most difficult for the listener to follow. It is practically unbroken in imitative texture from beginning to end; it makes almost continuous use of a single motive. It not only lacks clear breaks at the ends of sections and phrases but also has no regular grouping of measures (such as the four-measure groups in the F-minor Fugue) to help locate interior points of reference. Even the measures themselves are not convenient guides, for the rhythms, while metrical, are not sufficiently so on enough levels to follow easily by regular counting.

In return for being hard to grasp in its outlines, the D-major Fugue is very rich in sonority and lyricism. Its intricate contrapuntal texture invites ever-fresh appreciation of details of harmony and line. At higher levels, this Fugue has a way of changing our minds about its design: its sections (insofar as we can make them out), its proportions, and the location of its climaxes, seem to shift around from one hearing to another. We will come to slightly different conclusions about the piece as we examine it from various points of view.

The Fugue is consistently contrapuntal, with four lines or voices (soprano, alto, tenor, and bass) that maintain their identity throughout. This Fugue can, in fact, be sung with very fine effect (a recorded performance is listed in Appendix A).

The Fugue in D major is consistently imitative—more so than the Fugue in F minor. That is, the subject or theme appears in imitation not only at the beginning but also in each of a series of entrances throughout the Fugue. These sets of imitative entrances (eight in all) will provide the best reference points for understanding the interior plan of the Fugue. After examining the subject, we will need to map out the entrances and to identify them in the music.

The theme or subject has a distinctive beginning of three repeated notes (see Ex. 14-21). These are followed by a leap downward to a longer note, then by an even longer and more accented note, followed by four shorter ones. The subject seems to fade out with no firm conclusion. The three faster notes at the start of the subject are very prominent in entrances. The four faster notes at the end form a motive (*b*) heard almost constantly throughout the Fugue—less prominent, but more pervasive.

The shorter notes of the subject represent the fastest pulse of the Fugue. These pulses add up in

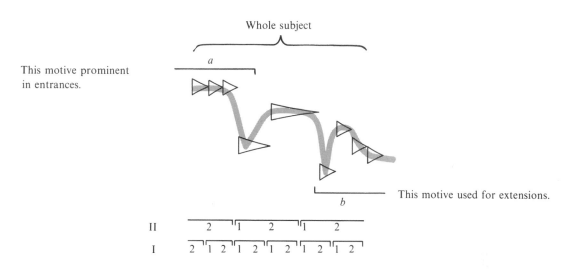

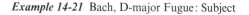

Example 14-21 Bach, D-major Fugue: Subject

twos to form the longer notes, so that there are at least two metric levels. Metric levels higher than that, while present, are not very significant for the listener.

This subject fits together in counterpoint with itself in a variety of ways, revealed by successive sets of entrances. Each set of entrances differs from the one before in the number of voices participating (two to four), in the intervals of time between successive entries, or in the intervals of pitch between the entries. This is best understood by examining the sets.

The first set of entrances is shown in Ex. 14-22, at 1. Between the entries is the metric scale from Ex. 14-21. All four voices—tenor, alto, soprano, and bass—participate, in that order.

The tenor enters first, presenting the subject alone. The alto follows at a higher pitch, as indicated. Before the soprano enters, motivic extension is heard in the alto; the time interval between alto and soprano is greater than that between tenor and alto. The tenor also shows motivic extensions but as counterpoint to the subject already sounding in the alto. The soprano enters on the same pitch as the tenor, an octave higher; the bass, similarly, enters on the same pitch as the alto, an octave lower.

These relationships as described may not be very

audible; more audible will be the sense of oscillation back and forth between the pitch content of successive entries—but that will be easier understood in connection with other harmonic matters.

The soprano and bass are separated by a time interval different from that between the tenor and alto, as can be seen in Ex. 14-22 by noting the place in the soprano that coincides with the bass entry and comparing it with the corresponding place in the tenor. This difference is heard as a subtle acceleration of entrances, not unlike the stretto encountered in the F-minor Fugue. We will find much more striking examples of stretto in later sets of entrances.

As each voice enters and completes the subject, it turns to motivic extension, always of motive *b* from the subject (see Ex. 14-21). These four faster notes seem to lend themselves well to extension by virtue of their less distinctive nature and by their position at the end of the open-ended subject. The fabric of the Fugue seems to be woven with motive *b* as the main thread. Since this motive is part of the subject, there is little element of contrast in the Fugue: either the whole theme is sounding, including the motive *b*, or just motive *b* in counterpoint with itself.

Listen to the whole Fugue several times, following

Set 1

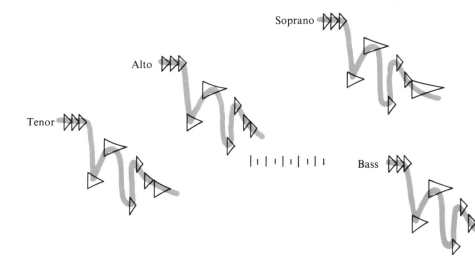

Set 2

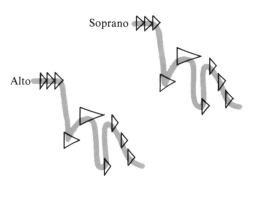

Set 3

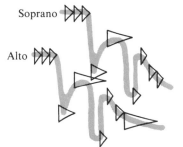

Set 4

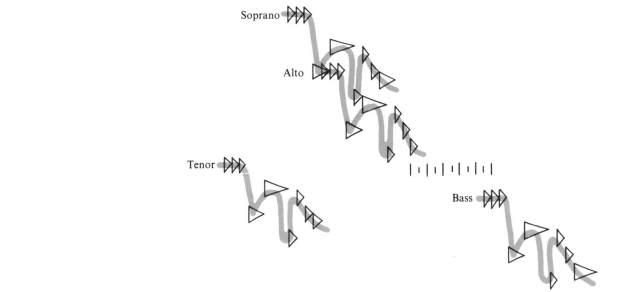

Example 14-22 Bach, D-major Fugue: The eight sets of entries

Ex. 14-22, which contains all the entrances, in eight sets (numbered 1 through 8). Example 14-22 contains *only* the entrances of the subject; it does not contain the motivic extensions between one set of entrances and the next. Since the time interval between sets of entrances varies greatly in this Fugue and since there is no regular upper-level rhythm to follow, you can locate the next set only by hearing it.

Within any given set, the entrances, as shown in Ex. 14-22, are at the correct time interval from one another: but only the voices having entrances are shown; the others (which are often carrying on motivic extension) are omitted. In other words, you must hear which of the three or four voices sounding has the subject.

On your first attempt, you may find that the Fugue is over before you have gotten, say, to the fifth set of entrances on the diagram, for the entrances are not easy to hear. Keep trying nonetheless, for contrapuntal texture responds well to increased concentration and familiarity. There is a definite skill to hearing imitative entrances; once learned, the skill greatly increases your sense of space within musical texture.

The second set of entrances brings alto and soprano into much the same relationship occupied by tenor and alto in the first set. The pitches are different (and so is the harmonic area, to be discussed later), but the subject is intact; the intervals in time and pitch between the two voices are the same as in set 1. The other two voices, however, do not enter as they did in set 1; there are only two entrances in set 2.

As if to make clear that set 2 had only two entrances, those same two voices (alto and soprano) enter soon again to form set 3. This time, they are separated by a much shorter time interval. The soprano enters before the alto has barely cleared the first half of the subject. This is one of several strettos in this Fugue; even closer, more elaborate strettos will soon be encountered. In addition, the two voices are slightly closer in pitch than before. As a result of both proximities, the subject produces friction as it binds against itself.

Set 4 of entrances brings back all four voices, but they are spread out unevenly over a relatively long phrase. The tenor enters first, followed by the soprano at a time interval not used so far between

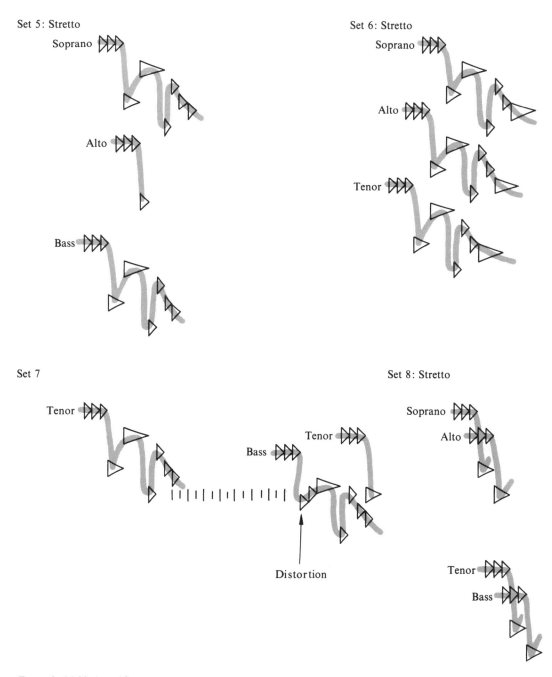

Example 14-22 (cont'd)

315

entrances and much further away in pitch than usual. The soprano, in turn, is followed by the alto, which enters on the same pitch the soprano is sounding. This puts the subject at two different pitch levels, to be sure, but ties them up into a very tight knot—especially notable after the relative distance between the soprano and the preceding tenor entry. After an even longer wait, the bass enters, almost as an afterthought.

Set 5 of entrances is another stretto. The soprano enters just two short pulses after the bass; two short pulses after the soprano, a third entrance is started in the alto but is not continued. Here, the rhythmic closeness of the voices is made to stand out by the pitch distance: the soprano is much higher than the bass (two octaves), the largest interval encountered in entrances so far. The truncated entrance in the alto is an octave below the soprano and an octave higher than the bass.

In set 6 the three entrances (tenor, alto, and soprano) maintain the same close rhythmic relationship as in the fifth set and draw closer together in pitch. This time, all three entrances are completed.

Set 7 is a relaxation of the entrance pattern, although an intensification in other ways. The motive from the end of the subject appears here in soprano and alto in a peculiarly intense form, effectively covering up the sole entrance (tenor) below. After a relatively long time interval, the bass makes an entrance, with expressive distortions of the line, as we will note later.

Stretto returns at set 8. The voices enter in order from high to low, at the close time interval introduced in set 5 and at a pitch interval so close (without being in unison) that the entrances are scarcely distinguishable, so tightly woven has the texture become. We hear a cascade of sound—feeling, rather than hearing, the presence of the subject.

There are, obviously, no clear section breaks: the continuous motion of the rhythmic pulse expressed in the omnipresent motive permits no breaks. But you can hear something new begin with each set of entrances of the subject; you can identify and remember each set according to the behavior of the voices in presenting the subject. Furthermore, in this respect the sets show a progression, during the Fugue,

toward increasing stretto. Also, the most elaborate entrance patterns come at the end, the simpler ones—excepting the first—toward the beginning.

HARMONIC MOVEMENT OF ENTRANCE SETS. The entrance patterns, once heard, provide a relatively explicit way of understanding the progress of the piece. Long before you were clear about the entrance patterns themselves, however, you probably reacted more strongly to the harmonic contexts in which they appear—even if you were not consciously aware of these contexts. With the subject itself now clear, the different ways it sounds in the different sets of entrances can profitably be compared.

In the first set of entrances, the major key of the Fugue is plainly audible in all four entrances (Ex. 14-23). The same major key returns at set 3—indeed, at that point the alto and soprano entrances are identical in pitch to what they were in set 1; and tenor and bass, while not entering with the subject in set 3, support the original harmonic area.

Sets 2 and 4 are in minor—two different minors, each closely related to the original major; the Fugue does not, in fact, move far away from its original key. Set 4, however, moves further than set 2, as is apparent from the feeling of instability at the moment the soprano and alto enter close upon one another.

Set 5 is a clear return to the opening key. The section begun at set 4 eventually finds its way to a stable area and to a cadence (about which, more in a moment); but, with set 5, the music seems abruptly to leave off what it was doing and to emphasize instead the original harmonic area. This emphasis is accomplished by having all three entrances insist on the same note in different octaves, with the accented leap down from this note arriving in each case at the central pitch of the opening key. Actually, it is probably the first note of the subject that sticks in the ear in set 5, especially the highest pitch, whose prominence here is supported further on, at the beginnings of sets 7 and 8.

Minor keys are absent for the rest of the Fugue, and the entrances, at least, stay close to the original key. The tenor entrance in set 7 is identical with the very first entrance of the piece. The following bass entrance, however, is strangely different: here (and

only here), the intervals of the subject and also its rhythm have been altered. The harmonic context reinforces these alterations, giving a momentary remoteness to the sound that is dispelled only by the entrances at set 8.

Set 8, in stretto, seems to imply a suddenly strong motion away from the central harmony. No real change of area takes place, however, and the effect is curiously reminiscent of the harmonic digression and return at the close of sections *A* and *B* in the Prelude.

OVERALL SHAPE OF THE FUGUE. Beyond identifying something of the harmonic quality of the entrance sets, we can go on to trace roughly the harmonic quality of each of the sections marked out by the sets—as we just did with the section that begins with set 8. We also noticed something about the harmonic shape of set 7 (namely, the sense of remoteness in the middle of the section), because it happened that one of the entrances, the bass, was postponed until the middle of the set. In the other sets, we will not often be able to refer the harmonic motion to an entrance of the subject.

After all entrances have been made in set 1, for example, the section goes on to make at its end a brief but clear move to another harmonic area (just before set 2). No complete statement of the subject is involved; the move is prepared with material formed completely from the pervasive motive of the last half of the subject. This move is summarized in Ex. 14-23, below "Harmonic motion," in order to include it in the overall plan of harmonic motion.

In the brief time between the end of the last subject entrance in set 2 (soprano, as in Ex. 14-22) and the first entrance in set 3, another clear harmonic move is made, from the minor of set 2 back to the major.

After set 3, there is a very clear division between the subject entrances, all in the original major key, and a long motivic extension that eventually cadences firmly in a closely related key. The leisurely way the cadence is prepared and approached is one of the most important aspects of this section.

In set 4 (as in set 2), a minor quality predominates. Set 4 ends on another firmly prepared cadence, with the subject (in the bass) playing an important part in the cadence. The cadence itself is in minor and, while

Example 14-23 Bach, D-major Fugue: Plan

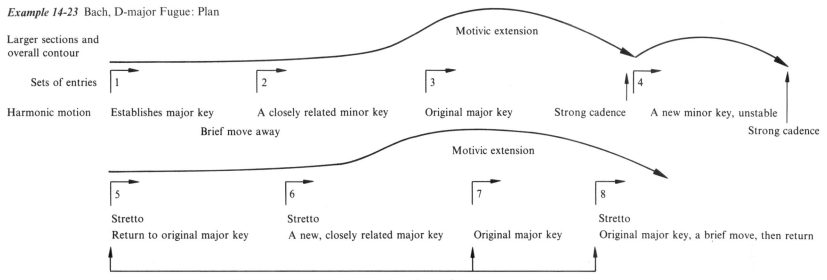

Larger sections and
overall contour

Motivic extension

Sets of entries | 1 | 2 | 3 | 4

Harmonic motion | Establishes major key | A closely related minor key | Original major key | Strong cadence | A new minor key, unstable

Brief move away

Strong cadence

Motivic extension

5 | 6 | 7 | 8

Stretto | Stretto | Stretto
Return to original major key | A new, closely related major key | Original major key | Original major key, a brief move, then return

The same high pitch appears at these three points.

not so very far away from the original major, still makes the original major sound fresh when it returns immediately after the cadence, at the start of set 5. We already noticed how the music seems to break off abruptly at the end of set 4 to make the return. The abruptness is largely a result of the solidity of the cadence in minor.

Set 5 does not move harmonically in any striking way; indeed, from here to the end of the Fugue, the harmonic motion concentrates increasingly on the original key, moving away only briefly in order to emphasize it more.

TWO IMPORTANT EXTENSIONS. You may eventually conclude that the entrance sets are not the most decisive events in the piece and that the way they divide the piece does not properly reveal its shape. We have mentioned at least two other kinds of events that may eventually seem much more significant as shaping factors; these are cadences and motivic extensions.

The two longest extensions (one after set 3, the other after set 6) can both be regarded as high points in the Fugue. The first one far overshadows the brief, simple entrance set (3) that precedes it. (This

passage is distinguished by the two-measure absence of the bass voice.) The motivic extension lifts quickly out of the subject, arching in a long, eloquent line that extends all the way over to set 4. In this case, the motivic extension culminates in the firm cadence—the firmest, best-prepared cadence so far in the Fugue. In other words, we could understand this climactic line, backed up by the cadence, as marking the end of the first large section of the Fugue, including within it three complete sets of entrances entries (see Ex. 14-23).

The second firm cadence comes soon after, at the end of set 4; it is the big cadence in minor. This, too, could mark a section—large in importance even if short in duration—for this section embodies the strongest harmonic contrast to the rest of the Fugue. The differentness of this section is confirmed by the abruptness of the return at set 5, with its insistent stretto.

The long line of the second motivic extension, beginning after set 5, rises more slowly, reaching its peak after set 6. Here, the line has the effect of driving the Fugue on past any divisions that might be indicated by sets of entrances. The long line works together with the three strettos (5, 6, and 8) to fuse

the latter part of the Fugue together with gathering momentum. It links the high note in set 5 to the same high note in set 8, in such a way as to make it a limiting, climactic event in the Fugue.

In this Fugue, dense, contrapuntal texture and virtually incessant use of a single motive combine to produce a high degree of musical continuity. Rhythm here has little to do with sectional division; rather, rhythm in this Fugue seems to be a matter of flow. By referring to different aspects of line, texture, or harmony, we can divide the flow into compartments; but the fact that we can do it in several different ways should encourage us to take none of them as definitive but instead to trust our own intuitive impression that the piece is essentially continuous, not sectionalized.

The fact that the Fugue is continuous, however, does not necessarily mean that it is amorphous. The Fugue assumes articulate, effective form; we can grasp its sense of phrasing even if the end of one phrase is identical with or overlaps the beginning of the next. Just as an intensely lyrical poem can have several meanings depending on how we group its lines and images, so a piece of music such as this one can be understood in several configurations without denying any one of them.

CHAPTER 15 BARTOK'S STRING QUARTET NO. 6

IN CHAPTERS 15, 16, AND 17, we will discuss the overall plans of a string quartet and two symphonies. Each of these works consists of several movements. We have already studied many of the movements separately, since almost every one of these movements is some kind of distinct entity with a shape of its own. Now we will concentrate upon the overall design of each of these multimovement works.

Such multimovement forms make special demands upon the listener's comprehension. This is not just because they are long, since Schubert's song cycle *Die schöne Müllerin* is longer; nor just because each consists of several distinct sections or movements, for this also is true of *Die schöne Müllerin*. The main problem is that the listener must understand the relationships among the movements of each piece without the help of a text. Relying on purely musical factors, the listener must try to hear how the several movements make a single, unified musical experience.

Understanding relationships among movements often requires understanding each movement as a unit in terms of only its most prominent characteristics. You may have to single out those few characteristics that are true of each movement as a whole, ignoring for the time being the variety and complexity evident within the movement.

To take the simplest, most immediate example, successive movements in a multimovement work usually vary in tempo—some being faster, some slower. Understanding the shape of the whole work may involve (among other things) hearing that one movement is in general slower than another—even

though the slow movement might contain passages with relatively fast motion. The same kind of general distinction might have to be made for timbre, texture, rhythm, or pitch.

As another, more complex example, it is frequently important to note whether successive movements are in the same harmonic area or in different areas; but an individual movement may move among several areas, forcing us to select—for purposes of comparison with other movements—one of these areas as the principal one. As a second step, we can of course refine the comparison by taking into account the secondary harmonic areas as well.

It is not too difficult to note *differences* or contrasts between two movements; it is perhaps more difficult to understand how these contrasts contribute to the unity of a work. It seems much easier to understand how *similarities* among movements contribute to unity. Bartók's Quartet No. 6 provides a convenient beginning to a discussion of overall shape in multimovement works, since its plan presents obvious, striking use of similarity among the movements as an expression of the unity of the quartet.

The movement plan of the quartet is given in Ex. 15-1. The composer has numbered the four movements of the quartet I, II, III, IV. Each of movements I, II, and III has a slow introduction labeled Mesto; these Mesto sections are shaded in Ex. 15-1. Movement IV is all in the Mesto tempo.

As you listen to the quartet straight through—even for the first time—you will notice the similarity of the Mesto sections. The first Mesto is relatively short and

is heard merely as an introduction to the long, complex Vivace that makes up most of movement I; but when the tempo of the first Mesto, together with its melody, appears at the beginning of movement II, the sense of return is prominent. The return is enhanced by the complexity of the intervening Vivace; and even though the second Mesto, like the first, is only an introduction to a much larger section, still these Mesto sections begin to acquire importance beyond that of introduction.

This subtle but essential shift in the role of the Mesto at the beginning of movement II may be associated with the curiously soft, light, "up-in-the-air" ending of the Vivace. Its final chords (indeed, its whole fourth section) are much less conclusive than such a tightly argued movement would lead us to expect; but perhaps the real function of the fourth section is not to end the Vivace but instead to prepare for the return of the Mesto.

In the second Mesto and also in the third, the original melody is set in substantially different ways (to be studied soon); yet it is the similarity among these sections that you notice. If the Mesto introductions were played one right after another without the

Example 15-1 Bartók, Sixth String Quartet: Plan

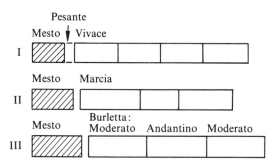

(Tempo marks are shown here only to identify the largest sections: other tempo marks have been omitted.)

rest of movements I, II, and III, then you would be much more impressed by their differences. However, alternating as they do with the longer, more complex sections—which are very different among themselves, going from I to II to III—the Mesto sections seem primarily to convey a sense of sameness; and, in so doing, they become the easiest aspect of the overall plan to hear and hold in mind. Without the Mesto introductions, you might at first think you were hearing merely a succession of pieces by the same composer. The more deep-seated affinities that bind the movements together are difficult to identify and describe. The return of the Mesto (even if heard only as a return of tempo) makes it immediately obvious that these movements belong together as parts of a single work.

It comes as no surprise, perhaps, that movement IV is given over entirely to the Mesto tempo. No longer just an introduction, the Mesto has established its importance in the quartet sufficiently so that in movement IV it can fill up the entire movement as if it belonged there—which, indeed, it does, having become the central theme of the quartet. Here again, the original melody is treated in substantially different ways in order to fill out movement IV; but our first impression is one of similarity and return.

DIFFERENCES AMONG THE MESTO SECTIONS. While the sameness of the Mesto sections provides a structural framework for the whole quartet, the differences among these sections give the quartet a specific sense of progress and expansion. In order to understand the larger shape in these terms, we do not need to take into account the inner structure of the fast portions of I, II, and II (except that we do need to refer briefly to the thematic structure of I, as discussed in Chapter 9). These fast portions are, of course, of great importance in the quartet—indeed, they provide most of its bulk. Paradoxically, however, they can be left aside in tracing the shape set out by the introductory Mesto sections; it is sufficient to remember that these long fast sections intervene among them.

The melody played by the solo viola at the beginning of the quartet reappears more or less intact at the beginning of movement II (Ex. 15-2). Here, it is played by the cello (at a slightly lower pitch level),

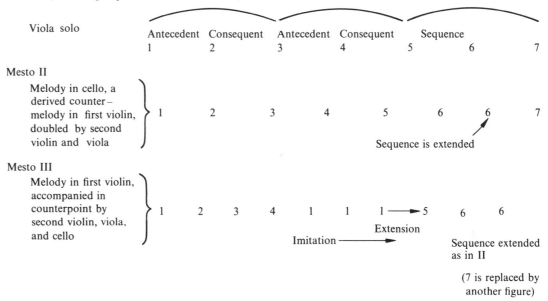

Example 15-2 Bartók, Sixth String Quartet: Linear relationships among the Mesto sections

accompanied by the other three instruments. They all play a single line—a countermelody—in octaves; the second violin and viola play the notes of the countermelody in a nervous, quivering timbre. The countermelody is derived from motives of the melody and sometimes seems to imitate it; more often the two melodies move in opposite directions, generating linear tension as they do so.

One important change has been made in the melody as it appears in II: the melodic pattern at 5, which is repeated at 6 to form a sequence, is repeated again, extending the sequence. This change, together with the thickening of the texture, begins a process of dissolution of the opening melody. Presented at the beginning of the quartet as a single compact line, the melody is gradually pulled apart in the succeeding Mesto sections, expressed more and more as fragmented motives in a contrapuntal context.

Mesto III begins with three parts, second violin and cello accompanying first violin. Then the texture becomes slightly more imitative, and viola is added.

At this point, the Mesto has reached the full texture normal to the quartet as a whole.

In Mesto III, the original shape of the melody is interrupted after group 4 (Ex. 15-2). Here, the melody returns to group 1, repeating and extending it in a generally upward direction. The motion is urged on by imitation in the second violin and later in the viola. When the line reaches a new high point, it ceases the repetitions of the motive from group 1 and picks up group 5, playing it three times in descending sequence (as in Mesto II). At the end, group 7 is omitted; in its place violin 2 has a new rising figure.

MESTO IV. One of the reasons Mesto IV seems such a natural development in the quartet is that in it the treatment of the original melody follows the trends already evident in Mesto II and Mesto III. The melodic groups of the melody appear at first more or less in order but become increasingly interrupted by motivic repetitions and extensions. The interruptions seem to discourage the completion of the melody; in fact, it never gets beyond group 5; and subsequent attempts are stalled even earlier. It is interesting that the complete statement of the melody appears in Mesto I (the shortest), while Mesto IV (by far the longest) contains the least complete statement of the melody.

The melody, along with other important melodic material, continues to be heard primarily in the first violin, although the other instruments have more and more to say as the texture becomes increasingly contrapuntal. Imitation in particular is one of the important means of extending the melodic material.

As shown in Ex. 15-3, the first half of Mesto IV is a presentation of the original melody, expanded and interrupted to a degree far beyond that of Mesto II or Mesto III. The first phrase (groups 1 and 2) is immediately repeated, then group 1 by itself is repeated several times. For the time being, the melody gets no further. The repetitions of the opening motive give way to a pianissimo interlude for violin and cello, to be played *senza colore* ("without color"; that is, in as neutral a timbre as possible). The opening motive then returns but subjected to such intense development that no overall resemblance to the shape of the original melody can be detected.

When group 3 of the melody appears, the sense of resumption is entirely clear; everything between this group 3 and the previous presentation of groups 1 and 2 as a phrase is shown to be an expansion interpolated into the original melody. Groups 3 and 4 proceed in order, leading to group 5; but here again the melody is interrupted by repetition of 5—not in descending sequence any more but rather on exactly the same pitch, as if hindered from going on. The line actually breaks off, then goes all the way back to the beginning to try again, now playing the original melody pianissimo and senza colore. This is the start of the second half of Mesto IV.

So far, Mesto IV could be understood as a more extreme application of the procedures heard in Mesto II and Mesto III and could even serve as an introduction to a faster section, as in II and III. At this point in IV, however, a different kind of event takes place, one that makes explicit the leading role of the Mesto in the quartet. Into Mesto IV are introduced, in order, the principal themes from the Vivace in movement

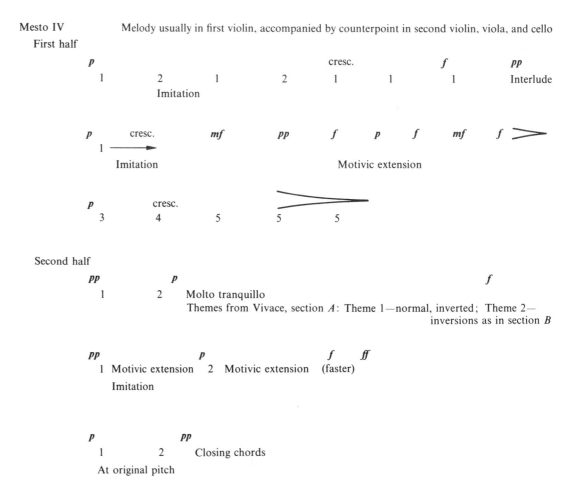

Example 15-3 Bartók, Sixth String Quartet: Linear relationships among the Mesto sections (compare Ex. 15-2)

I—theme 1, normal and inverted; theme 2; and the climactic inversion from section *B* of the Vivace (see Ex. 15-3; compare Ex. 9-12).

This recall of themes from movement I is not hidden within the context of intricate motivic development: there is no danger of missing the recall, if you are familiar with the themes in the Vivace, for they are clearly set apart in movement IV as quotations. The listener is supposed to identify them immediately as reminiscences from movement I and to feel a sense of

return, of binding up movement I with movement IV into a musical whole.

Recall of themes from an earlier movement is, of course, not the only way to unify a multimovement work. In fact, it might not even be a very convincing way. Simple thematic recall might seem contrived if it were not supported by some deeper kinship among the movements. The recall of a theme is made, not just for the sake of that theme, but rather for the sake of its whole context—the movement with which it is identified. In this particular case, Bartók wants us to remember the beginning of the quartet as we listen to the end; for this purpose, quotation of movements II and III would be irrelevant. Then, too, the actual quotation of themes from movement I must seem musically appropriate in movement IV. If the inner musical integrity of movement IV were broken by the quotation, the effect would be hard to justify simply on the basis of an external thematic relationship. Indeed, there does seem to be a specific connection between the Mesto melody and the themes of the Vivace from movement I, a connection that can be traced through the Pesante of movement I (see Ex. 9-10).

Ultimately, the quotation of themes from the Vivace of movement I seems secondary to the pervasive role of the Mesto—and dependent upon the Mesto for success. It is significant that the thematic recall takes place within a Mesto section, directly after a simple statement of groups 1 and 2; the Mesto mood and melody thereby assume ever greater importance, becoming almost personified like a narrator in a story or a protagonist in a drama. It is easy to push such personifications or analogies too far; what we hear in Bartók's quartet is a purely musical phenomenon, not a literary or dramatic one. Still, the analogy may have some value in calling attention to the extraordinary sense of identity that can become attached to a theme when it persists through a sufficiently broad and varied context.

The Mesto melody, returning throughout the quartet, acquires this kind of identity—not because of its own qualities, but because of the way it participates in the overall shape. The very end of the quartet, for example, may seem at first strangely inconclusive. That first impression is important and should not become effaced through familiarity. Perhaps the breaking-off at the end becomes more meaningful if heard as a response to the last abortive attempt of the Mesto melody, here very close in actual pitches to the beginning of the quartet but briefer than ever.

THE FASTER SECTIONS OF THE QUARTET. The Mesto melody has an effect on the quartet out of proportion to its actual length. As already mentioned, however, the Mesto makes its effect only little by little

as the quartet unfolds: Mesto I and Mesto II (perhaps even Mesto III) still sound introductory, while increasing in importance. We need to consider now the faster sections of movements I, II, and III, not only because they provide most of the bulk of the quartet, but also because it is their alternation and interaction with the Mesto that feed its growth.

In dealing with the faster sections of movements I, II, and III—Vivace, Marcia, Burletta (see Ex. 15-1)—we encounter the more difficult problem of hearing and evaluating differences (rather than similarities) among successive movements. The Mesto sections offer easy access to the overall plan of the quartet precisely because of their similarities; and their differences can be easily evaluated on that basis. Among the faster sections, however, there are no obvious similarities; their differences must be evaluated without reference to a common mood or melody. Furthermore, the faster sections in movements II and III (Marcia, Burletta) show no obvious similarity to their Mesto introductions, while the Vivace from movement I, as we saw, is closely related to its Mesto through similar motives. Whether we seek relationships among the faster sections or between them and the Mesto melody, we are faced with difference as a prevailing mode of relationship.

Here, we need to deal with relatively long, complex sections as if each were a homogeneous unit. For purposes of comparison at the highest level, all of the Marcia in movement II should be considered as a unit; similarly, all of the Burletta in movement III—and even the Vivace of movement I can be so considered. Yet the Vivace is not homogeneous, and movements II and III contain strongly contrasting middle sections. These can be taken into account by discussing the overall shape at the next lower level.

MARCIA. One of the most striking features of the Marcia ("March") is its uniformity of musical character—especially when compared to the preceding Vivace of movement I. The Marcia as a whole produces a single effect, as opposed to the varied effects of the Vivace. It is true that the Marcia has an $A_1 \, B \, A_2$ plan and that the B section is very different from its surroundings; yet this B section is so short, so erratic and unstable, that its function seems to be

limited to that of providing a relief to the overall effect produced by the A sections.

The uniformity of the Marcia is due to the prevalence of a single theme and to the persistence of one particular rhythmic pattern. In the Vivace, there were two distinct themes; and even though a swinging rhythmic pulse ran throughout at the lowest level, still there were several distinct rhythmic motives that kept the Vivace from being uniform. Furthermore, the Vivace had a sense of dynamic change, of development, so that the movement took on a different character as it proceeded. The Marcia, by comparison, seems to return again and again to the same theme and the same rhythmic motive; any other themes or motives (and there are a few others) provide only temporary contrast and soon merge into the persistent marchlike rhythm.

The prevailing theme of the Marcia and its characteristic short-long rhythm are quite unlike anything in the Vivace. Since this one theme and rhythm do characterize the whole Marcia, they serve to make the Marcia distinctly different from the Vivace.

How should the differentness of the Marcia be interpreted in terms of the plan of the whole work? At this level, differentness is sometimes hard to understand: that is, at this point, you may wonder why the Marcia should be part of the same work as the Vivace. Eventually, such differentness encourages a thoughtful listener to seek latent similarities—perhaps having to do with harmonic area or with motivic relationships—that could provide a bridge between the two movements.

Another kind of consideration is so obvious that it often goes unnoticed—and should be mentioned just for that reason. In live performance, the Marcia is played by the same four players sitting just as they were for the Vivace. There has been no "change of scene," no change in the source or the overall kind of sound. Such similarity is so gross that it would have little artistic value in comparison, say, to a strong thematic connection between movements. However, in the face of thematic difference (such as that between Marcia and Vivace), the gross similarity provides a basis of continuity, a bias toward hearing the two movements as part of the same work. Source of sound, as well as kind of sound, can, after all, be changed from one section of a work to another, and such changes would have a profound effect upon the continuity of a work.

After taking into account these possible bases for similarity (the one subtle, the other obvious), the differentness that was the first, strongest impression should be recalled as the primary mode of relationship. Works of art must employ differentness in some way; what might puzzle us in the case of the Marcia (as in many a multimovement work) is that the differentness is manifest at the movement level. The differentness of the B section of the Marcia, for example, presents no such problem of interpretation. In this particular work, of course, continuity at the movement level is made immediately obvious by the recurrence of the Mesto (as we have seen); and the Mesto has made its first return—the return that establishes the Mesto as a recurrent element in the quartet—just before the Marcia. The differentness of the Marcia, then, can be understood as a natural reflex from the sameness of the Mesto. From their juxtaposition, it becomes apparent that in this work sameness and differentness will alternate in concentrated blocks at the movement level.

BURLETTA. Assessing the differentness of the Burletta in movement III is more difficult, for the Burletta produces no such clear-cut effect as the Marcia.

At the highest level, the Burletta has the same kind of plan—$A_1 B A_2$—as the Marcia; in fact, the presence of this plan in both Marcia and Burletta and the clarity and literalness with which it is carried out set these two inner movements off against the Vivace on one hand and the concluding Mesto in IV on the other.

The $A_1 B A_2$ plan is, however, realized in the Bur-

letta differently than in the Marcia. Perhaps most obvious is the much greater claim the B section—the Andante—has on our attention. Softer, slower, now lyric and nostalgic, it seems to contradict the title "Burletta" and its implications of sarcasm or irony. In any case, the B section is not only a contrast to the Moderato A sections, but maintains a distinct identity alongside them. Unlike the Marcia, then, the Burletta has two main ideas, not just one.

Does the independent B section enter into the larger design of the quartet through thematic or motivic connections? The question, prompted by the strong contrast between the A and B sections, does not have a clear answer. On first hearing, you may have the distinct impression that the B section is using melodic or rhythmic motives previously encountered; on repeated hearings of the B section of the Burletta, you may have a deepening conviction that the source of these motives is to be sought in the first or second themes of the Vivace—especially in the second theme. However, close comparison with the themes of the Vivace will fail to show any literal connection. It seems to be a fact of listening that, when confronted with strong differences, the ear seeks out any similarities, no matter how farfetched.

Within its A sections, the Burletta is much less uniform than the Marcia; yet its variety is not that of the Vivace, for the Burletta does not grow or progress like the Vivace. Instead, the Burletta (as we saw in Chapter 5, pages 80–85) begins each of a series of subsections with a relatively clear statement of rhythmic motives, then proceeds to get increasingly involved in its own complexities, finally abandoning that line of argument to start another.

More specifically, the A sections of the Burletta have a wider variety of kinds of articulation (including

some striking effects of timbre) and stronger contrasts of dynamics than the other movements. They also have a greater variety of textures, from forceful unison statements to the strong rhythmic counterpoint over an ostinato (see page 84).

One of the important functions of the Burletta seems to be to provide relief from the persistence of the Marcia. As a relief, the Burletta (that is, its A section) seems tangential to the main line of the quartet. This in turn might suggest that the B section, contrasting as it does with A, is by reflex a return to the main line, thus strengthening our earlier impression of a thematic reminiscence in B. These, at any rate, are the kinds of considerations that arise as soon as the attempt is made to understand a series of contrasting movements as a unified whole. There are ways to deal with differentness as a mode of relationship, ways that are more difficult, less conclusive, than those of similarity but just as important.

In the case of Bartók's quartet, the problem of differentness is readily resolved by the recurring Mesto. At the beginning of movement IV, it has become so clear that the Mesto is the main theme of the quartet that its preemption of the whole of movement IV seems perfectly natural. In spite of their length, Marcia and Burletta are now understood as subsidiary, their differentness subsumed under the Mesto identity; and to confirm the relationship, Mesto IV quotes the themes from the Vivace (as described on pages 320–321), showing the close relationship of the Vivace with the Mesto theme. Vivace and Mesto IV are more than just frame, beginning and ending of the quartet. While the Mesto is the dominant personality of the quartet, the Vivace is its alter ego—in some mysterious way that may never be entirely clear.

SOMETIME EARLY IN YOUR STUDY of Haydn's Symphony No. 100 (or of any multimovement work), you should listen to the whole work straight through, without interruption and preferably without any prior information. You may not retain much from such a hearing; nevertheless, what you do retain may well be an essential foundation for your future understanding of the work.

If you listen for "whatever is there" in Haydn's Symphony No. 100, your first complete hearing will be especially bewildering, since the symphony contains so much. Some filtering of less noticeable details takes place automatically. Indeed, control over the largely unconscious process of filtering details (remembering some, forgetting others) is probably one of the composer's most important means of giving his piece a shape. That is too complex a proposition to explore in general; but you can, and should, encourage the process of filtering by letting those details or aspects that *seem* important for the overall shape register more strongly in your mind, meanwhile letting slip other details that (at the moment anyway) seem to have only passing significance. Apparently unessential details may, of course, ultimately turn out to be important: if so, the composer will probably take pains to remind you of them; if not, the details are always there to be found again.

At right is the kind of summary you might make after one or two complete hearings of Haydn's Symphony No. 100. Some items (such as meter) are identified absolutely; others (such as length) only relatively, in an attempt to gauge the effect of one movement in terms of those preceding it. Hearing the functions of individual parts of the symphony as it unfolds is one of the most important aspects of grasping its shape.

When you first listen to the symphony, you do not know that the opening Adagio is going to be relatively short; for that matter, even when the Adagio is over and the Allegro has begun, you still do not know that the Adagio was shorter until the Allegro has gone on for a long time. While you listen to the Allegro, it gradually becomes apparent that it is the more stable, the more substantial of the two, and that the Adagio functioned as an introduction to the Allegro. This

CHAPTER 16 HAYDN'S SYMPHONY NO. 100

becomes even more clear when the Allegro comes to a solid ending.

Similarly, it is not clear from just the first section (Menuetto) and the second (Trio) of the Moderato that the Menuetto will return. You might think that a succession of shorter movements had begun. When the Menuetto does return, it has the important function of binding up Menuetto and Trio into a larger unit (with a common moderato tempo and a common

Adagio

slow

relatively short

duple meter

no sections; open-ended

Allegro

fast

long

duple meter

sections too long for ready comprehension; subsections often obscured by a feeling of rhythmic continuity; sometimes phrases are clear, but often not; a varied flow of melodic materials, with a complex use of both themes and motives

Allegretto

moderate

shorter than Allegro

duple meter

marchlike character; simple, regular rhythms; clear sections, clear phrases; much more repetition than

key) roughly the size of the preceding Allegretto but with a much more sharply differentiated section plan.

Each part of the symphony has its own distinctive rhythmic motion. The Adagio, in duple meter at all levels, has a broad motion as well as a slow pace. The following Allegro, also in duple meter, has a more insistent kind of motion with the beats grouped firmly in twos and with more vigorous accents. The rhythms have a strong tendency toward higher-level groupings

in Allegro; less variety, except for a fortissimo blast near the end

Moderato (Menuetto and Trio)

moderate

roughly same length as Allegretto

triple meter

very clear sections—two completely independent sections arranged in an *A B A* plan (Menuetto, Trio, Menuetto); clear subsections, in spite of occasionally intricate rhythms; phrases usually clear and regular

dancelike character

Finale—Presto

fastest of all

seemingly elaborate but over fairly soon

triple meter at lowest level, duple at higher levels

a combination of a very clearly phrased theme with long stretches in headlong, uninterrupted rhythms; no clear sections except as marked by returns of the theme in fours, but there is an equally strong counter-tendency to upset these fours (once established) with irregularities. Rhythmic interest in the Allegro tends to be found at a level higher than the measure.

The Allegretto, in duple meter with two moderate beats per measure, is rhythmically the simplest, most regular, movement. It tends strongly toward metrical organization in groups of four or eight measures each.

The Moderato (Menuetto and Trio) is in triple meter at the principal level—the only movement of the symphony to be so organized. This fact by itself sets the Menuetto off from the other movements. In addition, the Menuetto has some of the most intricate lower-level rhythms, as well as some of the most complex groupings of measures (see the discussion on pages 77–79).

The Finale (Presto) has triple meter at the lowest level, duple meter at the second level. This is another unique metrical combination in the symphony. The triple meter at the lowest level produces a distinctive effect very different from the triple meter in the Menuetto; the Finale is, if anything, closer in rhythm to the Allegro, with a strong tendency to generate high-level regular groupings of four and eight measures.

Although contrasting in rhythm, the two inner movements—Allegretto and Moderato (Menuetto and Trio)—share a sense of restricted dimensions that differentiates them from the expansive outer movements. The Allegretto stays too close to regular four- and eight-bar phrases and phrase symmetry to generate expansive rhythmic energies. The Menuetto's rhythmic energy seems directed inward rather than outward, congesting the phrase structure instead of opening it into a long arc. In both cases, sectional plans of the central movements unfold clearly within relatively limited dimensions, whereas in the outer movements it is very difficult to perceive sectional plans at all on first or second hearing. These relationships among the movements can be made more specific after we are more familiar with the plan of the first movement and can compare it with the plans of the other movements already studied. Even on first hearing, there is a clear difference between the inner movements on one hand, and the outer movements on the other. In this, as in tempo and meter, the slow

introduction stands apart, with a seemingly indeterminate, or at least inconclusive, structure.

THEME AND MOTIVE. All the movements have themes, all have motives; different movements make use of thematic recall and motivic development in different ways. To summarize first impressions that can be made more specific later, we can say that the relationship among theme, motive, and overall substance of the movement is simplest in the Allegretto, involute in the Menuetto, most complex in Allegro and Finale. In these two outer movements, thematic recall seems to play an important role in our perception of the shape of the work from the start of our listening experience with it. We are aware equally early of the pervasive motivic extensions in those same movements, even if much study is required to understand how the extension operates.

We should note, also from first listening on, that there are no *obvious* thematic or motivic links among any of the movements. That is, in no case does the composer seem to say (like Bartók in his Quartet No. 6), "Do you hear this? It comes from a previous movement." Whether there are latent or obscure relationships among movements and what role such relationships might play in the unity of the whole symphony are questions you can consider later. At that later time, however, you should recall that links among movements were not an obvious feature of the work on initial hearing.

HARMONIC SHAPE. An aspect of the work difficult to perceive and assess at any stage of experience is the unity of harmonic area. The work as a whole is organized closely around a single harmonic center, as you can hear by listening to the first and last measures of the symphony. The result is a stability that seems so natural as to make it difficult to be aware of harmony as an organizing factor. We seem to respond more consciously to the harmonic contrasts—the differences, rather than the samenesses.

All movements save one are in the same key; the variant, the Allegretto, is in a very close key, the one whose leading harmony is the central harmony of the others (Ex. 16-1). These relationships should be easily apparent in the connections between movements: the

first movement leads to the second as smoothly as two movements can; the beginning of the fourth movement should be clearly perceptible as being in the same key as the end of the third. The connection between second and third movements is less obvious at first and less clear in its implications; we will consider it again later. The identities of first, third, and fourth movements will certainly be felt right off, but you probably will not be aware of these identities until after you are better acquainted with the whole.

Furthermore, in exploring remote harmonic areas, each movement seems to seek out some of the same alternatives to the central harmonic area. In ways unexpected—and certainly not obvious—a movement will touch upon a remote harmony that seems to have resonance with similarly remote events in a preceding movement. Such relationships, abstruse yet by no means inaccessible to the attentive listener, constitute a great source of richness at the highest levels of the work. We will discuss these remote harmonic shifts after we have worked with the Allegro.

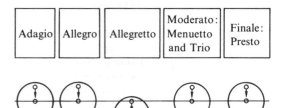

Example 16-1 Haydn, Symphony No. 100:
Plan of movements
and their key relationships

THE ALLEGRO. Try to approach the Allegro the same way you began with the symphony—as a whole, on the highest level, noticing the effects that result from all factors operating together, without trying at the moment to separate them.

On first or second hearing, the Allegro will not yield a clear overall plan because, for one thing, it is not clearly sectioned; that is, there are sections, of various kinds, but they do need pointing out. Your first impression is likely to be one of prevailing continuity: the Allegro rushes along through a variety of themes and motives, with occasional cadences and frequent thematic returns that do not fall into any obvious pattern.

Even on first or second hearing, however, you may become aware that various areas of the Allegro differ in their degrees of stability. The middle of the Allegro is noticeably less stable than either the beginning or the end. Perhaps you can best sense this difference in comparing the middle to the end. As it approaches its end, the movement proceeds more and more steadily; there is only one digression (which we will consider more carefully later)—and that comes as a great surprise, partly because by that time we sense that the end is near and do not expect any more departures. In the middle of the movement, on the other hand, so unstable is the basic motion that we would never expect the piece to end soon and are not surprised by the appearance of one new development after another.

For the time being, do not worry about whether you can identify the precise moment when the motion becomes stable or unstable; simply try to be aware of the prevailing difference between the middle of the Allegro and the end.

In terms of this rough comparison, we can also say that the beginning of the movement is more like the end than like the middle; that is, the beginning is relatively stable when compared to the unstable middle. It is harder, of course, to judge the stability of the beginning because it is the first term of the comparison, to which the middle is referred. Here, you might best gain an insight into the relationship of beginning and middle by listening for the moment when the music seems to strike off in a really different direction. Then, thinking back, you can perceive that what came before was relatively stable.

The beginning, middle, and end of the movement (as we have been discussing it) are actually sections, marked off precisely from one another in various ways that will be taken up soon. Haydn indicates an optional repeat for the first section. In some performances, therefore, the beginning section will come twice—which will make a difference in the way you hear the overall plan (Ex. 16-2).

One of the most obvious ways in which the end is made to seem stable relative to the middle is that it consists of a return of material from the beginning. This material turns up in the last section more or less as it was at first, giving the end of the movement the feeling of a return to things relatively well known and familiar. Some of the same material—especially the motives—turns up in the middle as well; but there it is strangely distorted, not sounding at all as it did in the beginning. We can add another dimension, then, to that of stable-unstable-stable: beginning and end of the movement are relatively similar; the middle is different (Ex. 16-2).

First section	Middle section	Last section

Harmonic motion: Stable   Unstable   Stable

First and last sections similar

Middle section different

When performed with repeat:

First section	First section repeated	Middle section	Last section

Example 16-2 Haydn, Symphony No. 100, Allegro: Sectional plan

THE FUNCTIONS OF THEMES. After one or two hearings, you may begin to become aware of the importance of themes in the overall plan of the Allegro. Of all the elements in this movement, themes, perhaps, are what strike the listener most clearly. Later, we will want to place these themes in their proper perspective by stressing the importance of the nonthematic elements, but let us begin with the most obvious elements—the themes—to hear how they guide us through the movement.

When we studied the Finale to this symphony (pages 156–168), we encountered a main theme whose literal returns shaped the whole movement; a second theme recurred at various times between the appearances of the main theme. A similar arrangement is found in the first movement, except that there is more of a balance between the two themes: the first one does not reappear so persistently, while the second, on the other hand, is more independent (hence more easily identified) and has a more important role in the overall plan. The result is a less obvious, more complex plan.

The music at the very beginning of the Allegro functions as a principal theme. This function is made clear in two ways—first, by the mere return of the theme and its distinctive woodwind timbre; second, by the clear, stable melodic shape of the whole theme. We will consider these two aspects separately.

With the broad outline of the movement in mind, locate more exactly the literal returns of the first theme; these all involve the distinctive woodwind timbre in a high register, as heard at the start of the Allegro (Ex. 16-3). In order to grasp the significance of each return, we need to describe the second aspect of the theme—its clear, stable, melodic shape.

As heard at the very beginning of the Allegro, the theme consists of an antecedent-and-consequent pair of phrases; the antecedent (*a*) is played by woodwinds, the consequent (*b*) by strings (Ex. 16-4). The theme remains throughout in a single harmonic area, with a half cadence at the end of *a* and a full cadence at the end of *b*. The effect of this full cadence is partly obliterated, however, by the boisterous entrance of the tutti right on top of it: the pitches are there, but the change of timbre is strong enough to make that point sound more like the beginning of a phrase than the end of one.

Thematic statements	First section 1 2	Middle section 3	Last section 4

1—First theme
2—Antecedent of first theme at a new pitch level
3—A modified fragment of the first theme in minor
4—First theme at the original pitch level

Example 16-3 Haydn, Allegro: Statements of first theme

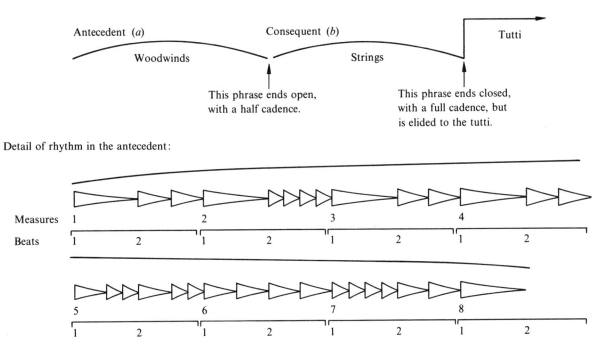

Antecedent (*a*)   Consequent (*b*)   Tutti

Woodwinds   Strings

This phrase ends open,   This phrase ends closed,
with a half cadence.   with a full cadence, but
                                is elided to the tutti.

Detail of rhythm in the antecedent:

Measures   1   2   3   4

Beats   1   2   1   2   1   2   1   2

         5   6   7   8

         1   2   1   2   1   2   1   2

Example 16-4 Haydn, Allegro: Phrase structure of first theme

In spite of the tutti's entrance, the basic impression given by the first theme is one of balance and stability. The melody could almost exist by itself as a brief song (except for its melodic and rhythmic insistence). It does not need the rest of the Allegro—unless it wants to go beyond the limits of a brief song to participate in more lofty musical excursions. The Allegro, however, needs this moment of clear, stable theme to provide a reference point elsewhere in the movement.

Now return to Ex. 16-3 to see the different functions of this theme in the movement as a whole. The theme appears for the second time very soon after the beginning. The return is literal, as far as it goes: only the antecedent returns, and that never reaches its half cadence. (Thereafter the music proceeds differently, as we will discuss later.) The woodwind timbre is the same and is still placed in a high register, but at a different pitch level. This last aspect may be difficult to hear; but is worth concentrating on, for

the change of harmonic area involved in reaching this different pitch level is an important feature of the movement.

This second statement of the theme has several important functions. Coming early in the movement (yet after something definitely different), it establishes the first theme as an element that returns. The return brings with it the sense of stability experienced in the theme in its first appearance—but with important qualifications. Only the antecedent returns, so the sense of stability is less than would be produced by a full return; and, coming at a new pitch level, the stable theme gives a sense of movement away from the stable harmonic area established at the beginning of the movement.

It is a long way from the second statement of the theme to the next *complete* statement. (If the performance repeats the first section of the Allegro, then of course you will hear what Ex. 16-3 calls the first statement of the theme, followed by the second, then

by the first, then the second, before going on to the middle of the movement.) The fragmentary, modified statement of the first theme halfway along in the middle section is noticeable chiefly because it has the woodwind timbre played softly, following the conclusion of a loud tutti and a pause. It is a moment of high contrast; a mere hint is sufficient to suggest the melody of the first theme, even though it does not establish a return. Furthermore, the fragment of theme that is identifiable is temporarily in minor, rather than the original major.

In contrast to this fragmentary reference, the next statement of the theme is much more like the first (Ex. 16-3). Interestingly enough, this literal return is not preceded by a complete break (as was the fragmentary reference) but instead seems to grow unobtrusively out of a long motivic extension in the same high woodwind timbre. The consequent of the theme (*b*) is played by loud tutti instead of soft strings; it does not come to a full cadence but leads

Example 16-5 Haydn, Allegro: First theme, statements 1 and 4 compared

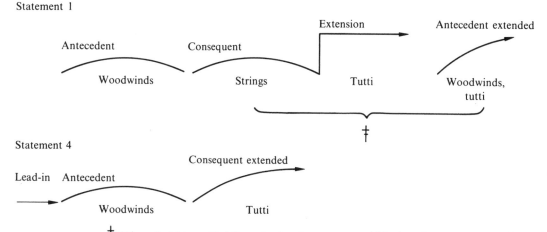

Statement 1

Antecedent   Consequent   Extension   Antecedent extended

Woodwinds   Strings   Tutti   Woodwinds, tutti

Statement 4

Consequent extended

Lead-in   Antecedent

Woodwinds   Tutti

† This material is omitted from the fourth statement, which gives the consequent to the tutti, then goes immediately to the material previously used to extend the antecedent.

on in the fashion of the *second* statement of the theme (Ex. 16-5).

This last complete statement of the theme has several important functions. First, it is *the* important literal return of the theme—the one time, after the beginning, that we hear this theme more or less as it was in the beginning. For this reason, the theme can here announce the major structural return of the whole movement: it begins the last section, which as we saw is similar to the first in material and stability of motion. The return of the theme is the specific element that marks off the final section from the middle one, even if it is preceded by no break or pause.

That much might have been accomplished with a mere reference to the theme—or just to the antecedent. But there is more involved than just the return of the melody. When the theme was first heard, it was closed and stable. When it returns in this literal form, it brings the same sense of stability with it. It is essential, in other words, that more than just the opening notes of the melody return; the whole song-like shape presages the broader stability that will characterize the whole last section.

As another aspect of this high-level function, the return takes place at the exact pitch level of the first statement. This identity of pitch level involves an identity of harmonic area or key. It should be emphasized, here as elsewhere in this book, that most people do not automatically identify the key of the return as the same as the key of the beginning—either absolutely, as one recognizes the color red when seeing it in a new context, or relatively, as when comparing two red patches in separated places in a painting. The last statement of the theme is too far from the first statement for us to remember the original key. With concentration and practice, however, a listener can become more sensitive to that sense of harmonic "rightness" of the return of the theme (perhaps present already in his first hearing) to the point where the key of the return seems to be the original key, even without a basis for direct comparison.

One last function of this return has to do with the fact that it is not entirely literal but is slightly changed. As we noted, the consequent phrase is for loud tutti (not soft strings) and does not reach a full cadence but instead leads on. The sense of this change seems to be that this appearance of the theme combines in one statement three features of the beginning section—the first theme in its first appearance, the first theme in its second appearance (just the antecedent with no cadence), and the loud tutti that comes between these two statements (Ex. 16-5). The change in the return

of the theme tends to accelerate the section as a whole toward the conclusion of the movement. Events we first heard as widely separated come here in such rapid succession as to seem a single event; suddenly we find ourselves much further along in the last section than we thought we were.

FUNCTIONS OF THE SECOND THEME. To some degree, we can follow the progress of the movement through the first theme alone; for this reason the first theme can be called the *main* theme. Even though it is actually present a relatively small portion of the time, its appearances—specifically the last one—are placed where they have the most decisive effect upon the shape of the whole movement.

The other theme prominent in the movement is in many ways as important as the first (and, in fact, is present, through its motives, a much longer portion of the time, as we will see); yet this other theme does not seem quite as decisive as the first. It is a *second* theme in order of appearance, as well as a *subsidiary* theme in final significance.

The second theme appears (at 1 in Ex. 16-6) soon after the second statement of the first theme, which is followed by a brief, loud tutti and a full cadence. The central, concluding harmony of the cadence is then played softly in a rapid accompaniment figure in

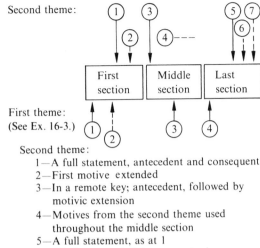

Second theme:

First theme:
(See Ex. 16-3.)

Second theme:
1—A full statement, antecedent and consequent
2—First motive extended
3—In a remote key; antecedent, followed by
   motivic extension
4—Motives from the second theme used
   throughout the middle section
5—A full statement, as at 1
6—Motive extended in a remote key
7—First motive extended, as at 2

Example 16-6 Haydn, Allegro: Statements of first
and second themes

strings. The melody that enters over this accompaniment is the second theme (Ex. 16-7).

Like the first theme, the second provides on each of its returns a moment of clarity and stability, and its first statement is marked by this stability. Also like the first theme, the second has a clear antecedent-and-consequent structure at the highest level and at lower levels too. In order to keep track of its manifold symmetries, we need a detailed diagram of the rhythm of the second theme (Ex. 16-8).

Example 16-7 Haydn, Allegro: Preparation
for the second theme (statement 1)

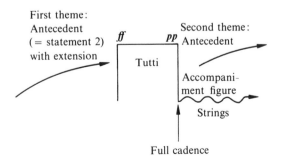

The rhythm of the theme at the lowest level consists of a three-note motive with two short upbeat notes and a longer downbeat note. This lively upbeat motive gives the second theme a markedly different character from the first theme, which begins with a clear downbeat (Ex. 16-4). The upbeat motive pervades not only the second theme but also the whole middle section of the movement, as we will see.

The persistent low-level rhythm of the motive is molded into phrases by line and harmony. A clear rise and fall of the line creates the subphrase structure (Ex. 16-8), subphrases 1 and 3 rising, 2 and 4 falling. These four subphrases lead to a cadence that is full and therefore a closed ending on the lower harmonic level; but, during this first part of the theme, a smooth shift of harmonic area has taken place, so that in context of the whole theme this cadence at the end of subphrase 4 is open. Thereafter, the theme moves gradually back to its central harmony (Ex. 16-9). The open ending halfway through the theme separates it clearly into antecedent and consequent phrases.

16-6. Numbers 2, 4, 6, and 7 in the diagram (with dotted lines) show the use of motive just discussed. Numbers 1, 3, and 5 (with solid lines) show the appearances of the theme as a theme.

The return of the second theme at 3 is the most striking one. Between 2 and 3 is the loud tutti that begins with the upbeat motive in the bass line. This tutti continues, full and strong and very stable harmonically; it comes to a clear full cadence (the clearest so far in the movement), followed by a pause. Then comes the soft, rapid accompaniment figure and the second theme—just as in Ex. 16-7. The harmonic area, however, is drastically different.

This sudden departure into a remote key is the most striking harmonic event in the Allegro up to this point. Coming as it does after a full cadence and a clear break, it sets off everything that follows from everything that came before. This harmonic departure, indeed, marks off the first section of the movement from the middle.

The harmonic departure at the start of the middle

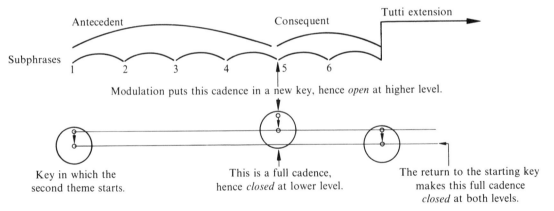

Example 16-9 Haydn, Allegro: Modulation and phrase structure in the second theme

The first motive from the second theme is put to work immediately in the following tutti; its persistent repetitions appear in the bass, generating a lively, rising line. For much of the rest of the movement, this motive is used in various ways that will require our attention later. For now, we need to notice the returns of the second theme as a theme, not just the appearances of its motives. These returns are shown in Ex.

section could have been made without the second theme; but the return of the second theme as the vehicle for the departure greatly enhances the effect. For one thing, the second theme has just provided (on its first appearance) a very clear expression of a different harmonic area. To have this same theme return right away in a remote area makes the shift especially apparent. The two statements are close

Example 16-8 Haydn, Allegro: Rhythm and phrase structure of second theme

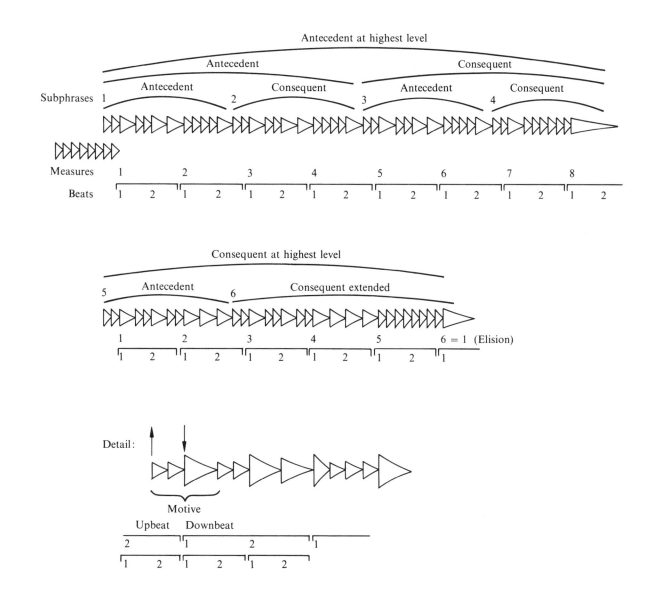

enough that we can almost compare them directly as we listen to the piece.

The return of the second theme starts off the middle section in a way more striking than, say, a return of the first theme could have. In addition, there is something arresting about the appearance of the second theme rather than the first at this point. A more common-sense layout of the piece would have given the first theme its expected turn, instead of letting the second theme come twice in succession. Haydn, however, has a more refined plan in mind: the return of the first theme can more effectively mark off the final section—and establish a sense of overall return for that section—if it does not appear here at the start of the middle section.

The second theme makes its other return in due course after the appearance of the first theme, in the final section (Ex. 16-6, No. 5). In this case, the second theme marks no sectional division; its function is rather to consolidate the feeling of stability of the final section. It does this, first of all, just by returning: the second theme followed the first at the beginning of the movement and must do so at the end if all is to be present and accounted for.

More than that, the second theme now returns in the same key as the first theme, thereby strengthening the sense of stability in the final section. As we heard, the first section involves a modulation between the two statements of the first theme (Ex. 16-10). The second theme, when it appears in the first section, is in the new key. First and second themes mark out a progression from one key to another and suggest a tension between them. In the last section, on the other hand, first and second themes appear in the *same* key; even if they are not close enough to permit direct comparison by ear, still we sense the way one confirms the other. Moreover, they are much closer to each other than they were in the first section.

We can follow the course of the movement with the help of both themes much better than just with the first. (It is worth noticing that we could not follow it very well just with the second theme). Still, however, we leave out a great deal if we listen only for themes. It is good to start with the themes: the composer put them there so we would have clear reference points early in our experience with the piece. In this respect,

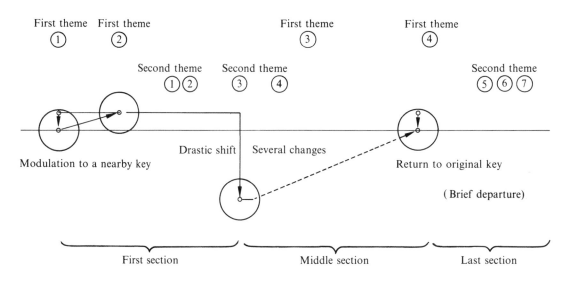

Example 16-10 Haydn, Allegro: Key relationships and thematic statements

the themes fulfill a general function not unlike that of the text in, say, *Le Nozze di Figaro* or *Les Noces*. Eventually, however, we want to grasp the piece as a whole, which includes all the nonthematic passages as well as the thematic ones. Nor should the nonthematic passages be regarded merely as filler, as bridges from one beautiful theme to the next. A moment's reflection will show that just the themes, if excerpted from Haydn's Allegro and placed in succession on a tape, would scarcely provide the sense of the whole piece. We draw close to this sense when we listen for the themes *in context*; we draw even closer when we take into account the context as well.

Certain elements of the outline of the Allegro as sketched so far reappear frequently in the first fast movements of symphonies and some other kinds of pieces such as string quartets or sonatas (a multi-movement work for piano solo or some other solo instrument, with or without piano accompaniment). Musicians commonly use certain standard terms for the large sections we have called first, middle, and last. The first section of a movement with this plan and character is called an *exposition*, because it displays the themes and principal keys to be used in

the movement. The middle section is often called the *development* section, because it is likely to contain much thematic and motivic development. Development does, however, occur at any other place in the movement the composer wishes. The middle section is also (but less frequently) called a *fantasy* section, because of the way remote keys follow one another in unexpected succession and because the themes may assume new and different shapes. The third section is called a *restatement* or *recapitulation*, because it restates or recapitulates the themes and other material from the exposition, without exactly repeating it. The whole plan is traditionally called *first-movement form,* or *sonata-allegro form*, or simply *sonata form*; but these last two terms are misleading, since, on the one hand, the form of any particular sonata (or symphony) includes all the movements, not just the first; and, on the other hand, insofar as sonata form is common to a number of works, it is as characteristic of symphonies and string quartets—if not more so—than of sonatas. In any case, we are concerned in this book with the shape of a particular piece, not with what that piece has in common with certain other pieces.

THE FIRST SECTION. Almost all the passages of the first section that are not thematic are for tutti—usually a loud tutti (Ex. 16-11). The thematic statements are all in reduced timbre and texture. The first theme is played by woodwinds or by strings. The second theme is played primarily by strings; and, even though the winds also play a little, they do not raise the sound to the level of a tutti.

The tutti sound is always there, waiting for the softly understated themes to finish so that it can dominate the conversation by boisterously echoing something in the theme, then expanding on it. Although the movement is written for full orchestra, the themes are for smaller groups. This fact alone should indicate that the themes are not the only important parts of the movement.

The first tutti has the very important function of moving from one key to another. As we heard, the second appearance of the first theme is at a new pitch level, in a new key (compare Ex. 16-10). The key is not changed abruptly, but rather by a smooth modulation that takes place within the first tutti. Later we will pinpoint this change even more closely.

In addition to changing key, the first tutti provides a contrast to the first theme in many ways: while the theme is stable in key, the tutti is unstable; while the theme is closed, with clear antecedent and consequent phrases, the tutti is open-ended and asymmetrical in phrase shape. More than that, the tutti is driven forward with continuous motion; it does not really have any clear phrases. Because of these aspects (as well as more subtle ones), the tutti's melodies do not become themes, nor do its rhythmic or melodic figures become motives.

In order to understand the musical process involved in the first tutti, we need to refer to a detailed diagram. Ex. 16-12 shows the first fifty-two measures of the Allegro, beginning with the theme (for orientation) and going on through the tutti, up to the first return of the first theme. We cannot indicate everything to be discussed on this one diagram; but matters discussed in connection with the more detailed diagrams to follow can be located on this one. As when using all such diagrams, listen through once or twice while counting just to match up the diagram with the music.

The harmonic components of the tutti are simple.

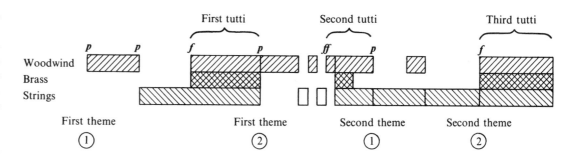

Example 16-11 Haydn, Allegro: Tuttis in the first section

There is an initial pedal note on the central pitch (measures 16 through 26). Then we have a series of three-measure groups (27 through 29, 30 through 32, 33 through 35) that contain similar material at different pitch levels—somewhat like a sequence, except that the overall motion is neither descending nor ascending, and the material is not exactly repeated. A real sequence (35 through 39) follows. Finally, there is another pedal (39 through 50) on the leading harmony of the new key. The modulation is effected specifically in the three-measure groups, shown in the detail of Ex. 16-12.

This modulation is accomplished without much ado; your attention is more likely to be engaged in the rhythmic processes of the tutti. At first, you will hear what might be the start of a soaring line in the violins over the pedal. This line soon develops a good deal of rhythmic repetition (in two-measure groups) but yet does not seem about to stop for breath—it does not form phrases, at least in the manner of the first theme. As the line becomes increasingly motivic and less tuneful (measure 26), it dispenses with even slight inflections that might articulate the line into phrases. Only the motivic groupings themselves or the groupings provided by harmony (as in the three-measure groups) remain effective, and they tend to become very short. In the descending sequence, the groups are one measure long; over the following pedal they become two measures long.

None of these groupings is long enough to be a phrase; yet none of the means used to make phrases in the first theme is used here in the tutti. The result is a long continuous arch that stretches from the end of the first theme all the way to the return of this theme. The relationship between the rhythmic continuity and the harmonic modulation is complex, for the rhythm helps sweep us along through the change of key, while the change, for its part, helps keep the sound of the insistent rhythm fresh and interesting, lest it degenerate into something mechanical.

Besides a specific function (here, change of key), nonthematic passages such as this have much broader functions in large movements. A collection of clearly phrased themes could not attain the stature and dimensions of this Allegro, with its subtle blend of unity and variety. The nonthematic passages are an essential means of extending the dimensions and significance of the movement beyond the limitations of clear phrase and stable harmonic area as found in the theme. We could, in fact, regard such a movement as consisting mainly of open-ended continuity, interrupted occasionally by a relatively closed, static theme.

SHAPE OF THE MIDDLE SECTION. We noticed (page 328) that the second theme appears at the very beginning of the middle section in a remote harmonic area, as if to suggest the harmonic departures and more intense harmonic motion to follow. The most obvious aspect of the harmony in this section is its instability: clearly central harmonies are infrequent; the *direction* of the passages leading from one area to another is not always clear. We are, however, given some clues of a linear nature (similar to the bass line studied on page 121) with which we may follow the long-range harmonic motion.

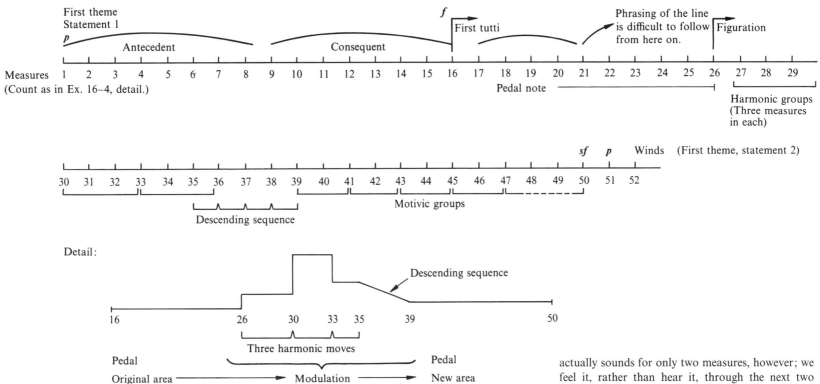

Example 16-12 Haydn, Allegro: Modulation in the first tutti

Certain harmonies seem to establish themselves over relatively long stretches—one harmony for four measures, say, or even for eight. These harmonies seem as if they rested on pilings sunk deep into the subsoil of the orchestra, sometimes showing as pedal notes, sometimes only intermittently perceptible through the persistent motivic repetitions. If we focus on these reference pitches and follow their slow progression, we discover the special kind of harmonic direction that binds the development section together and sets it off from the rest of the movement.

The reference tones for the harmonic motion of the first half of the development section are shown in Ex. 16-13, which of all the diagrams for this movement is probably the most difficult to follow. The difficulty lies in hearing the note—or implied note—represented in the diagram. Begin by merely following the measures (using the key at the bottom of Ex. 16-13). Listen for the dynamics, which not only serve for orientation but also are closely correlated with the long-range harmonic motion. After one or two hearings, begin to follow the long notes indicated in the diagram, listening—more intuitively than analytically—for sustained or reiterated pitches that might correspond to these notes. The first note (centered on the measure-counting line for convenience) is heard merely as the intermittent bass note in the accompaniment. The second note (measure 111) is also in the bass, but alternates in a rocking motion with a pitch a semitone higher (not shown on the diagram). The third and fourth notes, forte and sforzando, are clearly audible. The sforzando note

actually sounds for only two measures, however; we feel it, rather than hear it, through the next two measures, then can follow the semitone motion up and down again (measures 121 and 122).

From measure 123 on, there is a repetition of the motivic material first heard in 111. Measures 111 through 122 and 123 through 135 constitute a descending sequence in line and also in harmonic motion, as shown in Ex. 16-13. The harmonic descent to the sforzando in measure 117, repeated in sequence at measure 130, shapes the first half of the development section. If you can hear this colossal harmonic sequence, you can grasp harmonic motion at relatively high levels.

The last prolonged note in Ex. 16-13 (measure 142) is part of a harmonic progression from a leading chord to a central chord, shown in the enclosure; the prolonged note in the bass (sounding in several other registers too) can be said to leap up to the bass note in the central harmony. The resolution to the central harmony takes place after the break that precedes the fragment of the first theme, so that the mighty

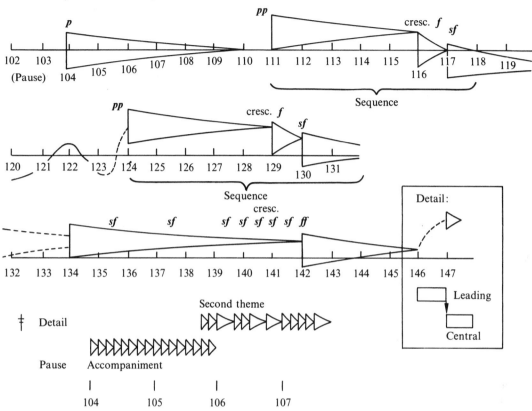

Example 16-13 Haydn, Allegro:
Plan of harmonic motion
in the middle section (first half)

progression up to that break can be said to have an open ending. The rest of the development section follows as natural consequent.

THE FINAL SECTION. The restatement of material from the first section is not literal: some things heard in the exposition are now omitted. One event is added —a sudden, startling departure into a remote key at the end of the second theme.

The basic difference between recapitulation and exposition has to do with their respective functions in the movement. The exposition presents two themes in two different keys; the transition from one key to the other is important and is given prominence by the modulating tutti (the first) and the repetition of the first theme. The second theme, in turn, is well prepared. The third tutti is relatively brief, since by then the function of the exposition is nearly done, and more important things lie just ahead.

In the recapitulation, on the other hand, the main purpose is closure of the movement with reestablishment of the opening mood and character after the departure of the middle section. By way of accomplishing this with dispatch, the first theme is followed (after a very brief extension) directly by the second, which enters with no special preparation. The second theme is now in the original key (see Ex. 16-10), which is firmly maintained until the end of the move-

ment—except for the single sudden departure after the second theme. Clearly, the function of such a departure (number 6) is to provide harmonic relief and freshness without an actual modulation, which would unsettle the overall harmonic plan and hinder the thrust toward conclusion.

The tutti material, then, is rearranged to help carry out the function of the recapitulation. Besides being all in the same key (the original one), the tutti material is grouped all together, making one continuous tutti at the end of the movement. The plan in Ex. 16-14 compares the order of events in the three sections, showing specifically how the recapitulation reorders the material of the exposition.

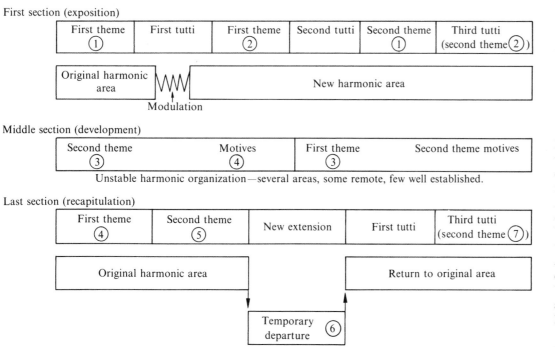

First section (exposition)

First theme ①	First tutti	First theme ②	Second tutti	Second theme ①	Third tutti (second theme ②)

Original harmonic area	Modulation	New harmonic area

Middle section (development)

Second theme ③	Motives ④	First theme ③	Second theme motives

Unstable harmonic organization—several areas, some remote, few well established.

Last section (recapitulation)

First theme ④	Second theme ⑤	New extension	First tutti	Third tutti (second theme ⑦)

Original harmonic area	Temporary departure ⑥	Return to original area

Example 16-14 Haydn, Allegro: Comparison of the three sections

THE SYMPHONY AS A WHOLE. With the shape of the large Allegro movement in mind, we can return to the shape of the whole symphony. One way to appreciate this shape is to imagine the movements of the symphony played in some other order. Some of the other possible orders distort the intent of the individual movements drastically: for example, if the Adagio introduction were placed at the end of the work (*after* the Presto) instead of at the beginning, there would be a blatant contradiction between the open-ended nature of the introduction and its position in the symphony. You probably do not need to imagine such an order to appreciate the function of the introduction; some of the other possible orders, however, involve more subtle adjustments in the inner balance of the symphony and can give us insight into that balance.

For example, the slow introduction might have a reasonable function when placed before one of the other movements. In Ex. 16-15, plan (*a*), the introduction remains first in the symphony, followed by the Presto; the Allegro is transferred to the end as Finale; and the two inner movements are exchanged. What would be the effect? There would be very high contrast of character between solemn introduction and mercurial Presto—so high as perhaps to be comic. Then the intricacies of the Menuetto, coming *after* the Presto, might have the effect of making the Presto sound even lighter and less substantial. The Allegro at the end would reinforce that effect and would in addition make the work harder to grasp as it went along, rather than easier.

The placing of the Allegretto third instead of second would have the least noticeable effect upon the whole; in plan (*a*) of Ex. 16-15, this position of the Allegretto would be the least change. But suppose the Allegretto came first, as in plan (*b*). The idea of a march would be perfectly appropriate at the start of a large work; but this particular march would begin the symphony with an air of nonchalance, even diffidence. The Adagio would then be restricted in function, serving only as an introduction to the Allegro, rather than to the symphony as a whole; or else the symphony would seem to have another beginning after the Allegretto. This effect would be the stronger because of the harmonic plan: the Allegretto is the odd movement, the only one in a different harmonic area; placed by itself at the beginning, *before* the weighty introduction, it might actually split off from the other movements and seem like a separate work.

There are, of course, many other possible arrangements of these movements. Consideration of any one plan might yield additional insight into the mutual relationships of the movements. We would not necessarily conclude that any one plan (including the plan Haydn chose) is *better* than the others. Haydn's plan suited his intent better than any other—but that puts the matter differently. The important thing is to become sensitive to the different effects produced by different arrangements, so as better to appreciate (in this or any multimovement work) the effect produced by the arrangement actually used. While you should be on the lookout for any insight specific enough to be stated as a "reason" for the construction of the work or for its unity, such reasons are hard to

Example 16-15 Haydn, Symphony No. 100: Other possible orders of the movements

(*a*)	Adagio	Finale: Presto	Menuetto	Trio	Menuetto	Allegretto	Allegro

(*b*)	Allegretto	Adagio	Allegro	Menuetto	Trio	Menuetto	Finale: Presto

discover and harder to formulate. You should hope to hear that the work *is* unified, without necessarily expecting to be able to demonstrate why.

Tempo, key, rhythmic nature, and character were considered as gross factors in the plan earlier (page 323); we could continue to consider them, at the movement level, in more and more refined ways. There is a tendency to think that profound insight into a work can occur only at the level of detail and that questions involving large units such as entire movements are by nature superficial. But Johannes Brahms (1833–1897), a great symphony composer, thought long and hard about completely replacing the first movement of his beautifully lyric Symphony No. 2 (after it was all finished)—presumably for reasons having to do with tempo, rhythm, and character. Beethoven did in fact replace movements in completed works. Such decisions are hardly to be considered superficial. The larger outline of a work (rather than details of inner construction) is a matter about which the educated listener can most appropriately be expected to have sensitive perception and ultimately intelligent judgment.

In Haydn's Symphony No. 100, the role of the Adagio is the easiest to understand: it has to be an introduction to *something*; that is, because of its nature it is going to sound like an introduction no matter where it is placed. The other movements are more difficult to appreciate. It seems clear, however, that the Presto is indeed a Finale; that is, considering all the movements, no other seems more apt for an ending. The Allegro is going to be the center of gravity of the symphony wherever it appears, and its position (if changed) will determine to a large extent the balance of the whole. For the sake of the integrity of the key plan, the Allegretto must be an inner movement, not an outer one. The most subtle question of order concerns the Allegretto and Menuetto: if only these two were exchanged, the basic economy of the symphony would be only slightly changed—but it would be changed.

We have not yet considered the sectional plans of the individual movements in order. We have studied two of the movements (Menuetto and Trio, Chapter 5; Finale, Chapter 8); we will summarize without discussion the plans of the Adagio and the Allegretto

(Ex. 16-16). The plans of all the movements are included in the same example. It is immediately apparent from this example that no two movements are alike in their overall plan; the differences are substantial.

The Adagio introduction has no sectional plan; it starts to display a phrase plan, but that soon becomes indeterminate through irregular extensions and harmonic changes. The introduction offers, as it were, a *tabula rasa*, a null state, as far as sectional plans are concerned. It prepares us to hear more acutely whatever comes next.

If we can say little, in context, about the plan of the Adagio introduction, we cannot say much more—again *in context*—about the plan of the following Allegro, simply because it is the first sectional plan we meet in this symphony. It is a difficult plan to grasp, in that it continues to unfold for a relatively long time before revealing what kind of a plan it is going to be. In fact, we discover many things about the movement

(its tempo, rhythm, principal keys, themes, and motives) before we notice the plan, before enough sectional divisions or returns have occurred to inform us about the plan. On the one hand, we are encouraged by the music to listen to developmental process, not plan; on the other hand, insofar as we do hear a plan (especially toward the end of the movement), we notice its large dimensions and complex inner constructions.

The Allegretto brings not so much a different plan as a different feeling about plan. The Allegretto is laid out (considered abstractly) in the same $A_1\ B\ A_2$ arrangement as the Allegro; but, because of the much shorter dimensions, as well as the regularity of phrase structure, the plan of the Allegretto is perceptible as the movement unfolds—indeed, the plan is an important part of the way it unfolds.

As the plan of the Allegretto shows, the A_1 section consists of a first phrase group, a_1, that ends open and is immediately repeated; then a phrase group b,

Example 16-16 Haydn, Symphony No. 100: Overall plan of movements

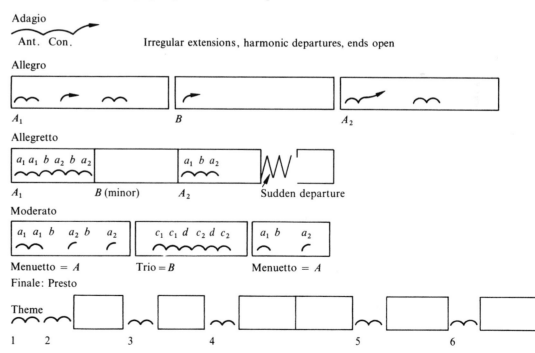

335

followed by a_2, which is very similar to a_1 except that it ends closed. The combined group $b\ a_2$ is immediately repeated.

These phrase groups are relatively short and simple; they are easily perceived—which is what makes the piece as a whole seem naïve. The repetition of a_1 is set off by a change of timbre from strings to woodwinds; the repetition of $b\ a_2$ is set off in the same way.

Most important for our purposes is the fact that section A_1 is made up completely of these clear phrase groups and their literal repetitions. The melody of section A_1 has a structure that many people could be taught to sing from memory in a relatively short time. The rhythm throughout the A_1 section proceeds in regular groups of four measures. Melodic patterns are repeated often, in simple ways. The harmonic progressions either remain very clearly in one area or move directly to a nearby area. (Phrase group b makes a very clear move to the area whose central harmony is the leading harmony of the original key; this phrase group presents an excellent opportunity to practice hearing this particular modulation.) There is nothing else in section A_1 except these clearly constructed phrase groups.

If we think back to the Allegro, a contrast becomes immediately apparent. In the Allegro, there was a clear antecedent-consequent phrase group at the beginning; but right after that came an extended tutti in which clear phrase groups were deliberately avoided. In this tutti and in the first section as a whole, clearly defined phrase structure was the exception rather than the rule: the bulk of the section was not clearly phrased. Indeed, one of the main functions of clearly phrased themes was a contrast to the rest of the section. Now that you can compare such a procedure to the Allegretto, where clear phrase structures account for *all* of the A_1 section, you can perhaps appreciate the significance of those relatively unphrased tuttis in the Allegro; they serve to spring the whole section loose from the closed effect of clear phrases.

Section B of the Allegretto provides a contrast to section A_1 in harmonic color and key: it shifts immediately to minor, then modulates to another key for a short time. The melodic material, however,

is derived from that of section A_1; furthermore, the phrase structure of section B continues to be regular, although not shown in Ex. 16-16. We must make a relatively refined qualification of section B: we must say that insofar as its melodic material is an extension of the material of the A_1 section, section B is something like a development of A_1—and, to that extent, has a certain similarity to the middle section of the Allegro. The similarity, however, is one of procedure, not of size. We must add that the B section of the Allegretto has phrases far too regular and short to reproduce the effects of the hard-driven extensions and far-flung phrase shapes of the Allegro. In other words, if we indicated the phrase structure of the B section of the Allegro in Ex. 16-16, it would completely fill up the box representing the section, just as in the box for the A_1 section. To put it still another way, the B sections of Allegretto and Allegro are as different in effect as are the A_1 sections. The Allegretto as a whole has a sense of symmetry, of limit and closure, that makes it basically different from the Allegro.

As if to compensate for this sense of closure, Haydn provides one startling departure in the movement. Toward the end (at the jagged lines in Ex. 16-16), there is a trumpet call, then an abrupt shift to a remote harmony, hammered home with a barrage of percussion; the whole event is alien to the rest of the movement. Immediately afterward, the movement returns to its regular rhythmic movement and clear, closed melodic shapes—but not completely, for something of the surge of the Allegro has been mysteriously introduced into the Allegretto. This last effect is admittedly very subtle. The harmonic shift, on the other hand, is obvious, and will be discussed further when we consider harmonic areas in the symphony as a whole.

In general, the phrase structure of the Moderato, movement III, and its relationship to the section plan, recalls the Allegretto. These two central movements are similar in basic construction, even if dissimilar in key, meter, and character. The Moderato has a section plan $A\ B\ A$ (Menuetto, Trio, Menuetto). In this case, the second A section is a literal repeat of the first, except for the omission of the repeat ($a_1\ a_1\ b\ a_2$ instead of $a_1\ a_1\ b\ a_2\ b\ a_2$). The B section, or Trio,

consists entirely of short, regular phrases ($c_1\ c_1\ d\ c_2\ d\ c_2$). As in section A_1 of the Allegretto, the phrase structure completely fills out the section; there is no extension or development that overrides the regular limits established by the opening phrase.

The same kind of clear phrasing is heard at the beginning of the A section or Menuetto ($a_1\ a_1$ in Ex. 16-16). The A section begins with an antecedent-consequent phrase group (a_1) that ends closed, then is immediately repeated in slightly different timbre.

At the point marked b in Ex. 16-16, a different kind of phrasing appears—a kind much more reminiscent of the Allegro. Through the various procedures described in Chapter 5, regular phrasing is here overridden by rhythmic intricacy at the lower levels. The result is a sense of continuity that carries over all the way to the return (a_2), with but only one obvious break. Even though a_2 brings with it the clear phrasing of the start of the movement, this too is overridden by the extension that follows it.

In this one passage, then, the Moderato reminds us of the procedures of the Allegro—but on a much smaller scale. In fact, it seems that the passage at b does not really break out of the regular phrasing already established; instead, it merely obscures it, creating a sense of involvement at the level of detail that makes it difficult to perceive what is happening at the level of phrase. Our initial impression of the Moderato—as a movement in which phrase groups filled out sections—still holds.

We can say, then, that while both Allegretto and Moderato momentarily revert to the procedures characteristic of the Allegro, they have in general a different sense of motion, one in which each successive phrase comes to some kind of ending (either open or closed) at regular intervals. These intervals of time are short enough (most often four measures) that they are easily held in the ear. Each section is heard as a summation of regular phrases. What is most interesting about the symphony as a whole is that the movements with regular phrasing follow, rather than precede, the movement with greatly extended, almost unphrased passages. The more irregular kind of music comes first; the more regular, more easily perceived kind comes afterwards. Insofar as we compare one against the other, we do so retroactively: we remember, while listening to the Allegretto and Moderato, that they were preceded by something far more complex and irregular. As we get further from the Allegro, we become increasingly aware that it contained the most difficult, challenging music of the symphony.

Against this background, the structure of the Finale (Presto) turns out to be especially interesting. When we studied this movement in detail (Chapter 8), we noticed the discrepancy between the very simple, square theme and the increasingly complex, extended passages between the returns of this theme (summarized in Ex. 8-1). We noticed even a certain triviality in the theme considered by itself; it possesses little that would elevate it above a common dance tune. Now we can hear that this simple tune is designed to be the most extreme expression within the symphony of clear antecedent-consequent phrasing. It exceeds in simplicity anything found in the Allegretto or Moderato. On the other hand, the rest of the Finale (that is, the passages between the returns of the theme) rivals passages of the Allegro in degree of motivic development. In fact, even though we identified a second theme in the Finale, that theme is not nearly so obvious as the second theme of the Allegro. The developmental passages of the Finale tend to fuse together, then spill over in new, ever-changing shapes even more than those of the Allegro. Thus, the Finale presents in extreme form the two procedures found in the symphony. Appearing side by side as they do in the Finale, the two procedures seem to be in greatest contrast; no matter how extensively motives from the theme are used in development, the theme seems to retain an absolute integrity; it returns again and again with almost comic obstinacy, ultimately untouched by the elaborate transformations that occasionally threaten to overwhelm it in the developmental excursions.

HARMONIC RELATIONSHIPS. As we noticed briefly (Ex. 16-1), three of the four movements of the symphony are in the same key, the other movement (the Allegretto) being in a closely related key. There is, in other words, one principal harmonic area for the whole symphony. This is expressed technically by identifying this symphony as being in "G major"; "G" refers to the pitch level at which all movements except the Allegretto are *notated* (see Appendix C); "major" indicates the harmonic color, as we have been using the term.

A work of twenty or thirty minutes' duration, however, cannot remain strictly in one or even in two keys without risking monotony. And, indeed, harmonic changes of various kinds have appeared in all the movements. The curious aspect of these changes—especially the more drastic or remote ones—is that they tend to involve the same remote areas. They do not, in other words, go off each in a completely different direction; or, at any rate, there is a strong tendency for the more striking changes to form their own common area, a pole opposed to the pole represented by the principal area.

We can express these two poles in the diagram shown in Ex. 16-17. The principal area is the horizontal band that includes the bulk of the four movements (the Allegretto being slightly out of line). Striking harmonic shifts are shown by vertical lines leading to the numbered circles. All the circles in Ex. 16-17 lie below the principal area, because all these keys are closely related, constituting an area of their own (labeled "other area" in the diagram). There is no inherent reason why a circle should not appear in some other place, for example above the principal area; it just happens that in this symphony all the striking harmonic shifts go in the same direction, the one represented here *below* the principal area. There is, in fact, harmonic movement through areas lying above the principal one, but such movement occurs smoothly and inconspicuously.

The harmonic shifts shown in Ex. 16-17 occur as follows:

1. At the beginning of the middle section of the Allegro
2. The deceptive cadence at the end of the second theme in the last section of the Allegro
3. Section *B* of the Allegretto
4. The blast toward the end of the Allegretto
5. The second appearance of the second theme in the Finale (see Ex. 8-16)
6. The digression between theme statements 5 and 6 in the Finale (see Ex. 8-15)

Harmonic shifts 2, 3, and 6 are to the same key; shift 1 is to the key whose central harmony is the leading harmony of 2, 3, and 6; the key in shifts 4 and 5 has as leading harmony the central harmony of 2, 3, and 6. Thus the three keys involved in the shifts are closely related.

Analysis of this kind becomes increasingly remote

Example 16-17 Haydn, Symphony No. 100: Harmonic areas

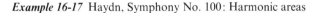

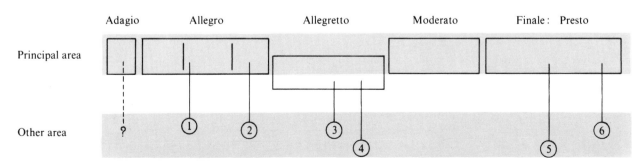

from the listening experience: most listeners do not hear the "other" area as a continuing dimension of the symphony in the spatial way suggested by Ex. 16-17. As a matter of fact, many listeners are perhaps not continuously aware of the principal area. (We might be aware of it in a poorly constructed piece that irritated us by its monotony.) What we hear is momentary change. At the moment of change, a particular change may recall another somewhere in the same piece. That is, it may if we are attending to such matters and if the composer encourages us to notice it by many subtle manipulations of the material.

For example, shift 1 (Ex. 16-17), at the beginning of the middle section of the Allegro, comes as a mere surprise. There is almost nothing in the symphony so far that would suggest the possibility of a move to this harmonic area. (We have to say "almost," because included in the slow introduction—as one of its seeming vagaries—was a brief move to the other area. This brief move might be regarded as sufficiently important to count as 1, but different listeners will ascribe different degrees of importance to it.)

The second shift, at the end of the last appearance of the second theme (2), is made startling largely by its placement as a deceptive cadence. At that particular moment, any shift could be a surprise. Probably no connection is made at that point specifically to the harmonic area of 1. You will probably be reminded at 2, however, that another shift had taken place earlier; and you may be dimly aware that shift 2 feels like the earlier shift (1)—that the quality of harmonic movement was similar.

In the Allegretto, shift 3 follows so smoothly from the change to minor at the beginning of the B section that it does not seem to involve a special harmonic area. You will, however, notice the harmonic area at 4; the accompanying fanfare makes it difficult not to notice. Here, too, your awareness is probably one of a similar kind of move, rather than of a return to a previously established destination.

Nonetheless, we should not ignore the fact that abstract, analytical examinations show a common destination or closely related set of destinations to all these shifts, including 5 and 6 in the Finale. This common destination of all the drastic harmonic moves in the symphony adds to its sense of purpose as a whole. The symphony does not merely have a principal area, a place to depart from and return to; it has the other area as a place to depart *to* (and return *from*).

Do not be alarmed if these polar areas are not immediately evident in your listening experience. They are the kind of fact that operates on a long-range basis to shape the work in very subtle ways, sometimes rising to consciousness but usually remaining unnoticed. Concentrating on long-range key relationships is an exercise (like reaching for the sky) that one does in order to stretch awareness, without necessarily expecting to succeed. In any case, long-range key relationships do not constitute the whole form or the whole meaning of the piece. They are only one set of factors, whose effects properly come to fulfillment in the successive moments of our listening.

One danger in concentrating too hard on long-range factors such as key relationships is a tendency to hear similarities among movements as the most important aspects of a work. That tendency easily misleads us into *listening* only for similarities. For example, in trying to understand the symphony as a whole, we may try to find thematic or motivic similarities—even the use of the same theme—among the various movements. Some symphonies do use the same theme in two or more movements. But it would be wrong to conclude that because Haydn's Symphony No. 100 does *not* use the same theme or the same motives in different movements, it is thereby less of a whole.

The important point is that finding relationships does not consist entirely or even mostly in finding similarities. Finding differences is just as much a part of comparing two or more movements. In comparing movement plans in Haydn's symphony, for example, the important facts were that the plans were different and that these differences, taken in order, had a definite effect. In many works, the *way* in which successive differences are ordered is one of the primary features of the work. Perceiving similarities is fruitful only when undertaken together with concomitant perception of differences.

UNDERSTANDING AN ENTIRE SYMPHONY by Beethoven is one of the most difficult challenges in listening to music. All other factors aside, the mere size of his Symphony No. 7 is enough to tax one's powers of comprehension. There are, to be sure, many works that are longer, but few in which the relationship of the overall length—as well as other aspects of the whole work—is so intimately related to detail. We must, in other words, try to grasp the work as a whole, not just sit through it. If this seems too ambitious a task for a listener in an introductory stage, remember that college students (even high school students) are encouraged to read and understand a play by Shakespeare as a whole.

We can begin by making a rough list of the relative qualities of the individual movements, as we did for Haydn's symphony (page 323). As before, the list considers the movements in order, comparing them as it goes along. For each movement, the list begins with very simple things, such as pace, a subjective impression of length, and meter. The list then goes on to first impressions of the overall shape of the movement, the prominence of themes or motives, and the character of the movement compared to those that precede it. By this time, you should be able to perceive aspects such as these on first or second hearing.

One way to approach Beethoven's Symphony No. 7 is to think of it as a larger version of the plan Haydn used in his Symphony No. 100. There are differences, but these come out clearly in the comparison and bring with them insights into the large design of Beethoven's symphony.

The similarities, expressed in Ex. 17-1, are obvious: both symphonies have a slow introduction followed by a large, complex, fast movement. The second movement in each case is a subdued marchlike piece in moderate tempo: the third movement is a faster movement in triple meter. These two central movements are the most obviously sectional ones and also the least developmental. The last movement is less obviously sectional and is as fast as or faster than any of the others. In neither symphony can the last movement be called completely clear or simple; on the other hand, neither of these last movements is as difficult in its inner construction as the first movements.

CHAPTER 17   BEETHOVEN'S SYMPHONY NO. 7

One of the most obvious differences between Haydn's symphony and Beethoven's is the much greater length of Beethoven's slow introduction. Along with the greater length—in fact, demanded by it—is a sectional structure not apparent in Haydn's Adagio. Both introductions have open endings—or

Poco sostenuto

somewhat slow; relatively long; in duple meter
contrasting interludes produce a clear sectional structure; but overall effect is cloudy, due to complex treatment of harmony and theme in main sections
ends open (with a transition leading directly to the Vivace) as an introduction; not self-contained

Vivace

lively but not too fast; relatively long; in triple meter at one low level, duple at other levels
seemingly continuous—at least, sections are not clear at middle levels, and so long as to be hard to grasp at highest levels
themes and motives seem important
complex, with a sense of growth and development as it goes on; strong ending

Allegretto

moderately slow: relatively long; in duple meter, except for some figuration
contrasting interludes produce a sectional structure that is clear in some respects, complex in others
two themes prominent throughout the main sections, alternating with interludes (roughly *A B A B A*)
starts simply and softly, becomes sometimes loud,

rather do not end at all, properly speaking, since each leads directly into the following fast movement. Yet, in the case of Beethoven's Poco sostenuto, you may feel (even after many hearings) that something more than an introduction is involved; and certainly on first hearing the Poco sostenuto could easily be a

sometimes complex, ends softly with reminiscence of the beginning
on the whole, more subdued than the Vivace

Presto/Assai meno presto

very fast (the Assai meno presto slower)
the shortest movement so far, but still long; in triple meter at lowest level, duple meter at the higher levels
very clear sections—by far the clearest in the symphony; the contrasting interludes are slower and completely different in material; at the sectional level the movement is very repetitive (*A B A B A*), with apparently exact repeats of whole sections
each section thematically and motivically homogeneous
on the whole, a bright, lively contrast to the Allegretto, and the least complex movement so far

Allegro con brio

fast; longer than the Presto; in duple meter
occasional repetitions of blocks of material; has the continuity, but less of the growth and development of the Vivace; is more like the Vivace than any other movement; has more rhythmic drive and momentum than any other

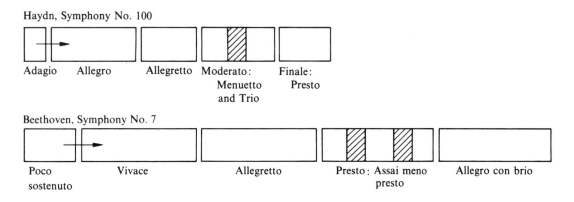

Haydn, Symphony No. 100

Adagio   Allegro   Allegretto   Moderato: Finale:
                                      Menuetto   Presto
                                      and Trio

Beethoven, Symphony No. 7

Poco   Vivace   Allegretto   Presto: Assai meno   Allegro con brio
sostenuto   presto

Example 17-1 Beethoven, Symphony No. 7: Movement plan compared to Haydn

principal event in its own right, at least up until it leads into the Vivace.

In comparing Haydn's Allegro with Beethoven's Vivace, you are probably most aware of the much more monumental effect of the latter. As will be clear when we discuss the Vivace in greater detail, its basic plan is very similar to that of Haydn's Allegro; but, because this plan is complex and because Beethoven's treatment of it in this particular symphony is so large and powerful, the differences seem at first more important than the similarities.

Another striking difference lies in the much greater weight of Beethoven's final movement, the Allegro con brio. Haydn's last movement is labeled Finale; and the movement does indeed bring the symphony to a clear, brilliant conclusion but one that reveals the center of gravity to be located back in the first movement. In spite of the great weight of Beethoven's Vivace, his Allegro con brio seems to rival it: in this case it is not so certain where the center of gravity lies.

The shape of Beethoven's symphony can be understood as two lesser movements framed by two greater ones (the whole preceded by the slow introduction), with the structural weight of the whole symphony shared equally by first and fourth movements. Distribution of weight or importance is an aspect impossible to diagram adequately; Ex. 17-2 attempts to suggest some intuitive comparisons of such differences between Haydn's symphony and Beethoven's. You can probably make diagrams that are more

meaningful to you with the help of some other kinds of shapes.

It is clear that such broad impressions of the shape of a symphony depend greatly on the shapes of the constituent movements. We have studied much of Beethoven's Symphony No. 7 at the movement level: we have discussed in detail the second movement (in Chapter 3) and the third movement (in Chapter 2); the Poco sostenuto was discussed in Chapter 7. We need now to work more closely with the first and fourth movements.

SOME WAYS TO APPROACH THE VIVACE. It is possible—and in some ways fruitful—to listen to the Vivace in terms of the large sections sketched out for

Example 17-2 Beethoven, Symphony No. 7:
        Distribution of weight in the
        movement plan, compared to Haydn

Haydn, Symphony No. 100

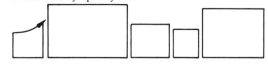

Beethoven, Symphony No. 7

Haydn's first movement, Allegro (page 325). One can find in Beethoven's Vivace a first, relatively stable section (exposition); a middle, less stable section (development); followed by a third that resembles the first (recapitulation; Ex. 17-3).

So far (and with qualifications to be discussed soon) the plan for Haydn's first movement holds for Beethoven's as well. But then Beethoven's Vivace goes right on into a large fourth section—one that is at first unstable, then very different, then finally similar again to the third section. This fourth section, a striking feature of the Vivace, represents a substantial difference from the plan of Haydn's Allegro. (This kind of section has a special name—*coda*, or "tail.") One of the advantages of having Haydn's plan in mind is the feeling of exciting expansiveness you will experience as Beethoven's Vivace plunges on past the expected end into a whole new section.

You may or may not be able at first to hear Beethoven's Vivace in terms of these sections. Two kinds of difficulties stand in the way. First, Beethoven goes on at considerably greater length than Haydn, putting a real strain on your ability to grasp the sections as self-contained units. Such sections seem to lie right on the breaking point between areas we can comfortably comprehend as units and those we automatically hear as consisting of two or more smaller units.

The other kind of difficulty (which reinforces the first) is that each section is less homogeneous, more disjointed than those of Haydn's Allegro. The disjointed quality is especially noticeable in the first section of Beethoven's Vivace—and right there is the cause of the problem. Even on repeated hearings, it is hard to distinguish between the seeming disjointedness of the first section and the instability of the second. Similarly, the third section does not seem to bring with it a return of stability as strong as that in the analogous place in Haydn's Allegro. The function of the sections become less obvious as the sections themselves (especially the first one) become more complex.

Differentiation of sections is made yet more difficult by an opposite tendency in the second section (Haydn's middle section) and in the fourth: these two sections have long stretches of repeated rhythms,

Haydn, Symphony No. 100, Allegro

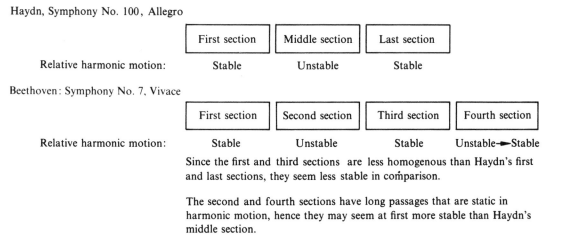

	First section	Middle section	Last section
Relative harmonic motion:	Stable	Unstable	Stable

Beethoven: Symphony No. 7, Vivace

	First section	Second section	Third section	Fourth section
Relative harmonic motion:	Stable	Unstable	Stable	Unstable→Stable

Since the first and third sections are less homogenous than Haydn's first and last sections, they seem less stable in comparison.

The second and fourth sections have long passages that are static in harmonic motion, hence they may seem at first more stable than Haydn's middle section.

Example 17-3 Beethoven, Symphony No. 7, Vivace: Sections and harmonic motion compared to Haydn

motives, and harmonies that create a feeling of stability simply because they go on for so long. You may mistake static passages in the second and fourth areas for stable passages in the first or third. Actually, the static passages in the second area, considered as huge building blocks, are juxtaposed in the same kind of unstable relationships heard in Haydn's development section; but this is difficult to hear at first.

Approaching Beethoven's Vivace with the plan of Haydn's Allegro in mind brings both difficulties and advantages. The difficulties are due, not to any irrelevance of Haydn's plan, but simply to the fact that Beethoven's piece is complex when considered from *any* point of view; no other plan offers an approach any less difficult. The same is true of other kinds of approaches we might derive from Haydn's Allegro—for example, theme as a clue to overall shape.

Beethoven makes extensive use of theme in his Vivace. There is no lack of thematic clues; rather, there are too many clues for an immediate understanding of the overall shape. The actual number of separate themes is very small: there are, in fact, only two; and of these only one (the first theme) is used extensively as a theme, the other being principally a source for a motive. In this respect, Beethoven's procedure is similar to Haydn's.

Example 17-4 Beethoven, Vivace, first theme

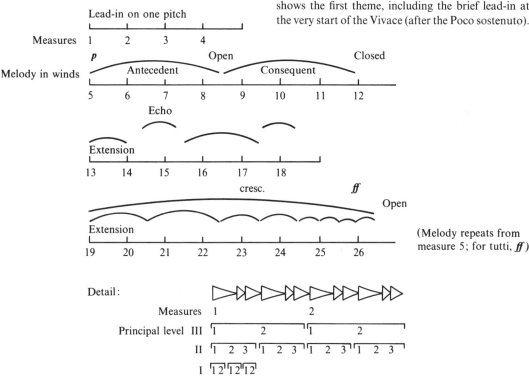

In Beethoven's Vivace, there is generally less difference between thematic and nonthematic material than there was in Haydn's Allegro. Theme or thematic material seems present a much larger percentage of the time. Motives drawn from both themes are used more persistently than in Haydn's Allegro—especially in the first section. Then too (as you will hear), the first theme returns in something more than merely motivic form in different places and with different functions, even within the first section.

In listening for the first theme in its high-level functions, you must have to distinguish among a hierarchy of kinds of appearances. You can profitably listen to the movement straight through two or three times, noticing each time a less obvious kind of appearance of this theme, as outlined here.

Full, literal returns of the first theme are actually very few—as in Haydn. In order to identify such returns, you must have a clear idea of the full extent of the theme in its first appearance. Example 17-4 shows the first theme, including the brief lead-in at the very start of the Vivace (after the Poco sostenuto).

341

The whole theme consists of:

an antecedent phrase with an open ending (half cadence in measure 8)

a consequent phrase with a closed ending (full cadence in measure 12)

an extension with echo in the accompaniment (measures 13 through 15)

the same extension repeated (measures 16-18)

a closing phrase formed from a motivic extension (measures 19-26)

We encounter ambiguities already in measure 26, for the cadence in this measure is obviously open. Is this the end of the theme? What follows certainly seems like a repetition of the theme for tutti (as opposed to the solo winds heard before). We can say, on one hand, that the complete theme ends in measure 26, then is repeated; on the other hand, we can say that measures 5 through 26 are a huge antecedent that ends open, followed by a huge consequent. This consequent (as it turns out) does not end at all, but leads directly into something else. Whichever interpretation you choose, note that the ambiguity is inherent in the music, not in the approach. Even if you do not hear a huge antecedent and consequent, be assured that Beethoven is quite capable (elsewhere if not here) of asking you to hear such long-breathed phrase structures.

Only one return of the first theme includes enough of the material just outlined to be called a complete return—and even this return is not literal, involving as it does some important changes. This return has a very important high-level function: it marks the beginning of the third section and the return of the original key, together with much of the material of the first section (Ex. 17-5). The return of the theme, in other words, is the principal shaping feature of the movement, from the point of view of sameness in the movement; other shaping features tend to lead toward difference, toward expansion or digression. At the return of the first theme, there is a mighty pulling together of the forces in the Vivace into a new focus.

In case you do not hear the four areas outlined earlier, you will find the return of the first theme slightly more than halfway through the Vivace.

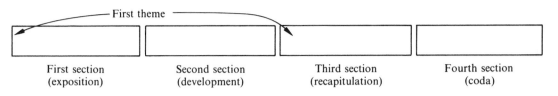

Example 17-5 Beethoven, Vivace: Main appearances of the first theme

Beethoven wants you to hear this return; and, while Beethoven is frequently obscure or complex, when he really wants you to hear something, you will hear it. After what seems interminable groping in the dark with no firm grasp on anything, the orchestra finally lays hold first of the right key, then the right motive, then—after one last stumble—breaks through into the full light of the theme. So intense does the thematic process become in Beethoven's hands that it seems here to take on the quality of dramatic gesture.

The set of thematic appearances next in order of importance involves the adaptation of the first theme as a closing theme for the first section. To some degree, this use of the first theme helps locate the end of the first section; at the same time, however, one needs to know roughly where to find this appearance of the theme, simply because motives from the theme occur so frequently throughout the movement. We need to digress briefly to locate the end of the first section more precisely.

Beethoven has left a clear landmark at the end of the first section—one that you may already have noticed. The first section ends with a pause for the whole orchestra, the only complete pause in the Vivace up to that point. Since the pause interrupts a fortissimo tutti, it is very noticeable. Just before the pause, the tutti comes to a resounding cadence, emphasized by the whole orchestra playing a great stammering figure in unison. This figure, a very distinctive one, is immediately repeated (with different pitches), then broken off again by another complete pause (Ex. 17-6).

The first theme is used as a closing theme in the seven measures immediately preceding the stammering figure, that is, during the fortissimo tutti. Only the beginning of the first theme (measures 5 through 7 of the antecedent) is used. It appears

several times in quick succession, however, for it is treated in imitation between soprano and bass. The line has also been modified to make it more suitable for the close of the section. In Ex. 17-7, you can compare the two versions of the line. You might listen through the first section, following the first theme at the beginning, then at the close, in Ex. 17-7.

The whole procedure—closing theme, stammering figure, complete pause—reappears at the end of the third section, marking off the third section from the fourth just as clearly as it marks off the first from the second. We can add one more appearance of the first theme—or at least its first few notes—as the closing theme for the entire movement, in the last few measures. All these appearances are shown in Ex. 17-8, from which it might seem that the first theme delineated the broad areas of the movement very clearly. The catch is that motives from the theme permeate the rest of these areas so much that the theme itself, especially when used as a closing theme, is not sharply differentiated from its surroundings.

Example 17-6 Beethoven, Vivace,
end of the first section

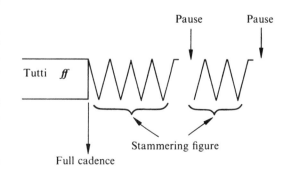

First theme at the beginning of the first section

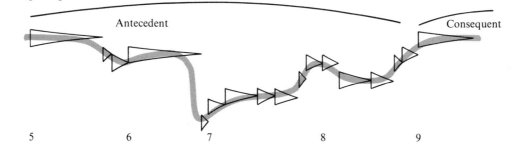

Antecedent

Consequent

5   6   7   8   9

At the end of the first section

From the antecedent

From the antecedent, condensed

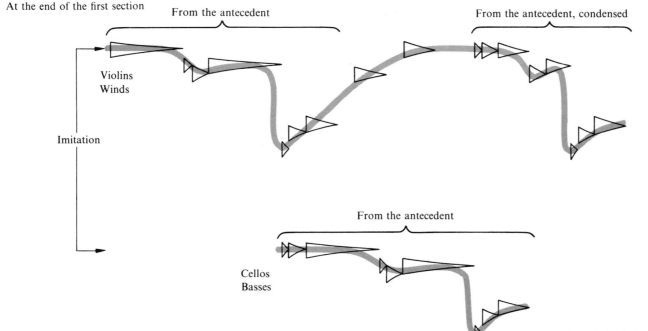

Violins
Winds

Imitation

From the antecedent

Cellos
Basses

Example 17-7 Beethoven, Vivace: First theme as closing theme

Example 17-8 Beethoven, Vivace: Appearances of the first theme as closing theme

One can, indeed, approach the whole movement from a purely motivic point of view. This approach, however, has a definite danger—or rather, a definite consequence. The process of motivic extension or motivic development found in pieces such as this depends upon tiny changes in pitch and rhythm to give a sense of continuity to relatively long stretches of music. The changes are by nature so subtle that they often go unnoticed; the emphasis is on sameness,

not difference. When you listen to a piece exclusively from a motivic point of view, you are apt to emphasize the similarities perceptible through the motives in all areas of the piece. With these prevailing similarities firmly in mind, you may have a more difficult time perceiving the differences that have such an important role in shaping the movement. You might, for example, become so involved in the sameness of rhythmic motive throughout the second

First theme as closing theme

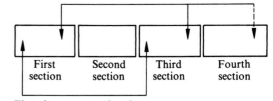

First section | Second section | Third section | Fourth section

First theme as opening theme

343

section as to neglect the return of line and phrase shape that announces the third section. That perhaps is unlikely; but it is likely that you will miss the function of the closing theme if you start by following only the motives in the first section.

The first theme—or better, its opening motive—functions in one more capacity to shape the movement at its highest level. No substantial return of the theme is involved; but the placement is so important as to raise the motivic reference to the stature of a thematic return.

At the end of the first section, after the second of the two pauses associated with the stammering figure (Ex. 17-6), you hear the lead-in from the very beginning of the Vivace. The return of this lead-in is literal, except that it is transposed to a different pitch. The presence of the lead-in makes one expect the first theme; only the first measure of the theme actually sounds, but after the lead-in that much is enough to create the feeling of a real thematic return. The passage continues with imitative entries of the first measure of the theme.

A similar passage, involving the lead-in and first measure of the theme, follows the pauses at the end of the third section. The effect is to make the fourth section, the coda, begin like the second, the development. Since the development involved far-reaching excursions, we are led to believe the coda may too. How the fourth section manages to turn into a concluding section is another matter, which we will take up later.

The sense of continuity furnished by the motivic processes at work in the movement makes it necessary to be cautious in laying out sections and subsections. Even if the four sections already discussed can be located with the help of thematic appearances (as in Ex. 17-8), these appearances account for relatively little of the bulk of the sections. Somehow, this movement does not make much sense when we consider only isolated thematic appearances. The music seems to demand being heard in its own succession: there seems to be in this work, more than in any other studied in this book, a train of thought that must be followed step by step.

For this reason, we need to follow through the first section of the Vivace at the phrase level. Once that

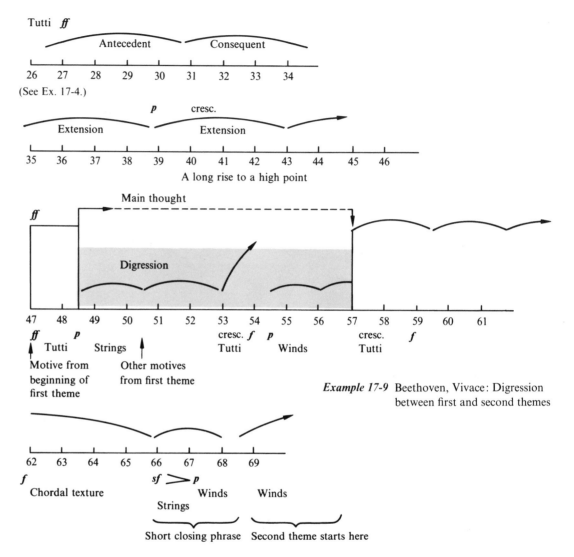

Example 17-9 Beethoven, Vivace: Digression between first and second themes

section—and the special kinds of phrase structure found in it—are clear, the other sections can be understood in somewhat broader terms. In this movement, the first section seems really to be an exposition: we must be familiar with the material as set forth in this section before we can follow the subsequent argument.

We have already discussed the phrase structure of the first theme through the first phrase group, up to the half cadence (Ex. 17-4). At that point, the tutti starts to repeat the first theme fortissimo. The ensuing passage contains a difficult but instructive digression—instructive in the kind of suspended phrase structure that must be understood in order to follow this movement. Example 17-9 starts at the fortissimo repeat of the first theme and continues until the entrance of a second theme. Listen from the beginning of the Vivace, following Ex. 17-4, then Ex.

17-9, to hear the entire first theme, then the digression; concentrate first on keeping your place in the diagrams.

The repeat of the first theme that starts in measure 27 is literal (except for the fuller timbre) through the antecedent and consequent phrases. The extension is the same as before, except the echoes in the accompaniment are lacking; this makes the measure groupings fall into twos instead of threes and pushes the rhythmic motion ahead.

After the extension from 35 through 38, the close similarity to measures 5 through 26 ceases. Instead, persistent extension at the *motivic* level carries the line up and forward with increasing urgency over the pedal note, which has been sounding steadily since measure 26. Added to the motivic drive and to the rising line is a long crescendo that culminates in a brief fortissimo outburst (measures 47 and 48) of the opening notes borrowed from the first theme.

The first theme, which was never really closed on its first presentation, has been sprung wide open on the second, for the return of its opening motive in measures 47 and 48 is set over new harmonies that effect a modulation. Within those two measures, the harmonic motion of the Vivace has been lifted up and set down in a new area, markedly different from the area associated with the long pedal note. The shift of area, while immediately perceptible, is too abrupt to be immediately absorbed. The measures that follow the shift have the important function of providing time for the shift to sink in.

It is difficult to follow the line of thought that leads from measure 47 to measure 57; the ear must accept the intervening measures as a digression—or even as a parenthesis. Considered at the highest level, the sense of line and harmony goes directly from measure 47 and the beginning of measure 48 to the beginning of measure 57. This connection is shown by the dotted line in Ex. 17-9; the digression is placed inside a shaded area.

Two aspects complicate the digression. All the melodic material within the digression is derived from motives of the first theme and sounds very familiar; from a thematic point of view, it sounds like simple extension. Also, in the middle of the digression the melody makes an abortive move to return to the main

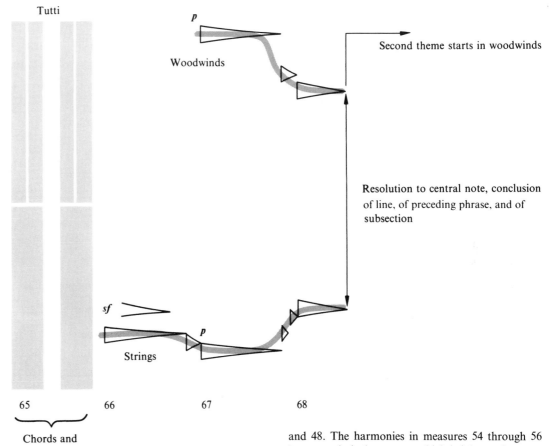

Example 17-10 Beethoven, Vivace:
Detail just before the second theme

line of thought (measures 53 and 54), with a brief crescendo to forte.

The digression is best understood by listening to timbre, dynamics, and harmony. Except for the brief crescendo in measures 53 and 54, the digression is piano; the timbre is reduced to strings for the first pair of phrases, to woodwinds (with strings unobtrusively accompanying) for the second pair. The whole digression involves harmonies different from those expected because of what has gone before— different even from the abrupt shift in measures 47

and 48. The harmonies in measures 54 through 56 become relatively remote, which heightens the sense of return to the main thought in measure 57; there the harmonies pick up the sense of the shift started back in 47 and 48 and carry it to its logical conclusion. The modulation begun in measure 47 is confirmed between measures 57 and 68, and the ear fully understands it only during those measures.

In measures 66 through 68 (Ex. 17-9), we encounter another difficult procedure, understanding of which is essential for this movement. Measure 66 begins with a strong accent—a sforzando on a relatively long, unison note low in the strings; nothing else is sounding, and this unison note (actually doubled in two octaves) is in contrast to the chordal texture immediately preceding (Ex. 17-10). The next measure, 67, is soft again; and the unison line rises easily and quickly in the strings to reach its central note—the central note of the new harmonic area just established and confirmed. The line, the phrase, the subsection—all come to their proper conclusion on the first note of measure 68; but this is not at all obvious, because Beethoven has twisted the sense of line and harmony by the abrupt change of texture and the sforzando accent in measure 66; by the use of a new melodic figure in 66 and 67 apparently unrelated to anything yet heard in the Vivace; and by the entrance of the woodwinds, which seem to start something new in measure 67. At the concluding moment in a phrase and subsection, when we expect all to proceed smoothly to the end of the sentence, a new thought seems to have been suddenly introduced. We must learn to understand these measures as merely a new inflection of the line of thought that is indeed proceeding to its conclusion as it should.

SECOND THEME AND ANOTHER DIGRESSION. Yet another difficulty follows immediately: a second theme starts in the second half of measure 68, but this second theme often goes completely unnoticed because of the effect of the two measures preceding. The second theme is heard in the woodwinds; the passage is marked *dolce* ("sweet"), as if it were an interlude in a piece for marching band.

The start of the second theme is overshadowed, not only by what went before, but also by what comes after. The theme has an antecedent-and-consequent phrase; the consequent is deflected by a striking harmonic shift followed by another digression. Here again, we must learn to listen over a number of measures to follow the main line of thought.

Example 17-11 shows the second theme starting halfway through measure 68. The antecedent contains a graceful rise and fall of the line, played by woodwinds. This is not an obtrusive theme; in fact, it is easy to miss altogether. The consequent starts forte in measure 72, played by strings; it rises like the antecedent, then falls, using the same motive as the antecedent. At the moment when the line of the consequent has reached its peak, at the beginning of measure 74, the harmonic shift takes place, the digression begins, and the fall of the line is turned into a new harmonic area.

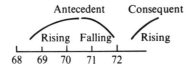

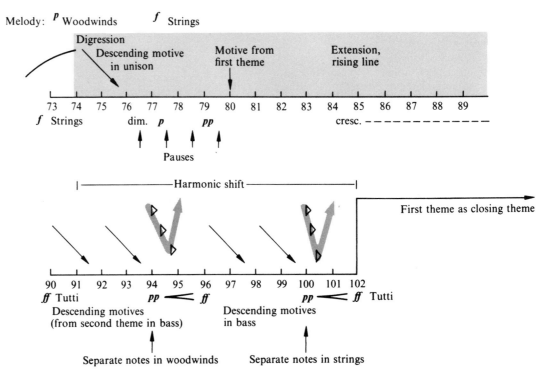

Example 17-11 Beethoven, Vivace: Digression in the second theme

This shift is much more striking than the shift in the previous digression (Ex. 17-9); the new harmonic area is more remote, and the move to it is more precipitous. As if to give us time to digest the shift, the line pauses and almost stops completely (measures 77 through 80). Into this moment of suspense is introduced the beginning motive from the first theme, high in the violins, with a little answering figure in the bass. The motive is repeated four times at the same pitch, then extended into a rising line. We scarcely have an opportunity to notice that the consequent phrase of the second theme was never completed.

We can notice, however, that the goal of the rising line, a strong arrival at a fortissimo tutti, marks the end of the digression and the return to the line of thought started by the second theme. In this tutti, the bass makes long, downward sweeping lines out of the motives found originally in the falling part of the second theme. The succession of events is similar to that in Haydn's Allegro, where the tutti following the second theme was built on a bass line using a motive from that theme. The difference between Beethoven's and Haydn's pieces is the striking digression and harmonic shift Beethoven has interpolated into the second theme.

One would imagine that to be enough; but Beethoven is still reluctant to let the tutti pound to a completely foreseeable conclusion. After two downward sweeps of the bass line (measures 90 through 94), three strangely remote notes in the woodwinds, suddenly pianissimo, finish the phrase. The pattern is immediately repeated in measures 96 through 100. The materials contained in this phrase are so disparate in dynamics, line, and harmony that the ear has difficulty hearing measures 90 through 96 or 96 through 100 as a unified phrase; yet that is what Beethoven seems to intend.

The reason for studying the phrase structures of the first return in such detail is that you must understand them if you are to perceive the basic stability of the first section. The digressions have the function of breaking up the flow and highlighting certain details; they perform this function so effectively that you are likely to notice only the details and miss the larger design. An understanding of nothing but detail would leave you helpless before the vast reaches of the next section.

The second section has no digressions; it uses on a grander scale the extended phrase groups and long-breathed harmonic progressions already encountered in Haydn's middle section. Such progressions are most obvious at the beginning of the second section. The lead-in and set of imitative entrances on the first-theme motive discussed before (page 344) all unfold within a simple harmony, relieved only briefly by its leading harmony. Then come a pair of imitative entrances in soprano and bass on the motive from the *second* theme—still on the same prolonged harmony. Finally (after 24 measures), the harmony makes a move. This is the pace of harmonic motion we can expect in the second section.

The long stretches between harmonic moves are filled in with manifold repetitions of motives. For the most part, these are motives already encountered from the first theme and the second. These two motives (indeed, the two themes) have similar if not identical kinds of rhythms (Ex. 17-12). As a result, the second section is dominated by what seems to be one persistent rhythmic pattern, which in combination with the slow-moving harmonies builds up tremendous momentum.

The second section is interrupted only once, about

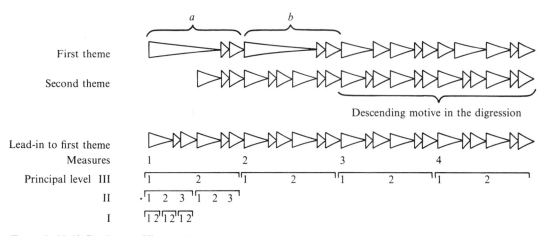

Example 17-12 Beethoven, Vivace: Rhythm in first and second themes

a third of the way through. At that point, there is some rapid antiphony between winds and strings (still in the prevailing fortissimo dynamics and in the persistent rhythm) and, at the same time, a violent wrench in the harmonic motion. Then a sudden soft chord for woodwinds alone divides everything that came before from everything that is yet to come. The second section seems to make a new beginning: it becomes concerned with soft imitative entries, only gradually returning, through a long crescendo, to the fortissimo dynamics, pounding rhythms, and giant-like harmonic progressions. These culminate in the return to the first theme that marks the beginning of the third section.

The second section is basically unstable in its overall sense of harmonic motion, but this harmonic motion goes so slowly that its instability is not readily apparent. Each harmony lasts for so long it seems stable just from not moving—more stable than the first section with its confusing digressions.

There is another confusing moment at the start of the third section when the first theme, having just been played through once by the tutti in the original key and ending on the half cadence, is repeated by the oboe in a closely related, but different key. The key relationship is such as to make you doubt for a while which key really is the original one. Is this the real return of the first theme? (The first theme, after all, was introduced originally by woodwinds, not tutti.) It gradually becomes apparent, as the repeat turns

out not to be literal, that the fortissimo tutti was indeed the real return and that the solo oboe led us astray.

The most striking harmonic departure is reserved for the start of the fourth section. After the third section, you might expect this long movement to come to an end; but then it goes on. From the composer's point of view, the construction of a coda to follow the final-sounding recapitulation is full of difficult choices. There must be something striking enough at the start of the coda to indicate that the piece is really going to continue in earnest. There must be something spectacular enough in the coda to justify this reopening of a form ready to close. Yet the form must close soon, and more decisively than it might have before; otherwise the extension will not be convincing.

As already heard, the fourth section is announced by the great stammering figure and by pauses; it begins with the lead-in from the beginning of the Vivace, somewhat modified. The harmonic area is suddenly remote—more remote than anywhere else in the movement. Having made a giant step to a faraway key, Beethoven immediately returns to the original area in two more giant steps; but so swift is the return that it is some time before you realize you are home. Meanwhile, the beginning motive of the first theme echoes mysteriously back and forth across the vast harmonic distances. It is a moment of wonder.

Then, still pianissimo, comes another mysterious passage, bringing a new mood—and at this particular point in the Vivace a new mood has great structural importance. The procedures of the second section, for example, would be redundant here. Two motives (are they new? where did they come from?) start a curious dialog in soprano and bass, while woodwinds sustain a single harmony. The bass is an ostinato, the soprano gradually expands and varies its insistent repetitions. A very slow crescendo completes the hypnotic effect. Afterward, the Vivace concludes quickly with familiar motives from the first theme.

THE SYMPHONY AS A WHOLE. If we reflect on the overall plan of Beethoven's symphony in the same way we reflected on the plan of Haydn's symphony (pages 334–337), we come to some of the same conclusions, simply because the same kinds of movements are involved (see Ex. 17-13). Beethoven's Vivace movement is going to be the center of gravity of the symphony no matter in which position it appears. The slow introduction is going to have to be an introduction to something; and because the Poco sostenuto is so solemn and so sustained, it would produce a possibly comic contrast if followed immediately by one of the less serious movements. Also, if the Poco sostenuto were to appear in any position except the beginning, it would tend to split the symphony in two.

As we already mentioned (page 340), Beethoven's Allegro con brio assumes great importance as the conclusion of the symphony. Relocating this movement would involve a fundamental redistribution of weight in the overall plan. The position of the two central movements, on the other hand, is a much more subtle matter: Allegretto and Presto could be interchanged; it would make a difference, but not a drastic difference. One of the most important results would be in the succession of harmonic areas.

For many reasons, Beethoven's Poco sostenuto seems to be an introduction more to the whole symphony than just to the first movement. The Poco sostenuto can perhaps best be understood as having two separate functions. Insofar as its net structural effect is oblique and its main sections are less clear than its interludes, the Poco sostenuto is a foil for the Vivace. The Poco sostenuto makes broad motions around the principal key, while the first theme of the Vivace lands squarely on it. The Poco sostenuto

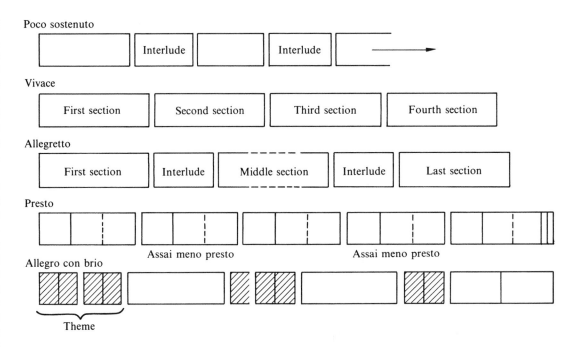

Example 17-13 Beethoven, Symphony No. 7: Overall movement plan

moves slowly and ponderously; the Vivace presents its clear melody in a bright timbre and in decisive rhythms.

This first function, comparable to the function of Haydn's Adagio, could have been accomplished without the interludes. Their specific function is different: they are windows on other harmonic areas —remote areas whose relationship to the principal one is not at all clear at the start and is to be explored throughout the symphony. We can sketch the most striking appearances of the other areas in a diagram (Ex. 17-14) similar to the one used for the two areas of Haydn's symphony (Ex. 16-18). Instead of discussing the harmonic aspect of Beethoven's symphony separately, however, we will refer to Ex. 17-14 as we go along.

The two functions of the Poco sostenuto touch briefly in a single decisive moment, a single progression that becomes characteristic of the whole symphony. In discussing the harmonic organization of the Poco sostenuto, we located the end of the second

interlude and the motion of the bass a semitone down to the pedal note that prepares the beginning of the Vivace (page 122). The progression over that semitone tends to reappear at decisive moments in the symphony; the two harmonies involved—the first being part of the remote interlude, the second being central to the principal key—represent the two poles of harmonic movement throughout the symphony.

A comparison of the sectional plans does not become significant until we are past the Vivace, for while the Poco sostenuto is sectional, it offers little basis for comparison with the Vivace; and the Vivace, in turn, gives us plenty to think about without our trying to perceive high-level relationships to what came before. We may, however, start to pick up reverberations of the other harmonic areas indicated by the interludes in the Poco sostenuto.

In the digression that interrupts the second theme of the Vivace, there is a swift harmonic move to a remote key (see page 346 for the description), which is the key of the first interlude of the Poco sostenuto,

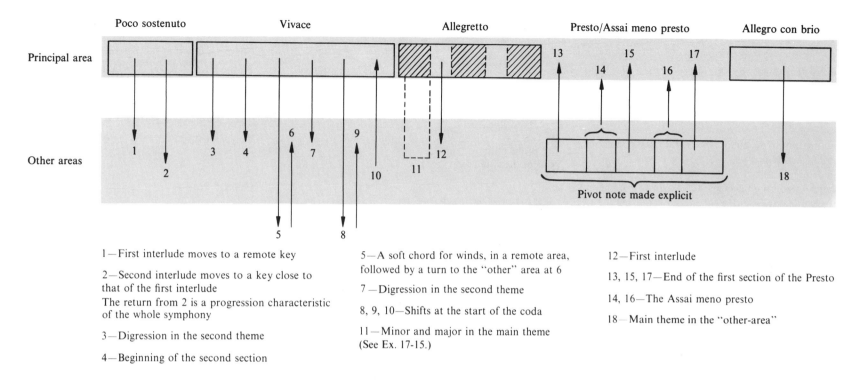

Principal area

Poco sostenuto | Vivace | Allegretto | Presto/Assai meno presto | Allegro con brio

Other areas

Pivot note made explicit

1—First interlude moves to a remote key

2—Second interlude moves to a key close to that of the first interlude
The return from 2 is a progression characteristic of the whole symphony

3—Digression in the second theme

4—Beginning of the second section

5—A soft chord for winds, in a remote area, followed by a turn to the "other" area at 6

7—Digression in the second theme

8, 9, 10—Shifts at the start of the coda

11—Minor and major in the main theme (See Ex. 17-15.)

12—First interlude

13, 15, 17—End of the first section of the Presto

14, 16—The Assai meno presto

18—Main theme in the "other-area"

Example 17-14 Beethoven, Symphony No. 7: Harmonic areas

as shown in Ex. 17-14. As in Haydn's symphony, there would be little reason to mention this identity of key if it was the result of gradual modulation through many keys. It is only because the key is reached in both instances through an abrupt shift that we notice it, wonder about it, ask ourselves what could have been the preparation for such a seemingly unprepared move. Finding no satisfactory answer in the immediate neighborhood, we might be pushed back all the way to the first interlude of the Poco sostenuto.

In the Vivace, the key of the digression soon returns at the beginning of the second section (4 in Ex. 17-14). Here, too, the remote key is reached by an abrupt shift, so that we again notice the new key. From that point on, we probably do not notice specific keys in the same way. Yet there is a connection among keys and among movements; alert to this connection, we may be encouraged to hear others, at least when unexplained harmonies occur in prominent positions.

Halfway through the second section, for example, is a soft chord for winds (discussed on page 347). Details make the chord prominent—change of timbre, reduction of texture and dynamics, absence of figure and rhythmic motive. The moment seems to be far more significant than these largely negative factors would suggest. If we listen to the kinds of harmonic motion used in approaching and leaving the chord, we find them to have the same quality as the progression at the end of the Poco sostenuto.

At the beginning of the fourth section of the Vivace, the same quality of harmonic motion leads several times in succession from one remote area to another. These remote shifts occur close together in time, taking up relatively little time in the movement as a whole; yet they are far more prominent than other progressions, attracting attention and directing it to a comparison with other similar features elsewhere.

The plan of the Allegretto is basically different from

that of the Vivace; the difference is apparent at several levels. The theme of the movement has the phrase structure *a b b* (see Chapter 3)—distinctive, if not unique within this symphony. This theme is repeated immediately three times, varied in some respects but retaining exactly the same phrase structure—a procedure sharply contrasting to that of extension or digression in the Vivace. Insofar as the rest of the Allegretto carries out the idea of variations on a theme, it has a movement plan different from the preceding movement. Only in the imitative passage in the middle of the movement are we reminded of the Vivace and its sense of growth and development.

The interludes in the Allegretto suggest those in the Poco sostenuto. There might be a real similarity of design between Allegretto and Poco sostenuto, except for the effect of the key relationships. The Allegretto as a whole is in the same area as the Vivace, but in minor—a change of color. The interludes are in the

349

same area, in major. That is, the most obvious effect of the interludes is that they reestablish the principal key of the symphony. There are other effects, however, that bind the Allegretto to the preceding movements in more complex ways.

The theme of the Allegretto moves very easily from its opening minor to a closely related major at the end of its phrase *a*. Phrase *b* then begins in that major key and returns to the minor (Ex. 17-15). The modulation is so smooth that you may scarcely hear it. Yet the odd thing is that this theme has moved across the same broad span that separates the principal area of the symphony from the other area generated out of the interludes of the Poco sostenuto and reinforced in the digressions of the Vivace. The reason the theme of the Allegretto can make this move so easily is that it starts in minor, not major; by starting in the minor of the principal area—a large contrast in harmonic effect—the theme has already jumped most of the way across the gap. In this way, the Allegretto explores and partially fills in the key relationship opened up in the Poco sostenuto.

As in Haydn's symphony, the mechanics of these long-range key relationships are not immediately apparent in the listening experience. But is there not something puzzling about the opening theme of the Allegretto? Why should such a simple march tune have such a haunting effect? We search in vain for the answer within the confines of the tune itself; but as we become sensitive to the harmonic reverberations picked up by the theme from the rest of the symphony, we begin to understand how simple things can become musically meaningful.

It should be mentioned that the first interlude does contain a strikingly beautiful modulation to the other area (Ex. 17-14). This modulation, starting as it does from the major of the interlude (rather than the minor of the theme), has the sense of surge and breaking crest implicit in the shifts of the Poco sostenuto and gradually exploited throughout the symphony. The treatment of this shift in the first interlude of the Allegretto (12 in Ex. 17-14) is the most eloquent so far.

The Presto/Assai meno presto, with its strict alternation of two independent sections, presents a plan that also is unique in the symphony. In the

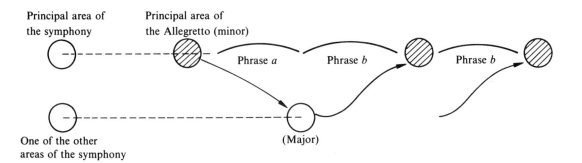

Example 17-15 Beethoven, Symphony No. 7, Allegretto: Harmonic areas in the first theme and their relationship to areas of the whole symphony

Allegretto, the returning element—the theme—was varied each time it came back; there was a sense of change throughout the movement, even without the dynamic development of the Vivace.

In comparison to the sections of the Vivace, each section of the Presto is extremely homogeneous. The Presto itself has a very short opening subsection, hardly more than a phrase group (see page 19). Brief as it is, we should notice it here, first, because in its concentrated brevity it is characteristic of the Presto as opposed to the preceding movements; second, because in its harmonic movement it connects the Presto to the rest of the symphony.

The other subsection of the Presto is much longer and, in its developmental expansion, might recall the Vivace. It is much more homogeneous than the Vivace, however, carrying out the single-mindedness of the first subsection. Attention is brought back again and again to the sectional alternation at the highest level as the main point of the Presto/Assai meno presto.

The Presto is in the other harmonic area. At this point in the symphony, the other area is represented by a main event rather than by an interlude—unless we regard the whole movement as an interlude, as we probably should.

As is evident from Ex. 17-14, harmonic shifts in the Presto are turned back toward the principal harmonic area of the whole symphony. Beethoven could have

used the new key of the Presto as a staging area for even more remote excursions. Instead, he has made the harmonic structure of the Presto as a whole into a mirror image of the rest of the symphony, with subtle but remarkable effects upon the long-range relationships.

The first short subsection of the Presto begins abruptly in the new key and just as abruptly makes its move—back to the principal area of the symphony. For a moment, there is real doubt as to what key the Presto is in. The ambiguity is eventually straightened out, but it leaves a feeling of wonder and richness that pervades the whole movement.

The Assai meno presto is in a key very close to the principal key of the symphony—so close as to be part of the same area for all practical purposes. The connection is made even closer through a detail, a single note that occupies a pivotal position in the scheme of the symphony. We already noticed this note as a pedal note sounding in the whole orchestra at the end of the Presto, then in the violins (and eventually other instruments) throughout the Assai meno presto. Even without going into the detailed relationship between this note and the various harmonies in which it participates, you can certainly hear how it echoes back and forth between Presto and Assai meno presto, and perhaps you can hear its relationship to the previous movements. It is, in fact, the central note of the symphony.

The plan of the Allegro con brio, once again, is different from the plans of the other movements. The Allegro con brio combines a clearly phrased, obstinately returning theme with a whole procession of other things.

The theme appears at the very beginning of the movement. It consists of fourfold repetitions of a strong rhythmic figure, set in regular phrases and simple, stable harmonic motion. There is little sense of melody such as one might sing; yet the closed, regular phrase structure is extremely clear. The effect is that of a marching band, playing a bright, quick march this time instead of the more somber kind of march used in the Allegretto.

It is perhaps the manifold repetitions within the theme that most strike the ear; and you certainly notice these repetitions when they occur in the various returns of the theme throughout the movement. Many aspects of the Allegro con brio—the key, the tempo, the prevailing brilliance of sound, and the driving character of motion—recall the Vivace. The obstinate repetitions in the theme, however, especially in later returns of the theme, do not recall the Vivace, indeed seem quite different.

Because of these repetitions, you can easily identify the literal returns of the theme, as shown in Ex. 17-13. These returns mark out the large sections of the movement. You are less apt to hear sections, however, and more apt to hear just the thematic repetitions, because of what comes between.

After playing the first theme, the orchestra seems to strike up one tune after another. Sometimes the motive from the theme reappears, often it does not—the feeling of motivic extension being here much less strong than in the Vivace. If we worked through the movement in detail, we would discover the modulations that guide the course of the procession; we could eventually identify a second theme and find the first theme motive used as closing material for the first section. However, the primary impression is one of stable, repetitious theme followed by varied succession. (If the first section is repeated, the theme becomes even more firmly entrenched as the stable element.)

Eventually, after some false starts, there is a full literal statement of the theme in another key (shown in Ex. 17-14). This other key is part of the remote area of the symphony. Because of the strength and stability of the thematic statements, the keys in which they appear emerge as poles of harmonic motion. But if the other area is given a strong expression in the middle of the Allegro con brio, the rest of the movement hammers away at the principal key, as if the main function of the movement, the goal of all its great rhythmic momentum, was a statement of the original key strong enough to make it absolutely clear what key the symphony was finally in.

APPENDIX A

SUGGESTIONS FOR FURTHER LISTENING AND READING

FURTHER LISTENING. The pieces listed here can be used as further examples of timbre, texture, rhythm, melody, harmony, theme, motive, and aspects of music related to these, as discussed in Part One (Chapters 1 through 9).

In several cases, reference is made to specific recordings that present material in a unique way. Otherwise, no discography is supplied, primarily because of the speed with which a discography goes out-of-date. Current information on recordings is easily accessible in the *Schwann Long Playing Record Catalog*, published monthly and found generally in libraries and record stores.

It should be noted that no suggestions for further listening are provided for Part Two (Chapters 10 through 17). This is because the discussion in those chapters is directed toward each of a series of individual pieces with the purpose of exploring the qualities unique to each piece as a whole. Clearly, none of these chapters would apply to any other piece; no other piece would illustrate any of these chapters. The authors hope that these chapters will suggest techniques and ideas useful in approaching other pieces; but the specific applicability of one of these techniques to another piece will involve a decision that can be made only by the listener.

CHAPTER 1: INTRODUCTION

Bach, Johann Sebastian: Brandenburg Concerto No. 1 in F major, B.W.V. 1046. Menuetto: Allegretto (fourth movement).

Mahler, Gustav: *Songs of a Wayfarer* (*Lieder eines fahrenden Gesellen*): "Wenn mein Schatz Hochzeit macht" (song 1).

Mozart, Wolfgang Amadeus: Symphony No. 40 in G minor, K. 550. Menuetto (third movement).

Stravinsky, Igor: *In Memoriam Dylan Thomas*.

Telemann, Georg Philipp: Fantasia No. 1 in D for harpsichord (1. Douzaine).

CHAPTER 2: QUALITIES OF SOUND

Berg, Alban: *Lyric Suite*. Presto delirando (fifth movement).

Berlioz, Hector: *Requiem*: Dies Irae.

Couperin, François: *Messe pour les paroisses*: Dialogue sur la trompette et le chromhorne.

En la basilique Saint Marc de Venise (record: Erato STE 50274). Works by Giovanni Gabrieli, Vivaldi, Cavalli, and Caldara.

Guillaume de Machaut: *Plus dure que un dyamant* (virelai). On record: *Machaut: Motets, Ballades, Virelais, and Rondeaux* (Westminster XWN 18166; conducted by George Hunter).

Ligeti, György: *Atmosphères*.

Liszt, Franz: *Les Prèludes* (all, or just the beginning).

Mahler, Gustav: Symphony No. 10. Adagio (first movement).

Stockhausen, Karlheinz: *Momente*.

Strauss, Richard: *Also sprach Zarathustra* (beginning).

Varèse, Edgard: *Déserts*.

CHAPTER 3: TEXTURE

Bach, Johann Sebastian: *Well-Tempered Clavier, Book II*. Fugue No. 5 in D major. On record: *Bach's Greatest Hits* (Philips PHM-200-097; Swingle Singers).

Berlioz, Hector: *Requiem*: Sanctus—Osanna—Sanctus.

Brahms, Johannes: *Ein deutsches Requiem* (*A German Requiem*), op. 45. "Herr, lehre doch mich" (third movement).

Buxtehude, Dietrich: *Jesu meine Freude und Lust*.

Froberger, Johann Jakob: Fantasia I sopra ut, re, mi, fa, sol, la (for organ).

Hindemith, Paul: *Nobilissima visione* (suite). Marsch und Pastorale (second movement).

Leonin: *Haec dies*.

Messiaen, Olivier: *Quatuor pour le fin du temps* (*Quartet for the End of Time*) (movements V-VI-VII as a group).

Mozart, Wolfgang Amadeus: Piano Concerto in F major, K. 459. Finale (third movement).

Mozart, Wolfgang Amadeus: String Quartet in G major, K. 387. Molto allegro (fourth movement).

Mozart, Wolfgang Amadeus: Symphony No. 40 in G minor, K. 550. Menuetto: Allegretto (third movement).

Schubert, Franz: Piano Trio No. 2 in E^b major, op. 100, D. 929. Scherzo: Allegro moderato (third movement).

CHAPTER 4: RHYTHM AND METER

Bach, Johann Sebastian: Violin Concerto in E major, B.W.V. 1042 (third movement).

Brahms, Johannes: Symphony No. 3 in F, op. 90. Allegro grazioso (third movement).

Gabrieli, Andrea: *Ricercar del 12° tuono*. On record: *Renaissance Festival Music* (Decca DL 9419; Noah Greenberg, conductor).

Scarlatti, Domenico: Sonata in C major, L. 303, K. 170.

Schumann, Robert: *Papillons*, op. 2, for piano.

Tchaikovsky, Peter Ilyitch: Symphony No. 6 in B minor, op. 74 ("Symphonie pathétique"). Allegro con grazia (second movement).

Tempo contrasts

Beethoven, Ludwig van: Piano Sonata, op. 31, no. 2 in D minor. Largo—allegro (first movement).

Janáček, Leoš: String Quartet No. 2, "Listy dùvěrné" (all, the second movement only, or the third movement only).

Webern, Anton: *Five Movements for String Quartet*, op. 5.

CHAPTER 5: REGULAR AND IRREGULAR RHYTHM

Monteverdi, Claudio: "Lamento della ninfa."

Mozart, Wolfgang Amadeus: *Le Nozze di Figaro*. Act IV, scene 9 (Susanna's and the Countess's recitative) through Susanna's aria "Deh vieni, non tardar." (Metrical versus nonmetrical rhythm.)

Perotin: *Sederunt principes*. (Metrical versus nonmetrical rhythm.)

Purcell, Henry: *Dido and Aeneas*: Dido's aria, "When I am laid in earth" (Act III).

Unit pulse

Hindemith, Paul: String Quartet No. 3, op. 22. "Fast eighths" (second movement).

Stravinsky, Igor: *Le sacre du printemps* (*The Rite of Spring*).

No pulse (or pulse difficult to hear)

Carter, Elliott. Double Concerto for Harpsichord, Piano, and Two Chamber Orchestras.

Lutoslawski, Witold. *Trois poèmes d'Henri Michaux*.

Martirano, Salvatore. *Underworld (1965)*.

Rhythmic figuration

Beethoven, Ludwig van: *Variations on a Waltz of Diabelli*, op. 120.

Brahms, Johannes: Intermezzo, op. 117, no. 2 in B^b minor, for piano.

Chopin, Frédéric: Preludes, op. 28, for piano.

Corelli, Arcangelo: *La follia* (Sonata for Violin and Continuo, op. 5, no. 12).

Satie, Erik: *Trois morceaux en forme d'une poire* (*Three Pieces in the Form of a Pear*).

Syncopation

Gabrieli, Giovanni: *Canzona 9° toni à 12* (from *Symphoniae Sacrae,* 1597). On record: *En la basilique Saint Marc de Venise* (Erato STE 50274).

Hindemith, Paul. *Nobilissima visione* (suite). Passacaglia (third movement).

Messiaen, Olivier. *Quatuor pour le fin du temps* (*Quartet for the End of Time*). Danse de la fureur (sixth movement).

Phrase groupings

Bach, Johann Sebastian: Violin Concerto in E major, B.W.V. 1042 (third movement).

Brahms, Johannes: *Variations on a Theme of Haydn*, op. 56a. Theme.

Handel, Georg Friedrich: *Semele*. Semele's aria, "No, no, I'll take no less" (Act III).

Scarlatti, Domenico: Sonata in C major, L. 303, K. 170.

Schumann, Robert: *Papillons*, op. 2, for piano.

CHAPTER 6: LINEAR ORGANIZATION OF PITCH

Berlioz, Hector: *Romeo and Juliet*, op. 17. Andante malinconico (beginning of second part).

Chopin, Frédéric: Mazurka No. 45 in A minor, op. 67, no. 4.

Debussy, Claude: *Pelléas et Mélisande*. Act III, scene 1, beginning to no. 4.

Fauré, Gabriel: *Requiem*: Libera me.

Guillaume de Machaut: *Douce dame jolie* (virelai). On record: *Machaut: Motets, Ballades, Virelais, and Rondeaux* (Westminster XWN 18166; conducted by George Hunter).

Hindemith, Paul: *Das Marienleben* (revised version), no. 11, "Pietà."

Mahler, Gustav: Symphony No. 10. Adagio (first movement).

Messiaen, Olivier: *Quatuor pour le fin du temps* (*Quartet for the End of Time*). Danse de la fureur (sixth movement).

Stravinsky, Igor: *Canticum Sacrum*: Surge Aquilo.

Wagner, Richard: *Tristan und Isolde*. Act I, sailor's song; Act III, shepherd's song.

CHAPTER 7: HARMONIC ORGANIZATION OF PITCH
Static harmony

Riley, Terry: *In C.*

Wagner, Richard: *Das Rheingold*. Prelude to Act I.

Contrast of stable and unstable harmonies

Berlioz, Hector: *Requiem*: Sanctus.

Mozart, Wolfgang Amadeus: String Quartet in C Major, K. 465 ("Dissonant"). First movement: slow introduction and beginning of Allegro.

Wagner, Richard: *Siegfried*. Act I, scene 2.

Central pitches or harmonies as reference points

Bach, Johann Sebastian: Partita No. 2 in C minor, B.W.V. 826. Rondeaux.

Schubert, Franz: Piano Sonata in B^b major, op. post., D. 960. Molto moderato (first movement).

Schumann, Robert: *Papillons,* op. 2, for piano.

Webern, Anton: Piano Variations, op. 27. Second movement (Sehr schnell).

Various uses of cadences

Brahms, Johannes: *Variations on a Theme by Haydn*, op. 56a. Theme.

Chopin, Frédéric: Prelude in E minor, op. 28, no. 4.

Fauré, Gabriel: *Requiem*: Libera me.

Guillaume de Machaut: *Douce dame jolie* (virelai). On record: *Machaut: Motets, Ballades, Virelais and Rondeaux* (Westminster XWN 18166; conducted by George Hunter).

Scarlatti, Domenico: Sonata in A minor, L. 429, K. 175.
Verdi, Giuseppi: *La Traviata*. Violetta's aria, "Sempre libera" (Act I).

Contrasts of major and minor

Chopin, Frédéric: Prelude in D^b major, op. 28, no. 15.
Handel, Georg Friedrich: *Semele*. Semele's aria, "No, no, I'll take no less" (Act III).
Mahler, Gustav: *Lieder eines fahrenden Gesellen* (*Songs of a Wayfarer*). Songs 1 and 4.
Mozart, Wolfgang Amadeus: Symphony No. 40 in G minor, K. 550. Allegro molto (first movement). (Compare second theme in exposition and recapitulation.)
Schubert, Franz: String Quartet in G major, D. 887. Allegro molto moderato (first movement).
Telemann, Georg Philipp: Fantasia No. 1 in D for harpsichord. (1. Douzaine.)

CHAPTERS 8 AND 9: THEME AND MOTIVE IN HARMONIC CONTEXTS

Beethoven, Ludwig van: Symphony No. 5 in C minor, op. 67. Allegro con brio (first movement).
Brahms, Johannes: Symphony No. 2 in D major, op. 73. Allegro non troppo (first movement).
Scarlatti, Domenico: Sonata in C minor, L. 407, K. 115.
Schoenberg, Arnold: String Trio, op. 45.

Thematic transformation

Berlioz, Hector: *Symphonie Fantastique*.
Debussy, Claude: *Jeux*.
Liszt, Franz: *Les Préludes*.

FURTHER READING

DICTIONARIES AND ENCYCLOPEDIAS
Biography only

Baker, Theodore: *Biographical Dictionary of Musicians*, 5th ed., completely revised by Nicholas Slonimsky, G. Schirmer, Inc., New York, 1965.

Biography, historical articles, and terms

Grove, Sir George: *Dictionary of Music and Musicians*, 5th ed., Eric Blom (ed.), Macmillan & Co., London; St Martin's Press, Inc., New York, 1954. 10 vols.
The International Cyclopedia of Music and Musicians, Oscar Thompson (editor in chief), 9th ed., Robert Sabin (ed.), Dodd, Mead & Company, Inc., New York, 1964.

Historical articles and terms

Apel, Willi: *Harvard Dictionary of Music*, 2d ed., Belknap Press, Harvard University Press, Cambridge, Mass., 1969.

THE LISTENING EXPERIENCE

Meyer, Leonard: *Emotion and Meaning in Music*, University of Chicago Press, Chicago, 1956.
Sessions, Roger: *The Musical Experience of Composer, Performer, and Listener*, Princeton University Press, Princeton, N.J., 1950.

HISTORY AND CRITICISM

Boyden, David D. *An Introduction to Music*, 2d ed., Alfred A. Knopf, Inc., New York, 1970.
Cannon, Beekman Cox, Alvin H. Johnson, and William G. Waite: *The Art of Music: A Short History of Musical Styles and Ideas*, Thomas Y. Crowell Company, New York, 1960.
Crocker, Richard L.: *A History of Musical Style*, McGraw-Hill Book Company, New York, 1966.

Late eighteenth, early nineteenth centuries

Pauly, Reinhard J.: *Music in the Classic Period*, Prentice-Hall, Inc., Englewood Cliffs, N.J., 1965.

Nineteenth century

Abraham, Gerald: *A Hundred Years of Music*, Aldine Publishing Co., Chicago, 1964.

Twentieth century

Salzman, Eric: *Twentieth Century Music: An Introduction*, Prentice-Hall, Inc., Englewood Cliffs, N.J., 1967.

Opera

Kerman, Joseph: *Opera as Drama*, Alfred A. Knopf, Inc., New York, 1956.

MUSICIANSHIP AND NOTATION	Chapman, Roger: *Essentials of Music*, Doubleday & Co., Inc., Garden City, N.Y., 1967. Read, Gardner: *Music Notation: A Manual of Modern Practice*, 2d ed, Allyn and Bacon, Inc., Boston, 1969. Shanet, Howard: *Learn to Read Music*, Simon and Schuster, Inc., New York, 1956.
CONDUCTING	Bamberger, Carl (ed.): *The Conductor's Art: Essays on Conducting*, McGraw-Hill Book Company, New York, 1965.
QUALITIES OF SOUND (CHAPTER 2)	Baines, Anthony (ed.): *Musical Instruments through the Ages*, Penguin Books, Inc., Baltimore, 1961. Rogers, Bernard: *The Art of Orchestration: Principles of Tone Color in Modern Scoring*, Appleton-Century-Crofts, Inc., New York, 1951.
RHYTHM AND METER (CHAPTER 4)	Cooper, Grovesnor, and Leonard Meyer: *The Rhythmic Structure of Music*, University of Chicago Press, Chicago, 1960.
LINEAR ORGANIZATION OF PITCH (CHAPTER 6)	Erickson, Robert: *The Structure of Music: A Listener's Guide* (a study of music in terms of melody and counterpoint), Noonday Press, Inc., New York, 1955.
HARMONIC ORGANIZATION OF PITCH (CHAPTER 7)	Mitchell, William: *Elementary Harmony*, 3d ed., Prentice-Hall, Inc., Englewood Cliffs, N.J., 1965.

APPENDIX B GLOSSARY

a battuta	*See* battuta.
a cappella	Choral music without an accompaniment.
a piacere	("At pleasure," Ital.) Freely performed, free tempo.
a tempo	*See* tempo.
accelerando	Getting faster (Ital.).
accidental	A sharp, flat, or natural not in the key signature.
accompaniment	Musical background to a main part.
act	Largest division of an opera.
adagio	Slow (Ital.).
adagissimo	Very slow (Ital.).
affettuoso	Warmly, affectionately (Ital.).
agitato	Excited, agitated (Ital.).
al fine	To the end (Ital.).
al segno	("To the sign," Ital.) Play as far as the sign.
alla	In the manner of (Ital.).
alla breve	A quick 2/2 meter.
allargando	Broadening (Ital.).
allegretto	Slower than allegro, faster than andante.
allegro	("Happy," Ital.) Fast.
all'ottava	At the octave, above or below. Abbr., 8va.
all'unisono	At the unison (Ital.).
alto	The lowest female voice.
alto clef	A C clef which indicates that the middle line of the staff is middle C.
amabile	Lovingly (Ital.).
anacrusis	*See* upbeat.
andante	Going, moving (Ital.).
andantino	(Diminutive of andante, Ital.) A little slower or faster than andante.
antecedent phrase	The question phrase of a pair of question-and-answer phrases.
antiphony	A dialog between different timbre combinations.
appassionato	Impassioned (Ital.).
appoggiatura	("Leaning note," from Ital. "appoggiare," to lean.) A non-chord tone appearing on an accented beat and resolving by step on a weak beat.

arco	Bow of a stringed instrument (Ital.). After a passage played pizzicato, *coll'arco* means "play with the bow again."
area	*See* harmonic area.
aria	An elaborate solo song, with orchestral accompaniment, found in operas, cantatas, and oratorios, and also as a separate concert piece.
articulation	The way a performer attacks and releases sounds.
assai	Rather (Ital.).
attacca	("Begin," Ital.) Play the next movement or section without a pause.
attack	The beginning of a sound is its attack.
augmentation	The statement of a theme with its note values lengthened.
authentic cadence	*See* full cadence.
band chord	(Not a standard term.) A large cluster formed of many pitches sounding simultaneously through a wide range.
bar	*See* measure.
bar line	A vertical line marking off each measure on a score or part.
baritone	A male voice with a range lower than the tenor, higher than the bass.
bass	The lowest male voice.
bass clarinet	A single-reed woodwind instrument, sounding an octave lower than the clarinet.
bass clef	A clef which indicates that the next-to-top line of the staff represents the F below middle C.
bass line	The lowest sounding line, whether vocal or instrumental.
bass viol	*See* double bass.
bassoon	A double-reed woodwind instrument, of a low to medium register.
battuta	Beat (Ital.); *a battuta*: return to normal tempo.
beam	A notational symbol.
beat	Beat is the metric pulse at the principal level.
belebend	Becoming animated (Ger.).
binary form	The shape of a piece containing two sections, each repeated. It can be expressed by the letters *A A B B*.
Blockflöte	Recorder (Ger.).
brace	A vertical line which connects two or more staves together into a "system."
brass instruments	A class of instruments typically made of thin brass in some hornlike shape; sound is produced by blowing on a cupped mouthpiece (for example, trumpet, French horn, trombone).
Bratsche	Viola (Ger.).
bravura	Boldness, skill (Ital.).
brio	Spirit (Ital.).
broken chord	A chord presented as a figure, one note at a time instead of all the notes simultaneously.
burletta	("Burlesque," Ital.) In a playful manner.
C clef	*See* alto clef, soprano clef, tenor clef.
cadence	The conclusions of a phrase or section; the sense of falling to a state of respose.
cadenza	A passage, generally improvised, played by the soloist(s) in a concerto, just before the final cadence of the soloist(s).
calando	Slackening (Ital.).
calmato	Calm (Ital.).
canon	A type of imitative, contrapuntal piece in which one part is imitated exactly by another part (or other parts) in successive entries. The imitation continues strictly throughout the work.
cantabile	Singing (Ital.).
cantata	A work in several sections (such as recitatives and arias) for one or more solo voices and sometimes chorus, with instrumental accompaniment; the text may be sacred or secular.
canzonetta	A little song (Ital.).

capo	*See* da capo.
cello	(Violoncello.) A bowed stringed instrument of low to high register.
central harmony	(Tonic.) One of a group of harmonies that seems to provide a "center of gravity" for the others; the one to which the others can most easily be referred.
central pitch	A pitch around which the other pitches gravitate.
chamber music	Music written for a small number of performers, each performer playing or singing a separate part.
chant	A kind of vocal monophony.
chord	A block of simultaneous sounds; the opposite of line.
chordal texture	A texture dominated by chords.
chorus	A group of human voices, more than one voice singing each part.
chromatic scale	An arrangement of pitches, in ascending or descending order, with a semitone between any two consecutive pitches.
circle of fifths	An arrangement of keys by the interval of a perfect fifth (such as C–G–D–A, etc.) so that they form a circle, the key with six flats being enharmonically equivalent to the key with six sharps.
clarinet	A single-reed woodwind instrument of a medium to high register.
clarino	Trumpet (Ital.).
clavichord	A small, soft keyboard instrument on which sound is produced by strings struck by a thin bronze "tangent."
clavier	Keyboard instrument (Fr.).
clef	("Key," Fr.) A notational symbol that indicates which specific pitches the lines and spaces of a staff are to represent.
closed ending	A complete stop at the end of a phrase or section.
cluster	Several pitches within a narrow range, sounding simultaneously.
coda	("Tail," Ital.) A concluding section of a work, especially a section placed after one that might have been the end.
col legno	("With the wood," Ital.) Play with the stick of the bow on the strings, instead of with the hair of the bow.
coll'arco	With the bow (Ital.), as opposed to pizzicato.
coloratura	An elaborately ornamented melody line. (Usually used in reference to vocal music.)
colore	Color, tone color (Ital.).
come prima	As at first (Ital.).
come sopra	As above (Ital.).
common time	A meter of 4/4.
comodo	("Convenient," Ital.) At a convenient tempo.
composite meter	A regular alternation of duple and triple metric groupings at the principal level.
compound meter	If the metric level below the principal level is grouped in threes (the principal level being either in twos or threes), the meter is said to be compound.
con	With (Ital.).
concerto	A work for solo instrument(s) and orchestra.
conductor's beat	Motions the conductor makes with his right hand to indicate the meter.
conjunct melodic motion	Motion by step.
consequent phrase	The answering phrase of a pair of question-and-answer phrases.
consonance	The pitch relationships between two sounds which blend together smoothly.
contrabass	*See* double bass.
contrabassoon	A double-reed woodwind instrument, sounding an octave lower than the bassoon.
contrafagotto	Contrabassoon (Ital.).
contralto	*See* alto.
contrapuntal texture	*See* counterpoint.
cor	Horn (Fr.).

cor anglais	English horn (Fr.).
cornet	A brass instrument of medium to high register.
corno	Horn (Ital.).
countermelody	A secondary melody in counterpoint with a principal melody.
counterpoint	A type of polyphonic texture in which two or more relatively independent lines are combined.
countersubject	A line combined in counterpoint with a subject, as in a fugue.
countertenor	The highest male voice, above the tenor.
crescendo	Growing, getting louder (Ital.); abbr., *cresc.*
crotchet	British for quarter note.
cymbal	A percussion instrument consisting of a brass plate that is struck; often used as a pair struck together.
D.C.	*See* da capo.
D.S.	*See* dal segno.
da capo	From the beginning (Ital.): abbr., *D.C.*
Dämpfer	Mute (Ger.); *mit Dämpfer*: with mute; *Dämpfer weg*: without mute.
dal segno	From the sign (Ital.); abbr., *D.S.* Go back as far as the sign and play from there.
damper pedal	*See* sustaining pedal.
deceptive cadence	A cadence that ends somewhere other than expected.
decrescendo	Diminishing, getting softer (Ital.); abbr., *decresc.*
development	The middle section of a movement in "sonata form" or "first-movement form," whose function is to develop the themes and motives presented in the exposition. *See also* motivic development.
diatonic system	An arrangement of pitches in the following intervallic pattern, ascending (S, semitone; T, tone): . . . T T S T T T S T T S T T T S . . .
dim.	*See* diminuendo.
diminuendo	Getting softer (Ital.); abbr., *dim.*
diminution	The statement of a theme with its note values halved.
disjunct melodic motion	Motion by leap.
dissonance	The pitch relationship between two sounds which do not blend together smoothly.
divisi	Divided (Ital.).
dolce	Sweet (Ital.).
dominant	*See* leading harmony.
dominant seventh	A type of chord.
dopo	After (Ital.).
doppio movimento	Twice as fast (Ital.).
dot	A notational symbol.
double	To double is to play or sing a line at a set interval, such as a third or an octave, from another part.
double bass	(Bass viol, contrabass.) A bowed stringed instrument of low register.
double flat	A notational symbol that lowers the pitch of a note a whole step.
double sharp	A notational symbol that raises the pitch of a note a whole step.
downbeat	At the principal metric level, the count of one. The beat on which the conductor brings his hand down.
duet	A composition for two singers or instrumentalists.
duo	*See* duet.
duple meter	Meter in which the beats are grouped in twos.
Dur	Major (Ger.).
dynamics	The degree of loudness or softness of a sound.
eighth note	A notational symbol.
elision	Two phrases run together so that the end of the first coincides with the beginning of the second.

English horn	A double-reed woodwind instrument of a moderately low to high register.
enharmonic	Two different spellings for the same pitch.
ensemble	("All at once, together," Fr.) A group of performers, as distinct from a soloist. Also, the music performed by such a group.
entrance	Same as entry.
entry	Each successive statement in an imitative texture.
equal temperament	An adjustment of the tuning of keyboard instruments so that all the semitones are equal (at least in principle).
espressivo	Expressive (Ital.); abbr., *espress.*
etwas	Somewhat (Ger.).
exposition	The first section of a movement in "sonata form" or "first-movement form." The function of this section is to set forth the themes and principal keys to be used in the movement.
f	*See* forte.
F clef	*See* bass clef.
Fagott	Bassoon (Ger.).
fagotto	Bassoon (Ital.).
fantasy section	*See* development.
fermata	Hold, pause (Ital.); symbol, ⌒.
ff	*See* fortissimo.
figurated chord	*See* broken chord.
figuration	The consistent use of a figure or figures.
figure	A recognizable pattern of notes, especially of faster notes that are subdivisions of a beat.
final	The concluding note of a piece or section of chant.
finale	The end of an act in an opera, or the last movement of a multimovement instrumental work (Ital.).
fine	End, close (Ital.). *See also* al fine.
first-movement form	*See* sonata-allegro form.
flag	A notational symbol.
flat	A notational symbol that lowers the pitch of a note a half step.
Flatterzunge	Flutter tongue (Ger.).
flautando	An instruction to string players to "play like a flute."
flauto	Flute (Ital.).
flauto piccolo	("Little flute," Ital.) Piccolo.
Flöte	Flute (Ger.).
flute	(Transverse flute.) A "woodwind" instrument, generally made of silver, of medium to high register.
flutter tongue	A rapid tremolo on a wind instrument, produced by rolling the tongue in the sound, 'drrrrr.'
forte	Loud, strong (Ital.); abbr., *f.*
fortissimo	Very loud (Ital.); abbr., *ff.*
forzando	Accented, forced (Ital.); abbr.: *fz.*
frame	In this book, two pitches that serve as reference points for a line.
French horn	*See* horn.
fugue	A type of piece characterized by imitative counterpoint, especially noticeable at the beginning.
full cadence	(Authentic cadence, dominant-to-tonic cadence.) The cadential progression from a leading to a central harmony.
full score	A score in which all the parts appear, aligned one above the other, on separate staves.
fuoco	Fire, speed, force (Ital.).
fz	*See* forzando.
G clef	*See* treble clef.
G.P.	*See* Generalpause.

Generalpause	A rest for the complete orchestra (Ger.); abbr., *G.P.*
geschwind	Fast (Ger.).
giocoso	Playful (Ital.).
giusto	Appropriate, just, proper (Ital.). *See also* tempo.
glissando	("Sliding," Ital.) A slide, encompassing all the pitches between the beginning and the ending notes of the glissando.
grace note	A type of ornamental note.
Gradual	A kind of Gregorian chant.
grave	Very serious, solemn (Ital.).
grazioso	Gracefully (Ital.).
great staff	A system of two staves, the lower staff with a bass clef, the upper staff with a treble clef.
Gregorian chant	A repertory of ancient chant used in Roman Catholic Church services.
guitar	A stringed instrument on which sound is produced by plucking or strumming.
half cadence	A cadence ending on the leading harmony.
half note	A notational symbol.
half step	*See* semitone.
harmonic area	A group of several harmonies closely related to each other and giving a feeling of stability. Same as "key."
harmonic center	*See* central harmony.
harmonic color	*See* major, minor.
harmonic progression	A succession of harmonies.
harmonic rhythm	The relative speed at which the harmonies of a piece change.
harmonic shift	*See* modulation.
harmony	In a most general sense, the quality of whatever pitch relationships are perceptible in a piece, including those in a line, but also—and especially—those not in a line; more specifically, relationships within a chord and among a succession of chords. Sometimes limited to triads and their derivatives.
harp	A stringed instrument on which sound is produced by plucking or strumming.
harpsichord	A keyboard instrument on which sound is produced by strings that are plucked mechanically.
hautbois	Oboe (Fr.).
head (of a note)	A notational symbol.
homophonic texture	*See* homophony.
homophony	A type of polyphonic texture in which the sounds are heard as blocks, rather than as separate lines. Same as "chordal texture."
horn	(French horn.) A brass instrument of medium-low to high register.
imitation	A type of contrapuntal texture in which each voice in turn states the same or similar material.
incidental music	Music for stage plays.
instrumentation	The art of writing for instruments.
interval	The distance between any two pitches. For a list of intervals, see Appendix C, Exs. C-29 and C-30.
Introit	An "entrance song" in Gregorian chant.
inversion	Melodic inversion is the statement of a melody "upside-down," so that the inverted melody moves downward when the original melody moves upward, and vice versa.
kettledrum	*See* timpani.
key (1)	*See* harmonic area.
key (2)	*See* keyboard instruments.
key signature	One or more sharps or flats, placed at the beginning of a piece to indicate the key.
keyboard instruments	A class of instruments in which the sounding element—of whatever kind—is activated through keys, as on a piano. Keyboard instruments include the pipe organ, which has a set of pipes comparable to woodwinds;

the harpsichord, on which a set of strings is plucked in the manner of a guitar; the piano, on which the strings are struck by little hammers; as well as other kinds.

Klarinette	Clarinet (Ger.).
kleine Flöte	Piccolo (Ger.).
langsam	Slow (Ger.).
largando	Broadening out, slowing down (Ital.).
larghetto	Somewhat broad, slow (Ital.); faster than largo.
larghissimo	Very broad; slower than largo (Ital.).
largo	Broad, slow (Ital.).
leading harmony	(Dominant.) A harmony that leads to or causes the listener to expect the central harmony (tonic).
leaning note	*See* appoggiatura.
leap	A relatively large melodic interval.
ledger line	A notational symbol.
legato	("Bound," "connected," Ital.) Smooth articulation in which the notes of a line are connected.
leger line	*See* ledger line.
leggiero	Light, detached (Ital.).
legno	*See* coll'legno.
lento	Slow (Ital.).
level	A way of perceiving the structure of a piece. At a low level, perception is directed toward detail only; at a high level, perception is directed at overall aspects of structure.
librettist	The author of a libretto.
libretto	The text of an opera or other dramatic musical work.
Lied	("Song," Ger. Plural, *Lieder*.) A song with a German text.
line	A succession of pitches heard in relation to one another.
litany	A repeated prayer of intercession.
lungo	Long, for a long time (Ital.).
lyric	Songlike.
M.D.	*See* mano destra.
M.M.	(Maelzel metronome.) A metronome marking, for example, *M.M.* $\downarrow$ = 60.
M.S.	*See* mano sinistra.
ma	But (Ital.).
madrigal	A particular style of part-song, usually in four or five voices, with sections of varying texture.
mässig	Moderate (Ger.).
maestoso	Majestic (Ital.).
maggiore	Major (Ital.).
major	A particular kind of harmonic color, contrasted with minor.
major second	*See* tone (2).
mano destra	Right hand (Ital.).
mano sinistra	Left hand (Ital.).
marcato	Marked, stressed, emphasized (Ital.).
marcia	A march (Ital.).
martellato	(From Ital., "hammered.") In string playing, incisive, detached strokes of the bow.
Mass	The Roman Catholic Holy Communion service.
measure	A measure is a metric group at the principal level.
melisma	Many notes sung to a single syllable.
melismatic	A type of text setting using melismas.

melody	In a most general sense, quality of pitch relationships among single pitches in succession. Sometimes restricted to a succession of pitches that seems tuneful or melodious.
melody and accompaniment	A type of polyphonic texture in which a single line stands out against an accompaniment. Sometimes (but not in this text) used synonymously with homophony.
meno	Less (Ital.).
menuetto	Originally a court dance in triple meter.
mesto	Sad, mournful (Ital.).
meter	In this text, an exactly equidistant pulse, or system of pulses, that the listener infers from the music, and that he expects to continue.
meter signature	In notation, a numerical indication of the metric grouping and of the type of note which represents a beat.
metric group	A group of pulses as found in a particular meter.
metric level	A low metric level is one on which relatively fast pulsations are grouped; a high metric level is one on which are grouped relatively slow pulsations. A high level typically subsumes several lower levels.
metrical rhythm	Rhythm that is regular.
metronome	A device that can produce equidistant ticks or flashes of light at a variety of tempos.
mezzo	Half, middle, moderate (Ital.).
mezzo-forte	Moderately loud (Ital.).
mezzo-piano	Moderately soft (Ital.).
mezzo-soprano	A female voice with a range lying between the soprano and the alto.
microtone	An interval smaller than a semitone.
miniature score	A small score used for study purposes.
minim	British for half note.
minor	A particular kind of harmonic color, contrasted with major.
minor second	*See* semitone.
minore	Minor (Ital.).
minuet	*See* menuetto.
misura	Meter, measure (Ital.).
mode	The difference between major and minor harmonic color is called a difference in mode.
moderato	Moderate, moving at a moderate pace (Ital.).
modulation	A shift from one harmonic area (key) to another. In a modulation, the previous central harmony (tonic) is supplanted by a new one.
Moll	Minor (Ger.).
molto	Very, much (Ital.).
monophonic texture	*See* monophony.
monophony	A type of texture with only a single line of music—one note at a time.
mosso	Animated, moved (Ital.).
motive	A short musical fragment used extensively in the construction of a particular piece; shorter than a theme, and apt to be used in such a way that it loses its original identity.
motivic development	Development that takes place at the motivic level, involving a progressive modification of motives.
moto	Motion (Ital.); *con moto*, with motion, with animation.
movement	The largest division of a symphony, or other extensive instrumental work.
musical rhyme	Same or similar music at the ends of different phrases or sections, in the manner of a poetic rhyme.
natural	A notational symbol that restores a note previously altered by an accidental to its original pitch.
neighbor (1)	(Not a standard usage.) In this text, a pitch just above or just below the central pitch.
neighbor (2)	A non-chord tone which is a step or a half step above or below the chord tone from which it has moved and to which it resolves.

nicht zu	Not too (Ger.).
non-chord tones	Pitches that are not part of a given harmony. *See also* appoggiatura, neighbor (2), pedal note.
nonet	A composition for nine performers. Also, the performers of such a work.
nonharmonic tones	*See* non-chord tones.
note	In this text, a single, distinct musical tone, with a specific pitch and duration.
obbligato	Required (Ital.).
oboe	A double-reed woodwind instrument of medium to high register.
octave	If two pitches are an octave apart, their respective frequencies are in the ratio of 2:1. Such notes sound almost the same but are in different registers.
octet	A composition for eight performers. Also, the performers of such a work.
offbeat	A rhythm occurring off (between) the beats. An accented offbeat is an accent occurring between the beats.
open ending	An incomplete stop at the end of a phrase or section.
opera	A dramatic work set completely to music (for singers and instrumentalists) and staged, with costumes and sets. Operas typically contain arias, recitatives, and ensembles.
oratorio	A large dramatic work for soloists, chorus, and orchestra, often on a sacred subject and usually not staged or acted.
orchestra	A large group of instrumentalists, several performers doubling on each part. The conventional symphony orchestra is divided into groups or "families" of instruments: woodwinds, brasses, percussion instruments, and strings.
orchestration	The art of combining timbres.
organ	(Pipe organ.) A keyboard instrument on which sound is produced by pipes similar to woodwinds.
organ point	*See* pedal note.
ossia	Alternate, or (Ital.).
ostinato	(From Ital., "obstinate.") The repetition of a figure many times, at the same pitch level.
ottava	Octave (Ital.); abbr., 8va.
overture	An instrumental composition which forms an introduction to a stage work (a play or an opera) or which is an independent concert piece.
p	*See* piano (1).
parallel	Two lines in parallel motion maintain a constant interval (such as an octave) between them.
part (1)	(A contrapuntal part.) *See* voice (2).
part (2)	The written or printed music for only a single performer or group of performers playing the same notes.
pedal (of a piano)	*See* sustaining pedal.
pedal note	A note that is sustained through changing harmonies, forming a dissonance with some of them.
pedal point	*See* pedal note.
pedal tone	*See* pedal note.
percussion instruments	A class—or rather, several classes—of instruments. The name "percussion" expresses the principal class, on which sound is produced by striking (as on a drum); the resulting sound may have a distinct pitch (as timpani) or may not (as a cymbal). Almost any instrument that produces a nonpitched sound is for convenience grouped under "percussion."
pesante	Heavy (Ital.).
phrase	A basic musical unit, comparable to a sentence.
phrase group	A division larger than a phrase and smaller than a section.
pianissimo	Very soft (Ital.); abbr., ***pp***.
piano (1)	Soft (Ital.); abbr., ***p***
piano (2)	(Pianoforte.) A keyboard instrument on which sound is produced by strings struck by felt hammers.
pianoforte	*See* piano (2).

piano-vocal score	A score which contains all the vocal parts of a work for voice(s) and orchestra, but in which the original instrumental parts have been arranged for piano accompaniment. Operas are frequently published in this format.
piccolo	(Ital., *flauto piccolo*.) A small flute with a very high register.
pieno	Full (Ital.).
pipe organ	*See* organ.
pitch	The quality of "highness" or "lowness" of musical sounds. Pitch is measured in terms of the number of vibrations per second, or frequency in cycles per second (cps), of the sound that produces the pitch.
più	More (Ital.).
pizzicato	(Ital.) Plucked, as opposed to bowed, strings.
pocket score	*See* miniature score.
poco	Little (Ital.); *un poco*, a little.
polyphonic texture	*See* polyphony.
polyphony	A texture in which more than one pitch sounds at the same time.
portamento	Carried over, smooth, very legato (Ital.).
Posaune	Trombone (Ger.).
pp	*See* pianissimo.
prelude	A piece played as an introduction to something else, such as a prelude to an opera.
prestissimo	As fast as possible (Ital.).
presto	Very fast (Ital.).
prima	First of all, formerly (Ital.).
prima volta	("First time," Ital.) Take the first ending when there is a repeat indicated.
primo	The upper part of a piano duet. (The lower part is marked *secondo*.)
principal level	The metric level at which it is most convenient to count or to conduct.
program music	Music provided with a "program"—a literary or pictorial description, clue, or analog of the ideas or events the composer intended to include in the music.
Prose	A kind of Latin chant.
quarter note	A notational symbol.
quartet	A work for four performers, vocal or instrumental. Also, the performers of such a work. *See also* string quartet.
quasi	Almost (Ital.).
quaver	British for eighth note.
Querflöte	Flute, transverse flute (Ger.).
quintet	A composition for five performers. Also, the performers of such a work.
quintuplet	(Also quintolet.) A notational symbol.
rall.	*See* rallentando.
rallentando	Slowing down gradually (Ital.); abbr., *rall.*
range	The extent of all the pitches capable of being played by an instrument or sung by a singer. For a list of instrumental and vocal ranges, see Appendix C, Exs. C-36 and C-37.
recapitulation	The third section of "sonata form" or "first-movement form," which restates the themes and other material from the exposition.
recitative	Musical declamation of text in relatively fast rhythms and relatively slow-moving lines and harmonies; used in opera and other types of dramatic works.
reciting note	A frequently occurring pitch, on which a large portion of a text is recited.
recorder	A end-blown type of wooden flute made in several sizes, with various ranges from low to high.
reed instruments	A group of woodwind instruments. Single-reed instruments include the clarinet and saxophone, double-reed instruments include the oboe, English horn, and bassoon.
register	The average pitch level of a musical passage. Also, part of a range.

relative major	The major key which has the same key signature as a given minor key.
relative minor	The minor key which has the same key signature as a given major key.
release	The manner in which a sound ends.
represa	Repeat, repetition (Ital.).
rest	A written or printed symbol for silence.
restatement	*See* recapitulation.
retrograde	The stating of a melody or other musical material in reverse order.
Rf, ***Rfz***, *rinf.*	*See* rinforzando.
rhythm	In the most general sense, the temporal aspects of a piece of music; the way a piece unfolds in time.
rhythmic group	A group of notes that seem to belong together in time.
rhythmic level	A low rhythmic level is one on which relatively short notes are grouped in relatively short groups; on a high rhythmic level the shorter notes of a piece will be subsumed under relatively long groups, and groups of groups.
rinforzando	Suddenly accented, stressed (Ital.); abbr., ***Rf***, ***Rfz***, *rinf.*
rit.	*See* ritardando.
ritardando	Slowing down gradually (Ital.); abbr., *rit.*
ritenuto	Slowing down immediately (Ital.).
ritornello	("Little return," Ital.) An instrumental refrain, in a vocal or an instrumental composition.
rondo	An instrumental composition with a recurring section or theme.
root	The lowest note of a triad in its simplest position.
rounded binary form	A sectional arrangement which could be expressed as $A_1\ A_1\ B\ A_2\ B\ A_2$.
rubato	("Robbed," Ital.) Freedom of tempo.
saltando	("Leaping," Ital.) The bow is to bounce lightly on the strings.
saxophone	A reed instrument constructed of brass, made in several sizes with ranges from low to high.
scale	A set of pitches, arranged in an ascending or descending order, normally conjunct.
scene	A division of an act, in an opera.
scherzando	Playfully (Ital.).
schmachtend	Yearning (Ger.).
schnell	Fast (Ger.).
scordatura	("Mistuning," Ital.) Unusual tuning of a stringed instrument.
score	The format in which a whole piece of music (as opposed to a single part) is written or printed. Each part is aligned directly over or under the other parts.
score order	The conventional order in which instruments appear on a page of score.
scorrevole	Flowing along (Ital.).
secco	Dry (Ital.).
seconda volta	("Second time," Ital.) Often used in scores to refer to the repeat of a section.
secondo	The lower part of a piano duet. (The upper part is marked *primo*.)
section	A large division of a piece or a movement.
segno	("Sign," Ital.) A sign (·𝄋·) indicating the beginning of a section to be repeated. *See also* al segno, dal segno.
semibreve	British for whole note.
semiquaver	British for sixteenth note.
semitone	(Minor second, half step.) Half a tone; the smallest interval used in the traditional Western system.
semplice	Simply (Ital.).
sempre	Always (Ital.).
senza	Without (Ital.).
septet	A composition for seven performers. Also, the performers of such a work.

septuplet	(Also septolet.) A notational symbol.
sequence (1)	A melodic and/or harmonic pattern immediately repeated at another pitch level.
sequence (2)	A kind of Latin chant.
sextet	A composition for six performers. Also, the performers of such a work.
sforzando	Reinforced, suddenly accented (Ital.); abbr., *Sfz*.
sharp	A notational symbol that raises the pitch of a note a semitone.
signature	*See* key signature, meter signature.
simple meter	If the metric levels below the principal level are all consistently grouped in twos (the principal level being either in twos or threes), the meter is said to be simple.
sixteenth note	A notational symbol.
slur	A curved line joining notes to be performed in a legato manner.
slurred notes	Notes joined by a slur in the score.
smorzando	Dying away (Ital.).
solo	("Alone," Ital. Plural, *soli* or *soloists*.) Music for a single performer, playing or singing entirely alone or with accompaniment. In the plural it refers to a group of performers, each playing or singing a different part.
sonata	A work for piano or other solo instrument with or without piano accompaniment, usually in two or more movements.
sonata form	*See* sonata-allegro form.
sonata-allegro form	A standardized description of the treatment of themes and keys for first movements of symphonies, quartets, and sonatas.
song cycle	A group of songs based on a set of related poems, generally by the same poet.
sopra	Above, other (Ital.).
soprano	The highest voice type.
soprano clef	A C clef which indicates that the lowest line of the staff is middle C.
sordino	The mute (Ital.), of a stringed instrument, a brass instrument, etc.
sostenuto	Sustained (Ital.).
sotto	Below, under (Ital.).
spacing	The relative position of notes sounded simultaneously. Notes can be spaced closely, in the same register, or far apart, in different registers.
spiccato	Light, detached bowing (Ital.).
spirito	Spirit (Ital.); *con spirito*, with spirit, fast.
staccato	("Detached," Ital.) Detached articulation, separating notes from one another.
staff	(Plural, *staves*.) A system of five horizontal lines, used in notation to indicate pitch.
stem	A notational symbol.
step	A relatively small melodic interval, as opposed to a leap.
stesso	Same (Ital.).
stretto	("Narrow," Ital.) An acceleration of entries in a contrapuntal texture.
string quartet	Usually, a composition for two violins, viola, and cello. Also, the performers of such a composition.
stringed instrument	A class of instruments on which sound is produced by a vibrating set of strings stretched over a wooden case (or "sound box"); the strings may be set vibrating by means of a bow or by plucking. The colloquial term "strings" usually refers to the bowed instruments: violin, viola, cello, and double bass.
stringendo	Speeding up (Ital.).
strophic	A type of text setting in which the same music is repeated for each successive stanza of the text.
subito	Suddenly (Ital.).
subject	Musical material, usually melodic, which functions as the main idea of a piece (especially a fugue); similar to a theme.

sustaining pedal	A device on a piano which releases the dampers and enables the strings to continue sounding.
syllabic	A type of text setting employing one note per syllable.
symphony	A work for large orchestra, generally in several movements.
syncopation	An accented note that starts on an offbeat and continues through the following beat.
system	Two or more staves connected together.
temperament	A special kind of tuning.
tempo	("Time," Ital.) Pace, rate of speed; *a tempo*, resume the previous tempo; *tempo giusto,* normal speed, strict tempo; *tempo primo*, resume the first tempo; *tornando al tempo*, return to the previous tempo.
tempo indication	A verbal direction (such as "allegro") or a metronome marking (such as "*M.M.* ♩ = 60"), placed above the staff at the point where the (new) tempo begins.
tenor	A high male voice.
tenor clef	A C clef which indicates that the next-to-top line of the staff is middle C.
ternary form	A sectional arrangement that could be expressed by the letters *A B A.*
terzett	*See* trio (2).
text setting	The manner in which words are set to music.
texture	Metaphorically speaking, the way the "fabric" of a piece of music is "woven."
thematic statement	Each recognizable appearance of a theme is sometimes called a statement.
theme	A group or pattern of pitches with a strong, distinctive identity, which returns to shape a larger piece.
threnody	A song of lament.
tie	A notational symbol.
timbre	In a general sense, quality of sound; tone color.
timpani	A set of large drums ("kettledrums") each of which is tuned to a specific (low) pitch.
tone (1)	*See* note.
tone (2)	(Whole step, whole tone, major second.) The next smallest interval of the traditional Western system.
tone cluster	*See* cluster.
tonic chord	*See* central harmony.
tonic note	The central note of a major or minor key.
tornando a	Return to, resume (Ital.).
transposition	The writing or performing of a piece or a passage at another pitch level than originally written or performed.
transverse flute	*See* flute.
treble clef	A clef which indicates that the next-to-bottom line of the staff represents G above middle C.
tremolo	(1) In singing, a wide fluctuation of pitch; (2) in string playing, the rapid repetition of the same pitch; (3) in piano music, the rapid alternation of two notes an octave apart.
triad	A chord formed of three notes, generally built of two superimposed thirds.
trill	An ornament consisting of the rapid alternation of two notes a tone or semitone apart; abbr., *tr.*, 〜〜.
trio (1)	A kind of piece originally scored for three winds and grouped with a minuet, as in a minuet and trio.
trio (2)	A composition for three performers, vocal or instrumental. Also, the performers of such a work.
triplet	A notational symbol.
tromba	Trumpet (Ital.).
trombone	A brass instrument of low to medium register.
troppo	Too much (Ital.).
trumpet	A brass instrument of medium to high register.
tuba	A brass instrument of low register.
tuning	A system of relationships among a set of pitches, expressible in mathematical terms.
tutti	("All," Ital.) A passage in which all the performers play and/or sing, usually with more than one performer on a part. Opposed to "solo."

tympani	*See* timpani.
unison	Pitch relationship of identity. To play or sing in unison means that more than one voice or instrument performs the same part at the same time.
unit pulse	A pulse at the lowest metric level, not grouped regularly at any higher level.
upbeat	A beat that immediately precedes the downbeat and that is very closely linked to it.
veloce	Quick, fast (Ital.).
vibrato	A minute fluctuation in pitch.
viola	A bowed stringed instrument of medium low to high register.
violin	A bowed stringed instrument of medium to very high register.
violoncello	*See* cello.
virtuoso	A performer who can play or sing technically difficult passages with ease.
vivace	Lively, quick (Ital.).
voce	Voice (Ital.).
voice (1)	The human voice, as opposed to instruments.
voice (2)	Each separate, independent line in a contrapuntal texture is called a voice, whether the music is written for human voices or for instruments.
voice type	A particular range and quality of male or female voice. *See* alto, baritone, bass, countertenor, mezzo-soprano, soprano, tenor.
white-key scale	The scale represented by the white keys on the piano; the diatonic system in its untransposed or "natural" position.
whole note	A notational symbol.
whole step	*See* tone (2).
whole tone	*See* tone (2).
wind instruments	*See* woodwind instruments, brass instruments.
woodwind instruments	A class of instruments on which sound is produced by blowing on a pipe, as on a flute or recorder. In several kinds of woodwinds, the blowing sets vibrating a "reed" or thin sliver of flexible material; such instruments (for example, oboe, clarinet) are also called "reeds," and may be "single-reed instruments" (clarinet) or "double-reed instruments" (oboe.)
ziemlich	Rather (Ger.).

APPENDIX C MUSICAL NOMENCLATURE AND NOTATION

MUSICAL NOTATION. The conventional system of notation for music is primarily a way of telling a performer what pitches and durations to play and how to play them. To put it another way, conventional notation does not immediately present to the listener a picture of how the piece sounds; that is not its purpose. Considerable experience is required in order to form a reliable mental image of a piece merely from looking at its notation. Even if you just follow the notation while listening to a piece, you are likely to encounter many details that—while essential to the performer—are irrelevant or misleading to the listener.

For this reason, we do not recommend that the listener study conventional notation until he has had some experience listening to pieces and has developed skill in understanding the musical shapes that he hears. Eventually, however, many readers may wish to know something about conventional notation, so we include here an introduction to notation designed for the listener who has worked his way through at least part of this book. We will use as illustrations of conventional notation portions of core pieces that have been studied earlier in the text; the meaning of the conventional notation can be more easily understood by comparing it to the sound of the piece and to its representation in the special notation used in the text itself.

Conventional notation is particularly difficult to learn because it is the result of convention rather than of a carefully thought-out system. This kind of notation is the product of more than a thousand years

of continuous modification. Many of its features are the way they are simply because that is the way they developed. Often theorists suggest more rational or more systematic ways of notating certain details; but these suggestions are usually ignored, and changes come (if they come) primarily through the day-to-day use that musicians make of notation.

The format in which a whole piece is written down or printed is called a *score*; in a music library, for example, you would ask for the score of Beethoven's Symphony No. 7. Music is also written down in other formats, since the score of a symphony (needed by the conductor) may be a large, expensive book; the flute player does not need the score, which contains all the instrumental parts, but only his own part. Symphonies, string quartets, and many other kinds of music are also published in *parts*—a separate part for each kind of instrument. But you need the score to see the whole piece. Many works are available in pocket-size *miniature scores* for study purposes.

A score contains many different kind of directions to the performers: directions about pitch, dynamics, tempo, the articulation of sounds, and the duration of both sounds and silences. These directions take the form of words as well as of the symbols peculiar to musical notation. Directions about dynamics and tempo usually appear as words (or as abbreviations of words); the most commonly used words are given in the glossary, Appendix B.

Throughout the book, we have used *note* to mean a single, distinct musical tone, with a specific pitch and duration. Our English cousins frequently speak

of this as a *tone*, reserving the word "note" for the written or printed symbol used in musical notation. American usage (which we have followed) confounds the two. Ordinarily that does not matter, but at this point it will cause some difficulty, since we must now distinguish carefully between the sounding tone and the graphic symbol.

Each separate note—that is, tone—of a piece is indicated by a symbol of the kind shown in Ex. C-1. The elements of this symbol have to do with its duration (as will be explained soon). In addition, such symbols may be located relative to a system of *vertical* lines called *bar lines* (compare page 65), which further define the coordinates of duration. The duration of silence is indicated by the shape of *rests*.

To indicate pitch, each note symbol is located relative to another system of *horizontal* lines; these lines are grouped in fives, each group of five being called a *staff*, to be shown in Ex. C-19. (The individual note symbol itself includes no indication of pitch.) These two systems of lines—horizontal and vertical—are superimposed one on top of the other.

Example C-1 Note shapes

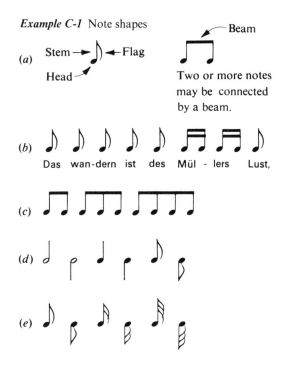

The articulation of a note, that is, the manner in which sounds are begun (*attack*) and ended (*release*), is shown by additional symbols added to the note symbols, shown in Ex. C-35.

DURATION: RHYTHMIC NOTATION. Example C-1*a* illustrates the separate elements of a note symbol. All notes that have a specific pitch have a *head*, for even though the head itself does not indicate the pitch, the placement of the head on the staff shows what pitch is to be played. (Nonpitched percussion is sometimes written in headless symbols.)

Stems, flags, and *beams* indicate relative duration; they are added to a head to modify the duration of the note. Beams and flags are alternate forms of notation. There is no absolute rule concerning the choice of beams or flags. In vocal music, pitches sung to different syllables are usually notated with flags; those sung to the same syllable are usually notated with beams (Ex. C-1*b*). Beams are sometimes used to show certain kinds of rhythmic groupings (Ex. C-1*c*).

Stems may go upward or downward from the head. If they go up, they are written on the right side of the head; if they go down they are written on the left side (Ex. C-1*d*). Whether stems go up or down depends sometimes on the location on the staff, sometimes on other, more complex factors; but the direction of the stem does not affect the duration. Flags are always attached to the right side of the stem (Ex. C-1*e*).

Duration. The durations expressed by the system of notation are completely *relative*. The symbols do not indicate that a note is, say, half a second long, but only that one note is, say, half as long as another.

Durational symbols come in basic denominations and are related to each other in a *binary* system. That is, unless modified in ways described further on, each note has a durational value twice as great as the next smaller denomination or half as great as the next larger one. (A long time ago, there was also a ternary system in which a basic denomination could be one-third the value of the next larger one, but that system was dropped for the sake of simplicity.)

For purely traditional reasons, the basic denominations are named from a symbol without a stem called a *whole note*. The binary system derived from the

whole note is shown in Ex. C-2. The smallest values in common use are sixty-fourth notes. Rests are arranged in a parallel system, shown at the right of Ex. C-2.

While many durational patterns can be notated using only these basic denominations, many more require different note values—values that are not exactly twice as long or half as long as other values. The relative lengths indicated by the symbols can be altered in several ways.

A *tie* creates a longer value out of two shorter ones by indicating that the second symbol does not have a separate attack (Ex. C-3). In addition to providing for notes of irregular length, ties are used for a variety of complex reasons springing from conventions of metrical notation. Rests are never tied.

Ties closely resemble slurs (page 13) in appearance, but do not have the same meaning (see Ex. C-35). Ties are for duration, slurs for articulation.

A *dot* lengthens the value of the note to which it is attached by half of that note's value (Ex. C-4*a*, *b*, and *d*). Dots are often used to notate a long-short pattern (Ex. C-4*e* and *f*). Sometimes such a pattern is

Example C-2 Values of notes and rests

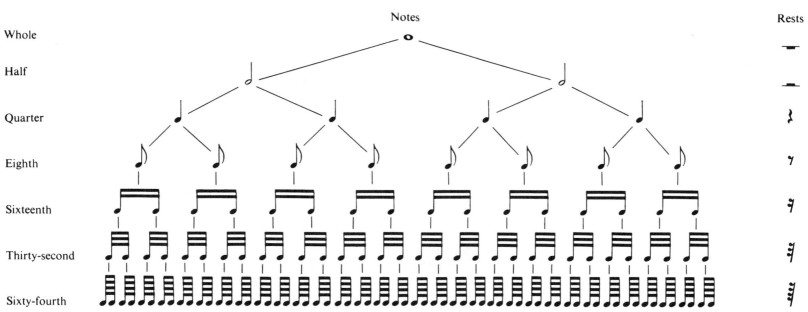

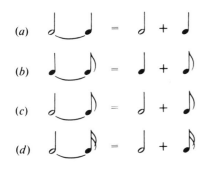

(a)   *(b)*   *(c)*   *(d)*

Example C-3 Ties

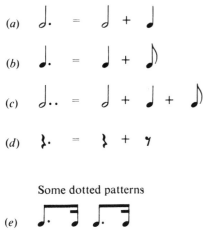

Example C-4 Dots

(a)

(b)

(c)

(d)

Some dotted patterns

(e)

(f)

(g)

(a) Triplet of eighths

(b) Triplet of quarters

Example C-5 Triplets and other subdivisions

(c) Triplet of sixteenths

(d) Quintuplet of sixteenths

(e) Alternate form for quintuplet of sixteenths

5:4

Example C-6 Some examples of rhythmic notation. (Parts *g* and *k*, Bartók, Sixth String Quartet. © 1941 in U.S.A. by Hawkes & Son, Ltd. Copyright for all countries. Used by permission of Boosey and Hawkes, Inc.) (Part *j*, Stravinsky, *Les Noces*. © 1922 by J. & W. Chester Ltd. Used by permission.)

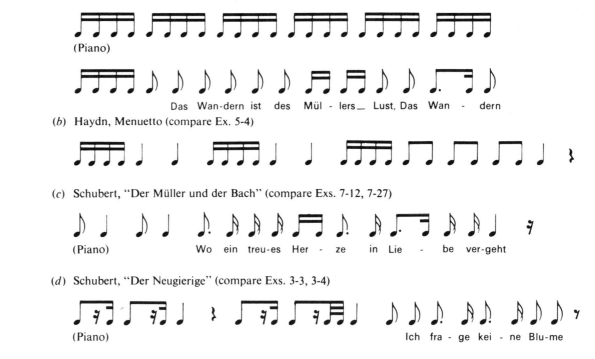

(a) Schubert, "Das Wandern" (compare Exs. 4-10, 4-16)

(Piano)

Das Wan-dern ist des Mül - lers___ Lust, Das Wan - dern

(b) Haydn, Menuetto (compare Ex. 5-4)

(c) Schubert, "Der Müller und der Bach" (compare Exs. 7-12, 7-27)

(Piano)   Wo ein treu-es Her - ze in Lie - be ver-geht

(d) Schubert, "Der Neugierige" (compare Exs. 3-3, 3-4)

(Piano)   Ich fra - ge kei - ne Blu-me

Example C-6 (*cont'd.*)

(e) Beethoven, Allegretto, interlude (compare Ex. 3-23)

Clarinet
Bassoon

Violins

(f) Monteverdi, "Chiome d'oro" (compare Ex. 2-10)

Chio - me d'o - ro bel te - so - ro, tu mi leghi in mil - le mo - -

(g) Bartók, Mesto (compare Ex. 6-1)

(h) Bach, Prelude in D major (compare Ex. 14-13)

(i) Gregorian Chant, "Resurrexi" (compare Ex. 6-11)

Re - sur - re - xi_____ et__ ad - huc te - cum sum _____

(j) Stravinsky, *Les Noces* (compare Ex. 2-4)

(Grace notes ♪ are subtracted from the preceding value.)

(k) Bartók, Burletta (compare Ex. 5-20)

double-dotted, which has the effect of making the long note even longer and the short one even shorter (Ex. C-4c and g).

A series of consecutive dotted half notes (or of half notes each tied to a quarter note) would represent values each equivalent to three quarter notes. In this way dots or ties can be used to adapt the essentially binary system of notation to a ternary grouping. Used in other combinations, dots or ties can produce a wide variety of irregular patterns.

Another way of varying the binary system is provided by a temporary division of a value into something other than half. For example, a quarter note can be divided into three equal parts instead of two; the group of three is called a *triplet*, each of the three notes being written as an eighth note, even though the value of each of these notes is less than an eighth (Ex. C-5a). Triplets can occur in any denomination (Ex. C-5b and c). Subdivisions other than triplets are also possible; the most common are *quintuplets* (or *quintolets*) and *septuplets* (or *septolets*) (Ex. C-5d). These are sometimes notated with the aid of a ratio, such as 5:4 for quintuplets (Ex. C-5e) to make it perfectly clear that five sixteenth notes are here supposed to occupy the time of four normal sixteenth notes.

A good way to understand the use of these durational symbols in notating rhythms is to listen to a rhythm while looking at the notation. The selections in Ex. C-6 have all been studied in the main part of the book; these rhythms should sound familiar to you. You can compare their sound and their appearance in the notation used in the main part of the book with their conventional notation as shown here.

Meter. In addition to indicating relative durations, notation also indicates metric groupings, together with principal level and beat. Metric groupings were discussed in general in Chapter 4; here we will describe specific ways of notating these groupings. Remember that musical notation is the composer's way of directing the performer how to play the piece: the composer chooses a particular notation for the meter, principal level, and beat so that the piece will sound the way he originally imagined it. Often a composer must choose among several approximately

375

Example C-7 Simple duple meter. Schubert, "Das Wandern" (compare Ex. C-6*a*)

(a)

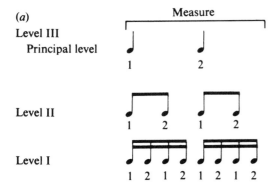

Level III
Principal level

Level II

Level I

(b)

Mässig geschwind (moderately fast)

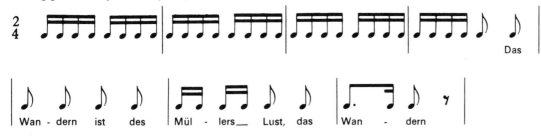

Wan - dern   ist   des   Mül - lers___ Lust, das   Wan - dern

(c)

2 indicates number of beats per measure
4 indicates kind of note used for beat

(d)

(fast)

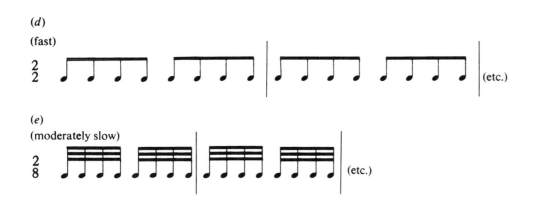

(etc.)

(e)

(moderately slow)

(etc.)

equivalent notations offered by the notational system.

The composer must decide what denomination to use for the beat at the principal level and how to notate the metric grouping of beats. Having made his selections, he writes the rhythms of the piece within the framework of vertical lines called *bar lines* and indicates both the beat and the measure at the beginning of the piece by a *meter signature*. He also places a tempo indication (such as "allegro") at the beginning of the piece, to indicate the speed of the beat.

For "Das Wandern," Schubert wanted to indicate a beat at level III grouped in twos. (See Ex. 4-10 in Chapter 4.) Example C-7*a* shows the levels of Ex. 4-10 in the traditional note symbols Schubert used. Example C-7*b* shows the traditional notations for the rhythms of the piano introduction and first phrase of the voice part with the bar lines, meter signature, and tempo indications used by Schubert (compare Ex. 4-16). In the meter signature (which should not be thought of as a fraction), the lower number indicates the denomination chosen as beat, the upper number indicates the number of these beats in each measure (Ex. C-7*c*). In this case, Schubert chose quarter notes for the beat ("4" represents quarter notes) and made the measures each two quarters in duration. The piano accompaniment begins with its fastest notes written as sixteenth notes, which are grouped eight to a measure, since eight sixteenth notes are arithmetically equivalent to the two quarter notes indicated by the meter signature. When the voice starts, it sings in eighth notes at first (written with flags instead of beams because each eighth note goes with a separate syllable). There are four eighth notes in each measure, since that is the equivalent of two quarter notes. Having chosen a combination of symbols and bar lines, the composer notates whatever rhythms he wants to use within this metrical framework—either for the rest of the piece or until the rhythm changes sufficiently to require a different metric framework.

The tempo indication (in this case *Mässig geschwind*—"moderately fast") is important. Since the symbols indicate only relative, not absolute, duration, the performer must be told how fast to go—although the meter signature gives him some clue, for the beat (here, the quarter) will fall within the limits described on page 64. By using a different tempo indication,

376

Schubert could have notated the piece in different denominations, as shown in Ex. C-7d and e.

Example C-8a, b, and c shows three alternate ways of notating another of Schubert's songs, "Der Müller und der Bach"; Schubert used the first way. In addition, Ex. C-8d includes the identical patterns of duration notated in still another way, whose metric grouping completely changes the sense of the original rhythm. It often happens that a particular pattern of durations can be fitted into more than one metrical framework. As a corollary, a composer may occasionally introduce a drastic change of rhythm into the middle of a piece (by his choice of note values), without changing the meter signature to conform to the new rhythm.

Example C-9 shows more of the excerpts from Ex. C-6, with meter signatures, bar lines, and tempo indications added. Here, as in most scores, the space on the page between individual notes or rests is not exactly proportional (sometimes not even remotely approximate) to their audible duration. The first and third measures of "Der Neugierige" (Ex. C-9b) take more space on the page than measures 2 and 4, but the beats in each of these measures move at the same rate in performance. This is an important difference between conventional notation and durational notation (such as the notation used in this book), where the length of the symbols on the page is exactly proportional to the audible duration.

Simple meter. If the metric levels *below* the principal level are all consistently grouped in *twos* (the principal level being either in twos or threes) the meter is said to be *simple*. The more common signatures for simple duple meter are $\frac{2}{2}$ (also written $\mathۇ{C}$), $\frac{2}{4}$, and $\frac{2}{8}$ (see Ex. C-9b and c); for simple triple meter, $\frac{3}{2}$, $\frac{3}{4}$, and $\frac{3}{8}$ (see Ex. C-9b). Signatures such as $\frac{2}{16}$, $\frac{3}{16}$, and $\frac{2}{32}$, and the like, are possible but not often found. In other words, signatures for simple meter indicate the grouping of beats at the principal level *only*; groupings at lower levels are understood to be duple.

Two groups of beats in simple duple meter are frequently combined into *quadruple meter*. The more common signatures for this meter are $\frac{4}{2}$, $\frac{4}{4}$ (also written **C**), $\frac{4}{8}$, and—more rarely—$\frac{4}{16}$. In this case, the "4" in the upper number of the signature indicates

Example C-8 Simple triple meter. Schubert, "Der Müller und der Bach" (compare Ex. C-6c)

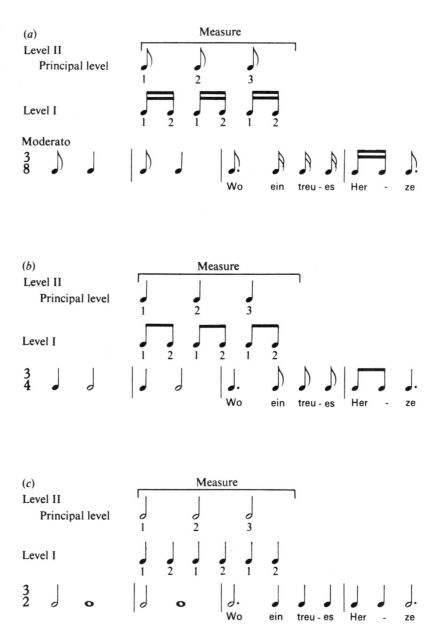

Example C-8 (*cont'd.*)

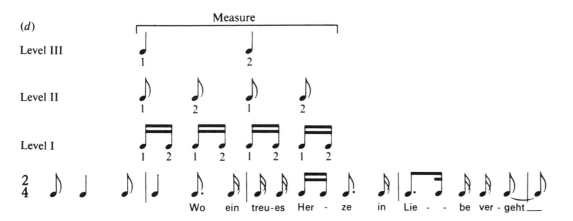

(d)

Level III

Level II

Level I

Wo ein treu-es Her - ze in Lie - - be ver - geht

Example C-9 More examples of metric notation

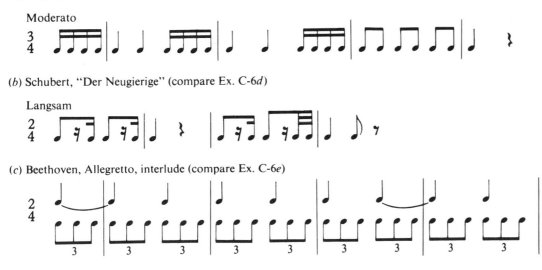

(a) Haydn, Menuetto (compare Ex. C-6b)

Moderato

(b) Schubert, "Der Neugierige" (compare Ex. C-6d)

Langsam

(c) Beethoven, Allegretto, interlude (compare Ex. C-6e)

two metric levels, both duple. Example C-10 shows the rhythm of the beginning of the vocal line from Monteverdi's "Chiome d'oro," notated in quadruple meter.

Compound meter. When the level next below the principal level is *triple*, the rhythm is usually notated in a *compound meter*. The need for compound meter springs from the binary nature of the notational system. If the beat at the principal level is to be subdivided in threes at the next lower level, this beat must be represented in some way other than a regular note value, since regular values are all subdivided in twos. (It is possible to accomplish the subdivision by triplets, but this is not usually done for a whole piece or for long sections.)

The usual way is to represent the beat at the principal level by a dotted value, then to include in the signature a metric system—in threes—for the level next below the principal one. The result is a *compound meter*, which indicates that the principal level is either duple or triple *and* that the level next below is triple. Frequent signatures for compound duple meter are

$\frac{6}{4}$ that is, the level next below the principal level is triple and written like $\frac{3}{4}$; each of these groups represents a beat on the principal level; they are grouped in twos to make $\frac{6}{4}$;

$\frac{6}{8}$ that is, the level next below is triple and written like $\frac{3}{8}$; each of these groups represents a beat at the principal level; they are grouped in twos to make $\frac{6}{8}$ (see Ex. C-11).

Another frequent compound duple meter is $\frac{6}{16}$. Frequent signatures for compound triple meter are $\frac{9}{4}$, $\frac{9}{8}$, $\frac{9}{16}$; these work the same way, except that the principal level is triple, being composed of groups of three of the measures implied at the next lower level.

Compound quadruple meter—four groups of threes—is also found, frequent signatures being $\frac{12}{4}$, $\frac{12}{8}$, $\frac{12}{16}$. Since quadruple meter itself indicates groupings at two levels, compound quadruple meter indicates groupings at three levels (Ex. C-12).

Composite meter. A regular alternation of duple and triple groupings at the principal level is sometimes

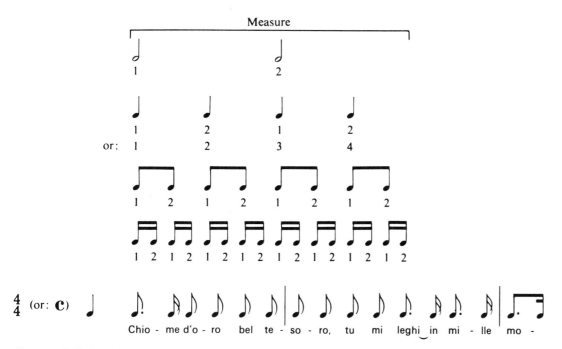

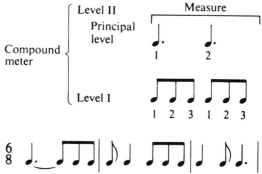

Example C-11 Compound meter. Bartók, Mesto (compare Ex. C-6g). (Sixth string quartet. © 1941 in U.S.A. by Hawkes & Son, Ltd. Copyright for all countries. Used by permission of Boosey and Hawkes, Inc.)

Example C-10 Quadruple meter. Monteverdi, "Chiome d'oro" (compare Ex. C-6f)

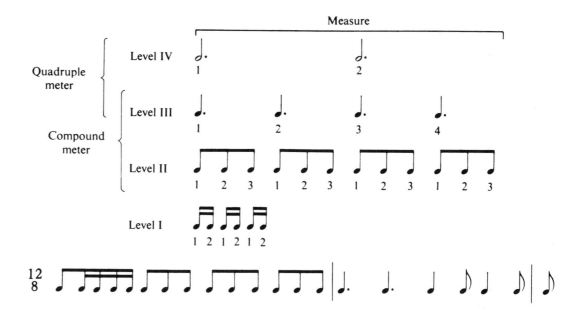

Example C-12 Quadruple compound meter. Bach, Prelude in D major (compare Ex. C-6h)

called *composite meter*. The most frequently found groupings are those of *five* and *seven*. A composite meter of five may be indicated by signatures like $\frac{5}{4}$, $\frac{5}{8}$, and $\frac{5}{16}$; similarly, meters of seven may have signatures like $\frac{7}{4}$, $\frac{7}{8}$, and $\frac{7}{16}$.

Composite meters are regular at each level except the principal level (Ex. C-13). The composer may wish to indicate the irregular principal level groupings by means of the signatures. Instead of a signature of $\frac{5}{4}$, for example, he can write $\frac{3+2}{4}$. Or he can write a double signature such as $\frac{3}{4}\frac{2}{4}$, which indicates regular alternations of measures of $\frac{3}{4}$ and of $\frac{2}{4}$.

The table in Ex. C-14 shows the more commonly found meter signatures and the metric groupings that they indicate at a moderate tempo. The relationship between metric groupings and signatures depends greatly upon tempo: a fast-paced rhythm notated in simple triple meter may sound like compound duple meter. Conversely, a slow-paced rhythm notated in a compound meter may sound like simple triple meter.

Notation of music with a unit pulse. Music that has a regular low-level pulse, or *unit pulse*, but no regular grouping of these pulses at any level, may be noted in several ways.

1. Without any meter signature and without bar lines.
2. With changing meter signatures (see Ex. C-15).
3. With a regular meter signature and bar lines, *as if* the music were metrical. In such cases, the performer has to realize that the metric notation is only for convenience, and tells him little or nothing about the actual rhythmic groupings of the music. (See Ex. C-16; refer to pages 65–66 for a discussion of the *rhythmic* upbeats and downbeats.)

Notation of rhythm without regular pulses. The conventional notational system is inadequate for music lacking a regular pulse at any level. Composers writing music with such a rhythmic structure have had to invent new systems of notation.

In Penderecki's Threnody, for example, events in the piece are referred to clock time, measured along a scale at the bottom of the score marked off in seconds. Each important change in attack, dynamics,

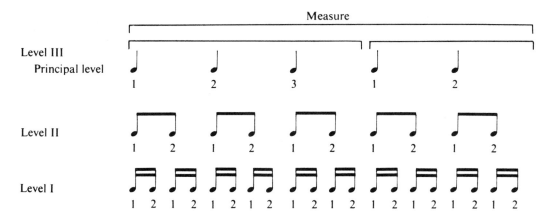

Example C-13 Composite meter

and the like, is plotted against this scale. Less important events are located only approximately on the time scale (Ex. C-17). Other composers have evolved a variety of ad hoc notations to cover situations for which conventional notation does not work.

NOTATION OF PITCH. The pitch component of music comes to us in a form far more conventionalized than the temporal component. As a result, pitch notation is more arbitrary than the notation of rhythm and meter. In order to make sense of pitch nomenclature and notation, we must take considerable account of the conventions that produced them. Specifically, in order to explain traditional Western notation, we must refer to the conventions of Western music dominant during the thousand years up to 1900—even though many of these conventions may no longer be operative in musical composition today.

Any single piece of music uses a selection of pitches, rather than all conceivable pitches. Audible pitches occur in a continuum from very low sounds to very high ones, and there are an unlimited number of distinct pitches in the continuum (just as there are an unlimited number of points on a line). The selection itself comes about by convention, varying from one age and culture to another—or even from piece to piece within the works of a single composer.

The octave. There are, however, several objective (or at least easily understandable) factors in the selection, factors that tend to turn up again and again in pitch systems of different cultures. The most important such factor is the octave—the paradoxical relationship between two pitches that sound "the same," even though one is higher than the other (see page 20). This striking relationship has become the basis of Western notation and nomenclature.

Since pitch is produced by some form of vibration (such as the vibration of a piano string or of your vocal chords), it has become customary to measure pitches in terms of the number of vibrations per second or more precisely in terms of the *frequency in cycles per second* (cps) of the sound that produces the pitch. Sounds that you can hear extend from very low frequencies of 20 to 30 cycles per second to very high frequencies of 15,000 to 20,000 cycles per second. One of the most striking applications of this way of measuring pitches and their relationships is the demonstration of the size of the octave: if two pitches are an octave apart, their respective frequencies are in the ratio of 2:1; for example, 200 cps for the higher pitch to 100 cps for the lower or any other two frequencies in the ratio of 2:1. The simplicity of the ratio 2:1 (as compared to ratios such as 4:5, or 27:32, or $1:\sqrt{2}$) is a mathematical expression of the simple relationship we

Example C-14 Metric groupings and meter signatures

	Metric groupings			Common meter signatures
Cases in which the meter signature indicates the grouping at the principal level *only*. Lower levels are understood to be duple. Groupings reflected by the meter signature are marked here "MS." Horizontal brackets indicate measures.	Principal level is duple (*simple duple meter*)	MS ⌐1 2 ⌐1 1 2 1 2 1 121212121..		$\frac{2}{2}$ (¢) $\frac{2}{4}$ $\frac{2}{8}$
	Principal level is triple (*simple triple meter*)	MS ⌐1 2 3 ⌐1 1 2 1 2 1 2 1 1212121212121..		$\frac{3}{2}$ $\frac{3}{4}$ $\frac{3}{8}$
	Principal level contains alternate groups of 2s and 3s (*composite meter*)	MS ⌐1 2 1 2 3⌐1 (fives) 12121212121..		$\frac{5}{4}$ $\frac{5}{8}$ $\frac{5}{16}$
		MS ⌐1 2 1 2 1 2 3⌐1 (sevens) 121212121212121..		$\frac{7}{4}$ $\frac{7}{8}$ $\frac{7}{16}$
Cases in which the meter signature indicates groupings at two or more levels. Lower levels are understood to be duple. Groupings reflected by the meter signature are joined by vertical brackets and marked here "MS." Horizontal brackets indicate measures.	Two principal levels, each duple (*quadruple meter*)	MS { ⌐1 2 ⌐1 1 2 1 2 1 121212121		$\frac{4}{2}$ $\frac{4}{4}$ (c) $\frac{4}{8}$ $\frac{4}{16}$
	The level below the principal level is triple (*compound meter*)	The principal level is duple	MS { ⌐1 2 ⌐1 1 2 3 1 2 3 1 1212121212121	$\frac{6}{4}$ $\frac{6}{8}$ $\frac{6}{16}$
		The principal level is triple	MS { ⌐1 2 3 ⌐1 1 2 3 1 2 3 1 2 3 1 121212121212121 21	$\frac{9}{8}$ $\frac{9}{16}$
		Two principal levels, each duple	MS { ⌐1 2 ⌐1 1 2 1 2 1 1 2 3 1 2 3 1 2 3 1 2 3 1 121212121212121212121212	$\frac{12}{8}$ $\frac{12}{16}$

Example C-15 Unit pulse notated in changing meters. Stravinsky, *Les Noces* (compare Ex. C-6*j*). (© 1922 by J. & W. Chester Ltd. Used by permission.)

(Grace notes ♪ are not counted in the meter, being subtracted from the preceding value.)

Example C-16 Unit pulse. Bartók, Burletta (compare Ex. C-6k). (Sixth string quartet. © 1941 in U.S.A. by Hawkes & Son, Ltd. Copyright for all countries. Used by permission of Boosey and Hawkes, Inc.)

hear between the two pitches—of the fact that they sound "the same." In general, the more complex is the ratio between the two frequencies, the more complex is the relationship in sound between the two pitches. Such ratios are used extensively in music theory, but not in notation.

The diatonic system. In the Western tradition of distinct pitches selected from the continuum, the interval between two pitches an octave apart is subdivided by six more pitches (remember that an unlimited number of pitches could be sounded between these two an octave apart). It is as if six particular shades of color—a particular shade of red, of orange, of yellow, and so forth—were selected from the spectrum, and all other shades were either not used or were referred to one of the six already selected. Naturally the basis for such an important selection is an important theoretical concern, but not one that we can pursue here.

Ascending from a given pitch, then, there are a total of seven pitches, before reaching the pitch that sounds "the same" as the first. In other words, the pitch that sounds "the same" as the first pitch is the eighth pitch in order away from it—which is how the interval between the first and the eighth got its name, octave. The seven pitches that constitute the foundation of the Western notational system are designated with letters of the alphabet, starting with A and proceeding upward through seven pitches to G. The eighth pitch is again called A, as an expression of the fact that it sounds "the same" as the first A. Similarly, the pitch next above

this second A is called B, and sounds "the same" as the first B; and so for the rest, as far up as you care to go, as shown in Ex. C-18a. The several pitches called by the same letter, for example, each of the A's, are of course in a different register; there are a number of systems used for designating these differences.

The pitches represented by the seven letters A to G are not all the same distance apart; there are two distinct sizes of intervals between adjacent letters— tones and semitones (see page 105). Most of the letters are separated by tones. Semitones appear in two places, between B and C and between E and F, as shown in Ex. C-18b. This specific arrangement of tones and semitones within the octave, which is the foundation of traditional Western notation and nomenclature, is called the *diatonic system* (*diatonic scale*). It has as its essential features the succession of intervals shown in Ex. C-18b. This is most easily remembered as a series of tones punctuated by single semitones in such a way that a group of two consecutive tones alternates with a group of three consecutive tones (proceeding either up or down in pitch).

The keyboard. The structure of the diatonic scale is reflected in the way that the keys on a piano are laid out (Ex. C-18c). Indeed, the piano keyboard is the easiest way of understanding the diatonic system —even if you have never played a piano. Play the white keys on a piano, starting anywhere but proceeding consistently upwards (from left to right on the keyboard) without skipping any white note (do

not play the black keys); you have played the diatonic scale going forward in the alphabet. Proceed consistently downward (from right to left on the keyboard); you have played the diatonic scale going backward in the alphabet. Find two white keys *not* separated by a black key; you have found either B and C or E and F. By counting the number of white keys between one such semitone and the next and comparing with the keyboard diagram in Ex. C-18c, you can determine whether it was B and C or E and F; from there it is an easy matter to find the other letters and not too difficult to memorize the letters that go with each white key on the keyboard.

Since the white keys on the piano constitute a diatonic scale, it is often convenient to speak of the *white-key scale* when we wish to refer to that position of the diatonic scale in which its pitches are named by the unmodified letters A through G. For, as we will soon see, the diatonic system can be located in other positions and its pitches named differently.

Sharps and flats. As is evident from the arrangement of the piano keyboard, there are more pitches in the traditional system than just the seven (per octave) designated by the letters A through G. The black keys on the piano represent an additional five pitches in each octave. These five have no letter names of their own, but rather each is designated as a variant form of one of the adjacent white keys. For this purpose, the terms *sharp* and *flat* are used respectively in the sense of higher and lower: the black key a semitone above C is called C sharp; the black key a semitone below A is called A flat (Ex. C-18d).

On the piano, there is only one black key between two white ones, and each black key can have two names, depending on which adjacent white key it is referred to. The black key between C and D can be called C sharp or D flat. On many instruments (for complex reasons having to do with the whole structure of the pitch system), C sharp and D flat would be different pitches (remember that between C and D there are an unlimited number of possible pitches). But for purposes of nomenclature and notation, C sharp and D flat are regarded as two

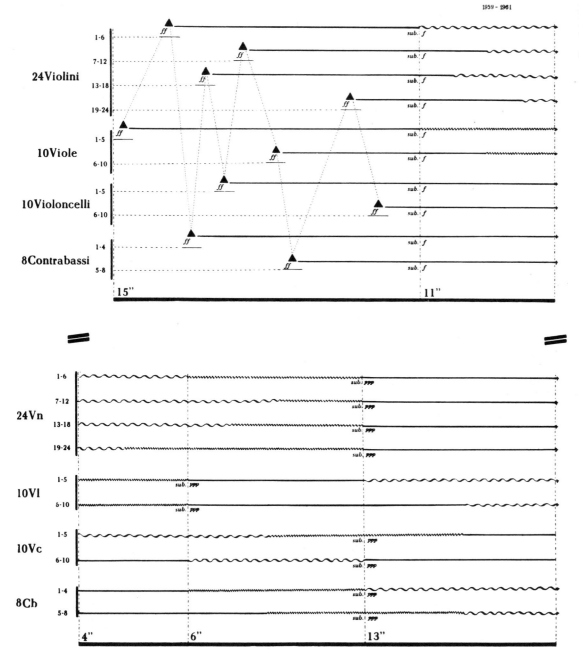

KRZYSZTOF PENDERECKI
1959 - 1961

24Violini
10Viole
10Violoncelli
8Contrabassi

24Vn
10Vl
10Vc
8Cb

Example C-17 Penderecki, To the Victims of Hiroshima: Threnody. (Copyright 1961 by P. W. P. Przedstawicielstwo Wydawnictw Polskich, Warszawa, Poland. Printed in Poland. Copyright assigned to SESAC, Inc., N.Y.)

Example C-18 Diatonic system and the keyboard

(a)

Ascending pitch ⟶

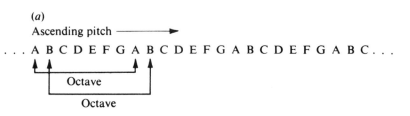

. . . A B C D E F G A B C D E F G A B C D E F G A B C . . .

Octave

Octave

The distance from any letter to its next appearance is one octave.

(b)

Ascending pitch ⟶

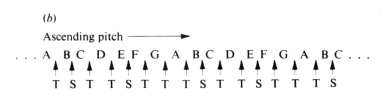

. . . A B C D E F G A B C D E F G A B C . . .

T S T   T S T   T   T S T   T S T   T S

(c)

Ascending pitch ⟶

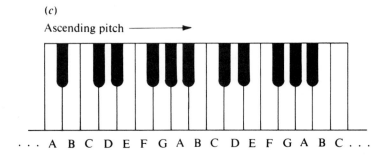

. . . A B C D E F G A B C D E F G A B C . . .

(d)

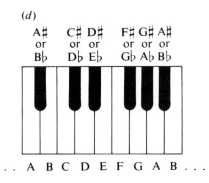

A♯   C♯ D♯   F♯ G♯ A♯
or   or or   or or or
B♭   D♭ E♭   G♭ A♭ B♭

. . . A B C D E F G A B . . .

names for the same pitch; similarly D sharp and E flat; F sharp and G flat; G sharp and A flat; A sharp and B flat. The word *enharmonic* is used to refer to such double names; F sharp is said to be an enharmonic equivalent of G flat.

In a general sense, then, the term *sharp* means that a pitch has been raised, while *flat* means that it has been lowered. By extension, the two white notes that have no black note above them—E and B—can also be raised, or sharped. The results are a pitch named E sharp, identical (on the keyboard) to F, and B sharp, identical to C. Similarly F flat equals E, and C flat equals B. By yet another extension, a black note can be raised or lowered: if F sharp is raised, or sharped, the result is a pitch named F double-sharp, enharmonic with G; if G flat is lowered, the result is a pitch called G double-flat, enharmonic with F. Such complex nomenclature has a very practical application (to be seen later) necessary for the sake of preserving consistency in the whole system of naming pitches.

The chromatic system. The seven pitches of the diatonic system, expanded by the five accidentals, or remaining pitches (on the keyboard), constitute the *chromatic system* (or *chromatic scale*), containing twelve pitches per octave, each a semitone from the next. You can play a chromatic scale by playing in succession the black *and* white keys on the piano. When naming the pitches of the chromatic scale, sharps are used in ascending, for example, A, A sharp, B, C, C sharp . . . ; flats in descending, for example, A, A flat, G, G flat, F, E, E flat . . . .

The staff. Letter names are used constantly by musicians to refer to pitches, yet hardly ever to write music down in a score. Instead, pitches are indicated with the note symbols already described for rhythmic notation. These symbols—specifically, the note *heads*—are located on a system of five horizontal lines called a *staff*. As mentioned, the note head itself contains no indication of pitch; the location of the head on the staff shows the pitch. Example C-19*a* shows three whole notes placed on a staff. Note 2 is higher in pitch than 1, note 3 is lower in pitch than 2, but higher than 1. Note heads can be placed on

Example C-19 Staff and clefs

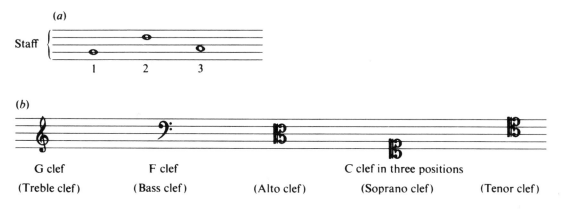

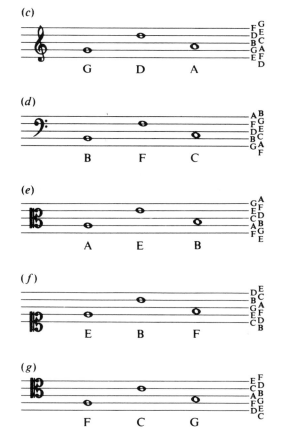

lines or in the spaces adjacent to the lines (as in 3).

Clefs. Adjacent lines and spaces of a staff represent consecutive letters of the pitch alphabet A to G. At least one line or space must be labeled with its letter to show where to begin. (The bottom line, for example, does not always represent the same letter.) The labels take the form of *clefs* (French, "key," used here in the sense of "clue"). Three traditional clefs are in common use; they are shown in Ex. C-19b.

The present shape of these symbols has evolved from old forms of the letters G, F, and C. The line on which the clef is placed gives the "key" to the letter names of the lines and spaces of the staff. In Ex. C-19c, the G clef (or *treble clef*) is curled around the second line from the bottom of the staff. This line represents G, and the letter names of the entire staff (from bottom to top, beginning with the space below the staff) are D, **E**, F, **G**, A, **B**, C, **D**, E, **F**, and G. (The letters in boldface here are the names of the lines, the others are the names of the spaces.) The three notes from Ex. C-19a have been reproduced in Ex. C-19c: their letter names in the treble clef are G, D, and A.

In Ex. C-19d, the two dots of the F clef (or *bass clef*) surround the fourth line of the staff (counting upwards). This line therefore represents F, and the letter names of the entire staff, from bottom to top, are F, **G**, A, **B**, C, **D**, E, **F**, G, **A**, and B. The three notes from Ex. C-19a are shown in Ex. C-19d; their letter names in the bass clef are B, F, and C.

In Example C-19e, *f*, and *g*, the letter names of the lines and spaces of the staff are indicated for three positions of the C clef, called respectively the *alto clef*, *soprano clef*, and *tenor clef*. In each case, the line that the clef centers around is C. The three notes from Ex. C-19a are shown in each clef.

Clefs and registers. The various clefs do more than indicate the letter names of the lines and spaces of the staff: they also show the octave register in which notes with these letter names occur. For example, the note B in Ex. C-19d is an octave lower than the note B in Ex. C-19e and two octaves lower than the B in Ex. C-19f. The pitch indicated by the C clef is always *middle C*—the C found roughly in the middle of the keyboard. The F of the bass clef is the F below middle C, and the G of the treble clef is the G above middle C.

The different clefs are used to notate music in different registers. Music for high voices or instruments (such as the violin) is usually notated in the treble clef. Music for low voices or instruments (such as the double bass) is usually written in the bass clef. The alto clef is customarily used for the viola, an instrument of medium register; the tenor clef is used for the highest notes of the cello and other low instruments.

Ledger lines. It is often necessary to notate pitches that lie too high or too low to be placed on a staff. Such pitches are notated with the help of *ledger* (or *leger*) *lines*, shown below and above each staff in Ex. C-20. These short horizontal lines are just extensions of the staff upward or downward; together with the spaces they form, ledger lines are given letter names as continuations of the staff on which they are placed.

Example C-20 shows the pitches of five consecutive octaves, notated in bass, alto, and treble clefs. Notes

Example C-20 Ledger lines

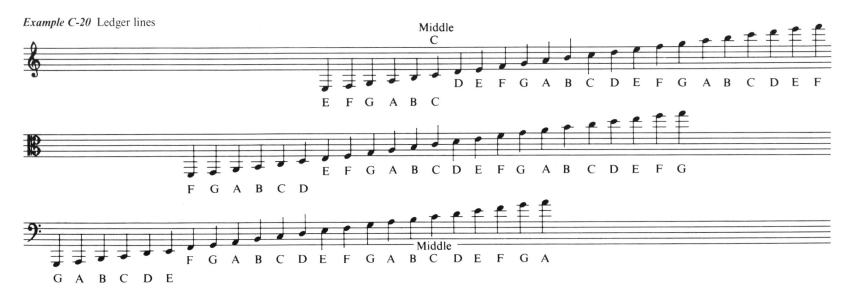

aligned in this example directly over or under each other represent the same pitch as notated in different clefs. Example C-20 also shows that any one staff (even with ledger lines) is too narrow to encompass all the pitches used in vocal or instrumental music;

this is why parts for different voices and instruments are written in different clefs.

Great staff. Instruments with a very wide range, such as the piano, require two staves, the upper one

with a treble clef, the lower one with a bass clef, as shown in Ex. C-21. The first ledger line above the bass clef is the same pitch as the first ledger line below the treble clef; this pitch is middle C. This combination of staves is called the *great staff*.

Example C-21 The great staff and the piano keyboard

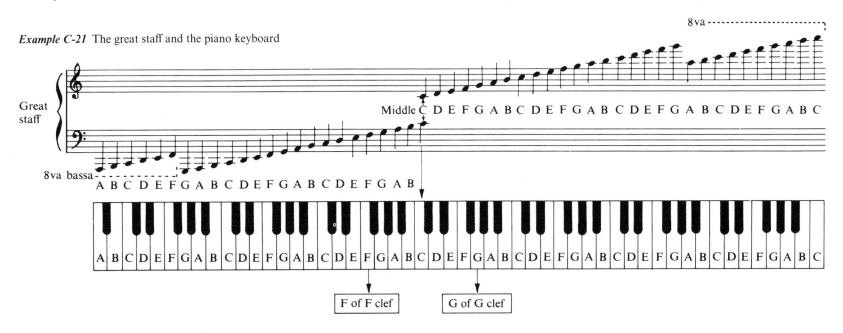

386

Below the great staff in Ex. C-21 is a diagram of a complete piano keyboard. The notes on the great staff show the pitches of the *white* keys of the keyboard; each note is aligned over its key. The notes at the very bottom of the scale are to be played an octave lower, as indicated by *8va bassa* ("an octave lower"); those at the very top are to be played an octave higher (indicated by just *8va*).

Accidentals. Sharps and flats are notated on the staff by placing the sign for a sharp (♯) or for a flat (♭) in the line or space corresponding to the letter name of the pitch to be raised or lowered, directly before the note head. A double sharp is indicated by ·✘·, a double flat by ♭♭. A natural sign (♮) restores the pitch of that line or space to what it was before the raising or lowering. Various accidentals are shown in Ex. C-22.

Transpositions of the diatonic system. Suppose you were to accompnay a singer at the piano, in a melody that began and ended on C and used only white notes (as many do); and suppose that the singer asked you to play the piece a little lower so that she could sing it more easily. You could, of course, play exactly an octave lower, but that would probably be much too low for her to sing and, in any case, would not be what she meant by "a little lower"—in other words, one or two tones lower. As you can easily see from the diagram of the keyboard in Ex. C-21, if you were to start playing the melody that originally began on C, on B, or on A (or on any note other than C) and used only white notes, the semitones would come in different places

relative to the first note, and the sound of the melody would be changed. (You can actually try this with some very simple tune that you can pick out at the piano.) Some adjustment must be made in order to play the original melody starting from some pitch other than C, and this adjustment involves the use of the black keys, of flats and sharps.

In technical language, what the singer asked you to do was to transpose the diatonic system to some other pitch level. This is often done, either for a whole piece or for part of one. *Transposition*, used in complex ways, is the basis of modulation (as discussed on pages 133–134). One of the most important uses of accidentals, including double sharps and double flats as well as enharmonic letter names, is in notating pitches in transpositions.

Try to imagine what happens if you transposed part of the diatonic system, say A B C D E F G A B C up one tone, starting on B, but preserving the succession of tones and semitones found between the letters as originally given (that is, *T S T T S T T T S*). Example C-23a shows the letters that will be needed and how some of these letters have to be modified with sharps. In its new position, the scale will read B, C sharp, D, E, F sharp, G, A, B, C sharp, D.

Example C-22 Accidentals

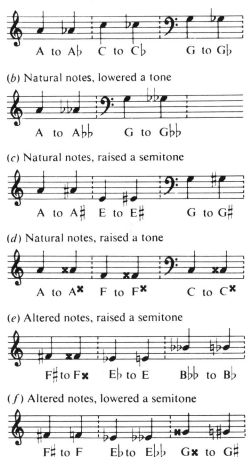

(*a*) Natural notes, lowered a semitone

A to A♭   C to C♭   G to G♭

(*b*) Natural notes, lowered a tone

A to A♭♭   G to G♭♭

(*c*) Natural notes, raised a semitone

A to A♯   E to E♯   G to G♯

(*d*) Natural notes, raised a tone

A to A✘   F to F✘   C to C✘

(*e*) Altered notes, raised a semitone

F♯ to F✘   E♭ to E   B♭♭ to B♭

(*f*) Altered notes, lowered a semitone

F♯ to F   E♭ to E♭♭   G✘ to G♯

Example C-23 Transpositions of the diatonic system

(*a*)

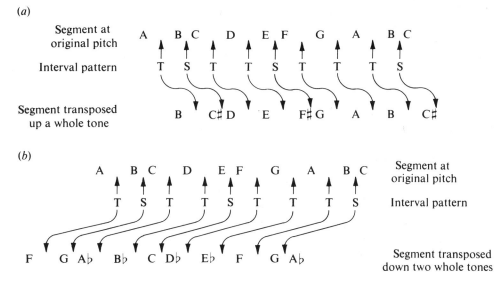

Segment at original pitch: A   B C   D   E F   G   A   B C

Interval pattern: T   S   T   T   S   T   T   T   S

Segment transposed up a whole tone: B   C♯ D   E   F♯ G   A   B   C♯

(*b*)

Segment at original pitch: A   B C   D   E F   G   A   B C

Interval pattern: T   S   T   T   S   T   T   T   S

Segment transposed down two whole tones: F   G A♭   B♭   C D♭   E♭   F   G A♭

387

Or, to take another example, imagine this same segment of the diatonic system transposed down two whole tones, beginning on F. The pitches would then be: F, G, A flat, B flat, C, D flat, E flat, F, G, A flat (Ex. C-23b).

The original convention of naming pitches assigned a new letter to each successive pitch in the diatonic system. By way of preserving this convention, every transposition of the diatonic system also requires a different letter name for each pitch of the scale. For example, the first three transposed pitches of Ex. C-23b must be spelled F, G, A flat, *not* F, G, G sharp.

Note that one of the accidentals from Ex. C-23b— D flat—is an enharmonic spelling of another accidental—C sharp from Ex. C-23a. If you worked out many transpositions of the diatonic system, you would eventually have to use all the enharmonic equivalents, as well as several double flats and double sharps.

Key signatures. In the transposition of the diatonic system in Ex. C-23a (up a whole tone), two accidentals occur, F sharp and C sharp. (Even if we were to extend the length of the segment, no further accidentals would be needed.) Instead of writing the accidentals each time they recurred throughout a piece or section, it is more convenient to indicate those accidentals at the beginning by means of a *key signature*. (It is called a *key* signature because it is also used to indicate a specific kind of transposition for keys, as will be discussed soon; here we are dealing with a simpler, more general kind of transposition.) For example, a piece using the transposition of the diatonic scale shown in Ex. C-23a would have a key signature of two sharps, F and C. The key signature is written after the clef sign and before the meter signature, as shown in Ex. C-24. All F's and C's that occur in a piece with this particular signature will be sharped unless they are preceded by a natural.

Example C-24 The same key signature in three clefs

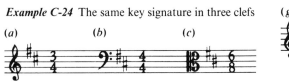

Example C-25 Key signatures

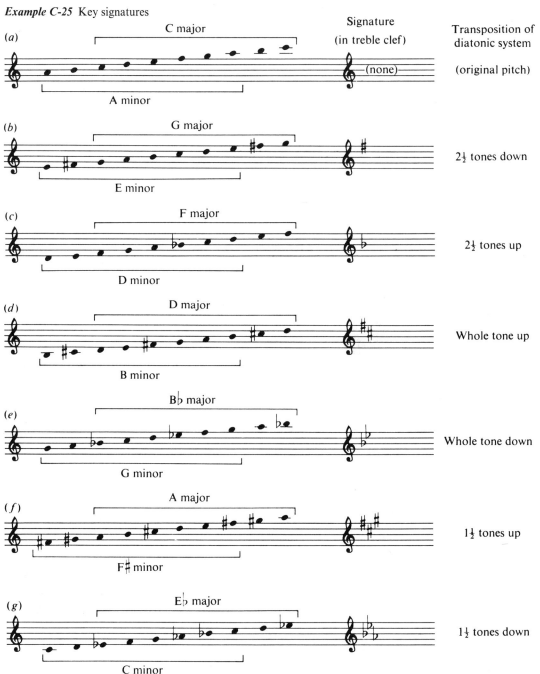

388

Example C-25 (cont'd.)

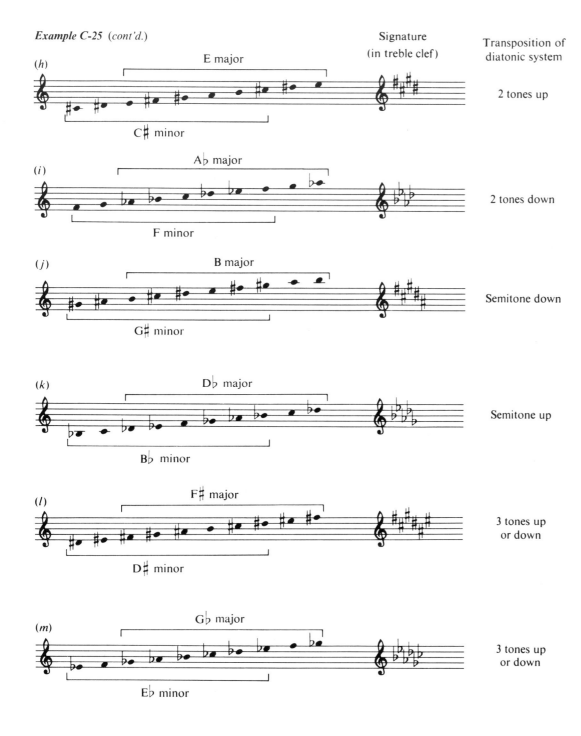

Signature
(in treble clef)

Transposition of
diatonic system

(h) E major / C♯ minor — 2 tones up

(i) A♭ major / F minor — 2 tones down

(j) B major / G♯ minor — Semitone down

(k) D♭ major / B♭ minor — Semitone up

(l) F♯ major / D♯ minor — 3 tones up or down

(m) G♭ major / E♭ minor — 3 tones up or down

Similarly, the key signature for the transposed segment in Ex. C-23b would be four flats—B flat, E flat, A flat, and D flat. Sharps are always added to the signature in the following order: F, C, G, D, A, E, B; flats are always written in the order B, E, A, D, G, C, F.

All of the key signatures (up through seven sharps and seven flats) are shown in Ex. C-25. In the left-hand column is the same segment of the diatonic system found in Ex. C-23a and b, transposed to different pitch levels. In the middle column are the required key signatures. The right-hand column shows by how many half steps and whole steps up or down the diatonic scale has been transposed in each case. Transposition 25*l* is an enharmonic equivalent of 25*m*; 25*n* is an enharmonic equivalent of 25*k*, and 25*o* is an enharmonic equivalent of 25*j*. Disregarding these notational duplications, there are twelve different positions of the diatonic system possible within the chromatic system. Such indications as "A minor" and "C major" will be discussed later.

Circle of fifths. Example C-25 is arranged by increasing the number of accidentals. Another way of arranging the same twelve transpositions is in a circle, as shown on the outer circle of Ex. C-26. Each key signature indicated on the outer circle represents a transposition $2\frac{1}{2}$ tones, or a fifth, higher or lower than the one adjacent, as indicated by the arrows. Hence, this arrangement is called the *circle of fifths*. (The inner circle and the terms "major" and "minor" will be discussed later.)

Special notations. As indicated before, the notational system just described is based upon the historical convention of the chromatic system. Traditional notation offers no way of notating pitches not found in the chromatic system. Pitches that lie between the semitones of the chromatic system (and there are an unlimited number of them) must be indicated by some special notation. For example, Bartók places an arrow above certain notes in the Burletta of his Sixth Quartet, indicating that these notes are to be played a quarter tone lower than notated (Ex. C-27). Intervals smaller than a semitone

Example C-25 *(cont'd.)*

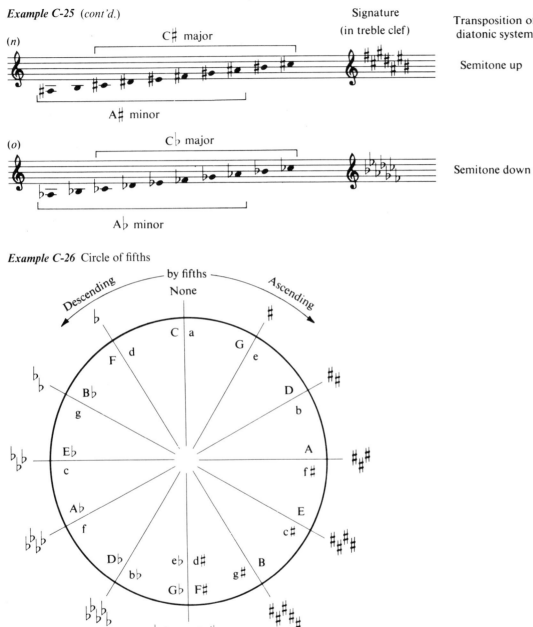

(n)

C♯ major

A♯ minor

Signature (in treble clef)

Transposition of diatonic system

Semitone up

(o)

C♭ major

A♭ minor

Semitone down

Example C-26 Circle of fifths

by fifths
None

Descending   Ascending

♭   ♯

(Capital letters indicate major keys; lowercase letters indicate minor keys.)

are sometimes called *microtones*. Example C-28 shows a kind of notation used by Penderecki in his Threnody.

Intervals. Standard nomenclature exists for all the different kinds of intervals found between any two pitches of the chromatic system. We have already encountered the intervals named *tone, semitone,* and *octave.*

The system of naming intervals is based upon intervals smaller than the octave; intervals larger than an octave can be regarded as compounds of one or more octaves with the corresponding interval smaller than an octave. For example, the interval between an A and the B just above the next higher A (A B C D E F G A B) can be regarded as an octave and a tone. (An alternate nomenclature, used for some intervals and certain purposes, calls this interval a *ninth.*)

Like other aspects of pitch nomenclature, the naming of intervals is derived from the letter names (the white-key scale) and makes most sense in terms of the diatonic system. The table in Ex. C-29 shows the naming and sizes of intervals up through the octave. The table in Ex. C-30 shows the same intervals, all reckoned upward from the note C and also downward from the note C, for purposes of comparison in their *sizes.* You should study Ex. C-30 in conjunction with Ex. C-29, which is primarily intended to explain the derivation of the *names.*

The name of each interval (as shown in Ex. C-29) is derived directly from the number of consecutive letters included in the interval; but note that the

Example C-27 Bartók's notation for quarter tones

mf

↓ indicates a quarter tone lower.

╱ indicates slide from one pitch to the other.

390

interval itself is the distance between only *two* pitches. For example, the interval between A and C includes *three* consecutive letters, **A B C**, therefore is called the interval of a *third*. In actual sound, this interval would consist only of the pitch A and the pitch C.

The smallest interval found in the diatonic system is the semitone (as between B and C, E and F); the next smallest is the tone (as between A and B,

C and D, D and E, F and G, G and A). Each semitone and tone is called an interval of a *second*, because each includes two consecutive letter names. Obviously, some distinction must be made between the seconds that are semitones (like B to C) and those that are tones (like C to D); this is done by saying *minor second* (that is, "smaller" second) for one, *major second* ("larger" second) for the other.

The terms "major second" and "minor second"

Example C-28 Pitch notation for a tone cluster (in Penderecki's Threnody)

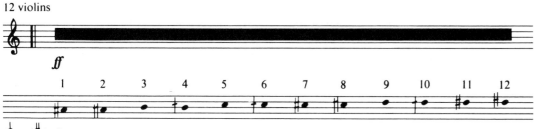

12 violins

†and‖ indicate quarter tones.

Each of the 12 violins plays one pitch as indicated in the lower staff. All 12 pitches are sounded simultaneously, producing the cluster indicated by the thick black line in the upper staff.

Example C-29 Naming and sizes of intervals

The outer pitches of any	2	adjacent letters of the diatonic scale form the interval of a	second	if 1 semitone, a *minor* second if 2 semitones, a *major* second
. . .	3	. . .	third	if 3 semitones, a *minor* third if 4 semitones, a *major* third
. . .	4	. . .	fourth	if 5 semitones, a *perfect* fourth
. . .	5	. . .	fifth	if 7 semitones, a *perfect* fifth
. . .	6	. . .	sixth	if 8 semitones, a *minor* sixth if 9 semitones, a *major* sixth
. . .	7	. . .	seventh	if 10 semitones, a *minor* seventh if 11 semitones, a *major* seventh
. . .	8	. . .	octave	if 12 semitones, a *perfect* octave

Example C-30 Examples of intervals

Size in tones	Ascending	Descending	Name
½	C to C♯ C to D♭	C to C♭ C to B	Augmented unison Minor second
1	C to D C to E♭♭	C to B♭ C to A♯	Major second Diminished third
1½	C to D♯ C to E♭	C to B♭♭ C to A	Augmented second Minor third
2	C to E C to F♭	C to A♭ C to G♯	Major third Diminished fourth
2½	C to E♯ C to F	C to A♭♭ C to G	Augmented third Perfect fourth
3	C to F♯ C to G♭	C to G♭ C to F♯	Augmented fourth Diminished fifth
3½	C to G C to A♭♭	C to F C to E♯	Perfect fifth Diminished sixth
4	C to G♯ C to A♭	C to F♭ C to E	Augmented fifth Minor sixth
4½	C to A C to B♭♭	C to E♭ C to D♯	Major sixth Diminished seventh
5	C to A♯ C to B♭	C to E♭♭ C to D	Augmented sixth Minor seventh
5½	C to B C to C♭	C to D♭ C to C♯	Major seventh Diminished octave
6	C to B♯ C to C	C to D♭♭ C to C	Augmented seventh Perfect octave

serve as models for some of the others in the table—thirds, sixths, and sevenths. In each case, major intervals are distinguished from minor ones by the number of semitones included—just as the minor second had one semitone; the major second, two.

Fourths and fifths are not called major or minor; instead, one size of fourth (with 5 semitones) and one size of fifth (with 7 semitones) are called *perfect*. If perfect or minor intervals are made smaller by a semitone, they are said to be *diminished*, as a diminished fifth; if perfect or major intervals are made larger by a semitone, they are said to be *augmented*, as an augmented fourth. These two intervals—diminished fifth and augmented fourth—happen to be the same size (six semitones or three whole tones—whence the name *tritone*); the terms "augmented" and "diminished" are used here (and elsewhere) to preserve consistency with the letter names. For example, the interval B (C D E) F is a fifth because it includes five letters; yet it is smaller in size than a perfect fifth. And even though the interval F (G A) B has the same size, it includes only four letters, hence must go by a different name.

Consonance and dissonance. Different intervals may vary not only in size but also in degree of *consonance* or *dissonance*. In some intervals, the two pitches, when sounded simultaneously, blend together smoothly. In the interval of an octave, for example, the two pitches blend so well they sound "the same." Such blending is called *consonance* ("with-sounding"). Even more consonant than the octave is the unison, as when two singers sing the same pitch in the same register. A unison is not an interval, strictly speaking, since there is no distance between the two pitches; but the unison, being the most consonant relationship conceivable, is a convenient starting point for the continuum of blending.

The different kinds of intervals can be arranged roughly in a continuum going from unison or complete consonance toward increasing dissonance. Individual judgment enters in, however, and the context in which these intervals are actually used plays a very important role. Furthermore, in many cases it is difficult to discriminate among certain pairs of intervals as to the degree of dissonance.

Example C-31, therefore, is only an approximate indication of degrees of consonance and dissonance. Intervals larger than the octave have more or less the same degree of dissonance as their counterparts within the octave—but with some differences that can be significant under certain conditions.

Triads, scales, and keys. Up to this point the matters discussed in this appendix have been concerned strictly with notation and nomenclature. A few other terms used in the text should be defined. These terms, however, involve matters of harmonic theory that go beyond objective nomenclature and bring up questions that are open to discussion among theorists. We do not intend to go into these matters here, but simply to provide working definitions of the few terms involved. More adequate treatment of harmonic theory can be found in the books listed in Appendix A.

The terms to be defined all involve—directly or indirectly—the notion of a central note or central harmony, as discussed in Chapters 6 and 7; without the auditory experience of a central note or central harmony, the definitions will make little sense. For a period of Western music roughly represented by Monteverdi, Bach, Haydn, Mozart, Beethoven, Schubert, and Wagner (in round figures, 1600–1900), central notes and harmonies were associated with the specific kind of harmonic area called *key*. Key is usually defined in terms of *major scales* or *minor scales*, and *triads*.

Major and minor triads. A triad is a particular kind of harmony, expressed in its simplest form as a three-note chord of the type found in Ex. C-32a. The pitches of a triad are so arranged that the top pitch forms the interval of a fifth with the bottom one (called the *root*), while the middle pitch forms the interval of a third with the bottom one. This simplest form of the triad appears often; but more often the equivalent intervals are found in more complex distributions over a wider range, as shown in Ex. C-32b.

If the middle note forms a *major* third with the bottom note (hence a minor third with the top one), the triad is called a *major triad*. When the middle note forms a *minor* third with the bottom one (hence a major third with the top one) the chord is called a *minor triad*. A change from major color to minor or vice versa, as in Schubert's "Der Müller und der Bach" (pages 123, 134), involves principally a change of the *central* harmony from major to minor or vice versa (some of the other chords in the key are also changed in the process).

Example C-31 Consonance and dissonance

Consonance ⟶ Increasing dissonance ⟶

Unison	Octave	Perfect fifth Perfect fourth	Major and minor thirds	Major and minor sixths	Major second, minor seventh	Minor second, major seventh	Tritone

Example C-32 Major and minor triads

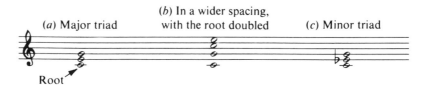

(a) Major triad — Root (b) In a wider spacing, with the root doubled (c) Minor triad

The close relationship of triads to the diatonic system can be seen in the fact that if, starting on any note of the white-key scale, you add the third and fifth white notes above it, the result is a major or minor triad in all cases save one (the triad starting on B, called a *diminished triad*). In other words, any segment of the diatonic system designates a specific set of triads built upon the notes of that segment. Keys are defined with the help of such segments and their associated triads.

Major scales. A *major scale* is that segment of the diatonic system with the interval configuration *T T S T T T S*, as found in the ascending octave segment from C to C on the white keys (called the *C-major scale*). This particular configuration can, of course, be found starting on any other note by using the appropriate sharps and flats, as shown in Ex. C-25.

The C-major scale has a major third above its bottom or *tonic* note (C–E), and the triad built on this bottom note is a major triad (C–E–G). The fact that a major scale has a specific bottom and a top (C to C, in this case) does not mean that a piece using this scale is restricted in range to this octave, but merely that the bottom note, the tonic, functions as the central pitch of the piece. In other words, the octave scale is a theoretical abstraction used for classifying a piece according to its central pitch and the set of pitches used in conjunction with the central pitch. Pieces (using the triadic conventions prevalent from 1600–1900) that make exclusive or predominant use of the pitches in the C-major scale (that is, the white keys, rather than the black ones) and have C as a central pitch with the triad on C as a central harmony, are said to be in C major, or in the key of C major. If a piece uses the pitches of some other octave scale, with the triad on the bottom note of that scale as the central harmony, it is said to be in that scale or key. A piece can be in any one of the twelve major scales shown in the transpositions of Ex. C-25 or Ex. C-26. A piece in a particular scale or key will have a *key signature* showing the appropriate flats or sharps, as discussed previously. The key signature, however, is not by itself a complete indication of the key of the piece.

Minor scales. There is no diatonic segment that corresponds exactly to the set of pitches used in minor keys—that is, keys whose central harmony is a minor triad. The segment A to A of the white-key scale is the closest approximation; it is called the *natural minor scale*. But pieces using the A-minor triad as a central harmony usually use accidentals (especially G sharp) as *essential* notes of the key—essential, that is, to the triads needed to establish the key. (In practice, then, a key is more a set of triads than it is an octave scale.) There are twelve minor scales paralleling the twelve major ones, as shown in Ex. C-25. Each signature (for example, one sharp) is used for a major key and also a minor one (in the case of one sharp, G major and E minor; see Ex. C-26).

Modulation. When a piece *modulates* (see pages 133–134), it changes key. This change will appear in the score as a change in the number of flats and sharps—expressed either as a new key signature or, more frequently, as one or more accidentals appearing in the music wherever appropriate.

The twelve major and twelve minor keys are related to each other by various degrees of closeness or remoteness. The degree of closeness between two keys can be most simply expressed in terms of the number of notes held in common by the two major or minor scales. Several kinds of key relationships are shown in Ex. C-33. Each circle represents a major or minor scale, containing seven pitches, as indicated by the letters. Two overlapping circles will share a greater or lesser number of pitches. At Ex. C-33a, the two circles share six pitches (A, B, C, D, E, G); each circle has only one pitch (F or F sharp) not found in the other circle. These two keys are very close, differing in only one pitch. The right-hand circle represents the key of G major, the left-hand circle the key of C major (compare Ex. C-25a and b). Their central pitches, C and G, are a perfect fifth apart. The kind of relationship shown in Ex. C-33a is that in which the central harmony of one key (here, G major) is the leading harmony of the other. The same kind of relationship can be heard in the middle section of Schubert's "Der Müller und der Bach" (see pages 132–133) or in the first tutti of

the Finale and the first section of the Allegro of Haydn's Symphony No. 100.

Example C-33f shows a pair of keys remote from each other. These two keys, C major and G flat major, share only one pitch, F. Their central pitches are a tritone apart.

Minor keys, because of an inherent instability in their pitch structure, cannot be represented as precisely as major ones. Still, you can compare Ex. C-33g and h: in 33h, representing C major and C minor, the central pitch is held in common but two other pitches are not. In Ex. C-33g, A minor and C major have a different central pitch, while all pitches but one are held in common. Example C-33h is the kind of relationship found in Schubert's "Der Müller und der Bach."

Example C-33c and d, in which the two central pitches are a third apart, shows the kinds of striking relationships often encountered from one song to the next in *Die schöne Müllerin*. Such keys share enough pitches to have much in common, yet differ sufficiently so that the transition from one to the other has a fresh sound.

Tonic and dominant chords. Among the whole set of triads involved in any one key, two are preeminent in establishing the key and in forming cadences in it. These are the two we called central harmony and leading harmony. Their standard names are *tonic (chord)* and *dominant (chord)*, respectively. As we have seen, the tonic chord is the triad built on the bottom note—the tonic—of the octave segment. The dominant is the triad built on the fifth note of the octave segment (that is, on the top note of the tonic triad), as shown in Ex. C-34a. When the dominant leads to the tonic, these form a full cadence that helps establish a key.* Sometimes the dominant triad is enriched with another note a seventh above its bottom (or root) note, as in Ex. C-34c; then it is called a *dominant seventh chord*.

Use of nomenclature and scores. Throughout the foregoing discussion, we have been moving steadily

---

*These triads must be expressed in more complex forms with doubling and wider spacing in order to make the progressions work, as shown in Ex. C-34b.

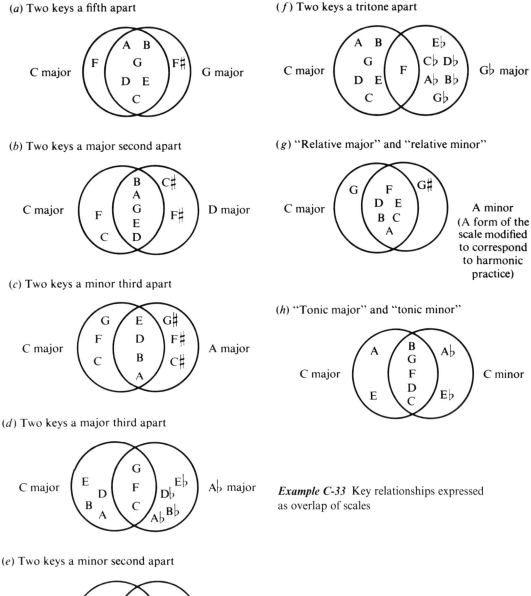

(a) Two keys a fifth apart

C major — G major

(b) Two keys a major second apart

C major — D major

(c) Two keys a minor third apart

C major — A major

(d) Two keys a major third apart

C major — A♭ major

(e) Two keys a minor second apart

C major — D♭ major

(f) Two keys a tritone apart

C major — G♭ major

(g) "Relative major" and "relative minor"

C major — A minor
(A form of the scale modified to correspond to harmonic practice)

(h) "Tonic major" and "tonic minor"

C major — C minor

Example C-33 Key relationships expressed as overlap of scales

from nomenclature to practice, from things that are true by definition to things that are the way they are for artistic reasons. Standard nomenclature is valid only as long as the conventions that produced

it remain static—and then only as long as the composer chooses to observe them. Reconciling standard nomenclature to actual music is frequently very difficult. The listener should go by the axiom that what he hears is probably far closer to the truth than what standard nomenclature or standard notation might lead him to believe.

Understanding the structure of a piece *solely* from looking at the score is a difficult, hazardous procedure requiring professional experience; listeners without such experience are not advised to try it. A far more reliable way is to develop aural sensitivity to aspects of musical design such as key and modulation.

If you have begun to develop such sensitivity, however, you may find that a score helps to fix in your mind the plan of these and other aspects, making it easier to grasp the structure of the piece. In other words, with a little training and experience, a score can be used in much the same way as one of the plan diagrams in this book.

It is essential to decide *by ear*—first and last—whether a particular concept is applicable to a particular piece. Only when you are satisfied from listening *whether* a piece is in one or more keys or has a central harmony, is it fruitful to try to find out from the score *which* keys or harmonies it uses.

The key of a piece or section can often be determined from the end of the piece or section. Look at the last, lowest sounding note; it will probably be the root of the tonic triad—if the piece uses triads! (The beginning of the piece does not necessarily provide a definite indication of the key.) If the letter name of this note is A, the piece is probably "in" A. From the sound of the piece and also from the key signature, you can tell whether it is A major or A minor. Then listen carefully throughout the piece for perfect cadences at sectional divisions; locate these cadences in the score; determine the key *at that point* by inspecting the lowest note. In this way you can construct a key plan of the work, showing the modulations and returns to the principal key. *Check constantly with your ear.* Correct identification of the name of a note at a place that is not a cadence or is not an important structural point may produce totally meaningless results.

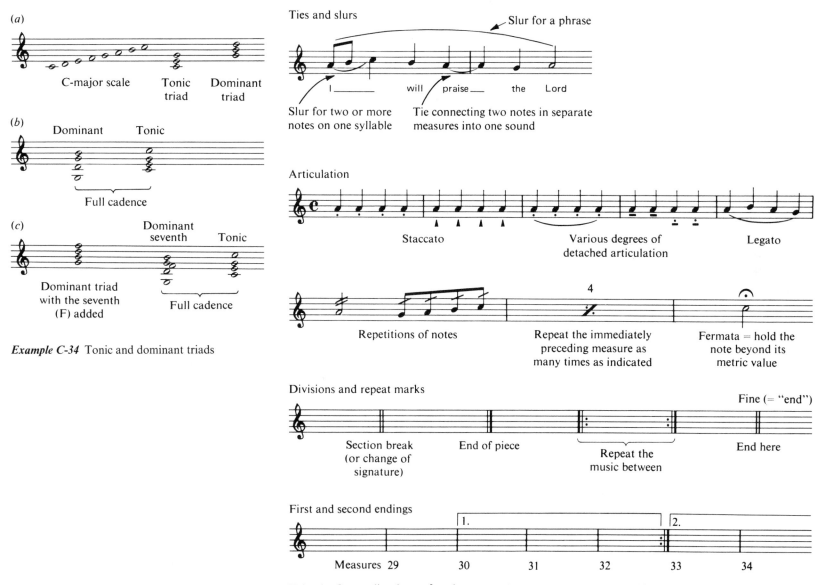

(a)

C-major scale   Tonic   Dominant
triad   triad

(b)

Dominant   Tonic

Full cadence

(c)

Dominant
seventh   Tonic

Dominant triad
with the seventh
(F) added   Full cadence

Example C-34 Tonic and dominant triads

Ties and slurs

Slur for a phrase

I _____ will praise ___ the Lord

Slur for two or more   Tie connecting two notes in separate
notes on one syllable   measures into one sound

Articulation

Staccato   Various degrees of   Legato
detached articulation

Repetitions of notes   Repeat the immediately   Fermata = hold the
preceding measure as   note beyond its
many times as indicated   metric value

Divisions and repeat marks

Fine (= "end")

Section break   End of piece   End here
(or change of   Repeat the
signature)   music between

First and second endings

1.   2.

Measures 29   30   31   32   33   34

Take the first ending by performing up to the repeat sign (measures 29, 30, 31, 32), then return to the beginning of the section and play measures 1 through 29 a second time; omit the first ending and take the second ending (measures 33 and 34), going on as indicated.

At the words Da Capo (meaning "from the start"), go back to the beginning.

Example C-35 Miscellaneous notation

At the words Dal Segno (meaning "from the sign"), go back to the sign (usually 𝄋).

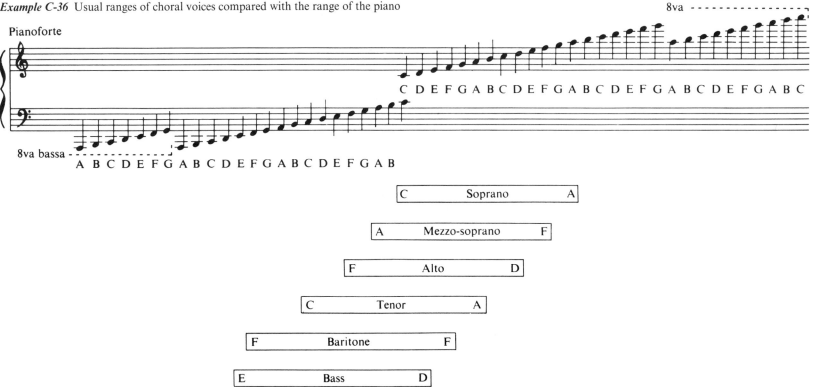

Example C-36 Usual ranges of choral voices compared with the range of the piano

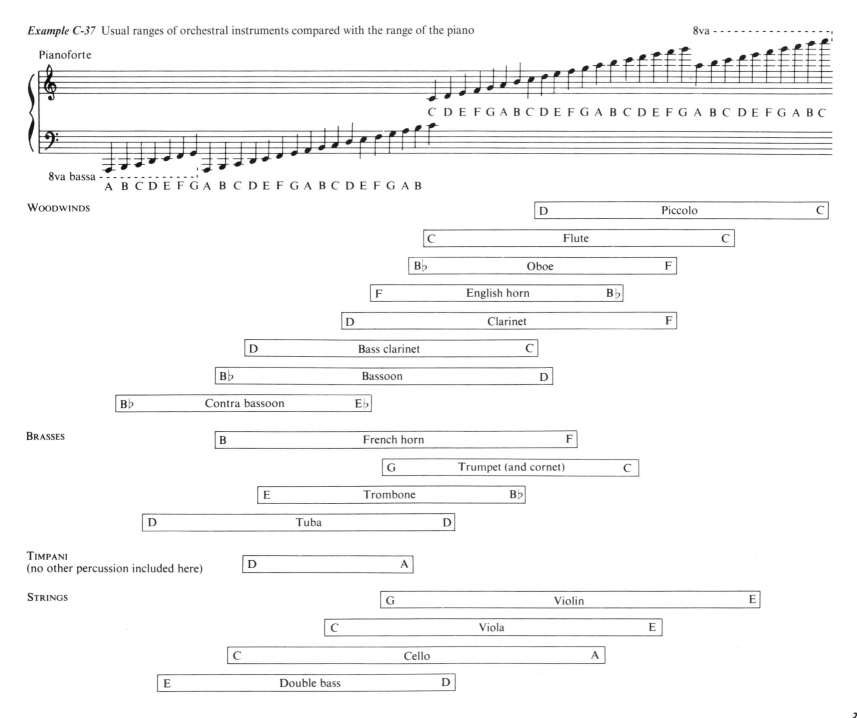

Example C-37 Usual ranges of orchestral instruments compared with the range of the piano

APPENDIX D

HISTORICAL OUTLINE OF WESTERN MUSIC FROM 700 TO THE PRESENT

THE FOLLOWING OUTLINE is designed to be used *after*, not before, the material in the main part of the text, since it makes use of concepts developed in the text. The outline can be used as an introduction to a subsequent study of music history or merely to help the reader see how the works that he has studied separately fit together in historical sequence. The reader is urged, however, not to read the outline as preparatory "orientation" to the pieces discussed in the text—especially those in Part One.

In order to make intelligent use of the outline, it is necessary to realize what it contains and what it omits. Its primary purpose is to give an account in the most general terms of the changes that have taken place in Western music since about 700 and of the principal musical forms these changes have produced. Once the reader has followed the historical continuum described in the outline, he should be able to locate on it individual composers and works as he meets them. Since it is extremely brief and very selective in its reference to specific materials, the outline is no substitute for a full-length historical text. Relatively few composers are mentioned; there is practically no discussion of their lives or of individual works. A restricted number of technical terms are introduced but are not usually described or defined in full, since to do so would shift the emphasis from history to terminology, from an outline to a dictionary. The music encyclopedias and history texts cited in Appendix A should be consulted for more detailed information.

This historical description, like many others, uses chronological periods, which are best considered as conveniences in grasping an essentially continuous process. As the materials of history become familiar to the reader, he can and should dispense with periods.

Periods are used here on two or three levels: it is important to notice the headings—for example, 1150–1600 as opposed to 1150–1300—in order to know at what level the discussion is aimed. These periods are built on a simple 150-year module. Indication of locales is given where appropriate.

The outline makes no attempt to relate music to other cultural events. Establishing such relationships is one of the most rewarding aspects of a study of history but is properly undertaken after some familiarity with the musical materials themselves has been gained. Brief comments are made, however, in connection with the period labels such as "Renaissance" or "Baroque," since these are in common use and would be soon encountered in further study. Some readers, indeed, may have encountered them already in other fields (since most of the labels are borrowed); in that case, clarification is often necessary.

EUROPE: 700–1150. Most of the music composed and performed throughout this period was monophonic in texture; but after 900, there was increasing interest in experiments in polyphonic texture.

Within monophonic texture, many different timbres were possible, including high and low adult male voices (tenor and bass), as solos or in small or large choral groupings, as well as boy sopranos. These timbres could be used to double each other so as to render a single line simultaneously in several registers—still monophonic in texture but much richer in timbre. In addition, various instruments could participate in the doubling or could provide unwritten accompaniment such as a drone.

Monophonic music went through a long, elaborate development, producing a wide variety of forms, for several different purposes and environments. Sacred monophony is often called *chant*. During this period, chant was most often composed in monasteries for use in the extensive sacred ritual usually carried on there. Secular monophony was most often associated with a courtly environment.

Europe: 700–850. From this period come the earliest written records of chant repertories used in Rome, Milan, Spain, and various parts of France. It is not known when these repertories were created; but by 800 they reflected a high state of development—especially the Roman chant, which was imported around 800 into France under the name *Gregorian chant* (named for Pope Gregory I, died 604).

Gregorian chant, whose texts are in Latin and are mostly taken from the Psalms, became the standard traditional music for the Roman Catholic Mass (Holy Communion Service) as well as for other traditional services (called *Offices* and including, for example, *Vespers*) performed in cathedrals and monasteries. Gregorian chant was composed in a variety of forms, ranging from very short, simple melodies to long elaborate ones. Introits such as "Resurrexi" represent moderate dimensions. The most elaborate chants, including graduals such as "Haec dies," or the Alleluia "Pascha nostrum," are in a highly melismatic, convoluted melodic style.

France: 850–1000. From around 850—or earlier—monastic composers in northern France began producing chant in a style markedly different from that of Gregorian. The new style had clear, forceful melodic shapes capable on one hand of tunefulness and on the other of great expansive power, in which repetition of well-marked phrase shapes was an important factor. Strophic hymns were the simplest forms of the new chant; a more elaborate form was called a *sequence* or *prose*, with a typical plan *a* b_1 b_2 c_1 c_2 d_1 d_2 . . . ("Victimae paschali laudes" is a relatively short sequence). Elaborate chants for *Kyrie, Gloria in excelsis, Sanctus,* and *Agnus Dei* (texts for the Mass) were composed during this period. *Kyries* and sequences are often striking examples of the tendency to break out of songlike shapes and dimensions (as used in hymns, for example) into larger, more challenging designs. Their far-ranging melodies have a clear sense of melodic direction and often make extensive use of motivic relationships. A bridge between the new chant and the old was provided by *tropes*—short, often hymnlike compositions interpolated into a Gregorian chant.

Most of the music preserved from this period is sacred (there are a few secular examples), but that may be due to the fact that written records in general were kept primarily by sacred agencies such as monasteries. Improvised singing of tribal epics can be assumed, and probably popular songs and dances as well.

France: 1000–1150. Monastic composers continued to be very active, producing large quantities of new chant, even though (as in the preceding period) they rarely put their names on their works. They also continued to develop new styles, now showing particular interest in refined control over detail. In writing texts (still in Latin), this meant making great use of rhymes and scansion to build strophic designs of exceptional variety and complexity; in writing music, it meant increased use of melodic ornament but, more important, a closer relationship among all the notes of a melody. The results were often strikingly tuneful, providing a foundation for Western European folk song. The new style of chant infiltrated existing forms such as hymn and sequence and in its purest form was called *versus* (which means simply "verse"). The versus often had a *couplet* (a pair of rhyming lines sung to the same melody) and a refrain.

Experiments in polyphonic texture were often carried out during this period, most often in con-

nection with the versus, showing that polyphony was felt to be an extension of the most recent musical developments in monophony. Many examples of polyphonic versus are preserved from the years 1050–1150, most of them from Aquitaine (central to southern France). By 1150, basic problems of polyphonic sonorities had been given some initial solutions. For another hundred years, however, monophony (sacred and secular) provided the bulk of the current musical repertory, polyphony still being a special—and often experimental—kind of music.

By 1150, large repertories of secular monophony, modeled on the rhyming, strophic versus, were in process of formation. The composers, usually associated with a court environment, were called *troubadours* in Aquitaine, *trouvères* in northern France, *Minnesingers* ("singers of love") in Germany. These vernacular repertories, encompassing hundreds or even thousands of songs, extended up to 1400.

Also by 1150, medieval musicians had developed (indeed, virtually created) the bases of Western notation and theory of pitch relationships—including staff notation with clefs (for polyphonic as well as monophonic music), letter nomenclature, and a scalar construct called *hexachord* that remained in use up past 1600 (it went out of use after 1600, but profoundly influenced succeeding constructs such as the major scale). Three more basic aspects—metric notation, completion of the chromatic scale, and a theory of relationships among two-note chords (but not yet triads) were accomplished by 1400.

The period 1000–1150 corresponds roughly to what art historians call *Romanesque*, and the term is sometimes used in music as well. It is perhaps clearer in music, however, than in art that this period is the logical continuation of the preceding one.

EUROPE: 1150–1600. During this period, polyphony became predominant in Western music—so much so that at the end of the period we no longer need to speak of polyphony as distinct from monophony.

With the predominance of polyphony, variation in texture became extremely important in musical shape.

Vocal and instrumental timbres were combined with polyphonic textures in many different ways, although the specific combination of timbres in a given piece was left up to the performers rather than being firmly controlled by the composer. A relatively small number of pieces were intended for instruments alone (including keyboard instruments), but a greater number were performed instrumentally on occasion. The overwhelming majority of pieces were to be performed by a combination of voices (solo or choral) and instruments.

Concomitant with the rise of Western polyphony was a development of precisely measured rhythm (and of systems of meter with which to notate and perform the measured rhythm). Chant—as, indeed, all music—had rhythm and could be performed "precisely" in the sense of involving extremely refined, artistically appropriate renditions of sounds in a rhythmic context. What was new was the composer's desire to fix the duration of all notes of a piece relative to each other in some precise way that would be binding upon the performer. This fixation came about only gradually and was never completely achieved; there was always a larger or smaller residue of rhythmic freedom left to the performer. Speaking roughly, the degree of precision and control in notation of measured rhythm was greatest toward the middle of the period and less at the beginning and end.

The predominance of polyphony brought with it an intense exploration of the effects produced by a simultaneous combination of pitches. Some of the factors to be considered were various degrees of consonance and dissonance, doubling, spacing (whether compact or open), as well as the effects of chords on lines and the relationships among all the chords in any given piece. As the period wore on, composers tended away from high contrast between consonances (such as octaves and fifths) and dissonances (such as seconds or sevenths), moving gradually closer to a consistent use of harmonic triads, in which the consonant fifths and octaves were enriched with major and minor thirds. Up to 1600, however, composers used triads for the sake of their harmonious sonority rather than as structural elements in the shape of the piece, so that we do not properly speak of music before 1600 as "triadic" in the same sense as music after 1600.

It is possible to see in the development of polyphony from 1150 to 1600 a gradual shift in the kind of shape used for individual pieces, especially as expressed in the kind of harmonic organization. This shift can be outlined in a very general way by these three stages.

1. Between 1200 and 1250, composers characteristically tended toward very short, compact structures. Each piece might involve—to some degree—a structural principle peculiar to itself; and each piece had a high degree of internal consistency, with little variety.
2. Later, between 1325 and 1375, composers tended to make use of more universal principles of pitch organization (evolved in the interim). Individual pieces might have considerable variety and flexibility; yet they also had a high degree of coordination between clear overall plan and detail, as well as a strong sense of direction running through the pitch organization.
3. Finally, from 1450 on, composers created very long, complex structures, exceedingly rich in detail, organized now in relatively oblique or diffuse ways.

Paris: 1150–1300. During the 1100s, a decisive shift took place in the locale of polyphony (as in other arts) from the monastery to the urban cathedral. After 1150, new cathedrals were being built in a monumental style called *Gothic*, a term often applied to polyphony as well.

After 1150, the repertory of polyphonic versus grew tremendously. Now called *conductus*, the polyphonic versus was usually written for two or three voice parts, singing the same text at the same time. Toward 1200, the low-level rhythms of the conductus were increasingly coordinated into a consistent long-short pattern called a *rhythmic mode; modal rhythm* was the first clear manifestation of the trend toward a precisely measured rhythm.

The center of conductus composition from 1150 to 1200 was Paris; but the conductus, being now a relatively conservative form of polyphony, did not represent the most progressive accomplishments of Parisian composers. In the decades after 1150, new forms of polyphony were developed at the cathedral of Notre Dame of Paris. The new forms, which were to be decisive in the future course of polyphony, were first apparent in the works of two composers, Leonin (active 1160–1180) and Perotin the Great (active about 1200); other composers were presumably working with them to produce the large repertory of "Notre Dame polyphony."

Using an ancient Gregorian gradual or alleluia chant as a ground plan, Leonin erected—literally on top of the chant—a vast polyphonic superstructure. Thus one distinctive feature of this kind of polyphony (sometimes called *organum*) is the use of a preexistent chant (called a *cantus firmus*) in the lowest voice part (called *tenor*). Leonin used modal rhythm extensively in his polyphony. The use of precisely measured rhythm in polyphony that included a cantus firmus was a most important combination of factors for the next two centuries of polyphony. This was especially true of certain portions of Leonin's works in which the two voices moved at about the same speed and were closely synchronized in their rhythms (called *discant* style). The sense of pitch direction provided here by the cantus firmus, together with the sense of coordination provided by the rhythm, gave polyphony a strong point of departure for new developments.

Perotin the Great carried the development of discant in modal rhythm much further. Perhaps his most decisive step was in giving the tenor a repetitive rhythmic pattern of its own and the upper voice an independent phrasing, while otherwise maintaining the very close rhythmic relationship between the voices. By this step, he began to exploit some of the great structural possibilities of precisely measured rhythm.

Perotin's discant style led eventually to a kind of piece called a *motet*. The tenor of a motet drew its melody from a preexistent piece of chant (following the practice of Leonin), usually from a chant melisma, with the result that the tenor might have only one syllable of text or at most a few syllables. As the motet developed, the tenor part was soon played on an instrument rather than sung.

Above the tenor there might be one, two, or three newly composed sung parts, each with its own text different from the others. This was a significant difference with respect to the conductus, in which all voices sang the same text at the same time. The part above the tenor was called *motetus*, the parts above that *triplum* and *quadruplum*. Thus a three-part motet (the most common kind) would have an instrumental tenor and two upper voices, each with its own text. These might be Latin sacred texts or French secular ones. By 1300, a large, varied repertory of motets had come into being, and motets were the leading form of polyphony.

Toward 1300, the rhythmic relationships between the voices of the motet loosened, the tenor going relatively slower, the triplum relatively faster and moving in patterns more intricate and irregular than those customary in modal rhythm. Motets by Pierre de la Croix (thirteenth century; exact dates unknown) illustrate this stage of development.

Europe: 1300–1450. During this period, polyphony, which was rapidly replacing monophony in both sacred and secular music, attained a remarkable integration of large overall plan with finely wrought, graceful detail. Composers executed large plans as well as small ones with clarity of form, yet greatly increased rhythmic variety. Song forms and textures—especially a solo voice with instrumental accompaniment—prevailed after 1350. The sacred repertory increased significantly in bulk, but the center of gravity of polyphony remained in secular music written for a restricted court audience. Courts and urban cathedrals continued to be the principal centers of musical activity. (The term *ars nova*, "the new practice," is sometimes used to designate the period 1300–1400 but is more properly restricted to the decades 1310–1350.)

France: 1300–1350. The motet continued for a while as the leading form, with its instrumental cantus-firmus tenor moving through regular repetitions of a now longer rhythmic pattern, under two sung parts each with its own text. As in the motets of Pierre de la Croix, there was a pronounced difference in pace between the tenor and the rapid upper parts. In the motets of Philippe de Vitry (1291–1361), however, these different rhythmic levels were combined in an integrated fashion, producing a graceful combination of animated detail with clear phrase shapes. Philippe gave the motet a distinctive shape that persisted through various modifications almost to 1500. His procedures for integrating the regular tenor repetitions with the rhythms of the upper parts were imitated and eventually stereotyped by composers late in the 1300s (these procedures are sometimes called *isorhythm*).

Other composers, mostly anonymous, began setting portions of the Mass such as *Kyrie, Gloria in excelsis, Credo, Sanctus, Agnus Dei* (these texts, which did not change from day to day, were later referred to collectively as the *Ordinary of the Mass*). The texture, usually in three parts, was sometimes simple discant, with the three voices singing the same text at the same time. Sometimes there was a difference of rhythmic pace among the voices, as in a motet, and sometimes the tenor was textless and instrumental, but usually such settings lacked the cantus firmus, the repeating tenor pattern, and the polytextuality characteristic of the motet.

Motets with French secular texts showed a tendency to take on delightfully whimsical features such as imitations of bird calls—the musical counterpart of a sophisticated rusticism in certain of the texts. Shapes inherited from monophony, especially those involving couplet and refrain, sometimes controlled the music as much if not more than did the tenor structure. A very special kind of piece (not a motet) was called a *chace*, that is "chase"; it combined mimesis of pastoral sounds with the musical technique of strict imitation.

Toward 1350 (and on for the rest of the century), composers set French poems to polyphony with more attention to the shape of the poems (as expressed in couplet and refrain structures), and correspondingly less attention to rhythmic structures typical of the motet. The results were the polyphonic song forms *ballade, virelai,* and *rondeau*, each having a distinctive musical shape for the couplet-refrain structure of a particular type of poem. Unlike the motet, settings of song forms typically had one sung part with two accompanying instrumental parts. One of these was called *tenor*, even though it had no

cantus firmus and no repeating pattern such as those found in motets; the other was (most often) a *contratenor*, similar to the tenor in behavior and range.

Guillaume de Machaut (died 1377) wrote numerous songs, both texts and music. The texts, while technically brilliant, have a certain uniformity of theme (so-called courtly love), but the music shows great rhythmic variety and tonal richness. In Guillaume's songs, the animation and lyricism of French music of the 1300s found perhaps its most convincing form.

Italy: 1300–1350. Italian composers followed much the same path from motet to song form but showed almost no interest in the motet itself. During the first part of the century, they composed a kind of piece called a *caccia* (same as French *chace*) and another called a *madrigale*, which was usually for two roughly equal voices. Delicate figuration was prominent, while the underlying structure was relatively simple. By midcentury, interest shifted decisively to the more poetically shaped *ballata* (same as French *virelai*). Francesco Landini (1325–1397) brought Italian forms to their culmination; already in his works, musical line and texture showed an increasing tendency to resemble French models of the time of Guillaume de Machaut. By the end of the century the distinctive Italian style of the 1340s had disappeared.

France: 1400–1450. Throughout these years, the emphasis on songlike shapes persisted as the single most important guiding principle in an otherwise confusing stage of development. Motets had expanded in size to the point where the cantus firmus and repeating rhythmic pattern in the tenor no longer provided effective control. On the one hand, songlike phrase structure appeared increasingly in the motet as a means of making musical sense; on the other hand, composers of sacred music neglected the large motet, pursuing instead the variety of polyphonic styles first used for sacred purposes during the preceding century—and these styles, too, were increasingly animated by songlike shapes. As a result of both these tendencies, in place of the traditional

large sacred motet there now appeared a smaller kind called a *song motet*; musically it was a song, for it lacked the distinctive structural features of the motet, but it had a sacred Latin text.

The duality of expanded traditional motet and the newer song motet is still present in the works of the English composer John Dunstable (died 1453), whose influence on the continent was largely responsible for a wave of fresh lyricism and rich sonority in French music after 1425. In the large, varied output of Guillaume Dufay (died 1474), the lyricism of the time found its strongest expression.

Dufay's personal accomplishment is so great that it is sometimes taken as the start of a new period. In a broader view of forms and styles, however, it seems clear that the changes to come around 1450 went far deeper than those that took place, say, around 1425. The most progressive aspect of Dufay's work was the development (along with Dunstable and others) of the *cyclic mass*, a musically unified setting of the five Mass texts *Kyrie, Gloria in excelsis, Credo, Sanctus, Agnus Dei*. Being the logical extension of the large motet as well as of the growing interest in sacred polyphony, the cyclic mass became the leading form in the decades after 1450.

Europe: 1450–1600. At the start of this period, composers worked for a new intricacy and density for polyphonic sound. Rhythmic figuration was a little less varied than in the decades 1380–1450, but was used more evenly throughout a piece, often with subtle but nearly continuous syncopation. Similarly, composers now used the rich sounds of harmonic triads—or at any rate thirds and sixths—consistently in almost every chord.

Overall plans became further extended, then veiled by the continuously intense detail. Clear sections and phrases tended to become obscured. Traditional song forms gradually disappeared as did the distinction between song motets and larger motets.

Traditional voice functions, such that of tenor, and clear distinctions between vocal and instrumental parts were merged into a rich profusion of sound. Choral timbre tended to replace the solo voice, and the chorus was often doubled by instruments (especially trombones). The resulting quality of sound, which had important structural implications, persisted through various changes in other aspects right up to 1600.

The overwhelming majority of leading composers and performers during this period came from an area along what is now the Franco-Belgian border and are commonly referred to as Franco-Flemish composers. After 1500, important composers emerged in other countries, too, especially in Italy; but, until almost the end of the century, they remained under strong Franco-Flemish influence.

The most characteristic locale of the new style was the ducal chapel—a special combination of the traditional locales of court and cathedral. The best composers were hired to provide masses and motets at the chapels of dukes and princes in France and Italy, as well as those of the Pope, the Emperor, and the King of France. Such composers also provided secular works for the court, but sacred music was their principal occupation. Later in the period, their achievements filtered down to the level of parish church and educated music lover.

Because of its coincidence, more or less, with the period in painting and literature known as the Renaissance, music of this period (sometimes including the decades from 1420 on) is often called Renaissance music. This terminology requires a certain caution, however, for many of the features commonly thought to characterize the Renaissance or Humanism are not clearly present—or even present at all—in music. Rebirth or imitation of classical models, for example, has no clear analog in music before 1550. As already pointed out, the leading styles were northern and sacred, not Italian and secular (even though the northern sacred music was highly prized in Italian courts). Finally music, without being any less progressive than the painting of the same period, shows a clear continuity with its Gothic past.

Franco-Flemish music: 1450–1500. The cyclic mass as developed by Dufay and others around 1440 became in the hands of Johannes Ockeghem (ca. 1430–1495) the leading midcentury form, temporarily eclipsing both motets and songs. Each of Ockeghem's masses unified the five sections (*Kyrie, Gloria in excelsis, Credo, Sanctus, Agnus Dei*) in a different way—sometimes by using the same cantus firmus in each section but often in more subtle or obscure ways. Ockeghem's mature style is marked by almost continuous elision or overlapping of phrases, producing a feeling of suspension that can last throughout a long section.

In its density and continuity, Ockeghem's style represented an extreme; less extreme positions were taken by Jacob Obrecht (ca. 1450–1505) and especially Josquin Des Pres (ca. 1440/1450–1521), who so perfectly combined the expressive flow of Ockeghem's music with such a wide variety of other, clearer phrase shapes that his music became a standard against which that of all other composers of the time was judged.

In addition to a number of cyclic masses, Josquin greatly developed the motet, giving it a definitive shape for the rest of the 1500s. Cantus firmus and repeating tenor patterns, although still used occasionally, were no longer relied upon to unify the motet. In place of such purely musical modes of organization, the phrasing of the music was now made to correspond more closely to the phrasing of the text, each new line of text receiving a new phrase of music, varied in texture from the preceding phrase. Frequent imitation among the voices bound them together. All voices sang the text but often (as in imitative passages) at slightly different times, increasing the density and intricacy over that of a simple discant texture. All voices moved at about the same pace with about the same rhythmic character, producing a smoothly homogeneous flow. This flow and the control of sonority to produce a succession of harmonic triads were the main ingredients of what was known in the 1500s as the perfect style.

Franco-Flemish music: 1500–1600. The importance of this style in the hands of Josquin and his contemporaries was that it remained the basis of musical composition throughout the 1500s. Succeeding composers contented themselves for the most part with making relatively minor adjustments or rearrangements, just sufficient to produce music with an identity of its own.

Masses and motets continued to be composed in increasing quantities, including very many beautiful masterpieces, but interest gradually shifted to secular forms again—first to compositions with French texts, called *chansons*, then after 1520 to compositions with Italian texts, called *madrigals* (no stylistic connection with the madrigale of the 1300s). There also existed an increasing quantity of simple strophic songs in polyphony (the result of gradual popularization of medieval song forms and their derivatives); but the essence of the madrigal was that it was *not* strophic, rather that—like the motet from which it sprang—it provided new and different music for each new line of text. As the madrigal developed during the 1500s, composers took increasing pains to make each phrase of music depict or express, by texture, line, or rhythm, the meaning of its line of text. The term *madrigalism* has come to designate this kind of "word painting" in music.

The madrigal was created by the northerners Philippe Verdelot (died ca. 1540) and Jacques Arcadelt (1505–1567), who moved easily from motets and chansons to similar settings of Italian texts. Other northerners such as Cipriano da Rore (1516–1565) and Giaches de Wert (1535–1596) provided abundant models, and native Italians all the way from Costanzo Festa (1490–1545) to Luca Marenzio (1553–1599) cultivated the madrigal with enthusiasm and imagination. Also in sacred music, Italian composers such as Giovanni Pierluigi da Palestrina (1525–1594) showed that they could write masses and motets comparable to those of the Franco-Flemish masters Jacques Clément (Clemens non Papa, ca. 1500–1556), Philipp de Monte (1521–1603), and especially the versatile, prolific Orlando di Lasso (1532–1594).

While the perfect style remained the core of musical composition, it was adapted in many ways to a wide variety of vocal and instrumental combinations, extending from a growing solo keyboard repertory to magnificent *polychoral* ("many-choir") works. Giovanni Gabrieli (1557–1612) at the very end of the century at St. Mark's in Venice, composed polychoral motets with a colorful abundance of instruments actually indicated in the score; he was one of the first to indicate specific instruments, thus marking the transition from the old *ad libitum* use of instruments to the new practice adopted after 1600.

EUROPE:1600 TO THE PRESENT. Changes in texture, which had become important in musical shape between 1150 and 1600, continued to be so; and, by process of accumulation, composers had an ever-growing stock of textures on which to draw. From 1600 on, control over timbre—especially of instruments—became an equally important part of the composer's resources. This control was exerted gradually, reaching a peak in the art of orchestration of the 1800s and in even more refined form in certain kinds of music in the 1900s.

The search for rich sonority in the preceding period had by 1600 established the harmonic triad as the normal sound of polyphony. After 1600 and up until 1900, pitch organization was increasingly carried out in terms of the triad and of chords derived from it. This is the triadic period of Western music.

As in the period 1150–1600, the kinds of shapes resulting from pitch organization after 1600 can be sketched roughly in three stages.

1. During the 1600s, pitch organization was most evident in relatively short, compact units of song-like dimensions; but these units were combined into much larger aggregates by various other means (such as text).
2. Toward 1800 and after, pitch organization was steadily extended over longer dimensions, producing a sense of harmonic area or key, then extended still more until several harmonic areas were brought under refined control, making possible the organization of very large works by primarily harmonic means (as in the works of Beethoven and Wagner).
3. This use of extended harmonic areas, which during the 1800s was associated with highly directed motion or modulation, was often replaced after 1900 by a sense of harmonic stasis or sometimes by a greatly retarded kind of harmonic motion in oblique (as opposed to straightforward) directions. When the harmonic motion becomes nil (sometimes, indeed, the pitch content seems irrelevant to shape), then pieces often revert to much smaller dimensions.

Europe: 1600–1750. The end of the 1500s had produced such a broad spectrum of vocal and instrumental possibilities that scarcely anything immediately after 1600 seems really new. Yet certain new emphases indicate a decisive turn towards a new style.

Perhaps the most widespread impression gained from music after 1600 is the strong sense of projection from performer to listener, as opposed to the richly veiled effects of masses and motets of the 1500s or the sense of involvement through participation, as in the madrigal, which was designed more to be sung than listened to.

Musical aspects of this strong projection include accentuation of soprano and bass lines—the profiles of the sound—through use of a high solo voice of brilliant timbre (such as soprano or tenor) on top and a battery of stringed and keyboard instruments playing the bass line and the harmonies between bass and soprano. Inner contrapuntal lines—very important during the 1500s—were often completely absent *as lines* after 1600 (they came into evidence again toward 1700). The battery of instruments on the bass line, known as the *basso continuo*, usually included at least one instrument to play the line and another to add the chords; but often several instruments were involved.

The seamless continuity typical of music in the 1500s now gave way to a series of relatively short sections, each contrasting sharply with the one before in tempo, rhythm, and line, sometimes in timbre and texture, too. As harmonic area became clearly defined toward 1700, change of area became yet another frequent means of contrast between sections.

Within any one section, tempo and rhythm tended to be uniform. At the same time, the smoothly flowing, pervasively syncopated rhythms of the 1500s, which had been veiled in complex contrapuntal texture, were now replaced by much more vigorous, dancelike rhythms, clearly projected by the much more homophonic textures.

The principle of musical shape so generated—that of a series of sections each set off from the preceding by a contrast of pace and rhythm—lasted throughout the period 1600–1750 and beyond; it is

responsible, for example, for the fact that each largest section of a symphony is called a movement. Furthermore, the sectional contrasts in rhythm were one of the composer's most important means of projecting meaning, especially in a song or music drama in which he wished to convey the affect of the text.

Music of this period is often called *baroque*, a term meaning among other things "bizarre" or "grotesque"; the term is used by art historians for stylistic tendencies at the end of the 1500s and in the 1600s. In music, it has come to refer to the period from 1600 to the death of J. S. Bach (1750), which is an arbitrary use. There is a stylistic continuity to the period 1600–1750, but it is based upon musical factors not specifically baroque; furthermore, this period includes much music—especially after 1680—that is definitely not baroque. Stylistic application of the term is most appropriate, in music as well as in art, during the 1600s and generally earlier rather than later.

Italy: 1600–1680. Italian composers led the way to the new music, developing not only forms and styles but also a new format, music drama. Songs had often been used in stage dramas during the 1500s; what was new was the idea of a drama set to music from beginning to end. To put it differently (and more accurately), the new art work was essentially a long, complex piece of music with a dramatic shape and intent.

Music drama (or *opera*, as it became generally called) consisted of sections that alternate in timbre among vocal solo, instrumental, and choral—mainly the solos—and among the various singers that are the protagonists in the drama. The sections contrasted in rhythm between declamatory *recitative* and more songlike or dancelike *arias*. Although the declamatory recitative was widely used and persisted as an operatic style up past 1900, it did not develop significantly. Musical development took place primarily in the aria, where repetitive rhythms (often taken from dances such as the *sarabande*, *ciacona*, or *passacaglia*) opened the way to great rhythmic expansion, and clear, songlike phrasing provided a foundation for the emerging sense of harmonic area.

Opera was developed by Jacopo Peri (1561–1633) and Giulio Caccini (1545–1618) at Florence and especially by Claudio Monteverdi (1567–1643) at Mantua. Monteverdi worked out the new styles in a brilliant series of madrigals dating from about 1590 to 1620, by which time he had gone to Venice, the nerve center of the new music. "Si ch'io vorrei morire" shows the madrigal in its traditional five-voiced imitative texture, but infused with a new impassioned feeling; "Chiome d'oro" and "Amor che deggio far" show the new emphasis on soprano and bass lines, combination of voices with instruments, repetitive rhythms, and dancelike phrases. In Rome, Girolamo Frescobaldi (1583–1643) developed solo keyboard styles and forms (for harpsichord and organ) comparable to Monteverdi's vocal forms; and Giacomo Carissimi (1605–1674), also in Rome, did the same for church music, creating a dramatic sacred form that came to be called *oratorio*. Composers such as Luigi Rossi (1598–1653), Francesco Cavalli (1602–1676), and Marc'Antonio Cesti (1623–1669) further developed and refined operatic composition after Monteverdi's death in 1643.

Northern Europe: 1600–1680. Composers in Germany, France, and England followed Italian models in a variety of ways, more successfully in works for solo keyboard or smaller dramatic works, both secular and sacred, than in opera, which had a precarious existence north of the Alps.

Heinrich Schütz (1585–1672) wrote a great many sacred *concertos* (throughout this period, a *concerto* was a combination of voices with instruments) in Latin and especially in German, attaining a depth of conception unmatched even by Italians. Johann Jakob Froberger (1616–1667) continued the accomplishments of Frescobaldi, and a whole school of French keyboard composers brought dance forms such as the *allemande, courante,* and *sarabande* to a state of high refinement. Italian opera was represented at the court of Louis XIV by Jean Baptiste Lully (1632–1687), writing more or less in the style of Cavalli but adapted to French taste and language.

Italy: 1680–1750. Opera continued to flourish in Italy, every winter season bringing numerous new works as well as many revivals of old ones—but never very old, since styles continued to change. Productions were expensive, involving brilliant soloists, spectacular sets, and often lavish choreography, all accompanied by an orchestra as large as conditions would allow. The core of the orchestra was the first and second violin parts, and the basso continuo grouped around the harpsichord; winds (flutes, oboes, and bassoons) could be used as needed, with trumpets and drums for martial or regal effects, and perhaps trombones for scenes in hell.

Musical development took place primarily in the aria, leading to an increased clarification of harmonic area and greatly expanded dimensions. Repetitive rhythms, sometimes of great force and vigor, moved the aria forward through its grand designs, and now tended to overrun the previously clear, songlike phrase shapes. The musical result was long, stable, uniform sections of music; the dramatic result, a slowing down in the rate of change of affect and action. As it acquired grandeur, serious opera tended to deepen and darken, while more animated, flexible forms of musical theatre developed alongside, especially after 1700.

Alessandro Scarlatti (1660–1725) was perhaps the greatest (but not the most popular) opera composer around 1700. The next generation included Leonardo Vinci (1690–1730), and the next, Giovanni Battista Pergolesi (1710–1736), whose few mature works in serious opera as well as in sentimental comedy show the increased rhythmic variety and disjunction of phrases apparent after 1730.

The solo keyboard virtuoso was less in evidence, as composer, in Italy during this period. The most brilliant instrumental music was found in the *trio sonata* for two violins and basso continuo, and especially in the *concerto*, now written for a purely instrumental ensemble—first and second violin parts (with perhaps a dozen players on each part) plus the basso continuo battery. Instead of contrast between voices and instruments, these concertos exploited contrasts between a small group of instruments and the tutti or between a solo and the tutti. Both sonatas and concertos consisted of a series of sections or movements contrasting in tempo and rhythm but usually unified in key. The best sonatas, as well as some of the first of the new concertos, were written by Arcangelo Corelli (1653–1713); Antonio Vivaldi (ca. 1678–1741) wrote numerous concertos, including very important ones around 1715.

One of the few manifestations of Italian keyboard music—but a brilliant one—was in the harpsichord sonatas of Domenico Scarlatti (1685–1757, son of Alessandro). These short pieces in binary form reveal a wealth of invention and the same increase in rhythmic variety found in the vocal music of Pergolesi.

Northern Europe: 1680–1750. Two composers, Johann Sebastian Bach (1685–1750) and Georg Friedrich Handel (1685–1759) have come to represent—if not overshadow—the host of composers active in northern countries between 1680 and 1750. Actually, Henry Purcell (1659–1695) might be considered more representative of English dramatic music than Handel, and François Couperin (1668–1733) embodies ideals of continental keyboard music better than Bach; Friedrich Wilhelm Zachow (1663–1712) and Christoph Graupner (1683–1760) stood at the center of German sacred music, and Georg Philipp Telemann (1681–1767) was probably more popular, and prolific, than any of those mentioned. But Bach and Handel have survived into the modern repertory.

Although Bach wrote much sacred vocal music (especially in the form of concertos, or *cantatas*, as they are commonly called) his most distinctive works, in his time as in ours, are those for keyboard—organ or harpsichord. Works for organ include very large, sometimes rhapsodic, sectional pieces called *toccatas* or *preludes*, extended *fugues*, and pieces built upon a *chorale* (that is, a German hymn) called *chorale preludes*. Works for harpsichord (or clavichord) include toccatas, *suites* (or sets) of dance forms (for example, allemande, courante, sarabande, bourrée, minuet, gigue) and the more compact kind of preludes and fugues found in the two books of *The Well-Tempered Clavier*.

Handel, a German, wrote what was essentially an Italian style in England. He composed a wealth of Italian operas, then turned to (or better, established) the category of English oratorio. In his works the grandeur of the Italian style of 1700 found one of its best expressions, coupled with a humanity and depth of affect peculiarly his own. As with Bach, Handel's uniqueness involved isolation from the progressive continental style of 1720, which was moving in a new direction having little to do with these two composers.

During the 1700s. During the 1700s an important shift took place in the locale of music (that is, of music embodying the most serious ambitions of a composer, for functional music making can be assumed throughout history at any social level). Wealthy merchants—leaders of the bourgeoisie— became increasingly active in sponsoring musical performances in their homes, supplementing and eventually replacing the nobility as patrons and the court as locale. Even more important, public concerts open to large audiences drawn ultimately from all social classes presented the composer with new opportunities—and new problems. Simultaneously, religious institutions withdrew to a significant degree as sponsors of progressive music.

Centers of musical performance, then, tended to be increasingly localized in the largest cities—London and Paris in western Europe, Vienna in the east— and composers also were drawn to these centers.

As often happens toward the latter part of a period, smaller forms and intimate styles coexist with larger, more imposing ones, often outstripping them in inventiveness and popularity. Indeed, such smaller forms usually arise as a reaction to the natural expansion of the period's central forms. Thus, after 1700 smaller forms were increasingly popular in both vocal and instrumental media, and although they contained no structural novelties, they often had an ingratiating charm and smartness that made them preferred over the more serious operas or concertos. Such music is sometimes designated by the term *rococo*, borrowed from art history; a better term, widely used in the 1700s for manners as well as art, is *style galant*.

Considered in broader terms, music during the 1700s developed a common language that made a most efficient use of harmonic triads and the clear phrase shapes of song and dance. Cosmopolitan and urbane (although sometimes adopting a rustic pose), this language could be used anywhere in Europe with only slight differences in regional inflection. It forms a base from which the individual achievements and often strongly personal styles of Haydn and Mozart can be gauged.

Europe: 1750–1900. During this period, German composers emerged as leaders of Western music, especially of instrumental music in the symphonic forms to be mentioned. Opera continued to flourish, but in instrumental music composers found the best medium for expression of personal affect—a side of music very prominent during the 1800s.

A strong tension now existed between small forms (and their songlike or dancelike phrase structure) and larger ones. The best works involved a careful integration of opposing forces—of large-scale stability with the kind of intimate or exciting detail associated with self-expression, or else a treatment of smaller forms that made it possible for them to contain this self-expression. In general, a trend toward large, integrated works can be found from 1750 up past 1800, another trend toward small forms to 1850, then ambivalence to the end of the century.

In many different ways, stability was evident at higher structural levels, flexibility and variety at lower ones. The most characteristic instrumental ensemble, the symphony orchestra (a descendant of both the opera orchestra and the instrumental concerto), was capable of remarkably varied effects of timbre and texture. These effects were most noticeable as detail; considered at higher levels, the symphony orchestra provided an integrated sound, a universe of sound that encompassed and unified the wealth of varied detail to be found in a symphony. During the 1800s, the symphony orchestra became standardized to a remarkable degree.

Rhythm, too, was susceptible of great flexibility and variation of detail, often from one phrase to the next; yet the variation usually took place within a stable framework represented by the use of a single meter and tempo for large sections (with some important exceptions).

Finally, varied or unexpected treatment of harmonic detail was one of the composer's most potent means of expression. On the other hand, large-scale stability of key was perhaps the most distinctive feature of the period as a whole.

Germany-Austria: 1750–1830. In the years around 1750, several German composers, especially Carl Philipp Emanuel Bach (1714–1788, second son of J. S. Bach), composed instrumental music that was unusually forceful in expression through its idiosyncratic treatment of the common language. Sometimes this involved special use of dynamics (which from that time on were yet another aspect closely controlled by the composer), sometimes more thoroughgoing twists of harmony and rhythm.

A new kind of keyboard instrument was developed to enable the performer to change dynamics and produce sudden accents at will (which he could not do on the harpsichord); this instrument was called a *fortepiano* ("loud-soft"), which after eventual modifications became the instrument known to us, curiously enough, as a piano. The piano virtuoso, succeeding the harpsichord virtuoso of the preceding period, soon embodied one of the most concentrated expressions of the new music.

Between 1760 and 1790, Joseph Haydn (1732–1809) gradually transformed the *sinfonia* from a nondescript common-language piece into a large, impressive kind of concert work. It rivaled serious opera in its demands upon the listener, and at the same time possessed the power of self-expression and strong individual character previously found in smaller, more erratic forms used by the young Germans around 1750. Simultaneously, Haydn transformed another common-language form, the *divertimento*, into an even more challenging, serious kind of work we know as a *string quartet*. There had been pieces for two violins, viola, and cello before; what Haydn did was stabilize the medium, define the individual functions of the instruments, and above all give them something significant to say. Both sinfonia and divertimento had had a variable number and order of movements; Haydn standardized both into a four-movement plan, greatly expanding the dimensions of the first movements especially. These had started out as binary or rounded binary forms; then dimensions were expanded, key areas stabilized, functions of the various sections clarified, and traditional section repeats dropped to leave the three-section plan of exposition, development, and recapitulation known to us as *sonata-allegro form*. For the faster of the two middle movements, Haydn adopted the minuet-trio-minuet plan and for the finale often a sonata-allegro or a rondo or a combination of the two. For the slower of the two middle movements (sometimes very slow, sometimes of a moderate tempo) Haydn used a variety of shapes, often *A B A B A*. In addition to providing strong, standard shapes for symphony and string quartet, he also found ways to make each work individual—demonstrating that integration of plan and detail mentioned before. His twelve "London" Symphonies (of which Symphony No. 100 is one) became models for the next generation.

Haydn's achievement was the basis for German leadership and for the subsequent developments of Mozart and Beethoven. From the point of view of stylistic development, the important mature works of the prolific Wolfgang Amadeus Mozart (1756–1791) are of two kinds—those that build directly on Haydn's models and those that show Mozart finding his own individual solutions. In the first group are symphonies and string quartets, deepened and enriched, but following Haydn's plan. In the second group are string quintets, piano sonatas, piano concertos, and operas, for all of which he developed a wealth of new ideas and a distinctive personal style. (The Finale from Act II of *Le Nozze di Figaro* is one of the best-known examples of Mozart's special treatment of complex operatic ensemble.)

Ludwig van Beethoven (1770–1827) carried the thrust of Haydn's development to its logical conclusion. Without essentially changing Haydn's concept of symphony or string quartet, Beethoven expanded them to dimensions that were now truly heroic, developed an inexhaustible supply of fresh, expressive detail, and all the time maintained a faultless integration at all levels of structure. Each work has an individual character: his nine symphonies are as clearly distinguished from each other as if each had its own plot and personages, like an opera.

Indeed, the themes of Beethoven's symphonies become so bound up with the musical structure that the interaction of the two often has distinctly dramatic qualities. This is especially true of Beethoven's development sections, which tend to become increasingly important in the overall design.

Himself a piano virtuoso, Beethoven also gave the piano sonata a consistently larger stature. Numerous early sonatas helped prepare his innovations in symphonies and quartets, while his "late" sonatas similarly prepared the profound, remote language of the last symphony and quartets.

Beethoven's music, even more than Haydn's or Mozart's, set standards for succeeding composers, who on one hand tried to continue from where he left off, and on the other found that exceedingly difficult, if not impossible, to do. Thus, there is both a strong continuity and a discontinuity between Beethoven and the next generation.

Franz Schubert (1797–1828), most of whose output falls within Beethoven's lifetime, reached a point at the end of his short life where he could control the large forms used by Beethoven in symphony, sonata, and string quartet. Schubert also, however, found a fruitful alternative to these forms in the song (German, *Lied*, plural *Lieder*) for solo voice with piano accompaniment. The song accomplished an integration of opposing forces in ways very different from those of symphony or sonata. A relatively simple voice line set forth clear phrase shapes, while the piano accompaniment, rich in harmonic detail and sometimes complex in texture, added a great depth of expression. A single song could stand by itself as a brief lyric insight; or a number of songs could be linked together—on the surface by text, underneath by a complex harmonic plan—into a song cycle as extensive as a symphony. (*Die schöne Müllerin* is one of Schubert's most famous cycles.)

Even though Hector Berlioz (1803–1869) was a Frenchman working in Paris, he was so profoundly impressed by Beethoven's music that his own can in certain important respects be grouped with it. Sensitive to the power of Beethoven's music to generate images in the mind of the listener, Berlioz sometimes provided his own symphonic works with *programs*, literary analogs or guides to the inner content of the music. Yet Berlioz's symphonic shapes continued to be predicated on those of Beethoven. Berlioz also developed forms midway between symphony and drama, again by way of spelling out some of the expressive qualities of German instrumental music.

Germany: 1830–1850. Music right after Beethoven—or sometimes including him—is often called *romantic* and set in opposition to music of the *classic* period, here meaning roughly 1750–1800. This terminology can be very misleading. In the first place, the opposition is not so clearly present in the minds of "romantic" composers and observers, who often felt much more kinship with Haydn, Mozart, and Beethoven than the terminology would indicate. In the second place, use of the term "classic" is extremely unfortunate; this term is quite incommensurate with "romantic," which has much firmer connections with historical reality in musical as well as literary sources. "Classic" is used in *at least* two senses: (1) as a style-period term peculiar to music history, it is presumed to include Haydn and Mozart but, as actually used, refers rather to the common language of the 1700s; (2) when legitimately applied to Haydn, Mozart, or Beethoven, it takes on its more common meaning of aesthetic judgment, designating works whose style and form are handled with exceptional discrimination and propriety. These two applications are incompatible; neither is historically useful here.

Most important in the objection to classic-romantic is that as a period division it obscures an underlying continuity from 1750–1900 based upon a drive toward self-expression and individual character. If the polarity is put as one between an interest in form and an interest in content (as it often is), then it must be said that Haydn and Mozart were deeply concerned with content, Schumann and the romantics just as deeply concerned with form. Musical excitement and intimacy, produced throughout the period by the drive for self-expression, did indeed surface in self-conscious form in Schumann and were embodied in concentrated musical fragments in Chopin's Preludes, but these same qualities could just as well be integrated into long, complex concertos by Mozart—or appear in a number of other ways in the works of other composers.

Differences between Beethoven and succeeding composers are better understood in terms of specific musical features, such as the preference for small forms found already in Schubert's songs and continued especially in a great number of small piano pieces produced by composers of the next generation. While sometimes successful in symphonic works, these composers wrote truly distinctive music, full of imaginative ideas and new sonorities, in smaller forms—either singly or in large sets corresponding to song cycles. Robert Schumann (1810–1856) and Frédéric Chopin (1810–1849) developed a whole repertory of such pieces, creating brilliant styles for the piano. As forms got smaller, harmonic, rhythmic, and textural density tended to increase, giving small pieces a concentration that greatly heightened their power of evocation.

Both Schumann and Chopin were active mainly during the 1830s and 1840s. Franz Liszt (1811–1886), although about the same age, did his most important composing toward the end of the 1840s and revealed a turn toward larger dimensions. Becoming interested in symphonic music, Liszt (primarily a piano virtuoso) developed the *concert overture*, or, as it was soon called, the *symphonic poem*, which had the dimensions of a single movement of a symphony, a strong sense of character or content, and a title or program to make the content more explicit. Liszt's style put great emphasis upon harmonic power, especially the power of individual chords. Along with Beethovenesque dimensions came also a new emphasis upon themes and motives as unifying factors.

Germany: 1850–1900. A return to the symphonic spirit of Beethoven can be felt even more in the music of Richard Wagner (1813–1883), even though almost all his work took the form of music drama. Perhaps the most distinguishing feature of Wagner's music is its massiveness, a striving for huge dimensions that made Wagner's music so different from that of the years 1830–1850. For Wagner, the concept "romantic" seemed somehow limited; he used it, for example, with reference to his own

operas before 1850; and while those that came after 1850 continue many of the same specific features, they refuse to be contained in the romantic world, creating their own instead. Wagner wrote a relatively small number of mature works, each large, each with a unique character (*Tristan und Isolde* is one such work).

The combination of text and music in Wagner's music dramas raises many questions that must be passed over here. It is important for us that purely musical aspects played an ever more important role in his works and that these aspects were intimately connected with the symphonic accomplishment of Beethoven. The flexibility and variety of symphonic timbre and texture—and especially its power—found their way into Wagner's music either directly or through the work of Berlioz.

In keeping with its massiveness and large dimensions, Wagner's music disdained the fragmentary forms used earlier, using instead very long-range key plans and a high degree of integration between plan and detail. Themes and motives once again played a central role in coordination with the key plan; indeed, themes became especially charged with dramatic significance at the same time that they clarified the musical structure. The resulting shapes, however, are not those of the symphony: there are no sonata forms or even movements in Wagner's dramas. Instead, the interplay of theme and key generated new, unique forms.

Another very distinctive feature is the slow pace of Wagner's harmonic rhythm. In general, the significant rhythms are very large, stretching over immense durations and moving with a slow pulse. In terms of this pulse, many of the musical-dramatic shapes turn out to be lyric ones; Wagner's formal solutions, in other words, have perhaps as much to do with the songs of Schubert as with the symphonies of Beethoven.

Beethoven's legacy to Wagner can be fruitfully compared with his legacy to Johannes Brahms (1833–1897). Brahms grew up in the musical world of Schubert and Schumann, writing (for example) many romantic songs. Then he set out to compose symphonies on the scale of Beethoven. His four symphonies—each very individual in character—

integrate large-scale plan with detail in a way unique after Beethoven. Unlike Wagner, Brahms often followed closely Beethoven's concepts of specific forms but was able to infuse them with his own distinctive textures, figures, and harmonies. Alongside these monumental symphonies, Brahms placed a series of very intricate, concentrated, small piano pieces, and a variety of chamber works.

Europe: 1850–1900. After 1850, there were increasing tendencies in other European countries to produce music that was independent of Germany—of Beethoven, Wagner, or Brahms. Sometimes the independence was achieved through use of indigenous elements of folk song, sometimes through long-standing national traditions of art music, sometimes by an indefinable national character. Many composers were involved; the most distinguished were Modest Musorgski (1839–1881), one of several important Russian composers; Giuseppe Verdi (1813–1901), who raised Italian opera once more to a position of European eminence; and Claude Debussy (1862–1918), whose music, while unlike anything previously composed in France (or anywhere else), has an extraordinary Frenchness.

Debussy is often taken as the first composer of a new period that extends into the 1900s. His treatment of harmony avoids both clearly stated keys and directed modulations, thereby eliminating the bases of forms in common use for two centuries. Still, harmony plays an essential role in his music, because of both its expressive potential and its structural function. Debussy's use of harmonic organization represents a tendency, increasingly apparent throughout the 1800s, to group harmonies in obscure or unexpected ways.

Debussy wrote for a wide variety of instrumental and vocal media, from small piano pieces to music drama and works for symphony orchestra (but more like symphonic poems than symphonies). Whatever the medium, his works show a one-of-a-kind approach to form, and a veiled quality of sound that has often been called dreamlike. It is the richness of the sound, perhaps, that links Debussy more closely with his past than with his immediate future, when a very different kind of sound was soon to become essential in the new style. The veiled quality seems to have the function of concealing other features that connect Debussy to the much more emphatic language of Wagner.

Europe and America: 1900 to the present. Music since 1900 has produced a very wide variety of sounds and shapes—wider, it may seem to us, than at any other time in history. Furthermore, the locale of music has become dispersed to an unprecedented degree, with some attendant loss of exchange among composers and between composers and listeners. Nonetheless, it would be premature to conclude that music since 1900 shows no such patterns of development as are apparent in previous centuries, or that development—significant development—has gone on at a very much faster rate than before, or finally that its only guiding principle has been that of reflecting an "anxious age."

One revealing fact is that some of the most radical experiments and extreme kinds of sound were first produced early in the 1900s, especially between 1910 and 1925, and that development since those early years has in some respects not been so rapid after all. For example, the two distinctive techniques of the 1950s—an *aleatory*, or (loosely speaking) "randomized," approach to shape, and electronic generation of sounds—have not produced musical results so very different from those produced by more conventional contemporary techniques. From a historical point of view it is possible to treat music since 1900 in the same continuum as music before 1900, although of course various accounts may differ from each other considerably. The present extremely brief account is concerned with only a few of those composers whose works seem to indicate the development of style, ignoring (as in the rest of the outline) the larger number of more conservative or derivative composers, as well as the diffusion of various kinds of functional music throughout Western society.

One of the clearest aspects of the early 1900s was the desire on the part of progressive composers to avoid the musical sounds and shapes current in the preceding decades. Such avoidance does not account completely, of course, for the new music; understanding the avoidance is merely a convenient way of following the development from old to new,

while perceiving the new shapes in their own right is more a matter of immediate experience in hearing new pieces.

Particularly avoided (speaking always of the more progressive music) was the rich, varied, but unified sound of the symphony orchestra. One of the most striking developments around 1920 was that of music for relatively small instrumental groups emphasizing solo winds and sometimes percussion. Bright, fresh, hard timbres became for a while a trademark of new music. Since 1940, ideals of sound have mellowed, sometimes toward the sound of a symphony orchestra, sometimes in the direction of newly developed sounds, most notably those produced by electronic means.

Also generally avoided is metrical rhythm, that is, a regular, consistent grouping of pulses. Other elements of rhythm are present in abundance, but because of the increasing absence of meter, rhythms often do not generate a hierarchy of levels, tending to be perceived on only one level—a high one or a very low one. Unit pulse, for example, is common. A regular phrase structure is also avoided, although irregular phrase structures are often very clear.

The use of triadic harmonies has been increasingly avoided but in different ways. Most avoided of all is the sense of remaining in a stable key—already often absent from the music of Wagner and Debussy. However, many composers have continued to use triads (in one form or another), without linking them together in stable keys or clearly directed modulations. Often triadic harmonies lie just concealed beneath a layer of dissonance, whose specific function, indeed, may be that of concealment. Other composers, while more or less eliminating triads (and other traditional chord combinations), have retained a sense of directed motion through implied harmonic areas. Still others avoid even this kind of motion. (There is also music that does not use twelve semitones to the octave or does not use distinct pitch for structural purposes; such music, of course, avoids traditional pitch organization completely.)

Themes, very important factors in symphonic shapes, have generally been minimized or avoided altogether. Motives, traditionally less obvious and more pervasive in nature, have been used more,

but they too are tending to disappear. In general, it might be said that traditional modes of organization through rhythm or pitch have been avoided as now too obvious or, if used, then used in a covered or diffused manner; when musical shapes are clear, they are often made so through timbre and texture rather than through rhythm or pitch.

Of several composers whose artistic personalities have dominated the first half of our century, Béla Bartók (1881–1945) has made the most consistent use of traditional shapes—especially in string quartets and in concertos and other orchestral works of various kinds. Bartók overlaid traditional shapes with rich, often pungent, qualities of sound, and with a consistently dissonant treatment of chords. But stable areas comparable to keys and directed motion between them are clearly apparent. Themes and especially motives regularly appear to guide the musical flow. Rhythms vary greatly from rhapsodic, almost unmeasured, ones (which are usually slow) to fast, extremely insistent, rhythms with very strong, irregular accentuation; but meter is often present underneath for long stretches.

Bartók's works were among the first to represent a style characteristic of the twentieth century and, in spite of a brusque exterior, soon established themselves in the modern repertory. His six string quartets occupy a central position in twentieth-century chamber music.

The relationship of Igor Stravinsky (born 1882) to traditional music has often seemed more difficult to assess. He frequently uses ready-made sounds and idioms—triads, or common-language idioms from the 1700s—but in new, unfamiliar ways. His use of preexisting materials is deceptive, for they lead the ear to expect the shape with which they have been traditionally associated; but Stravinsky uses the materials independently of such shape, making instead his own, often unique shapes.

In timbre, rhythm, and harmony, Stravinsky has been less colorful, less violent than Bartók but paradoxically has effected a greater separation from the past. There is, for example, much less sense of meter or of directed harmonic motion in his music. Instead, he characteristically creates passages that are static in harmony and are prolonged by intricate repetitions of a rhythmic figure (often with a unit pulse). Harmonic motion is likely to take place by an abrupt shift to another static passage. Out of the rhythmic figuration often springs a new kind of line, disjunct and strangely phrased but lyric. *Les noces* is one of the first of Stravinsky's major works to show these features clearly.

Stravinsky has composed a very wide variety of kinds of pieces, each externally different from the others and often in response to musical demands and opportunities as they arose. This has become characteristic of twentieth-century composers, who tend to compose works one of a kind.

The development of Arnold Schoenberg (1874–1951), while easy to follow in its historical logic, soon (by 1912) led to a kind of music that was for decades virtually excluded from the concert repertory because of its seeming extremity. Schoenberg, working in Vienna around 1900, began with the hyperexpressive symphonic style of Richard Strauss (1864–1949) and Gustav Mahler (1860–1911) and like them wrote intense, continuous modulation in a basically triadic context. Then, Schoenberg progressively stripped away both the triadic context and the symphonic sounds; his new music, instead of staying in easily recognizable harmonic areas or moving with a perceptible sense of direction, moved at will anywhere and everywhere. In this harmonic frame of reference (called *pantonal* or less appropriately *atonal*), individual chords and lines are not to be heard in relationship to a triadic framework, but rather in relationship to each other. The relatively high degree of dissonance, for example, has to be judged differently—and, indeed, produces a very different effect—from dissonance in Bartók's music.

In spite of all, Schoenberg maintained close connections with the past through a strong sense of developmental continuity (as found especially in traditional symphonic "development" sections); this is most apparent in line and rhythm, which if translated into a triadic context would sound surprisingly traditional.

If Schoenberg's music represents the tendency toward developmental expansion, the music of Anton Webern (1883–1945) represents the opposite tendency toward songlike shapes or toward fragmentary pieces of intense individual character. Working closely with Schoenberg, Webern moved even more quickly (by 1910) to what appeared then as completely alien music. After 1950, however, it came to represent progressive twentieth-century style to a far greater degree than did the music of Bartók—or even of Schoenberg.

The initial impression made by Webern's music is one of extreme discontinuity. Details such as the timbre, the attack, the duration, and the pitch of individual notes are often isolated by means of discontinuity in texture, line, or rhythmic flow, so as to be better perceived and individually more expressive. Avoidance of traditional sonorities, meters, lines, and especially keys and modulations is thorough: the elements of a piece can be referred only to each other. Indeed, they usually turn out to have a high degree of intrinsic cohesiveness, even though it is more easily intuited than demonstrated. A unique lyricism pervades Webern's works—not merely his songs but also his pieces for smaller or larger instrumental ensembles.

The elimination of a triadic framework in the music of Schoenberg and Webern is often accomplished by *serial* techniques, in which pitches are used according to a series that prevents any one group of pitches from establishing itself through repetition as a harmonic center. Since this results in a more or less equal use of all twelve pitches in the octave, serial techniques are also called *twelve-tone* or *dodecaphonic* techniques. The most important result is an overall sense of harmonic stasis. This in turn eliminates reference to the forms and especially the dimensions of traditional harmonic design (as found, say, in the symphony), so that even though relatively short, Webern's pieces can have the effect of weighty if not profound content.

Serial techniques, applied not only to pitch but to rhythm and timbre as well, have often been used since 1950. Simultaneously others, called *aleatory* ("chance") techniques, were developed; and, although these would seem to be the exact opposite of the refined control possible through serialism, the two go hand in hand, producing under certain conditions similar results. As a simple example of an aleatory technique, a composer might provide the performer with a set of notes or of phrases that the performer could play in any order or in any register or on whatever instruments he wished. Relatively elaborate aleatory procedures have been developed.

Techniques for generating sound electronically have also been developed since about 1950. Besides making possible (at least in principle) a variety of new timbres, such techniques enable the composer to use an unlimited number of pitches (rather than just twelve to the octave) and free him from reference to metrical subdivisions in notating rhythm. As with serial and aleatory techniques, however, the method of generating sound is artistically neutral; what is significant to the listener is the effect in and on the musical shape.

Mario Davidovsky (born 1934) is one of several composers who have incorporated electronic sounds into successful musical shapes. He has also found ways to combine electronic sounds with those of traditional instruments to their mutual benefit.

Broader definitions of "musical shape" and of "music" have been put forward in recent decades; for example, that music is a communal awareness of sounds and that musical shape is whatever happens, accidentally or on purpose, during a period of communal awareness. Some compositions make use of "mixed media," including, say, film strips or lights. Other compositions make provision for active audience participation on an improvisatory basis.

Alongside the kinds of music just described, the mid-1900s have produced intense cultivation of all kinds of traditional styles: examples are the widespread concert life based upon German music of the 1800s (but including more and more music from earlier repertories), as well as increased interest in "folk music"—meaning anything from commercial country-style music to genuine ethnic repertories.

A broad spectrum of ways of making music has opened up since 1950. At the same time, no longer under pressure to react violently against music of the preceding century, some composers have moved toward a common language of the later 1900s, with what might be called the "apotheosis of Webern" after 1950 as a point of reference. Even more significant, from some points of view, is the fact that a composer such as Krzysztof Penderecki (born 1933) can write music whose shapes and emotional content have proved accessible to a relatively widespread audience, while still using sounds distinctly belonging to twentieth-century musical style.

 **NDEX**

For performance terms (dynamics, tempo, etc.), names of instruments, and note values, see glossary.